THE COLLECTED WRITINGS OF
ROBERT DUNCAN

The publisher gratefully acknowledges the generous contribution to this book from the Jess Collins Trust and the ongoing efforts of its trustees.

The publisher also gratefully acknowledges the generous support of the Humanities Endowment Fund of the University of California Press Foundation.

The H.D. Book

Robert Duncan

The H.D. Book

Edited and with an
Introduction by
Michael Boughn and
Victor Coleman

University of California Press
Berkeley   Los Angeles   London

University of California Press, one of the most distinguished university presses in the United States, enriches lives around the world by advancing scholarship in the humanities, social sciences, and natural sciences. Its activities are supported by the UC Press Foundation and by philanthropic contributions from individuals and institutions. For more information, visit www.ucpress.edu.

University of California Press
Berkeley and Los Angeles, California

University of California Press, Ltd.
London, England

Frontispiece: Jess (1923–2004), "his mind / ours a sublime community," from *Emblems for Robert Duncan,* 1989, paste-ups, 6¼" x 5⅞". Seven ovals (with seven alternates) were created by Jess especially for this edition. Courtesy of the Jess Collins Trust.

For acknowledgment of previous publication, see credits, page 659.

Library of Congress Cataloging-in-Publication Data

Duncan, Robert, 1919–1988.
    The H.D. book / Robert Duncan ; edited and with an introduction by Michael Boughn and Victor Coleman.
        p.   cm. — (The collected writings of Robert Duncan ; 1)
A collection of 17 essays, composed from 1959 to 1964.
    Includes bibliographical references and index.
    ISBN 978-0-520-26075-7 (cloth : alk. paper)
    1. Poetry, Modern—20th century—History and criticism—Theory, etc.   I. Boughn, Michael.   II. Coleman, Victor, 1944–   III. Title.
    PS3507.U629H3   2011
    814'.54—dc22   2010005640

20   19   18   17   16   15   14   13   12   11
10   9   8   7   6   5   4   3   2   1

Contents

Illustrations

Acknowledgments

All the manuscripts for *The H.D. Book* are housed at the Poetry / Rare Book Collection at the State University of New York at Buffalo. We would like to thank the staff at the Collection, and especially the curator, Michael Basinski, and the assistant curator, James Maynard, for making us welcome and for their help in locating Robert Duncan's materials and making them available to us. James Maynard, in particular, not only quickly provided all the materials we asked for, but used his extensive knowledge of the collection to go out of his way to suggest material we would have taken weeks or months to otherwise locate. Without his generous assistance this project would have taken much longer than it did. Christopher Wagstaff, Mary Margaret Sloan, and the Jess Collins Trust have also been extremely generous and timely in their support of this work.

In addition, Mr. Maynard generously read an early draft of our introduction. His support and criticism were essential in helping us shape it into its final form. Peter Quartermain also took valuable time out from his own editorial tasks to offer us support and criticism. For that we are deeply grateful.

We would also like to thank our respective spouses, Elizabeth Brown and Kate Van Dusen, for their patience and support during our various trips to Buffalo and the cottage.

Without Laura Cerruti's trust, we would never have had the opportunity and the privilege to live so closely with Robert Duncan's mind and language for so long. And without Rachel Berchten's patience and dedication, we would never have gotten this far.

Michael Boughn and Victor Coleman

Introduction

Today I will allow myself whatever projects of what might come of this mining (You've to dig and come to see what I mean / where I, in that poem, almost wanted to point to that word "come"; because there is something about real thought that is as autonomous as ejaculation; and has the further mystery of the orgasmic if it have spirit). —Robert Duncan to Norman Holmes Pearson, July 2, 1960

The H.D. Book is one of the great "lost" texts in the history of American poetry. In 1959, when he began writing the book, Robert Duncan was already an accomplished and well-known poet, connected with the Berkeley renaissance and the San Francisco renaissance, as well as Black Mountain College and the Beat poets. He had published a number of important works—including *Heavenly City, Earthly City; Medieval Scenes; Fragments of a Disordered Devotion; Caesar's Gate; The Venice Poem;* and *Letters*—and was about to appear in Donald Allen's groundbreaking anthology, *The New American Poetry.* His mature work, however, had yet to come. *The H.D. Book* would be the alembic in which that work was gestated.

Composed from 1959 to 1964, various chapters of *The H.D. Book* appeared in little magazines between 1966 and 1985 (see appendix 2). It was never published as a completed book, however. Perhaps *lost* overstates the case, since it was never forgotten, but for some forty years, the only access to the text was photocopied assemblages of the various magazine publications, treasured—and sometimes passed from hand to hand—by Duncan's loyal readers. In 2001, we posted a transcription of the magazine publications on the internet; while this made the existing text available to those who did not have the photocopies, it did not include the many revisions Duncan had made over the years to his ever-changing text. A complete, edited version of the book remained elusive, the stuff of endless complaint and speculation.

Duncan began writing *The H.D. Book* when H.D.'s friend and literary executor, Norman Holmes Pearson, asked him for a short homage to present to H.D. on her birthday in 1960. Duncan had long admired H.D.'s work. As he tells the story in the opening chapter of *The H.D. Book,* her poem "Heat," read to him by a high school English teacher, was his first experience with the magic of poetry, an experience that led him into his life-long devotion to the art. What began as a simple homage quickly turned into an epic meditation and exploration of what Duncan felt were the hidden springs that fed the roots of modernism and the work of the poets and writers he took on as masters: H.D., Ezra Pound, D. H. Lawrence, William Carlos Williams, Edith Sitwell, among others.

Duncan's early work on *The H.D. Book* coincided with his correspondence with H.D., which lasted for about two years (not including an early letter from 1950), from July 1959 until her death in September 1961.[1] Much of the thinking that began to take shape in *The H.D. Book* was echoed in these letters. Their talk of myth and Hermetic philosophy mixed with and informed their talk of other poets. Both shared a history of connection to outsider or repressed spiritual knowledge and practices. H.D. had been raised in the Moravian Church of Count Zinzendorf and had traveled in circles during the 1920s that engaged with magic and various occult practices. Duncan had grown up in a family with connections to Theosophy and spiritualism. This, too, bound them together.

Both had also turned away from such practices. H.D. wrote in a letter (October 27, 1960) to Duncan how Yeats and his wife, Georgie, had invited her to Oxford—presumably to participate in some Rosicrucian ritual—but "something held me back." Duncan interpreted this as "the disinterest of a growing thing for possibilities outside its law, its real" (October 31, 1960) and proposed that Yeats (unlike H.D.) seemed not

Robert Duncan and H.D., circa 1960, at the time of their meeting.

Photo of Robert Duncan by Helen Adam, courtesy of the Poetry/Rare Book Collection, State University of New York at Buffalo. Reproduced by permission of the Jess Collins Trust. Photo of H.D. by Islay Lyon. Courtesy of the Beinecke Rare Book and Manuscript Library, Yale University.

to have known "the numinous woodland and shoreland, the events of god outside the ritual." Duncan, an inveterate anarchist, was always loyal to the sense of an inner law, often, if not always, in the face of an outer law, a demand by society to conform to its practices, even when they were the rituals of obscure cults. What Duncan (and H.D.) derived from that youthful experience was not a set of beliefs or practices dictated by churches or cults, but a deep sense of the possibility of other modes of thinking the world.[2] These modes of thinking, grounded in the freedom of the imagination, were fed by hidden or lost or excluded material, material deemed silly or superstitious or heretical by a society whose forms of life dictated a totalitarian "normality." For both poets, the matrix for poetry was in the spaces between those given forms. They shared a commitment not to the *this* or the *not this,* not to the *self* or the *other,* but to the fissure from which such forms arise into the conditioned contingencies of the given.

Such recognitions held important political implications for Duncan, whose anarchism arose from an Emersonian commitment to a further self,[3] a self whose moral perfectionism led Duncan toward the recovery of what had been lost or forgotten, as part of his commitment to the fullness of the world—what he called "What Is."[4] His sense of the world's wildness was linked to his resistance to the suffocating culture of bourgeois conformity he knew well from his youth in Bakersfield. His pacifism—which went hand in hand with his anarchism—grew out of that, as did his attention to what was not known, or not allowed to be known; among other things, say, the obscured sign of his homosexuality in the official constellations of the culture. The hidden from sight. The occult.

If there is a master word that haunts the thinking in *The H.D. Book,* it is, in just this sense, *occult.*[5] In, call it *Bakersfield,* modernity had realized itself in a social world of drastically constricted possibility.[6] Its collective imagination of its own "virtue" gave it permission to impose a strict sense of the "normal" (not to be confused with the "ordinary") on the community.[7] Part of that normality is a given world without depth, what some have called a *disenchanted world,* referring to the Enlightenment's legacy of equating the "real" with the material and the commensurable, a world restricted to measurable quantities.[8] It is also a world whose restricted vision gives rise to a counter-impulse of illicit traditions of cults with elaborate theologies and ritual practices.

"Occult" is a loaded word in such a culture. The illicit theologies and ritual practices are identified as "the Occult" and deemed ridiculous superstitions. But beyond the organized ritual cults lay all that is outside the "normal"; the worlds of hidden fact, hidden history, hidden mind, hidden body, as if all of us live on the edge of an occult reality that is really quite ordinary. Duncan's reading of Freud located Freud's unconscious as just such an occult reality. The traditional knowledges of Eros rooted in ancient human experience and banned and repressed by Judeo-Christian doctrine were also, for Duncan, part of that occult reality. One of the crucial issues for Duncan in this regard, an issue central to *The H.D. Book,* was the dismissal of the authority of both actual women and that range of human experience identified as the feminine, occulted beneath layers of patriarchal authority, and reflected in the repression of the knowledge of the leading role of women writers in the invention of modernism. At a time when anthologies and university reading lists contained almost entirely male authors, Duncan argued for the centrality of women in those ranks. He was a pioneer in singling out and tracking down the work of Edith Sitwell, Mary Butts, Djuna Barnes, Dorothy Richardson, Mina Loy, and Laura Riding and arguing for their importance as the hidden inventors of modernism.

H.D. was the main focus of this revelation. At the time Duncan began writing *The H.D. Book* in 1960, H.D. had been dismissed from the ranks of serious poets by the official arbiters of literary taste and had largely disappeared from public recognition. Until the 1950s her reputation had rested, however incorrectly and fragilely, on her ongoing identification as the quintessential "Imagist," a hangover from her work of some thirty-five years previously. Then Randall Jarrell and Dudley Fitts dismissed H.D.'s *Tribute to the Angels* (1945) and *The Flowering of the Rod* (1946) after their publication, characterizing her visionary poetry, as Duncan notes several times in *The H.D. Book,* as "silly." Following that, Karl Shapiro and Richard Wilbur dropped H.D. completely from the 1955 edition of Louis Untermeyer's influential anthology *Modern American and Modern British Poetry,* thus banishing even her Imagist poems from the halls of academically acceptable poetry. She became lost, hidden to the official world of poetry, her work out of print, her memory kept alive by a few dedicated readers.

The H.D. Book in one sense was an effort to undo that injustice, that occultation. A number of times Duncan humorously imagined himself as a knight coming to rescue H.D.'s honor with her scarf tied on his arm. But in the process of unpacking the hidden assumptions and judgments that led to Jarrell's condemnation of H.D. as "silly," Duncan found himself increasingly caught up in the revelation of further lost or hidden dimensions in the history of modernism. Duncan's recovery of an occulted H.D. began specifically with a poem, "Heat," which, like the scent of the madeleine in Proust's novel *À la recherche du temps perdu,* opened into a cosmos, as if it were a seed, and that cosmos, that world, was hidden in it. In his revisions to Chapter 1 of Book 1, Duncan eventually added an epigraph by A. E. Waite from his book on the Rosicrucians:

As regards the Lost Word, it is explained that the sun at autumn has lost its power and Nature is rendered mute, but the star of day at the spring tide resumes its vital force, and this is the recovery of the Word, when

Nature with all her voices, speaks and sings, even as the Sons of God shouted for joy in the perfect morning of the cosmos.

This invocation of the "lost word" marked Duncan's entrance into a world of hidden things—lost words—coming to light, the light of a recovered Word, a perfect morning:[9] the hidden memory of Miss Keough's classroom, the hidden (esoteric) writing presented by the teacher to the few students worthy of it, the hidden intensities of feeling brought to mind by the poem, the hidden worlds of thought behind the stultifying bourgeois superficialities of Bakersfield, and the hidden meaning of "image" behind it all. "The poem had a message, hidden to me then," Duncan wrote, "that I felt but could not translate, an unconscious alliance that made for something more than a sensual response. . . . More than sensation then, more than impression, gave force to the image. It was not only a vivid representation of sensory data but an evocation of depth" (1.1). The depth of the world was a hidden thing that Duncan's meditation on "image" and "imagism" brought forth. "There is a crucial difference between the doctrine of the Image where Poetry itself is taken to be a primary ground of experience and meaning in life, and the image which is taken as a fashion in the literary world" (1.1). This thinking then led him to a tradition that goes back to Renaissance and medieval Hermeticism, the Troubadours and the *trobar clus,* Hellenistic neo-Platonism, Gnosticism, and Arabic angelology, in which Images (and the Imagination which is their ground) mediate between another world and this, open this world to hidden powers.

Occult histories, occult teachings, occult memories, occult mind, occult inheritances, occult language, and above all, occult meanings—Robert Duncan unfolded them all in *The H.D. Book* in a kind of proliferating, symphonic performance of, as he puts it in his letter of July 2, 1960, to Norman Holmes Pearson, thinking as orgasm, thinking as an explosive release linked to Eros, rather than the traditional notion of a disciplined exposition, Logos, with footnotes and citations. The importance of *hiddenness* itself unfolded along with them, orchestrated into a weave of shadow and light—in corners and at the far edges of the mind where a certain kind of light or enlightenment cannot, or at least will not, reach, playing itself out in shadows dancing. What is hidden is constantly brought into the light of the language of the poet, a frail light, finite, playing over the face of what is hidden, bringing it to attention. That is, after all, the poet's craft—to bring what is hidden to our attention while honoring its hiddenness.

At the heart of this concern with the occult was Duncan's quest for, as he puts it, a poetics. Duncan was pushing his sense of "a poetics" far beyond a concern with literary criticism and literary theory. The *Oxford English Dictionary* has *poetic* as "the branch of knowledge that deals with the techniques of poetry." This notion of knowledge and technique is closer to Duncan's intent, but even here knowledge must be understood in the fullness of its etymon, *gna,* the *gna* that leads to gnosis and knowing, as having to do with coming into the recognition of what is beyond the Logos, what the Logos necessarily excludes, leaves hidden. Technique follows from that. Allen Ginsberg's mantra (via Chogyam Trungpa)—"first thought best thought"—resonates here. Duncan was uninterested in Ginsberg's temporal focus—he worked, reworked, and then revised his reworkings, some might say obsessively, always pushing toward a more finely honed articulation. But the *first* remained shining through all that. For Duncan it was more specifically a question of opening to the occult dwelling in the first, of responding to what is hidden in every moment in order to reveal the plenum of the world, both what is visible and what informs that visibility. If Ginsberg found that in the spontaneous, the unedited, Duncan found it in the immersion of mind in the process of creative release—thinking as orgasm.

In this sense, knowledge and technique are inextricably wed to vision as it extends beyond the visible, the materially commensurable to, say, the visionary. Duncan's sense of a poetics was rooted in the recognition that what is seen is always already informed, full of form that determines what is seen and how it is seen, even though the forms may remain hidden. His proposal here had to do with the claim that arose from the Enlightenment's argument with the *ancien régime* that the knowable is limited to the commensurable, and that the incommensurable is what came to be called "superstition." Only in the late eigh-

teenth century did "superstition" move from a sense of idolatrous reli-
gious practice to a sense of any "irrational" belief (including religion).
This grounding of knowledge in the material and rational was part of
a vision of the cosmos as matter in motion bound by laws, a vision that
went on to determine the culture of the West in modernity. Duncan's
quest for a poetics was a quest to extend his vision beyond those limits
to include all that such a culture excluded or hid from itself, as well as
what those selves who were formed in such a culture were blind to.

In Book 1 of *The H.D. Book,* Duncan pursued this opening through
its multiple implications, sketching out the great themes that run
through the book by tracing them in H.D.'s work: hidden or lost tradi-
tions of thinking about Eros, hidden or lost modes of conceiving of
time and space, hidden or lost ways of representing the self or person,
hidden or lost understandings of the source and nature of form, and
finally the profound sense of exile that is the lot of the poet who under-
takes to recognize and recover these lost things. Duncan was led on in
these inquiries by his ongoing argument that the dismissal and occulta-
tion of H.D. arose from the unexamined belief, in fact the delusion,
that the terms of Realism, as an aesthetic doctrine grounded in and
grounding the culture of modernity, were "real," where "real" marks a
reduced and utterly measurable world.

Duncan argued for an expanded sense of the "real": "The crux for
the poet is to make real what is only real in a heightened sense. Call it
his personal feeling, or the communal reality, it exists only in its dance,
only to its dancers" (1.6). Again and again, Duncan comes back to
Randall Jarrell's judgment that H.D.'s great visionary poems of World
War II, written in London during the Blitz, were "silly." In what came
to be known as her war trilogy, H.D. presented the violence of the
war as rooted not in politics or economics, but in a cosmic spiritual
war. The forces of light and darkness, life and death, battled it out over
London in H.D.'s poems, resembling the powers described in ancient
Gnostic gospels. Gods played out eternal struggles. Angels came and
went bearing messages of hope. Old narratives of death and resurrec-
tion reasserted themselves in mundane events. And through it all, the
poet asserted the experienced reality of the vision, identifying herself
with the prophet John of the Book of Revelations, and his simple dec-

laration: "I, John, testify." It was this testimony that Jarrell dismissed as "silly." Duncan located that word in its etymological roots and used that to reveal the shallowness of Jarrell's philosophical-cultural grounding. Jarrell became in that sense, along with his cohort, representative of modernity's arrogant superficiality, its insistence that only the visible, not the visionary, is *real*.

In Book 1 of *The H.D. Book,* these themes are explicated in the form of digressive essays which identify what Duncan calls the stars and their potential patterns, a metaphor he develops in Book 2, through which hidden forms will emerge in the sky, the constellations of the mind, forms that will bind Tiamat, the dragon of chaos. H.D., Pound, and Williams, that marvelous configuration of poets, that constellation of stars, who led Duncan into the permissions of poetry, are at the heart of it. Around them circulate the lights of others—Freud, Joyce, Arnaut, Blavatsky, Lawrence, Yeats, Dante, Frazer, Stein, Mead, Harrison, Nietzsche, Browning, Avicenna, Malraux, Plutarch, Plato, Iamblichus, Corbin, Apuleius . . . the circle keeps expanding in its complexities as Duncan tracks the relationships that defined the emergence of this particular possibility of poetry not to "describe" the world, but to ground it in "the dissolving of boundaries of time" (1.6), to rouse the form and content of the world "as the ritual devotee seeks to arouse the content and form of the god" (2.4).

In Book 2 Duncan left the essay behind and moved to a new form (and the idea of form is central here), the day book. The day book reintroduced time as an element of form, locating thinking in its temporal fragility—its finitude—even as it subverted the temporal by repeatedly returning to the same issues from different angles. This repetition, which some have criticized as if it were a question of "style," was an expression of Duncan's growing sense of the open-ended nature of his undertaking as his quest for a poetics began to absorb the lessons of his first essays into what he called the *Opus.* To return again and again was his method. With each return, new facets of meaning were revealed, new depths of thought plumbed. His understanding of *palimpsest* was crucial here. In the opening of Chapter 7, which is dated with multiple dates (October 8, 1964, and March 20, 1961) in his last revision, he wrote:

I seek now in working upon the later draft of the book not to correct the original but to live again in its form and content, leaving in successive layers record of reformations and digressions as they come to me. The form realized then is not to be a design immediately striking, like those housing developments and landscapings that rise where disorderly areas of a city have been cleared away, but it may be like an old city—Freud's picture of Rome upon Rome—in which in the earliest remains, in the diary of March 10th to March 15th, March 20th to March 29th, then May 25th of 1961: later additions may appear, anachronistically like the Gaudi restorations in the gothic cathedral of Palma or the Casa Guell's art-nouveau romanticism in the midst of old buildings, where we are aware of periods of creative activity and conservative inertia. (2.7)

These accretions are revelatory. Each passage opens the work to the further emergence of still-hidden form and content. There is no singular "meaning" to be recovered, only the potentiality for further meaning to be encountered. Meaning is not a sum to be arrived at, but an ongoing engagement unfolding in the poet's language. As Emerson, anticipating Duncan by some 125 years, pointed out in the address to the Harvard Divinity School that got him banned from speaking at the university for thirty years, "Men have come to speak of the revelation as somewhat long ago given and done," going on to argue that like the "refulgent spring" (which is of the mind as the mind is of the world) with which he opens the address, only a continually renewed opening to the "moral sentiment," a commitment to knowing rather than knowledge, can keep the revelation alive and full of meaning.[10]

Book 2, then, became an enactment of the dynamics discussed in Book 1, or more accurately, the discussions of Book 1, the essays, were converted into the form of their contents, form that goes on to continually recast and renew the contents, or perhaps to resituate the contents as emerging form.[11] Duncan's analysis of Roheim's Freudian study of the ritual practices of the Aranda in Book 1 became an opening into an actual ritual invocation of the forms and powers hidden within Duncan's thinking of H.D., forms and powers that day by day and moment by moment erupted into the poet's consciousness, emerged from his language.

Dream became increasingly important as a channel for hidden information, unconscious content, occult meaning, roiling to the surface of thought, as in the Sally Rand episode that runs through Chapter 8. Emerging from sleep, Duncan jotted down the remnants of a dream of which he remembered only an image—caressing H.D.'s naked back—and the words SALLY RAND, words that left him feeling uneasy, even repulsed. Sally Rand, the name of a notorious fan dancer, initially seemed to offer Duncan nothing. But working and reworking the material, the words began to yield. What they yielded was a field of thinking in which each moment bloomed with a new significance, a new form erupting from the language that had unknowingly contained it. It was a masterful performance of the very ritual engagement Duncan had written about in Book 1.

When Duncan began *The H.D. Book,* much of the literary history that he recovered had been lost to the official protectors of Literature. His concern, especially with the work of the women who were so central to high modernism, was unprecedented. The writing of Edith Sitwell, Laura Riding, Djuna Barnes, Mary Butts, and Dorothy Richardson had largely disappeared into the mists of time, ignored by the almost entirely male cohort of professors who collected anthologies and wrote literary histories, patrolling the boundaries of Literature. That history was part of the occult content he sought to bring to light. And while his discussions of the work of Pound and Williams, of Yeats and Eliot and Lawrence were a significant contribution to the criticism of modernism, his focus was not on the literary, but again on those aspects of the work and its context that were considered out of bounds by the strict moralisms of the New Criticism.

The H.D. Book is not fundamentally a work of literary criticism or literary history. Nor is it, as some have proposed, an attempt to articulate a literary theory. In fact the book is deeply anti-literary in just about every way possible. In the same vein, although it delves into the thinking of various esoteric cults including Theosophy, Hermeticism, Rosicrucianism, neo-Platonism, Gnosticism, and psychoanalysis, it is neither a Theosophical nor a Hermetic nor a psychoanalytic text. Duncan's concern throughout was to create a space, an opening, into which the hidden, the occult, could emerge. Long before the wave of postwar European philosophies entered the awareness of North American academics, Duncan was already exploring the significant moves they were to make to reopen the world to the multiple realities foreclosed by modernity's singular Real. The indeterminacy of meaning, readerly texts, the diversity and multiplicity of the truths of the world, the fluid boundaries of "time" and "space," the fictionality of the subject, all these openings into those dimensions of the world rendered occult by the disciplinary institutions of modernity, were the playgrounds of his thinking.

His goal there was straightforward—to discover a poetics. For Duncan, the idea that poetry could arise from a theory—be it a theory of linguistic production, a theory of economic production, or a theory of psychic production—was not only ridiculous, it was profoundly damaging to the spirit of poetry. Poetry for Duncan was always inextricably implicated with What Is, his designation of the world's plenum. And that plenum was fully determined at any given moment only with the admission of what was outlawed, repressed, excluded, ignored— what was hidden. This is the occult reality that defines the unfolding engagement of *The H.D. Book*. No theory can approach that. Instead, a poet, a maker, must find/forge a methodology that allows What Is to emerge, to find forms. Just as there is no singular Truth that can be theorized, there is no singular methodology. Each poet must find her/ his own way into that process.

As he pursued this quest through the writing of *The H.D. Book*, Duncan published *The Opening of the Field* (1960) and began to compose what many feel are his mature works—*Roots and Branches* (1964) and *Bending the Bow* (1968). Out of impatience with the distractions of the competitiveness and careerism that came to the fore in "the poetry scene" in the 1970s, Duncan vowed not to publish for 15 years, even as he continued to work on his final masterpieces. In 1984 he finally published *Groundwork—Before the War,* but died before its companion volume, *Groundwork—In the Dark* made it into print in 1987. All of this work springs from the remarkable quest for a poetics recorded in *The H.D. Book*. "The poet and the reader," Duncan wrote, "who if he is intent in reading becomes a new poet of the poem, come to write or to read in order to participate through the work in a consciousness that moves freely in time and space and can entertain reality upon reality" (1.6). *The H.D. Book* is a unique record of such a journey.

•

We began this editorial project with a firm belief that Robert Duncan wanted *The H.D. Book* to be made into a book. As open-ended as his compositional method was—constantly writing and rewriting and then rewriting again—his goal was always clear: publication. "I build even as I prepare the book for the publisher at last," he wrote in Book 2, Chapter 7, "living once more as I copy, and take over wherever I see a new possibility in the work." Circumstances conspired against him and he never got to see *The H.D. Book* published, but he left us, his editors, with a clear goal. We wanted to make the book that Robert Duncan wanted to make, at least as far as that is possible. That is the principle that has guided this undertaking.

It was not always easy. The initial occasion for the book, the invitation from Norman Holmes Pearson in 1960 to write a little piece on H.D. for her birthday, almost immediately began unfolding into something much larger. Duncan never settled on a definitive sense of the final form of the book. Even as he typed up a version for publication, he was still thinking of some further form—another three chapters for Book 1, a twelfth for Book 2. The process of composition was a process of allowing form to arise, to make itself evident in the act of creation. So in one sense it could never finally be settled.

Robert Duncan was an accretive writer, and *The H.D. Book* was a constantly evolving entity. He began with notes on scraps and pieces of paper, few of which survive, although he refers to them in correspondence with Pearson as a method for avoiding a totalizing relation to his materials. He rewrote those notes into notebooks, then rewrote that again with a typewriter, revised in hand on the manuscript, then rewrote again with the typewriter. With each passage the text expanded and changed. Sometimes the changes were minor punctuation issues, sometimes they had to do with diction, often they were substantive textual additions. It was a process that coincided with his understanding of the palimpsest as he articulated it in Book 1, Chapter 4, mind as palimpsest. As with the mind, nothing is ever lost. One layer forms

The H.D. Book

Part I

Beginnings

Chapters 1-6

Robert Duncan

Black Sparrow Press   Los Angeles   1971

Duncan's typed title page for the aborted
Black Sparrow edition.

Acknowledgement is made to Aion, Caterpillar,
Coyote's Journal, Stony Brook, and Tri-Quarterly
where sections of this book previously
appeared.

Black Sparrow Press
P.O. Box 25603
Los Angeles, California
90025

SBN 87685-029-8 (paper)
SBN 87685-030-1 (signed cloth ed.)

Duncan's typed copyright page for the aborted
Black Sparrow edition.

on top of another, but the lower continues to make itself felt, and each layer, as it changes from what is before and after, exists in a complex web of modulated meanings.

In addition to the published versions, multiple copies exist of each chapter of *The H.D. Book,* none of which is dated. In the case of some chapters like Book 1, Chapter 6, up to seven copies exist in various forms. Some are done on different typewriters, some are carbon copies, some are photocopies of carbon copies, some are whole stand-alone copies of individual chapters, some are partial copies, some are included in manuscripts of the entire Book 1. Changes exist on almost all of them.

For Book 1, Chapters 1–5, the problem of dating was solved by circumstance. In 1971, after Duncan had tried and failed to get the book published by Scribner's and others, John Martin of Black Sparrow Press proposed to do it. By that time all of Book 1 and Chapters 1–5 of Book 2 had been published in various little magazines. The copyedited typescripts from which the magazine versions were set are easily identifiable in Duncan's papers (though even some of these contain holograph corrections that were made after publication). Based on the deal with Martin, Duncan proceeded to retype the entire book. Most of those manuscripts, all done on the same typewriter in the same run, are also identifiable. After retyping them, Duncan then edited them by hand. Here it gets a little tricky. He went completely through Book 1 making changes by hand. He also apparently made some changes in Book 2 as well. There Chapters 4, 5, and 6 show significant changes; 1, 2, and 3 have minor changes; and Chapters 7–11 have almost no changes. Many of the changes appear to have been done at different times.

Duncan then began to type Book 1 yet again. His goal this time through was to produce a typescript that would serve as the typeset copy for the Black Sparrow edition. It has a very particular look. It is typed on an IBM Selectric using an elite typeface so that he could make actual italics. It is also done on typesetting paper, unlike anything else in the files. Once again, though, he added significant material as he worked through the text. This was particularly so in Chapter 1, the earliest work in the book, where he added several pages of text, mostly having to do with developing his thinking about the "image" and

H.D.'s identity as "Imagist." The relation with John Martin, however, soured when Duncan was working on Chapter 5, and the publication deal fell through. Duncan finished retyping more than half of Chapter 5 before dropping the project. He apparently continued to make small changes to existing copies of the manuscript after that. He also apparently skipped ahead to retype/rewrite parts of Book 2, Chapter 5 in the same format with the same Selectric typewriter.

So, for Book 1, Chapters 1 to halfway through 5, we have Duncan's final revisions before what he thought was going to be publication, including a typeset typescript of the title page and the copyright page. For Chapter 6 we have the stage before that—a retyped manuscript with many holograph revisions on different manuscripts. The same typescript done on the same typewriter exists for the rest of the chapters, although there are fewer holograph revisions, with the exceptions of Book 2, Chapters 4, 5, and 6. There are also, as noted, a few diction, punctuation, and grammatical changes in Chapters 1–3, and almost none in Chapters 7–11.

Our goal was to arrive at a manuscript that was as close as possible to the state it was in when Duncan stopped working on it. Our procedure was to begin with the magazine publication as the basic copy text for all chapters, knowing that Duncan had prepared those early texts, then to interpolate *all* changes that were made after that on all available manuscripts. Duncan seems to have been somewhat indiscriminate about which pieces of paper he made his changes on. Since there were in most cases multiple copies of each chapter in a file, all undated, there's no way to identify when the changes were made. If it's clear that the changes were made after the magazine publication, we included them regardless of which manuscript they were on. If there was a conflict, we tried to identify the last change by looking at the process of Duncan's thought, and finally by applying the rule, "in the last resort go for the change that is most condensed and elegant," since that was his general mode of revision.

Only once did we have to actually collate two different manuscripts. In Book 2, Chapter 5 there are four separate manuscript versions that include three separate versions of the beginning of part 2, done on three different typewriters. Manuscript A is from the primary typescript for

*

We may see the deeper significance of the role translation has had for Pound as a poetic task, when we think of how in psychoanalysis dreams and daily life have begun to appear as a language we must learn to read in order to translate something we have always to say that we do not know yet to hear. "The dream-thoughts," Freud writes, "and the dream-content are presented to us like two versions of the same subject-matter in two different languages." As, too, we see the importance of the ideogram for Pound, for it is his route towards--"as it were a pictographic script"--the condensare of the dream.

II

Poems are events of Poetry, of our consciousness of making a universe of feeling in language. Celebrating, is it? or praying for? Of singing, of dancing, What Is.

*

As our concept of What Is changes, our concept of form changes, for our experience of form is our experience of What Is. As I begin to see, in terms of William James's pluralistic reality, a sense of the total world emerging from many kinds of apprehension, and, in terms of Freud's exploration of one kind of psychosexual reality with its sense of the divine will as Eros and Thanatos, the three things Dante named as worthiest concerns in the poem--"safety, love, and virtue"--and their three appropriate forces--"prowess in arms, the fire of love, and the direction of the will", whatever their meaning in the thirteenth century and in Dante's life, take on new and troubled meanings when they are taken as primaries in our own lives. Dante understood "safety" as having to do not with the interests of his city Florence primarily but with the good of humanity as a whole, and so, he took the Emperor as against the city, and he was condemned to death, a traitor, in Florence. As today, for the sake of "safety" our own "prowess of arms" would have to be given, were we to take Dante's

A page (173) from Book 2, Chapter 5
(Manuscript C) showing Duncan's early wording.

174

politics, to the union of all nations, against the contention
of those who govern the United States in the name of private
enterprise against communal goods and who are engaged in a
disastrous struggle for domination against their counterparts
in Russia and China. We live today, as Dante lived in the
13th century and in Florence, in a crisis of just these three
worthiest subjects that must have their definition not in our
personal interests or we find ourselves at war with the commune,
not in our national interests, or we find ourselves at war
with other nations, but in our human interests, our understanding
of the universal term that is Man. "Of all civilizations,"
Dante argues in De Monarchia, not of Florence or of Rome alone.
The goal of politics he discerns is "the realizing of all the
potentialities of the human mind." "And this demands the
harmonious development and co-operation of the several members
of the universal body politic."

  *

  All thru the body of our nation, where men are fighting
for the realization of all the potentialities of the human
mind, against exploitation and discrimination, for the
potentialities that have been denied ~~negroes~~ _blacks_ and for our own
potentialities of community with ~~negroes~~ _blacks_, of brotherhood,
companionship in work, and marriage, that have been denied,
they are fighting, we are fighting, for our true "safety" and
have that "prowess of arms" that poets would praise. "I too,"
Whitman answers the Phantom, genius of poets of old, who
challenges him that he does not sing the theme of War:

> I too haughty Shade also sing war, and a longer and
>   greater one than any,
> Waged in my book with varying fortune, with flight,
>   advance and retreat, victory deferr'd and wavering,
> ....the field the world,
> For life and death, for the Body and for the eternal Soul

  *

  Living in the warp of a capitalistic oligarchy, we begin
to realize that the potentialities of human mind lie hidden

A page (174) from Book 2, Chapter 5
(Manuscript C) showing Duncan's holograph revisions.

Book 2, Chapters 1–4 and into Chapter 5, done on the same type-writer with the Courier face that Duncan usually used. It has the large decorative chapter number done in Duncan's hand that the rest of the typescript has for each chapter. In the upper right hand corner is the identifier, "II-5-1" (for Book 2, Chapter 5, page 1) with subsequent page numbers following after that. At "II-5-16" Duncan begins using a new typewriter, double-spaced in a new typeface. This is manuscript B, which goes through "II-5-19," then stops. II-5-19 contains the opening paragraphs of part 2 of Chapter 5. A new manuscript follows, done on the same typewriter as Manuscript A, but with the simple page number in the upper left hand corner beginning at "173," suggesting it was part of a different retyping of the entire book paginated from the beginning of Book 2. This is Manuscript C. It too begins at the opening of part 2 (marked with the roman numeral II and without the immediate sub-division in our final version). There is a further one-page manuscript done on the typewriter and typesetting paper and in the style of the first five chapters of Book 1 that Duncan did for Black Sparrow. This is Manuscript D (which begins the section with a roman numeral I). Each of these texts differs significantly from the others.

Our analysis is that manuscripts A and B were done at the same time. They are identical to the magazine publication of part 1 and are continuous. Why Duncan changed machines in the middle of retyping the manuscript is a mystery. Perhaps he had a different machine at the house in Stinson Beach north of San Francisco where he and his partner, Jess Collins, often stayed (he sometimes refers to hearing the sea as he writes) and worked on the manuscript during a stay there. In any case, there are holograph changes to the manuscript that post-date magazine publication. In the first paragraph of the chapter, "usurious standards" (which appears in the magazine version) is changed to "usurious sys-tem." Part 2 seems to have been started later and went through several versions after it was published as a fragment in 1975. Manuscripts B, C, and D all revise the opening paragraph, reducing it from 110 words as it appeared in *Stony Brook,* to 27 (B), 28 (C), and 30 (D). The moves are all toward a more concise and elegant statement. Similar changes were made in the second paragraph. The *Stony Brook* publication reads at one point: "As I begin to see in terms of William James's pluralistic proposition of reality." B reads " . . . William James's pluralistic projection of realms of reality." C and D both have " . . . William James's pluralistic reality." Given Duncan's push toward concision and elegance, C and D would seem to be the later versions, a judgment upheld by other evidence.

The real problem comes up in the third paragraph, which begins, "All through the body of our nation. . . . " In his discussion of Dante's concept of "Prowess," Manuscript C is rewritten with reference to the then current civil rights and black power movements. Duncan had originally typed "where men are fighting for the realization of all the potentialities of the human mind, against exploitation and discrimination, for the potentialities that have been denied negroes and for our own potentialities of community with negroes, of brotherhood . . . "; he then crossed out "negroes" in both places and wrote in "blacks" by hand. In Manuscript D he has further changed the text to read, " . . . against exploitation and discrimination, for the potentialities that have been denied blacks, women, xicanos—but we are more and more aware of how many subservient groups have been defined by the establishment of society based on the supremacy of[.]" He breaks off there, unable to follow through with that particular rhetoric.

Clearly Manuscript D is the last version of the opening of part 2 of Chapter 5. All the changes indicate that, as does the appearance of the text, which was evidently done at the same time as the typeset version of Book 1, Chapters 1–5. The problem is that the text is incomplete, and Duncan was apparently uncomfortable with where the passage was going. In this case, we have chosen to integrate the two latest manuscripts (C and D), recognizing the direction of Duncan's thought, while trying to maintain textual continuity. Our edited version reads: "against exploitation and discrimination, for the potentialities that have been denied blacks, women, xicanos, and for our own potentialities of community, of brotherhood."

Other than that, our only changes have been formal. In general we have followed and made consistent Duncan's predominant styles in spelling and punctuation and in formatting of text. Duncan's early

March 14, Tuesday, 1961 [1963]

[*section one* appeared in *STONY BROOK* 3/4, 1969, pp 336-347]

I

    Poems are events of Poetry, of our consciousness of *making* a universe
of feeling and thought in language. Celebrating, is it? or praying
for? Of singing, of dancing, What Is.

    *

    As our concept of What Is changes, our concept of form changes, for
our experience of form *is* our experience of What Is. As I begin to see,
in terms of William James's pluralistic reality, a sense of the total
world emerging from many kinds of apprehension, and, in terms of Freud's
exploration of one kind of psychosexual reality with its sense of the
divine will as Eros and Thanatos, the three things Dante named as the
worthiest concerns in the poem--*safety, love,* and *virtue*--and their
three appropriate means--*prowess in arms, the fire of love,* and *the di-
rection of the will*--whatever their meaning in the thirteenth century
and in Dante's universe, take on new and troubled meanings when they are
taken as primaries in the creation of our own world. Dante understood
safety as having to do not with the interests of his city Florence pri-
marily but with the good of humanity as a whole, and so he took the
cause of the Emperor and the government of the Empire as even against
the party of the city, and he was condemned to death, a traitor, in
Florence. As today, for the sake of the safety of humanity our own
prowess of arms would have to be given, were we to take Dante's sense
of true government, to the union of all nations, against the contention
of those who direct the United States in the name of private enterprise
against communal goods and who are engaged in a disastrous struggle for
domination against their counterparts in Russia and China. We live
today, as Dante lived in the 13th century and in Florence, in a crisis
of just these three worthiest subjects of the poem that must have their
definition not in our personal interests, or we find ourselves at war
with our human commonality, not in our national interests, or we find
ourselves at war with other nations, but in our human interests, our
understanding of the universal term that is Man, the term not of a given
reality but of a creation in process. "Of all civilizations," Dante
argues in *De Monarchia*, not of the city of Florence, not of Rome, nor
even of Christendom alone. The goal of the governing art he discerns is
"the realizing of all the potentialities of the human mind." "And this
demands the harmonious development and co-operation of the several mem-
bers of the universal body politic." It is a body that extends not only
thruout the global space of Man but thruout the time of Man.

    All thru the body of our nation, where men are fighting for the real-
ization of all the potentialities of the human mind, against exploita-
tion and discrimination, for the potentialities that have been denied
blacks, women, xicanos--but we are more and more aware of how many sub-
servient groups have been defined in the establishment of society based
on the supremacy of

*A page from Book 2, Chapter 5 (Manuscript D) showing Duncan's
revisions to the paragraph beginning "All thru" compared to
Manuscript C. Note that this version is typed on typesetting paper.*

Photo courtesy of the Poetry/Rare Book Collection, State University of New York
at Buffalo. Reproduced by permission of the Jess Collins Trust.

manuscript italicized all quotations. He changed that in his version for Black Sparrow, and where he did not complete those changes, we did, although quotations in languages other than English are in italics. We have also regularized capitalizations and spellings that were not important to Duncan's style: neo-Platonist for neo-platonist, Gnostic for gnostic, etc. Titles of works are given in their standard bibliographic form, using italics or quotation marks as appropriate. When *Cantos* refers to Pound's book, we have italicized it; when it refers to individual poems, we have followed Duncan and not italicized it. Duncan, who coined the term "The War Trilogy" to refer to the three long poems of H.D.'s World War II epic (*The Walls Do Not Fall, Tribute to the Angels,* and *The Flowering of the Rod*), sometimes italicized it, and sometimes did not. We have kept the capitalization, but eliminated the italics throughout. Occasional misspellings and typos have been corrected.

Three other issues require some explanation. The first has to do with a parallel text derived from *The H.D. Book.* In 1960, Duncan proposed to Cid Corman to excerpt sections of Book 2 for publication in *Origin.* Duncan sent Corman an initial selection in January 1961, which Corman edited and sent back to Duncan. Duncan then continued to work on it, typing and retyping, adding and deleting selections, and even expanding and rewriting passages. The result was published in 1963 in *Origin* 10 (Second Series) as *The Little Day Book.* Although closely related to *The H.D. Book, The Little Day Book* is a separate text. There is no indication that Duncan ever envisioned them being published together, and we have elected not to include it in this edition.

The second issue has to do with Book 3, Duncan's reading of *Helen in Egypt.* All that exists is a notebook filled with initial observations made during 1961. It is difficult to say what Book 3 would eventually have looked like. Duncan was literally only in the first stages of working on it, and given the transformations that took place to the other two books, there's no doubt that the early notebook version would have become something radically different. For this reason, we have included it as an appendix rather than as a part of the body of the main book.

The third issue is the question of whether or not to provide an apparatus to locate and explain Duncan's references. Deeply learned

Hilda Doolittle

Sept. 10, 1886 born in Bethlehem, Pa.
daughter of Charles L. Doolittle and his second wife
Helen Eugenia Wolle

1895 when she was nine Doolittles moved to
Philadelphia; her father became Director of the
Flower Observatory.
educated at Gordon School, Friends' Central School,
and Bryn Mawr College, leaving in her sophomore
year because of ill health.

1911 went to Europe, expecting to stay for the summer.

1912 spring — Pound, H.D. Aldington agree on principles
given in Retrospect

1913 first poems printed in POETRY magazine
married Richard Aldington
editor of the Egoist, succeeding Aldington

1914   The Egoist

1915

1916 Sea Garden   Aldington enters war at 24

1917 D.H. Lawrence

1918

1919 moved to Berkshire (Aldington)

voice

But hysteria is the very prophetic
of Cassandra; cries woe and ruin of
cities, and ravens for what it most
fears. War-hysteria, love-hysteria.

maged and rayed with the word "beautiful"

In areas of science that most avoided
such thought, even the psychoanalytic
subconscious of Freud much less the
subliminal self of Meyers — men,
as if they did not know what they
were doing, invoked the great
hysterical possibility of our time —
the increase of pressures and
explosion in the atom bomb, the
radioactive aftermath that would
riot in the chromosomic structure of man,
that most would increase to a new
power the meaning of this hysteric
thing, this suffering in the womb.
Oppenheimer and Fermi, Teller
and Vannevar Bush enact two
stages of one operation: in the first

A page spread from Duncan's notebook containing his
preliminary notes for Book 3.

he knows what does but his judgment of the consequences is perverted.

The hysteric cannot see the consequences to which he contributes — he knows not what he does. ~~Yet~~ In the second, the hysteric is possessed by the sight of what he ~~does~~ and his greatest enemy is the ~~sight~~ at all of the consequences to which he contributes. Or they take on the lens of fate, and all that leads away from those consequences appears malicious and hysterical.

•

Wherever an "enemy appears" as now in the United States an enemy has appeared in Russia and even in the Castro regime in Cuba; or as in Russia an enemy has appeared in the United States, an hysterical crisis impends. All things about us become organized and useful to our hidden "mate" or "enemy" or "holocaust"; life takes on tendency.

•

"hist — enough — " Achilles says.
"I was afraid of evil,

and widely read, often in texts that are off the beaten path for most people, Duncan moved freely from the pre-Socratics to Renaissance Hermeticists to quantum physicists, from Medieval Church polemicists to modern poetic polemicists to nineteenth-century spiritualists. He was at home among them all and carried on a conversation with them all. Some readers have suggested that this material needs to be identified and explained in order to help the "uninitiated" into the text. We have opted not to do so for a couple of reasons. We feel strongly that the book Robert Duncan wanted was one designed to be read without the interruption of footnotes and various other scholarly apparatuses. Duncan was clear that he was not a literary scholar, nor was he trying to produce a work of literary scholarship. "For I am not a literary scholar nor an historian, not a psychologist, a professor of comparative religions nor an occultist," he wrote in *The H.D. Book* (2.4). "I am a student of, I am searching out, a poetics."

But beyond that is the question of whether annotating the references is even a reasonable undertaking. Duncan struggled with the idea that he might be seen as making H.D. salable in the literary marketplace. Did engaging her occultation and defending her against the misunderstandings of the professors mean he was trying to facilitate her into some literary celebrity? Some commodification? That was the last thing he wanted to do. His "rescue" mission was first of all a quest for a poetics. As a corollary to that, it was an attempt to reclaim from obscurity the world he shared with H.D. This quest was grounded in a conversation, not in assertions and truths about the "real." If it began as a conversation between H.D. and Robert Duncan, that *between* opened into a vast exchange of other voices, other minds.

A conversation is a particular kind of event. The central responsiveness—the back and forth—is also always, in a true conversation, a *further,* an opening beyond. Duncan's and H.D.'s conversation opens into further conversations with Dante, Avicenna, Freud, Arnaut, Browning, Iamblichus—the company keeps expanding, opening the conversation to further and further marvels of mind. Duncan's so-called references in *The H.D. Book* mark the expansive contours of this marvelous conversation. The presence of the names is itself an opening and an invitation to each reader to join in. Finally, though, the entrance into the conversation cannot be given. The Given is, in this sense, the problem. It must, as Arakawa and Madeleine Gins have so eloquently argued, be Taken.[12] *The H.D. Book* opens the door and points toward the world of companions that waits. All the reader has to do is take up the invitation and join in.

Michael Boughn
Victor Coleman

NOTES

1. H.D. / Robert Duncan, *A Great Admiration: Correspondence 1950–1961,* ed. Robert J. Bertholf (Venice, Calif.: The Lapis Press, 1992).

2. This is akin to Henry Corbin's description of the Active Imagination in the work of Ibn 'Arabi as an "organ of prophetic inspiration which perceives, and at the same time confers existence upon a reality of its own, whereas for us it secretes only 'imaginings.'" *Creative Imagination in the Sufism of Bin 'Arabia,* trans. Ralph Manheim, *Bollingen* Series XCI (Princeton: Princeton University Press, 1969), p. 88.

3. "This one fact the world hates, that the soul becomes . . . ." Ralph Waldo Emerson, "Self Reliance," in *Essays and Lectures* (New York: Library of America, 1983), p. 271.

4. "Moral perfectionism challenges ideas of moral motivation, showing (against Kant's law that counters inclination, and against utilitarianism's calculation of benefits) the possibility of my access to experience which gives to my desire for the attaining of a self that is mine to become, the power to act on behalf of an attainable world I can actually desire." Stanley Cavell, *Cities of Words: Pedagogical Letters on a Register of the Moral Life* (Cambridge: Harvard University Press, 2004), p. 33. See especially chapters 1 and 2 on Emerson and George Cukor's *The Philadelphia Story* for more on perfectionism.

5. "I want to compose a poetry with the meaning entirely occult, that is— with the meaning contained not as a jewel is contained in a box but as the inside of a box is contained in a box." From Notebook 5 at Berkeley. This is a transcription from a letter to James Broughton.

6. "The agreement of reasonable men was to quarantine the fever of thought." Robert Duncan, "Ideas of the Meaning of Form," in *Fictive Certainties* (New York: New Directions, 1985), p. 99.

7. "Normal" in this sense is a demand for what Emerson calls conformity,

the abrogation of Self. "Ordinary" refers, as Stanley Cavell has it, to "the missable, the unobserved, what we would call the uncounted, taken not as given but for granted." *Cities of Words,* p. 332. This "ordinary" is identical with Duncan's sense of the occult.

8. During the Occultation the loss of energy to
   universal negentropy as the Imagination died
   under the image to Pan (Sirius), then Venus, Moon &
   finally Sun . . .

   —John Clarke, "HAWK OR HARP?" *The End of This Side* (Bowling Green, Ohio: Black Book, 1979), p. 20.

See also, for instance, Charles Taylor: "Let me start with the enchanted world, the world of spirits, demons, moral forces which our predecessors acknowledged. The process of disenchantment is the disappearance of this world, and the substitution of what we live today: a world in which the only locus of thoughts, feeling, spiritual élan is what we call minds; the only minds in the cosmos are those of human beings . . . ; and minds are bounded, so that these thoughts, feelings, etc. are situated 'within' them." *The Secular Age* (Cambridge: Harvard University Press, 2007), pp. 29–30.

9. Duncan's epigraph from A. E. Waite, *The Brotherhood of the Rosy Cross* (New York: University Books, 1961), p. 430. Both Waite and Duncan are playing the idea of Morning against the notion of Enlightenment here: "The crisis of the Enlightenment was the crisis Keats saw recapitulated in Coleridge's collapse from the inspiration of 'The Ancient Mariner' and 'Cristobel' to the psychic despair, the rationalist obsession, of later years." Duncan, "Ideas of the Meaning of Form," p. 100.

10. Emerson, "An Address to the Senior Class in Divinity College, Cambridge, July 1, 1838," in *Essays and Lectures,* p. 75.

11. "We do not make things meaningful, but in our making we work towards an awareness of meaning; poetry reveals itself to us as we obey the orders that appear in the work." Duncan, "Towards an Open Universe," in *Fictive Certainties,* p. 82.

12. Arakawa and Madeleine Gins, *The Mechanism of Meaning* (New York: H. N. Abrams, 1979).

The H.D. Book

Book 1 *Beginnings*

Chapter 1

As regards the Lost Word, it is explained that the sun at autumn has lost its power and Nature is rendered mute, but the star of day at the spring tide resumes its vital force, and this is the recovery of the Word, when Nature with all her voices, speaks and sings, even as the Sons of God shouted for joy in the perfect morning of the cosmos. —A.E. Waite, *The Brotherhood of the Rosy Cross*

I.

It is some afternoon in May, twenty-five years ago as I write here—1935 or 1936—in a high school classroom. A young teacher is reading:

Fruit cannot drop
through this thick air . . .

The patience of her voice, where hope for a communion in teaching still struggled with a resignation to institutional expediencies, the reaching out of her voice to engage our care where she cared, had a sad sweet lure for me. But now, as she read the poem, something changed, became more, transformed by her sense of the poet's voice, impersonating the poet H.D.

. . . fruit cannot fall into heat
that presses up and blunts
the points of pears
and rounds the grapes.

To recall the poem, blunted and rounded in the heat, is to recall the first reading, and leads me back to that early summer of my sixteenth or seventeenth year. Just beyond the voice of the poem, the hum and buzz of student voices and the whirr of water sprinklers merging comes distantly from the world outside an open window.

Inside, in a room that was hers and an hour that was hers—for each period in the schedule of my school day still in those years would become a realm of expectancy for me—the poem came as an offering. It may have been a diversion or a reward after duties in our course of instruction. She had presented it as something more, a personal communication. "I have brought a poem today, not as part of your required reading," did she say? or "not belonging to English Literature, but to my own world, a confidence, a gift, or share?" It was clear, anyway, that for her as for us, much of what we had to read was the matter of a prescribed course and not of our own explorations. We were a group set apart from the mass of those attending high school, a few by their special aptitudes, but most of us by our being the sons and daughters of college graduates, and all of our courses of study were designed to prepare us for entrance examinations for college. We were in the proving ground of the professional middle class, where we were to learn by heart the signs and passwords of that class. Not only cases and tenses, histories and zoologies, but news reports and musical appreciations and the reading of novels and poems were to become critical tests in the would-be initiate's meeting the requirements of a cultural set.

Books had opened in childhood imaginations of other lives, dwelling in which the idea of my own life to be had taken on depths and heights, colors and figures, a ground beyond self or personality in the idea of Man. In fairy tales and in romances, old orders overthrown by the middle class lived on in the beginnings of an inner life, kings and knights long deposed by merchants and landlords, peasants and craftsmen swept aside by the Industrial Revolution, once powers and workers in the realities of the actual world passed now into the subversive realm of the irreal. In each of our histories, we were to repeat the historical victory of the Rise of Capitalism. Were there "Charm'd magic casements, opening on the foam / Of perilous seas, in faery lands forlorn," we were schooled not to be taken in by them but to take them in, to appreciate the poet's fancy, even as our forefathers no longer worshipped grove and fountain but exploited wood and water power as public utilities. English Lit with its reading lists, its established texts and tests, was to map in our minds the wilderness yet to be converted to our proper uses from the already developed areas of our real estate. Work by work, author by author, the right roads were paved and marked, the important sights were emphasized, the civic improvements were pointed out where the human spirit had been successfully converted to illustrate the self-respectability of civil men, and the doubtful, impulsively created areas or the adventuring tracks into back-country were deplored. If we, in turn, could be taught to appreciate, to evaluate, as we read, to improve our sensibilities in the ground of other men's passions, to taste and to regulate, to establish our estimations of worth in the marketplace, we were to win some standing in the ranks of an educated middle class as college graduates, urbane and professional, as our parents had done before us.

But there were times when Miss Keough all but confided that the way of reading required by our project was not only tedious but wronged what we read; and there were other times when—even among these things we were supposed to acquire among our cultural properties—she would present some poem or story as if it belonged not to what every well-read person must know, the matter of a public establishment, but to that earlier, atavistic, inner life of the person. Scott's *Ivanhoe* and Thackeray's *Vanity Fair* would be essential to our picture of English culture and society, but Emily Brontë's *Wuthering Heights* or Thomas Hardy's *Tess of the D'Urbervilles* were of a different order—the whole confidence and tone of her speaking was of an other order when she came to these works that she took as revelations of a life back of culture or society, of a life she wanted us to find. All the status of appreciation and knowing about things, of reading skillfully and remembering points that were important for tests in what you read, seemed nothing at all when compared with the alliance one's own life might make in love with other lives revealed in men's works that quickened such a sense of kinship. She would introduce certain writers, reading aloud in class or lending a book for us to read at home, with some hesitation and decision that gave the lending or reading aloud an importance in my personal relation to her, fearfully and in that bravely, as if, were I to come to the heart of the matter of them, I would come too to the matter of this woman's heart and to my own too.

This poem "Heat," by H.D., I understood was offered so. It belonged not to the order of poems and stories that we must know all about if we were to be accomplished students. It belonged to the second order that seemed to contain a personal revelation. It was the ground for a possible deeper meeting with her. At times like this, reading to us, she had the shy confidence of a child searching out her companions, sharing with us corners of a garden that were secret or magic places, risking our blindness or rejection of the gift, bringing forward treasures or keys, taking us to see her familiar animals or friends, in order to place her life in our keeping. She was trying us, not demanding response but testing for an affinity.

"This is the fine thing"—was that part of the transformation of the reading voice? a serious regard? "This intense care that can so distinguish its feeling of thickness and pressure, this is the rare courage?" There was her admiration for the sensitivity and the intensity that the poem made available, but there was her shyness too, as if what had been disclosed in the poem touched upon a similar disclosure in herself. The voice told us that something was at issue. The way the poet H.D. admitted—let in—to her self through the poem, and then, in a double sense, admitted to the listener or reader, being almost a victim of the thickness of air, the bluntness of fruit, to let life use you like this, was not shameful but heroic. To reveal, even if it be shameful in other eyes (as crying out, "O wind, rend open the heat,"—being intense that way about trivial things like pears—threatened the composure of household, gang, school, and city or state, and was shamed, put down, as one must put away childish things), to propose the truth of what was felt, to articulate just the emotion that was most vulnerable and in need, took courage.

Courage, yes—but there was something more. This poem in itself was necessary in order for what it evoked to be kept alive as a living power. It was the sense of the necessity that what was felt be kept that filled the poet in writing. To find out feeling meant to evoke a new power in life. To feel at all challenged the course of everything about one. To articulate the feeling, putting it forth in a poem like this, brought others into the challenge. To strengthen response was to strengthen and enlarge not only the resource but the responsibility of life ahead. It was something larger than being courageous then—a trust in living, not only to use things but to be used by them, a drive that broke through the restrictions and depressions of spirit whereby men were shaped to a conventional purpose.

Falling in love, a conversion or an obsession—these were close to what the poet knew in the poem, seeing the world in the light of a new necessity, a being in-formed. "O wind, rend open the heat, / cut apart the heat," meant that the poet submitted her will to be shaped by what happened. A longing? Or prayer? Addressed to a natural force in a world in which inner and outer nature were one?

In the heat of the afternoon. Outside, the whir of sprinklers, the glare, the blur of voices. Inside, from that murmur, there was a place of refuge, a silence created in our attention. Classrooms were for us—certainly for me—in high school meeting rooms. What I was to become was there for me in the presence of a few teachers, as it never had been at home, it seemed, as it never was to be later in university lecture halls until after ten years I was to return to study with Ernst Kantorowicz. Yes, there were others, but this one, this grave young woman in my adolescence, attended the possibility of a poet in me. She could be a task mistress where the preparation for college entrance exams was concerned. She had, after all, to project an authority over us. She was paid to carry out the intentions of an educational system that was devoted not to the discovery of self but to self-improvement. She must have endured, as we endured, a tedium then, but the dreary tasks of accomplishment and graduation could vanish in moments when work itself took on another meaning.

What I was to be grew in what she was. "I want to know what you will make of this," she would say, giving me Lawrence's *The Man Who Died* or Virginia Woolf's *The Waves* to take home with me. I was not to sum them up, not to know something about them so that I could do well in an examination, but I was to grow through them and toward them in some hidden way. What I would make of *The Man Who Died* or *The Waves* would be what I would make of myself, the course of a life. These works were keys at once to responsive chords in myself and to the music they belonged to, to the company of a larger life, and to my work there. A larger life—*la vita nuova,* Dante had called it—may be opened to us in some such way, because we fall in love, as I surely was in love with her, discovering in a teacher that which awakened an objective for ardor. *"La gloriosa donna della mia mente,"* so Dante addresses Beatrice. It was a responsibility to glory that she touched in me.

For my teacher brought me, where I sought to find our meeting ground in these books, not to some estimate of their literary worth but to the love of a way of being that they had known. H.D., Lawrence, Virginia Woolf, had found a realm most real or most alive or most individual in their writing. Wasn't it that they intensely showed what they were? Daring the disregard or scorn of conventional readers, if they might find the regard of the true reader? What other men kept to themselves, reserving certain thoughts and feelings as private properties, these sought to reveal, not as public property, but as belonging to a community of feeling.

The intensity of my own spirit was lifted from the shame it had seemed to incur in adolescence—for intensity, in itself, in the genteel household was uncouth—lifted toward a worth, a share, a fire or flame out of a fire, that through my teacher's eyes I saw disclosed in these writers was a thing—*the* thing—to be loved. The ardor for the truth of what was felt and thought, the faith in passion, was a virtue, a power of man: to search out a life within life.

The thick air of adolescence, the thick air of Bakersfield, the heat of the valley town where I grew up from the age of eight until I went to college, the pervasive oppressing atmosphere everywhere of social forces seeking to govern and direct a maturation of their purposes in me, blunting the edges, pressing up, gave substance to the immediacy of the poem as she read. There was the charged most real sensual image in the poem of a feeling of my self.

She must have said something about "Imagism." Certainly she had talked about imagism in discussing another poem—"Patterns"—by Amy Lowell. But Amy Lowell's garden had been descriptive in its appeal, leading us to picture the scene. Images there had illustrated the area of the poem, words chosen to call up visual representations, smells, and sounds. It was not far from Keats where we had learned to observe the sensual loading in which the picture evoked by the poem was enriched. Amy Lowell was flat work, it seems now to me. It did not sound the depths.

In the poem of H.D.'s, the image stirred not only pictures from my knowledge of a like world, from the shared terms of orchard, pear, and grape at the stem, and the shimmering medium of air in the heat; but it stood too for another statement, arousing and giving a possible articulation to an inner urgency of my own to be realized, to be made good. The poem had a message, hidden to me then, that I felt but could not translate, an unconscious alliance that made for something more than a sensual response. We were directed to imagine the scene, but the actual poem involved something we almost forgot in the sugges-tion of pears and grapes, of air so thickened and shaped in the heat that it cunningly fitted thickness and shape of fruit so that the suggestion shaped the poem itself. The idea of this being a perfect lyric, an ecstatic, a memorably shaped, moment, drew us away from recognition of the opening and closing address of the poem that cried out for release from such perfection.

We had heard of the heat of composition or inspiration that was like a forge in which words or metal yielded to man's shapings. It was a good thing, like the heat that brought pears to their shape and ripe-ness. And this poem had been shaped, hammered or cut, but it had too, not perfection but the organic irregularities of being felt out from within that life forms have. It had not the regularity of an imposed system, of repeated patterns of stress and syllable, alliteration and rhyme conforming to a prescribed scheme; but its form grew, as living forms do, in the faith or feeling of its own being, transforming itself, using inheritance and environment, tones and cadences, as they happened, toward its melody. Just beyond the threshold of our untrained ears were the rhymes built up in the tone-leadings of vowels and the variation of consonant groupings: "it" to "thick," "fruit" to "through," "air" to "pears," "rounds" to "plough," and the *r*, the *d*, the *p* of "rend open" to "drop" to "presses up." The short lines of the verse forming had their rhythm by the measures of changing numbers. The poem was finely conditioned, felt along the track of some inner impulse. It had form that was H.D., as the leaves of an oak have a form that is the signature of the oak. It had form not by convention kept but by the pulse of its own event.

There was another expression we had read or heard of that was echoed in the poem: a cry that rent the air. Something about to happen that would challenge inheritance and environment. "Rend it to tatters," H.D. asks of the wind in the poem. The address and the evoked image in their message concentrated a likewise hidden prayer of adolescence, that this intensity, this threatening to come to a conclusion, this susceptibility to be shaped, not be rounded in the oppressive thick air of home and town toward homeowner and townsman, but be broken or break forth into something yet to be known. The thickness and heat that ripened was the intensity's own medium of life. All about one, one saw the process of the town's shaping unruly youth into its citizens, pressing desire into the roundness of available civic enterprise, thickening the fire of the spirit into energetic figures that would be of public use. O, let my youth be rent open by some new force, the soul prayed: let a path be made, like a wind rending what cohered toward an end of energies into even, if need be, an incoherence, to free movement from its impending goal, enlarging the demand for form—

Cut the heat—
plough through it,
turning it on either side
of your path.

More than sensation then, more than impression, gave force to the image. It was not only a vivid representation of sensory data but an evocation of depth. Image in Amy Lowell's poem had meant that words could illustrate and give mood. But in this poem "Heat," image conveyed not only the appearance of things or the sensual feel of things and moods, but experience, the reciprocity between inner and outer realities. There was another working of the image, more than Amy Lowell proposed, back of sense and mood, partly conscious and partly unconscious. I was aware that sensual intensity in this poem of H.D.'s, like the sensual intensity in Lawrence's work, demanded some new beginning in life from my own intensity. Such images were more immediate and real than likenesses of seeing, hearing or smelling were. I was unaware that the poem "Heat" was the matrix of two statements in one. I did not know that this intense image of fruit, heat, and longing for a force that would break the ripening perfection, had a significant concentration for me. I could not, after all, have articulated the significant concentration of my own adolescent experience, for I did not realize that my own human life was an image, that my self was the persona of a poem in process of making, in which many levels of meaning were to be incorporated before the form of that life be realized.

The power of subtle, hidden organization, inbinding all elements to its uses, toward an early conclusion of free movements, a last judgment: such a shaping was the directive of all simple urgencies—toward the pear, toward the poem, toward the person of a man. But simple ends, direct uses of possible things, closing the opportunity in one, threatened the realization of some wholeness beyond. I thought not of the fruit of the tree but of the life of the tree, turned ring upon ring, the years gathered toward the spread of its roots and branches. I felt I must be, the world must be, something more various and full, having more of flux and experience than the immediate terms of achievement around me disclosed. Let me not come into my fulfillment until the end of all things, so the soul secretly resolved.

The poem had something to do with keeping open and unfulfilled the urgencies of life. Men hurried to satisfy ends in things, pushed their minds to make advances, right answers, accomplishments, early maturations. They contrived careers that they fully filled. They grew round and fat upon the bough in the heat that kept them where they were, and they prayed that they not fall from their success, that no wind come to break them loose.

•

Yet this very poem "Heat," I came to learn, stood in the fixed ideas of literary history as an example of a kind of early perfectionism. As it had appeared first, in *Some Imagist Poets* of 1915, it had been not a poem in itself, as anthologists came to present it, but the second part of the poem "Garden." It was preceded then by the statement of another image, a rose seen as if cut in rock, and by the poet's counterstatement, "If I could break you . . . if I could stir":

You are clear
O rose, cut in rock,
hard as the descent of hail.

I could scrape the colour
from the petals
like spilt dye from a rock.

If I could break you
I could break a tree.

If I could stir
I could break a tree—
I could break you.

The imagist thing in the poem, the hard "cut in rock" rose and the thick heat, contained the suggestion of a tense suspended awareness that was to be an ideal of modern sensibility in the second decade of the century and to find its expression in works of that generation in the nineteen-twenties. This experience hung upon its bough, and these poems were like moments brought to and kept in a perfection, roses, fruits or cut stones, valued for their implied discrimination. But the poet's dramatic statement of the wish to be freed from this keep of the perfect moment was not imagist, was romantic, and marred the example that readers searching for H.D. the Imagist sought in the poem. The poems most anthologists have taken, the poems that have been selected to label H.D., are few and were written in the brief period between 1912 and 1916. Even these have been mis-taken, removed from the total context of poetic experience to which they belong, for the work of these years included also "The Shrine" and "The Gift," which are not imagist but dramatic in intent, and poems like "Cities" or "The Tribute," which plead the cause of Beauty against the squalor of commerce or lament the death of young men in the war. So too, the second section of the poem "Garden" has been set apart from its original intent, to become exemplary of clarity, finish, hardness—self-containment, and to stand not as part of H.D.'s creative consciousness but as an example of Imagism. The poem "Heat" now, presented by the anthologist's picture, appears to have been written in order to capture the very image of stasis of heat and fruit that the poet longs to be shattered. But when we go back of the anthology establishment to contemporary reviews of H.D.'s *Collected Poems* in 1925, we find that Marianne Moore, William Carlos Williams, and Edward Sapir—or, earlier, John Gould Fletcher, reviewing the volume *Sea Garden* in 1917—see her work as a whole, having its vital import beyond and even outside of the Imagist program.

It was Ezra Pound who had first scratched that word at the end of a manuscript of hers—*"H.D. Imagiste."* Later he was to say that he had started the Imagist idea to launch the poetry of H.D. In the directives Pound drew up—the credo of 1912—the "A Few Don'ts" of 1913, included again in "A Retrospect" of 1917—the new idea of the image goes along with a new idea of poetic form, of composing in the sequence of the musical phrase, and with another idea of—"economy," he calls it—purification of the poem. The waste of tone color and ornament is to be cleared away; abstraction, whatever diffuse suggestion, must go. It is an imperative toward perfection that haunts the aesthetic propositions of Imagism.

So too, in Pound's idea of the image itself the perfectionist drive appears, for, though the image Pound proposes is "an intellectual and emotional complex," the complex does not proliferate but is realized "in an instant of time." Here, though the perfect and the complex would seem to be of different orders, Pound projects the aesthetic, even moral, suggestion of a perfected experience or epiphany: "It is better to present one Image in a lifetime than to produce voluminous works." They were working toward an intensity, a concentration of poetic force. Pound had brooded from a poem of thirty lines, he tells us, striving to render an emotion that had arisen in the sight of beautiful faces seen crowded in the Paris Metro:

> Six months later I made a poem half that length; a year later I made the following *hokku*-like sentence:
>
> > The apparition of these faces in the crowd;
> > Petals on a wet, black bough.

For Pound, H.D. in certain poems had realized the ideal of purity demanded; her poetic line pruned and tried toward the hardness of an utter economy exemplified "craftsmanship," and in the address of her poems she praised the beauty of flowers, trees, stones, or grains of sand, that had been tried by the elements. She had perfected her name Hilda Doolittle too, leaving the bare initials, the essential signature that might be cut in stone. It was as Ezra Pound wanted her. That first Imagist poem, she tells us, after his reading, had been "now slashed with his creative pencil, 'cut this out, shorten this line'." And Pound was the first to write, when the poems of H.D.'s Lawrencian period began to appear in *The Egoist* in 1917—"The God," "Adonis," "Pygmalion," "Eurydice"—that she had "spoiled the 'few but perfect' positions which she might have held on to."

The definition of the image in the talk of Pound, H.D., and Aldington, in the tearoom of the British Museum in 1912, had led to the declarations of a literary movement, and it gave an advertising label to the work of new poems appearing in *The Egoist,* where Richard Aldington had become an editor in 1913, and in the United States in *Poetry,* where Harriet Monroe might be responsive, it was hoped, to Pound's advice. After Pound's anthology presenting the group, *Des Imagistes* of 1914, what had been a working program in poetry was fully launched as a literary fashion, and the idea of H.D.'s being the most perfect craftsman of the new Perfecti who had received that *consolamentum,* the "one image in a lifetime," was to be a central tenet. The original proposition of the Image had harkened back to intellectual and emotional overtones of the Symbolist era even as it moved forward toward a functionalism that was in the Modernist aesthetic to be anti-Symbolist. Like Symbolism, Pound's Imagism had been conceived as a cult of the elect in art. But with the Imagist anthologies of 1915, 1916, and 1917, edited by Amy Lowell, H.D., and Aldington, the Imagist movement became generalized and popularized. The ideas of image, composition by musical phrase, and verbal economy were let go into the lowest common denominators of impressionism, *vers libre,* and everyday speech. By 1937, twenty-five years after the birth of Imagism, all reference to the word *image,* once defined as presenting an intellectual and emotional complex, had been dissipated, and the term had come to indicate whatever in a poem brought a picture to the mind of the reader.

It was not only in "Amygism," as Pound dubbed the heretical popularization, that the first character of the Image as epiphany was lost, for Pound himself was to take as his project the work of small m modernists whose use of the image was profoundly anti-Imagist. For T. E. Hulme, whose work had already been published by Pound at the end of the volume *Ripostes* in 1912, and often in Eliot's poems, the image had not been the nexus of an experience but the opportunity of an expression, of a striking figure in the author's rhetoric. Whatever else they were, the images—in Hulme's poem "Autumn," the ruddy moon that may be like a red-faced farmer peering over a hedge, or in Eliot's "The Love Song of J. Alfred Prufrock," the evening that may be like a patient etherized upon a table—are not mythopoeic in their operation or intent, not deepening our sense of the reality of moon or of evening, but present extension of their author's wit, personal conceits. In the work of Amy Lowell, the image was imitative of sensory appearances informed by mood, a kind of literary impressionism. The persuasive personal conceit and the sensual personal impression were what most critics and readers readily accepted as the range of the image.

The modern sensibilities of Hulme, Eliot, and Wyndham Lewis excited Pound, and he sought to identify his work with theirs, but as Lewis saw in *Time and Western Man,* Pound was "A Man in Love with the Past," and for all his efforts to make of *The Cantos* a dynamic ideogram, *The Cantos* remain a post-Symbolist work. For Pound, as for H.D., as for Lawrence or for Williams, the image was not an invention but a numinous event in language, a showing forth of a commanding Reality in the passing personal real. Like James Joyce, they sought epiphanies. "Image," for Pound, was carefully so set off by quotation marks and spelled with the capital. Although he would disarm us with his reference to "the technical sense employed by the newer psychologists, such as Hart" (the reference to Dr. Bernard Hart, Fellow of University College, London, perhaps to exorcise the thought of Dr. Sigmund Freud of Vienna, when speaking of the term *complex*), there is, for those readers who are wary of the context of Pound's thought immersed as it is in the tradition of Poetry and the Spirit of Romance, a beckoning suggestion in the "intellectual and emotional complex" of that Intellect in which man comes close to the Creative Intent, of the *"Et omniformis omnis intellectus est"* from Psellos, which remains from the beginning thematic in *The Cantos,* or of that "apprehension by means of the potential intellect," which Dante tells us is Man's true mode of being. "Did this 'close ring,' this aristocracy of emotion," the youthful Pound writes in the essay "Psychology and Troubadours," "evolve, out of its half memories of Hellenistic mysteries, a cult—a cult stricter, or more subtle, than that of the celibate ascetics, a cult for the purgation of the soul . . . ?" The "complex" then was a node involving not only the psyche, as that term is used by modern psychologists, but the soul, as that term is used by esoteric schools. So too, the quotation marks and the capitalization, setting the word "Image" apart, carried for the knowing reader the sense that the word had a special meaning beyond the apparent. "Image" and "Intellect" in the framework of Gnostic and neo-Platonic doctrines that haunt Pound's cantos to the last are terms of a Reality that is cosmic and spiritual; they are terms of a visionary realism.

Reviewing H.D.'s volume *Sea Garden,* John Gould Fletcher, a fellow Imagist, wrote:

> It is really about the soul, or the primal intelligence, or the *Nous,* or whatever we choose to call that link that binds us to the unseen and un-created. . . . To penetrate H.D.'s inner meaning, it is only necessary that we approach her poetry with an open and responsive mind. . . . But this state of mind, receptive, quiescent, is also necessary if we are to under-stand Plotinus, or Dionysius the Areopagite, or Paracelsus, or Behmen, or Swedenborg, or Blake.

That Image and Intellect may have been in the first phase of Imagism charged with more than a literary meaning begins to be clear.

Pound in his study of Dante and in his conversations and read-ings with Yeats had come into what was to be a lifelong admiration of Iamblichus and Proclus, late neo-Platonists, in whose imaginations the Image had taken on powers of person and angelic being. Fletcher's early review of H.D. would indicate that for others too in the Imagist circle—the "School of Images" Pound calls it in his "Prefatory Note" to Hulme's poems—for H.D. then, and for some contemporary readers of H.D.'s work, the image of the Imagists was associated with the Image, with Eidolon and Idea as they appear in Hellenistic and again in late Medieval and Renaissance speculation. "One must consider that the types which joined these cults survived, in Provence," Pound writes in "Psychology and Troubadours": "and survive, today—priests, maenads, and the rest—though there is in our society no provision for them."

The very movement of the line might be a magic then, theurgic in its intent, in which the Image was specially evoked. The line was to be expressive—that was the demand of the modern aesthetic, and Pound and H.D. were acutely sensitive to the style that the age demanded; but it was also to be efficacious—it was not to express the Image but to call up its Presence, to cause it to happen. We may read H.D.'s proposal in the *Imagist Anthology* of 1915 with a gathering suspicion: "A new cadence means a new idea" takes on a special meaning when the word *idea* is colored by the poetic lore of neo-Platonic theurgy. Pound's injunction "to compose in the sequence of the musical phrase" may not only be a departure from literary conventions but a conversion to heresies of a spiritual order. There was no thing that was not, given the proper instant in time and intent in vision, Image. There was no image that was not, properly rendered, the nexus of divine and elemental orders in the human world. Anguish and ecstasy gave presence to, and were aroused by a presence in, the natural world. Rocks and sea, thunderous surfs, gardens and orchards actually exposed the soul to the spiritual presence, flooded it with the presence—all but unbearably—and yet, at the same time, sheltered it within the presence.

"To use absolutely no word that does not contribute to the presentation"—this second commandment of Pound's Imagist manifesto was essential in the high art that lay back of the famous rapture of H.D.'s early work, the root in practice of her lyric genius. The line of her verse grew taut, tempered to keep an edge naked in experience, tense to provide a mode in which reverberations of these presences might be heard. The image and the voice or dramatic mask provided the nexus of a mystery in Poetry corresponding to the outer and inner worlds in which the poetess, now a priestess in the mysteries of the language, worked toward higher and finer modes of participation in a mystery in Life Itself.

The new poetry was not to be a commodity, a negotiable sensibility in literature or culture, but an instrument in a process of spirit. Pound in his Cavalcanti essay during this early period of Imagism describes such a spiritual process in the contribution of Provence to poetry:

> The whole break of Provence with this world . . . is the dogma that there is some proportion between the fine thing held in the mind, and the inferior thing ready for instant consumption. . . . You deal with an interactive force: the *virtu* in short. . . . The conception of the body as perfect instrument of the increasing intelligence pervades.

We find in H.D.'s early work the evocation not only of presences of Nature but of the poet's own nature, her temper or virtu. In the poem "Toward the Piraeus" she pictures her own poetic virtu, contrasting her power with that of another who may have been—for this is one of her Lawrencian poems—D. H. Lawrence:

> my own lesser, yet still somewhat fine-wrought,
> fiery-tempered, delicate, over-passionate steel.

It is an image of an instrument prepared for experience that is at once the image of her physical body, her spirit, and the temperament of the verse itself. It was an image too of tension in passion that appealed to the sentiments of the modernist generation. Not the erotic sensualities of the poem "Hymen" or the intoxications of "Heliodora" came to stand for H.D.'s special quality as a poet among her admirers, but the tenseness itself, the almost frigid apprehension of the passionate that in the poem "Wash of Cold River" she had characterized as most hers, was taken as her primary attribute:

> *all the sheer rapture*
> *that I would take*
> *to mould a clear*
> *and frigid statue;*

We might read "carve" for "mould," for the fiery tempered steel of the poet's self-projection is the steel of the sculptor's chisel, shaping the resistant stone. The art that H.D. projects is haunted by Gaudier-Brzeska's messianic doctrines of sculptural energy and sculptural feeling that swept Pound up into his Vorticist period. Gaudier-Brzeska sought the expression of challenge and intensity that found modelling insipid. "He cut stone until its edge was like metal," Pound tells us in his work on Gaudier: "The softness of castings displeased him and so he cut the brass direct."

The matter is of marble, not of clay:

rare, of pure texture,
beautiful space and line,
marble to grace
your inaccessible shrine.

So H.D. concludes "Wash of Cold River." Her art, and her sense of the passionate, demanded fineness of feeling, exactness, that was not soft or compliant but hard and resistant. She suggested in poems like "Sea Rose," "Sea Lily," "Sea Violet," or "Pear Tree," an exquisite sensibility, leaf and petal delicately cut, "precious," "like flint / on a bright stone," "fragile as agate," "from such a rare silver," at once "precious," "fragile," "rare," the bane of critics-to-be, and yet to be shaped only by elemental energies, by sea and wind, furrowed "with hard edge."

Pound, too, in his Cavalcanti essay refers to the stone and the stone-cutter's art in order to illuminate the poet's art:

The god is inside the stone, *vacuos exercet aera morsus*. The force is arrested, but there is never any question about its latency, about the force being the essential and the rest 'accidental' in the philosophical technical sense. The shape occurs.

It is along these lines that, in "Pygmalion" (published early in 1917), H.D. presents the poet as the sculptor questioning the vitalities at work in his art beyond the mastery of the craft:

am I master of this
swirl upon swirl of light?

In the magic of the stone's being carved, the Divine and the human meet; the force of the work is interactive. That demonically inspired restless spirit of the sculptor Gaudier-Brzeska haunted not only Pound but H.D., for, in the few years before his fateful death in the First World War, charged with the vision of a vortex of energies to be released in matter toward form in which the drive of his own genius might be consummated, he had had evenings too with the Aldingtons, talking on and on to pour out the message of his Vortex. Possessed by his spirit, or married to his spirit, the sculptor in H.D.'s poem works in stone and light, even as the poet works in the densities of the given meanings of words and in the aura of a gathering music, a breath informing the poem, until an image emerges in the work, working the medium until the work itself is immediate to the mind. But this "work" is both a power and, the artist begins to realize, a person. The work of art is itself a living presence in which its creator stands. Man, stone, and light, cooperate in the event. "Am I the god?" Pygmalion asks:

> or does this fire carve me
> for its use?

Just as there are certain events in actual life that are so charged with the information of a content that is to be realized in the maturation of the soul or form of the total lifetime, and as there are certain dreams that flood our active consciousness with the forms of unconscious, as yet unborn, facts of our identity, so, for the poet, there are poems that are prophetic of a poetry that is to be realized only in the fullness of the poet's life, as for H.D. this early poem stands as a foreknowledge, a foreacknowledgment, of the major task she is to undertake in poetry. *Ion,* her version of Euripides' drama, twenty years later, will mark the re-entry of the forces that for a moment she had seen at work toward fulfillment beyond the psyche in the advent of creative form in "Pygmalion"—of light, of heat, of fire, of stone and god. In the poetry of H.D.'s major phase, particularly in *Helen in Egypt,* the sense increases that as the artist works to achieve form he finds himself the creature of the form he thought at first to achieve. The role of the poet, his craft, is to seek out the design in the carpet, to come to know and then to acknowledge his identity in the terms of a poetry he but belongs to. The fire is indeed to carve the poet for its use.

·

As we come into the fullness of our sense of a life work, it is as if we were recovering or rescuing the import of what had always been there. We make good our earliest readings, make real what even we failed to see present at the time, transforming the events of our earlier life in a process of realizing what our work and life comes to mean. Creating meaning we create work and life, and, in turn, for meaning is the matter of the increment of human experience which we come to recognize in the language, we unite our individuality with a vision of its communal identity.

Over thirty years, my sense of that first reading of "Heat" has grown along lines of recognition and discovery of affinities to inform my return to those lines. Unconscious of the content that made for that imprint and awakened in me the sense of a self-revelation or life-revelation in the pursuit of Poetry, I was conscious only of my excitement in the inspiration—the new breath in language—and of a vocation. Whatever my abilities, it was here that I had been called to work. Beyond that, I had no more information than the uninformed account of what Imagism was as it was taught in literature classes of the late nineteen-thirties, where I came to learn that Amy Lowell's "Patterns," Pound's "Metro," Flint's "Swan," Joyce's "I hear an army charging upon the land," and this poem "Heat" of H.D.'s were examples of Imagism. Their titles come in a list as if learned by rote. They had become set in the textbooks and classrooms of the late nineteen-thirties from the anthologies and arguments of the Imagist period itself. In the literary establishment Eliot had won the day—he had, indeed, designed that literary establishment in his essays; and H.D., along with Lawrence and even Pound (for Eliot had dismissed from serious consideration the "Religio" and the later Confucian conversion), belonged with those who had departed from what reasonable men consider of concern and had lusted after strange gods. Eliot had the charge of bringing his own poetic imagination into the circumscription of a Christian orthodoxy; but even in literary ranks where Eliot's own god was considered strange,

Imagism was dismissed as if it were a false religion. The Imagist fallacy was not an inherent weakness but a danger. In textbooks on poetry, the schoolmasters of the rationalist orthodoxy strove to establish Imagism as an aberration, a kind of insanity of the poem, in which imagery, which properly was a means in the poet's presentation of his picture, became an end, as if image carried a meaning in itself.

There is a crucial difference between the doctrine of the Image where Poetry itself is taken to be a primary ground of experience and meaning in life, and the image which is taken as a fashion in the literary world. With H.D.'s "Heat" or with Joyce's "I hear an army charging upon the land," I cannot separate the poem from its operation as prophecy or prayer in the shaping of my own life, the efficacy of the poem to awaken depths in me. The key lies in a rhetoric which is magic in its intent and not literary. This is its heresy.

Pound had presented his Imagist manifesto as an attack on rhetoric. He had sought a cure of tongues in the discipline of the eye, some restraint that would keep words grounded in meaning. The pomp of Milton or the sensual indulgences of Swinburne had led men to take effect and enthusiasm as in themselves poetic—the more effect, the more enthusiasm, the more poetic. There had been an inflation of language. Protesting against the "prolix" and "verbose," against words "shoveled in to fill a metric pattern or to complete the noise of a rhyme-sound," against "decorative vocabulary," Pound's insistence that there be "absolutely no word that does not contribute to the presentation" was the expression in poetics not only of a modern aesthetic demand for the functional but also of a demand that was moral and economic. If we think of Pound's later concern for a monetary credit that is grounded in an actual productive order, "the growing grass that can nourish the living sheep," and his outrage at the great swindling of confidence represented by usury, commodity speculation, money changing, and inflation, we find a basic concern for the good credit of things. Both words and money are currencies that must be grounded in the substance of a credibility if they be virtuous. Abstraction from the actual guarantee of experience meant manipulation of the public trust, as, in the United States, demagogues had long established by their misuses of language the common sense that what was "rhetorical" was for effect only, a persuading with words that were not truly meant, empty or worse, a hiding of the real meaning in order to make a sell.

In *Guide to Kulchur,* in 1938, relating his own Cantos to the quartets of Bartók, Pound saw in these works "the defects inherent in a record of struggle." *The Cantos,* designed, as we see them, to bear the imprint of Pound's experience of man's history, contain as their condition and express the troubled spirit of our times as no other work in poetry does. It is his impersonating genius that, even where he presents flashes of eternal mind—*veritas, claritas, hilaritas*—they do not appear as a sublimation of the poem but remain involved, by defect, in the agony of the contemporary. A profound creative urge—"So-shu also, / using the long moon for a churn-stick"—churns in the sea of Pound's spirit everywhere, even as it churns in the sea of our own history. We have our moment of truth just where contention will not allow our reason to rest undisturbed. The figure we seek is revealed in fragments in the path of a moon that troubles the waters in which the path of its light is reflected. It is part of the polemics of his time that is also ours that Pound juxtaposes his insight of the good and his prejudice of the bad. We are lost if we take his uses as having an authority other than the truth of how the world is felt and seen by the poet if he keep alive in him the defects inherent in a record of struggle. We, as readers, must enter the struggle and contend with the drama of defects. When Pound writes "Consider the definiteness of Dante's presentation as compared with Milton's rhetoric," all is not *claritas.* In the contention, our sense of the good of definiteness and of Dante is to be the greater; but he means also that our sense of the good of rhetoric and of Milton is to be the less. Where Pound uses the popular pejorative demeaning of the word "rhetoric," voiding its base in the likeness between the flow of speech and the flow of a river, he troubles the currents of meaning. Working with the debased currency of the word, he forces us to search out for ourselves the good credit of the word in man's experience.

Hretor (ῥήτωρ, orator) comes from the Greek verb *hreo* (ῥέω, to say) that had, if not a root in the strict etymological sense, the association of a pun, in common with the verb *hreo* (ῥέω, to flow). The flow of speech was for the Greeks, as for us, an expression that could refer to words running glibly off the tongue being like a babbling brook, and likewise to the elemental power of fluency in saying. The poet must be fluent in speech. There must be currents of meaning as well as particularities of meaning. Speech was a river. The Greek lexicon of Liddell & Scott tells us that "*hoi hreontes* was a nickname for the Heraclitean philosophers who held that all things were in a constant state of flux." The mistrust that men had of speech was their mistrust of rivers that swept men along, that persuaded.

Pound was a man of inner conflicts. At once to convey a complex of emotions and to perfect an art. So too, his persuasion was against persuasion. It is characteristic of Pound's nature in saying, of his river of speech, a currency he has in the common sense where it is most disturbed and disturbing, that words that come up in his contentions— "abstraction," "rhetoric," "jew," or "shit,"—appear deprived of their good sense. "Rhetoric" became a term of derogation in his criticism, just as in *The Cantos* his great river of voices began, sweeping all conflicts up into the persuasion of its Heracleitean flux, having mastery through its triumphant rhetoric. The "one Image in a lifetime," defined "in an instant of time," in the life-flow of time is no longer discrete and unique but leads to and inherits depths from other times and places. In each instant of time, the tide of its river impended.

Imagist poems are charged with the drama of this arrest of a time that is like the force of a powerful current in arrest. In the suspended tension of H.D.'s poem "Garden," there is the threat of movement. So too, in Joyce's "I hear an army charging upon the land," which had appeared in Pound's anthology *Des Imagistes,* the intellectual and emotional complex does not exist in an instant of time, in a flash of the essential reality, but it is charged with the portent of associations to come. Say that Joyce presents the waves of the sea, made the more vivid because he sees them as the horses and men of an army—these horse-men of the surf are an old Celtic idea—and that, in the close, his cry of despair and loneliness conveys the retreat of the wave. It still remains that what the poem presents leads us as readers on to something that the poem "says" beyond the image. Joyce is also telling us he hears (and everything we know of his genius in the story *The Dead* or in *Ulysses* or in the closing pages of *Finnegans Wake* verifies this sense of his language) the armies of the dead and the unborn at the shores of consciousness, swarming invasions from a sleeping reservoir that press upon Joyce's waking mind, as all things of the waking world press upon his sleeping mind. What appears, whatever we see there, answers the call of his declaration of listening: "I hear. . . . " The beginning of the saying reaches out from the proposition of what it says, and hearing rushes in to illustrate the proposition. The speaker, speaking of his hearing, hears; the hearer sees. Clairaudient to the voice of the poem and then beyond, Joyce becomes clairvoyant. It is all in the medium of saying: second-speech begins; the second-hearing or second-sight comes to meet it.

This complex does not exist in an instant of time but in a language or history out of an increment of times. Where these hosts are also (and all that we remember of what was about to happen in that year 1914 fulfills the prophecy) intimations of the actual armies of the First World War. "I hear an army charging upon the land" is not only an image of the sea breakers but an omen of war, ready to take on reverberations from history, fitting, preparing as it does, our own immediate knowledge of how a world that is now all a sea of armies grew. Place Joyce's poem alongside of Arnold's "Dover Beach" or Hardy's "Channel Firing," and its rhetoric rings out as of the same order.

It was the rhetoric too, the undercurrent of her speech, that gave meaning to H.D.'s poem. "O wind, rend open the heat—" if we respond in the mode of its address, persuades us to a need in our own being to break the perfection of the instant and restore the disturbing flow of time.

In Pound's "Metro," the immediate presentation may be enough, the interchange or correspondence of blossoms wet pressed to a black bough with faces in a crowded subway station. We may grasp the sense in being struck by the likeness. "The proper and perfect symbol is the natural object," Pound writes in the Credo of his essay "A Retrospect": "so that a sense, and the poetic quality of the passage, is not lost to those who do not understand the symbol as such, to whom, for instance, a hawk is a hawk." If we ask further, what does the image mean? what are these faces upon what "bough"? why "apparitions"? if we grant that the immediate image is *a* sense of the poem and yet, following the lead of Pound's italicizing the indefinite article, we search beyond for an other sense of the poem, are we reading more into the poem than there is there?

In H.D.'s poem "Heat," the images presented become propositions of a language that spoke of something hidden from me in hearing the poem, an ideogram I could not read yet. Everything that was felt was clearly rendered; what was felt was that something more impended. Not that I knew more than was there but that there was more there than I knew. We, the poet and those of us readers who have the commitment, must, like the knight who would heal the wound of the Fisher King and revive the Waste Land, ask the meaning of "fruit that cannot fall," of "thickness of air," of "heat," and that meaning has only one place in which to gather—our life experience. We must discover correspondences and come in reading the poem to read our own lives.

It may be a sufficient issue of "Metro" or of Flint's "Swan" to have read the image in the terms of its first instance, to have seen vividly the very clustered faces that are also the crowded blossoms or the swan passing into the dark of an archway. But now, turning back to the poem, I see that Flint would add "into the black depth of my sorrow." Does it mar the image? "Don't use such an expression as 'dim lands *of peace*'," Pound had instructed the would-be imagist: "It dulls the image. It mixes an abstraction with the concrete. It comes from the writer's not realizing that the natural object is always the *adequate* symbol."

We may do well enough with "Patterns" to follow the Lady in impersonation and see the scene of the garden with its too-planned patterns as we go, as if it were a sequence from a costume movie of the period, scenario by Sabatini. The poets may have meant these images to satisfy us in their being seen. I have never returned to read Amy Lowell's poem in any event since high school, here, at least, taking the Pounding prejudice against Amygism as my own.

Let these ratiocinations stand as they are. They present an account of what the propositions of Imagism have come to mean to me as far as they have gone. But a new way of seeing, related to Pound's later concern with the ideogram, colors my thought of the direct object, the symbol, or the image. The great art of my time is the collagist's art, to bring all things into new complexes of meaning, mixing associations. I am the more aware that the figures of wet pale faces that are blossoms upon the black bough of some Tree, that the Swan, that the Lady in the Garden, are not only immediate images struck of particular things in their instant seen by Pound, Flint, or Amy Lowell, proper each to its poem, but are parts now of a composite picture, belonging to one passion in me of Poetry. "Only passion endures," Pound writes somewhere, "the rest is dross." And these images are part of an enduring memory. Just so, they have been claimed by my mind among the illustrations of my own life, fitting its vision. My vision then may mistake the poems in part to fit. They have waited there long among the shades of memory, and now perhaps that we have recalled them, the course of this study will bring them forward to a new account, until we must read again the actual texts in the present light. But in the case of Joyce's poem, as with H.D.'s, the memory and the text have been deeply imprinted with the scene of its first reading. Joyce's poem belongs to one of the decisive events of my actual life.

•

It may have been in 1938, one of those radiant days that October brings to Berkeley after the fog and even cold of the summer. I sprawled on the grass, the little Black Sun Press book with pages printed in blue italics, lovely and most precious, in my hands; and, as I turned for the first time to read Joyce's poems, cutting the pages as I went, I read aloud to two girls—young women—whose sense of the world was deeper than mine, I felt, so that I was supported by their listening. For they had known poverty and loneliness in an alien land (the one Italian, the other Jewish, coming from immigrant families). They came from working-class households, close to the burden of labor, it seemed to me, that furnished the essentials of life, food, and clothing, so that they had in my eyes a more immediate sense of the human lot.

Athalie was the young Jewess. Let her be a "Jewess"—for she impersonated a racial elegance, knowingly referring to old ideas of beauty from the Middle East, Levantine or Persian hints that had a mock seductiveness, exciting our sense of the exotic and taunting us in that sense. At the same time she had a bitter knowledge of what to be Jewish meant—it gave reality to her despair. And, being Polish, she had known the scorn not only of Germans but of German Jews. She would bring to play in Eliot's "Sweeney Among the Nightingales" overtones of a menace that the history of our own time with the rise of the Nazis seemed but to illustrate, where "Rachel née Rabinovitch / tears at the grapes with murderous paws," reciting the lines with a terrible kind of humor, an imminent threat, so that the poetry and the history we might have associated with the poem became her own revelation to our company that adored her of the reality of some inner risk. "A woman runs a terrible risk," she would quote by heart. She had barely made—did not finally succeed in making—the transition from her family, dominated by a fanatic orthodox father, from the folk-world of a Polish ghetto and a poetry world out of ancient Hebrew traditions, to the shores of light she thought to find in philosophy. The mind! Her mind was a fire. James and Dewey might be a new testament, and Pragmatism a new dispensation, but the Old Testament and the Covenant remained. Truth she knew by its disaster. Terror of her mad father, pity for her enduring mother, madness and enduring in her self, the old tribal law that put women among contaminated beings, the old mystery that exalted her as an object into the bridal glory of the Shulamite, the old wisdom way that looked deep into the vanity of all things and cried "Fear God! There is *no* end."

"Of making many books there is no end"—all was caught up into a wave of hysteria, inspired, impersonating, daemonic in part, with a sense of its own caricature, with a sense of its social outrage. She had histrionics then, delighting in tirade and dramatic gestures. Lighting it all, so that she is still a power in my memory and love, she had intense joys and despairs, a vitality that leaped—as later I was to discover the Hasidim had leaped and danced before the glory or joy of the Lord in the most grievous of times—before the fact of a painting like Picasso's *Woman in the Mirror* or some scene in reading Dostoyevsky's *The Idiot*, celebrant, before whatever was expressive of a passionate, troubled human soul. And she had a wild affection for whatever in us showed response. To suffer, to undergo, to understand anything, danced in a frenzy. Her consciousness rose, as the consciousness of the world rose in the last years of the Depression toward the mania of the War. The lot of the Jews, the lot of women—these stood for her as symbols of the real lot of mankind. Imitating Madame Croiza's inspired howling as Electra in the recording of the Claudel-Milhaud *Oresteia* that we used to listen to ritually in those days, she was projecting something she felt prophetic of herself; and as we came to the ebb tides of the night, she would acclaim Céline's *Voyage au bout de la nuit,* where she had seen in the furies that maddened the young doctor working in the slums of Paris those furies that pursued her own mind. Something had been revealed in the heart of Paris that was prophetic of our own lot to come. Long before her anticipation of human disaster was illustrated in full in the actual world at Belsen and Buchenwald, before at Nagasaki and Hiroshima we were to see that the evil was not German alone, Athalie had passed from the brilliant wave of her despair and joy, and the wave had gone out, back into the miseries and infantile recesses of dementia praecox. Something once acted had become most actual.

Or, we may say, something set into action. We were, it seems to me now, trying the scene and ourselves to find the plot and our roles therein. We imagined a life as passionate, as full of depths and heightened colors as we found in works of art. The lawn, the sun, the two full-bodied young women with their flowing hair and their sandaled feet, and my reading there, had the command the stage has over all other events when we attend. They were my audience as I read— yes—but they were also—the whole little scene was built up with their composition of it—a chorus. Let these things be fates over me, I had resolved. As I read on, leafing through the pages of Joyce's *Collected Poems,* which I had just found in a bookshop that day, past the bronze crayon portrait by Augustus John, past poems that did not key in, I was looking for poems that would belong to our own scene. Lines or words in scanning would give the clue: "A merry air,"—no—"Welladay! Welladay!"—I all but despaired finding the voice I wanted. There was a self-mockery in the book, where the title *Chamber Music* had a double meaning in which its author mocked his own sentiment with a possibility of parody, the too-muchness of the song's manner. One had known something like this in adolescence we were only too close to, striving to cover for shyness and passion and ignorance, enacting one's painful self-consciousness as if it were a deliberate sophistication, anticipating social rejection by a self-rejection incorporated in the feeling itself, a safety of irony or not caring that disavowed the fatal original importance of that feeling. The voice I sought was a different voice. There were glimmers of it in certain poems where for a moment Joyce had the courage of his sentiment:

Because your voice was at my side

That sprang into life for me, immediately speaking for what I wanted to say.

There is no word nor any sign
    can make amend—

came direct from the emotion of the artist as a young man without the later Joyce's self-knowing and dissembling pose, and it spoke too as if from my own emotion to say something I had to tell my two companions. Poetry was a communal voice for us—it spoke as we could not speak for ourselves. And there was a voice in me that sought such a communal speech in order to come to feel at all.

"All day," I continued, "I hear the noise of waters / Making moan, / Sad as the sea-bird is, when going / Forth alone," acknowledging in reading—what I could not otherwise acknowledge in myself or in them—that we too, each, had gone, and now went forth, in such a loneliness.

The Italian girl, Lili, had a kind of laughter of eyes, of the curve of her lips, as if even one's loneliness was reflected there in an amusement. Did she pretend to be a Muse? She walked as if there were a music within which she walked, with an air, a reverie, that set her everywhere apart. Hesiod tells us that the Muses, hinting at their art, said: "We know how to speak many false things as though they were true; but we know, when we will, to utter true things." And then he tells us: "They moved with vigorous feet. . . . Thence they arise and go abroad by night, veiled in thick mist, and utter their song with lovely voice." Everything Hesiod tells of the Muses might tell of Lili. She, like them, a serious spirit who was at the same time playful. She was amused, as if there were some womanly strength and wisdom in her countenancing life that came out of shared weaknesses and sorrows in which she had her self-humor, where compassion was part of appreciation. She had humanity; and to have humanity was harder and, at the same time, richer, than what was needed to be a woman or what was needed to be Italian or Jewish in a social world where this was foreign. But it was not that life was hard or that it was rich. Life was, I think, in itself, some kind of inner joy to her, not only human life but the life of a geranium or of the grass could awake in her a response that touched that inner music. As I read from Joyce that day, she had a sympathy for the inner music of the poem that in our consciousness of that sympathy made music all, as a sustaining current.

They were, in their audience, these two women, my nurses, as, with a nurse's delight in the free vitality, they caught up the spirit of Joyce with that love in which we find most dear some earnest candid need or weakness—no—the vulnerability in itself that shows bravely forth as a condition, not for our commiseration but for our sympathy, feeling with it, as in Joyce's poem, a vital information.

Or they were playing nurse, for we were all children of ourselves, and writers like Joyce or Dostoyevsky or painters like Picasso and Matisse, artists we admired, seemed to us children of their arts. Or we hoped to be children, for what we meant by "child" had little to do with what we had been. It was, rather, some potential we felt within us. It was the secret alliance with life that we saw in artist or saint that we admired.

Lili had come from a land and a language of saints. "Dearest Brother," she would address me, laying her hands upon me with an expression of intimate care and love that may have emulated Saint Francis, for he was one of our heroes. The man Joyce, because his poem had that vulnerability and candor, in the midst of his self-consciousness and pose, would be "Brother." I had no knowledge then of Francis of Assisi's *Canticle of Brother Sun;* but, just as Athalie evoked her person at times from furies and lamentations out of the Songs and Wisdom of Solomon, so Lili's joy in pathos had its counterpart in the litanies of Francis. The poem was a lament, a confession or a hymn that showed forth sympathy with what was otherwise alone. In truth the poet-voice was isolate, alone with its own music. *"All day, all night, I hear them flowing / To and fro,"* I read aloud and paused before turning to the next poem.

From the Campanile bells sounded, announcing with their render-ings of popular tunes that the change of hours was about to come. Turning from my book with dismay, I cried, "There is the bell, I have to go."

In the jostling streams, lowerclassmen, some in uniform, some still to change into uniform, went from all parts of the campus toward the gymnasium. It was the hour for R.O.T.C. classes that impended.

"You don't have to go," Lili commanded, raising her hand in a dra-matic gesture that had been delegated its powers by the conspiracy of our company. "Stay with Joyce." What we had been enacting, the reader and the listeners—the Muses, perhaps, for some serious amuse-ment or enchantment had been worked through our cooperation—celebrating this most high reading of the poem, was to become real. "Rejoice with Joyce," Athalie commanded. A poem was to take over.

Away toward duty, the one command of the State over us, the duti-ful students went. In time. Toward the eleven o'clock drill. To march in time.

There had been the arrogance of Joyce, or the intelligence of Joyce, or the inspiration of Joyce, that had exiled him from church and state, from Ireland, from place and time, so that Dublin was finally to be all his own creation, transformed. For the poet, too, had been going forth alone. The moment was an eternal, an isolate thing. A moment of a poem was an eternal thing, from which many phases of itself radiated into time, where we might enter our share in a man's isolation.

The students obeyed the orders of the day. Military at eleven, Tues-days and Thursdays. Some, I knew, got excused by doctor's recom-mendations, escaping from the boredom of it, disqualified by virtue of some physical defect, bad eyesight or flat feet, or by psychiatric warrant. Doctors were liberal in providing the out.

I, too, did not like the boredom, the surrender of mind and body to obey compulsory authority in order that there be such an authority over me. There was an eternal conflict between these orders, forcing us into conformations, surrendering self and awareness in order to endure the tedium, and the other obedience we had just begun, to an inner order of spirit, or the obedience to the beauty of a thing or the fitness of the time. Nerves that must be kept the edges of a vulnerable everlasting consciousness, kept raw and yet fine, our nerves that must serve us if we were to be artists, strained and recoiled at each session of drill, barely allowed for the numbness necessary to get through.

I hear an army charging upon the land,

I read out of Joyce. Going on to the following poem from where I had stopped, taking up the words that rang out now, not of onerous classes and marches, but of *war*.

And the thunder of horses plunging, foam
    about their knees!

War! We were supposed to hate the thought of it but to embrace the fact of it, as if only there we would prove our manhood. Some students were opposed to whatever fact of war. I knew there were pacifists, students who challenged the order to take Military and had gone on strike, as if they had a right to education that they did not owe to the State and its army. They were expelled from school, if they did not dodge the issue. They had conscience. For the State, to be prepared did not mean to be prepared for life but to be prepared for War. It was a condition of our being educated at all at a state university, we were told, that we subscribe to that position, that we be prepared, that we march. Keep time. I, too, believed that back of the army was a cult of War or a business or profession of War, an evil—for it stood against all hope of peace. But I had no sufficient righteous conviction to take a stand. I despaired myself of peace. I was afraid of vested authority.

Away from me the disconsolate students went as I read. It was too late. I could never make it. I would be late. Without an excuse. This poem of Joyce's was not an excuse; it was an affronting fact. The time was gone.

It's that moment I wanted to remember, turning, not without panic, but with relief too, away from the Military hour that had been a bother, a burden, and then, because I felt there was something wrong about the submission, a shame, and somehow, because there had been in those other students a strength of conscience that there was not in me, a guilt—turning away from bother, burden, shame, guilt, to the orders of the poem. Attended by two radiantly beaming women who had won me so into their company, their conspiracy, against the army, against the university finally. For I never took getting a degree seriously then. I never went to Military classes again. I ceased going to other classes that I had found a sham. I had come into a poetic order more commanding than my fear of military and school authorities, but I had lost too the reality of graduating from a course of studies, of going on to take my place as a member of some professional caste. Toward an other reality where the poem, the little book of Joyce, the reading, and the listening women had a commanding power stronger than the demand of time.

On the fields below, the troops were marching in ranks. Between eleven and twelve o'clock. The students flooded out, breaking and eddying, released, upon the noon bells, hurrying toward their fraternities and dorms and public eating places. I had let them go from me.

With panic, with the benediction of my muses, with guilt and with joy, I had come from the orders of the day, a deserter from my prescribed career where I was to have been assured of a steady living, from literary strategies and fellowships to be, into the reading of a poem. A member of the cast in a play that now would be autonomous—my idea of a drama of a poetry would rule my life. Now the melody of events was stronger in me, "carried away," so the common sense of it is, I was carried away by the mood of our scene, transported into the authority of the impulse of a poem from the authority of parents, faculty advisors, and the R.O.T.C.

The authority of the poem was a voice of the spirit. To be a poet meant an even fanatic allegiance to a vision or dream, in order that there be Poetry. Men commonly spoke of vision or dream with mistrust. To be a dreamer was ambivalently respected, for dreams rendered men uneasy in their conventional pursuits. A poet must follow his own ideas or feelings wherever they led. In a way, instead of having ideas or feelings, the poet lets ideas or feelings "have" *him*. Seized by an idea.

Turning from the authority that the requirements and grades of the university or the approval of my teachers had once had over me to a new authority in the immediacy of what I had come to love, I came into a new fate. The quickening of vowels and consonants, the breath or spirit that moved beneath the meaningful, the sequence and hidden design of voice and image that followed the sequence of emotion and intellection belonged now to an eternal order that challenged all other orders.

"They come out of the sea and run shouting by the shore," I read.

In time, Athalie was to be a mumbling, cackling thing, as Lili or her sister Mary told me later, gobbling down chocolates and then, slyly, as if her visitor did not see, storing them away in her shoes. I saw her once in an interval before all was lost. She had been released by the hospital, shocked into a kind of conformity. But they had cured the jagged edge of her vital being back from its disturbed contact with the knowledge of a terrifying reality.

Lili, working in canneries in the summer, was converted in those years to a Trotskyite politics. Her dream and her imagination must have been won by the vision of unreleased powers that lay in the work of fields and factories still untranslated into ideal and action. But now, not only the expressions of compassion and vision won her, but she became partisan too in the political strategies and revolutionary stands in which the orthodox Trotskyites strengthened their commitment to the ultimate claim of the party.

It is toward what I have called the eternal that time is disturbed to awaken the workers of the world to the virtue, the power, that lies in their labor. The poet, too, is a worker, for the language, even as the field and the factory, belongs to the productive orders and means in which the communal good lies. All that is unjust, all that has been taken over for private exploitation from the commune, leaves us restless with time, divorced from the eternal. If I had come under the orders of poetry, I saw too that those orders would come into their full volition only when poetry was no longer taken to be a profession and when the poet would be seen to share in the daily labor toward the common need.

But the great vision of such a communism in which old dreams of a brotherhood of man survived, the acknowledgment that all goods belonged to a creative order, the gospel that the socialists of the nine-teenth century had raised in terms of a new idealization of the working class, has gone into its ebb; and from the salvation and justice that were all ideal imagined themes for a new life, men's minds have turned to strategies and expediencies and then to their defeat there. Workers were to be awakened not to the good that was in labor, to the true community that lay in the creation of social goods, but to the political and economic power that might lie in organization. To become leaders! To bargain in the market where labor was not a work but a commodity! Not to increase our common share in labor but to monopolize toward power. Over dinner tables and in living rooms with Picasso's *Guernica* presiding on the wall the flame of inspiration disappeared in the heat of contentions and political ambitions for the seizure of power.

Those young men struggling back to their boarding houses, breaking away from their ordered ranks, released into their crowd or their individual selves, were to go on into the ranks of armies and industries and professions made real upon that other field of lies and ambitions, fears and hopes—a war that only gave rise to a wider breach between nations and peoples, preparing in its waste for war upon war.

My heart, have you no wisdom thus to despair?

It was before the outbreak of the First World War that Joyce had written that close of his poem, of the war that we have come to know was not a last conflict but the continuum, the meaning of our nations, our politics, our labor unions, our leaders and masses.

Come, let us have a lasting sentence! the heart resolved. What is there lasting but our human condition, but what is most vivid in our imagination of what our life has been? The threat is part of that then. And the green lawn in the sun. The radiant women—Etruscan beauty, as we had seen it in Picasso's archaic mode, Semitic beauty as in Matisse's odalisques. The poem transforming loneliness and despair into lovely measures of song. The feet, feet, feet of young men marching. The distant shouting of orders in the playing field that in turn becomes the issue of orders in battlefields and war offices, warehouses and shipyards and laboratories, new classrooms and political parties and factories of mind. The war, too, defines eternal measures.

Chapter 2

Writing these opening pages of a book "On H.D." or "For H.D.," a tribute and a study, I came at this point to see this first part or movement of the book as relating how I had found my life in poetry through the agency of certain women and how I had then perhaps a special estimation not only of the masters of that art but of its mistresses, so that certain women writers came to be central in importance for me. Miss Keough reading to us in that high school English class long ago the poem "Heat," so that there was an actual voice that I loved in the voice of the poem for me; Athalie and Lili listening as I read aloud "I hear an army charging upon the land," so that there was the voice of my own loving that found itself in the voice of the poem—these had emerged as first awakenings to the informing and transforming powers of Poetry. In the very beginning, in the awakening of childhood back of this later awakening of the man I was to be, there had been my mother's voice reading the fairy tales and myths that were to remain the charged ground of my poetic reality.

I have written elsewhere that I am unbaptized, uninitiated, ungraduated, unanalyzed. I had in mind that my worship belonged to no church, that my mysteries belonged to no cult, that my learning belonged to no institution, that my imagination of my self belonged to no philosophic system. My thought must be without sanction. Yet to be a poet is to be reborn—to be baptized, initiated, graduated, analyzed. The Muses—for me in my adolescent days, these women, my teacher and my companions—admit the poet to their company. But we are drawn to them, as if in the beginning we were of their kind, kin of Poetry with them.

Back of the Muses, so the old teaching goes, is Mnemosyne, Mother of the Muses. Freud, too, teaches that the Art has something to do with restoring, re-membering the Mother. Poetry itself may then be the Mother of those who have destroyed their mothers. But no—The image Freud projects of dismembering and remembering is the image of his own creative process in Psychoanalysis, which he reads into all Arts. Mnemosyne, the Mother-Memory of Poetry, is our made-up life, the matrix of fictions. Poetry is the Mother of those who have created their own mothers.

Given the memory of Miss Keough reading "Heat" and then of Athalie and Lili attending my reading of Joyce's "I hear an army charging upon the land," a third memory claimed its place, and in the relations of these three scenes the formal image of the book comes: the first part developing along the lines of three stages and their attendant women—my falling in love or conversion, my loving or company in the art, and then, something quite different it would seem, setting all into a new motion, my first intimations of an historical task with the modernist imperative. For my directive to *The Cantos* of Ezra Pound, and at the same time a directive to work not from preconceived form but toward a form yet to be created, came from another woman. She was a poet, perhaps what is called a poetaster, for nothing came of her writing later, but, importantly, she was an arbiter of the modern. She had taste, an autocratic sense of the right things—Stein, Sitwell, Proust, Joyce. They were the set fashionable authors for a literary snobbism of the time, but they were also to be formative and lasting sources for my life as a poet. "What should he read—" her paramour asked as we walked toward the campus the day of our first meeting—"Should he read Eliot—?" "No," she made her pronouncement, speaking of me in the third person—it was as if he had enquired on my behalf at Delphi of the oracle: "His work is too melodramatic as it is. He should read Pound."

Just here, with this memory, a third scene, I had the sense of a missing element of my story coming into the picture. It was at once the weakest in its claim to being a living reality—just as the claim of a stylish mode in itself can seem a weak ground indeed. But the reality of art was to be for me always a matter of love *and* taste, Eros and Form. Had that arbiter not been so purely a creature of taste or fashion, of an even snobbish sense of what was *right,* and so little—it was my entire impression of her—a creature of *soul,* I might have mistaken taste for liking. Liking, being fond of like things and people, was itself a mimic of love, and could be then a mimic too of judgment. But taste—even the snob's presumption—excited in me another apprehension, the lure of a quality in a work in itself that demanded something of me, beyond the recognition of my own feelings expressed in an artist's work, the recognition of feelings that were demanded by the form of the work itself. Love and the sense of Form or Judgment—passion and law—know nothing of liking or disliking. The modern taste, the exacting predilection, beyond likes, was, just here, a third aspect—my involvement with the structural drama of H.D.'s art. I was as a poet to be not only a Romantic but also a Formalist.

Form is the mode of the spirit, as Romance is the mode of the soul. In liking and disliking there was a beginning of creating one's soul life, determining in recognizing what would be kindred and what alien to one's inner feeling of things, making a likeness of one's self in which the person would develop. In taste, almost the vanity of taste, there were intimations of the formal demand the spirit would make to shape all matter to its energies, to tune the world about it to the mode of an imagined music.

In my conversion to Poetry I was to find anew the world of Romance that I had known in earliest childhood in fairy tale and daydream and in the romantic fictions of the household in which I grew up. I had set out upon a soul-journey in my falling in love with my teacher in which she set me upon the quest of the spirit in Poetry, that reappeared later disguised in this foolish, even vain, presentation of a lady of fashionable tastes who demanded of me the secret of form hidden in the modernist style. The high adventure was to be for me the romance of forms, haunted by its own course, its own secret unfolding form, relating to some great form of many phases to which it belonged. The crux of my work was still to be melodramatic—if we remember the meaning of that word as being "a stage-play (usually romantic and sensational in plot and incident) in which songs are interspersed, and in which the action is accompanied by orchestral music." But the elements of stage and play, of romance and sensation, that are usually taken to belong to the psyche-drama, were to come more and more to be seen to belong to, to illustrate and accompany, the musical structure. So the world of the spirit hidden in the experience of soul and body becomes dominant, informing romance and sensation with a third possibility, even as soul dramatizes or enacts body and spirit, or as body incarnates as a living idea propositions of spirit and soul. The orchestration no longer accompanies but leads the dance.

.

A kindred earnest regard, ready and with the joy of self-discovery, had leaped up towards a life, a larger play of vitalities, quickened in the ardor with which a young teacher—in her early thirties perhaps when I was sixteen—read and loved the work of H.D., of D. H. Lawrence, and of Virginia Woolf. It was, wasn't it, that in these the inner consciousness saw a clue to its part or work in the world? The intense truthfulness to conception, the communication of self, because she had so loved this, was to be the key, the way.

I drew now upon my teacher's own romance, her hero worship or daydream of the role of the writer. The important thing for her was that the writer awakened a greater demand in life, that the tips of consciousness, the nervous susceptibility, be kept bare, sympathetic, ready, as a condition for reality. Coming to realize something is a creative imperative, for we must ourselves make it real. She was not wrong that truth was romantic, that the life of the writer was a romance. There is no physical reality that is not a psychic or spiritual creation, for the universe has just that reality for us that we extend to it as the dreams of body, soul, and spirit become one dream; and what is most terrible about the world that men have made is that it so embodies the dreams, the soul and spirit, of mean and vain imaginations. She was not wrong to daydream of the writer. The hero, the saint or poet, moves in such a confusion or cooperation of modes in one great mode that we call Reality or Vision, a romance that must create its own terms of existence in the midst of dreams of empire and commerce that seem to most men patently realistic.

"The study of literature is hero-worship," Pound writes in *The Spirit of Romance.* Carlyle's vision of the poet haunts Pound's thought here. But "hero" for my teacher did not mean the sublime ego, the great man that figured in Carlyle's thought of Dante or Goethe. It meant the courage to live with sensitivity. All that was sensitive to qualities and finenesses in impulse most needed courage, heroic resolve, in towns like Bakersfield where I was growing up. It needed daring to live by the imagination.

Miss Keough was Irish. She was consciously Celtic. She found me out, tried me with James Stephens's *Deirdre* and *Crock of Gold,* with books of Fionn and of the old world of glamors and wishes. "Escape literature" such works are called by those who patrol the borders of our realities to keep us grounded in the viabilities of practical reality, and even border guards of the realm of imagination would draw a line where fancy began and true imagination ended. Such official boundary lines grow confused before the eye when we enter the territories of the Celtic twilight. Pound will acclaim the gods and crystalline body of light "come forth / from the fire," but he won't take Yeats's "spooks." And even for some of those who will go along with Yeats wherever Red Hanrahan or Michael Robartes lead, Dunsany's King of Elfland's daughter will be beyond the pale.

Folklore, myth, and phantasy shared a territory with the reality of the personal imagination of Lawrence's *The Man Who Died* or Virginia Woolf's *The Waves.* There was in all the element of pretend turned most serious. We must take in earnest the Christ and priestess of Isis in Lawrence's story, even as their reality grows confusing upon the borderline of his story-telling and his being. Do they illustrate something he has to tell us, or do they impersonate his true being more intensely than his actual personality, as if Lawrence had his life in his writing? "I have survived the day and the death of my interference, and am still a man." Is this Christ, Lawrence? He indwells in his Christ, but also in his priestess of Isis in that story. He takes presence in what he creates for us, as the Celtic bard Taliesin claimed presence wherever he sang of the time of Man: "I have been in the firmament with Mary Magdalene," he sings. In Virginia Woolf's or H.D.'s imagination the scene is filled with presence, so that flowers, rocks, sea, night and day, seem to embody self, a revelation of identity, more potent than the writer's proper personality. The proprioceptive grows hallucinatory, for the proper body of the author presents itself in the surrounding scene. The cooperation of fantasy and reality, the correspondence and then the identity felt between one's being and the events of the outer world, the interchange of being, is very like the affinity that Celtic art has for interweaving forms, shape-changings, letters that are alive with animals and flowerings, reincarnations, in an art where figure and ground may be exchanged as the artist works. H.D. addressing the "meagre flower, thin, / sparse of leaf" in the poem "Sea Rose" is also addressing some person, we realize, and, beyond that, this figure of the sea rose is meant to present the image of some self-creation both of her art and of her own being, an idea or ideal in the image, "caught in the drift"—it is a witchcraft or spell.

Let these things be terms of your life, and you will come into the things that I love—that was what my teacher seemed to say in her presentation of the poem or novel. She had come herself to Bakersfield from Berkeley, from what was for me the outside world, leaving behind associations where she had been close to the community of poets or at least at the margins of poetry. She had had a link among her friends in a gaunt, beautiful, touched, old woman, Ella Young, whom I in turn as a student at Berkeley once heard tell of those Irish circles, of poets who practiced magic, of women who saw into what was beyond the common sense, of that folk who dwelt upon the margins of fairy. But all men are "folk" in their dwelling there, as men are businessmen in their dwelling upon money and its affairs. Professional men lived on the margins of their careers; literati upon the margins of the world of letters; public figures upon the margins of public affairs. As poets lived upon the margins of poetry. For "folk," "money," careers," "letters," "the public," are all realms that men in their phantasies invest with reality.

This was the operation of what was called a "story." "A story" in childhood meant a fib. "That was just a story" meant it wasn't true or that it wasn't worth worrying about. "You made it up," that, too, meant it was a falsehood. But "story" meant also an entertainment, in the afternoon or evening, close upon naptime or bedtime, close upon dreaming then.

Miss Keough had left behind some time of her life when she had dreamed of living in a world of writers and artists. And on vacations from college, she had gone to Carmel and to Taos, because Jeffers and Lawrence were there, that she had been to *their* places was part of her story. The fame of the poet was an actual presence or power for her, a charm. The town she had come to teach in was protestant against charm. It knew no news nor wanted to know any of an other life. Yet, just in this, it was most like those towns in fairy tales, where men are always blinded by greed and realistic ends to the vision of a world beyond their ken. The burden of the 1930s, the hardship she must have known during Depression years to support her mother and to finish her education—these too were terms of the old stories. She had, along with her resignation to the terms of her job, a romance of teaching. She enacted her role in a folk rite of the soul's awakening. She brought news and waited for news of any who had known or might come to know the life of the poets. Just beyond the news, just beyond the troubled vision of an *other* life raised by the poets who were heroes for her, lay the old questions of the mysteries: "Do you know who you are?" "Do you know where you are going?"

There may have been a wish, a power of that god *Wunsch* that the folklorist Grimm believed must have existed. I was to go forth then, from a wish she had, the hero—not the hero of Carlyle's essay, but the other, unlikely younger brother or little one or silly one of the fairy tales, following a hint given by a maiden or a lady, and I would come some day under the protection of the Moon's grandmother, of the Sun's grandmother, of the Wind's grandmother, or the Devil's grandmother, whose book this is to be.

She had left behind a wish. And, coming to Bakersfield, in her teaching she had had that inspiration to open for me the wish that underlies, informs, and directs, the writer's way toward a pouring out of self that turns out to be an opening up of self in the light of men's love. A wish, and a desire. It was desire, Eros, that, unknowing, I knew attended my awakening.

"You were a wonderful boy," she told me years later. But I was a miserable boy. I had found the wonder in her.

Love showed me the way and bid me to follow. My work in life must be likewise to reveal inner forces, to make articulate what pulse, nerve, and breath knew. Shame or guilt, weakness or sin—these were lifted up to be the very material, despised among men, that gave the gold of experience. Hiding what others might scorn or revile, showing forth what others might value or reward—all this was the very misery of life in that town where hidden indulgences grew and values dwindled to fit shop-front presentations. Where truth is the root of the art, to come to fullness means to let bloom the full flower of what one was, the truth of what one felt and thought—a flowering of corruptions and rage, of bile and intestines, as well as of sense and light, of glands and growth. For it was not the ideal or the model of feeling that I saw as my work, but the revelation of the nature of Man in my own being. I knew nothing of Baudelaire, but I knew that the heart must be stripped bare. But so much of what I felt and thought sickened me or frightened me. I longed to come into the trust of mankind but what in me trusted? The wish and the trust were what I must search out.

I was to undertake the work in poetry to find out—what I least knew myself—what I felt at heart. But in the beginning the work was a gift to my teacher. I was to undertake the work to present what I felt at heart to someone who had a trust I did not have in the heart, who wished for just that gift for love's sake. I was to undertake the work in order that Eros be kept over me a Master.

"Folks expect of the poet to indicate the path between reality and their souls," Whitman writes in his 1855 "Preface." There was, anyway, a path between Miss Keough's reading that poem of H.D.'s, a path taken because of love, and the reality of this book that is my soul way. Not because I read everything H.D. wrote, as I read all that I could of Lawrence in those early years. It was not until *The Walls Do Not Fall* that H.D. would take her place, along with Ezra Pound and William Carlos Williams, as a Master for me in my art and as one of the few primary authors among moderns in my reading. Then, recognizing in her writing a gospel of Poetry, I was to read everything in a new light. So that, when, in the third book of The War Trilogy, *The Flowering of the Rod*, I came to read the lines:

I go to the things I love
with no thought of duty or pity;

I go where I belong, inexorably,

the very lines themselves, even as they spoke for my own intense feeling of so taking in the things I loved the path between reality and my soul, belonged too to those things. They fitted. I had an old sense in which my life was involved, in which there was an alliance with H.D.'s sense. Between that first poem heard as a gift of love and as news of the gods, a secret then of what the path was to be, and charged with that portent, between the poem "Heat" and *The Walls Do Not Fall,* there had been a way. What had been loved had, along some path, come to be most valuable. The path of H.D.'s work, between that poem and the many levels of consciousness mastered in The War Trilogy, and the path of my own recognitions in poetry and life, between that classroom where I had resolved to devote my life to poetry and the first formative crises when I began to see what that poetry was to be, had their coordinations.

A classroom had been a meeting room. I had come at the appointed hour with a lover's joy in her company who had given me the most gracious of gifts, these things she loved she gave me to love. Books were the bodies of thought and feeling that could not otherwise be shared. There was more. Certain writers so revealed what a human being was that each of us had a share in that being. Love and Poetry were so mixed in the alembic that they coinhered in a new experience. "When in the company of the gods," H.D. writes in that passage of *The Flowering of the Rod,* "I loved and was loved"—That was long ago in childhood hours of Mother's reading myths and fairy tales in which that world appeared. In the new experience old layers of being found a pathway and welled up into the present:

> never was my mind stirred
> to such rapture,
>
> my heart moved
> to such pleasure,
>
> as now, to discover
> over Love, a new Master:

Every resonance had been prepared, for I had found—as when I was sixteen I had found a new teacher who brought me to Love—a new Master over Poetry in the work of H.D. In these things my mind likewise was stirred to rapture, my heart moved to such pleasure. My first teacher had given me a key to my future resource. She had presented the work that was worthy, and the work was to be the ground of Eros. For that winged bright promise that the soul seeks in its beloved appeared to me in the life that the inner sensitive consciousness of Lawrence, Virginia Woolf, or H.D., had found for itself in their writing, thriving there, hidden from the careless reader, surviving the scorn and even hatred of the antipathetic reader, a seed that would chance somewhere, sometime, upon the ground that awaited its revelation, for the reader who would not misunderstand or revile but who would come to find therein his own kindred life.

Chapter 3 *Eros*

The work, the ground, and Eros lie at the heart of our study here. The work itself is the transformation of the ground. In this ground the soul and the world are one in a third hidden thing, in imagination of which the work arises. It is the work of creation then. It is Poetry, a Making. It is also the *opus alchymicum* of Hermetic and Rosicrucian alchemy. The rhymes of this poetry are correspondences, workings of figures and patterns of figures in which we apprehend the whole we do not see. The path that poetry creates between reality and the soul is the path of a conversion. Our path here must often come close to the path of depth psychologies and of theosophical schools, but we are tracing the path of Psyche and her Eros as workers of a fiction in the art of poetry, projecting not a cure of souls or an illumination of souls, except as the secret of fictions may cure or illumine, but the inner works of the poetic opus. Our work is to arouse in a contemporary consciousness reverberations of old myth, to prepare the ground so that when we return to read we will see our modern texts charged with a plot that had already begun before the first signs and signatures we have found were worked upon the walls of Altamira or Pech-Merle. *Mythos* Aristotle defined as the plot of the story. The plot we are to follow, the great myth or work, is the fiction of what Man is.

Soul and Eros are primordial members of the cast. To imagine ourselves as souls is to become engaged in all the mystery play, the troubled ground, of a poetry that extends beyond the reaches of any contemporary sense. Eros and Psyche are personae of a drama or dream that determines, beyond individual consciousness, the configurative image of a species. Just as the source of the song lies in an obscurity back of the first writing on the wall, so, in my own childhood, in the dawn of story, before I could read or write, there was a tale told to me of Cupid and Psyche. In the beginning I heard of this god Eros and of the drama of loss and search. I understood only that there was a wonder in this tale.

If the Work has to do with Eros—and for the poet the poem is a return to the work in the charged sense we would pursue here—the would-be poet stands like Psyche *in the dark,* taken up in a marriage with a genius, possessed by a spirit outside the ken of those about him. That there be gold or wonder or the beloved in such a blind matter, no one else can believe. So the poet William Carlos Williams in *Paterson* Four sees the work of poetry in the chemistry where Madam Curie works the pitchblende:

A dissonance
in the valence of Uranium
led to the discovery

. . . .

by the hour, the day, the week
to get, after months of labor .

a stain at the bottom of the retort
without weight, a failure, a
nothing. And then, returning in the
night, to find it   .

LUMINOUS!

For my middle-class parents the work I was to undertake was as fearful and doubtful as that calling that Psyche, in the story Apuleius tells, knew in the dark. The genius of Poetry appeared to them "not a son-in-law of mortal birth but a dire mischief," "a winged pest." They, like Psyche's parents, were dismayed and strove to dissuade me. They tried to make me see this alien calling in the light of common sense. And there was every reason to mistrust, for I had no sure talent. I was in the dark about what poetry was. How badly first poems turned out! If one looked at them at all in a critical light, the charm might be broken. What garbled and even monstrous expressions stood for the first articulations of poetic feeling! *"Knowledge, the contaminant,"* Williams writes. Luminous in the dark, and so Madame Curie works—it haunts Williams that it is a woman—for she is the poet, but also, here too, she is Psyche:

> And so, with coarsened hands
>   she stirs
>
> And love, bitterly contesting, waits
> that the mind shall declare itself not
> alone in dreams   .

Hints of the old story appear in the workings of the new.

.

There was the Palace of Eros. Psyche was to inherit all, on the one condition that she not seek to see her Eros in the light. Her mind must not become involved in the knowledge of love. "When well inside the palace she came upon splendid treasure chambers stuffed with unbelievable riches; every wonderful thing that anyone could possibly imagine was there." This Palace, as it appears in the beginning of the story, is like the wealth of works the imagination has left us, that we call our Culture. Writing, painting, architecture, and music seem to exist to enrich our appreciations, to furnish forth our taste, to suit or not our predilections. Some men believe that mountains, streams, animals, and birds, that the plenitude of the world, exists like this, a storehouse of commodities for human improvement and uses. And the Palace of Eros has another likeness to the world that exists in works of art—"No single chain, bar, lock, or armed guard protected it," the story tells us. It lay an open secret for those who discovered it to live in.

Psyche, before her sin, is a dilettante. To read, to listen, to study, to gaze, all was part of being loved without loving, a pleasure previous to any trial or pain of seeking the beloved. The light must be tried; Psyche must doubt and seek to know; reading must become life and writing;

and all must go wrong. There is no way then but Psyche's search, the creative work of a union in knowledge and experience with something missing. At the end, there is a new Eros, a new Master over Love.

Eros, like Osiris, or Lucifer (if He be the Prince of Light whom the Gnostics believe scattered in sparks throughout the darkness of what is the matter), is a Lord over us in spirit who is dispersed everywhere to our senses. We are drawn to Him, but we must also gather Him to be. We cannot, in the early stages, locate Him; but He finds us out. Seized by His orders, we "*fall* in love," in order that He be; and in His duration, the powers of Eros are boundless. We are struck by His presence, and, in becoming lovers we become something other than ourselves, subjects of a daemonic force previous to our humanity, that, as the poet Hesiod pictures Eros, "unnerves the limbs and overcomes the mind and wise counsels of all gods and all men within them." This Eros is a primal authority, having the power of a cosmic need. Men knew His terrors before they knew anything of Him as Cupid with his darts, before men had invented arrows.

There was an Eros before there were Titans or Gods. But then there is a second Eros. After the Titanic Kronos cuts away the genitals of the Father Uranus, the Great Sky, and casts them away behind him upon the raging sea (that may be the sea of the act itself), "they were swept away over the main a long time: and a white foam spread around them from the immortal flesh, and in it grew a maiden"—Aphrodite—and, with her, Eros and Himeros. A transformation has taken place. In this Greek figure the Father's parts, the essential "Father," reappear in three persons: his penis becomes the goddess Aphrodite or Beauty, and his testicles become the attendant gods, Eros and Himeros.

In the *Zohar* of Moses of Leon in the thirteenth century A.D., there appears another figure of the Father that may be related to his Greek figure from the Hesiod's *Theogony* of the eighth century B.C. In the Kabbalistic lore, the Glory of En Soph is a womanly power of God, the Shekinah. And we learn too that there is a mystery of the two sides, the Left and the Right, that are testicles from which the souls of the living come. Souls, in Kabbalistic thought, are seminal.

Love, desire, and beauty, in the poet's *Theogony,* precede mankind. They were beings before they were human feelings. The meaning of things seems to change when we fall in love, as if the universe were itself a language beyond our human language we had begun to understand. It is the virtue of words that what were forces become meanings and seek form. Cosmic powers become presences and even persons, having body to the imagination. We fall in love with Love.

In the old rites, Eros appeared as an unwrought stone. And from our childhood, for some of us dim, for some of us vivid, memories remain of the way a stone could seem to be alive. The presence or protective genius of a stone could become a secret ally of oneself. For the sculptor the stone "speaks" and his work emerges along the lines of a colloquy between his listening and—out of a dumbness or meaninglessness of matter, were it not for this listening—a language of space which the stone has evoked for him. For what we call our common sense, for the consensus that is even contemptuous of being influenced by mere things, the stone is properly inert. But for the imagination, for the mind seeking communication, to create in its life a serious play, even inert matter is alive with person. So, for the Orphic poets, the seed or egg of the universe is created by *Hyle*, the primal chaos of matter.

Again and again in our lives we find our vital sense of the universe must return to this muddle, to begin again in the unspeaking obstruction of the stone. It is the artist's block that heightens his awe of the other power in which his material speaks to him. The block itself is the blockage of a breath. The inspiring stone "breathes" as the artist awakens to his work.

From the unwrought Eros, once the work begins, the form of a vital spirit flies up. Chaos itself, the abyss—but it is a block—is alive with that personal possibility. In its obscurity, Chaos corresponds to the psychoanalytic unconscious, for the idea of the unconscious is also that of a vitality that, unless a man enter a colloquy with what cannot sensibly speak and take instructions from what he cannot know, may show itself as a deadly and deadening matter. But once he take faith in what he cannot see, from a World-Egg, where once there was demonic Chaos, the universe of Creation comes forth, and, as Jane Harrison observes in her *Prolegomena to the Study of Greek Religion*, "it is almost inevitable that there should emerge from the egg a bird-god, a winged thing."

Hidden, Eros is the very vitality felt by the sculptor in the stone.

Revealed, he is shown to be an idea, a youth flying up from the head of a Titanic Mother or Matter awakening or come alive in the ground, the Earth-goddess, Γη or Gaia. This Earth is also the artist's content, the subject of the conversation with an otherwise speechless matter, the ground of potential identity in which he works. In the figure shown by Jane Harrison on page 639 of the *Prolegomena,* attendant upon the work, are two satyrs with pickaxes, breakers of the ground; the giant female head uprises. And from the aroused head two *erotes* spring—the primal Eros and Himeros.

In Hesiod's *Theogony,* the second Eros and Himeros appear as transformations of the Father's testes, and back of this erotic replacement, there is the scene of a chaotic or psychotic episode—the castration of the Father. In the mysteries of the Mother, the awakening of Chaos giving rise to Love and Desire seems also to follow upon such an attack, but here it is upon the Mother. One satyr holds his pick swung high for a blow; the other has completed his stroke. Describing an earlier figure shown on page 279 of the *Prolegomena,* Jane Harrison sees this as the *anodos* or calling-up of the Maiden: "The colossal head and lifted hands of a woman are rising out of the earth. Two men are present. Both are armed with great mallets or hammers, and one of them strikes the head of the rising woman." It may be the same rite as that of the breaking of the world-egg. We see them attacking the stone, breaking the ground or egg—it is the mothering head—to release from its container the ideas of a new order: Eros and his other.

•

In Athens, Jane Harrison tells us, the cult of Aphrodite gave way to the cult of the male Eros. "There is no Aphrodite," the poet Alcman sang:

> Hungry Love
> Plays boy-like with light feet upon the flowers.

The power of Love that had been a woman in an other phase is impersonated by youths.

"O Menexenus and Lysis, how ridiculous that you two boys," Socrates says at the close of Plato's dialog *Lysis,* "and I, an old boy, who would fain be one of you, should imagine ourselves to be friends—this is what the by-standers will go away and say—and as yet we have not been able to discover what is a friend."

In the aristocratic cult of the homo-Eros, the winged images we saw drawn upon the vases become winged ideas in full. The daemonic force of Eros remains, but within the created world of Plato's book the cosmos itself has been idealized. Empedocles had called Eros *Philia;* and now in *Lysis,* Plato's Socrates speaks of a first principle, a higher Eros, the πρῶτον φίλον. In his *Hexameters,* Xenophanes had remarked:

> If oxen and lions had hands or could draw with hands and create works of art like those made by men, horses would draw pictures of gods like horses, and oxen of gods like oxen, and they would make the bodies in accordance with the form that each species itself possesses.

In the idealizing philosophy of Plato the true form of God is the ideal of the Good. Whatever of the old divine world cannot be incorporated in the ideal of the Good must be put down as the falsification of Art or Poetry. Just as men may imagine themselves to be friends but cannot come to discover what is a friend, so men may imagine immortal gods with immortal bodies, but

> no such union can reasonably be believed to be; although fancy, not having seen or surely known the nature of God, may imagine an immortal creature having both a body and also a soul which are united throughout all time.

The young men flying in a sexual rapture now are called to school their bodies, serving a new rapture of the rational mind. For them, there is to be a rational Eros, the Love because of Whom men try to love, the First Beloved, the most dear, because of whom men hold life dear and would imagine themselves friends. Caring in itself becomes an adventure of the imagination that is wed here to the great adventure of Eros and desire.

But the old power of the old Eros haunts the new love of friends. We do not quite know what makes us find things most dear. Just here, in the unknowing, Plato must call upon the primal force to make real the idea. The Good has power in men's minds, but it comes not in their knowledge but in their desire that there be good. Eros and even Dionysos, desire and intoxication, Plato argues are daemons of the Good.

But then the story turns, as life itself turns. The light spills. Eros is burned or betrayed. Some five hundred years after Plato, a Christian contemporary of Apuleius, Ignatius of Antioch, said, "crucified"—"My Eros is crucified." It is the beginning of our era.

Eros, in Apuleius's story, when he comes to Psyche in the dark, is something she knows not what. He is what the oracle at Miletus said he was—a monster that belongs to the old order, an unwrought stone. But he is also an other, for he carries arrows. She is curious about those arrows; her investigating hand trembles and she wounds herself. She bleeds. Psyche becomes soul; the figure of the human Eros comes to light—the Divine Bridegroom to be. Who might have been a dilettante becomes an exile from delight. What might have been pleasure is to be joy, that is the new faith. It is in exile from Eros that this love and this faith appear depending upon a promise that is unbelievable. In the new myths, Orpheus turns to look, and Eurydice is lost. "Woman, what have I to do with thee?" the Christ says to his mother or bride or woman. In the Gnostic interpretation, the spirit loses or puts away the soul. Psyche disobeys the law and raises the light to know Eros, and the separation of soul and spirit follows. Something like this happened in our history in the Western World, so that, for men of the second century after Christ, that there was a Life within life, a Love within love, became a promise only faith could believe. Eros had been seen in the flesh, a figure the light drew out of the old dark to husband the soul. The great dark reality in which body, soul, and spirit had been one in unknowing was reft. "Knowledge, the contaminant"—and then—"Uranium, the complex atom, breaking / down." Men revile the body they had seen. Psyche is set to those tasks by an offended Aphrodite. Life and history appear to travail in punishment that is necessary before the restoration of paradise. The spirit retreats from its incarnation and is removed to states of ecstasy and despair, heaven and hell.

The god had said: "Today shalt thou be with me in paradise." As H.D. tells of Him in *The Flowering of the Rod*:

> He was the first to say,
> not to the chosen few,
>
> his faithful friends,
> the wise and good,
>
> but to an outcast and a vagabond,

The passers-by jeered at Him, so Matthew tells us. We remember, that for Plato too, there had been the sense of what "by-standers" would say, mocking the Eros of those who imagined themselves to be friends. "Even the robbers who were crucified with Him," so Matthew testifies, "abused Him in the same way." There may then have been mockery when one said, as Luke testifies he did, "Remember me when you come into your kingdom!" Eros, being taunted, would have replied likewise—"I say unto thee, today shalt thou be with me in Paradise." For Paradise is the inexorable power of Eros.

In Greece, in Plato's lifetime, the virtue of boy-love in men's eyes had come to be suspect, and the faithful friends lost the ground in Eros they had imagined to claim as philosophers. He who had immortalized the Symposium was to condemn symposia in his *Laws,* where, in his old age, Plato sees the State as the stronghold of Reason:

> Now the gymnasia and common meals do a great deal of good, and yet they are a source of evil in civil troubles; as is shown in the case of the Milesian, and Boeotian, and Thurian youth, among whom these institutions seem always to have had a tendency to degrade the ancient and natural custom of love below the level, not only of man, but of the beasts. . . . Whether such matters are to be regarded jestingly or seriously, I think that the pleasure is to be deemed natural which arises out of the intercourse between men and women; but that the intercourse of men with men, or of women with women, is contrary to nature, and that the bold attempt was originally due to unbridled lust.

The Platonic and Sapphic lovers are driven not only outside the law or the rational State but outside of the natural order into the criminal chaos from which Eros had first come.

In Jerusalem, the Temple was to fall and the Jews go scattered among the gentiles into the Diaspora. Gnostic cults taught that the Light Itself had been in the beginning scattered so into a Darkness, sparks or seeds of light imprisoned in matter. All men were to become outcasts and vagabonds. There was in Christ's "today," because of the promise, no end of time in the actual world.

He had also said: "The time is coming when you will worship the Father neither on this mountain nor at Jerusalem." Man had retracted his worship from place and time. The old cosmic gods, and the Elohim among them, withdrew from mountain and temple to men's minds. We saw in Plato's teaching the old cosmology replaced by a new ideology. Now, everywhere, cosmology and ideology give way to psychology.

Hesiod, like the Old Testament, speaks of a beginning that was Earth and Sky. And Heraclitus says of Hesiod: "They think that he knew many things, though he did not understand day and night. For they are one." And then: "God is day and night, winter and summer, war and peace, surfeit and hunger. But he undergoes transformations—just as fire, when it is mixed with spices, is named after the savor of each." This was the ancient world, where, if God was man, He was also day and night, beast and sun, wind and tree; where before there was man, there was Beauty, Eros, and Himeros.

But with the Gospel of John—is it six hundred years after Heraclitus?— a Book begins to take the place of the Old Testament that had been a spoken word, what-they-said or myth, passed from man to man. The new written testament knows nothing of Earth or Sky, of day or night, of summer or winter. "In the beginning was the Word," the new Book tells us: "Everything came into existence through Him, and apart from Him nothing came to be." The universe had once, almost, spoken to man. Now, a language that originated in the Word, the speech of man, was to be the true universe. The *vis imaginativa* in which the things of men's souls and the things of the actual universe dance together, having concourse and melody, the magic world of resonances and freely associating rhymes—is disowned. And what appears is a world of two opposing possibilities—dogma and heresy.

The primal Eros rages in the division. Sex witches brew their ointments in Thessaly. Devils and lamiae swarm about the bodies of saints in the desert, familiar animals that were once dear to the household come now as familiars with messages from beastly hell. The old reverences die out or are scattered out from their centers to flare up in new woods and fountains, in the hearts of guilty lovers or upon pagan hearths, in the hinterlands where groves are too close and wheat too dear to be denied the worship of men. "In Benedict and Gregory," Henry Osborn Taylor tells us in *The Medieval Mind,* "the salvation which represented the true and uncorrupt life of man on earth, as well as the assured preparation for eternal life with God, had shrunken from the universality of Christ, and even from the fullness of desire with which Augustine sought to know God and the soul." But the Christ had not been more universal at first than Galilee in the midst of Judea was—He had been a god of a division among Jews, of a tribal dispute. The universal Christ is the god of an Empire and has that universality. The salvation which represented the true and uncorrupt life of man on earth had its counterpart in the Roman law which represented the civilized life of man on earth.

The universality and the fullness had, as had the Roman organization, boundaries beyond which was disorder. Clovis in the fifth century crossed the Rhine not only into the Romanized world but into humanity, for, as Gregory of Tours tells us, his ancestor was a dragon or demon of the other side. The Eros within was Christ; the Mother within was a Virgin. The Eros without or beyond the pale was "a monster Bridegroom," was Pan and then Satan; the Mother without was Nature, was Aphrodite, was a Witch, was Lilith. The Church was a bulwark against them—against the unification of man with his other nature—even in marriage. The Nature without was lawless and false. The Church recognized a Nature within and defined what was outside that recognition as *contra naturam.*

The Palace of Eros, where once Psyche had known every imagined thing, had fallen into the darkness of a perishing civilization, and Psyche's tasks had begun. Driven by dogma, threatened by excommunication, she must harrow Hell before she come again into the light of the upper world.

Pound, in *The Spirit of Romance,* recalls another contemporary of Apuleius and Ignatius of Antioch in the second century—the author of the *Pervigilium Veneris.* When we put together the spiritual world projected by the magician, the Christian saint, and the pagan poet as they portrayed the dream content of their time as it were, we begin to gather that not only Christians but others too experienced the loss of a Divine Power in their history, and the promise in which Time, the time of history, became the stage of a spiritual drama, and in which there was to be a Resurrection, a Reunification of Paradise. In the division, there was not only the Christ, Jesus of Nazareth, or the Christ Enthroned, God of the Roman Empire, but there was an other Christ of the mystery cults, who had His place with Isis and with Aphrodite, the Venus Genetrix, and with the Virgin Without.

"Yea, hers is the song, and the silence is ours!" so the poet of the second century sings in prophecy of the Dark Ages ahead:

Ah, when shall mine own spring come?
When, as a swallow long silent, shall my silence find end?

Then Pound tells us: "The song did not again awake until the Provençal viol aroused it." The song, the "spring," the consort, the Sun, the Son— these seem to belong to the complex of one spiritual experience, once we read beyond the limitations of the permissions and prohibitions of the particular church.

The Church was a husk of the divine realm. The medieval synthesis was also the ground of a winter in which seeds of a new transformation worked, crossings-over and minglings of spirit where it had been scattered and gathered now toward new growth and species. In the eleventh century, poets again appear, as if spring, nine centuries underground, had returned from the *Pervigilium Veneris*. "High and low among the first come leaves," Arnaut sings: "The boughs and sprays are new with flowers, and no bird holds mute a mouth or throat, but cries and sings."

The Spring genius breaks through the husk everywhere in the twelfth and thirteenth centuries, within the Church and without. In Poictiers and Champagne, the trouvères sang once more of a Lady and of an *ars amatoria* that was the secret of an *ars poetica*. There were courts of a law that was Love's or Amor's, where certain ladies sat in judgment, and poets avowed they knew no other law over their hearts. Pound, writing for G. R. S. Mead's journal *The Quest*, suggests that the Lady "serves as a sort of *mantram*" and he quotes from a code of Amor's law: "The lover stands ever in unintermittent imagination of his lady (co-amantis)." It was perhaps the Law Without, for the ladies commanded duties of love or proofs that were acts *contra naturam*. "I am Arnaut," Daniel sings, "who swims against the current,"—*nadi contra suberna*.

There was some inner rite; there was a *trobar clus*. There was a forbidden matter, a going against the current so Pound tells us, that needed a poetry that would carry more than one current of meaning. For some it was a matter of alternative meaning; for some, of double meanings. The poetry of Provence was divided into an orthodox language of single meanings and an heretical language where meanings were united in a spiritual double-entendre. "We find this poetry divided into two schools," Pound writes:

> the first school complained about the obscurities of the second—we have them always with us. They claimed, or rather jeered in Provence, remonstrated in Tuscany, wrangle today, and will wrangle tomorrow—and not without some show of reason—that poetry, especially lyric poetry, must be simple; that you must get the meaning while the man sings it.

Where there was, some objected, a willful obscurity, there was for others a matrix of meanings. In Provence, in castles on the Rhine, up from the hinterlands of the Pyrenees or of Wales, poets began to sing of hearts or of a land that had long lain waste and desert, of a Lady who is Queen of Love, of Fairy, of an Island or a Wood. There is a requirement of adultery or a condition of adultery; things are mixed or must be mixed. But also, the hero of the new mysteries must transgress the sacraments of the Church to come into the environs of the Eros Without; he must *prove* his Love. Forbidden sexual acts are bidden as proofs. There is no service that is not ordered.

While in the courts of the feudal order there appeared those other courts of Poetry and Romance, at large in Provence another movement was at work—or perhaps another phase of the same happening? Out of Bulgaria, from the margins of Christendom in the East, had come preachers of a Manichean Christ—so the Church says—and they won converts everywhere. There are echoes of the Hellenistic gnosis in their legend. They kept certain laws of the spirit—they would not eat meat nor would they kill; they would not take oath; they volunteered poverty. There were rites of purgation, catharsis, to free the spirit from its bondage to the body of this world. They were exiles from Paradise and sought return, purification. They had revived the old order of Spirit, Soul, and Body, as the Hellenistic culture had pictured them, as separate and contesting identities, and they had turned against the Incarnation. This heresy we know because these things had become spiritual scandals in the eyes of the Church, which brought them to trial. Not only the Albigensians but Waldenses and Spiritual Franciscans—those who kept the terms of Saint Francis's will and testament and who embraced Poverty—"the Lady Poverty," he had called her—were hunted down and exterminated.

Christ, *verus imperator mundi,* in the person of His vicar, Innocent III, out of His *plenitudo potestatis,* His fullness of power in this world, released the horrors of the Albigensian crusade upon Provence, where the specter of an other Christ had invaded the Empire. If we do not believe, as the Albigensians were said to have believed, in a dualism throughout the universe between forces of light and forces of dark, eternally alien to each other, what we see here is a God divided against Himself. The Eros within Christendom was permitted or gave His permission only in the orders of generation; all other Eros was forbidden. So, from outside the Empire, from the margins where things mix, a Christ returns, and an Eros too, whose law is now the verso of the law of the established Church. In this new Law, the generative order is forbidden; all other Eros is permitted. An echo of the Church's accusations against the Cathars or Bogomils—they were, originally, *Bulgars*—is left in our word today for one of these forbidden sexual acts that is still outside the law of the established State: *buggery.* In this feature of transgression in Eros, the cults of the Perfecti resembled the courts of Amor.

There was another likeness between the code of the Troubadour and the creed of the Cathar, for in each there was a cult of the Lady. If the heresy of Provence was of the Gnostic-Manichean tradition, it would have taught that the secret of the Light or Spirit that was imprisoned in the world had something to do with a Woman—a Helen or Sophia. There was at Montsegur, so the twentieth-century Albigensian devotee Maurice Magre writes, a Lady Esclarmonde. But when we seek out her legend, we find there were two—Esclarmonde de Foix, the chaste, who keeps the castle, and, wandering with the outcasts in the forests and mountains, Esclarmonde d'Alion, the bastard, *l'amoureuse*. Where does the story come from? It comes, one suspects, made to fit the romance of the Gnostic Helen or Sophia who had been "Light of the World," yet was found by the Magus Simon in a brothel in Tyre. Once fitting, it becomes part of the story. There was then a Lady. However close, whatever correspondence there was or was not, between the heresy and the *ars amatoria* of the poets and their Lady, the *trobar* of Provence came to an end when the Cathar came to an end.

But the infection was abroad, the signs of a new time continue. On the Rhine they refused to take oath; at Lyons they gave their goods to the poor and went out to preach, inspired by the Spiritus Sanctus—or was it the "Santa SPIRITA, breather, life, / Beyond the light," as the New World poet Walt Whitman is bold to name Her in his "Chanting the Square Deific." At Assisi, Saint Francis in his Testament said that God Himself commanded him and his brothers give all to the poor and to be content with but one patched cloak. "And I labored with my hands," he wrote, "and I wish to labor; and I wish all other brothers to labor." Labor, that, like woman, had been designated a necessary evil, was proclaimed in the new vision a great good. Poverty itself was taken to be good. There was too close a likeness perhaps between the vows of poverty that the Cathars made and the love Saint Francis proclaimed for his Lady, his *sancta paupertas*. After the death of the saint, from the infallibility of His dogma, Pope John XXII declared the love of poverty to be heretical. The Saint was to be established Within; his Wish was to be banished Without. In 1318, at Marseilles, four who kept their vows to Saint Francis's Rule were burned.

In his *Frederick II*, Ernst Kantorowicz sees Francis as a poet, for he lived in this world, it seems to the historian as if it were in the eternal presence of all things; he lived in metaphor as if it were not a mere device of rhetoric but were a reality of what was. He was, Kantorowicz writes, "the first open-eyed soul who spontaneously experienced Nature and Life as magic and emotion, and traced the same divine *pneuma* in all that lived." Francis lived in the Palace of Eros then, in the fullness of the imagination, and, receiving the stigmata, he received too the burn from the oil of Psyche's lamp—he impersonated Eros.

If Saint Francis can be seen so, to be not only a saint but a poet, and his very sanctity to be a verity of his poetic imagination, we too begin to experience "Nature and Life as magic and emotion." A story or mythos of many myths begins to unfold in history itself that has poetic organization. Actual men become dramatis personae of a stage beyond the actual. Again and again, in eternal return, the old orders will not behave themselves, but move to speak in the new.

So, not only the song of the minnesingers sounds in the religious poetry of Mechthild of Magdeburg's *Flowing Light of God,* so that we recognize in the language of the Catholic mystics' illumination erotic terms that may be traced to a theophany that once belonged to the troubadours of Provence, but we may see too in the Catholic devotee's address to Frau Minne ghostly parallels to the old story of Cupid and Psyche that Apuleius told in the Hellenistic second century in which the mythic identities of Logo, Light, and Love, were compounded. "My Lady Love," the Soul in Mechthild's poem pleads, "Thou hast hunted and taken, bound and wounded me; never shall I be healed." It is Christ who is the all-but-lost Bridegroom of the Soul, in love of Whom the Soul is wounded. The terms are Christian, but we remember that Christ, too, like the Bridegroom in Apuleius's tale, was Love wounded for the sake of Love, and was taken up into heaven, because of a Disobedience. Dimly, but, once we suspect its presence, persistently, elements from an earlier story show through the later writing in the palimpsest. When Frau Minne answers the Soul, saying: "It was my pleasure to hunt thee; to take thee captive was my desire; to bind thee was my joy," behind her figure another seems to stand—Venus in her wrath upbraiding Psyche. "I drove Almighty God from His throne in heaven, and took His human life from Him, and then with honor gave Him back to His Father," she continues, "How couldst thou, poor worm, save thyself from me!"— even so we may remember another god driven from his palace and his bride, his human life, by Venus, and removed into the realm of immortal Zeus, beyond Psyche's reach. Psyche, who in her beauty was yet but a soul-worm, yet to become the soul butterfly herself. The story of one Eros we find entering the story of the other Eros.

Provence was laid waste, but out of the cult of its poets the *ars amato-ria* went as a poetic tradition, from Toulouse to Palermo and Florence. In that tradition or teaching, Dante was to discover in his Beatrice a magic having to do with the vision of God; His Lady was to lead him until she drew him "Within the yellow of the eternal rose"—*Nel giallo della rosa sempiterna*—"which doth expand, rank upon rank, and reeketh perfume of praise unto the Sun that maketh spring for ever." Such is the inspiration of Dante, and such his vision therein, that in *Commedia,* as in Saint Francis's legend and his Canticle of Brother Sun, it almost seems as if the separation of and from Eros were to be healed.

Out of the Celtic world, in the twelfth century, from the extreme Western borderlands of Christendom, possibly first by a Welsh prince, Bledri ap Cadivor, who was, so Jessie Weston tells us, "*Latinarius*" or "translator" and who had come over to the Norman side from the pagan Welsh world, a story came over to the Christian side, a magic is trans-lated into the content of a religion, and again, the Eros Without comes over into the Eros Within. Francesca, who whirls in the hellish storm of the Eros Without, tells Dante that she and Paolo were seduced by the enchantment of reading the story of Lancelot, seduced by Romance. The Celtic genius in a poetry that was not a rational melody but the weaving of a spell so intertwined and elaborated its figures that now we see the one Eros and now the Other, Within and Without dance in interchanging patterns. Which came first? the scholars still ask. Fertility cult, folk lore, or Christian mystery—however we read—the hallows, the Grail, the Lance that drips its blood into the Dish, the Wound, the Question that is not asked, the Lamenting Women that attend, are *feyrie, phanopoeia.* The sacra of the Church and the magic treasures of ancient kings, the sexual emblems and ritual objects of chthonic cults, have been stolen to furnish the changeling mysteries of a Romance in Poetry. They have become properties of an other stage that presents a play within the play.

Romance has appeared, and there may have been, in this, a new Eros. Not only the primal cosmic power, but also the Platonic ideal, the First Beloved, but also the most human god that Psyche sought in her quest, but also the Eros that Church fathers, Catholic and heretic, had named an evil, but also now the power of a cult that remains as a mode in poetry. Eros had become a tradition of the poem. Garden and rose, bird and dawn, dew and paradise, are notes now of a melody that first troubadours sang.

I too may be Celtic, and a spell be felt to be necessary to the works here, for weaving *is* necessary as I go, to keep many threads and many figures so that every thread is central and every figure central to threads and figures, with none coming to its conclusion but leading further into the process. But in this return of the *erôtes* of the verso as active elements of our own time, we are heirs of work done in the first decades of this century. In *The Spirit of Romance* Pound related the tradition of Eros from Apuleius to "the consummation of it all in Dante's glorification of Beatrice" and "the final evolution of Amor by Guido and Dante, a new and paganish god, neither Eros nor an angel of the Talmud." The poetic tradition of the Grail was related to this tradition by Jessie Weston in two books, *The Quest for the Holy Grail* (1913) and *From Ritual to Romance* (1919). The cult of the gods as it is found in the Hellenizing poems of D. H. Lawrence, H.D., and Pound in the Imagist period cannot be separated from the reawakened sense of the meaning and reality of the gods as facts of human experience that we find in contemporary studies of the mystery cults, in Jane Harrison's *Prolegomena to the Study of Greek Religion* (1903) and *Themis* (1912), in Cook's *Zeus* (1914), in the Orphic studies of Robert Eisler, and the Gnostic studies of G. R. S. Mead, whose lectures Pound attended in 1916 finding, as he tells us, "in the legend of Simon Magus and Helen of Tyre a prototype of chivalric love." In scholarship as well as in poetry there is an insistence that the contemporary world must call up within itself the old gods, that there must be a return of the Underworld into this world. "I know, I mean, one man who understands Persephone and Demeter," Pound writes in *The Spirit of Romance,* "and one who has, I should say, met Artemis. These things are for them *real*." Edward Sapir, reviewing H.D.'s *Collected Poems* in 1925, saw rightly, beyond the question of Imagism, "the rediscovery of ancient and beautiful ways made apt once again for the hungering spirit." Along these ways, Eros and Psyche come to reveal their meanings—here, now; there, then. "All ages are contemporaneous," Pound proposed, but it was by the poetic genius that these terms were created—"all ages" and "the contemporaneous" are perspectives of time that belong to the imagination. *The Spirit of Romance* was not a history of the actual past but an instruction in the nature of the high art that was to be contemporary poetry.

"Earth's fallen kingdom contains its original face," a fellow poet, M. C. Richards, writes in a poem that arrived today in a letter. "Dante found it in a dream," H.D. writes in "The Guest" in 1946, a companion work to *The Spirit of Romance.* Where Pound had taken the story of the Spirit of Romance from what he calls "the phantom dawn" in Apuleius to the Latin Renaissance after Dante, H.D., "remembering Shakespeare always, but remembering him differently," follows the proliferation of the Spirit in Elizabethan and Jacobean poetry. Theosophic insights lie back of Pound's study; Freudian learning informs H.D.'s—but these poets bring us to see the theosophic and the psychoanalytic anew as hints of a primary poetic vision and experience that returns where it will in man's history. Of certain men, Pound wrote, "their consciousness is *germinal.*"

> Their thoughts are in them as the thought of the tree is in the seed, or in the grass, or the grain, or the blossom. And these minds are the more poetic, and they affect mind about them, and transmute it as the seed the earth . . . the strength of the Greek beauty rests in this, that it is ever at the interpretation of this vital universe, by its signs of gods and godly attendants and oreads.

This image of seed and influence, consciousness and germination, reappears in H.D.'s account of a Spirit of Romance brought into the ground of Poetry in England:

> The lesser and the greater poet alike met in the unanimous acceptance of one article of faith . . . The dream was greater than reality. Out of it, they built a city, comparable to Augustine's *City of God,* or a fortress as formidable as the *Castle* of Teresa. Francis himself might have learned much from the blossoms of Robert Herrick or the *lilies of all kinds* of that *Winter's Tale.*

The images of the poem, then, were not impressions translated from the given reality of the poet into words but were evocations of a dream greater than reality, a New World coming into existence in the *opus* of the poem itself. In that New World an Old World reawakened. "The spiritual inheritance, substantially absorbed by Rome, was not lost," H.D. tells us:

> It had been carried, not in iron chests guarded by the vanguard of a conquering army, but it had blown on the wind, as the jongleur, the jester, the beggar wandered, himself suspect, from court to court. He gathered sometimes as he went, strange flowers, it is true, but the seeds of the faith, in the end, blown by the tempest or carried in the dowry-chest of the girl from the south, took root.
>
> An exotic flower—it blossomed only in the queen's tiring-room or later, in the king's banquet-hall. Then it was hewn down. But the roots of that flower still flourished and sent out thorny branches.

The seed and the roots here are seed and roots of a poetic faith in which Eros and Poetry, Romance, Rite, and Lore, have become One in the Imagination. Poetry Itself becomes for the new heresy of Poetry a primary experience of the Divine Order. "An aristocracy of emotion," Pound calls it in 1916—evolving "out of its half memories of Hellenistic mysteries." "A Dream greater than Reality," H.D. calls it in 1946. Whatever we are following here, it is not the heresy of Spirit against Matter or against the Incarnation—for in the Imagination, there is no contradiction between the Radiant Body and the actual physical body: the one is seen in the other, or imagined in the other. What we attend is the unification of visions of the world and its reality once held to be in conflict.

It is of the essence of Poetry that sexual rites, fertility rites, Christian rites, and Celtic rites, may be confused, transmuted in an alembic to yield the stuff of a poetic reality, until we cannot divide the magic from the religious ingredients. The ritual objects of the Grail romance are entirely properties of the Imagination. So H.D. traces in *The Guest* how in Shakespeare's lifetime the imagination in the poetic theater took over into a higher reality the things of the church and the things of the court.

Henry VIII had ransacked the monasteries. "The church was plundered by the palace; the palace became the background for new ritual."

In the masques and plays acted in the throne-room or the antechamber, the objects from the world of religion became stage properties. "Sumptuous plate and linen, looted from the Cardinal's palace, was shared alike by Montague and Capulet. Juliet's tomb was, no doubt, magnificently draped in violet. The candle-sticks recalled another canopy, another burial." In the reality of actual life, Christendom and Kingdom both fell. But the "original face" remains, for just here, in the fall, Christendom and Kingdom fell into the Imagination. In the reality of what exists only as it is created in the Imagination, Christendom and Kingdom had begun.

That one image may recall another, finding depth in the resounding, is the secret of rhyme and measure. The time of a poem is felt as a recognition of return in vowel tone and in consonant formations, of pattern in the sequence of syllables, in stress and in pitch of a melody, of images and meanings. It resembles the time of a dream, for it is highly organized along lines of association and impulses of contrast toward the structure of the whole. The impulse of dream or poem is to provide a ground for some form beyond what we know, for feeling "greater than Reality."

Chapter 4 *Palimpsest*

The first great era of Romance is born in the fictional civilization that follows the world conquest of Alexander, as the Hellenic becomes the Hellenistic in an empire of Orientalizing Greek and Hellenizing Orient that eventually has its capital in Rome. When again in the eighteenth century, the Western World would conquer India, the dream of Vishnu returns to infect the West, so that in the nineteenth century even in America, with Emerson and Whitman, the synthesizing Romanticism of a new world-mind is under way. And it is to this Romantic movement that Pound, H.D., and Lawrence, in the Imagist period, belonged. Essentially anti-modernist, in the Credo of 1912 with its insistence upon the ultimate reality of the image in itself and upon the magic of a cadence that corresponded with that image—what Pound called an "absolute rhythm"—the Imagists seek a return to Hellenic purity, even to the archaic Greek, in reaction to the theosophy and Hermeticism of the Symbolist movement typified by Yeats. But soon Pound with the neo-Platonism and light-gnosis of *The Cantos* and Lawrence with the sexual mysteries of his *Fantasia of the Unconscious* clearly have returned to the Hellenistic basis of *The Spirit of Romance*. And with a series of prose works—*The Hedgehog* (1925), *Palimpsest* (1925–26), the story "Narthex" (1927) which appeared in the *Second American Caravan,* and the novel *Hedylus* (1927)—H.D. makes her own full presentation of a commitment to Hellenistic syncretism.

Palimpsest, the central work here, consists of three stories:

1. HIPPARCHIA. War Rome (circa 75 B.C.)
2. MUREX. War and post-War London (circa 1916–1926 A.D.)
3. SECRET NAME. Excavator's Egypt (circa 1925 A.D.)

as they are presented in the table of contents.

She may have had in mind Flaubert's *Trois Contes,* which had been a touchstone in Pound's proposition of the new aesthetic, the new poetry was to measure up to the best in prose: "Flaubert is the archetype," he writes in *ABC of Reading.* And earlier, in *How to Read:* "Flaubert, by force of architectonics, manages to attain an intensity comparable to that in Villon's *Heaulmière,* or his prayer for his mother." Like Flaubert's *Trois Contes,* the three stories of H.D.'s *Palimpsest* present juxtapositions of the modern with ancient time. Like Flaubert's Félicité and Julian, Hipparchia, Raymonde Ransome in "Murex," and Helen Fairwood in "Secret Name," are drawn to illustrate phases of ecstatic experience, the special psychologies of states of fever or abnormal apprehension. The story "Herodias" from *Trois Contes,* a modern critic writes, "justifies Hugo's comment that Flaubert combined 'the real, which exhibits life, with the ideal, which reveals the soul'."

But the form of the whole in H.D.'s work was not only that of contrast and parallel between persons as in *Trois Contes.* The key was given in the title—*Palimpsest*—and underlined by H.D. in her subscript to the title: "i.e., a parchment from which one writing has been erased to make room for another." Each of the three stories of H.D.'s *Palimpsest* presents a consciousness in which some underlying suppressed consciousness shows through, and, in turn, in each story the attentive reader will find traces or ghosts of the other stories—of Hipparchia in Raymonde or of Raymonde in Helen Fairwood. *Palimpsest* is a study in reincarnations.

The image of a parchment from which one writing has been erased to make room for another may also be the image of an identity where one person has been erased to make room for another, a life or lives erased to make room for another life. The doctrine of reincarnation is itself not only in the context of our contemporary scientific orthodoxy but in the earlier context of Christian orthodoxies a belief that, where it comes to the surface, leaks through as an erased writing. Even in the world of fictions, the theme of reincarnation can demote a work as being ultimately beyond the pale of serious concern. But that what once was has an objective existence in what is, is a concept current in the thought of science and philosophy as well as in the possibly vagrant imaginations of certain poets. Whitehead pictures the personal identity of a man so, as "a matrix for all transitions of life" that "is changed and variously figured by the things that enter it." "If we talk of the tradition today," W. H. Auden writes:

> we no longer mean what the eighteenth century meant, a way of working handed down from one generation to the next; we mean a consciousness of the whole of the past in the present.

To come into such a continuum of human life in which our identity contains the past is to find a new dimension of personal life. As we drew the figures of successive stages of Eros in history, we had to do with reincarnations of Eros in writing upon writing, a palimpsest of scriptures entering our thought, to change and figure what we are then once we entertain the mere idea, and becoming the working force, in reading, of an objective reality.

The sensory clues or cues that lead Proust in his *Remembrance of Things Past* to the images from which the fullness of a lost life flows back into consciousness, or the dream data and double meanings which Freud follows to bring up into consciousness events of a repressed—erased— experience, these are sought out as one might seek out the underlying script in reading a palimpsest. To reclaim life's first content. As Freud detects or calls up primal scenes of man's prehistory in *Civilization and Its Discontents* and in *Moses and Monotheism* to picture, as before he had pictured the return of the repressed in the individual life, the return of the murder of the father in the life of a collective unconscious, and as Jung proceeds to elaborate the eternal return of the dramatis personae in the theatre of the imagination, which he sees as archetypes of the unconscious, back of these ideas of a recapitulation of primal experi- ence in the experience of each individual of the species there is a rein- carnation of an everlasting identity in changing events and forms. The figure of Eros, then, is not only that of an idea in evolution but also that of an identity constantly revealing itself, reinstating itself. As we begin to take our identity, beyond the fiction of personality, in the idea of Man, the variety of persons Man has been may begin to inhabit what we are as we impersonate Him. Divine or daemonic forces appearing in dreams seem to appear as illustrations of the depths of our own being—a being now that includes all that we have come to know Man to have been—and behind their faces we read the faces of father or mother, sister or brother, actual figures of our own *erased* lives within our present lifetime. Their appearance within us is more significant than their appearance before our imagination.

In Poetry, between the *Dramatis Personae* of Robert Browning and the *personae* of the Imagists' dramatic lyrics, the mask comes to reveal the poet's inner self. The mode of Pound and of H.D., and probably of D. H. Lawrence, is derived from that of Browning. In reviewing Charlotte Mew's *The Farmer's Bride* in 1916, H.D. writes:

> In this, our present day, literary Alexandria, even the most 'original' among us may take a sort of perverse delight in finding a new writer daring to discard his personality to follow, remotely or unconsciously perhaps, the tradition of an earlier generation. . . . In England there have been few masters among the poets, but those few so supreme that they stamped, created as it were, a mould for generations of frailer, if not less beautiful, spirits to follow. We have Dekker and Fletcher, and countless others, but the summits and depths of the English language is Shakespeare. And so, drawing nearer to our own generation, the dramatic poem is Browning, and Browning the dramatic poem.

Where she sees her own time as "Alexandria," H.D.'s classicism is that of Plutarch and Philo Judaeus, and her lyricism is dramatic, not personal, where she would take Shakespeare and Browning to be masters of her art. The writer "daring to discard his personality" not only follows a tradition but is created in it; he must take on personality now as an actor does from the theater in a drama of Poetry. The idea of generating masters or fathers casting a stamp or mould upon generations of spirits, like the idea Imagists had of expressing their generation or time, is related to older religious concepts of reincarnation—the *metempsychosis* or transmigration of soul, the *metangismos* or transfusion—the pouring of soul from one body into another—of the Greeks, or the *gilgul* of the Jewish tradition, in the Alexandrian world. But it is also here the author of the play giving the actors their parts.

Browning is such a generating master, for he had developed a form for the poet's dramatic participation in other personalities in other times. It was a magic of affinities. "Remotely or unconsciously perhaps," the poet reincarnated himself along the lines of a tradition or spiritual family tree. So, there would appear correspondences between poems of which the poets might be unaware and unintending, for poems were related generically and images came from the fountains of a collective imagination as souls were drawn from the fountain of life. "One is particularly obsessed with this idea in first reading Mr. Ford Madox Hueffer's beautiful poem 'Heaven'," H.D. continues, referring to Robert Browning as the source of the dramatic poem:

> But Mr. Hueffer says that he never read Browning. Therefore Mr. Hueffer has followed the Browning mould unconsciously—as unconsciously and inevitably as Miss Charlotte Mew in her poem "The Fête," and in her other poem, the wracked, tortured "Madeleine in Church." When one reads of 'the white geraniums in the dusk' one feels that Madeleine has wandered in that same garden where the moth and moth kiss brushed the heavy flower petals—and the 'portrait of my mother at nineteen' brings to one's oversophisticated imagination the Duchess with her unappreciated, wan smile and her branch of cherries.

"It is part of our pleasure in art in these days to imagine such things," H.D. concludes, "and the lines lose none of their poignancy, none of their personal flavor for this fine, subtle association." But it is also something more than a cultivated association, for the idea lingers that "that same garden" comes into the poem by Charlotte Mew that came into Browning's poem and that the portrait of the poetess's mother at nineteen and the portrait of Browning's poem "My Last Duchess" are significantly related, that there is, back of poetry, some collective poetic unconscious.

In the voices of Pound or H.D., the poet's personal identity is involved in the projection of the poem, and, in this, they are different from the dramatic monologs of Robert Browning. Pound derives his own personal legend from Odysseus, Peire Vidal, Homer, Kung; he identifies with them in impersonating them. So too H.D. is to be confused with Sappho or Helen, with the priestess of Artemis in whom Artemis speaks. D. H. Lawrence undergoes a self-conversion in his poetic projection of Dionysos. In this the poets are most contemporary with the psychologists who begin to see the work of art as well as the dream as a projection of the individual psyche in which an unconscious content seeks to reveal itself.

The masks of Robert Browning's *dramatis personae* lead directly to the masks of the Imagists, but the poetic persona is no longer discrete. The concept of person itself has undergone a crucial change in the work of Symbolists, and, for all of their reform of Symbolist ways the Imagists are heirs of their work. Where the poem was once theatrical, it is now more and more viewed as a process of psychological information, related to dream-work.

In his magic-lantern art, Robert Browning calls up Verona, as in the poem *Sordello,* not out of his subconscious but by virtue of his theatrical power, and:

Lo, the past is hurled
In twain: up-thrust, out-staggering on the world,
Subsiding into shape, a darkness rears
Its outline, kindles at the core, appears
Verona . . .

The darkness that rears and kindles at the core, in which the scene is evoked, suggests to us the unconscious; but for Robert Browning it remains a machinery of a stage midway between the phantom-shows of Doctor Faustus, where we but see Helen of Troy as a display, and the shadow-screens of the motion picture to come. So Browning also dismisses his phantoms: "The ghost is gone, and the story ends." This is an art in which the poet calls up *image* and *persona,* keeping at the same time his distance, and our own, the magician's pentacle within which he stands.

"The consciousness of some seems to rest," Pound says in "Psychology and Troubadours," "or to have its center more properly, in what the Greek psychologists called the *phantastikon.* Their minds are, that is, circumvolved about them like soap-bubbles reflecting sundry patches of the macrocosmos." Here image was *phanopoeia,* "a casting of images upon the visual imagination." The Imagists in the beginning worked towards a new *phantastikon.* We are not to underestimate the role that this magic of reflections has in even the later works of Pound or H.D. But there was another, higher poetic power, it seemed to Pound, in the "germinal" consciousness. The image or persona—what is seen in the world "outside" or in the mind's world "inside"—no longer is a show of that world only, but is a seed, a generative point of the inner and outer. This is a world not of mere appearance, but of a vital process.

•

The images and persons of *Palimpsest* work through each other, as if story were written over story. So too the sequence of times works in a set of superimpositions. The palimpsest is not only that of image over image or person over person, but of time over time. Within London 1926 is wartime London of 1916. But also, within the Hellenistic world of wartime Rome in the story "Hipparchia" is the underscript of wartime London. It is the palimpsest of a layered consciousness in which all times and worlds are to be found. Not only may the past be back of the present, but the present may be back of the account of the past. So too as Edward Sapir, reviewing H.D.'s poetry, pointed out, back of her Hellenism is the subscript of an American experience and character:

> Personal and remote as are her images, there breathes through her work a spirit which it would not be easy to come upon in any other quarter of the globe. The impatience of the rhythms and the voluptuous harshness and bleakness of the sea and shore and woodland images manifest it. Such violent restraint, such a passionate pleasure in the beauty of the denuded scene and the cutting thrust, themselves but inverse symbols of caress, could only develop in a culture that hungers for what it despises.

Sapir is reading H.D. in terms of what he sees the American spirit to be—at once the expression of a Puritan heritage and of the physical environment of a forbidding continent. Hipparchia, exiled from Greece, dreaming of her lost homeland in wartime Rome, reminds us of H.D. in wartime London, haunted by dreams of lost or forgotten coasts of New Jersey. For the generation of the twenties abroad, the American spirit was thought of as being in exile; and the America of the childhood late nineteenth-century, "lost." Raymonde Ransome in the story "Murex," an autobiographical portrait, sees her room in post-war London as a palimpsest in which memories survive:

> such a tiny room to hold so much, so many superimposed people. And she was happy alone here and didn't want to go away. They were passing, would always be passing and she would remember them; as an *American* she would remember them.

Helen Fairwood in "Secret Name" presents another autobiographical portrait, moving through an Egyptian scene haunted by overscripts or underscripts of Greece and America:

> This was Egypt. America had been wiped out, she had thought, even before the heavy down-weight of London's five war years . . . But it wasn't. It stared at her in an English country-house bedroom, in a New England seaside village bedroom with four-poster draped with white of mosquito gauze, with strip of rug, and pottery Devon-like jugs.

"I spent most of my childhood," she tells Captain Rafton, "(although you won't accept it that I'm American) along the gigantic stretches of New Jersey. Sand and scrub-bushes. So the incurve of the sand about these sphinxes is familiar." The scene itself, as she walks by moonlight to visit the ruins of Karnak, is a palimpsest:

> Her past merged, moon eclipse, black crystal; the marshes of New Jersey low-flowering wax and wortle-berry brushed the shimmer of the robe of dragon-fly blue texture of some incredibly slender Graeco-Egyptian. A Graeco-Egyptian was wandering across New Jersey marshes in search of those famous (even in Egypt) ivory pointed, saffron centered lily lotuses.

Raymonde Ransome's mind in "Murex" searches out along currents of association to draw a magic, a poem actually, out of the depths. But they are depths not only of her own life, the memory of a labor and the loss of her child at birth, while behind the scenes there was her lover's adultery and desertion during her pregnancy, but depths also of human history that must be healed. The interior monologue itself provides a medium into which all things can flow as into one sea, from whose depths the murex may be brought up, and Raymonde Ransome's mind returns again and again to the thought of the writer James Joyce, hinting that back of this writing—another sense of the name *palimpsest*—is the writing of Joyce's *Ulysses:* "Art was magic—but it had lost— had lost—its savour. Joyce was right. It had lost." In *Ulysses,* back of Bloom's day in Dublin, magically, had been earlier Greek presences, a writing we almost read through the print we actually read. Signs appear in the stream of consciousness that back of Bloom's personality is that of Odysseus. Back of the stream of consciousness mode is Robert Browning's dramatic monolog. Faces and masks are interchanged in a masque of identities. "Faces, people, London," Raymonde Ransome recalls:

> People, faces, Greece. Greece, people, faces. Egypt. James Joyce was right. On, on, on, on, and out of it like some deep-sea jewel pulled up in a net squirming with an enormous catch of variegated squirming tentacled and tendrilled memories, just this, this—

She cannot name it, but the painful "purple" or *murex* is the birth of the child that dies in birth. In the conscious mind it is a poem coming into form: "Verses were the murex. They dyed all existence with their color. Small verses, things that in no way matter." Back of the poem that is coming up in her mind there is something she is listening to, the sound of feet passing up Sloane Street on the way to Victoria Station outside the room where she sits at tea facing a visitor who racks up the memory of Raymonde Ransome's old life. But it is the sound of young men in that old life, marching to the War. Brzeska, Hulme, Wilfred Owen. *The Egoist* listed the artists and writers newly fallen with each issue in the war years. And there was another, an equally painful death of love. *The Death of a Hero,* Aldington, H.D.'s young husband had entitled his portrait of those years. The war and the adultery are written one on the top of the other, or one obliterating the other, erased to make room for the other. She has lost her child or her lover to the war. "Layer and layer of pain, of odd obliteration had forbidden Raymonde Ransome to see into the past that to her was further than an Egyptian's coffin. The past of somewhere about 1917." The marching feet of the young men on their way to the troop trains, the feet of the lost young men, are, we begin to realize, the measuring feet of the poem itself.

Raymonde is very much Hilda or the writing of a portrait in the place of Hilda. In the autobiographical portrait, the person of the author has been erased to make room for the story of the self revealed in a secondary personality. Just as Hilda Doolittle erased her name and wrote in its place the enigmatic H.D., so Raymonde Ransome has the writing name *Ray Bart*.

> Behind the Botticelli, there was another Botticelli, behind London there was another London, behind Raymonde Ransome there was (odd and slightly crude but somehow 'taking' nom-de-guerre) Ray Bart. There was Ray Bart always waiting as there was behind the autumn drift and dream-anodyne of mist, another London. A London of terror and unpremeditated beauty. A London of peril and of famine and of intolerable loveliness. Behind London there was the London of darkened street lamps (of 'doused', Freddie used to say, 'glims') behind a mist and drift of anodyne in an Italian background of small and precise little pincushion pink roses, there was another Italy, another Venus, another realm of beauty never to be apprehended with the senses.

Recalling in "Murex" the stream of consciousness mode of Joyce's *Ulysses* or, as in "Secret Name," Algernon Blackwood's narratives of occult experience, the prose of *Palimpsest* is not, as contemporary reviewers tended to think it was, impressionistic. Language becomes throughout a ground of suggestion and association, a magic ground, a weaving of phrases echoing in other phrases, a maze of sentences to bind us in its spell, so that we begin to be infected with the sense of other meanings and realms within those presented. The style is obsessional. We must come back and back to the same place and find it subtly altered in each return, like a traveler bewildered by lords of the fairy, until he is filled with a presence he would not otherwise have admitted. Here it is not past time or present time but the blur, the erasure itself, that is the magic ground in which the necessary image may occur.

What we are to see needs a fused light, twilight or moonlight. What the eye must strain to see in the diminishing light takes on the imprint of inner phantasy and becomes newly significant to the soul. In the story "Hipparchia," Marius sees his mistress's eyebrows in such a light as a sign, "Black, like the inner hieratic marking on the honey-colored hyacinth," activating the magic of correspondences:

> He saw, in that thickening of the last glow of late sunlight, her eyebrows apart, separated from her being. As Greeks of the old days disregarded the sheer substance of the flower as they perceived (mysterious script) the aie, aie, that tells of lost Adonis or the wail for the dead Spartan. He saw why Greeks inordinately must rule forever, not Rome, but prophetically, the whole world.

"Your eyebrows, Hipparchia," he tells her then, "penciled for my dismissal are engraved somewhat on my spirit." Searching out from its dimness the detail, as for the reader, searching out what seems only dimly present in his text, Marius finds it comes to him at last as a content of his own inner experience. He has cooperated in what he has come to see.

Not only the dimness in which suggestion can arise but the circling repetition in which resistance is eroded and transformed is necessary for the author who would cast a spell. The mesmerist must call upon his reader's assent to a conversion in which words come to have an artistic identity of their own. Readers of Joyce's *Ulysses* before the impact of that work had been exorcised by the commentaries and appreciations of the professors of literature, where they were resistant to Joyce's art, often expressed themselves in angry, even hostile, terms regarding the boredom they had experienced. Corresponding to this boredom or pain of resistance experienced by the reader who refused to be taken in by Joyce is the creative fatigue which the reader who is to follow the author's lead must undergo. The ideal reader of his hypnogogic prose, Joyce suggests, must enter the realm of sleep as an insomniac.

In the story "Secret Name," Helen Fairwood finds herself prepared by fatigue for her experience of the numinous. The reiteration of the word "fatigue" and the play of the words "curious" and "peculiar" suggest that both the nervous state and the moonlight are elements of an aura surrounding the event:

> all the uncanny perceptions of the early morning, the fatigue, and the uncanny perceptions of the Tomb, nullified, smoothed away, eradicated by this curious moonlight; eradicated, sponged out . . . The intellect was to such an extent off guard, benumbed by her peculiar fatigue.

The prose demands that we yield to its wanderings, its reiterations; and when we yield, it brings us into such a fatigue of intellectual resistance that only an inner emotional acquiescence, and then an alliance with the shifting ground of things that is being prepared keeps us going and takes over, so that for us, as for Helen Fairwood, the sphinxes appear not foreign but most familiar. "Maryland is exactly the sort of child, more or less, I was," Mrs. Fairwood tells Captain Rafton, "when I first crossed." "And what kind of child do you think you are now?" he asks. To cross from America to Europe, to cross from childhood into womanhood, to cross from innocence into wisdom or mistrust? We have been confused and we are not sure. To be a child may mean more than we first thought.

What Helen Fairwood comes to feel as she stands with Rafton in the ruins of Karnak, in the blur or erasure of moonlight, is first the incarnation of Greek entities in the scene. Rafton appears to be Zeus as he turns to her who seems now to be "another Leda or Calliope." But then, deeper—"What kind of child do you think you are now?"—the two see together an appearance out of the moonlight of a "tiny temple or tomb or birth-house," a Greek shrine within the Egyptian: "It rose as if cut from one block of stone, at that little distance she could not tell of quite what material, with the moon too working its common magic." The miasma of phrases, drifts of meaning within meaning exhausting any literal reading until the prose swarms with seeds of meaning, may be to prepare for the image of a wish. As Mrs. Fairwood and Captain Rafton return from Karnak, it seems to her "as if they stood static and the thud-thud of hoofs was only the heart beat of some close, live body. As if they in some strange exact and precious period of pre-birth, twins, lovers, were held, sheltered beneath some throbbing heart." Egypt, the moon, the night, here, may be a mother, and the two, the man and the woman, are for a moment the twin King and Queen, the children in the womb of Egypt. This Egypt, this night, is the Mother, the Imagination, the Dream that—it is the presiding theme of H.D.'s later work—is not only revelatory of but creative of Reality.

Hipparchia, confused in her fever, hears an "odd insistent bird note of anguish" that may be out of the past or of the distance, "a voice from far and far and far webbed over with its pain of actuality." The pulse of the pain is actual, a condition of her fever. But it is also—the whole is a palimpsest—the script of an earlier pain, the pulse of labor pains that Raymonde Ransome knew in 1917. Hipparchia and Raymonde exist as twins in a womb of time where there is no before and after. They coexist. And Hipparchia in 75 B.C. remembers, as if it were in the past and also in the future, Raymonde's labor pains.

"But there is no such thing as a start and a finish of the whole circumference of a circle," the Hellenistic philosopher Porphyrius argues, and he refers then to the Hellenic philosopher Heraclitus: "Beginning and end in a circle's circumference are common." Hipparchia, Raymonde, Helen Fairwood, and their author H.D., like Heraclitus's mortals and immortals, "live in each other's death, die in each other's life." For H.D., as for the Greek philosophers, the reality of the world belongs to a unity of creative thought in which it has its origins, the circumference of a divine idea.

But the pain is an actual bird note, "outside," an insistence of a new figure working in the matrix where identity is in transition. Hipparchia's actual sickness we see now as something else, the condition in which a new state of consciousness is at work. The birth of a child, the birth of a poem, the birth of a spirit, the birth of self out of self—a host of experiences and fantasies, suffering and wish, gather to charge the epiphany of the little birth house with its particular force. They are rhymes, sounding in each other; so that a bass note accumulates. They are resounding identities belonging to the emergence in their unity of one person. Not only Raymonde in Hipparchia, and Hipparchia in Helen Fairwood, but each of these in turn in a mystery of person are more than a self portrait of H.D., whose personality now is not that of author but that of a member of the cast in the play. The autobiographical has become part of the fiction of the whole; H.D.'s own personality begins to appear, like the persons of the stories, as an extension of an identity in the process of revealing itself or creating itself.

It seems to Marius as he looks at Hipparchia "as if the very substance of the light webbed in that late sun, in that wanfaced, wild, thin woman was the very gay wedding garment (he searched his mind for a vague remembered image ah—) Medea wrought for Jason. A garment that as he drew it on, clung close and poisoned him with a thousand evil pricklings." Drawn into the web of associations, it seems to him at first that she is a witch—even as in H.D.'s late work, *Helen in Egypt,* Achilles will cry out at first, "Are you Hecate? are you a witch?" Then it seems to him Pallas Athene is present, only to give way in his mind to another figure out of myth, the weaver who challenged Athene in her art. "Was she simply, put it to the final test, some wayward voice personified?"

> He began again the old tiresome and boring circle. The web and web and web that was the illusion of Hipparchia. He said suddenly for, that he could see, no reason, 'Hipparchia is no Pallas but Arachne.'

In "Secret Name," the figure of the woman as Arachne, the web-spinner, appears again. Helen Fairwood's over-mind is Athenian, but, below, her thoughts wander and in the dusk of evening take over:

> It was utterly Athenian starkly to define, to outline in terms of thought every human emotion, not making allowance for this intermediate state where thought and emotion were delicately merged. Thought and emotion merged delicately now that she had let go, or now that her very evident fatigue had let go for her, that stark analytical hold on things of emotion, on things of intellect. Fire-flies (she couldn't help feeling) should have darted up, hung between her and the smudged-out smile of the oblong, seated cat-Sekmet, a veil, glimmering of dancing frenzied stars.

The under-mind wandering weaves a complexity in which the fatigue of the over-mind spreads until Athene succumbs to Arachne. Dressing for dinner, Helen finds that "she was in the un-Athenian dusk of the blurred over Luxor garden, making deep down a web, a fine and subtle surprise for Captain Rafton . . . when the blue slim creature with the heavy blue collar of blue stones should rise, '*you*'." Her upper-mind had thought about Greece and Egypt, about thought and emotion, but her lower-mind all the time had been conceiving how she would veil herself:

> She was planning this, in the spider part of her subconsciousness, all this, but her brain had not recognized the plan, had only starkly qualified the empty spaces of the garden with some image, 'there should be, why aren't there, knots and star jewels of flaming fire-flies?' Her brain had formed that precise image but her spider self was weaving, weaving down, down the very, very self she was to offer.

The reoccurrences are rhymes or knots in the web of reality. Suddenly, at the knot of it, we *realize* what is going on. If Pallas Athena may stand for the gnosis, the ultimate knowledge of the cosmic order, Arachne stands for the worker whose work is the realization of What Is. H.D. is to be concerned now—as her Hipparchia, Raymonde, or Helen Fairwood are—with "transitions of life," with things that enter not only her thought but her identity, which will be changed and figured anew. "Osiris was waiting to recall her," it seems to Hipparchia. Who the Osiris is still engages H.D.'s imagination twenty years later in *The Walls Do Not Fall*: "Osiris, / the star Sirius,"

> relates resurrection myth
> and resurrection reality
>
> through the ages . . .

In the Hellenistic synthesis, as Lord of the transitions of Life, Osiris stands for the order or intent in the work, and he is most experienced by the artist at the crossroads of his art.

A gloss of *The Book of the Dead* tells us: "*As for yesterday, that is Osiris.*" Osiris may be the "mutual immanence" of all events in the present that figures in Whitehead's *Process and Reality*. "Present and future equally," H.D. names him in *The Walls Do Not Fall*. What is his name? Can it be hidden (the earliest script in the palimpsest), erased, in:

O, Sire, is this the path?
over sedge, over dune-grass,

as H.D. hides or erases it in xlii of *The Walls Do Not Fall?*

O, Sire, is this the waste?
unbelievably . . .

as if the Way were hidden in the Wasteland. Freud reinforces H.D.'s Hellenistic leanings. In dreams and in the psychopathology of daily life, we are prepared to see the pun, as the name *Ra* may be hidden in *Rafton* of "Secret Name," or to hear the pun in "O, Sire, is." In the epigraph for "Secret Name" H.D. quotes from a hieratic papyrus of the XXth dynasty:

> But Isis held her peace; never a word did she speak, for she knew that Ra had told her the names that all men know; his true Name, his Secret Name, was still hidden in his breast.

The secret name of Greece is hidden in Egypt, and we must go to Luxor to read the hieroglyph of its birth-house, as the initiate in Freudian analysis must go to Yesterday to find the clues to his soul, or the Pacific Northwest Indian must go into the solitude of the forest to find his name. In her last great work, *Helen in Egypt,* again Egypt is the warp upon which the woof of the Greek weaves.

"You're always talking about the Greeks," Rafton says to Helen— he is addressing the high-minded Helen, the Pallas Athena Helen— "The Greeks came to Egypt to learn." To go deep within the self for Raymonde Ransome in "Murex" is to go deep within history where back of Greece Egypt was primal, the Depth to be sounded. Hipparchia in her fever sees the Greek Helios-Phoebus as the god of her anguished upper-mind; and then, back of or below the bird note of anguish, she sees or hears Osiris who waits to recall her. "Some god (Osiris loved her, but Life, Helios, cheated her.)" "She had said then, 'Phoebus speaks doubly and his word cuts doubly'."

"Phoebus had cut her doubly from herself so that she might regard an image of absolute peace that would recall her. Osiris to recall her."

The Greek Helios appears as the bird note of pain, the pains-taking upper-mind, the painful ambiguity of higher thought, the glaring light of the Sun, driving her to seek out the alien god who stands in the shadows of the room—Osiris. The voice within the pain is Egypt's. In the confusion of the fever, as in the confusion of Helen Fairwood's fatigue, Egypt begins to appear back of the Greek:

> A voice from far and far and far webbed over with its pain of actuality, its bird-note of insistent anguish, the pain of mental striving . . . something from far and far about some 'suave and golden Eros—' suave and golden. Osiris was waiting to recall her. [Then, later:] Helios, a god of poetry, did not forget her. Helios, a god of anguish, had not forgotten her. Helios, a god of Greeks, was insistent, bird anguish and song notes of unassailable desire. Osiris. Far and far and far, surrounded with a web of old illusion.

In the poem the music, the melodic *strain,* arises along some line of anguish. We hear it in the poet's voice, any poet's voice, as a mode of grief—lamenting the Mother, so the Freudian persuasion has it, wrapped round in the illusions of the restored Mother. The Helios, the upper poetic mind, opens in grief a window in which as poets we see the object of our "unassailable desire." The double play of the art, the gift of Helios that "cuts doubly," opens a wound in the pain of which we have vision. Osiris here is the vision of poetry. Egypt may be the fever in which Hipparchia sees at last her fever-vision—the islands of Greece restored.

Her mind in fever goes out in what we call its wandering or stream of consciousness, or, after Freud, its free association—but what we find is a wave in its fullness revealing an organization of time, in-bound throughout to its own particular tenor or pattern, a *gestalt*—free, but committed to a message that is not arbitrary, moving from the thought that haunts her—"Greece is now lost," towards a melody that releases the pain into beauty.

"Greece is now lost, the cities dissociated from any central ruling," her lover Marius had taunted Hipparchia. And now, from the seeming dissociation (her reviewers were to find H.D.'s prose in *Palimpsest* guilty of being "dissociated"), from the darkness of Egypt, a voice comes:

"My father collects everything that is Greek." It is the voice of a young girl attending Hipparchia in her illness. "Greece is now lost. Greece is now lost" had run in Hipparchia's head. But now in her delirium, Greek things appear: "Hipparchia had only to sink back, to drift out, out, out to tiny island upon wave-lapped tiny island. They were all in her head—an attendant lover to recall her."

To remember is Osiris but Hipparchia's *Yesterday* is Greece, Helios out of Osiris. "From far and far and far—some golden Eros some-time—." She had mistaken a statue in the room for Eros earlier. Then she begins to see that the actual figure is Egyptian. "Done in dark metal with a seated Eros; Horus precisely." But Eros and Horus in the Hellenistic mysteries were combined in one—Harpocrates. Just there or just beyond, the voice comes that releases her anguish into its rapture: "Some said *Greece is a spirit. Greece is not lost.* I will come with you."

The sentence, "My father collects everything that is Greek," which comes in the patterning of Hipparchia's interior monolog to define a dramatic crisis, has a possible origin in H.D.'s memory of her own father. The astronomer, Professor Doolittle, had, in a sense, such a col-lection in the stars and planets that were the objects of his profession. He was most familiar with them and would not have thought too con-sciously of the presences of the old gods that lay back of their names, but, in the father's talk, before she could read or write, H.D. heard the names—Mars, Venus, Mercury, Saturn. In the palimpsest, the Greek gods were behind the Roman names. They were her father's familiars.

Seven years after the writing of "Hipparchia," that line "My father collects everything that is Greek" was to echo again in H.D.'s life when Freud, who collected everything that belonged to another "Greece," another lost land, the dream, was to take H.D., back of the analy-sis room, his office, into his other room, his study, where he too—a father figure (in her *Tribute to Freud,* H.D. calls him throughout "the Professor," recalling deliberately her father's title)—had a collection of everything that was Greek, his own private museum of god figures. Art objects, but they were also cult objects in a time when psychoanalysis had brought all the divine images back as figures of a new psyche-cult. He brought "everything Greek" into the collective treasure of the valuable—the ivory Indian figure of Vishnu in the same room, the presence of the little bronze image of Pallas Athena. "He had said," H.D. writes of Freud:

> he had dared to say that the dream had its worth and value in translatable terms, not the dream merely of a Pharaoh or a Pharaoh's butler, not the dream merely of the favorite child of Israel, not merely Joseph's dream or Jacob's dream of a symbolic ladder, not the dream only of the Cumaean Sybil of Italy or the Delphic Priestess of ancient Greece, but the dream of everyone, everywhere.

•

The great Hellenistic source where the lore of Egypt and the lore of Greece are gathered together in the synthesis of a common religion as they are in the synthesis of H.D.'s creative imagination is Plutarch's "Isis and Osiris," dedicated to Clea, priestess of Apollo at Delphi, followed in the fifth book of the *Moralia* by his essay "On the *EI* at Delphi," in which he expounds the interpretations of the Delphic Epsilon for the poet Sarapion of Athens. Following the involutions of Plutarch's exposition, we begin to see how fully in Hipparchia's mind H.D. has portrayed the inner structures of emotion and intellect characteristic of the syncretizing Hellenistic spirit. Whatever else she is, Hipparchia is an authentic reconstruction or restoration of the Graeco-Egyptian devotee typical of the intellectual society of the post-Alexander "Roman world."

EI, Plutarch tells the poet, is the second vowel, the Sun is the second planet, and thus *EI* is the sign of Apollo. We may remember that in the Empire a cult of Helios as *Sol Invictus* was to become the cult of a state in its unifying and universalizing period. For Plutarch, *EI,* if it was the sign of the sun was the sign of a governing power, but it also, he reminds us, means "*if*" and is the mode of wishes and prophecy, of "If I only could" and of "If this is so, then that shall be."

The meanings of the word multiply as meanings within the Hellenistic Empire multiplied in the confusion of civilizations that deepened in the new cosmopolis of Rome or Alexandria. Not again until our own world which has emerged from the universalizing imperialisms of the nineteenth century will there be such a mixing of local identities and even of ancient cultures, East and West, South and North, to form the multiphasic language of Man in such a complex of associations. The sign *EI* multiplies in its significances. It is the sign of such proliferation. As the sign of the number five, Plutarch tells us, it is formed in the conjunction of two, the first even number, which resembles the female, and three, the first odd number, which resembles the male; so it is "generative" and was called "*Marriage*" by the Pythagoreans. "There is also," Plutarch continues:

> a sense in which it has been called *Nature,* since by being multiplied into itself it ends in itself again. For even as Nature receives wheat in the form of seed and puts it to its uses, and creates in the interim many shapes and forms through which she carries out the process of growth to its end, but, to crown all, displays wheat again . . .

so five reappears in its square, twenty-five, and likewise in its higher powers:

> It has a unique characteristic, when added to itself, of producing either itself or ten alternately as the addition progresses, and of doing this to infinity, since this number takes its pattern from the primal principle which orders the whole . . . as that principle by change creates a complete universe out of itself, and then in turn out of the universe creates itself again, as Heracleitus says, *and exchanges fire for all and all for fire* . . . .
>
> If, then, anyone ask, *What has this to do with Apollo?* we shall say that it concerns not only him, but also Dionysus, whose share in Delphi is no less than that of Apollo. Now we hear the theologians affirming and reciting, sometimes in verse and sometimes in prose, that the god is deathless and eternal in his nature, but, owing forsooth to some predestined design and reason, he undergoes transformations of his person, and at one time enkindles his nature into fire and makes it altogether like all else, and at another time he undergoes all sorts of changes in his form, his emotion and his powers, even as the universe does today.

In a Mediterranean world invaded not only by Egyptian and Near Eastern but by Hindu thought, a world that, following Alexander's period of conquest, had experienced wide-spread deep-going changes, the intellectual saw himself in the terms of a transitional identity. From the transformations of symbol in Plutarch's account, and then from the metamorphoses of the god, we begin to get a picture of a multiphasic psyche. Not only is the god the one called Apollo he tells us, "because of his solitary state, and Phoebus because of his purity and stainlessness," but he is also the one called Dionysus. His is not only the paean, "music regulated and chaste," but also the dithyramb, "laden with emotion and with a transformation that includes a certain wandering and dispersion":

> And as for his turning into winds and water, earth and stars, and into the generations of plants and animals, and his adoption of such guises, they speak in a deceptive way of what he undergoes in his transformation as a tearing apart, as it were, and a dismemberment . . . They construct destructions and disappearances, followed by returns to life and regeneration.

Osiris, Plutarch tells us in his study, may stand for the unity or truth of some wisdom text that has been dispersed and must be gathered together, as we gather what we know. Isis becomes the seeker of wisdom or the would-be knower, and Typhon the enemy of knowledge:

> He tears to pieces and scatters to the winds the sacred writings, which the goddess collects and puts together and gives into the keeping of those that are initiated into the holy rites . . . the end and aim of which is the knowledge of Him who is the First, the Lord of All, the Ideal One.

The robes of Isis are of many colors

> for her power is concerned with matter which becomes everything and receives everything, light and darkness, day and night, fire and water . . . [which robes] they use many times over; for in use those things that are perceptible and ready at hand afford many disclosures of themselves.

> But the robe of Osiris has no shading or variety in its color, but only one single color like to light . . . They lay it away and guard it, unseen and untouched, [for] the apperception of the conceptual, the pure, and the simple, shining through the soul like a flash of lightning, affords an opportunity to touch and see it but once.

•

From the pagany of her early poetry, with its gods evocative of wood-land and headlands of the sea, from the elemental Athena, Demeter, or Hermes of the Ways, by 1926 H.D. had come to be concerned, as we have seen Plutarch in his theosophical writings was concerned, with the gods as personae of states of mind, yes, but also as guides or messengers leading toward some gnosis of the universe. Here, the Image that comes in the poem is also a Sign of a reality beyond the poem. A content impends in everything and demands to be known. The stream of consciousness mode in writing, as Raymonde Ransome realizes, is a form of search for a further content in experience, predicated upon the immanence of meaning and self in the universe and of the universe in self: "It saw a world (James Joyce was right) in a grain, in nothingness; superstitiously in the fact that the fourth candle had burnt out, in the fact that the table needed dusting." This "superstition" may be the old doctrine of omens and signatures, or it may be the new psychoanalytic doctrine that asks, *What does it mean that the fourth candle had burnt out? Who are you that the table needed dusting?* Image and Fact are now presentations of Logos, revelations of a message that we must receive. The Universe is a book of what we are and asks us to put it all together, to learn to read.

Beyond or within the physical presence of the gods and elemental daemons in the world of H.D.'s early poetry, where the Image was the nexus of the individual consciousness and the Presence, and the *sense* (awareness as feeling) of Presence was all, now H.D. must search out the sense anew in the meaning *sense* has of import (awareness as knowledge of meaning); she must read the message the Presence presents.

To read the universe as a palimpsest, "from which one writing has been erased to make room for another," and yet to find the one writing in the other, is to see history anew as a drama in which the One is in many acts enacting Itself, in which there is an Isis in history, history itself being her robe of many colors and changes, working to restore in many parts the wholeness of *What Is* as Osiris. This is a form that exists only in the totality of being, a form in our art that exists only in the totality of that art's life; so that in any particular work this form appears as faith or on faith. In the study of the Epsilon at Delphi, Plutarch finds in the highest orders of meaning that his *EI* is *"Thou art"*—"the asser-tion of Being."

"The fact is," Plutarch continues: "that we really have no part nor parcel in Being, but everything of a mortal nature is at some stage between coming into existence and passing away." "He, being One, has with only one 'Now' completely filled 'Forever;' and only when Being is after His pattern is it in reality Being." So that Reality—of our selves and of the universe, is a *Thou*. We may look back from Plutarch's peroration at the close of his study to the philosophy that is also a poetry of Heraclitus, and we may also look forward to Hegel's vision of history as Spirit and God in process, just as we may look forward from Plutarch's exposition of Apollo and Dionysus to the vision of Nietzsche. The formal unity of history, like the formal unity of H.D.'s prose in *Palimpsest* is "laid away and guarded," hidden. Our experience of form throughout is a faith in the voice's telling that we follow. If we are not moved in faith, where we do not accept the voice and follow the presentation of images, then the prose, the history, and the universe are empty. What we follow is the Way of Isis, for in reading we must search and gather what we are searching for as we do so, even as H.D. followed the way of Isis, the path of a prose that is all the robe of Isis, the weaving of many disclosures in which there is some "apperception of the conceptual." *Palimpsest* is a book for Heracliteans.

In our time again the garment is riven. We had seen, pure and simple, our Christos or Osiris or resurrection, in the vision of a free society—"a voluntary state," Vanzetti called it—in which all properties were com-munal as in the vision of St. Francis, and the individual volition was the mover of government. Now Typhon has torn apart the sacred writings, and the search has begun. In the darkness of Bolshevist doctrine, the individual volition is denied, and the Communist Party is substituted for the communality. In the darkness of industrial capitalism, in the name of free enterprise, the communal goods are denied and mass-man or the statistical majority abstract is substituted for the individual. The Typhonic States, "communist" and "democratic" alike, prepare to destroy all possibilities of the Osirian dream in a storm of war and outrage. We had seen . . . it was one of those . . . the robe of Osiris, of Man's first Nature, "shining through the soul like a flash of lightning."

And those of us who saw and acknowledged what we saw came into a work or quest: to gather up out of the darkness the betrayal of the ideas of democracy and of communism the truth of that vision that was torn asunder. It was the new Adam, this individual man who was the brother of all men; this worker whose work was for the good of all. It was the new Eros that Psyche must now again seek even in Hell. Hipparchia may not have been mistaken then in taking Horus, the god of resurrection, to be Eros. For as Plutarch tells us in "Isis and Osiris," Horus is himself completed with the strength of Typhon whom he conquered; and Hermes, the patron of poets, cuts out the sinews of Typhon and uses them as strings for his invention of the lyre. Not only in Osiris but in Typhon is the secret of the new Eros hidden, the strength and sinews of whose song must gather from the war.

Chapter 5   *Occult Matters*

This is not the beginning of the book. That was later, or, coming later, it was written earlier. What was to become our study began surely long ago. In one sense it began before writing or reading began, when as a child I lay drifting in the environment of voices talking in the next room. I would be put to bed among the potted plants by the wall that was all windows of a sunroom or herbarium at my grandmother's, and, as my elders talked in the inner chamber, I, outside, could gaze at the night sky where some star was "mine" and watched over me, stars were eyes, or the first star seen was a wish or would grant a wish. My soul, they told me, went out to the stars or to other worlds. I laid my body down to rest in the bed as if it were a little boat and sailed on a voyage I pretended. "Wynken, Blynken, and Nod," the rhyme went:

> one night
> Sailed off in a wooden shoe—
> Sailed on a river of crystal light,
> Into a sea of dew.

"Where are you going, and what do you wish?"—so the old moon questions the voyagers. "I know where I'm going and who's going with me," another old song went. The rhyme was a child's fancy by Eugene Field, who was to become, when one was grown-up, a repressed, even despised, source, put away among childish things. In Maxfield Parrish's picture—"Show us the picture," we used to ask as Mother read—still glowing in memory, they go out into a sea of stars, into the blue of the night sky. "I pray the Lord my soul to keep."

The soul, my mother's sister, my Aunt Fay, told me years later, was like a swarm of bees, and, at night, certain entities of that swarm left the body-hive and went to feed in fields of helium—was it in the upper atmosphere of the Earth or in the fire-clouds of the Sun? The "higher" ascended nightly, and in its absence, the "lower" dreamed, flooding the mind with versions of the Underworld. "While the cat's away, the mice will play." There were not only pretend dreams or plagiarized dreams like making up the Wynken-Blynken-and-Nod Boat out of the poem by Eugene Field to be one's own, but there were rare dreams of the higher realms, instructions from angels of the Sun, and there were dreams of one's own "lower" nature, messages from the Underworld, rebellious images that flooded the mind in the absence of its King, when genitals or liver, heart or bowels, took over the imagining screens of the brain for their own drama.

My aunt's name—*Fay*—had to do with illusions or enchantments, bewilderings of the mind in which men saw an other world behind or under "reality," and at the same time it meant the enchanters them-selves, the folk who lived under the Hill. *Fate, faith, feign,* and *fair,* we find, following the winding associations of *fay, fey,* and *fairy,* in the Oxford English Dictionary, are closely related. From many roots, words gathered into one stem of meaning, confused into a collective suggestion. There is *fay,* too, from old Teutonic **fôgjan,* to join, to fix. In the American of the nineteenth century the word referred to the fit of a garment: "Your coat fays well," the O.E.D. gives us. The casting of the image is high fairy, *phanopoeia;* but the image itself, as Pound conceived it to be, a nexus—"an intellectual and emotional complex in an instant of time," he wrote in "A Stray Document," "which gives that sense of sudden liberation; that sense of freedom from time limits and space limits; that sense of sudden growth"—the image itself is *fay,* at once an apparition and a joining of two into one.

The little poem by Field was fay, for it cast its spell. And in the inner chamber, the adults, talking on, wove for me in my childish overhear-ing Egypt, a land of spells and secret knowledge, a background drift of conversation close to dreaming—spirit communications, reincarnation memories, clairvoyant journeys into a realm of astral phantasy where all times and places were seen in a new light, of Plato's illustrations of the nature of the soul's life, of most real Osiris and Isis, of lost Atlantis and Lemuria, and of the god or teacher that my parents had taken as theirs— the Hermetic Christos. This word *teacher,* as I first heard it, before I went to school, meant the same as a god. God was not a god, but from His Being He sent out teachers or gods. True teachers—Christ, Buddha, Hermes, or Lao-Tse—were Light Beings, messengers of the Sun Itself, a Sun to which our sun but referred. Hermes, Mercury, was the one with winged helmet and winged sandals I had seen in the bronze figure that stood on the piano at Aunt Fay's. He was the god of the high air, of those helium fields, carrying a rod around which two snakes twisted. This wand or *caduceus* meant, Aunt Fay explained, that he was god of Life, of the systole and diastole of the heart beat, and also of the ascent and descent of the soul. But the real image of the god was the picture Grandmother showed me in *The Book of the Dead.* In Egypt was the hidden meaning of things, not only of Greek things but of Hebrew things. The wand of Hermes was the rod of Moses, and my grandmother studied hieroglyphics as she studied Hebrew letters and searched in dictionaries for the meaning of Greek roots, to come into the primal knowledge of the universe that had been lost in the diversity of mankind. This god, the Egyptian Thoth, was Truth, the truth of what life intends that we know in death or judgment. He appeared not in the high air but was a Being of the Sun Below the Earth, a Lord of the Dead. He held the scales and weighed the soul; he judged between the fair and unfair. He had another title in *The Book of the Dead*—He-Who-Decides-In-Favor-Of-Osiris.

Fay from *fata* had to do with the dead. The fairies as fates or norns were spinners of the threads from which life was woven, who measured man's span and cut the cord to deliver him into his death as once they had cut the first cord or chord when the music began. But the word *fey* came too from another root that meant *fated to die, cowardly,* or *weak,* as the O.E.D. tells us—unmanned. In our common speech it meant "crazed," "touched," and then "clairvoyant," "in tune with the dead." The lords of the dead were, in the Egyptian writing, the ibis-headed

Thoth, the lady Isis with the disk crown, the lion-headed Sekmet, the winged-serpented Sun, showing the animal mystery in which our souls had evolved.

Just as, when that rhyme of Eugene Field's was all but forgotten, in the study of Pound's Cantos I was to come again to a "river of crystal light," and in the study of Yeats or André Breton, I was to come to hear of a "dew" or a "sea of dew," so in Whitman's "eidolon yacht of me," in D. H. Lawrence's "Ship of Death," and in the "caravel" that in *Helen in Egypt* carries the hero Achilles to the shore of dreams where his Helen waits, I was to come again to that "wooden shoe," the Wynken-Blynken-and-Nod Boat. When I was no longer a child but a boy in my early teens, I found it again in the fairy ship of Avalon. The Boat of Dreams, the Boat of the Dead, was one of the great vehicles or images of Poetry. In the late Cantos of Pound it has appeared as I saw it, almost as early as that other picture by Maxfield Parrish, in the Egyptian picture-writing my grandmother studied—the ship that makes its way on the journey in the other world—Ra-Set Boat. "And then went down to the ship," Pound had begun the established text of those Cantos, moving with the phantoms of Odysseus and his descent to the dead upon a sea of the imagination.

In the fairy-world, the otherness or alien nearness of the dead and of hidden elements, of illusion and delusion in our daily life, the witchcraft of phantasy and the bewitched obsessions of madness, all the psychological dangers, combined as if they were the heart's wish. The specter that haunts Europe Marx had called the hidden wish of the human spirit in history. The traumatic image Freud had called the repressed wish of the psyche, the primal scene. The underground uprises into the place of what is above-board. Justice demands it. The verso appears, so vivid that we see the surface of things had faded in the sunlight, and what we most feared we must now become. The living seem dead and the dead most alive. The words *fey, fay,* and *fairy* had a meaning I was to learn among schoolmates that in the common usage superseded all other meaning: "queer," "perverted," "effeminate." Old concepts of sodomy and of shamanism—the cult that Orpheus was said to have brought from the forest world of the North to corrupt Greece, a cult of mediumship, poetry, and homosexuality—carry over into our vulgar sense of the word *fairy,* where men's fear and mistrust of a sexual duplicity are most active.

The Above and the Below, the Left and the Right—in Hermetic doctrine the universe was itself, like sexuality, duplicit. Love, I was taught, had once been, in another life, hatred; and hatred, love. There were times when, in anger against my mother's domination, I could hate her. That was in the law of karma, my mother would explain, that hatred and love were so intertwined. This too was shown in the caduceus, in those two intertwined snakes on the magic wand, above which the wings of the mind hovered. Male and female were mixed too, for we who were men had been women in other lives and understood what to be a woman meant out of those depths of our human experience, the source of sexual sympathies and powers, the source too of antipathies. Thus, a poet like Shakespeare, calling upon his memory of lives beyond his own immediate life, had inner knowledge of a woman's soul in which to fashion a Lady Macbeth as well as his man's knowledge of Macbeth. Being was the ground of an ambivalence that was the key in turn of the universe hidden and disclosed in all things.

In the beginning I heard of guardian angels and of genii, of vision in dreams and of truth in fairy tales, long before Jung expounded the gnosis or Henry Corbin revived and translated the Recitals of Avicenna. For these ideas were properties not only of the mind above, the high thought of neo-Platonists or of Romantic poets, but they were lasting lore of the folk mind below too, wherever old wives told their tales. Gossip had preserved stories and brought rumors of the divine wisdom into American folk ways. From the popular movement of nineteenth century American spiritualism, where witch tradition out of Salem, shaman rites out of the world of the American Indian, and talking in tongues or from the spirit common in congregations of the Holy Ghost in the Protestant movement, mingled to become an obsession at large, so that in the last decades of the century, in town and in the country, groups met to raise the dead at rapping and levitating tables, new affinities with more ancient mystery cults of spirit and of a life beyond life were awakened. The theosophy of Plutarch, of Plotinus and Pseudo-Dionysius the Areopagite, the hermeticism of Pico della Mirandola, with *The Light of Asia* and the *Bhagavad-Gita,* joined in the confusion of texts and testimonies of libraries that could include accounts written by trance-mediums of travel to past time or far planets, manuals of practical astrology and numerology, or Max Heindel's *The Rosicrucian Cosmo-Conception* ("*Its Message and Mission: A Sane Mind. A Soft Heart. A Sound Body.*").

My grandmother, as a young wife of eighteen, so I remember the story, had lost two babies in a polio epidemic, and she came down to San Francisco from what is still backwoods Sierra country in California to go from one spiritualist circle to another, seeking consolation or communication, some continuity of her relation with the dead. The Indian guides must have seemed not out of place, for she had been born in Indian country in the wilderness of the Modoc territory in Eastern Oregon in the 1850s. My father's family had moved West too, first into Ohio at the beginning of the nineteenth century, and then on, at the frontier, or beyond the frontier, of America, into California. Tales of pioneer days, of Indian wars and of Indian sympathies, pacts with the Indians, lingered on, along with the new lore of strange ways, of pacts with the other world. From Modoc County in northeastern California, where she had gone as a young bride, my grandmother brought Indian baskets and beaded belts, feathered charms and *wampum* or strings of shells, her curios. In my childhood, there were still mediums who talked in Indian voices among those adults meeting in the other room. But my grandmother had gone on from the spiritualist circles, and, sometime in the eighties, she had joined with a group to form an Hermetic Brotherhood.

Their thought rose from a swarming ground that had been prepared by Helena Petrovna Blavatsky. *Isis Unveiled* had appeared in 1877; *The Secret Doctrine* in 1888. Sinnett's *Esoteric Buddhism,* the popular presentation of theosophical ideas, had appeared in 1883. Into her alembic or witch's pot, Blavatsky had stirred whatever hints, scraps, legends, lore, visions, phantasies, things she made up herself, into a muddle or stew. "Pot and Pan-theism" a contemporary wit dubbed it in scorn. Though she ransacked demonologies, histories of magic, studies of religion, encyclopedias of Gnosticism and neo-Platonism ("about 2100 quotations from and references to books that were copies at second hand . . . without proper credit," an angry critic wrote: "Nearly the whole of four pages was copied from Oliver's *Pythagorean Triangle,* while only a few lines were credited to that work"), the material of *Isis Unveiled,* H.P.B. insisted, was her own, not out of reference books she had read, a matter of her research and imagination, but was revealed to her in the Akashic or Astral Records. So her disciple Olcott describes how, in the evening when he would return from his office and sit opposite her as she wrote "with the vacant eye of the clairvoyant seer" (but we see it also as with the vacant eye of one recalling what she had read that day), she would "shorten her vision as though to look at something held invisibly in the air before her, and begin copying on her paper what she saw."

Did she pretend, as I used to pretend as a child, to sail out in the boat previous to dreaming? Why? Her references were actually all there in books that Olcott and she had gathered in their library in that very room or had borrowed from the libraries of occultist friends. She had an insatiable curiosity and energy in gathering information. She talked with everyone and read everything. In those very years (1875–77) when *Isis Unveiled* was conceived and written, she had drawn upon the learning of a friend, Alexander Wilder, an American occultist, who had edited and annotated Thomas Taylor's *Eleusinian and Bacchic Mysteries* and had translated the *Theurgia* of Iamblichus. Blavatsky insisted that her guides were spirits. "One such collaborator," Gertrude Williams tells us in her book on Blavatsky, *Priestess of the Occult,* "was the Old Platonist who, remaining invisible, talked by the hour, dictating copy, checking references, answering questions." "The spirit Old Platonist would be more convincing," Mrs. Williams comments, "if there had not been an Old Platonist in the flesh—Dr. Wilder, who also talked by the hour, checking references and answering questions."

But the work was not meant to be convincing. It was meant to be upsetting to the mind that would have tolerated Dr. Wilder as an authority in a curious field of thought but would balk at the pretension of a spirit as an authority in a revelation. Her purpose was not to convert but to overthrow the established orders of thought, to set up whatever was doubted, feared, or despised in the place of the ruling authorities. Yes, but mixed up with the hysterical impulse to insult and subvert the respectable and reasonable was—also a component of hysteria—the intense sense of how much the society itself was in need of some release of vital powers that had been repressed.

"I am solely occupied," Blavatsky wrote to her sister, "not with writing *Isis,* but with Isis herself":

> I live in a kind of permanent enchantment, a life of visions and sights, with open eyes, and no chance whatever to deceive my senses! I sit and watch the fair good goddess constantly. And as she displays before me the secret meaning of her long-lost *secrets,* and the veil, becoming with every hour thinner and more transparent, gradually falls off before my eyes, I hold my breath and can hardly trust to my senses! . . . Night and day the images of the past are ever marshaled before my inner eyes. Slowly, and gliding silently like images in an enchanted panorama, centuries after centuries appear before me . . . I certainly refuse point-blank to attribute it to my own knowledge or memory. I tell you seriously I am helped. And he who helps me is my Guru.

My "Daemon," Socrates had called him. Or Genius. My *Muse,* a poet might have called Isis. But Blavatsky was not, she insisted, musing. Whatever else *Isis Unveiled* might be, it was not to be taken as a scholarly study, a philosophy, or a work of the imagination. It was to be taken as revelation, a dictate of the unconscious. A new specter was raised to haunt the course of Western Civilization.

"The mind is the great Slayer of the Real," reads one of the aphorisms in *The Voice of Silence,* "translated" so Blavatsky declared, out of *Senzar,* the lost language of the world before Atlantis. The scholar, the philosopher, the poet, were all men of the mind, and in the critical distance of their disciplines or arts, slayers of the real. This "Real" was Isis naked, the Revealed Doctrine. We can read another message in the oracle, for the Mind, the idiotic or autistic dream and will, is also a great slayer of another "Real," the common sense of things. Blavatsky had set about to destroy what Freud calls the reality principle. John Symonds in his book on Blavatsky, *The Lady with the Magic Eyes,* comments: "The *Mind* is here used in the sense of consciousness, upon which all our Western scientific knowledge is based, but which the East regards as only part of the world of illusion." Blavatsky's Mind as Slayer of the Real may have stood for the Conscious then at war with the Unconscious, as Freud was to find it in his study of hysteria at the end of the century. Plagiarism, fraud, perversion by pun, by reversal of values and displacement of content, of above into below, of male into female, left into right, before into after—all these Freud saw as operations of the unconscious in the psychopathology of daily life.

She impersonated the Unconscious, but she also gave her ego over to unconscious—"invisible" or "occult," she called them—guides. She was unconscious of what she read or learned in talking with Dr. Wilder, and accepted the information only in a trance-like state from the unconscious where it had been banished from her consciousness.

She was a wishful thinker, and she flew into rages when her wishes were questioned. She did not rage at Nature. Nature seemed to cooperate with her powers. But she was savage when confronted by ways of the mind that others took for granted as proper, by what was right to think, reasonable to hope for. More, she was outraged by her own disciples, the credulous and ever-admiring Olcott, the reason-seeking Sinnett, for she wanted the mind in following her Doctrine to be converted by what it could not believe, to submit to the unreasonable. She did not want her Theosophic manifesto to be accepted; she wanted men to come by way of what they could not accept into the rebellious impulses that lay back of *Isis Unveiled*. "If you only knew what lions and eagles in every part of the world have turned into asses at my whistle, and have obediently wagged their long ears in time as I piped," she wrote to a confidante.

There is pathos in her scorn. She had wanted to awaken a disobedience in man that would restore the lion or eagle he must be. The hidden Adam restored, man transformed under the dictatorship of the unconscious. You have nothing to lose but your chains of belief and disbelief, she had wanted to say.

For she herself was bound in chains of belief and disbelief. The imagination was intolerable to her conscious mind. She denied that there was any truth or trust in what a man might create or initiate. Even her book, in order to be doctrine, could not be created by her or have any virtue in her own thought but must be dictated by the authority of Masters outside the work, just as the truth of Man could not be immanent in his evolution but must be established in a paradigm, an actual plan given in the beginning, recorded in the eternal—the "Akashic" or Astral Light—and lost. "I certainly refuse point-blank to attribute it to my own knowledge or memory," she had said then, as if such an attribution would have brought the authenticity of *Isis Unveiled* into question. She would have excluded the more vehemently any suggestion of her own phantasy or imagination as a source.

Whatever came from the individual inner volition was suspect. Over and over again she warns against the elemental and animal entities, the false impulses, that threaten any free life of the psyche as a medium. It is experience itself that she warns against. What does not come from a superior external authority, from Adepts "closely connected with a certain island of an inland sea," what does not come from the teachings of a primal and esoteric wisdom, comes from below, from the Left, from the swarming mass of a false science based upon the senses. All the imaging, voicing, personating, creating activity that characterizes the imagination in the ego was denied and mistrusted by her conscious mind. Only what was actual and imperative was permitted reality. Her ideas, her intuitions, her voices—the imagined teachers Morya and Koot Houmi—were illusions, if they belonged to her own creative life. The Universe itself was Maya, if it was created. The real could not be made up.

Given the chains of belief and disbelief, the alternative of illusion is delusion. The creative was the veil of Isis. To find the hidden thing one had to strip the creative veil away. The magic of Blavatsky, the fascination of her writing, was never then to be the magic of an enchanting prose, evoking its life in us to become most real in the weaving of a spell that is also a music with many images and levels of meaning—the illusion of an experience. Her magic was to be, on the contrary, the fascination of an argumentative delusion, the pursuit of proofs and laws behind appearances.

She searched in India and in Egypt, she drew portraits, and, finally, she faked evidence, to prove that her Masters were not figures of a dream or fiction, creatures of the veil, but were actual persons. Antimaterialistic though she declared herself, she could not believe they might be spiritual beings "not of this world." She rejected all sublimations. Proofs lay in materializations—cups and saucers, gloved hands, bells rung, wafts of scent, actual letters received in a spirit post office.

Ideas, imaginings, reveries, were immaterial. She sought only the manifest. Yet she could live too in "a kind of permanent enchantment," as she writes to her sister, smoking hashish and having, not her own phantasies, but hashish phantasies. Given the manifest agency of the drug, so that any suspicion of her own psychic agency might be denied, she could dwell "with Isis herself."

In 1891, a month before her death, she closed her last essay with a quotation from Montaigne: "I have here made only a nosegay of culled flowers, and have brought nothing of my own but the string that ties them." The string she had brought of her own was the thread of her argument, a wish that she, and mankind with her, might be released from the contradictions of dream and fact, creative idea and actuality, volition and authority that tortured her spirit. But the string was also the quest for the end of dream, creative idea, volition—if only they could be proved to be their opposites, so that what we thought was moving would prove to be schematic and settled. The string was the obsessional winding of the thread—the double-faced words "mind" and "real," the inversion of evolutionary theory, the perversions of geological theory, the inversions that must not be conversions, the transference of fact into fiction and of fiction into the mode of fact, the subversion of accepted scientific thought, the plagiarism, the fraud—worst of all, the reasoning of a woman who knows she must be right and will take any means to prove it.

With pathos, she added: "Is anyone of my helpers prepared to say that I have not paid the full price of my string?" She had been attacked and exposed, vilified and ridiculed. Her own followers had come to doubt that her Masters "really" existed. But the pathos was Mercurial, for she had meant for her followers in all the stupidity of their conscious minds, bound by chains of Theosophic belief, like her defamers, bound by the chains of scientific or religious disbelief, to pay the full price of her string.

For the price of the string, the price of the wish, the quest, the obsession, lay in an oppressive state. She had gathered a pitchblende of suggestion, once her doctrine was mixed, in which some radium lay hid. In the mess of astrology, alchemy, numerology, magic orders and disorders, neo-Platonic, Vedic, and Kabbalistic systems combined,

confused, and explained, queered evolution and wishful geology, trans-
posed heads—the fact of her charged fascination with it all remains
genuine. It has the charge of a need, and her sense binds: that until man
lives once more in these awes and consecrations, these obediences to
what he does not know but feels, until he takes new thought in what he
has discarded from thought, he will not understand what he is.

Isis Unveiled and *The Secret Doctrine,* midden heaps that they are of
unreasonable sources, are midden heaps where, beyond the dictates of
reason, as in the collagist's art, from what has been disregarded or fallen
into disregard, genres are mixed, exchanges are made, mutations begun
from scraps and excerpts from different pictures ("2100 quotations . . .
without proper credit") to form the figures of a new composition. In
the conglomerate that Blavatsky gathered, things of disparate traditions
whirl and take on new shapes for the conscious imagination, separated
from their contexts and credits, tainted with foreign meanings. Her
conscious insistence that her work was dedicated to the immutable and
archetypal Reality of the esoteric wisdom hid or veiled her unconscious
wish—it was a vital intuition also of the meaning of science, religion,
and art—for a magic to take over nature, our own inner nature then,
from the Father, and to give birth to a new Nature, to prove *What Is*
to be an illusion in the light of What Must Be. The Isis, the Esoteric
Wisdom of What Is, appears in the imagination to keep alive the rebel-
lious writer's sympathies with her own nature, with Nature then—in
the presence of the would-be usurping wish.

So, Blavatsky saw vividly how Science, under the dictatorship of
Reason, had isolated itself from concern with any world of spirit or
psyche, and finally from human and animal sympathies, declaring only
that world to exist which could be positively known. "We must bravely
face Science and declare," she wrote in 1888, "that the true Occultist
believes in *Lords of Light*":

> that he believes in a Sun, which—far from being simply a 'lamp of day'
> moving in accordance with physical laws; and far from being merely one
> of those Suns, which according to Richter, 'are sun-flowers of a higher
> light'—is, like milliards of other Suns, the dwelling or the vehicle of a
> God, and of a host of Gods.

Behind the world that science had defined, she sensed intentions and potentialities that disturbed those definitions. There was no realm of matter that was not charged with spirit, and man's increasing knowledge in the material realm was filled with the karma or hubris of his unacknowledged spiritual content at work there. Blavatsky's chapter heading in *The Secret Doctrine*—"Modern Physicists Are Playing At Blind Man's Buff"— has not lost meaning but has gained in terror in our day. Again and again she portrays eras of desolation and loss in the history of knowing that seem at once to be myths of our present psychic state and ominous predictions of states yet to come. "There had once been," she tells us:

on the plan of the Zodiac in the *upper* Ocean or the Heavens: a certain realm on Earth, an inland sea, consecrated and called the 'Abyss of Learning'; twelve centers on it, in the shape of twelve small islands, representing Zodiacal Signs—two of which remained for ages the 'mystery Signs'—were the abodes of twelve Hierophants and Masters of Wisdom. This 'Sea of Knowledge' or learning remained for ages there, where now stretches the Shamo or Gobi Desert. It existed until the last great glacial period, when a local cataclysm, which swept the waters South and West and so formed the present great desolate desert, left only a certain oasis, with a lake and one island in the midst of it, as a relic of the Zodiacal Ring on Earth. For ages the Watery Abyss—which, with the nations that preceded the later Babylonians, was the abode of the 'Great Mother,' the terrestrial post-type of the 'Great Mother Chaos' in Heaven, the parent of Ea (Wisdom), himself the early prototype of Oannes, the Man-Fish of the Babylonians—for ages, then, the 'Abyss' or Chaos was the abode of Wisdom and not of Evil. The struggle of Bel and then of Merodach, the Sun-God, with Tiamat, the Sea and its Dragon—a 'War' which ended in the defeat of the latter—has a purely cosmic and geological meaning, as well as an historical one. It is a page torn out of the history of the Secret and Sacred Sciences, their evolution, growth and death—for the profane masses. It relates (a) to the systematic and gradual drying up of immense territories by the fierce Sun at a certain prehistoric period, one of the terrible droughts which ended by a gradual transformation of once fertile lands abundantly watered into the sandy deserts which they are now; and (b) to the systematic persecution of the Prophets of the Right path by those of the Left.

The psychic history of the Universe, Earth, and Man, was the drama of each in the drama of the other, written in traumatic scenes—the freezing of the Hyperborean continent, the submerging of Lemuria and Atlantis, the drying up of the Gobi centers. Just as in the bardic tradition, the poet claims to have lived in all times of history from the creation of the world, so in Blavatsky's theosophy, the individual psyche of the seer inhabits every place and time, every event in the history of the collective; everything survives in some way or other in man.

Gwion (Finn) in the thirteenth-century *Romance of Taliesin* not only tells us that he is the hero or godchild of the land of fairy, Fionn, but names himself also Taliesin, the ninth-century poet, and, again, suggests that he may be a power of the Cosmos, for he claims, "my original country is the region of the summer stars":

> I was with my Lord in the highest sphere,
> On the fall of Lucifer into the depth of hell.
> I have borne a banner before Alexander . . .

This "I," the poet's persona in his song, lives in whatever he sings, as Madame Blavatsky lives in whatever she knows. What they "imagine" has the autonomy of the given:

> I am a wonder whose origin is not known.
> I have been in Asia with Noah in the Ark . . .

—just as in the psyche-mysteries of Freudian psychoanalysis, the individual psyche was taken to recapitulate the psychic life of his species; the deepest psychic resources, to be found in the collective unconscious. "Since the time when we recognized the error of supposing that ordinary forgetting signified destruction or annihilation of the memory-trace," Freud tells us in *Civilization and Its Discontents,* "we have been inclined to the opposite view that nothing once formed in the mind could ever perish, that everything survives in some way or other, and is capable under certain conditions of being brought to light again, as, for instance, when regression extends back far enough." Tracing the history of "the Eternal City" Rome, Freud then turns to picture the psyche itself as such an Eternal City in one of those creative phantasies in which Freud works a kind of poetry:

> Now let us make the fantastic supposition that Rome were not a human dwelling-place, but a mental entity with just as long and varied a past history: that is, in which nothing once constructed had perished, and all the earlier stages of development had survived alongside the latest. This would mean that in Rome the palaces of the Caesars were still standing on the Palatine and the Septizonium of Septimus Severus was still towering to its old height; that the beautiful statues were still standing in the colonnade of the Castle of St. Angelo, as they were up to its siege by the Goths, and so on. But more still: where the Palazzo Caffarelli stands there would also be, without this being removed, the temple of Jupiter Capitolinus, not merely in its latest form, moreover, as the Romans of the Caesars saw it, but also in its earliest shape, when it still wore an Etruscan design and was adorned with terra-cotta antefixes. Where the Coliseum stands now we could at the same time admire Nero's Golden House; on the Piazza of the Pantheon we should find not only the Pantheon of to-day as bequeathed to us by Hadrian, but on the same site Agrippa's original edifice; indeed, the same ground would support the church of Santa Maria sopra Minerva and the old temple over which it was built.

To penetrate the depths of the psychic life, Freud resolved: "We shall have no hesitation in allowing ourselves to be guided by the common usages of language, or as one might say, the feeling of language, confident that we shall thus take into account inner attitudes which still resist expression in abstract terms." And in the study of languages, the same sense of all times indwelling in our time or of the essential person of each man indwelling in every period of man's history takes over. In the grand project of the Oxford English Dictionary, "on historical principles," undertaken in the latter half of the nineteenth century, the first volume appearing in 1882, the English language was revealed in layers of usage laid bare, even as the city of Rome had been excavated by archeologists or the Earth by geologists. "The past" of our words, once it was acknowledged, entered into the present of their meaning.

Like the detective hero of the murder mystery which was contemporary in its rise with psychoanalysis and the O.E.D., Freud reads in the dreams and life stories told by his patients searching for clues to a pre-history or metahistory leading to the disclosure of some past event that will make clear what really happened, parallel with the solution that satisfies the form of the popular mystery novel. So, in the Theosophic mystery, the traumas of Hyperborea or of Atlantis come as disclosures of shaping forces in our own lives—they are still with us. "*Those very Monads* which entered the empty, senseless Shells, or Astral Figures of the First Race emanated by the Pitris," Blavatsky writes, "are the same who are now amongst us—nay, ourselves, perchance." Pound, writing in a period when he was most conversant with Yeats's Kabbalistic lore, in Canto VII, hearing "Thin husks I had known as men, / Dry casques of departed locusts / speaking a shell of speech," must have had the presence of such *kelipot* in mind, evil, that are quickened only by the sin of man: "Life to make mock of motion"—

> For the husks, before me, move,
>   The words rattle: shells given out by shells.
> . . . .
> And the tall indifference moves,
>   a more living shell,
> Drift in the air of fate, dry phantom, but intact.

The bardic tradition may be recalled by Robert Graves in his "historical grammar of poetic myth," *The White Goddess,* or the primal scene of Titanic infants playing with fire may haunt Freud's *Civilization and Its Discontents,* as the Atlantean transgression of Nature's laws occupies Blavatsky's thought, because we live in a time into which all times are gathering. "The communion of saints is a great and inspiring assemblage," Whitehead writes in his *Aims of Education* in 1929: "but it has only one possible hall of meeting, and that is, the present." We find ourselves gathering what they were or drawn to the idea of them, for we have that wish for a great time or a great space—overpopulated as we are—to live in; and we call up the whole population of mankind and even, thinking of Darwin, of the living, to live in us.

"Before the mind's eye, whether in sleep or waking, came images that one was to discover presently in some book one had never read," Yeats tells us in *Per Amica Silentia Lunae:*

> and after looking in vain for explanation to the current theory of forgotten personal memory, I came to believe in a Great Memory passing on from generation to generation. But that was not enough, for these images showed intention and choice. They had a relation to what one knew and yet were an extension of one's knowledge. If no mind was there, why should I suddenly come upon salt and antimony, upon the liquefaction of the gold, as they were understood by the alchemists, or upon some detail of cabbalistic symbolism verified at last by a learned scholar from his never-published manuscripts, and who can have put together so ingeniously, working by some law of association and yet with clear intention and personal application, certain mythological images? They had shown themselves to several minds, a fragment at a time, and had only shown their meaning when the puzzle picture had been put together. The thought was again and again before me that this study had created a contact or mingling with minds who had followed a like study in some other age, and that these minds still saw and thought and chose.

With Yeats, we are close to Blavatsky's influence, for he had sought her out in 1887 when he was in his early twenties and he had gone on in other circles to devote his life to the esoteric wisdom cults. But it was the affinity that Poetry in the Romantic tradition has for the occult that moved him. For from the first Yeats had believed that Poetry had itself a secret tradition and doctrine. It was the study of Blake that had brought him to the threshold, leading beyond to Boehme and to the *Zohar* of Moses of Leon. It was Shelley who had set him on his way, for Yeats had read in that poet's poem "Hellas" of a Jew, Ahasuerus, of whom Shelley says:

> Some feign that he is Enoch: others dream
> He was pre-Adamite, and has survived
> Cycles of generation and of ruin.

"Already in Dublin, I had been attracted to the Theosophists because they had affirmed the real existence of the Jew, or of his like," Yeats tells us in *The Trembling of the Veil.* He demanded, like Blavatsky, that his images be verified. He had come in search of a Master in life who had appeared to him in Shelley's play—the Wandering Jew, Ahasuerus. "Mistake me not!" Ahasuerus had said in Shelley's poem:

All is contained in each. . . . Thought
Alone, and its quick elements, Will, Passion,
Reason, Imagination, cannot die;
They are, what that which they regard appears,
The stuff whence mutability can weave
All that it hath dominion o'er, worlds, worms,
Empires, and superstitions.

It was to increase the dominion of the poetic mind that Yeats pursued his studies in the occult. The doctrine of correspondences that he found there enlarged the mission of metaphor and simile. The concept of the *eidolon* inherited from Iamblichus in which primal and eternal images are the movers or powers of the universe, agents of reality, charged the poet's reveries and visions with a radical purpose, a directive towards the heart of the matter, taken in what the majority of men took to be a literary pastime—at best a function of cultured sensibility, at worst an idle and even childish indulgence in phantasy.

Yeats is often called a symbolist, but the symbol, for him, was a magic intermediate, having its efficacy in the route it made between the soul and the image, the objective. But, it was also . . . , it had . . . , it moved into the mind with . . . , intention and choice. It was also the subject; it presented itself to him. For Yeats, as for Blavatsky, the great images were not imagined in the sense of being thought up, but came to the imagination. There was a way, he tells us, in which men kept their bodies still and their minds awake and clear so that they became a mirror of the Real.

"I had no natural gift for this clear quiet," he continues: "and I was seldom delighted by that sudden luminous definition of form which makes one understand almost in spite of oneself that one is not merely imagining." It was to live in this as if it were more than imagined, as if it were a poetry that had its authors in eternity, as Blake said they were, and into which the poet entered in his art, projecting a like-poetry, a microcosmos of the Real in the medium of words, guided, like Freud later was to be guided, "by the *feeling* of language." The Universe was a great Work or Language, life itself its voice, and all that the poet felt, heard, saw, and sensed, in the world about him or in himself, was a language he must come to read, just as each art had its particular language of images, sounds, or movements in which meanings were evoked.

In an age when what we commonly call Science, the evocation of the use of the world, the presumption of mechanical imaginations in place of all other imaginations, defined its own realm as the sole Real and all other worlds as unreal, there were men in the arts too who attempted to define realistic claims, working purely in terms of semantic or cultural values, at war with unrealistic or animistic feelings of language. Turning to the pseudo-scientific or heretical concerns of the occultist, the evocation of a world in terms of a living language, Yeats was turning too from any purely literary or aesthetic interpretation of the role of poetry, to affirm the truth he had found in Shelley or in Blake as most real. He sought not only theosophy, god-knowledge, but theurgy, god-work; and there was magic too, daemonic experiment. Words were at once agents of personal feeling and composition in a poem and also bearers of knowledge felt, evokers of the real and casters of a spell.

•

The Hermetic Order of the Golden Dawn, the ritual cult to which Yeats belonged, begun by Dr. Woodman, Dr. Wynn-Wescott and MacGregor Mathers, after the publication of Mathers's *The Kabbalah Unveiled* in 1888, ten years after Blavatsky's *Isis Unveiled* and the same year as *The Secret Doctrine,* gave rise not only to new formations in occultist circles but also to new formations in the literary world. There was a first splinter group—as such mutinies were called in Marxist movements of the 1930s—when between 1900 and 1901 Mathers and Aleister Crowley left the party or were ousted from the party in a furor of legal battles, theoretic arguments, and black magic wars. Crowley, obsessed with the terror of the void since the trauma of the Chogo Ri expedition of 1902, when he was the sole survivor of a group attempting to climb that mountain, devoted the rest of his life to finding a sufficient nightmare to fill the emptiness. "The Abramelin demons, that

Crowley had invoked at Boleskine, would seem to have formed a secret alliance with their cousins of the Hamalayan heights," C.R. Cammell observes in his study of Crowley. After the Second World War (where certainly the void and terror opened in the death chambers of the Nazis or the radioactive holocaust let loose over Japan by the United States would seem a sufficient blackness), in the rise of a poetry of emptiness and black humor and in another poetry of spiritual rebellion, as in the works of Philip Lamantia or in the film-poetry of Kenneth Anger, the influence of Crowley began to appear as a force in the art of the new underground culture.

But we have here to do with a later division of the Order of the Golden Dawn into two distinct and even opposing groups among its members. Virginia Moore in her study of Yeats, *The Unicorn*, traces this history. The one, followed by Yeats and Algernon Blackwood, continued along the line of a pantheism in which all gods had reality in terms of the Anima Mundi below and the Great Mind or God above. The other, led by A.E. Waite, and including Arthur Machen, Charles Williams, and Evelyn Underhill, in 1903 broke with the parent body and formed a group which kept the Golden Dawn name but directed its study toward a Christian, even Catholic, mysticism. For this second group, the validity and verification of the esoteric tradition was determined by its devotion to the Christos—and outside the Christian reality, the esoteric was evil.

Algernon Blackwood, with Yeats and the elder Watkins, formed, Virginia Moore tells us, a Society of the Three Kings. In Blackwood's novels we find that he believes in or is drawn toward the idea of a mystical theurgy in the worship of the elements where the protagonist is united with the regions of the stars and a way is opened into the elemental realm of Nature that is also the restored childhood world and consciousness of *The Education of Uncle Paul*, *The Centaur*, or of *A Prisoner in Fairyland*. Yeats, as *The Trembling of the Veil* and *Per Amica Silentia Lunae* testify, sought a magic that might open his mind to invasions of sensation and image, uniting his imagination with the passionate and daemonic imagination of the Anima Mundi. They may have been—those three Kings devoted, we are told, "to the study of Mysticism not Occultism"—three Magi or Magicians too, studying the magic of the Child. Yeats in his *Autobiography,* like Blackwood in his novels, makes it clear that he seeks what he once knew in his childhood when he dwelt upon the thresholds of an enchantment or *faerie* in Nature, a closeness to the earth and to folk ways.

There was another movement after the death of Madame Blavatsky. This time not in the temple of a ritual cult but in the lecture hall of a theosophic school. G. R. S. Mead, who had been Blavatsky's secretary, followed the way not of magic rite nor of mystic ritual but of gnosis, the teaching in the divine mysteries. In 1896 he published his translation from a Latin version of the Coptic text the *Pistis Sophia;* in 1900 his study of surviving Gnostic texts and traditions, *Fragments of a Faith Forgotten;* in 1906 *Thrice-Greatest Hermes,* studies in Hellenistic theosophy and gnosis, with a translation of the Trismegistic literature; and then, the series of eleven texts: *Echoes from the Gnosis.* In the magazine *The Quest* edited by Mead, his purpose is clearly to establish all religions as one ground of man's search for a life in the Divine World, to free the mind of man in his quest for the Divine from the inhibiting forces of dogma and church views, and at the same time, to revive the sense of the Divine World as the Real, the source of man's vital life.

Along another path, at Oxford and especially Cambridge, following *The Golden Bough* of Frazer in 1890, both classicists and folklorists found themselves students of the mystery cults. The way led from Bergson's *L'Evolution créatrice,* Jane Harrison tells us in her Preface to *Themis* in 1912: "I saw that Dionysus was an instinctive attempt to express what Professor Bergson calls *durée,* that life which is one, indivisible and yet ceaselessly changing." From a second source, Durkheim's *Représentations Individuelles et Représentations Collectives,* she had gathered that not only was the mystery-god an agency of "those instincts, emotions, desires which attend and express life" but that "these emotions, desires, instincts, in so far as they are religious, are at the outset rather of a group than of individual consciousness."

The texts of the classicist or the folklorist began to take on contemporary meaning in the light of ideas of life forces and collective mind. "I was no longer engaged merely in enquiring into the sources of a fascinating legend," Jessie Weston writes of her conversion from the folklorist view in the Preface to *From Ritual to Romance:* "but on the identification of another field of activity for forces whose potency as agents of evolution we were only now beginning rightly to appreciate." Tracing the roots of the Grail legend to "the mysterious border-land between Christianity and Paganism," she tells us the path led from the Cumont to Mead where she found "not only the final link that completed the chain of evolution from Pagan Mystery to Christian Ceremonial, but also proof of that wider significance I was beginning to apprehend. The problem involved was not one of Folk-lore, not even one of Literature, but of Comparative Religion in its widest sense."

In the Quest Society, as in the person of its leader, G. R. S. Mead, the current of *The Golden Bough* and the current of *The Secret Doctrine* meet. In the pages of Mead's journal, *The Quest*, we find the new philosophy of Bergson along with Jessie Weston's Grail essays, Eisler's studies in Orphic cult and the Fisher King, Pound's "Psychology and Troubadours," along with essays on the Progressive Buddhism of Daisetz T. Suzuki. And there was not only the study of the *mythos*, the lore, but there was, so the testimony goes, back of these essays a revival of the *dromena*, of the actual rites. "I know, I mean, one man who understands Persephone and Demeter," Pound says, "and another who has, I should say, met Artemis. These things are for them *real*." The mysterious border-land between Christianity and Paganism that Jessie Weston sought knowledge of lay not only in the past but in the present London of 1909: "No inconsiderable part of the information at my disposal," she writes, "depended upon personal testimony, the testimony of those who knew of the continued existence of such a ritual, and had actually been initiated into its mysteries."

•

My grandmother was an elder in a provincial expression of this Hermetic movement, far from its center in London. Close to the woodlore of her origins in frontier life, she had some natural witchcraft perhaps. But then it may be too that all Grandmothers, as in fairytales, are Wise Women or Priestesses of Mother Nature. I was but a boy when she died, and with her death, my family's tie with the old wisdom-way was broken. There was no cult life for them after her death.

There is only what I remember out of childhood: the colored lithographs of Egyptian temples and the images upon the table, the voices talking of "Logos" and "Nous," the old women looking wisely into the Astral Light and telling what they saw there.

My father and mother had been initiates, but in their own lives the tenor of the initiation was lost. From the region of San Francisco, they moved to Bakersfield in 1929, obedient to the directions of the stars in the Zodiac, as now Zen converts are obedient to the *I Ching*—Fate and Chance. They were isolated from their Brotherhood, their studies changed to studies that were respected by the community into which they had moved. By the time I was adolescent, my father was involved in the study of botany and local historical sites. After his death, Mother was relieved, I think, that this way of studying things might be dismissed. New friends did not share her belief—that was part of it—but then, though her belief may have lasted, her interest did not last.

In my mind it has lasted. The lure is the lure of those voices weaving as I began to understand words a net of themes in which knots of meaning that refused any easy use appeared, glimpses from the adult world of words beyond them, as words were just beyond me, such a tapestry as Penelope is said to have woven that was never done but begun again each day, or as Helen wove, in which were all the scenes of the Trojan War. What was the hidden meaning of such a "Troy," of "War"? they would ask. It was not a dogma nor was it a magic that I understood for myself in the Theosophic world about me, but I understood that the meanings of life would always be, as they were in childhood, hidden away, in a mystery, exciting question after question, a lasting fascination.

The quest for meanings was a vital need in life that one recognized in romance where the hero must learn the language of birds, overhear the conversation of trees, call up even shadows to populate his consciousness. By associations, by metaphor, by likeness of the part, by fitting as part of a larger figure, by interlinking of members, by share, by equation, by correspondence, by reason, by contrast, by opposition, by pun or rhyme, by melodic coherence—what might otherwise have seemed disparate things of the world as Chaos were brought into a moving, changing, eternal, interweaving fabric of the world as Creation. It was the multiplicity of meanings at play that I loved in the talk of my parents in the 1920s. Two phases of the psyche's development in child-hood—the endless questioning and the timeless play—found their reflection or continuation in the adult world above and beyond.

We shall lose it all if it be not those voices talking over the evening fire. But the voices are gone. The waves throwing themselves down in ranks upon the shore are what I hear.

•

There had been catastrophe. There would be catastrophe. The time in which a man lived was a whirl or drift in a great sea that might rise out of itself into a roaring end of things. In the early years of the Depression, '30 or '31, when I was eleven or twelve, I would lie awake before going off to sleep at the summer cottage at Morro Beach, letting the crash of the surf take over and grow enormous in my mind which dwelt at times like this upon the last days of Atlantis, imagining again the falling of towers, the ruin of cities, the outcry of a populace swept under by the raging element. When would the long-awaited tidal wave, the advancing wall of water, sweep all before it? Even so the grownups talked of Atlantis and of America, as if it were a New Atlantis. The Atlanteans, even as we might, in their science had come to know too much, the grownups said. They had found some key to the universe and had unlocked forbidden, destroying, powers.

Taller than Morro Rock I would think the breakers of that catastrophe must be. I would try to picture the flood enormous enough to crash upon the mountains of the Coast Range as if they were but banks of sand, a wave to drown the San Joaquín. Or I would listen, curled up on the ledge back of the seat in the coupé, as Mother drove us home from the movies in San Luis Obispo, to the beach, for the fascinating sound above the fascination of the motor-sound, for the sea-roar. Now it will come, now it is coming, pouring in from the coast to meet and overwhelm us.

Born in 1919 at the close of the War, I belonged, I had been told, to an Atlantean generation that would see once more last things and the destruction of a world. There was a repeated dream I had as a child that came to be my "Atlantean" dream, for my mother told me it was a memory dream from that previous life. I belonged, too, to the generation that had been destroyed in a cataclysm before the world we lived in began. I had a part in the fabulous.

Sometimes in phantasizing, calling up pictures like this to illustrate an other life, I would rescue myself and set out upon the sea again in a boat. But the boat now was no longer charmed or charming, like the Wynken-Blynken-and-Nod Boat had been. Huddled in the wrappings of my bedclothes, I was never sure how the dark exposed rowboat or lifeboat had escaped the holocaust in which it had been said all was lost, but it had been said too that certain adepts escaped and I would be an adept. I was never sure how the boat was making its way now north and east over a grey and forbidding sea toward new land. The way was alien. I was never sure that this part, going on to rescue myself like this, would work out at all. My heart sank, for, even in a dream, I could but pretend to be an adept; I would be found out. On and on the boat sped toward some colony or destiny that had no such reality as the deluge, the sea itself, had, but lay ahead unseen and unreal.

We had moved from the Bay Region to the Valley in '28 away from the house my father as a young architect had designed in Alameda before I was born or was adopted by my parents, away from the towers of San Francisco where he had worked in a firm as a junior architect, and away too from the circle of Hermetic students. Back of what we knew as children, scenes were being shifted: from the big house with its parties, the garden and the studio, to the crowded little house in Bakersfield where my sister and I slept in the same room; from the conversation at table that was all fabulous history and fantastic science to the admonitions and explanations of the Depression years, the economic worrying and the things-to-be-discussed-later-but-not-in-front-of-the-children. What was left me from the talk of the elders in that antechamber of my childhood was now all my own. My parents, living far from the center of things, were concerned now with security and status, the politics and business opportunities of Bakersfield. Our religion became something we did not talk about to everybody. I talked to myself about it.

I would shake the mahjong table, and the palace of many gardens and courts, the majestic halls and ramparts, constructed by giant hands from another world, the corridor where the Queen walked in the evening to meet the King, would fall. It seemed as if distant almost real shouts of anguish rose among the tottering ivory walls, and, making my play of earthquake—for I was the genius of the scene—I almost heard the confusion of delicious dismay, grief, and fear, echoed in my heart as if bonds of human sympathy united me with the inhabitants of this world I created to destroy again and again. What I would see then was . . .

Yes, I would see the actual mahjong tiles. I had had to build with utmost care and grandeur my little piled-up city or kingdom with many levels, for in the care, piece by piece, a place for something to happen was prepared, an other realm was built up, each tile the immediate occasion of a life fated to come to its last day. What I would see then was the monolithic real building I was engaged in, coming into existence block by block and yet the blocks themselves coming into existence in the building, out of what they were—the imposing gleam of the red dragon and green dragon walls, the mysterious symbols of the Chinese game with its winds and flowers converted into ancient glyphs and signs of a fated citadel. The Queen again would walk in the shadowed colonnade, the priests would sound their alarms from the tower, the scenes of human panic would flare-up in the mind's eye, the pitiful consolation of the Queen in the King's embrace as the walls fell, the . . . No, he would not get to her!—the crashing house between, the grief and loss. Each time I would experience what the victims of the holocaust experienced.

In the Atlantis phantasy and the Atlantis game or play, the most real emerged only in terms of what was most unreal. It was an experience true and untrue to itself. I could call up these returns of a scene, but I had no will in calling them up that could go against the emerging pattern, given in the play. The intense reality, wherever I became arbitrary, as if I could alter the fate of my play, dissolved into unreal and unsure elements. I could not name for sure any place as my destination. I could not name for sure any time as my appointed time. So, though I read eagerly anything and everything about my Atlantis, it grew only more suspect in the obsessional proofs of Ignatius Donnelly—I didn't believe in an historical Atlantis—and yet, when geologists and reasonable historians scorned the would-be fact of Atlantis, the sinking land seemed real. Outside of history, there was an Atlantis—the shuddering earth, the engulfing waters that must have been, came into their own again.

"In other words, they are not poeticised versions of unique historical events in the life of any individual 'hero'," Jane Harrison writes of myths in *Themis:* "but reflect recurrent ritual practices, or *dromena.*" The things said over the fire long ago in my grandmother's rooms, or the talk at table in my childhood of planetary influences, elemental powers, lives before this life—the whole pictured island of lost consciousness under the sea waves that might rise once more: Atlantis—was not false history but spoke of a feeling about the course of life itself. My grandmother died in her drama, her *mise en scène* of the Hermetic cult, and those who had lived in the enchantment of her stage survived to defend, to prove, to suspect, or to put away, what, when she had been alive, had been the language in which her living was written.

It is in the dream itself that we seem entirely creatures, without imagination, as if moved by a plot or myth told by a story-teller who is not ourselves. Wandering and wondering in a foreign land or struggling in the meshes of a nightmare, we cannot escape the compelling terms of the dream unless we wake, any more than we can escape the terms of our living reality unless we die. There is a sense in which the "poet" of a poem forces us as writer or reader to obey a compelling form, the necessities of the poem, so that the poet has a likeness to the dreamer of the dream and to the creator of our living reality; dream, reality, and the poem, seem to be one.

The dream that was called my Atlantis dream was not something I thought up or that derived from the talk of my elders. The sequence remains emblematic and puzzling. Had my parents been Freudian instead of Hermeticists, they might have called it my birth-trauma dream. My first mother had died in childbirth, and in some violent memory of that initiation into life, she may be the mother-country that has been lost in legend. But, for me, the figures of the dream remain as if they were not symbolic but primal figures themselves of what was being expressed or shown. Memory of Atlantis or memory of birth-trauma, phantasy of Isis or play with words—these are not what the heart fears and needs, the showing forth of some power over the heart.

First there was the upward rise of a hill that filled the whole horizon of what was seen. A field of grass rippled as if by the life of the grass itself, yet I was told there was no wind. When I saw that there was no wind, it was a fearful thing, where blade by blade the grass so bowed of its own accord to the West. The grass moved toward the left. The seer or dreamer then was facing north. There may have been flowers—day's eyes—the grass was certainly in flower. The field was alive and, pointing that way, across the rise of the hill to the West, gave a sign.

Was I four or five when I first dreamt this dream? It came again and again as if to cut its shape for sure in what I would be. "For these images showed intention and choice," Yeats said of such primary things. When I heard the story of that nymph who fell hopelessly in love with the Lord of the Sun, Helios, I was drawn to identify with the sunflower that, rooted in her passion, turns her head to follow the Sun's way, for there was some faint reminder there of the grass I had seen in my dream bowing to the West. But in my dream there was no sun. The light was everywhere, and I can not be sure whether it was morning, evening, or high noon.

Then, in a sudden almost blurred act of the play, there was a circle of children—sometimes they were all girls or all boys, sometimes they were boys and girls—dancing in the field. They chose or had chosen someone who was "IT" in the center of the ring, but I saw no one there.

The Dreamer is in the center, the "I" or Eye of the Dream. And just here, I realize that this "I" is my self and second that I have been "chosen," but also that in dreaming I am the Chosen One, I have been caught in the wrong—a "King" or victim of the children's round dance. Ring a round of roses. Pocket full of posies. Or is it poses? for I had been proposed or I had posed as King, posed myself there. Ashes, ashes. All fall down!

In the third part—but it is the second section of the dream, for the Field and Its Dancers are two parts belonging to the one section—I am shown a cavern underground. A throne room? There is a stone chair on a dais. Seeing it is the King's chair or, even, in some dreamings of this dream, finding myself a lonely king in that chair, there is no one rightly there. A wave of fear seizes me. All things have gone wrong and I am in the wrong. Great doors break from their bars and hinges, and, under pressure, a wall of water floods the cavern.

The open field, the dance and the presumption, the seeing the dark throne and the flooding of the underworld (the dream that my mother believed to be memory of a past life) seem now a prediction of what life will be, now a showing forth of some content of what life is, as in the Orphic mysteries the story of Persephone was shown in scenes. The restless dead, the impending past life, what had been cast away—a seed—sprouts and in the vital impulse would speak to us. The head of a giant woman rises from the ground.

"I have seen Kore," the initiate Heracles says: "What face more terrible? I am initiate, prepared for Hades." Wonder and terror seem to be signs of the rite. But in my life dream, I have not seen the Maiden, for I stand in her place or in her way.

Chapter 6 *Rites of Participation*

The drama of our time is the coming of all men into one fate, "the dream of everyone, everywhere." The fate or dream is the fate of more than mankind. Our secret Adam is written in the script of the primal cell. We have gone beyond the reality of the incomparable nation or race, the incomparable Jehovah in the archetype of Man, the incomparable Book or Vision, the incomparable species, in which identity might find its place and defend its boundaries against an alien kind. All things have come now into their comparisons. But these comparisons are the correspondences that haunted Paracelsus, who saw also that the key to man's nature was hidden in the design of the larger Nature. We are a variation among variations in the music of a natural intent in which evil as well as our good plays its part, becomes a term of the good of the totality in process.

In the terms of Space, this has meant the extension of our "where" into a world ecology. The O.E.D. gives 1873 as the earliest use of the word in our language, appearing in the translation of Haeckel's *History of Creation:* "the great series of phenomena of comparative anatomy and ontogeny . . . oecology." The very form of man has no longer the isolation of a superior paradigm but is involved in its morphology in the cooperative design of all living things, in the life of everything, everywhere. We go now to the bushman, the child, or the ape, who were once considered primitive, not to read there what we once were but to read what we are. In the psychoanalysis of the outcast and vagabond, the neurotic and psychotic, we slowly discover the hidden features of our own emotional and mental processes. We hunt for the key to language itself in the dance of the bees or in the chemical code of the chromosomes. Likewise, it is the secret theme of a new music transforming the meaning of earlier themes in which the very thriving of Mankind has come into crisis.

The inspiration of Marx bringing economies into comparison and imagining a world commune, of Darwin bringing species into comparison and imagining a world family of the living in evolution, of Frazer bringing magic, rituals and gods, into comparison and imagining a world cult—these inspirations toward a larger community of Man belong to the nineteenth century of imperialist expansions. In Time, this has meant our "when" involves and is involved in an empire that extends into the past and future beyond times and eras, beyond the demarcations of history. Not only the boundaries of states or civilizations but also the boundaries of historical periods are inadequate to define the vital figure in which we are involved. "For the intense yearning which each of them has towards the other," so the witch Diotima tells Socrates in Plato's *Symposium,* "does not appear to be the desire of lover's intercourse, but of something else which the soul of either evidently desires and cannot tell, and of which she has only a dark and doubtful presentiment."

The symposium of Plato's time was restricted to a community of Athenians, gathered in the common creation of an *areté,* an aristocracy of spirit, inspired by the homoEros, taking its stand against lower or foreign orders, not only of men but of Nature at large. The intense yearning, the desire for something else, of which we too have only a dark and doubtful presentiment, remains, but our *areté,* our ideal of vital being, rises not in our identification with a paradigm in a hierarchy of higher forms but in our identification with the process of design beyond our own figure. To compose such a symposium of the whole, such a totality, all the old excluded orders must be included. The female, the lumpen-proletariat, the foreign; the animal and vegetative; the unconscious and the unknown; the criminal and failure—all that has been outcast and vagabond in our consideration of the figure of Man—must return to be admitted in the creation of what we are.

The dissolving of boundaries of time, as in H.D.'s *Palimpsest,* so that Egyptian or Hellenistic ways invade the contemporary scene—the reorganization of identity to extend the burden of consciousness—this change of mind has been at work in many fields. The thought of primitives, dreamers, children, or the mad—once excluded by the provincial claims of common sense from the domain of the meaningful or significant—has been reclaimed by the comparative and universalizing psychologies of William James, Freud, Levy-Bruhl, Piaget, or by the comparative linguistics of Sapir and Whorf, brought into the community of a new epistemology.

"Past the danger point, past the point of any logic and of any meaning, and everything has meaning," H.D. writes in *Bid Me to Live:* "Start superimposing, you get odd composites, nation on nation." Malraux in his *Psychology of Art* hears "a furtive colloquy in progress between the statuary of the Royal Portals of Chartres and the great fetishes" beginning in museums of the mind where all the arts of man have been brought into the complex of a new idea of Art and Man in their assemblage. "Our art world is one in which a Romanesque crucifix and an Egyptian statue of a dead man can both be living presences," he writes in *The Metamorphosis of the Gods:* "In our imaginary museum the great art of Europe is but one great art among others, just as the history of Europe has come to mean one history among others."

"Each civilization had its 'high places'," he concludes in the introduction to *The Metamorphosis of the Gods:*

> All mankind is now discovering its own. And these are not (as the nineteenth century took for granted) regarded as successive landmarks of art's long pilgrimage through time. Just as Cézanne did not see Poussin as Tintoretto's *successor,* Chartres does not mark an 'advance' on Angkor, or Borobudur, or the Aztec temples, any more than its KINGS are an 'advance' on the KWANNON at Nara, on the PLUMED SERPENTS, or on Pheidias' HORSEMEN.

If, as Pound began to see in *The Spirit of Romance,* "all ages are contemporaneous," *our* time has always been, and the statement that the great drama of our time is the coming of all men into one fate is the statement of a crisis we may see as ever-present in Man wherever and whenever a man has awakened to the desire for wholeness in being. "The continuous present," Gertrude Stein called this sense of time and history, and she saw the great drama as man's engagement in a composition of the contemporary. Man is always in the process of this composition. "The composition is the thing seen by every one living in the living they are doing," she writes in "Composition as Explanation":

> . . . they are the composing of the composition that at the time they are living is the composition of the time in which they are living. It is that that makes living a thing they are doing.

"Nothing changes from generation to generation," she writes later in her lecture "Portraits and Repetition," "except the composition in which we live and the composition in which we live makes the art which we see and hear . . . Once started expressing this thing, expressing any thing there can be no repetition because the essence of that expression is insistence. . . Each civilization insisted in its own way before it went away." To enter into "our time," she saw as "a thing that is very troublesome," for life itself was a disturbance of all composition—"a fear a doubt and a judgment and a conviction," troubling the waters toward some needed "quality of distribution and equilibration."

The first person plural—the "we," "our," "us"—is a communal consciousness in which the "I" has entered into the company of imagined like minds, a dramatic voice in which the readers and the man writing are gathered into one composition, in which we may find kindred thought and feeling, an insistence, in Plutarch or Dante, Plato or D.H. Lawrence, closer to our inner insistence than the thought and feeling of parents or neighbors. The discovery of self, time, and world, is an entering into or tuning to possibilities of self, time, and world, that are given.

"The single experience lodges in an individual consciousness and is, strictly speaking, incommunicable," Sapir writes in *Language:*

> To be communicated it needs to be referred to a class which is tacitly accepted by the community as an identity. Thus, the single impression which I have of a particular house must be identified with all my other impressions of it. Further, my generalized memory or my 'notion' of this

house must be merged with the notions that all other individuals who have seen the house have formed of it. The particular experience that we started with has now been widened so as to embrace all possible impressions or images that sentient beings have formed or may form of the house in question. In other words, the speech element 'house' is the symbol, first and foremost, not of a single perception, nor even of the notion of a particular object but of a 'concept', in other words, of a convenient capsule of thought that embraces thousands of distant experiences and that is ready to take in thousands more. If the single significant elements of speech are the symbols of concepts, the actual flow of speech may be interpreted as a record of the setting of these concepts into mutual relations.

There is no isolate experience of anything then, for to come into "house" or "dog," "bread" or "wine," is to come into a company. Eros and Logos are inextricably mixed, daemons of an initiation in each of our lives into a new being. Every baby is surrounded by elders of a mystery. The first words, the "da-da" and "ma-ma," are keys given in a repeated ritual by parental priest and priestess to a locus for the child in his chaotic babbling, whereby from the oceanic and elemental psychic medium—warmth and cold, calm and storm, the moodiness previous to being—persons, Daddy and Mama, appear. But these very persons are not individual personalities but communal fictions of the family cultus, vicars of Father and Mother, as the Pope is a vicar of Christ. The Child, in the word *child,* is himself such a persona, inaccessible to the personality of the individual, as the language of adult personal affairs is inaccessible to the child. To have a child is always a threat to the would-be autonomous personality, for the parent must take leave of himself in order to enter an other impersonation, evoking the powers of Fatherhood or Motherhood, so that the infant may be brought up from the dark of his individuality into a new light, into his Childhood. For the transition to be made at all, to come into the life of the spirit, in which this Kindergarten is a recreated stage set of the mythic Garden, means a poetry then, the making up of an imaginary realm in which the individual parents and infant participate in a community that exists in a time larger than any individual lifetime, in a language. For "Father," "Mother," "Child," are living words, deriving their meaning from thousands of distinct experiences, and the actual flow of family life, like the actual flow of speech, "may be interpreted as the setting of these concepts into mutual relations." The toys of the nursery are not trivia but first given instruments of an extension in consciousness, our creative life. There is a travesty made of sacred objects when the building blocks that are also alphabet blocks, the animal and human dolls, the picture books, are rendered cute or babyish.

"The maturity of man—" Nietzsche writes in *Beyond Good and Evil:* "that means, to have reacquired the seriousness that one had as a child at play."

In *The Zohar* of Moses of Leon, God Himself appears as Child-Creator-of-the-World:

> When the Holy One, blessed be He, was about to make the world, all the letters of the Alphabet were still embryonic, and for two thousand years the Holy One blessed be He, had contemplated them and toyed with them. When He came to create the world, all the letters presented themselves before Him in, reversed order. The letter *Tau* advanced in front and pleaded: May it please Thee, O Lord of the world, to place me first in the creation of the world, seeing that I am the concluding letter of *EMeTh* (Truth) which is engraved upon Thy seal.

One by one the letters present themselves. At the last,

> . . . the Beth then entered and said: O Lord of the world, may it please Thee to put me first in the creation of the world, since I represent the benedictions (*Berakhoth*) offered to Thee on high and below. The Holy One, blessed be He, said to her: Assuredly, with thee I will create the world, and thou shalt form the beginning in the creation of the world. The letter *Aleph* remained in her place without presenting herself. Said the Holy one, blessed be His name: *Aleph, Aleph,* wherefore comest thou not before Me like the rest of the letters? She answered: Because I saw all the other letters leaving Thy presence without any success. What, then, could I achieve there? And further, since Thou hast already bestowed on the letter *Beth* this great gift, it is not meet for the Supreme King to take away the gift which He has made to His servant and give it to another. The Lord said to her: *Aleph, Aleph,* although I will begin the creation of the world with the *beth,* thou wilt remain the first of letters. My unity

shall not be expressed except through thee, on thee shall be based all calculations and operations of the world, and unity shall not be expressed save by the letter *Aleph*. Then the Holy One, blessed be His name, made higher-world letters of a large pattern and lower-world letters of a small pattern. It is therefore that we have here two words beginning with *beth* (*Bereshith bara*) '*in-the-beginning He-created*' and then two words beginning with *aleph* (*Elohim eth*) '*God the*'."

In this primal scene, before the beginning of the world that is also here before the beginning of a writing, the Self contemplates and toys in a rite of play until the letters present themselves and speak; as in another primal scene, in a drama or play of the family, the child contemplates and plays with the sounds of a language in order to enter a world in which Father and Mother present themselves and speak. So too in the fullness of the imagination, blocks and even made-up playmates present themselves. The teddy bear was once in the shaman world of the great northern forests Grandfather or Folk-Father. The figures we play with, the members of our play world, given as they are, like the Katchina dolls of the Zuni child, are spirit figures. "My unity shall not be expressed except through thee," the Child-Creator promises. It is the first promise of love, "on thee shall be based all calculations and operations of the world."

These powers, the ambience in which all things of our world speak to us and in which we in turn answer, the secret allegiances of the world of play, the psychic depth of time transformed into eternity in which the conceptual persons of Father and Mother, Child and Play Thing, exist—these are pre-rational. Brother and Sister have such an existence in the unreal that, where actual brother and sister do not exist or are unwilling to play the part, imaginary brother and sister may appear.

For men who declare themselves partisans of the rational mind at war with all other possibilities of being, the prerational or the irrational appears as an enemy within. It was not only the Poet, but Mother and Father also, that Plato would exclude from his Republic. In the extreme of the rationalist presumption, the nursery is not the nursery of an eternal child but of a grownup, a rational man. Common sense and good sense exist in an armed citadel surrounded by the threatening countryside of phantasy, childishness, madness, irrationality, irresponsibility—an exile and despised humanity. In that city where Reason has preserved itself by retreating from the totality of the self, infants must play not with the things of the imagination nor entertain the lies of the poets but play house, government, business, philosophy, or war. Before the guardians of this state the voices and persons of the Child-Creator stand condemned as auditory and visual hallucinations a dangerous non-sense.

In the world of *The Zohar,* dolls were not permitted. The Child plays with the letters of an alphabet and Logos is the creator of the world. Man is to take his reality from, to express his unity in, the letter. But this letter is, like the doll, alive to the mind. *Tau* presents herself and speaks, just as the bear in our nursery does. To the extent that once for us too alphabet blocks were animate, all future architectures and worlds are populated, and we are prepared to understand the world-experience of the Kabbalist.

In this world-experience, rationality does not exist apart from the whole, but the understanding searches ever to picture the self in the ununderstandable. The human spirit draws its life from a tree larger and more various than knowing, and reason stands in need of a gift, "the gift of the queen to them that wander with her in exile."

There is a return in the imagination to the real, an ascent of the soul to its "root," that Hayyim Vital describes in his life work, *The Tree of Life:*

> The imaginative faculty will turn a man's thoughts to imagine, and picture *as if* it ascended in the higher worlds up to the roots of his soul . . . until the imagined image reaches its highest source and there the images of the supernal lights are imprinted on his mind *as if* he imagined and saw them in the same way in which his imaginative faculty normally pictures in his mind mental contents deriving from the world.

We seem to be in the description of the process of a poem, for here too the mind imagines, but then enters a real it had not imagined, where the image becomes informed, from above or below, and takes over as an entity in itself, a messenger from a higher real. In his ascent the mystic is irradiated by the light of the tree and in his descent the light finds a medium through which to flow back into the daily world:

> The thought of the prophet expands and rises from one level to another . . . until he arrives at the point where the root of his soul is. Next he concentrates on raising the light of the sefirah to *En Sof* and from there he draws the light down, from on high down to his rational soul, and from there, by means of the imaginative faculty, down to his animal soul, and there all things are pictured either by the inner senses of the imaginative faculty or by the outer senses.

Returning from *En Sof,* the unknowable, unimaginable God, from beyond sense, the imaginer, no longer imagining but realizing, carries a light from station to station, sefirah to sefirah, irradiating the imagined with reality, transforming the sense of the divine—the articulated Tree of Life—the cosmos, the rational soul and the animal soul, in light of a source that is a numinous non-sense or beyond sense.

This Tree, too, we saw each year, for at the birthday of the Child-Christos, we were as children presented with a tree from which or under which gifts appeared—wishes made real. This Christmas tree came, we know, from the tree cults of the German tribes, ancestral spirits. A burning tree. But it is also a tree of lights, and where, in the time of Jacob Boehme, in the early seventeenth century, the Jewish and the Germanic mystery ways are wedded in one, the Christmas tree may have also been the Divine Tree of *The Zohar,* lit with the lights of the Sefiroth.

In this ritual of the imagination of Hayyim Vital, there is not only the ascent by pretending, the "as if" of his text, the pretension then, but the mystic is pretender to a throne, a "source" or "root" in the Divine. In the descent a magic is worked and all the pretended way of the ascent is rendered "greater than Reality." Not only the deep dream but the day dream enlightens or enlivens. "Occasionally," Werblowsky relates from Vital, "the imaginative faculty may even externalize or project the effects of this 'light' so that the experience becomes one of external sense impressions such as of the apparition of angelic messengers, the hearing of voices."

This Tree of Life is also the tree of generations, for its branches that are also roots are male and female, and the light or life is a mystery of the Shekinah, the ultimate Spirit-Mother of Israel as well as God's Glory. The root or seed is a quickening source in the immortal or eternal womb, wherein each man is immortal.

·

In *The Eternal Ones of the Dream,* the psychoanalyst Géza Roheim draws another configuration of source, dream, and transformation of reality, that may cast further light on our way toward a picture of what is involved in poetry when the images and personae of a dream greater than reality appear as active forces in the poet's world:

> Strehlow, who as a missionary living for decades among the Aranda was certainly an authority on their language, tells us that he cannot explain the meaning of the word *altjira,* but it seems that the natives connect to it the concept of something that has no beginning—*erina itja arbmanakala,* him none made. Spencer and Gillen, however, have given another interpretation of the word. In their glossary, we find '*altjeringa:* name applied by the Arunta, Kaitish, and Unmatjera tribes to the far past or dream times in which their mythical ancestors lived. The word *altjeri* means dream.' Strehlow denies this; he says the word for dream is *altjirerama:* and gives the following etymology: *altjira* (god) *rama* (to see).
>
> For one thing, it is clear that *altjira* means dream and not god or ancestor (as Strehlow indicates) for I found that a folktale, a narrative with a happy end, is also called *altjira.*
>
> It is evident that Strehlow, from his preoccupation with *Altjira* (God) of the Aranda Bible, managed to miss the real meaning of the word. *Altjira* = dream, *altjireramaa* = to dream; *altjirerinja* = dreaming. This is as near as I could get to Spencer and Gillen's *altjeringa.* Moses thought it must be a mistake for either *altirerindja* or *altliranga.* There was no name for any mythical period. The time when the ancestors wandered on earth was called *altjiranga nakala,* i.e. 'ancestor was', like *ljata nama,* i.e. 'now is'. Other expressions were noted as equivalents of *altjiranga nakala;* these were *imanka nakula,* 'long time ago was', or *kutata nakala,* 'eternally was'. This led us to the explanation and etymology of the word *altjiranga mitjina. Mitjina* is equivalent to *kutata,* 'eternal'; *nga* is the ablative suffix *from;* therefore *altjiranga mitjina* = 'the eternal ones from the dream' or 'the eternal people who come in dreams'. This is not my explanation, but that

of the old men, Moses, Renana, and Jirramba. Another Aranda word for dream, ancestor, and story, is *tnankara*. It is not often used, and as far as I could see it means exactly the same as *altjira*. (Roheim, *op. cit.*, pp. 210–11)

In story and tribal rite, the Australian native seeks to convert time and space into an expression of his unity, to create a language of acts and things, of devouring and being devoured, of giving birth and being born, in which man and the world about him come into one body.

In an emu myth of the Aranda, Marakuja (Hands bad), the old man emu, takes his bones out and transforms them into a cave. . . . The kangaroo men take the mucus from their noses; it becomes a stone still visible now. The rocks become black where they urinate. (*Ibid.*, pp. 211–12)

Here the *altjiranga mitjina,* the ones living in a dream of time more real than the mortality of the time past, invade the immediate scene. For the Australians as for Heraclitus, "Immortal mortals mortal immortals, their being dead is the other's life." The things lost in time return and are kept in the features of the place. "Environment is regarded as if it were derived from human beings," Roheim observes.

In repeated acts—bleeding, pissing, casting mucus, spitting into the ground, or in turn, eating the totemic food and drinking the blood of the fathers—the boy is initiated into the real life of the tribe.

An old man sits beside him and whispers into his ear the totemic name. The boy then calls out the esoteric name as he swallows the food. The emphasis on the place name in myth and ritual can only mean one thing, that *both myth and ritual are an attempt to cathect environment with libido* . . . The knowledge of the esoteric name 'aggregates' unites the boy to the place or to the animal species or to anything that was strange before. (*Ibid.*, p. 216)

The "breast, anus, semen, urine, leg, foot" in the Australian song, chant, or enchantment, that are also hill, hole, seed, stream, tree, or rock, where "in the Toara ceremony the men dance around the ring shouting the names of male and female genital organs, shady trees, hills, and some of the totems of their tribe," are most familiar to the Freudian convert Roheim. He sees with a sympathy that rises from the analytic cult in which Freud has revived in our time a psychic universe in which dream has given a language where, by a "sexual obsession" (as Jung calls it), the body of man and the body of creation are united.

The "blood" of the Aranda, the "libido" of the Freudian, may also be the "light" of our Kabbalist text. "*En Sof,*" Gershom Scholem tells us in *Major Trends in Jewish Mysticism:*

> is not only the hidden Root of all Roots, it is also the sap of the tree; every branch representing an attribute, exists not by itself but by virtue of *En Sof,* the hidden God. And this tree of God is also, as it were, the skeleton of the universe; it grows throughout the whole of creation and spreads branches through all its ramifications. All mundane and created things exist only because something of the power of the Sefiroth lives and acts in them.
>
> The simile of man is as often used as that of the Tree. The Biblical word that man was created in the image of God means two things to the Kabbalist: first, that the power of the Sefiroth, the paradigm of divine life, exists and is active also in man. Secondly, that the world of the Sefiroth, that is to say the world of God the Creator, is capable of being visualized under the image of man the created. From this it follows that the limbs of the human body are nothing but images of a certain spiritual node of existence which manifests itself in the symbolic figure of *Adam Kadmon,* the primordial man. The Divine Being Himself cannot be expressed. All that can be expressed are His symbols. The relation between *En Sof* and its mystical qualities, the Sefiroth, is comparable to that between the soul and the body, but with the difference that the human body and soul differ in nature, one being material and the other spiritual, while in the organic whole of God all spheres are substantially the same. (Scholem, *op. cit.,* pp. 214–15)

"The world of the Sefiroth is the hidden world of language," Scholem continues, "the world of divine names." "Totemic names," Roheim calls the whispered passwords of the Australian rite. "The creative names which God called into the world," Scholem calls the Sefiroth, "the names which He gave to Himself." It is the alphabet of letters revealed to the initiate as at once the alphabet of what he is and what the universe is and the alphabet of eternal persons.

As Scholem hints, "the conception of the Sefiroth as parts or limbs of the mystical anthropos leads to an anatomical symbolism which does not shrink from the most extravagant conclusions." Man's "secret parts" are secret names or hidden keys to the whole figure of man, charged with magic in their being reserved. In the communal image, the human figure is male and female. Ass-hole, penis, cunt, navel, were not only taboo but sacred, words to be revealed in initiations of the soul to the divine body, as at Eleusis the cunt of a woman in the throes of birth was shown. In what we call carnal knowledge, in the sexual union of male and female nakedness, God and His creation, the visible and invisible, the above and the below are also united.

Ham, who sees the nakedness of his father, is the prototype of the Egyptian who in an alien or heretic religion knows the secrets of God. To steal a look, like the theft of fire, is a sin, for the individual seeks to know without entering the common language in which things must be seen and not seen.

"At the initiation ceremony the point is to displace libido from the mother to the group of fathers," Roheim writes. In the contemporaneity of our human experience with all it imagines, there may be not a displacement but an extension of libido: the revelation of the mother remains, the revelation of the male body is added.

> Some old men stand in the ring and catching hold of their genitals tell the boys to raise their eyes and take particular notice of those parts. The old men next elevate their arms above their heads and the boys are directed to look at their armpits. Their navels are exhibited in the same way. The men then put their fingers on each side of their mouths and draw their lips outward as wide as possible, lolling out their tongues and inviting the special attention of the novices. They next turn their backs and, stooping down, ask the novices to take particular notice of their posterior parts.

For Roheim, the images and magic of Australian story and rite are one with the images and magic of all dreams:

> After having withdrawn cathexis from environment, we fall asleep. But when the cathexis is concentrated in our own bodies we send it out again and form a new world, in our dreams. If we compare dream mecha-

nisms with the narratives of dream-times we find an essential similarity between the two. The endless repetitions of rituals and wanderings and hunting are indeed very different from a dream; but when we probe deeper we find that they are overlaid by ceremony and perhaps also by history. The essential point in the narratives as in the ritual is that man makes the world—as he does in sleep.

These natives do not wander because they like to . . . Man is naturally attached to the country where he was born because it, more than anything else, is a symbol of his mother. All natives will refer to their 'place' as a 'great place'; as they say 'I was incarnated there' or 'born there'. Economic necessity, however, compels him time and again to leave his familiar haunts and go in search of food elsewhere. Against this compulsion to repeat *separation,* we have the fantasy embodied in myth and ritual in which he himself creates the world.

Where the nursing woman and the countryside itself are both "Mother," and where in turn the men of the tribe man initiate and reveal maleness as an other Mother, "Mother" means unity, what Gertrude Stein called the Composition. What we experience in dreaming is not a content of ourselves but the track of an inner composition of ourselves. We are in-formed by dreams, as in daily life we experience that which we are able to grasp as information. We see, hear, taste, smell, feel, what can be drawn into a formal relation; to sense at all involves attention and composition. "It is very interesting that nothing inside in them, that is when you consider the very long history of how every one ever acted or has felt, it is very interesting that nothing inside in them in all of them makes it connectedly different," Stein writes in "Composition as Explanation":

> The only thing that is different from one time to another is what is seen and what is seen depends upon how everybody is doing everything. This makes the thing we are looking at very different and this makes what those who describe it make of it, it makes a composition, it confuses, it shows, it is, it looks, it likes it as it is, and this makes what is seen as it is seen.

The endless repetitions of rituals and wanderings and hunting as the pattern of life for the Australian is a living inside the Composition; and in their exhibiting the secrets of the male body to the boy, the men of the tribe are making a composition where what is seen depends upon how everybody is doing everything. In the ritual, song, parts of the body, parts of the landscape, man and nature, male and female, are united in a secret composite of magic names.

"One of the main sources of male creative power," Roheim tells us, "is the incantation itself."

> When I asked old Wapiti and the other chiefs what makes the animals grow? the spirits? the ancestors? O, no, they said: *jelindja wars,* the words only. The form of the incantation is an endless, monotonous flow of words, and actually the men urinate very frequently while performing the ceremonies. This parallelism between the words and the fluid is brought out in a description by Lloyd Warner: 'The blood runs slowly and the rhythm of the song is conducted with equal slowness. In a second or two the blood spurts and runs in a rapid stream. The beat of the song sung by the old men increases to follow the rhythm of the blood.'

We may begin to see, given Stein's concept of insistence that informs composition, and then thinking of the pulse of the living egg-cell itself, that beat, rhythm, underlies every pattern of our experience. Life itself is an endless, monotonous flow, wherever the individual cannot enter into it as revealed in dance and melody to give rhythmic pattern; the world about goes inert and dead. The power of the painter in landscape is his revelation of such movement and rhythm in seeing, in-formation, in what otherwise would have been taken for granted.

Gertrude Stein, reflecting upon permanence and change in the artist's vision, sees that "the only thing that is different from one time to another is what is seen and what is seen depends upon how everybody is doing everything." Close to the Cubist movement in Paris, she had experienced how painting or writing in a new way had revealed coordinations of what was seen and heard toward an otherwise hidden unborn experience of the world, so that one saw and heard with a profound difference. "A new cadence means a new idea," H.D. and Richard Aldington tell us; here too, cadence is how it is done. To make clear the meaning of cadence they refer to the choral line of Greek poetry that was also the movement of the choral dance, strophe and antistrophe. So too, Roheim, initiate of Freudianism, as Stein was initiate of Cubism, or H.D. of Imagism, sees in the narratives of his Australian informants how "in all of them environment is made out of man's activity," for he had himself experienced a conversion in which a new environment for man had been made out of analytic activity. The "man-made world" in which "environment is regarded as if it were derived from human beings" is the narrative itself—the unity of things in how the story is told.

Parts and operations of the human body, but also parts and operations of the cosmos, are related in a new ground, a story or picture or play, in which feeling and idea of a larger whole may emerge. The flow of sound from the throat and the flow of urine from the bladder, the flow of energy from the dancing feet, the flow of forms in the landscape, the flow of water and of air felt, translated in a rhythmic identity disclose to the would-be initiate what man is but also what the world is—both other and more than he is himself, than the world itself is.

Cézanne working at his vision of Mont Sainte-Victoire and Dalí at his paranoiac vision of the Catalonian landscape not only draw but are drawn by what they draw. From body and from world toward an other body and other world, man derives meaning in a third element, the *created*—the rite, the dance, the narrative; the painting, the poem, the book. And in this new medium, in a new light, "man" and "environment" both are made up.

The power of the poet is to translate experience from daily time where the world and ourselves pass away as we go on into the future, from the journalistic record, into a melodic coherence in which words—sounds, meanings, images, voices—do not pass away or exist by themselves but are kept by rhyme to exist everywhere in the consciousness of the poem. The art of the poem, like the mechanism of the dream or the intent of the tribal myth and *dromena,* is a cathexis: to keep present and immediate a variety of times and places, persons and events. In the melody we make, the possibility of eternal life is hidden, and experience we thought lost returns to us.

"The eternal ones of the dream," Roheim observes, "are those who have had no mothers; they originated of themselves. Their immortality is a denial of the separation anxiety. Separation from the mother is painful; the child is represented in myth as fully formed, even before it enters the mother . . . The *tjurunga* from which it is born is both a phallic and a maternal symbol."

The *tjurunga,* like the cartouche that encircles the Pharaoh's name as the course of the sun encircles the created world, is a drawing of the spirit being, an enclosure in which we see the primal identity of the person. But all primal identities are Adamic containing male and female, man and animal, in one. We are each separated from what we feel ourselves to be, from what we essentially *are* but also from the other we *must be.* Wherever we are we are creatures of other places; whenever we are, creatures of other times; whatever our experience, we are creatures of other imagined experiences. Not only the experience of unity but the experience of separation is the mother of man. The very feeling of melody at all depends upon our articulation of the separate parts involved. The movement is experienced as it arises from a constant disequilibrium and ceases when it is integrated.

"Composition is not there, it is going to be there, and we are here," Stein writes. Between "there" and "here" or "then" and "now," the flame of life, our spirit, leaps. A troubled flame—"The time in composition is a thing that is very troublesome," Stein tells us:

> If the time in the composition is very troublesome it is because there must be even if there is no time at all in the composition there must be time in the composition which is in its quality of distribution and equilibration. (Gertrude Stein, "Composition as Explanation," *Selected Writings* [1946], p. 461)

An anxious flame—"In totemic magic the destroyed mother is re-animated and in the totemic sacrament, eternal union of the mother and child is effected," Roheim tells us. But the eternal separation of the mother and child is also celebrated therein: "As a religion it represents the genitalization of the separation period and the restitution that follows destructive trends." *War,* Heraclitus called the flame, or *Strife.*

"All men are bringing to birth in their bodies and in their souls," Diotima, who here speaks as an Eternal One of the Mother, says to Socrates in Plato's dialogue:

There is a poetry, which, as you know, is complex and manifold. All creation or passage of non-being into being is poetry or making, and the processes of all arts are creative; and the masters of all arts are poets or makers . . . What are they doing who show all this eagerness and heat which is called love? . . . The object which they have in view is birth in beauty.

Beyond beauty—birth in the eternal and universal.

"According to the natives of the Andjamatana tribe," Roheim tells us, "children originate in two mythical women known as *maudlangami*":

> They live in a place in the sky. Their long hair almost covers them and on their pendulum breasts are swarms of spirit children who gather their sustenance therefrom. These women are the source of all life, each within her tribe producing spirit children of her own moiety.

The two *maudlangami* from whom all spiritual identities come are creatures of the story itself in which the germinal function of the story-telling is embodied. In the communion of the Story, the narrator and the listeners have their spiritual source, and all life has its source and draws eternal nourishment.

> Each Aranda or Juritja native has an immortal part or spirit double, whose immortality consists in eternally rejoining the Mother in the sacred totemic cave. From time to time they reidentify themselves with the eternal in them.

It seems to Roheim that in the story "they deny their great dependence upon Mother Nature and play the role of Mothers themselves." But Mother Nature in the eternal bond with Man is Herself, as He is, the member of the cast in a drama. In the rites that Roheim sees as denials of dependence, we see the dancers reviving the human reality in all that is disturbing to union, involving themselves in, insisting upon, and taking their identity in, the loss of their identity, keeping the rhyme of their separation alive in the sound of their unity, rehearsing their exile in the place where they are. The flame springs up in a confusion of elements, times, places.

For the Freudian, it all rests in a "psychical survival of the biologic unity with environment." "This 'oceanic feeling' (Freud) or 'dual unity situation,'" Roheim argues, "is something we all experience in our own lives; it is the bond that unites mother and child." "By taking the *tjurunga* along on his wanderings the native never gives up the original bond of dual unity which ties the infant to his mother."

From the unity once known between mother and child, the boy is initiated in a rite in which things once unified in feeling are shown as separated. This is the anatomization of the Australian scene, where parts of the body are exhibited as independent entities; but it is also the anatomization practices in which the poet is born, where words once unified in the flow of speech—the mother tongue which in turn had been articulated from the flow of sounds in the child's earlier initiation—are shown as articulated—separated into particular sounds, syllables, meanings—in order to be reorganized in an other unity in which the reality of separation is kept as a conscious factor. The "Mother" is now the World, and the "Child" is the Self. The World is revealed as a "Creation" or "Poetry" or "Stage," and the Self, as "Creator" or "Poet." The man or the hero begins his life that demands something of him, a wandering in quest of something known in the unknown. Taking with him the quest itself as his Mother—as the Australian takes the *tjurunga* or the devout Kabbalist the Shekina—he is to be most at home in his exile.

•

Roheim telling about his Australian natives does not mean to initiate us into the Aranda but through his creation of the Aranda in our minds to initiate us into the psychoanalytic fiction. The old men prancing, bleeding themselves, and showing their private parts; the emu ancestors, the eternal ones who come in the dream, the primordial Mother and Child, are people not of the Australian bush but of a creative book, haunted by "the wanderings of human beings from the cradle to the grave in a web of daydream," as the author of this mankind himself wanders in a web of psychoanalytic reverie.

"In the eternal ones of the dream it is we who deny decay and aggression and object-loss, and who guard eternal youth and reunion with the mother," Roheim writes in his coda:

> The old and decrepit men of the tribe become young and glorious once more. Covered with birds' down, the life symbol, they are identified with the eternally youthful ancestors. Mankind, the eternal child, *splendide mendax,* rise above reality . . . The path is Eros, the force that delays disintegration; and hence the promise held forth in the daydream and in its dramatization is no illusion after all. The *tjurunga* which symbolizes both male and female genital organ, the primal scene and combined parent concept, the father and the mother, separation and reunion . . . represents both the path and the goal.

This *tjurunga* we begin to see not as the secret identity of the Aranda initiate but as our own Freudian identity, the conglomerate consciousness of the mind we share with Roheim. "Above and below, left and right," the Kabbalist would have added in drawing his figure of the primordial man. The whole story is "daydream," a "web," and we are not sure of that because the path is Eros, the child, but he is also *splendide mendax,* a glorious maker of fictions, in which all the conglomerate of what Man is might be contained.

The *tjurunga* is not only the simple bull-roarer, a wooden slab with a hole in it, but, as *tjurung,* it is also the symbol of a complex relationship, the agency of a magic in which Man and Universe are identified. The *tjurunga* is not only then the instrument of Australian rites, but, as we begin to recognize the underlying intent, the instrument of our own initiations of meaning becomes likewise the *tjurunga.* The hammock and Calder's mobile, seen by Siegfried Giedion in *Mechanization Takes Command* as "deeply at one with the broad stream of modern evolution," are of such an order.

If, as in Malraux's *Psychology of Art,* we see painting and sculpture not only as discrete works but also as participants in a drama of forms playing throughout the time of man, so that what were once thought of as masterpieces of their time and place are now seen anew as moving expressions of—but more than expressions, creations and creators of—spiritual life, as acts of a drama of what Man is that has not come to its completion, but which we imagine as a changing totality called

Art; then poems too begin to appear as members of a hovering system "ever ready to change its poise," called Poetry. The draft of air or the touch of a hand reappears now as the inspiration or impulse of mind that will change states and interrelations. "Time in the composition comes now," Gertrude Stein puts it, "and this what is troubling everyone the time in the composition is now a part of distribution and equilibration"—"past the danger point"—throughout the history of Man. History itself, no longer kept within the boundaries of periods or nations, appears as a mobile structure in which events may move in time in ever-changing constellations. The effort of Toynbee's *Study of History,* beyond Spengler's comparison of civilizations, is toward an interpenetration of what before seemed discrete even alien areas of the life of man. Present, past, future may then appear anywhere in changing constellations, giving life and depth to time. The Eternal Return, no longer conceived of as bound to revolutions of a wheel—the mandala of a Ptolemaic universe or of a Jungian Self—beyond the "organic" concept Toynbee derives from Vico's life cycles, we begin to see order now as an insistence of figure in an expanding ground of many relations. The Composition is there, we are here. But now the Composition and we too are never finished, centered, perfected. We are in motion and our meaning lies not in some last or lasting judgment, in some evolution or dialectic toward a higher force or consciousness, but, in an Adamic content of the whole, the totality of mankind's experience in which our moment, this vision of a universal possibility, plays its part, and beyond, the totality of life experience in which Man plays His part, not central, but in every living moment creating a new crisis in the equilibration of the whole. The whole seen as a mobile is a passionate impermanence in which Time and Eternity are revealed as One.

Elie Faure in *The Spirit of Forms* (from which, as from Spengler's *The Decline of the West,* Malraux's thought would seem to develop) sees all ages and nations as one in a deeper universal art, a grand adventure of spirit in which men have envisioned Man:

We have reached a critical point in history when it becomes impossible for us to think profoundly—or to create, I imagine—if we isolate ourselves in the adventure of our race, if we refuse to demand a confirmation of our own presentiments from the expression in words or in the arts that other races have given themselves. . . . One of the miracles of this time is that an increasing number of spirits should become capable not only of tasting the delicate or violent savor of these reputedly contradictory works and finding them equally intoxicating [he speaks here of those fetishes and cathedral statues that Malraux in his work was to find "sinister" in their colloquy] . . . even more than that, they can grasp, in the seemingly opposed characters, the inner accords that lead us back to man and show him to us everywhere animated by analogous passions, as witnessed by all the idols, for all of them are marked by the accent of these passions. . . . The critical spirit has become a universal poet. It is necessary to enlarge inordinately, and unceasingly, the circle of its horizon.

This "we" was "an increasing number," but it was also, Faure saw, a few, an elite—a cult, then, of "the mobility of the spirit, favored by the exigencies of environment and the mixture of the species," projecting "a limitless visible field of emotion and activity," toward a cathexis of all that was known of man and the word, in terms of an open and expanding consciousness, as our Aranda initiates project their field of emotion and activity in terms of a tribal consciousness as an enclosure of time and space. For the Australian, the hardness of Nature herself drives him out from his home-place. The Aranda is a man of an actual waste land where he is again and again forced to wander in times of drought and famine when a man in want of water often opens a vein in his arm to drink the blood, and the brotherhood of the tribe must be kept in a constant imagination against the hunger in which men eat each other. Here the "we" is a term of survival itself. The creative fiction—the tribal narrative, the eternal ones of the dream, the spirit doubles, and the immortal sky-mothers—has its intensity of realization in the traumatic experience of the actual environment.

The esoteric tradition in Jewish mysticism again had its intensity in the loss of the home-land and in the long wandering in exile as children of a spirit-Mother, the Shekinah. She was the Glory, but She was also the Queen or Mother or Lady, and She might appear, as She does in *The Zohar,* as a great bird under whose celestial wings the immortal spirit-children of Israel nestled. The Jews, like the Aranda, lived in a threatening environment that called forth, if they were to survive, an insistent creation, the tenacity of a daydream to outlast the reality principle.

For the Imagists in London in 1912 there had already been exile. Pound, Eliot, and H.D. had sought a new spiritual home among eternal ones of the European dream, among troubadours or the melic poets, in refuge from the squalor and stupidity of the American mercantile, industrial, and capitalist world—"the American dream," it was called. Joyce had chosen a voluntary exile from Ireland, "dear dirty Dublin"; and Lawrence had fled from his environment in the industrial working class village to wander in exile in search of his own Kingdom of the Sun.

It was the World War that provided the traumatic crisis, the triumph of squalor and stupidity where the cult of profits and the cult of empire combined to exact their tribute, and the other cult-world of the poetic vision was challenged as unrealistic. Only in the imagination would beauty survive. *"I would bid them live,"* Pound sings in his Envoi to *Mauberley* in 1919:

> *As roses might, in magic amber laid,*
> *Red overwrought with orange and all made*
> *One substance and one colour*
> *Braving time . . .*

He addresses in the "Envoi" a "her," whose "graces give / Life to the moment"—a Lady "that sang me once that song of Lawes," but also a Mother that the Imagist poets had taken—Beauty. To survive in spirit men must be reborn in Beauty's magic amber, for the rest were revealed by War where

> Died some pro patria, non "dulce" non "et decor" . . .
> walked eye-deep in hell
> believing old men's lies, then unbelieving
> came home, home to a lie,
> home to many deceits,
> home to old lies and new infamy . . .

"Wrong from the start—" Pound describes himself: "No,":

. . . hardly, but, seeing he had been born
In a half savage country, out of date . . .

•

They did not "belong." In that feeling, their exile was not voluntary,
but a recognition of necessity. In the poem "Cities" published in *The
Egoist* in 1914, H.D.'s sense of a "we," a lonely few, isolated by their
common devotion to beauty, and to the goods of the intellect, in the
midst of a city of "them" who worship squalor, profit, and war, as the
"one god," is not a phantastic attitude assumed but a feeling rooted in
the social reality. "Can we believe," she proposes,

> . . . —by an effort
> comfort our hearts:
> it is not waste all this,
> not placed here in disgust,
> street after street,
> each patterned alike,
> no grace to lighten
> a single house of the hundred
> crowded into one garden-space.

Two ways of life—the one realized by the Protestant Capitalist cult
in its terms of usury, real estate, production for profit, and profitable
work, and the other realized by the Military cult, in which old orders
of Mithraic and Wotanic cult survived, in terms of Fatherland, death
in battle, holocaust, and the hero's reward in the Valhalla orgy and the
memorial days—these two had combined forces in 1914 to make a new
world. War was to become, as it is in our own day, the most profit-
able business, the foundation of the economy, and the economy was to
become the cause for which men fought. Not "Light," as it had been for
the Zoroastrian Mithraist, against "Darkness"; but the right of private
property in the sense of capitalism against communism or socialism.

H.D. sees war-time London of the First World War in terms of the
Platonic myth of the Golden Age and the Iron Age, and also, as in her
War Trilogy, London of the Second World War in terms of the Gnostic
myth of souls from a creation of Light surviving in a second creation

of Darkness. In "Cities," the maker of cities has made a second city and a second people. This is the hive of the modern metropolis, crowded with cells:

> hideous first, hideous now—
> spread larvae across them,
> not honey but seething life.

> And in these dark cells,
> packed street after street,
> souls live, hideous yet—
> O disfigured, defaced,
> with no trace of the beauty
> men once held so light.

Back of this world is the memory of another, first, city:

> with the beauty of temple
> and space before temple,
> arch upon perfect arch,
> of pillars and corridors that led out
> to strange court-yards and porches
> where sun-light stamped
> hyacinth-shadows
> black on the pavement.

It is the Poictiers or Verona of the first Cantos, and thirty years later in *The Pisan Cantos* it is "the city of *Deïoces* whose terraces are the colour of stars" and also *Wagadu,* the Mother-City of the Fasa, that four times in their wandering has been lost—"gone to sleep" the epic tale *Gassire's Lute* puts it, as given by Frobenius in the sixth volume of *African Genesis,* his collection of African folktales and poetry. In the prison camp at Pisa the memory of Wagadu, four times fallen asleep—"once through vanity, once through breach of faith, once through greed, and once through dissension"—with the chorus naming the cities of its four incarnations—"Hoooh! Dierra, Agada, Ganna, Silla—Hoooh! Fasa!"— returned to Pound as the lost city that is also the strength of those who live in the thought of her.

For in herself Wagadu is not of stone, nor of wood, nor of earth. Wagadu is the strength that lives in the hearts of men and that one time can be seen because eyes let her be seen, because ears hear the strike of sword and the clang of shield, and one time is invisible because worn out and beset by the untamable nature of men she has gone fast asleep.

"Now in the mind indestructible," Pound sings in "Canto LXXIV," and in "Canto LXXVI": "now in the heart indestructible." Wagadu may then be the first city of H.D.'s "Cities," the Mother that those who are devoted to Beauty remember. "For each man will salvage Wagadu in his heart," the African epic promises—"*bergen*,"—the German translates, which means *to salvage* or *rescue* and also *to give shelter to, to hold* or *to hide:* "and each woman will keep hidden a Wagadu in her womb."

The people of that city, the people of a dream of a kind of human life once known that perished as the dominant way and is yet carried forward in the minds and hearts of certain devotees, this people remains, like the "we" of H.D.'s poem, intensely aware of themselves in their allegiance to an invisible city more real than the city in which they are:

Can we think a few old cells
were left—we are left—
grains of honey,
old dust of stray pollen
dull on our torn wings,
we are left to recall the old streets?

To be a poet was to be disowned in terms of the reality values of the new city, to be outcast from the true motherland. In "The Tribute," published in *The Egoist* in 1916, the First World War and city of London are again seen in terms of an evil state that has taken the place of a good:

Squalor spreads its hideous length
through the carts and the asses' feet,
squalor coils and reopens
and creeps under barrow
and heap of refuse . . .

"Don't use such an expression as 'dim lands of peace'," Pound had commanded: "It dulls the image. It mixes an abstraction with the concrete." For a moment the word "squalor," if we take it as an abstraction, may abstract us from the immediacy of the poem, but the squalor of the city is itself the presentation of a person of the poem. A "personification" it is called by those who believe such things are mere devices of a poetic grammar. But this squalor is the face or mask of an actual entity:

> it lengthens and coils
> and uncoils and draws back
> and recoils
> through the crooked streets.

the Evil One Himself, the old serpent or worm, seen by the poet in the seizure of the poem as He has been seen in the vision of saints and Satanists or in the clairvoyance of seers, an astral shape pervading the ways of the city, so that the streets are "crooked," as in *The Mills of the Kavanaughs* Robert Lowell sees a path "snake" up its hill. Where He wounds us there are "our old hatreds," and in victory He may blacken the song upon singing lips. The dragon is *Neschek* as He appears in Pound's fragment of Canto LXXII or Jormungand, the Midgard Serpent, whose scales are the corpses of men and whose venom is a corrupting greed and ambition, in whose likeness is the squalor of the slums, the coils of usury, and the murderous arrogance of modern war. In "The Tribute," the tribute seems first to be the draft of young men into the armies of America and England, and the dragon has triumphed:

> with no voice to rebuke—
> for the boys have gone out of the city,
> the songs withered black on their lips . . .

The "larvae," the unawakened people of the poem "Cities," are now the people of the dragon, their "one god":

> They have banished the gods
> and the half-gods
> from the city streets,

they have turned from the god
of the cross roads,
the god of the hearth,
the god of the sunken well
and the fountain source . . .

and they show their enmity openly toward those who do not hold their
values and would oppose the tribute to their war:

Though not one of the city turned,
not one girl but to glance
with contempt toward us.

The few with convictions against the war really did face social
ostracism. "The world of men is dreaming," Lawrence wrote to Lady
Ottoline Morrell in 1915: "it has gone mad in its sleep, and a snake
is strangling it, but it can't wake up." Two years later, driven out of
Cornwall where they had been raided by the police, the Lawrences
took refuge with H.D. at 44 Mecklenburgh Square. "London is really
very bad: gone mad, in fact," he wrote Cecil Gray: "People are not
people any more; they are factors, really ghastly, like lemures, evil spir-
its of the dead." And young men who had already begun their work for
beauty's sake had died, "the songs withered black on their lips"—"*non
dulce non et decor.*" In the pages of *The Egoist,* war lists—first of young
French and German artists and writers, then of English—had begun to
appear.

The "we" of "The Tribute" is a remnant few very like the pitiful
group that in Aristophanes' anti-war *Lysistrata* hold the decimated city:

A few old men rose up
with a few sad women to greet and hail us,
a few lads crept to welcome . . .

And the song was "withered black" upon the lips in another sense. For
Pound, Lawrence, Joyce, H.D., Eliot have a black voice when speaking
of the contemporary scene, an enduring memory from this First World
War that had revealed the deep-going falsehood and evil of the modern

state. These had from their early years as writers a burning sense of the "they" that ran the war and that accepted its premises and of the "we" whose allegiance belonged to a Wagadu hidden in their hearts, among whom now were many ghosts or specters. Wilfred Owen had come as the first great English loss among poets and artists, but Gaudier-Brzeska and Hulme from the immediate circle of *The Egoist* had followed.

At the close of "The Tribute," a prayer for deliverance begins:

> May we know that our spirits at last
> will be cleansed of all bitterness—
> that no one god may trample the earth,
> but the others still dwell apart
> in a high place
> with our dead and our lost.

Now Wagadu no longer appears as an earlier city back of or surviving within the squalor of the contemporary city as in the poem "The Tribute," where those "who recall the old splendour await the new beauty of cities," but as a city in an other world evoked by a wish:

> That the boys our city has lost
> and the gods still dwell apart
> in a city set fairer than this
> with column and porch.

They appear here, the banished gods and lost boys, as the eternal ones who come in dreams, to whom the poet's tribute is offered:

> That the lads in that city apart
> may know of our love and keep
> remembrance and speak of us—
> may lift their hands that the gods
> revisit earth.

> That the lads of the cities
> may yet remember us,
> we spread shaft of privet and sweet
> lily from meadow and forest . . .

"And this we will say for remembrance," the poet continues: "Speak this with their names":

Could beauty be caught and hurt
they had done her to death with their sneers
in ages and ages past,
could beauty be sacrificed
for a thrust of a sword,
for a piece of thin money
tossed up to fall half alloy—
then beauty were dead
long, long before we saw her face.

"The Tribute" is not an easy poem to appreciate in terms of what came to be accepted as H.D.'s virtues in the modern aesthetic of the twenties—the ardor kept in restraint, the Hellenic remove, the hard-wrought art, the spare statement. The Imagist rules will not fit. But once we turn from "Cities" and "The Tribute," keeping the context of these poems, the seemingly "removed" Hellenism of "Adonis," "Pallas," or "Sea Heroes," written in the same period, proves to be a screen image in which another level of feeling is present.

Akroneos, Oknolos, Elatreus,
helm-of-boat, loosener of helm, dweller-by-sea,
Natueus, sea-man,

are lists of the war dead and lost from Homer. And now from our own sense of the experience of the War—and here her rites of remembrance have quickened in us the impact of what happened before we were born—we understand anew and in depth the agony of

But to name you,
we reverent are breathless,
weak with pain and old loss,
and exile and despair—

Since the dark, bitter, impassioned days of the First World War, even the words themselves—"beauty," "lad," or "boy"—have become uneasy words, smacking of the idealistic or the sentimental before what we call the Real, the pervading triumph of mercantile utilitarianism. The "architecture" of the utilitarian city is inspired by the display aesthetic of packaging and advertising art to put over shoddy goods, where a wealth of glass or cellophane, aluminum, copper, or gold paper facing takes over the city, presented in a poverty of imagination, housing the same old shoddy operations of whiskey, cigarette, or paper companies, and back of the sell, the demand for profit and increase, the exploitation of mind and spirit to keep the rackets going, the economy of wage-slavery and armed forces; over all, the threat of impending collapse or disastrous war. We too, in a hostile environment, taking our faith and home in our exile, live in creative crisis.

.

There is this sense, then, in which the Imagists—that group of poets printing in the pages of *The Egoist* between 1914 and 1917—stand at the beginning of a phase in poetry that has not ended. Pound, writing in 1914, felt that a break was necessary with the preceding generation in poetry: "Surely there was never a time when the English 'elder generation as a whole' mattered less or had less claim to be taken seriously by 'those on the threshold'."

For my own generation, our elders—for me, specifically Pound, H.D., Williams, and Lawrence—remain primary generative forces. Their threshold remains ours. The time of war and exploitation, the infamy and lies of the new capitalist war-state, continue. And the answering intensity of the imagination to hold its own values must continue. The work of our elders in poetry was to make—"a Dream greater than Reality"—a time-space continuum in which their concern for quality and spirit, for romance and beauty, could survive. Estranged from all but a few about them, they made a new dimension in which eternal companions appeared. As to the Aranda the ancestors came, or to the Kabbalist mystics dreams and even immediate presences of Elijah or of a *maggid* or angel came, so to Pound Plotinus appears or to H.D., in the orders of the new poetry, the Christos or the Lady.

In 1919 Pound published in *Quia Pauper Amavi* a first draft for the opening three Cantos of a new poem, addressing Robert Browning:

Hang it all, there can be but the one 'Sordello,'
But say I want to, say I take your whole bag of tricks,
Let in your quirks and tweeks, and say the thing's an art-form . . .

It was to be a realm in which Robert Browning and Arnaut, Brancusi and Kung could coexist; where Eleanor and Cunizza could come and go; and:

Gods float in the azure air,
Bright gods and Tuscan, back before dew was shed.

For the banished gods and for the heroes. And those lost. But not now, as in Dante, appearing each in his place in a set scene or architecture of Hell, Purgatory, and Paradise. For here, in *The Cantos* of Pound, the dead gather in as at a séance. "Ghosts move about me patched with histories," it seems to the poet. But there are not only voices speaking, *personae,* in this "catch" of time as Pound called it, there are also scenes— images of the poem, moving pictures. Where Dante had back of *The Divine Comedy* his magics to call upon—the magic of the poetic and of the mystic descent or ascent to the eternal world, but drawing also upon the practice of the dream-vision in not only Medieval Christian but in classical Roman tradition, but drawing also upon the practice of the *Mi'raj,* the spiritual transportations of the Sufi Recital, Pound had these and other magics—the séance tables of London mediums, the discourse of voices in which the rivers of many traditions came into a sea of humanity, and also, a new clairvoyance, the photomontage of times and places in the movies of Griffith.

In the three masterworks of this period—Pound's early *Cantos,* Eliot's *The Waste Land,* and Joyce's *Ulysses*—the contemporary opens upon eternity in the interpenetration of times. The literate public objected to or made fun of what they called their "references" or "quotes." "Say that I dump my catch," Pound had put it in the first draft of *The Cantos:*

shiny and silvery
As fresh sardines flapping and slipping on the
marginal cobbles?

and the image stands, for he was "fishing" and in it all working to catch something being said, about to be said, fishing along lines of metamorphoses in the beginning. Surely, knowing Mead and Yeats, Pound was aware of Eisler's *Orpheus the Fisher,* where the god appeared as a fisher of souls who was also the divine poet—the lyre was also a net or the poem a net of words. In the early *Canto* I, the poem itself appears as a fish-monger's booth:

> I stand before the booth (the speech), but the truth
> is inside this discourse: this booth is full of the
>   marrow of wisdom.

It may also be then the medium's cabinet. Our own net casts wider than Pound would, and we see that the shaman's tent is also such a booth. But Pound's intuition moves out, back of his evocation of Robert Browning's magic practice of the dramatic monologue, and So-shu churns in the sea,

> So-shu also,
> using the long moon for a churn-stick . . .

So Pound will give up the intaglio method and in the flux of a cinematographic art call in the swarming fish of the sea, where Robert Browning, Peire Cardenal, Catullus, gods, oak-girls and maenads, Metastasio, Ficino, Kuanon, Guido Cavalcanti, Botticelli, Mantegna are drawn into the nets of the first haul. These persons, like the place names of Wagadu—Dierra, Agada, Ganna, Silla—are loci of a virtu moving through time. Frobenius traces the wandering of the Fasa from Djerma of the Garama which he equates with Dierra, mentioned by Herodotus five hundred years before Christ, from the Fezzan of North Africa, to Tagadda on the ancient route through the Saliara, to Ganna and then to Silla of the Sahel. But the Wagadu of the Cantos is the lost city not of a tribe but of a kindred among all men, "an aristocracy of emotion" Pound called it.

It was the mixture of times and places, and especially the breakdown of all nationalistic distinctions that most angered the hostile critics and readers. Renaissance English or medieval Italian or modern French could enter into an all-American poem. Not only Dante but Kung and even Gassi were to be our heroes in the new legend. The new practice was most concentrated in the famous coda of *The Waste Land* in 1922:

London Bridge is falling down falling down falling down
Poi s'ascose nel foco che gli affina
Quando fiam uti chelidon—O swallow swallow
Le Prince d'Aquitaine à la tour abolie
These fragments I have shored against my ruins
Why then Ile fit you. Hieronymo's mad againe.
Datta. Dayadhvam. Damyata.

Children singing a round dance; Dante in Purgatory telling of Arnaut Daniel, master of the *trobar clus,* "Then he hid himself in the fire which refines them," and the voices of the poet—of the *Pervigilium Veneris,* of Gerard de Nerval, of Kyd in the person of Hieronimo, and of the thunder out of the Upanishads, speak one after another, taking over from Eliot's "own" voice, or speaking for Eliot, meeting through Eliot as through a medium. "Tiresias, although a mere spectator and not indeed a 'character'," Eliot notes, "is yet the most important personage in the poem, uniting all the rest. Just as the one-eyed merchant, seller of currants, melts into the Phoenician Sailor, and the latter is not wholly distinct from Ferdinand Prince of Naples, so all the women are one woman, and the two sexes meet in Tiresias." (Eliot, *Collected Poems 1909–1935,* p. 94)

For William Carlos Williams it was "the great catastrophe to our letters." "There was heat in us, a core and a drive that was gathering headway upon the theme of a rediscovery of a primary impetus, the elementary principle of all art, in the local conditions," he writes in his *Autobiography:* "Our work staggered to a halt for a moment under the blast of Eliot's genius which gave the poem back to the academics." Picturing himself as defending something betrayed by Eliot, and by Pound in his admiration of Eliot, Williams posed against the internationalism of *The Waste Land* the authenticism of the American speech. "Nothing from abroad would have the reality for me that native writing of the same quality would have," he resolves as an editor of *Contact* in 1922: "Eliot or Pound might say to me today—'Read Laforgue!' I might even be tempted to read because I had respect for their intelligence. But their words could not tempt me, force me, accompany me into the reading." Against the cinematographic time-flux, he meant to take with a vengeance the camera eye of still photography, the locality in time.

There was the studied disdain of silence on Eliot's part for Williams's work. It meant that Williams was never taken up in England; no influence could move Eliot who came to rule the informed taste abroad as Pound never did. And there was the increasing grievance on Williams's part. Not only Eliot but Pound and H.D. came to be seen as betrayers of the American thing in their exile, their "foreign" work. "When one's friends hate each other," the old man Pound as an old man would write in *Canto* CXV:

> how can there be peace in the world?
> Their asperities diverted me in my green time.

At heart, Williams's genius as a poet lay not in the local condition, in the isolated percept, the "American" thing or speech, but in the heritage Eliot—Jacob to his Esau—had stolen from him, in the world-poem where the wives of an African chief, a red basalt grasshopper recalling Chapultepec, Toulouse-Lautrec, Madam Curie working the pitchblende, Sappho, and Peter Brueghel were to enter into one cultural design. *The Waste Land* had stolen a march on *Paterson,* but, by the time the first volume of *Paterson* appeared twenty-four years later, Williams had brought his early poem into a fullness that was to be a challenge to the poets to come as *The Waste Land* was not.

In his Preface to *Selected Essays* in 1954 Williams tells us: "Poetry is a dangerous subject for a boy to fool with, for the dreams of the race are involved in it." He sought, he writes of *Paterson* in his *Autobiography* in 1951, "to find an image large enough to embody the whole knowable world about me." Between "the dream of the race" and "the knowable world," between the "idea" and the "thing" his river was to flow, the Passaic, yes, but also in the realized poem "the thunder of the waters filling his dreams!"

"The *subject matter* of the poem," he said in his lecture at the University of Washington in 1948, calling upon Freud's theory of the dream, "is always phantasy—what is wished for, realized in the 'dream' of the poem—but the structure confronts something else." "The Poem as a Field of Action," he titles that lecture, anticipating Charles Olson's "Projective Verse" with its proposition of composition by field. "The only reality we can know," he continues, "is *measure* . . . "

> How can we accept Einstein's theory of relativity, affecting our very conception of the heavens about us of which poets write so much, without incorporating its essential fact—the relativity of measurements—into our own category of activity: the poem. Do we think we stand outside the universe? Or that the Church of England does? Relativity applies to everything, like love, if it applies to anything in the world.

Williams's local condition and his "no ideas but in things" must ring true, find their resonance, in "the dreams of the race" and in a relativity of measurements that applies to everything, even as H.D.'s elect, the lovers or the writers, must somehow in their vision prove to keep the dream of "everyone, everywhere." The very heightened sense of the relatedness of everything set poets apart. The very secret of the impulse in poetry is the troubled awareness the poet has of meanings in the common language everywhere that those about him do not see or do not consider so important. "We," H.D. writes in *The Walls Do Not Fall,* "bearers of the secret wisdom," and then:

> but if you do not even understand what words say,
>
> how can you expect to pass judgment
> on what words conceal?

The ancient instruction "As above, so below" from the Smaragdine Tablet may be "the secret wisdom," but H.D. was an initiate of the Freud cult where she had learned in analysis that for the good of her soul she must bear the wisdom of "what words conceal." She tells us Freud said to her, "My discoveries are a basis for a very grave philosophy. There are very few who understand this, *there are very few who are capable of understanding this.*" But he might also have said "very few who are willing to understand," for the crisis of the new psychoanalytic wisdom lay in the resistance men have against knowing what is above or below, the strange refusal to see what they are doing or to hear what they are saying just when they are most engaged in their own self-destruction—"the untamable nature of men," the epic of Gassire's Lute says. So, Oedipus cannot and will not understand the vatic warnings of Tiresias or the fears of Jocasta but must pursue his blind course in order to expose the conflict within only at the cost of catastrophe for all. He seems to seek in the drama a compelling reason to make his blindness actual.

The great compulsion of our own states with their war economies and compulsory military servitude, the history that is now all written upon verges of a total war to come, about which we can do nothing and which we can imagine only in terms of total destruction, bears a curious resemblance to the hubris and fate of the Greek drama. *The People of the Truth* and *the People of the Lie* the Zoroastrians called the adherents of peaceful agricultural ways and the adherents of war; but Ahura Mazda, the Lord of Truth, was to become a War-Lord, for His was the *One* Truth, and all other truths were lies. "And now just look at what is happening in this wartime," Freud writes in a letter to Van Eeden in 1914:

> . . . at the cruelties and injustices for which the most civilized nations are responsible, at the different way in which they judge of their own lies, their own wrong-doings, and those of their enemies.

"The individual in any given nation has in this war," he writes in "Thoughts on War and Death" in 1915:

> a terrible opportunity to convince himself of what would occasionally strike him in peace time—that the State has forbidden to the individual the practice of wrong doing, not because it desired to abolish it, but because it desires to have the monopoly of it, like salt and tobacco.

For Freud, as for Lawrence, H.D., Pound, Joyce, or Eliot, the immediate experience of the First World War brought an intensified experience of the "we" and the "they." "The individual who is not himself a combatant—and so a wheel in the gigantic machinery of war," Freud writes, "feels conscious of disorientation, and of an inhibition in his powers and activities." So, in "Cities" H.D. in 1914 could still imagine the task of the "we" to be to awaken the "they" from their hideous larval life, to "recall the old splendor" toward a "new beauty of cities." In an essay on the work of Marianne Moore in August 1916, she speaks of Marianne Moore's work as if it were questionable: "these curiously wrought patterns, these quaint turns of thought and concealed, half-playful ironies" that readers "have puzzled over . . . and asked—what is this all about?" This poetry might be her own as well, with its curiously wrought patterns. Even among the literate, the few who made any pre-tense at all of being concerned with poetry, the Imagists were ridiculed and reviled. And among the less than few who appreciated, apprecia-tion was not the same as understanding. In the conclusion of that essay, the "they" that had been readers appear as the other "they" of "Cities," and likewise, the identification of herself with Marianne Moore in a "we" is outright: "She is fighting in her country a battle against squalor and commercialism. We are all fighting the same battle. And we must strengthen each other in this one absolute bond—our devotion to the beautiful English language."

The war experience had revealed a division in which one side could no longer communicate with the other. Freud writes in "Thoughts on War and Death":

> It rends all bonds of fellowship between the contending peoples, and threatens to leave such a legacy of embitterment as will make any renewal of such bonds impossible for a long time to come. Moreover, it has brought to light the almost unbelievable phenomenon of a mutual com-prehension between the civilized nations so slight that one can turn with hate and loathing upon the other.

But this abyss of incomprehension appeared not only between opposing states, but, within each state, between the few antipathetic to the war itself and those obedient to or sympathetic with the war. In the poem "The Tribute," H.D. sees the "we" and the "they" divided by a will on the part of the "they," not to hear, not to see—a resistance against beauty and any hope of peace, but also a compulsion toward ugliness and war, a conspiracy that these shall be the terms of the real. The City of the Gods, "set fairer than this with column and porch," no longer, as in the poem "Cities," what once was or what will be, the city of an historical task, is now in "The Tribute" a dwelling place of youths and gods "apart."

Augustine, when Rome fell to the Vandals in the fifth century and the Christians were accused of betraying the Empire in their disaffiliation from the war, answered in *The City of God* with the ringing affirmation of an eternity more real than historical time, a life eternal or supreme good more real than the good life of the philosopher. "And thus it is written," Augustine tells us: "The just live by faith, for we do not as yet see our good, and must therefore live by faith." For Augustine—as for Freud, there was the incomprehension between nations, or for poets the incomprehension between writers and readers, or for Sapir the incomprehension between the individual happenings and the language as communication itself—for Augustine too, in the world beyond the household and the city, the world of human society at large "man is separated from man by the difference of languages."

> For if two men, each ignorant of the other's language, meet, and are not compelled to pass, but, on the contrary, to remain in company, dumb animals, though of different species, would more easily hold intercourse than they, human beings though they be.
>
> But the imperial city has endeavoured to impose on subject nations, not only her yoke, but her language, as a bond of peace, so that interpreters, far from being scarce, are numberless.

He continues:

> This is true; but how many great wars, how much slaughter and bloodshed, have provided this unity! And though these are past, the end of these miseries has not yet come. For though there have never been wanting, nor are yet wanting, hostile nations beyond the empire, against whom wars have been and are waged, yet, supposing there were no such nations, the very extent of the empire itself has produced wars of a more obnoxious description—and with these the whole race has been agitated either by the actual conflict or the fear of a renewed outbreak.

For Augustine, convert of the Christian cult, Latin words themselves had a difference of meaning, and in that difference there was a disillusionment with all the values of the Roman world. Only in a total conversion could the "they," the would-be good and just men of the Empire, understand the "we," the little company of would-be saints. The rest—the whole "realistic" approach—meant utter misery.

> But, say they, the wise man will wage just wars. As if he would not all the rather lament the necessity of just wars, if he remembers that he is a man; for if they were not just he would wage them, and would therefore be delivered from all wars. For it is the wrong-doing of the opposing party which compels the wise man to wage just wars, and this wrong-doing, even though it gave rise to no war, would still be a matter of grief to man because it is man's wrong-doing. Let everyone, then, who thinks with pain on all these great evils, so horrible, so ruthless, acknowledge that this is misery. And if any one either endures or thinks of them without mental pain, this is a more miserable plight still, for he thinks himself happy because he has lost human feeling.

•

To write at all is to dwell in the illusion of language, the rapture of communication that comes as we surrender our troubled individual isolated experiences to the communal consciousness. But this "commune" is not, even in the broadest sense, the language of the human society at large. To write in English is not only to belong to a language-world different from French or Aranda but also to belong to a language-world different from, though within, the English-speaking world at large. Writing and reading is itself an initiation as special as the totem-dance of the Aranda, and just as the Aranda learns to read his own parts in the parts of the landscape about him, so that the body of the world becomes one with his own consciousness, so we learn to find our life in a literature, and, in turn, literature itself is valued as it seems true to life.

But once we would derive our life not in terms of tribe or nation but in terms of a larger humanity, we find our company in Euripides, Plato, Moses of Leon, Faure, or Freud, searching out keys to our inner being in the rites of the Aranda and in the painting processes of Cézanne. We must move throughout the history of man to find many of our own kin, for here and now those who think and feel in the terms we seek are few indeed. But from each of these the cry goes up—to whom other than us, their spiritual kin—from an intense solitude. Not only Freud's "There are very few who understand this," but Stein's "Do you know because I tell you so, or do you know, do you know. (Silence) My long life, my long life," or Joyce's "Thinking always if I go all goes. A hundred cares, a tithe of troubles and is there one who understands me? One in a thousand of years of the nights?" or Pound's plea from *Canto* CXVI:

> I have brought the great ball of crystal,
> who can lift it?
> Can you enter the great acorn of light?
> but the beauty is not the madness
> Tho my errors and wrecks lie about me.
> . . . .
> I cannot make it cohere . . .

Before war and death the whole world of the higher culture seems to be an illusion indeed. For Freud, the war evoked a powerful disillusionment. The cosmopolitan man, as Freud portrays himself in "Thoughts on War and Death," in peace-time dwelt in an "other" world, leaving the Mother-land or Father-land of the national state and entering a new Mother-land of an international dream:

> Relying on this union among the civilized races, countless people have exchanged their native home for a foreign dwelling place, and made their existence dependent on the conditions of intercourse between friendly nations. But he who was not by stress of circumstances confined to one spot, could also confer upon himself, through all the advantages and attractions of these civilized countries, a new, a wider fatherland, wherein he moved unhindered and unsuspected.

The generation of Joyce, Eliot, Pound, and H.D., living in the dream of European culture, or of Lawrence living in the dream of Western Indian culture, is the last to live abroad so. The generation of the twenties—the "lost" generation, as Stein called it—Hemingway, Fitzgerald, Mary Butts, Henry Miller, Katherine Anne Porter, Kay Boyle, Robert

McAlmon, live in Europe or Mexico as if in limbo, forerunners of the Jet Set and the New Wave. The cosmopolitan son of an imaginary world-father pictured by Freud had his roots in a time "before the War," in an illusion of peace, and thought of the achievement of the past as his spiritual heritage.

"This new fatherland was for him a museum also, filled with all the treasures which the artists among civilized communities had in successive centuries created and left behind," Freud continues:

> As he wandered from one gallery to another in this museum, he could appreciate impartially the varied types of perfection that miscegenation, the course of historical events, and the special characteristics of their mother-earth had produced among his more remote compatriots.

This dream of European Culture must recall the Palace of Eros. But Freud's heir of the ages and of the earth finds his reality not in day-dream but in an actual sea and actual mountains, in the treasure store of men's actual works. "Property is not capital. The increment of association is not usury," Ezra Pound insists in *Social Credit: An Impact* (1935) and prefaces his pamphlet with Jefferson's saying—"The earth belongs to the living." In the rites whereby man became cosmopolitan man, he came into an increment, an environment enhanced by his realization of the work and experience of others involved, into an increase that was not taken from things but taken in them.

In the cult-life of Freud's cosmopolitan man, as in the life of the Imagists, the gods and the heroes, the imagined beings and the men who in their creative work have increased the store of the imagination, are ancestral, Eternal Ones of the Dream. A new father-land is taken in the image of a world-father of man-kind. And a new kin is found in the ancestors—those who have contributed to the association of man "any and all of the qualities which have made mankind the lords of the earth."

"Nor must we forget," Freud concludes his picture of this illusion of the civilized man:

> . . . that each of these citizens of culture had created for himself a personal 'Parnassus' and 'School of Athens.' From among the great thinkers and artists of all nations he had chosen those to whom he conceived in

himself most deeply indebted for what he had achieved in enjoyment and comprehension of life, and in his veneration had associated them with the immortals of old as well as with the more familiar masters of his own tongue.

.

It is not the world of nature from which the poet feels himself alienated. One of the primaries of the poet is his magic identification with the natural world—"the pathetic fallacy" the rationalist-minded critics and versifiers call it. Freud's cosmopolitan man is a poet and a primitive mind, for in his pathetic union with the world, he "enjoyed the blue sea, and the grey; the beauty of the snow-clad mountains and of the green pasture-lands; the magic of the northern forests and the splendor of the southern vegetation . . . the silence of nature in her inviolate places." To find joy in the blue sea or beauty in mountains, magic in forests, splendor and silence in nature, is to live in an environment transformed by human sentiments; for these qualities are just that increment that would make man a lord. The joy and the splendor exist in a magic reciprocity—a property that is not capital; an increment that is not usury. Joy, magic, splendor, beauty, and the silence of *"inviolate places"* are pathetically present too in the language of the Aranda sexual organs and orifices, the "secret" organs of joy, magic, and splendor in the flow of blood and urine, the excitement and release of orgasm.

So too, the nature poems of H.D.—the early poems of sea and orchard, shell and tree in full blossom or fruit—betray, in their troubled ardor, processes of psychological and even sexual identification, and those critics who have rebuked her for these poems may be disturbed by content in the poem they do not want to recognize. In "Orchard," she writes: "and I fell prostrate / crying: / you have flayed us / with your blossoms." This flowering tree—it is the flowering half-burnt-out tree of *The Flowering of the Rod*—may also be the emotional tree of a sexual encounter; for this poem addresses the "rough-hewn / god of the orchard," "alone unbeautiful," "son of the god," and in its first publication in *The Egoist* was titled "Priapus (Keeper of Orchards)," and the "you" was then "thou," the too-intimate almost forbidden second person pronoun in English. The first pear falling, the thundering air and the honey-questing bees of the poem appear then in a poetic magic in which the natural environment and the sexual experience are fused. The intensity belongs neither to the tree as object nor to the priapic penis as object but to the evocation of the image in which they are fused.

Nor is it from the world of the ancestors that the poet feels alienated. The ultimate reality that the eternal ones of the dream have for the Aranda—the ultimate reality that our toys and imaginary playmates had for us in childhood—Moses, Michelangelo, Leonardo da Vinci, Hannibal have for Freud; and Sappho, Euripides, Shakespeare, or Browning have for H.D. They are forefathers of the work, but they seem also at times previous reincarnations of the spirit at work.

These poems where many persons from many times and many places begin to appear—as in *The Cantos, The Waste Land, Finnegans Wake,* The War Trilogy, and *Paterson*—are poems of a world-mind in process. The seemingly triumphant reality of the War and State disorient the poet, who is partisan to a free and world-wide possibility, so that his creative task becomes the more imperative. The challenge increases the insistence of the imagination to renew the reality of its own. It is not insignificant that these "poems containing history" are all products of a movement in literature that was identified in the beginning as "free" verse. *The Egoist,* where Pound, Eliot, Joyce, Williams, Marianne Moore, H.D., Lawrence, and Aldington first appeared together had formerly been *The New Freewoman;* free verse went along in its publication with articles on free love and free thought. And the "new" we find also as a demand. In his quarrel with Eliot, Williams could oppose the "new" to the "past"—as if all of the past were what Eliot meant by his "tradition." But the definition of the "new" was given by Ezra Pound from Confucius in "Make It New," and in *The Spirit of Romance* and the essay "Cavalcanti" he turns to the late Medieval reawakening of poetic genius not with the antiquarian's concerns but in search of enduring terms for the renewal of poetry in his own time. The study of literature, he wrote then, was "hero-worship"—"It is a refinement or, if you will, a perversion of that primitive religion."

The image, for the Imagists, was something actually seen. "At least H.D. has lived with these things since childhood," Pound writes to Harriet Monroe in 1912, "and knew them before she had any book-knowledge of them." In *ABC of Reading* he argues for a statement of Dante's as a starting point:

> because it starts the reader or hearer from what he actually sees or hears, instead of distracting his mind from that actuality to something which can only be approximately deduced or conjectured FROM the actuality, and for which the *evidence* can be nothing save the particular and limited extent of the actuality.

In the major phase of his last years William Carlos Williams, the poet who was to have "no ideas but in things," would relate poetry to dream and to phantasy, as H.D. in "Good Frend" would project the fictional life of Claribel who had no more actuality than her being mentioned in passing in Shakespeare's *The Tempest*—itself a drama of the poet's powers to enchant—and in *Helen in Egypt* H.D. would weave another fiction of persons who belong not to actuality but to an eternal dream. But the bias for what Williams called "the local conditions" as the primary impetus is strong and continues to haunt my own generation.

The immediate persuasion of Imagist poets was against the fantastic and fictional as it was for the clear-seeing, even the clairvoyant, and the actual, for percept against concept. The image as "that which presents an intellectual and emotional complex in time" or "the local conditions" could open out along lines of the poet's actual feeling. The poem could be erotic and contain evocations of actual sexual experience as in the poem "Orchards." And then, the image was also something actually seen in the process of the poem, not something pretended or made up. It was the particular image evoked in the magic operation of the poet itself—whatever its source, and it usually had many sources. In reviewing Fletcher's poetry in 1916, H.D. may be speaking too of her own art:

> He uses the direct image, it is true, but he seems to use it as a means to evoke other and vaguer images—a pebble, as it were, dropped in a quiet pool, in order to start across the silent water, wave on wave of light, of colour, of sound.

There was in the image a presentation that gave, Pound writes in "A Stray Document," "that sense of sudden liberation; that sense of freedom from time limits and space limits; that sense of sudden growth, which we experience in the presence of the greatest works of art." When he tells us that the total plan of Dante's *Commedia* is itself an image, there is a possibility that the image is something seen of or in the "other" world, a clairvoyance. Works of art here are works of a magic comparable to the imaginative practices of Vital or Ficino in which the imagination is thought of as a higher vision. In Pound's "Aux Etuves de Wiesbaden," Poggio says: "We are fortunate to live in the wink, the eye of mankind is open; for an instant, hardly more than an instant."

The *personae* of the Imagists had derived from the *dramatis-personae* of Robert Browning. Pound and H.D. wrote not in the tradition of the personal lyric, but they drew upon the dramatic choral lyric and the trance-voice of religious evocation to charge the actual with meaning. In this making the actual the condition of the true and the real, there was a curious consequence. For those elements of the imagination that are usually distinguished from what is actual—the impersonations, the projections, the creations of worlds and the speculations in ideas— return now in their higher truth and reality to be identified with the actual. In such an operation, H.D. suggests in her notes to *Ion,* for the devotee of Euripides, the actor of Hermes is indeed Hermes:

> Roughly speaking, there were two types of theatre-goers in ancient Greece, as there are today. Those who are on time and those who are late. The prologue is the argument or libretto; it outlines the plot. The ardent lover of the drama will doubtless be strung up to a fine pitch of intensity and discrimination from the first. The presence of this actor, who impersonates the god Hermes, will actually be that god. Religion and art still go hand in hand.

If poetry has to do with enchantment and the imagination has traffic with what is not actual but a made-up world, if indeed these would-be serious poets wove a romance of the actual itself, then religion and art may both be fictional and the intensity of their truth and reality is the intensity needed to make what is not actual real. The crux for the poet is to make real what is only real in a heightened sense. Call it his personal feeling, or the communal reality, it exists only in its dance, only to its dancers. Outside the created excitement, what we call the inspiration of art, the things done—the bleeding, the exhibition of private parts, the reiterated correspondences of the human world to the great world of nature and the eternal world of the dream—do not communicate. The reader of the poem must be just such an ardent lover as the communicant of the Mass, or the magic of the sacrament is all superstition and vanity. Christ is not actually there, even where He is most real.

The poet and the reader, who if he is intent in reading becomes a new poet of the poem, come to write or to read in order to participate through the work in a consciousness that moves freely in time and space and can entertain reality upon reality. "He has to begin as a cloud of all the other poets he ever read," Robert Frost says, comparing the poet to a water-spout at sea:

> . . . and first the cloud reaches down! toward the water from above, and then the water reaches up! toward the cloud from below—and finally cloud and water join together to roll as one pillar between heaven and earth: the base of water he picks from below, all the life he lived outside of books.

But, in eternity, there is a cloud below, a sea above, as well: books are real and also imagined, and they must be included if we would draw upon all the life we have lived. Life, a dream or a stage on which we act, is also larger than the life we have lived, for its reality is extended in all the poets we have read.

In this great poetry, "Today shalt thou be with me in Paradise" may have its resonance with "To-morrow, and to-morrow and to-morrow, / Creepes in this petty pace from day to day, / To the last syllable of recorded time"; for we have come in the comparison of languages to imagine one human Language from many tongues. If the language of Matthew be inspired, so is the language of Shakespeare. Christ and Macbeth have become personae of a world-poem. Not only this is true, but if it is, then also this is true. It has come to pass, anyway, that only in the imagination are Christ and Macbeth surely real.

Book 2   *Nights and Days*

Chapter 1

In Horace a man speaks to his own poetic faculty even as to another person; and they are not the words of Horace only but he says them as though reciting the words of the good Homer, here in his *Poetria: Dic mini Musa, virum,* etc. In Ovid Love speaketh, as he were a human being, in the beginning of the book named *Remedy of Love,* here: *Bella mihi, video, bella parantur ait.* And by this may all be made clear to one who finds a difficulty in certain parts of this my little book. —Dante Alighieri, *La Vita Nuova,* xxv

MARCH 10, FRIDAY. 1961. (1963)

Naming the stars out of the seas of heaven, men drew a net-work. The knots were suns, were burning. What the poets who bound the dragon of their confusion spun were lines of association where figures of light appeared, giving direction. All life is oriented to the light from which life comes. The bees in their dances are oriented to the sun and, if it is dark, will dance in relation to a candle flame. Men found at night a new orientation in the stars, found a heaven, a spreading mesh of lights, that became a projected screen of where and when they were as they danced, an image of another net that in memory we throw out over moment and place that are suns in time, the net of our selves. The bees dance to tell where the honey is.

They memorized as they realized. In turn, now, the surfaces and involvements of the brain were an imprint of the seas above; and the skydome above was the image of another configuration in the skull-dome below. So, a network there too bound the dragon of a confusion in constellations of living cells that made up a body or series of imaginary bodies a man was, is, would be.

.

It was a map. It was a great design of where they were and then of when. Night after night here in the country I have been learning my stars. The wavering cold of a mixed winter and spring, as if those distant lights were within the aroma of March blossomings, the lilac, lemon, and grasses, of the star-world, brings a fragrance of stars. Earth sparks of scent seem just to have flown up into those signs of the ancient ways in which the book of when-where sparkles and glows. As we come home from an evening with neighbors, Orion is in the high heaven.

.

The figure of the giant hunter in the sky brings with it, as often, the creative genius of Charles Olson for me. Since the appearance of *Origin* I a decade ago, my vision of what the poem is to do has been transformed, reorganized around a constellation of new poets—Olson, Denise Levertov, Robert Creeley—in which Olson's work takes the lead for me. This man, himself a "giant"—six foot seven or so—has been an outrider, my own Orion.

It was this same time of year, with Orion overhead, in 1955, when Olson read aloud to Jess and me the beginnings of a new sequence of poems, *O'Ryan*. The scene in the bare room at Black Mountain with its cold and the blazing winter sky at the window springs up as I write. The fugitive hero of that sequence was drawn from Robert Creeley, but he is also in the humor of the poem Hercules the Sun or Son who must pass the twelve houses of the zodiacal initiations: "Overall, mover of the unnumbered"—"who did twelve labors," Olson names him.

.

He's also—what else has he to be?—the rueful figure any of us are as the men we are:

                    who
            told you your flesh is

as rosy as your
baby's, as rosy as

Rosy, as, your
moth-er's, as who got you up

and to be up there, sky-high, is also to be "all lit up" as in *O'Ryan* 8,
and look down, as in 9, "you got a hard on / and it's / to be made." But:

I don't read your face. Or you mine.
By looking up or down. . . .

                •

Yet our roots are in the sky. Radical! The Milky Way appears, cross-
section of our galaxy. In the earliest news out of heaven, what they
said—the *mythos*—was that it was the slain body of the dragon, it was the
flow of everlasting mothering milk, it was light, it was rhetoric, river,
fluid. A stream of suns.

                •

Something of what we are is up in the air, beyond our grasp, and wher-
ever we are not sure of what is going on—as in the heavens then—a
phantasy of our selves appeared.

                •

Otherwise, other *ways* (as Charles Olson gave me the lead in his "Against
Wisdom As Such" that our wise is not more or less than our ways), if
there are not these roots in the sky, this place that is also a time of what
must be—otherwise poetry is a litter. "Litterature," Lewis Carroll called
his collection of bits and starts out of which he put together *Sylvie and
Bruno*. "The reader will overlook my spell," he added.

                •

In our time, Joyce, gathering up his mountain of litter, sorting and re-
sorting, accruing scraps upon scraps, took a patron in that "Dodge-son."

He too made out of the mound of twenty-five years' labor a pun upon literature and wrote a crawling language that must enter here, if only to play the adversary, for I have taken thought in this ground too. Like Milton, Joyce was blind. *Finnegans Wake* has its roots among letters and in the body, as if it were not moved by the stars. The work has intestinal fortitude, true to an internal chemistry. Its seasons are rounds of digestion. He had lost sight of the heavens.

•

In a man's guts there are no gods. There is agony, there is pleasure. Pain that binds the spirit to its own when-where. Pleasure that may be taken, as we may take thought.

In the flight of the imagination, in the reading of the stars, in taking thought, we go out of our selves. Flame out of the wet wood. Out of literature then. Out of matters of pain and pleasure.

•

The consciousness bent down to a literature lives on its wits in a sulfurous burning. And if we come under literary dictates, all is voluptuous or all agony, is a matter of what we like and do not like, of literary taste, of good-and-bad the tongue knows, is hell.

As the other consciousness we see in the light spread out in the heavens. Gods there; and in the darkness, daemonic stars.

•

In the map of stars we began to map our selves. Our projection of what we are was also a first poetry. A first making of a thing or image that projected a spiritual form in what we did not know. Well . . . There must have been another projected spiritual form—not only this but also this—when the adam named their things and kinds of the earth, another network of sticks and stones and names "that never hurt one." In our literary listings and groupings, we are doing all of that, nothing more. We make constellations in poetry that are, if they be anything, linked by gender, works of our selves then, ideograms of spirit, of when and where what we are is happening.

I.

This study of H.D.'s work is such an astrology, projecting a net of responses in which points in the sky and lines of feeling suggest figures in a plot at work from day to day. Here each opus is a sun, the locality of an event. An opus in itself—but I have in mind the *Opus* or Work as it appears in the imagination of certain alchemists, something undertaken in which we may discover the way of the soul, begin the romance of our spirit. A romance in Poetry that would be a counterpart of the alchemical romances of the seventeenth century.

So, when I think of H.D.'s later work: The War Trilogy, "The Writing on the Wall" *(Tribute to Freud),* the poem "Good Frend" and the historical essay "The Guest" that form *By Avon River,* and her "Madrigal"—the *roman à clef Bid Me to Live*—that these are masterpieces has a double charge. It means both that she is my master here in the art of writing; and, just in this, that she is my master here in spirit. That this book, in turn, is an apprentice piece. Where, trying my hand, a student, I must often miss and go on as best I can.

Jean Cocteau lists his *Oeuvres* as a king might list the states of his kingdom: *Poésie, Poésie de Roman, Poésie Critique, Poésie de Théâtre, Poésie Graphique, Poésie Cinématographique.* Drawings and movies are conceived as propositions of "Poetry." As we recognize that Blake's illustrations, not only of his own books but of Bunyan, Milton, and Dante, belong to the plot of his poetics.

Drawing a picture of his work in this way, articulating not only into prose and verse, but into formal entities—poem, novel, drama, critique, history, translation—the poet creates a syntax of the whole art in which individual works are jointures of a larger structure, not conclusions but functions. Each thing-in-itself is revealed anew as it is seen as the member of possible sequences.

So Joyce conceived *Chamber Music, Dubliners, A Portrait of the Artist as a Young Man, Exiles, Ulysses,* and *Finnegans Wake* as a deliberate series of forms in which his work is defined—as characteristic a design as the progress of parts in *Ulysses:* the book of songs, the book of short stories, the memoir, the drama, the book of the conscious mind or Dublin awake, the book of the dreaming mind or Dublin asleep. The sense of order in Joyce is simple-minded, comparable to that of César Franck; his inventive genius lay in the elaboration and illustration of one-dimensional, one-directional systems.

In Pound's work too we recognize the conceptual mind of the artist at work in the total design, but here that total design is not, as Joyce's is, a prescribed convention which the artist solves in a unique variation. Pound's total form, like the form of any poem or book, is not obvious but hidden, intuited by the artist then as a process, organizing and reorganizing the meaning of what he has done in what he does. "Years ago," he writes in the "Date Line" for *Make It New* in 1935, "I made the mistake of publishing a volume *(Instigations)* without blatantly telling the reader that the book had a design." Here design means also intent in an open possibility. In "The Chinese Written Character as a Medium for Poetry" Pound had found the inspiration of a moving syntax (as contrasted with the categorical syntax of Joyce, where parts of speech are things). "A true noun, an isolated thing," we read in the Fenollosa essay, "does not exist in nature. Things are only the terminal points, or rather the meeting points of actions, cross-sections cut through actions, snap-shots. Neither can a pure verb, an abstract motion, be possible in nature. The eye sees noun and verb as one: things in motion, motion in things, and so the Chinese conception tends to represent them."

As the works of the poet are articulated, so too his life is articulated. Phases appear, and immediate impressions and emotions are felt to belong to the ideogram of a body in time. The individual image operates as a manifestation of feeling, as the individual persona operates as a manifestation of identity. Projected in time from a series of works, there is an increment of design. Feelings take on the shape of a created life-experience, the lifetime in Poetry, and the personae take on the shape of a self, the poet.

Images, as the Japanese poet Kitasono proposed to Pound in 1937, take on another dimension in their assembly, and the poet, moving on from the evocation of the immediate image, in the "collection, arrangement and combination" of images becomes involved in a plastic apprehension. "That which we vaguely call poetical effect," he writes, "means, generally, ideoplasty, which grows out of the result of imagery." The shape of an imaginary geometry, an aesthetic intuition like the thinking out "to make a heart-shaped space with two right angles" it seems to Kitasono, begins to haunt the poet as he begins to be aware of the arrangements and combinations possible in his work. A sense of inner orders, of outline, arises. "The relation between imagery and ideoplasty," he continues, "makes us suppose the heart-shaped space which is born by the connection of the same mysterious two curves." In this process the aesthetic feeling arises and, in turn: "The phenomena in our life proceed, through our senses to our experiences, and intuitions. It is intuition rationally that provides the essentials for imagery, and it is the method of poetry that materializes intuitions perceptively and combines."

In H.D.'s early work the evocation of the Greek past and in the Greek past of the god-world, of nature and of her own life-drama in superimposed image and person, the identifications with Sappho and Euripides, and the development of the dramatic monologue and choral modes in sequences, the identification with the spirits of Sappho and Euripides: these are formal intuitions. In *Red Roses for Bronze* in 1931 the forms are clearly realized by the poet. And with *Ion,* translated from Euripides, and the notes to *Ion,* begun in Athens in 1920, there is a turning point—the crowning achievement of her first phase, but also the declaration of her later work. And in the very dedication of the book we see the poet's formalization of her own creative life. "For B. [Bryher] Athens 1920 / P [her daughter Perdita] Delphi 1932." In her novel *Palimpsest* in 1926 this suggestion of design in time first appears in the sequence of times given the component parts: "Hipparchia" (circa 75 B.C.), "Murex" (circa 1916-1926 A.D.), "Secret Name" (circa 1925 A.D.). From the flux of possible relationships she has begun to take certain keys in which her own life-experience is plotted and in turn to find between her own time affinities in history. Hipparchia and Raymonde Ransome are members with H.D. herself in a composite figure drawn from H.D.'s two confinements—the first in 1916 when the child died; the second in 1919 when H.D. herself almost died in the influenza epidemic. These identities and contrasts are correlatives of a third form, "a heart-shaped space," as Kitasono called it, imagined in time by the growing formal sense. These images rhyme with each other by factors of child-birth, of being deserted, of fever, of being found and nursed.

The transitions or notes which H.D. adds in her translation of the *Ion* of Euripides are initial to the major phase of her work that lasts from the inception of The War Trilogy with *The Walls Do Not Fall* in 1942 to the end of her life with *Hermetic Definitions* in 1960. From the vague sense she had had in 1916 that she was not interested in the image as a thing in itself but in something "moving, whirling, drifting," by 1932 she had come to see movement as inherent in the proportion of Euripides' work. It is part of H.D.'s interpretation in translation that she divides the whole into "nineteen divisions . . . sanctioned by the form of the play." It is not only that "each represents an entrance, an exit, a change in inner mood and external grouping of the characters," but we begin to be aware that back of H.D.'s conception of the play is a complex analysis—historical, ideological, psychological, as well as aesthetic. What is involved is the change from knowing how to do something that might be prescribed into knowing what must be done; from the mastery the craftsman has with his language to the obedience that the initiate must have who has come under the orders of meanings and inner structures he must follow. It is no longer *her* art but The Art.

So, when in her Translator's Note to *Ion*, H.D. writes: "It is significant that the word ION has a double meaning. It may be translated by the Latin word UNUS, meaning one, or first, and is also the Greek word for violet, the sacred flower of Athens," she may not only refer to Ion as initiating a new spirit in Athens but also to her own translated Ion as initiating a new spirit in her work to come.

Ion is the pivot. But then there is another aspect to the time of the work for it is a time of crisis. In the world at large between 1929 and the Second World War were years of economic depression and then the many crises and apprehensions in which the inevitability of the War was built up. In H.D.'s personal life there may also have been depression, the poet's coming to himself *"per una selva oscura,"* in a dark wood, *"che la diritta via era smarrita"*—where the straight way is lost. For H.D., the very increased consciousness of the structure, of significance and form, may have been the crisis. She sought and found her way in the psychoanalysis with Freud in 1933 and 1934.

For she stood upon the threshold of an art where she was to take her place with Ezra Pound and William Carlos Williams in the adventure of the higher imagination, in the full risk of the poem in which divine, human, and animal orders must be revealed. There had been an heroic resolve in *Ion*. "Especially . . . " Freud wrote H.D. in his appreciation of her notes, "where you extol the victory of reason over passions." But it is, too, in the play, an address to the passionate intellect.

There is a passion of mind that moves toward abstract beauty, the Ionian style, "the valiant yet totally unselfconscious withdrawal of the personality of the artist." That is part of it. "Let not our hearts break before the beauty of Pallas Athene," H.D. continues: "No":

> she makes all things possible for us. The human mind today pleads for all; nothing is misplaced that in the end may be illuminated by the inner fire of abstract understanding; hate, love, degradation, humiliation, all, all may be examined, given due proportion and dismissed finally, in the light of the mind's vision. Today, again at a turning-point in the history of the world, the mind stands, to plead, to condone, to explain, to clarify, to illuminate.

then: "each one of us is responsible." *then:* "What now will we make of it?"

In 1932, she had begun sequences of an Electra-Orestes play; in 1937 another section "Orestes Theme" appeared in *Life and Letters Today*. In 1935 two long sequences "The Dancer" and "The Poet"; in 1937 "In Our Town," "Star by Day," and "Wooden Animal"; in 1938 "Apollo at Delphi" in *Poetry;* in 1939 two fragments, "Saturn" and "Zeus-Provider" from a proposed "Temple of the Sun." From 1932 to 1942 only scattered essays in poetry appear.

There was the great work to undertake, but it was only in the experience of war-time London of the Second World War, where in the actual bombings life and death were so mixed, hope and despair, that the time ripened, the things of the poet's own inner life came due. The days of bombardment, the trials and crucible of the war, furnish a crucible of the poem where the long prepared art, the accumulated craft and knowledge fit or work. But it is the time too that fits, that works. In prophecy, this is the proof. It is the fulfilling of the word.

As at Pisa, uprooted from his study and his *idées fixes,* "a lone ant from a broken ant-hill," Ezra Pound was to come, in another part of the war, in the Summer and Fall of 1945, to a turning point, exposed, at the heart of the matter. Mussolini had been torn to pieces, like Cola di Rienzi his Renaissance counterpart. "Manes was tanned and stuffed," Pound remembers in the first Pisan canto. The poet had hitchhiked to Pisa and surrendered, given himself up to the army. Had he expected death? His fellow prisoners are led off to the firing squad each day. And, for the first time in *The Cantos,* in these Pisan Cantos, some attitude of authority, some self is surrendered, so that a pose seems to have fallen apart, exposing the genuine, confused, passionate mind. "A lizard upheld me," he testifies. He is in the condition of first things.

Not since the Imagist years, between 1912 and 1915, had Pound's and H.D.'s poetry belonged to a common movement. He had gone on from the Vorticism of Gaudier-Brzeska with its spirit of forms to the Vorticism of Wyndham Lewis with its blast at culture. The Pound of the thirties with his treatises on economics and his historical comparisons of Jefferson and Mussolini seems far indeed from the world of H.D. But when *The Pisan Cantos* appeared in 1949 how closely Pound's lines:

If the hoar frost grip thy tent
Thou wilt give thanks when night is spent.

recalled H.D.'s lines from *Tribute to the Angels* that had been published in 1945:

where, Zadkiel, we pause to give
thanks that we rise again from death and live.

In December of 1944, H.D. had finished her War Trilogy; she was 58. At Pisa, Pound was 60 when he finished *The Pisan Cantos.* William Carlos Williams at 62 in 1944 was working on *Paterson* I. For each there was to be ahead, in the last years of their lives, a major creative phase.

And "to reveal that secret and sacred presence"—there was to be *Paterson.* "It called for a poetry such as I did not know," Williams writes in his *Autobiography,* "it was my duty to discover or make such a context. . . ."

"'How deep is the water?' asked Paul. 'I mean at the deepest place?'" *Paterson* I (1946):

So you think because the rose
is red that you shall have the mastery?
The rose is green and will bloom,
overtopping you . . .

Paterson II (1948) "Sunday in the Park":

His anger mounts. He is chilled to the bone.
As there appears a dwarf, hideously deformed—

It is the genius of the place, of the falls—but the falls are the locus of the poem in the language; the river, the rhetoric. The dwarf then is the poet's own familiar:

The dwarf lived there, close to the waterfall—
saved by his protective coloring.

And in *Paterson* III (1949), "The Library," another image of the language but the poem itself also, and then of the poet, occurs:

An old bottle, mauled by the fire
gets a new glaze, the glass warped
to a new distinction, reclaiming the
undefined.

It seemed to me then that Williams, in the imagination, had come to the same place, under fire, that appears in *Tribute to the Angels* where:

then she set a charred tree before us,
burnt and stricken to the heart;

as if in London, in Pisa, in Paterson, there had been phases of a single revelation. Indeed, Williams saw that if his Paterson "rose to flutter into life awhile—it would be as itself, locally, and so like every other place in the world." Was it that the war—the bombardment for H.D., the imprisonment and exposure to the elements for Ezra Pound, the divorce in the speech for Williams—touched a spring of passionate feeling in the poet that was not the war but was his age, his ripeness in life. They were almost "old"; under fire to come "to a new distinction."

Where the fullness of their age was also the fullness of an historical age, as if the Second World War were a trouble of the times, unprepared or prepared for its old age?

They give, these three works out of the war, a text for the historian of our contemporary spirit; as Shakespeare gives text for the Tudor Renaissance; as Dante gives text for the thirteenth century catholic world.

In the light of these works I write today. Taking them as my immediate ancestors, as they in turn took Swinburne, the Pre-Raphaelites Rossetti and William Morris, and Robert Browning, as theirs. As Pound has his direct heritage from Yeats, carrying over the neo-Platonism, the Greek and Renaissance mystery cults, Plotinus and Gemistos Plethon—and even (*Section: Rock-Drill,* Canto XCI) the Rosicrucian John Heydon. Heydon had appeared first in the early drafts of Canto III:

> Another one, half-cracked: John Heydon,
> Worker of miracles, dealer in levitation,
> "Servant of God and secretary of nature,"
> The half transparent forms, in trance at Bulverton:

Pound owing as much of his medium to Yeats—how Pound becomes a medium himself—as Yeats owed modern measure to Pound.

In "Sagesse," the first ten poems of which were published in *Evergreen Review* 5, Summer 1958, H.D. comes round close to Yeats, for she takes the Kabbalist theurgy directly over from *La Kabbale Pratique* of Robert Ambelain as a poetic practice:

> An owl hooted out in the darkness,
> so the angel came—what angel and what name?
>
> is it Tara, *Dieu fontaine de sagesse*
> and the angel Ptébiou? it was his hour
>
> or near his hour, what did he say?

seeking to follow along the line of associations:

> into a mystery, the haunted mere of Märchen
> and old legends, or even Lethe or Eunoë, now and here.

She had never been, actually, close to Yeats, nor had she read his works. "Of course—what a tour de force," she writes in a letter in 1960 of Virginia Moore's study of Yeats: "that digging out the very 'secret' R. C. ceremonial! Odd, I met Yeats and 'Georgie,' as they first called her, & they invited me to Oxford—but something held me back. I did not know that 'Georgie' was a medium or he, what he was."

She did not know then that there had been a poet before her who tried to draw images from Hermetic cult and rite. Nor how close to the "Yeatsian" tradition she was in her own way in "Sagesse" as she asks,

> what am I doing? am I swept into a cycle
> of majestic Spirits, myself aspiring yet questioning
>
> my right to mention even one of the seventy-two regents
> of the right Temple of the Œdipus Ægyptiacus

And Pound in Canto XCI:

> that the body of light come forth
>   from the body of fire
> And that your eyes come to the surface
>   from the deep wherein they were sunken,
> Reina—for 300 years,
>   and now sunken
> That your eyes come forth from their caves
>   & light then
>   as the holly-leaf
>   qui laborat, orat
> Thus Undine came to the rock,
>   by Circeo
> and the stone eyes again looking seaward
>   Thus Apollonius
>   (if it was Apollonius)
> & Helen of Tyre

This nearness to Lethe or Eunoë, to shadow or light, to the astral or phantasmal world in which Simon Magus and his Helen still have their powers, is the daydream of old age. Which has no reality except in the imagination. As, too, in the "Coda" to "Asphodel," William Carlos Williams comes close to the myrrh and light of H.D.'s *Flowering of the Rod* when he writes of what it is like "after a lifetime":

Asphodel
> has no odor
>> save to the imagination
> but it too
>> celebrates the light.
>>> It is late
> but an odor
>> as from our wedding
>>> has revived for me

These three—Pound, Williams, and H.D.—belonged in their youth
to a brilliant, still brilliant generation that began writing just before the
First World War and publishing in *The Egoist* in London, in *Poetry* and
Others in America. They alone of their generation—and we must add
D. H. Lawrence to their company—saw literature as a text of the soul in
its search for fulfillment in life and took the imagination as a primary
instinctual authority. The generative imagination Pound called it. They
took the full risk of seeking to fulfill their vision of the poet as seer
and creator. It is the heroic concept of the poet that the Romantics had
had, Carlyle's Hero as Poet, whose "*musical* thought is one spoken by a
mind that has penetrated into the inmost heart of the thing; detected
the inmost harmony of it, namely the melody that lies hidden in it; the
inward harmony of coherence which is its soul, whereby it exists, and
has a right to be, here in this world."

At the outbreak of the Second World War Edith Sitwell was inspired
to write in the prophetic mode of high poetry. But the rest of that
company—Wallace Stevens, Marianne Moore, T. S. Eliot—remain
within the rational imagination and do not suffer from the creative dis-
orders of primitive mind, the shamanistic ecstasies and the going "after
strange gods." Following this generation that had made the breakthru
came not a creative but a reactionary period. There is one lonely ghost
light of poetry where Hart Crane is seized by his vision of the Bridge.
There is one lonely acolyte of poetry where Louis Zukofsky perfects
his art, wrapped in the cocoon of an "objectivism" derived from Pound
and Williams, a hidden *zaddik* in a thicket of theory, to emerge in the

myrrh and light of *"A"*, to keep the music, and in the working hive of his thought in *Bottom: On Shakespeare.*

For a new generation of young writers in the early fifties, *The Pisan Cantos* and then *Paterson* had been the challenge. But for me, The War Trilogy of H.D. came earlier, for searching out those first vatic poems of Edith Sitwell that Kenneth Rexroth had shown me in *Life and Letters Today* I had come across H.D.'s passages from *The Walls Do Not Fall.* Then came "Writing on the Wall" and "Good Frend." When the third volume of the Trilogy, *The Flowering of the Rod,* was published in 1946 I had found my book. From the beginning then, certainly from 1947 or 1948 when I was working on *Medieval Scenes* and taking H.D. as my master there among the other masters, there was The War Trilogy. In smoky rooms in Berkeley, in painters' studios in San Francisco, I read these works aloud; dreamed about them; took my life in them; studied them as my anatomy of what Poetry must be.

A new constellation was appearing in those days in the magazine *Origin.* It had started with a manifesto by a man called Charles Olson— he had come to see me once in Berkeley, but I did not know then that he was a poet—that was just after *Medieval Scenes* in 1947—it had started with Olson's "Projective Verse" essay of 1950, or it had started with a correspondence between this Olson and a Robert Creeley, a poet younger than myself. In Spring 1951 another poet Cid Corman published the first issue of *Origin.* There, for the first time in the work of any contemporary, I began to find a Call to Order. "I, Maximus, of Gloucester, To You" the first poem began:

> Off-shore, by islands hidden in the blood
> jewels & miracles, I, Maximus
> a metal hot from boiling water, tell you
> what is a lance, who obeys the figures of
> the present dance

In "The Gate & the Center" in that same issue Olson writes: "whatever be individuation, there are groupings of us which create kin ('hungry after my own kind'), limits of, say, Seven Tribes of man, or whatever—which same limits become vessels of behavior towards *use of* self, & recognition."

I have taken these as an imaginary kin and their works for me form a network of stars that influence me, as the willing astrologer believes his stars influence him; and hanging over me can seem even an evil at times, such powers I have given to the thought of them, in order perhaps to imagine a powerful kindred. Such a network appears in Olson's poem "As the Dead Prey Upon Us":

> they are the dead in ourselves,
> awake, my sleeping ones, I cry out to you,
> disentangle the nets of being!

nets, "which hamper at each step of the ladders," "The nets we are entangled in," that must be the tissues of life, the network of cells that is our flesh in which we exist. Is that it? to be released from the grievance and ache of the mother-flesh?

Stars, spirits, the dead. Some passage read years ago in Gertrude Levy's *The Sword from the Rock* had raised in my mind the idea that as men came to know the stars, to name them, and then to draw lines and inferences, netting the whole sky together in a sky-map of constellations, so they came to bind Tiamat, the Dragon of the Formless Heavens. The stars were, in that concept, knots of the net. That bound also, then . . . Tiamat, the Mother of our Formless Nature? the libido?

I had seen old pictures where Christ the Fisher of Men was Orpheus fishing for the fish of the Zodiac, Pisces, with a net. And I knew too that the sum of our wisdom was what the dead knew. Wise with what was dead in us.

But these poems of our first constellation: The War Trilogy, *The Pisan Cantos* and *Paterson* came as living stars. Works that were not only masterpieces, but striking fire that continues to burn and lead on—to the broken insistences, the sublimity, and the rant of Pound's *Rock-Drill* and *Thrones;* to the melodic distribution of phrases, the phrasing allowing for melodies within a melody, of Williams's *Desert Music* and *Journey to Love;* to the world-dream woven at the loom of *By Avon River, Tribute to Freud, Bid Me to Live,* and in the far-flung skeins and lights of "Helen and Achilles" (*Helen in Egypt*). "We have only one course:" Olson tells us in his song:

the nets which entangle us are flames

then:

O souls, burn
alive, burn now

As, in writing, deriving as I do, I burn the nets of my origins.

II.

An incident here and there
and rails gone (for guns)
from your (and my) old town square

"Here," "there" are suns, are loci. When-where points of the net. Actual fires. So, the Romans knew there was a genius of the place where we are. There was a point to it.

But "here," "there," the dedication of *The Walls Do Not Fall* makes clear are:

To Bryher
for Karnak   1923
from London   1942

A thread is spun out in the loom between two points of the design, two places, two times. Where Bryher appears as patroness.

This is the figure of the kneeling donor, a meaningful element of the rite in painting in the late Middle Ages—the one who makes possible the Opus.

H.D., deserted by Aldington, near death in a London hospital, had been rescued by Bryher, who found her there; and then, rescued from her life in London, from the grievous associations of her marriage with

Aldington, yes, but also from the other trials of her life as a poet in company with Lawrence and Pound. Bryher took her away, or made it possible for her to go away to the Isles of Greece. Athens 1920. Karnak 1923.

In the dedication verse of *Palimpsest* H.D. draws a likeness of Bryher as severe and unidealized as the portrait of the Chancellor Rolin in Van Eyck's painting of the Madonna. The great stars Hesperus, Aldebaran, Sirius, and Mars, are, we sense, where Bryher too has her star-nature, companions of H.D.'s who failed her in need, who "reel and fall."

To Bryher

Stars wheel in purple, yours is not so rare
as Hesperus, nor yet so great a star
as Bright Aldebaran or Sirius,
nor yet the stained and brilliant one of War;

stars turn in purple, glorious to the sight;
yours is not gracious as the Pleiads are,
nor as Orion's sapphires, luminous;

yet disenchanted, cold, imperious face,
when all the others, blighted, reel and fall,
your star, steel-set, keeps lone and frigid trist
to freighted ships baffled in wind and blast.

Pregnant with her second child H.D. had been stricken with double pneumonia. "The material and spiritual burden of pulling us out of danger," she writes in *Tribute to Freud*, "fell upon a young woman whom I had only recently met—anyone who knows me knows who this person is. Her pseudonym is Bryher, and we all call her Bryher. If I got well, she would herself see that the baby was protected and cherished and she would take me to a new world, a new life, to the land, spiritually of my predilection, geographically of my dreams. We would go to Greece, it could be arranged. It was arranged, though we two were the first unofficial visitors to Athens after that war."

"Anyone who knows me knows who this person is"—"She turned out to be the daughter of Sir John Ellerman, the heaviest taxpayer in England," William Carlos Williams puts it in his *Autobiography*. Years later. But the thought of H.D. irritates him; he wants to put her down. "'Wanna see the old gal?' I asked Bob. 'Sure. Why not?' So one afternoon we decided to take in the show. Same old Hilda, all over the place looking as tall and as skinny as usual." Wherever he remembers her this almost insulting, almost insulted affect colors his voice. He wants to brush Bryher off: "She had with her a small, dark English girl with piercing, intense eyes, whom I noticed and that was about all." And the thought of Bryher's proposing to Robert McAlmon and their marriage, McAlmon's "disastrous story," as he calls it, rankles. "She turned out to be the daughter of Sir John Ellerman, the heaviest taxpayer in England. Bob fell for it. When he told me, I literally felt the tears come to my eyes, whether from the anticipated loss of the man's companionship and the assistance of his talents, or joy for his good fortune, I couldn't decide."

The fortune itself rankled. Williams wasn't going to fall for it. Fall under the claim money made. The reality of money, the charm of money. "I could not imagine what to give the wealthy young couple as an adequate present," he tells us, "until Floss fell on the ideal gift: a box of the rarest orchids we could gather." "Imagine," Marsden Hartley laughed at the wedding supper, "what it would look like in the papers tomorrow, the headline: POETS PAWING ORCHIDS!"

Several days later, Williams continues, they received a post card "showing several actors, men and women with their hands in a pot of money, and signed, obscurely, D. H., in bold capitals." He means to get back at something—"I accused H.D. later of being the sender"—of being in on the scene then? "but she violently denied it. I never believed her."

The rancor is complex in William Carlos Williams; it flashes forth testily in his *Autobiography*. For us, for that constellation of new poets who began to appear in *Origin* in the fifties, where Charles Olson, Denise Levertov, Robert Creeley, Paul Blackburn, Larry Eigner, and I had our places, Williams was our immediate master. The poet of *The Wedge* in 1944 had broken a new way. The poet of *The Clouds* and then *Paterson* in the late forties had awakened us to our task in the language and had awakened us too to rediscover the poet of *Spring and All*. He seemed so wholly the poet in *Paterson,* the derisive, the defensive, the contending voice seemed so composed, to heighten the pathos of the ideal:

Go home. Write. Compose
Ha!
Be reconciled, poet, with your world, it is
the only truth!
Ha!
—the language is worn out.
And She—
You have abandoned me!
—at the magic sound of the stream
she threw herself upon the bed—
a pitiful gesture! lost among the words:

we saw him so as the hero, that it was hard to admit how close to hurt pride he could be, how he contended in his own mind for recognition.

But this place is New York, this year is 1921. There is already a disappointment not an appointment between these two poets who had once read their poetry together. A divorce of feeling. A refusal of recognition.

Looking back, *Spring and All* in 1922 stands a major realization of form. Its twenty-eight poems belonging to an open sequence of feeling, cohering, not in any plan or prescribed theme, but in the essence of their belonging to the pure intuition of the whole. As free as the new music of Webern or the new painting of Kandinsky. The work itself having the insistence of the formal. So much depended upon seeing what was being done. Charged with spring. With the spring of a new poetics. The sequence of discrete, sharply drawn, contrasting poems that are in turn parts of something else, elements thruout of a melodic structure. That can include (as the new art of the collage begins to include):

Wrigley's, appendicitis, John Marin:
skyscraper soup—

or after "The Sea," "Underneath the sea where it is dark / there is no edge / so two—," comes XXI "The Red Wheelbarrow." For upon the "so much depends" and upon the "red wheel / barrow" the imagination must have a heightened apprehension of what form means to take hold.

A year of achievement. Surely he must have known what he had done. But it was a year of rancor for Williams too, for what he had done in *Spring and All,* to give simple things a power in the imagination, to compose so in the pure exhilaration of a formal feeling, was not recognized by those closest to him in poetry. Pound, writing on "Dr. Williams' Position" in 1928, does not mention *Spring and All,* and he seems to be defending an art in its lapse. "Very well, he does not 'conclude'"; Pound writes: "his work has been 'often formless,' 'incoherent,' opaque, obscure, obfuscated, truncated, etc."

Williams had struck out to make a new claim for form and it had not been recognized. More than that, the impact of *Spring and All* was obliterated by the timeliness, the *mise en scène,* the very usable attitudes and conclusions of *The Waste Land.*

The Waste Land, as it seemed to the literati of 1922 to voice most to their time, appears now as a period charade; with put-on voices and some epitome of modernism-1922 played against cultural tones, orchestrated with Edgar Allan Poe and the Vedas. The "O O O O that Shakespeherian Rag—/ It's so elegant / So intelligent" we all recognize as a knowing touch of the artist, a stylish manoeuvre.

The modernism-1922 is there in *Spring and All,* in the hey-ding-ding tough-voice of "Shoot It Jimmy!" and "Rapid Transit"

To hell with you and your poetry—

cuts in. But it is there an authentic part of the conflict the poet knows, in its own rights, as the red wheelbarrow is. For what it is. An insistence in the poem.

Yet . . .

Eliot must be part of our picture. He worried about social forms, about being in good form. He was never quite sure about the form, the beginning and the end of that first long poem. About what belonged. As he worried too about who and what belonged in the right thing, in literature, in the true establishment. About what to include. "Do you advise printing 'Gerontion' as a prelude in book or pamphlet form?" he writes Pound: "Perhaps better omit Phlebas also??? Certainly omit miscellaneous pieces." "The *poem,*" Pound wrote Eliot, "ends with the

'Shantih, shantih, shantih'." A period charade? But it was the first poem in which the American mind lay so mediumistically open to the wastes of Europe's agony. "The great catastrophe to our letters," Williams recalls in his *Autobiography:*

> I felt at once that it had set me back twenty years, and I'm sure it did. Critically Eliot returned us to the classroom just at the moment when I felt that we were on the point of an escape to matters much closer to the essence of a new art form itself—rooted in the locality which should give it fruit . . . I had to watch him carry my world off with him, the fool, to the enemy . . .

Yet . . . "This is not to say that Eliot has not, indirectly, contributed much to the emergence of the next step in metrical construction, but if he had not turned away from the direct attack here, in the western dialect, we might have gone ahead much faster."

"He might have become our adviser, even our hero," Williams puts it. But he left the American language, the speech of childhood, the common speech—not for English, but for the language of English literature.

The footnotes may have done the damage, as Eliot believed later. They sent readers to look up the sources, not to find the fountain of feeling back of the poem, but to add to their know-all. For a new class in America that now fills our departments of English, bent upon self-improvement, anxious about what was the right book to refer to, Eliot, having his own like proprieties, became a mentor. "He returned us to the classroom." *The Waste Land* with its contrasts of an upper cultured world in its anxious aristocracy, "staying at the arch-duke's, my cousin's," to "go south in the winter," or sitting as the Lady does in "A Game of Chess," uneasily, in a movie set of traditional rich decor, with another world always threatening to show itself, to show the culture up—dead who will not stay buried, songs that are "'Jug Jug' to dirty ears"—this contrast fit and fed the literary needs of new young men in the Universities who were no longer climbing in society but climbing in culture, haunted by a world they had come from where their people had not read Kyd or Webster.

Eliot represented a high sophistication, as Noel Coward represented a low sophistication for those who were not serious-minded. He gave a histrionic remove. The poem suffered in its very success. It had been cut and reorganized to succeed, and had lost in its conscious form whatever unconscious form had made for the confusion of sequence, the "miscellaneous pieces" that did not seem to fit. "These fragments I have shored against my ruins." Out of whatever real ruin that threatened, Pound and Eliot had agreed finally upon the monumental artifice of a ruin, a ruin with an outline. "Complimenti, you bitch," Pound writes Eliot: "I am wracked by the seven jealousies, and cogitating an excuse for always exuding my deformative secretions in my own stuff, and never getting an outline. I go into nacre and objets d'art."

The heart of the poem was the unbearable mixing of things. The ruins were the ruins rising from adultery and rage, "when the human engine waits / Like a taxi throbbing waiting," of the cuckold cursing "Co co rico" and of finding the way thru, the meaning of what must be undergone. The agony of the adulterous marriage is seen as the agony of the earth in the corruption and desire of Spring. The curse burns the earth back and then in the waste land there is finally the prayer for rain. The Shantih shantih shantih at the close is the cry of the stricken heart.

In the fashionable reading the *mise en scène* took over. The fame of the poet itself had triumphed over the pain of the poem. Eliot was not, in the outcome, stricken but celebrated. The poem, once the Depression years were there, seemed to be an historical prophecy. And in the twenties, in circles like the little group that inhabits Mary Butts's *Armed with Madness,* the game of the poem was taken up in a social magic, the charging of things with symbolic powers, the ritual mixture of Christianity and another cult of adulterous suffering, with the help of the new cult of psychoanalysis. "The glasses turn to chalices," Pound had written off gleefully to Eliot in those initial letters:

> The glasses turn to chalices
> In his fumbling analysis

The Waste Land, anyway, is part of our story. In my first years at the University of California, in 1937 and 1938, when there was no knowledge at all—if there is any now—of H.D.'s post-Imagist work, *Palimpsest, Red Roses for Bronze,* or *Ion,* in the reading lists of modern lit., when William Carlos Williams was unknown, and Ezra Pound with his *Cantos* relegated to the dubious territory of the "experimental" along with Stein and *Finnegans Wake;* Eliot and *The Waste Land* were established, along with Archibald MacLeish and W. H. Auden. With the difference—and so it is part of our story—that back of the literary aspect of the poem was another aspect, back of the respectability there was something shady. A rite, a dramatization of life, that was something more.

William Carlos Williams could take Eliot as his challenge, and against the cult of Europe, in the year of *The Hollow Men* 1925, seek to define the issue with *In the American Grain.* Against the Old World. Red Eric. "Rather the ice than their way: to take what is mine by single strength," he begins. "The worst is that weak, still, somehow, they are strong: they in effect have the power, by hook or by crook."

Did he see his own lot in Edgar Allan Poe, an exile in his homeland? "But in poetry he was at the edge—there was nothing—":

> Here in poetry, where it is said 'we approach the gods,' Poe was caught, instead, in his time . . .
>
> Had he lived in a world where love throve, his poems might have grown differently. But living where he did, surrounded as he was by that world of unreality, a formless 'population'—drifting and feeding—a huge terror possessed him.
>
> Disarmed, in his poetry the place itself comes through. This is the New World. It is this that it does, as if—

That year H.D. published a *Collected Poems.* She had been known in *Poetry* and in *The Egoist* since that moment in 1912 when Ezra Pound had written off to Harriet Monroe "it is in the laconic speech of the Imagistes, even if the subject is classic," as an Imagist. She had been featured in Pound's *Des Imagistes,* and then with her husband, Richard Aldington, had taken part in the later Imagist Anthologies of 1915, 1916, 1917. The word was set in whatever public mind: H.D., Imagist. Miss May Sinclair had said in *The Egoist* that H.D. was *the* Imagist. That was 1914. It did not mean what it has come to mean. In the confusion of Amy Lowell's sponsorship, the movement came to include impressionism, not a heightening but a broadening of sensitivity. The taut line of H.D.'s verse was coupled now in the uninformed mind with the loosely conceived line of popularizers. Certain poems—"Sea Rose" or "Heat" or "Orchard"—became set pieces with "Patterns" among anthologizers. For H.D. in the public mind seemed a more refined Amy Lowell, capturing images.

Writing on *Sea Garden* in 1917, John Gould Fletcher said: "To penetrate H.D.'s inner meaning, it is only necessary that we approach her poetry with an open and responsive mind." Imagist, Imagist, Imagist—the cuckoo sang in the ears of the day from his anthology nest. "It is really about the soul," Fletcher warned, "or the primal intelligence, or the *Nous,* or whatever we choose to call that link that binds us to the unseen and uncreated." But the possibility that the image was no mere impression but had to do with the Platonic image or might come full round to the *Imago Christi* went unheeded.

Then there was, for those who saw beyond the "Imagism," the cult of something called Greece. Along with her earliest poems appeared translations from Euripides, *Iphigeneia in Aulis* and *Hippolytus.*

Artemis dominates: "She fronts the coast." Say it is no more than a translation, a task set to learn the lineaments and spirit of Euripides. The "we" in H.D. will always then be in part the choral consciousness of the Greek drama; the way "we" are a true folk, and our individual fates appear to us as if they were enacted upon a stage for our common sense as audience. There is an "I" each of us, as a member of a chorus of citizens, artists, or folk witnesses, has:

I crossed sand-hills.
I stand among the sea-drift before Aulis

a knowledge of the people. "At least H.D. has lived with these things since childhood," Pound says in that letter to Harriet Monroe. And the chorus tells "what happened"; the myth, the hearsay, comes from them. The heroes or the participants in the great fate do not see the myth—what the hearsay tells. They are projections of what the chorus fears will happen.

But Iphigeneia commanding the chorus:

Stand silent, you Greeks.
The fire kindles.

is also the inspired actor in the play. She is the genius, fired by the chorus, and thus hints go out of a likeness to the genius of the poem itself:

For I come to do sacrifice,
To break the might of the curse,
To honour the queen, if she permit,
The great one, with my death.

And out from Iphigeneia's "death," from her "fame":

. . . spears will clash in the contest,

the waves dash upon the coasts of Chalkis. Remembering, "She fronts the coast."

In 1916 "The Shrine" appeared in *Some Imagist Poets* with the subscription "She Watches Over the Sea." The "She" of the poem may be the lure, that has grandeur too, of a woman, a *femme fatale:*

It was evil—evil
when they found you,
when the quiet men looked at you—

Certainly the sequences of "shelter," "full and sweet," "tempting the quiet," "evil" and then:

But you—you are unsheltered,
cut with the weight of wind—
you shudder when it strikes,

. . . .
when the tides swirl
your boulders cut and wreck

all of this can, and does, once we recognize the possibility, more than an age of an exposed headland, refer to a persona or mask of the emotional regularity in women, of sudden "treacherous" moods and passions that make Scylla—or here may it not be Artemis-Scylla—a prototype. "She" of the Shrine does appear in all her savage splendor back of Iphigeneia.

> You brought me to the Greek light
> And I will not hold you guilty
> For my death

Iphigeneia says, addressing her father. But some ambiguous play may move here, for at first I mistook the address and had thought it was the Goddess she addressed:

> Alas, day, you brought light,
> You trailed splendour,
> You showed us god:

"Artemis, rejoicer in blood-sacrifice," the chorus calls the Goddess. As Iphigeneia volunteers to the sacrifice, she enters her "fate," which is also her "fame"; she becomes both the blood-sacrifice and the rejoicer in blood sacrifice.

"Alas," the chorus cries:

>   she steps forward
> To destroy Ilium and the Phrygians.
> . . . .
> She comes to meet death,
> To stain the altar of the goddess

Where we may also read: "In order that there be a stain on the altar of the goddess."

H.D. found her meter, drew her characteristic taut intense line from her translations, as she drew too upon the Melic poets for the lyric mode she wanted, as in painting Picasso drew upon classic sources. They were—Pound or H.D. or Joyce—most modern in their appropriation of the past. The stylization of their verse had its counterpart in Satie's *Socrate* or the Greek style of Cocteau. We have only to consider how close to the spirit of *Sea Garden* or *Heliodora* Braque's late drawings for Hesiod are. Or the "Alexandrian" portraits of Derain.

But H.D. found in Euripides not only form but content. They were one. And in Iphigeneia, Helen, Thetis, Artemis, Helios, Achilles she saw the personae or masks of her own life story. In the work of her old age, in *Helen in Egypt,* she weaves, as ever, the revelation of "these things since childhood" in the terms of Homer and Euripides.

Greece in the story is the homeland or mother-land, where, if we read as we do in dreams, we see that it is America that was H.D.'s Greece. She was most American in her "Hellenism," as Edward Sapir saw in his review of *Collected Poems* in 1926: "The impatience of the rhythms and the voluptuous harshness and bleakness of the sea and shore and woodland images manifest it. Such violent restraint, such a passionate pleasure in the beauty of the denuded scene and the cutting thrust, themselves but inverse symbols of caress, could only develop in a culture that hungers for what it despises." It was "in the American grain."

But there were few who read deeply. For most there was, past the "image" thing, the "Greek perfection" thing. She had found her style not only in translating but in pruning. "While the sense of the Greek has been strictly kept," she wrote in *The Egoist* in 1915: "it is necessary to point out that the repetition of useless ornamental adjectives is a heavy strain on a translator's ingenuity. This is only one instance from many where the Homeric Epithet degenerates into what the French call a *remplissage*—an expression to fill up a line. Such phrases have been paraphrased or omitted." And in her *Ion of Euripides* in 1937 she notes: "The broken, exclamatory or evocative *vers-libre* which I have chosen to translate the two-line dialogue, throughout the play, is the exact antithesis of the original."

There are times when she herself characterizes her art as cold and removed—what those who denigrated her Hellenism most accused her of—as in "Wash of Cold River":

to mould a clear
and frigid statue;

rare, of pure texture,
beautiful space and line,
marble to grace
your inaccessible shrine.

For most readers, the Hellenic thing in H.D. was all "clear," "frigid," "pure," "beautiful," "inaccessible." It set her apart.

•

Writing to Williams in 1916, H.D. pled against his impurities: "I trust you will not hate me for wanting to delete from your poem all the flippancies . . . I think there is *real* beauty—the real beauty is a rare and sacred thing in this generation—in all the pyramid, Ashur-ban-i-pal bits and in the Fiesole and in the wind at the very last . . . I feel the hey-ding-ding touch running through your poem a derivative tendency which to me, is not *you*—not your very self . . . "

The words rankled. "We look for deliverance," Williams came back, "from the desolation of a flat Hellenic perfection of style."

"Hilda Doolittle before she began to write poetry," he tells us in the 1920 Prologue to *Kora in Hell,* "or at least before she began to show it to anyone would say: 'You're not satisfied with me, are you Billy? There's something lacking, isn't there?' When I was with her my feet always seemed to be sticking to the ground while she would be walking on the tips of the grass stems."

When was that? "One in particular struck me," he writes home to his brother in 1905:

She is tall, about as tall as I am, young, about eighteen and, well, not round and willowy, but rather bony, no that doesn't express it, just a little clumsy but all to the mustard . . .

We went over fields, through woods, climbed fences, jumped streams, and laughed and talked till everyone simply had to get into the game. Well, this lasted hours, then Miss Doolittle, that's her name, found some flowers and sat down beside them to protect them from the rest of the party. I sat down beside her and the rest passed on. We began talking of flowers, when she said she knew a place where hepaticas grew so thick the ground was blue with them. I said I would like to see it, and we being at the tail end of the crowd turned aside and went into the woods. Needless to say we lost the crowd and had a great two hours walk by ourselves. Oh, Ed, but she is a fine girl, no false modesty and all that, she is abso-lutely free and innocent. We talked of the finest things: of Shakespeare, of flowers, trees, books, & pictures and meanwhile climbed fences and walked through woods and climbed little hills till it began to grow just dusky when we arrived at our destination. We had by this time, as you imagine, gotten pretty well acquainted. She said I was Rosalind in *As You Like It* and she was Celia, so I called her that, although her real name is Hilda . . . I got home at twelve, covered with some mud, a little glory and oceans of a fine comfortable happy feeling inside of me somewhere.

Williams was 22 that year. And in the manly earnest speech of the letter there is another youthfulness or innocence, of America itself before the War.

In the *Autobiography* in 1951 the picture has changed or something has been betrayed in the picture:

There was about her that which is found in wild animals at times, a breathless impatience, almost a silly unwillingness to come to the point. She had a young girl's giggle and shrug which somehow in one so tall and angular seemed a little absurd.

Ezra was wonderfully in love with her and I thought exaggerated her beauty ridiculously. To me she was just a good guy and I enjoyed, uncomfortably, being with her.

'For God's sake,' I told him, 'I'm not in love with Hilda nor she with me. She's your girl and I know it. Don't be an ass.'

Once I went alone for a walk with Hilda, one April I suppose, in that really lyrical Upper Darby country of those days. I particularly remember the grape hyacinths in a gully beside the road, deep blue, a flower with which I was completely unfamiliar. Hilda told me she was studying Greek and that she had heard that I too was writing poetry. That hurt. It wasn't something I wanted to talk about, for as a matter of fact I had in my own opinion produced nothing. Ezra, of course, was the hero.

Oh, well, she added, to help me along I suppose, I've been writing too. Some translations, she added—to escape blame. We wandered along. She with the back of her skirt dragging, no hips, no nothing, just Hilda, through the deep grass, over fences, barbed wire (I remember how Edmonson once told me, after a group walk one day, a fellow can't help but look sometimes! she was that careless).

As we went along—talking of what?—I could see that we were in for a storm and suggested that we turn back.

Ha!

She asked me if when I started to write I had to have my desk neat and everything in its place, if I had to prepare the paraphernalia, or if I just sat down and wrote.

I said I liked to have things neat.

Ha, ha!

She said that when she wrote it was a great help, she thought and practiced it, if taking some ink on her pen, she'd splash it on her clothes to give her a feeling of freedom and indifference toward the mere means of the writing.

Well—if you like it.

There were some thunderclaps to the west and I could see that it really was going to rain damned soon and hard. We were at the brink of a grassy pasture facing west, quite in the open, and the wind preceding the storm was in our faces. Of course it was her party and I went along with her.

Instead of running or even walking toward a tree Hilda sat down in the grass at the edge of the hill and let it come.

'Come, beautiful rain,' she said, holding out her arms. 'Beautiful rain, welcome.' And I behind her feeling not inclined to join in her mood. And let me tell you it rained, plenty. It didn't improve her beauty or my opinion of her—but I had to admire her if that's what she wanted.

"Hellenism," Williams wrote in the Prologue to *Kora in Hell,* "especially the modern sort, is too staid, too chilly, too little fecundative to impregnate my world."

The reproof of H.D. rankled. And the other sore spot of the *Autobiography*—Eliot's role—rankles here too. Before *The Waste Land* then. "T. S. Eliot and his *Love Song of J. Alfred Prufrock.*" Was it Pound's unqualified admiration for Eliot? "For what the statement is worth, Mr. Eliot's work interests me more than that of any other poet now writing in English," Pound had declared in reviewing *Prufrock* in 1917. And there may have been a cut-back that hit Williams more directly: "His men in shirt-sleeves, and his society ladies, are not a local manifestation; they are the stuff of our modern world, and true of more countries than one." "And there is always some everlasting Polonius of Kensington forever to rate highly his eternal Eliot," Williams exclaims.

III.

The first, the opening scene with its grouping, the three young would-be poets—H.D., Ezra Pound, Williams—remains a kind of announcement of the drama of modern poetry. Germinal, germane. Where we see these had their own Ion, firstness of spirit, and a flower. William Carlos Williams in "Postlude" with its

> O, prayers in the dark!
> O, incense to Poseidon!
> Calm in Atlantis.

or in "First Praise":

> Lady of dusk-wood fastnesses,
>   Thou art my Lady.
> I have known the crisp, splintering leaf-tread with thee on before,

is close indeed to H.D. Seems almost to answer or to belong to "Pursuit":

> this and a dead leaf-spine,
> split across,
> show where you passed.

"(which to me stands, a Nike, supreme among your poems)," H.D. wrote of "Postlude" in that letter of 1916.

"Oh, I have picked up magic in her nearness," Pound sings in "A Virginal." The volume the poem appears in, *Riposts,* 1912, is dedicated to William Carlos Williams.

> To sheathe me half in half the things that sheathe her.
> No, no! Go from me. I have still the flavour,
> Soft as spring wind that's come from birchen bowers.
> Green come the shoots, aye April in the branches,
> As winter's wound with her sleight hand she staunches,
> Hath of the trees a likeness of the savour:
> As white their bark, so white this lady's hours.

In the end, that germinal grouping will reappear. The War Trilogy, *The Pisan Cantos, Paterson*—and more especially later poems of Williams like "To Daphne and Virginia" or "Asphodel, That Greeny Flower"— can be compared because they are of a kind, having that common generation, that first spirit or Ion of the beginning scene, revealed at last.

So, "the box odor" from "To Daphne and Virginia" may be our first flower too:

> The box odor
>   is the odor of that of which
>   partaking separately,
> each to herself
>   I partake also
>   .   .   separately.

But meanwhile there are, "sanctioned by the form of the play," divisions, separations. In the Imagist period itself, when Pound, H.D., and Williams first appear as a group in *The Egoist,* there are new groupings. Pound is close to Yeats, as Williams and H.D. are not. H.D. is close to Lawrence, and Williams in time finds a kinship with Lawrence, as Pound never does. "Each represents an entrance"—Eliot enters the picture—"an exit"—H.D. leaves the picture—"a change in inner mood and external grouping of the characters."

In London, always keeping his correspondence with Williams, Pound goes on, after Imagism, to his "Vortex," a new grouping where Williams never fits. "If I am introducing anybody to Kulchur," Pound writes in *Kulchur,* "let 'em take the two phases, the nineteen teens, Gaudier, Wyndham L. and I as we were in *Blast,* and the next phase, the 1920's."

"The sorting out, the *rappel à l'ordre,* and thirdly the new synthesis, the totalitarian." For Ezra Pound in the twenties Eliot, Joyce, and Wyndham Lewis gave definition. *The Cantos, The Waste Land, Ulysses* and *The Apes of God* formed the *Quadrivium* of a modern education.

In New York another grouping appears, defined by their mutual sympathies. It was not a program. They were not concerned with culture, with a Kultur, but with the art of the poem. Amateurs in a sense. Looking back, we find them standing out in *Others,* the American anthology of 1917: William Carlos Williams, Marianne Moore, and Wallace Stevens. "One has to keep looking for poetry as Renoir looked for colors," Stevens writes to Williams after *Al Que Quiere* in 1920, "in old walls, wood-work and so on. Your place is"

> —among children
> Leaping around a dead dog.

The group in London were culture-heroes. Not only was the Imagism of Eliot, Pound, and H.D. an attack upon the literature but upon the deeper culture of England, forcing new roots in the revival of ancient matter. The counter-group in America were artists, relating themselves now to an aesthetic, to the poem as an art object. There would be the objectivism of Williams's work in the 1920s; there would be Wallace Stevens's fictive musics and still-lifes; there would be Marianne Moore's found objects and practised connoisseurship. Where Pound also always had a secret or not so secret aesthetic allegiance. The poem, for him too, was a work of art, to be compared with Brancusi or Bartók. For didn't he have, beyond the purposes of his *Kulchur,* his "nacre and objets d'art"? Where Eliot's verse had literary overtones, Pound's had luminosities and the musical phrase.

In the groupings of Eliot, Pound, H.D. in London, and Williams, Stevens, Marianne Moore in New York, I am led on by something else at play, a dynamic figure. Is there "a heart-shaped space," some all but intangible form that we sense as something happening in the separations and reformations, the overlappings and differences among the members. Once the whole play is there, with its prologue in America, "in that really lyrical Upper Darby country of those days," "before the War," where Williams, Pound, H.D. meet in one grouping, and Marianne Moore is near but not included, and then, its first scene in the Imagist Movement, in the four years or so between 1912 and 1914; with its epilogue in the second configuration in the Second World War, each of the members is seen in a new division between those who are to go on to a major phase in their old age that will change the ground or culture of Poetry itself, and those who are seen as having no dialectical role. Under fire of life's either coming into a new creative phase in old age, larger and deeper, challenging a new generation of poets, or coming to the summation of the work of a personal artist as a thing in itself, the work of Williams, like that of Pound and H.D., takes on new scope. Williams, in this second exposure, is revealed as no connoisseur of the poem as art object in itself but as a visionary, reawakening in poetry once more transcendent themes and implications. As if in the dynamics of some ideoplasty there were an exchange between the two superimposed configurations in which the heart of poetry appears, Eliot now belongs clearly on the side of Stevens and Marianne Moore. He regrets the Notes to *The Waste Land* that had suggested any involvement with Jessie Weston's *Ritual to Romance* or the cult of the Tarot cards, and in his *Four Quartets* we find that even religious matters are literary in their character, having the proper artistic distance. In the thing happening between the two figures is a central thread, a germinal figure, in which the emerging task of our own poetry is given.

Threads are spun out and are woven, from event into event. Hands work the dancing shuttles of a close net to make things real, to realize what is happening. A tapestry of a life appears in the mesh of many lives, a play. But just as when we weave a complex of lines a cloud or atmosphere appears, a texture or cloth, something more than the threads told, and out of that texture appear, not only the figures we were translating into our design, but other figures of the ground itself; so a "life" appears in the work itself. The weaving or the painting or the writing is "subjective," is an act out of however we can do it; the "subject matter" is "objective," is some thing or event as actual as ourselves which we reach out to capture, to draw into a texture with ourselves. In the medium, our work and this thing become mixed, changed then. A ground appears as a new condition of what we are doing.

Say we work loosely; we do not know quite how to secure our object, and gaps appear in the work. They have become, these makeshift elements, qualities of the whole, of the real. "The hey-ding-ding touch *was* derivative," Williams writes in his Prologue to *Kora in Hell*, "but it filled a gap that I did not know how better to fill at the time."

The stars are a fishing net, as men fish in heaven for what they are. The design was to fill in the gap of the sky, of space and time. But then, man has so shaped himself in his imagination of the stars, that

Astrology, even when we know more, know how falsely the stars are shown in its diagrams, shows us still a typology of character. "It might be said," Williams goes on about the hey-ding-ding touch, "that that touch is the prototype of the improvisations."

History is a close-weave. Fishing for the event.

The dragon is created in the creation of the net. It is as She is bound that we trace out the figure of Tiamat. So, too, the imagination is flung out to come into its figures. Naming actual things, persons, places, and times about us, we make our terms in which our design will be realized. Just beyond "our" design, because we do not ourselves name these things but come to these things thru names given in the beginnings of man's story, as the light of a star comes to us across "light-years," the thing in the word comes to us across "language-years." All the things of our lives came to us, first, before words, into focus, out of a commune of things, an already human world around us, where we were already happening; came out of a surrounding of words we did not understand but came to understand. Where there are meanings, here, too, we send the threads out towards one point, draw them back into another.

When we first come into the attraction of words in poetry, it is the craft of the net, the novelty of usage, the knot effect, often, that strikes us. We mistake the effect for the art. Style and signature most valuable, and the direct, uncharacterized speech, uninteresting. The "flippancy," the up-to-dateness or regular guy voice of Williams's language—the risk of those knots, the craft, the thing posed—appears interesting in itself. To be original. To challenge the communal thing. Will he make it?

To tie fancy knots and to contrive a greater show of our abilities. But all these original knottings are mistaken, are "hey-ding-ding"—"lead nowhere" the common sense is—if they are all novelty, things of 1920, not lasting forces. The knots that are flames are not originalities, but origins.

"I think you have the 'spark'," H.D. writes in her letter to Williams, "and when you speak *direct* are a poet." The *spark* lies in, is, the word wherever it is spoken direct, directs what we are then, for we involve ourselves in what is said. Direct. Even this being Bill Williams is a persona, a mask of a man. The interesting effects, the devices that give personality, are part of it; but they are not the work of the other, the poet, whose urgency it is to speak regardless of this person. In poetry we strive to make things real by working with every word as coming direct from an inner voice, as the immediate condition of or presence of the poem itself.

For the knots of the net are actual suns; are in poetry, as in dreams, directives in the imagination between actual events and man's self, are terms of the real, are when-wheres that co-existing in the word and in the world make actual events real. We sense the residue—the culture of Eliot, the slang of Williams, the pedantry of Pound, the remove of H.D.—as impediments in the individual nature to the imagined free voice.

A residue? or an impediment? But we move upon a stage where we must act our unknown "selves" in parts that are given by groupings, to hold our own and to correspond with other members of the scene. And the scene changes. In each grouping our part is somehow altered. What is our own and what is our correspondence we must dare as we can. The actor has his role given him. And the poet too has something given—what the poet is, how to enact the poet. The concept and the project is his creation. Analogous to the individual personality, but different, even contending, for the poet is a person of an order beyond the present scene or grouping. Attendant thereto. To the time and place. The poet of the company. The poet of the hour.

IV.

"Every hour, every moment," H.D. tells us in *Tribute to the Angels,* "has its specific attendant Spirit."

The Renaissance Platonist Ficino had designed a magic to evoke the powers of angelic orders, Regents of the Planets. Incenses, tones, colors, the feel of woods or stones, were organized in a music or rite to awaken the senses or open the senses to shapes and presences beyond the sensual. Each hour had its particular genius, became then a possible work of the art:

but *I make all things new,*
said He of the seven stars,

In the "Tribute," the seven stars are, as stars are in the Cabbalistic imagination of Ficino, angelic powers: *Raphael, Gabriel, Azrael, Uriel, Annael, Michael, Zadkiel.* They are, in their hours, guardians.

The clock ticking becomes the Lady knocking at the door of consciousness:

and she was standing there
actually, at the turn of the stair.

It does not seem so out-of-the-way when we take it that the thought of the Lady came to her:

that I lay awake now on my bed,
that the luminous light

was the phosphorescent face
of my little clock

and the faint knocking
was the clock ticking.

We are most familiar with this way of the subconscious to use things happening about us to project or to evoke its own forms. But in "Sagesse" IV, it is another time magic, not unconscious now but conscious; not using the clock, "this curious mechanical perfection," in itself, but using its hours in relation to the old orientation of the star map and the figures drawn from the stars that present themselves. Waking in the dark alone, she is not in the dark, she is not alone.

An owl hooted out in the darkness,
so the angel came—what angel and what name?

is it Tara, *Dieu fontaine de sagesse*
and the angel Ptébiou? it was his hour

or near his hour, what did he say?

This angel is an attribute of God. The old gods and the new, the Greek world and the Christian-Judaic world, have been found in the synthesis of a poetic-theurgy. As in the Cabbalistic system, the source of the voice, the self, is hidden. These angels-gods-guardians are attendants of the poetry itself, the voice in its manifestation. Patrons of the hour of writing, of naming the patron of the hour.

The thought of Ezra Pound might have come as an owl hooted in the darkness. Her mind was no nearer to that other grouping of the powers of poetry, to 1905 or 1912, no farther, than it was from this new grouping. In the poem "Stars Wheel in Purple" let the thought of Williams, Pound, Lawrence, and the ghost of her Roman lover Aldington come in the naming of Hesperus, Aldebaran, Sirius, Mars. I should be more bold, for anyone who is not with me here will long ago have ceased to read the book. They are not less real, more real, in the real of the poem than the stars, or these others, the powers that attend the poet.

Where angels appear in the orders of the poem—as they do in Rilke's *Duino Elegies* or in these poems of H.D.—we remember too in reading their dedications that patrons, Rilke's friend, the Princess Marie von Thurn und Taxis-Hohenlohe, or H.D.'s friend, Bryher, are also "angels." And we see between the higher angel of the imagination and the lower angel of our everyday world, some likeness. We see the figure of the medieval lord as donor kneeling in the presence of *his* Virgin and Child or *his* crucifixion, having a share, a donation, in the work of the artist.

Just as when we wake at some hour of the night and find ourselves not disoriented in the dark, but in the thought of some attribute of God, a particular angel, to see things in that light; so we may find ourselves in the course of a poem also in the thought of some attribute of our Life, a particular person, having also his or her particular time.

These dedications in The War Trilogy—to Bryher, to Osbert Sitwell, to Norman Holmes Pearson—form a part of the concept then, for they are human sponsors of the thought of the poem, just as the seven angels appear as supernatural sponsors of the thought of the poem. These patrons stand in turn as sponsors of the artist's soul, godmothers or godfathers we call them.

Pound had once stood as such a sponsor, when in the high baptism of poetry he named H.D. and a literary movement in one: "*Imagiste.*" Where she was born into a new identity, that lasted no more than four years—but the name stuck. In the despair and fever of her broken marriage, the still birth of 1915 "from shock and the repercussions of war news"—"the death of my father followed closely on the news of the death of my older brother in France"—and then the second confinement of 1919, close upon death, stricken with pneumonia, and in the birth of her child, Perdita: H.D., Imagiste, died, and was delivered to life again. Delivered from her old life by Bryher.

The *mythos,* the telling of it, how it is made up is part of our text; the *dromenon,* how it is enacted in the poet's life is part, what she went thru in the time of the poem. What they tell and what they do, the text and the action, form in turn a *rite de passage,* a way of survival for the poet in the personal life. In *Palimpsest* or in the novelette "Narthex" (published in *The Second American Caravan* in 1928) H.D. begins to tell the myth of what she went thru in 1915 and 1919.

"We travel far in thought, in imagination or in the realm of memory," she writes in *Tribute to Freud:* "Events happened *as* they happened, not all of them of course but here and there a memory or a fragment of a dream-picture is actual, is real, is like a work of art or is a work of art." Then, just beyond this I find: "For things had happened in my life, pictures, 'real dreams'"—thruout it is the *reality* of a dream, of a memory, of things that happened, that is H.D.'s concern. And that reality lay in a nexus of "actual psychic or occult experiences that were superficially, at least, outside the province of established psychoanalysis" and of psychoanalytic experiences—the novelettes of the mid-twenties, before her analysis, are psychoanalytic-minded; it was the reality of what poetry was. Life, itself, it seemed always to H.D. was "like a work of art" or was "a work of art"—a poetry. What is important here is that she took whatever she could, whatever hint of person or design, color or line, over into her "work." What was real was what entered the picture.

"Flagrantly creative, how could they endure you?" she addresses Rico (Lawrence) in *Bid Me to Live.* "Creative" here means making-things-up. "Key-of-heaven tree," Miss Kerr had told her Rico had named the tree in her garden. "Did you make it up, the name of that tree?" she asks in the letter to Rico that she will not send but is making up. "Did you make up Miss Kerr telling me the story, with the signed Henry James above her writing-desk and the petunia curtains?"

In the life of every "creative" writer some life they make up becomes more real than whatever was there before. "Rafe is not the Marble Faun, not even a second-rate Dionysus," Julia writes. Richard Aldington remains untouched by H.D.'s imagination. "I wrote that cyclamen poem for him in Dorset, at Corfe Castle, where I wrote your Orpheus. But you are right. He is not Dionysus, you are not Orpheus." But Lawrence, a creator himself, can be Orpheus; as H.D. can appear in the person of Eurydice.

So Bryher delivering H.D. from her old life into a new enters a picture, becomes one of the figures, not only in the personal life, but, because that life is the matter of a poetry, in the design of a poet. We recognize her in the young Roman, Julia Cornelia Augusta, who attends Hipparchia in *Palimpsest,* whose "small firm hand, detached and hard as ivory, dragged her back, back when she was lax and floating going—gone—." The old nurse had wakened her: "The young lady has been here the last three days to see you." "'*Young* lady?'" "Worse. She saw now. One of the preposterous new-rich who wanted to polish off (for court purposes) her accent."

In "Narthex," we see her as Gareth, sometime in the mid-twenties. "Say in the soul I want something," Raymonde Ransome thinks, "black or white, good or bad, anything just so you want it enough, up or down and something (with Faust it was Mephistopheles) will answer. Perversely at that moment Katherine answered." But Gareth too is an angel here, for she too had answered in a time of need. "Katherine, Gareth, they were two antique coin sides, Katherine one side, towered head, some Asiatic goddess, many breasted, something monstrous that yet holds authenticity, Gareth the other side, boy Emperor, slightly undershot little chin that gave a baby frailty to the hard clear profile . . . and that frightening intensity . . . late Greek, Graeco-Phoenician" or they are guardians of a door. "Two-fold initiation said the keeper of the gateway, you want to get through a door, doors are Janus-faced."

Gareth (Bryher) can seem to Raymonde like the angel driving Eve forth from the garden of her affair with the serpent and the apple, Katherine and Mordant, as Gareth rescues Raymonde from her London troubles. "Garry like a sword flashing through late London mist . . . had flayed her forth, out of the 'sticky drug of the Katherine-Mordant cycle' into the wilderness." He who has a servant has a master; so too liberating angels tyrannize. Garry orders Raymonde off to d'y Vaud to write and then after three months wires for her to join her in Venice "in order to take a boat (they would discuss that later) somewhere."

"She was connected with great wealth," Robert McAlmon writes, telling of his marriage to Bryher in *Being Geniuses Together,* and in his eyes, as he titles his opening chapter "Money Breeds Complications," there were complications.

There was, ever-present, in the Ellerman household the thought of "people knowing one only for money's sake, and artists seeking to be patronized and financed." But to be patronized or financed was not exactly the same as to find a patron or to receive a patron. It seemed to Robert McAlmon that Wyndham Lewis's manner "soon became patronizing." That was another sense of the word. To look down?

Lewis wanted McAlmon to get Sir John Ellerman to patronize him as an artist. McAlmon did get Ellerman to persuade certain editors to take drawings of Lewis's, but McAlmon could go no further. Lewis couldn't understand, McAlmon tells us, "that I was walking very carefully to avoid having Sir John plan my life."

Bryher had this way of taking things over, he tells us. "I managed to slip away, but she got at the Lump" (H.D.'s child, Perdita) "and through her at H.D. She got at me too, but I knew some day soon I'd go away for good." Earlier, we find: "Bryher, with her fervor for education, had taken on the upbringing of Hilda Doolittle's infant." Bringing someone up, taking someone *over,* is different from looking down. But our patron also may "look down," as "the angels look down."

Robert McAlmon, "a coldly intense young man, with hard blue eyes," as his friend Williams describes him, "an ideal youth's figure," would not have seen our angel, for his sights, as we come to know in his writing, would brook no such nonsense. The imagination itself is "nonsense," any imagination, as far as McAlmon was concerned. He disliked mysticism, he disliked "where Joyce goes Irish-twilighty and uses words for their isolated beauty," he disliked Mary Butts's "pretence," he disliked whatever hint of this malady called imagination and could be sarcastic or angry when confronted by it. "Oh, to hell with Yeats," he explodes, "and his sugared mysticism," or sneers when writing of H.D.'s "taking up" with Freud: "It appears that Doctor Freud discovered that the lady had been shocked upon discovering her father all but killed in a tram accident when she was but ten years old. It had left an impression upon her." "Such creative and astounding imaginative insight upon the part of these psychoanalysts," he concludes, "can only leave a layman such as myself breathless with awe."

He would not have seen—where if we follow here we must see—an angel of the hour present in Bryher's taking over. He would not have gone along with the idea that some attribute of God begins its work where a young woman may act as godmother. "Post war and late war eyes (unlike the very early shattered generation)," it seems to Raymonde Ransome, "had said 'hell, what's the use?' Robin Rockway with his cap tilted with remembered flying unit grace had flung his 'hell' and his 'hell' until even Garry, stoic and sympathetic, had recoiled."

Richard Aldington, Robert McAlmon, and Bryher too, have in common a certain stubborn literal mindedness; they are post-war or late-war eyes, Romans—Marius or Julia Augusta in "Hipparchia," Freddie in "Murex," Robin Rockway and Gareth in "Narthex"—Roman lovers, Roman patrons. Pound, Lawrence, H.D.—the poets—will always be Greek. William Carlos Williams too, McAlmon says, "was inclined to go literary and nostalgic about things Greek"; and Joyce had "a precious and literary nostalgia for the Greek poetizing, word-prettifying qualities dear to Pound's heart, *melopoeia, logopoeia, phanopoeia*. That is, an interest in words as words for their evocative and suggestive qualities to the extent of being indifferent to the larger qualities of material, content-concept. . . . "

H.D.–Raymonde Ransome–Hipparchia is a Greek in exile among Romans in a Roman world. And then there are others, not Roman or Greek, but Asiatic or Egyptian: the witch Mavis at her mirror, "the incense of some banished Circe that rose in spirals toward an enchantress' cedar roof so that Greeks (thinking men) were blurred over and forgot their Greek formula" in "Murex," or Katherine and Alex Mordant, "the late over-ornate winged Sphinx" and "some bearded bull" "Ninevah"—figures of old disastrous affairs, persons of a sexual magic. And in H.D.'s consistent translation into Hellenic parallels, they are figures of the orientalizing cults in the Roman world. "In this, our present day, literary Alexandria," she had written in 1916. It was

Gareth's role, not only to rescue Raymonde from death in 1919, but after "those diplomatic dodgings with poor Rockway," "after five years' separation," to rescue Raymonde from evil in 1925 or 1926, from the very midst of this mix-up with Katherine and Mordant.

Who were they? those others? "Once when I painfully unravelled a dingy, carelessly woven strip of tapestry of cause and effect and related to him, in over-careful detail, some none-too-happy friendships," H.D. writes of Freud, "he waved it all aside . . . But why,' he asked, 'did you worry about all this? Why did you think you had to tell me? *Those two didn't count'.*"

"*Those two didn't count,*" she continues: "There were two's and two's and two's in my life." And among these, "there were two countries, America and England as it happened, separated by a wide gap in consciousness and a very wide stretch of sea." The persons in "Narthex" belong also to two interlocking figures: "They were superimposed like two mystic triangles, the two triangles that make a star, the seal of Solomon. Triangle pointing up, triangle pointing down . . . the seal of utter wisdom. Alex Mordant, Katherine, Raymonde . . . " this is the triangle not only of what Gareth calls "evil," the evil in Raymonde, and of what Raymonde thinks of as the orientalizing Greek and the emotions, but also of the pre-war world—Katherine and Mordant and Raymonde, when in their company, are *demodé,* "PreRaphaelite." Then: "Raymonde again (the Ray Bart of Gareth's predilection) Gareth and Daniel."

Later the figure returns to Raymonde's mind: "The triangle Raymonde, Daniel, Gareth was a sort of platinum-white self-luminous white thing, you couldn't dissipate it. Iron frame work of burnt out triangle of Katherine, Mordant, Raymonde being burnt out leaves residue of suffering. Gareth was insufferable." The inner war with her angel has been rising all along, and now it speaks out: "What did Gareth know of the feeling of a burnt out frame work? What did Daniel? Alex Mordant knew things, Katherine was things. Why can't Gareth leave me alone to become something of the past? . . . Why can't Gareth leave me to be played out?"

Gareth and Daniel are late-war and post-war eyes. "Garry held true, fibre and valour but with strident inhibitions enough to drive any one, let alone poor nerve-shattered Rockway, to destruction. Garry had to be like that . . . " to survive. "Garry links me up to the post-war people," Raymonde thinks, "I link Garry up to the war people. We have held on sometimes hating each other . . . as now."

Two countries, two times: H.D. ambiguously American-English, before-the-war / modern, felt her life itself as a link of a larger design, an interweaving of two areas of pattern. Two continents: the Old World and the New World. But then there was also the duality of feeling. In "Narthex," as years later in The War Trilogy, she builds interlocking patterns of her two's and three's, of fours and sevens, to compose the complex of her feelings and thought. "Classic Venice, romantic Venice (Raymonde was debauched with the whole spectacle), poster Venice, post-card Venice, Othello Venice, clap-trap stage Rialto Venice became real . . . Elizabeth Barrett Browning and Wagner and Duse and George Sand Venice (she was frankly reeling with it) came true, became so many sets of feeling to cope with."

It is this very multiphasic association that alienates Raymonde from Gareth. "Garry saw in one dimension . . . outgrown trick of pre-war Raymonde's." "Ages kept coming up into ages where they don't belong, Raymonde was stricken with it, ghost ages like the dove in the light globe, Tintoretto swings, dove-sun into his barn annunciation in the Scuolo di San Rocco." And Gareth, who does not see this way, is left out. "Propitiate Gareth," Raymonde commands herself, "get her into it." "She had spread wide wings and Garry (this was the honor of it) hadn't. Garry was sulking visibly in sun-light."

"Garry was staring at her. Be decent, Raymonde. Garry sent you the wire, got you out of vibrant, weary, over-wrought loneliness and tension. Garry paid your fare here. You're the guest of Gareth. Be decent. You have behaved horribly." But the fact remained: "Garry couldn't know, odd dissociated half relationship with Rockway, emotion and all its tangled connotations. Garry moved in one cycle, had just one dial to go by . . . Garry didn't understand emotion and all its overlayers, the seasons so to speak, marked in zodiacal symbol like those seasons now part of a sort of coronal to the madonna . . . that blue garmented love-mother with time ticking away above it."

When we read Aldington's Life for Life's Sake, McAlmon's Being

Geniuses Together, or (this year, 1963) Bryher's *Heart to Artemis,* these have in common a one-dimensional seeing, no mind for emotion's overlayers. They seem to be rivals of the poet; both Aldington and Bryher putting down Pound, uninterested finally in the poetry to which H.D.'s work belongs.

"Let Zeus Record," the sequence in homage to her angel in *Red Roses for Bronze,* may also be in propitiation. For to get her into it, H.D. had made painful disclosures of her inner ambivalence of feeling. These are poems of praise too then, not only for Bryher's loyalty, her "one dimension," in the face of H.D.'s mixed emotions, but for her attendance in a time when Love seemed dead:

> yet when Love fell
> struck down with plague and war,
> you lay white myrrh-buds
> on the darkened lintel;
>
> you fastened blossom
> to the smitten sill;

The dedication of *The Walls Do Not Fall* in 1942 is not a propitiation. In a lifetime the poetess and her patroness had come to the understanding of old companions, living in some recognition of their differences. But it is perhaps a payment of a kind, "for Karnak," a gift in return for the gift of 1923. A return.

And the poem itself begins as a letter from H.D. in London to Bryher, who was still in Switzerland in 1942. Just here: "from your (and my) old town-square"; but then, imperceptibly, it continues to be written for us, for all her readers.

V.

"for Karnak 1923"

In 1920 Bryher had made real her promise that "she would herself see that the baby was protected and cherished and she would take me to a new world, a new life." She had made Greece possible, "a new world"—but *the* New World was America, the first mother-land. In the latter part of 1920, in fact, Bryher and H.D. had gone to America, to see, as if for a last time, the old New World. So Bryher had been guardian angel, but also nurse or mid-wife, taking H.D. from her old life into a new, a second mother-land that was Greece. "My mother's name was Helen," H.D. tells us in *Tribute to Freud*. And the psychoanalyst had interpreted her desire for Greece as a desire for union with her mother. "I was physically in Greece, in Hellas (Helen). I had come home to the glory that was Greece," H.D. writes.

Geographically, this Greece was Athens or the isles, as in translating, for H.D. it was Euripides or Sappho. But in time, Hellenism meant for H.D. not Athens, the classic period, but the great Hellenic dispersion after Alexander—the city of Alexandria then, and Egypt. Her Hellenic time belongs to the stage that Gilbert Murray in his *Five Stages of Greek Religion* called "The Failure of Nerve," in the orientalizing Greek world between the third century B.C. and the second century A.D.

"The world of Hellenism was a changed and enlarged world," Professor W. W. Tarn writes in his *Hellenistic Civilisation:* "Though the particularism of the Greek city-state was to remain vigorous enough in fact, it had broken down in theory; it was being replaced by universalism and its corollary, individualism. The idea emerges of an oecumene or 'inhabited world' as a whole, the common possession of civilised men." "It is a rise of asceticism, of mysticism, in a sense, of pessimism," it seems to Murray. "The personality of the individual has free scope," Professor Tarn observes, but Murray sees: "a loss of self-confidence, of hope in this life and of faith in normal human effort; a despair of patient enquiry, a cry for infallible revelation; an indifference to the welfare of the state, a conversion of the soul to God."

For the Hellenistic Greek, such as Plutarch, Egypt was the source of wisdom, at Sais, at Karnak. Helen, in H.D.'s *Helen in Egypt,* is hidden away in an Amen-temple that may be at Karnak, in a "mother" back of Greece, back of America. And in *Palimpsest,* the book in which H.D. in the mid-twenties sought to delineate her Hellenistic consciousness related to the modern period, Ermy in "Murex" is a Jew, but she is also "The East. The lotos of Buddha." She is "dead, unopened, unawakened"; she is "Egypt." What Murray called the Failure of Nerve was also the mixing of Greek with Jewish, Indian, and Egyptian civilisations—the reawakening of the ancient world in the birth of a new. So, in *Palimpsest* the third "chapter" or story is "Secret Name," "Excavator's Egypt."

We too are excavators. In the vulgar eloquentia of our day we have a valuable coinage "to dig," that may mean in the popular sense "to go in for"; that makes sense, deeper sense, in light of how archaeology has awakened our imagination of origins or sources in time past, as meaning to dig thru layers of what a thing is, to get back to the roots and to reconstruct from fragments. Back of that, the love one must have for the idea of Troy or the Mayan thing to go digging for it.

Here, anyway, is a last find for the day. Some glimpse of another previous world, though it was contemporary also, seen in the genre of "Secret Name." "Hipparchia" and "Murex" may be compared with the novels and short stories of Mary Butts, to the life of *Speed the Plough,* which appeared in 1923, or of *Ashe of Rings,* which was published by Contact Editions, closely associated thru McAlmon and Bryher with H.D.'s world. And in her later historical novels of the thirties, in *The Macedonian* and *Scenes from the Life of Cleopatra,* Mary Butts portrays the dawn and the height of the Hellenistic spirit. For the connoisseur of *The Little Review, The Dial, Pagany,* or *Life and Letters Today,* Mary Butts and H.D. appeared in one context and must have had their resonances.

In turn, "Secret Name" recalls another writer of the twenties—this time not a member of the avant-garde but a popular writer—Algernon Blackwood. I never asked H.D. if she had read Blackwood. He belonged to the same generation as Yeats, and in *The Centaur* in 1911 he had portrayed a Greece behind Greece itself, an elemental Nature that man knows in dream. If she had never read Blackwood, H.D. was to enter the same thought. "I've begun at the wrong end," O'Malley says in *The Centaur;* "I shall never reach men through their intellects . . . I must get at them *from within.* To reach their hearts, the new ideas must rise up from within. I see the truer way. I must do it *from the other side.* It must come to them—in Beauty . . . I can work it better from the other side—from that old, old Garden which is the Mother's heart."

Ghost stories have to do with our feeling about the presence of the past in the present where we are. Blackwood, like M. L. R. James before him, had a feeling of the evil of the past, the ecstasy of the past as a power over man. James in 1904 had published the first of a series of volumes of such stories that had their fascination, the very real impact, in the real terror and disgust which James, the scholar of heretical documents, had found in those "ghosts" of old ways that lasted on, behind the scenes, in Christian history.

But for Blackwood the beauty was greater than the evil. Like Yeats, he was at home in the occult and supernatural, most alive in the magic of the Eternal Return. To be possessed, in *The Promise of Air* (1918) or *The Bright Messenger* (1922), is to be inspired, flooded by a larger consciousness, an elemental but also an angelic Self. The horror of the orthodox Christian James gives way in the theosophical Hermeticist Blackwood to a floating sympathy with all spiritual imagination.

The story "Secret Name" may have an intermediate kind in the psychological ghost-stories of May Sinclair, but in its central revelation of an *other* world, we are, for the first time in H.D.'s work, clearly in the genre of the theosophical romance.

Memories of childhood and events in the past, and certain dreams, H.D. tells us in *Tribute to Freud,* are "retained with so vivid a detail that they become almost events out of time." Memories, dreams, and then—it is the core of her memoir—hallucination: the "writing on the wall," actually projected before her eyes on the wall of a hotel bedroom in Corfu 1920. It was for Freud, she tells us, "the most dangerous or the only actually dangerous 'symptom'." It was the essence of Imagism, the immediate presentation.

Not until the Second World War did H.D. come, as Blackwood and Yeats had, into theosophical circles. She may be speaking, in the Freud memoir of 1944, from her later view, but not necessarily, for the concept of second-sight belongs to folk lore at large and the idea of vision to poet lore, before whatever doctrine there may be in theosophical initiation. "For myself," H.D. continues: "I consider this sort of dream or projected picture or vision as a sort of half-way state between ordinary dream and the vision of those who, for lack of a more definite term, we must call psychics or clairvoyants." Then later: "I may say that never before and never since have I had an experience of this kind."

Helen Fairwood's hallucination or vision or presentational immediacy of the little birth-house or temple or tomb it seems to her, "set square with no imperfection or break in its excellent contour, like some exquisite square of yellow honeycomb" in the court at Karnak, is an effort to tell about this other actual presentation. Phantasy, tradition, surround it, and it almost seems a moment of what Cocteau so loves—the eternal return. But this is not, we realize, made up, as Helen Fairwood's surrounding associations are a make-up, but—that is the danger, the madness—come from a source independent of our creative mind, our conscious daydream. The word rhymes with all the surrounding pattern we had been weaving but it comes as if of itself.

Festugière in *La Révélation d'Hermès Trismégiste* comments that the evaluation of such presentations as a higher good or reality is a trait of the Hellenistic period, distinctly contrasting with our own sense of such presentations as mental disorders. Epilepsy, paranoia, or heatstroke in the Egyptian desert—the Mi'Raj, the visionary trance, the writing on the wall, has been declared beyond our ken, out of bounds.

Chapter 2

MARCH II, SATURDAY. 1961. (1963)

I have been reading recently along a line in the German romantic tradition, perhaps with a vague sense of relation to this search that has a beginning and an end in the entity H.D., but at the same time it seemed to me a rest or a change from my daily preoccupation to read these romantic tales and phantasies in the evening before sleep. Then I found myself following clues of what I sought for in these tales of man's psyche in the northern forest world. Long ago, as a child, I had known Tieck's *The Elves,* and after years I had read it again, but now—in the light, that for some must seem the shadow, of the *materia poetica* as I have begun to see it in my study—Tieck's fairy tale told its story anew. That folk that live in the fir-ground—"the dingy fir-trees with the smoky huts behind them, the ruined stalls, the brook flowing past with a sluggish melancholy," "as if bewitched and excommunicated, so that even our wildest fellows will not venture into it" it appears to most eyes—that is really the ground at once of an enchantment and of a fructifying source, seem now the people of a despised way of life, gypsies they appear in the story, pagan remnant or Albigensian outcasts they may be; now the people of some outcast area of the psyche itself, of a repressed content that to the conscious mind seems the home of "a miserable crew that steal and cheat in other quarters, and have their hoard and hiding-place here" but that is in the unconscious a wonderland, the hidden garden of an other nature; now the people of the romantic impulse, mistrusted and disowned—the romantic fallacy, the right-minded call it. The magic of this source, whether it be an actual company, of poets or heretics, or a hidden area of the psyche, or a source of the poem, lies in its being secret to all who have not entered into its inner life. Once it is explained, shown up for what it is, once the Secret is told that man's life has its abundance and blessing in this fearful, rejected ground, and that good fortune perishes. "Beware of telling any one of our existence; or we must fly this land, and thou and all around will lose the happiness and blessing of our neighborhood," the Elfin Lady tells Mary in the story. And in the end, in anger at her husband's injustice to those people that he sees as a nuisance to the country and their huts a blight, Mary cries out "Hush! for they are benefactors to thee and to every one of us," "and as Andres at every word grew more incredulous, and shook his head in mockery," she discloses the existence of the Elves.

Now all enchantment falls, and it is not only the Elvin world that disappears, illusion that it is, so that all night a host passes out of the neighborhood, and in the morning all is still. But also the illusion of the actual world fades:

> The freshness of the wood was gone; the hills were shrunk, the brooks were flowing languidly with scanty streams, the sky seemed gray; and when you turned to the Firs, they were standing there no darker or more dreary than the other trees. The huts behind them were no longer frightful; and several inhabitants of the village came and told about the fearful night, and how they had been across the spot where the gipsies had lived, how these people must have left the place at last, for their huts were standing empty, and within had quite a common look, just like the dwellings of other poor people.

The Square of Saint Mark's Cathedral in "Narthex" exists in Raymonde's seeing into it the way she does, not seeing thru it. "Crawl into Saint Mark's Cathedral like a bee into a furled flower head"; but "It was true that you could slit the thing to tatters, it had none of that quality Gareth liked . . . reality."

The dark and the light, the fearful and the lovely, belong to the romantic illusion and disillusion. The "O wind, rend open the heat" with which we began belonged to the same world of romance-living as Tieck and Wagner. My sense is that we are coming from what were once national traditions, "German" or "English" or church orthodoxies of belief and doctrine or progressive views into something else, a community of meanings, where we are to inherit—all things seen now as works of the imagination of what man is—a thread of being in which there are many strands. A psyche will be formed having roots in all the old cultures; and—this seems to me one of the truths I owe most to Charles Olson's poetry—the old roots will stir again. But this sense of impending inheritance is in the thought itself; for long before us, in the nineteenth century, Carlyle, Emerson, or George MacDonald took their thought in Novalis, Tieck, or Hoffmann as we do now.

So, last night, in this sequence of German Romantics—Tieck's stories translated by Carlyle, Wagner's *Ring* cycle, and then the "Helen Phantasmagoria" of Goethe's *Faust*—I went on to Hoffmann's *Don Juan* and with *Don Juan* this morning my thought takes its lead.

E. T. A. Hoffmann. It had been "E. T. W."; the biographical note by Christopher Lazare says that "the Amadeus, later substituted for Wilhelm, was a Mozartean afterthought." Hoffmann, we read, "yearned for some signal from the unknown."

In "Don Juan or A Fabulous Adventure That Befell a Music Enthusiast on His Travels," the narrator is an author (we take him for the author then) who wakes from deep sleep in a strange inn to the sound of an overture. He is told when he rings for the valet that a door opens from his bed-chamber into the theater itself, where *Don Juan* by the famous Maestro Mozart of Vienna is being presented. He attends then, sitting in this special visitor's loge that opens off of his room.

During the opera he hears in the loge beside him "the rustle of a silken garment," senses "a gentle, perfumed breath of air close to me." In the intermission he turns from his enchantment in the Mozart opera where he had been most drawn to the actress singing Donna Anna to find . . . to face the Lady of the play herself. "The possibility," the author of the story writes:

> The possibility of explaining how she could, at one and the same time, be both on stage and in my loge never occurred to me. Just as a happy

dream brings together the strangest events and our instinctive belief freely accepts it, in all its incongruity, as a phenomenon of life, so did I somnambulistically accept the presence of this marvelous creature. More than that, I realized, all at once, that there were secret bonds which tied me so closely to her, that she could not keep away from me even when she appeared on the stage.

Then:

> She said that music was her only reality, and that she often believed she could understand in song much that was mystically hidden or evaded expression in life.

There follows a moment of hallucinatory revelation in which Hoffmann, the author of the story ("the Amadeus, substituted for Wilhelm . . . a Mozartean afterthought") in a sleight of name is also the author of the opera, is Mozart. It depends upon the old afterthought, the possibility of the actual name *Amadeus* held in common:

> 'I know the frenzy and yearning of love' [Donna Anna confides] 'that were in your heart, when you wrote the part . . . in your last opera. I understood you. Your soul was laid bare to me in song! Yes,' (here she called me by my first name) 'Naturally, I have sung you. I am your melodies.'

Here again, as in Tieck's *The Elves,* the secret life is betrayed and the world of illusion dies. "As from a great distance, accompanied by the harmonica of an aerial orchestra" the author seems to hear Anna's voice: "*Non mi dir bell' idol mio!*"; then, in the *Epilogue,* Clever Man and Mulatto-Face, the Mid-Day critics discuss the death of the singer: "But that is what comes of overacting." "Yes, yes. I warned her time and time again! The role of Donna Anna always affected her oddly. Yesterday, she carried on like one possessed."

For the author the opera had been "as though the most esoteric thoughts of a bewitched soul had become fixed in sound and had taken form and shape, standing out in relief against a remarkable concept"; his very life seems to have its source in the stage. Writing to his friend,

Theodore, he says "This conflict between the divine and demoniac powers begets the notion of life on earth, just as the ensuing victory begets the notion of life above earth." But this "notion of life" we see is the story of a ghost, an afterthought, that appears between our being and the other life that we know on the stage, in the story, in legend, in the poem, in the vision of painting and sculpture.

I.

Our figures of the patrons in late medieval painting belong to two worlds. We know not in *The Madonna of Chancellor Rolin* whether the *Patron* is in *Her* presence or She is in *his* house. In Van Eyck's Ghent Altarpiece, Joos Vydt kneels in the life in contrast to the facing figure of St. John the Baptist who stands in the painting of stone, having the presence of a work of art within the Altarpiece itself. The patron, the donner, in the painting takes on flesh of flie, an illusion, in paint that seems life-like in contrast to the illusion of stone in the painting of the saint.

In back of that *Adoration of the Lamb,* the great central figure of the Ghent Altarpiece, is another play of images, a cult or afterthought of Philip, Duke of Burgundy, a fifteenth-century charade—the Order of the Golden Fleece, where his court played Knights of the Round Table and Argonauts in one mystery. The blood of Flanders shed at Ghent, out of which Burgundy had great wealth, flows from the Lamb into the Grail. Christian figures—the Lamb, John the Baptist, the Bleeding Heart, the Cup—become one with the wool that was the source of the wealth; with the theatrical ideal of chivalry; became one, in turn, with Greek legend.

It took wealth. It was in turn the creation of wealth. In this relationship between the artist and the patron, the artist—the true alchemist—transformed money into richness. For Colchis to be present in the court of Burgundy; for Karnak to be present in London or the glory that was Greece to be brought to Bryher. So, the Van Eycks painted for Philippe le Bon, tableaux of the chivalric mysteries, woven in turn into tapestries to transform the streets of Sluys where his bride Ysabel of Portugal landed in 1428, enhancing the actual world with another reality of the imagined world. And that imagined world of the Van Eycks takes on a solidity from properties of the patron's world: the jeweled crown, the sumptuous robe, the golden throne, the burnished chandelier, the laver and basin have a greater immediacy. For the artist himself, Jan Van Eyck, had been brought into such a world by his patron, as ambassador of Philippe to the court of Portugal must have worn such robes.

The reality that Gareth poses against Raymonde's other world of lure and involvement or enrichment is the seeing thru lure to the things of common sense and hard cash. It is the Protestant ethic described by Weber in *The Protestant Sects and the Spirit of Capitalism* that gives Gareth her one dimensional resistance. Putting together this picture of the patron Bryher, from "Narthex," from "Let Zeus Record"—but also now three years after my first draft, from Bryher's *Heart to Artemis—* I see how typically she resists luxury, phantasy; to keep money virtuous. It was the image of Artemis, the ardent spare beauty in which some ascetic necessity was satisfied that drew Bryher to H.D.'s poetry. For the artist it meant the beauty possible for one with limited means. For the patron it meant the beauty permissible for one who would maintain the responsibilities of capital, avoiding luxury and waste.

Remembering McAlmon's "Money Breeds Complications," we remember too that the artist breeds complications in order to enrich: the intertwining and doubled images of marginal illuminations, the underpainting and mixing of tones in the luxuriance of Titian, the elaborations of the poet worked in interchanges of vowels and consonants, undermeanings and overmeanings. So Joyce, presented with the largest gift of the century by his patroness Harriet Weaver, developed and complicated his *Finnegans Wake*—a jeweled, overworked texture that only the extravagantly endowed artist could venture. Miss Weaver was dismayed for she had wanted some reiteration of the solid achievement Joyce had secured in *Ulysses,* her money's worth; not this fairy gold or counterfeit of values.

"Compare the 'Phaedra' and the 'Hippolytus' series which were actually written in Greece," Bryher says in reviewing *Hymen* in 1922: "with 'Cuckoo Song,' 'Thetis,' 'Evadne.' Apart from an added intensity of color—the 'lizard blue' water, the 'red sands' of Crete" . . . but in

"Phaedra" there was not only the added intensity of color, there was also the appearance of a counter force, protestant to Phaedra's passion:

For art undreamt in Crete,
strange art and dire,
in counter-charm prevents my charm
limits my power:

that may be the same limit that Raymonde sitting in the Square of St. Mark's faces, the resistance the protestant ethic has against the alchemy, the transmutation of values, of the artist's impulse. The modern patron, the capitalist patron, may be loyal, generous, conscientious, but he must also be righteous, and the art he sponsors must be valid, credible, creditable. For all of "wish" and "touch," of "sea-magic" and Circe's longing for the glance of Odysseus, Bryher in reviewing the poem "Circe" sees her as "any woman of intellect who, with the very sincerity of her vision, turns lesser minds 'each to his own self'," an image of the higher capitalist mind. It is not by her inability but by the very strength of her character that Gareth is not taken in by the honeyhorn of St. Mark's cathedral with its saints and incrustations of wealthy suggestion. Bryher's H.D. is the high-minded priestess of Artemis—the poetess set apart. But in the twenties, H.D., in the milieu provided by Bryher, changes. Athens was integrity, but now there is not only Athens. Another H.D. emerges in kinship with Venice and finds herself alienated from the earlier "pure" H.D. She has a secret alliance with things and people that Gareth hates. "Mordant brought me those blue hyacinths . . . How Gareth hated Mordant." Phaedra in her passionate heat for Hippolytus offends Artemis: that is the play of the mid-20s, Hippolytus Temporizes. But also, between the artist and the patron, between the one who would transform reality and the one who would use reality, there is a difference of view and even truth that quickens another division within the self of two images where Phaedra and Artemis contend.

In "Narthex" we see for the first time the synthesis that will flower in her later work. In the composite image of St. Mark's H.D. reaches forward towards a fusion of oriental opulence and Greek spirit in images now of the Renaissance Christian world. "I had enough of Greek things, I said I wanted something . . . so-called Christian mysticism that finds complete co-relation with so-called classicism," Raymonde says to Daniel: "I have found it this time and with you, in Venice. I never really understood, accepted the renaissance till this time."

Entering more and more into the world of Bryher, H.D.'s major expression in this period is in the prose novelette that can provide elaborations and developments. Between 1925 and 1927 there are six published pieces: the three stories of *Palimpsest,* the children's book *The Hedgehog,* the novel *Hedylus,* and the story "Narthex." In 1928 and 1930 there are four more: two "Raymonde" stories "The Usual Star" and "Two Americans," then "Kora and Ka" and "Mira-Mare." There is a new—"precious" it could be felt—scene now: the cultivated love-life, the emotional transmutations of two's and three's, the divisions and multiplications of the authoring personality, the practised sensibilities belong to life in the higher circles of our society, the leisure class. Poems in *Red Roses for Bronze* appear not as works but as gifts or tribute. There is not only Raymonde's "Say 'Garry liked my writing,' what did it mean? It meant, Garry paid my fare here and I have behaved outrageously" but there is also H.D.'s pathos in "Chance Meeting":

Take from me something,
be it all too fine
and untranslatable and worthless
for your purpose,
take it,
it's mine;

In the drift of her writing in the twenties, she provides a picture of this world set apart by money from the common lot of working for a living, of the poet living from hand to mouth, and set apart by the post-war modernism from the traditions of the upper class. As the artist sees it: haunted by the unrealized wealth of associations, unreal then in the terms it has made for its reality. A fiction of sensibilities, these stories are related on the one hand to the art of Proust in the period before the war or of James in the golden age of American capitalism.

Raymonde and Daniel in their triangle with Gareth, we find, are like Kate Croy and Merton Densher in their triangle with Milly Theale: "They are far from a common couple, Merton Densher and Kate Croy, as befits the remarkable fashion in which fortune was to waylay and opportunity was to distinguish them," James writes in the introduction to *The Wings of the Dove:* "—the whole strange truth of their response to which opening involves also, in its order, no vulgar art of exhibition; but what they have most to tell us is that, all unconsciously and with the best faith in the world, all by mere force of the terms of their superior passion combined with their superior diplomacy, they are laying a trap for the great innocence to come."

A fiction of an emotional drifting, these stories related on the other hand to the literature of the "lost" generation, to the *romans-à-clef* of Mary Butts, especially *Armed with Madness, The Death of Felicity Taverner,* or *Imaginary Letters,* but also the popular novels of the day, Hemingway's *The Sun Also Rises* or Fitzgerald's *Tender is the Night.* The cult of the poem—Imagism—and the "we" H.D. had known in association with poets before the war was replaced now by the cult of the personality in other circles, verging upon the old orders of high society and upon the new orders of café society, little intense groups of ephemera having their day in the brief "modern" wave after the War that would run out in the "crack-up," as it was for Fitzgerald, of the Depression. "Something not very far off the deification of man is on us now," Mary Butts wrote in *Traps for Unbelievers* (1932):

> not, or not yet, of the kings and millionaires, but, and again, and this is primitive, of the conspicuous young men and women, our sexually desirable ones, whose nature it is to wax and wane and be replaced. Our Year-in-Year-out spirits, *eniautoi daimones,* whose beauty is no stronger than a flower.

So Daniel Kinouel, Gareth's husband, is an agonizing lure for Raymonde in "Narthex":

> the turn, she could almost feel it, of fine collar bone under the grey or under the dark blue or under the fawn-brown of his shoulders. She had

been so vivid, so certain of what had been there that there had seemed no reason for reaching across, drawing simply as one draws a curtain from before some holy statue, the cloth from those lean shoulders . . .

In the poem "Red Roses for Bronze" the avidity is not so tempered:

> but sensing underneath the garment seam
> ripple and flash and gleam
> of indrawn muscle
> and of those more taut,
> I feel that I must turn and tear and rip
> the fine cloth
> from the moulded thigh and hip,
> force you to grasp my soul's sincerity,
> and single out
> me,
> me,
> something to challenge,
> handle differently.

They turn, twist, test each other to produce flashes of higher emotion. The *noli me tangere,* that is so important a part of D.H. Lawrence's sexual design, is important here; there is also their living off of their nerves or their erotic excitement, living beyond their means, dependent as they are upon Gareth. Like Lawrence, they use the potentiality of homosexual attractions to heighten the heterosexual bond. In London, Raymonde had held Daniel up to her lover Mordant, as if she fired the one man like a crystal before the furnace heat of the other, it seems to her; and, sitting in Venice, she recalls "this sacrificial thing between them, great bulk of remembered (in London) male body, heavy thighs" of Mordant to key up the idea of Daniel as Hermes. The double triangle image of Katherine-Mordant-Raymonde / Ray Bart–Gareth-Daniel is the instrument of an erotic art. We remember from Williams's 1905 the naive magic of "She said I was Rosalind in *As You Like It* and she was Celia"; but now more terrible powers are called up to inhabit the drama of life.

Daniel follows to the Cathedral, where Gareth will not go, to fetch

Raymonde: "Gareth is waiting." They have just this place and time before they must return, before Raymonde says to Daniel "We must go back to Gareth":

> 'Look at the drinking fountain' meant 'and how is Garry?' Daniel knew that the 'whole renaissance is in this drinking fountain' meant 'I am worried about Garry.' The mind, a lily, rising on tall stem, rose out of confusion, out of hysteria . . . 'I loved her . . . terribly.'
>
> 'I mean,' a voice continued, her voice? 'I have loved . . . terribly. It's terrible to love and know oneself inadequate and helpless.' 'So she says.' 'So—?' 'Gareth. She says she is sorry for me if . . . I love . . . Ray Bart.' 'Being sorry does no good to any one, I am sorry for myself, harassed and lacerated loving . . . Daniel.' Sparks were drawn into one tall light. One candle burned where inappositely darkness had made cornice and square mosaic shine like gold fish.

The two hermetic lovers practice cruelty as if to strike a light, flint against flint. "I know why people hate you," Raymonde will flash out: "People hate you for the same reason that they hate me, Daniel." And Daniel will flash back:

> 'You have the tortured silly smile of some archaic statue.' 'I know.' 'Rather tight. Looking mincing almost.' 'I know.' 'You don't know, I'm rather glad you don't know.' 'Why—why glad Daniel?' 'It's—*horrible*.'

In "The Usual Star" (1928), the beauty of Daniel is thematic: "incandescence of swan features and the famous Swedish film star," it seems to Raymonde; it can also include her, for there is the "incandescence of the two of them, burning with their cerebral intensity"—an identification in beauty. "Raymonde wanted Marc de Brissaic to protect her from intolerable incandescence." In the twenties the great cult of beauty arises in those lights of the screen, gathering all possible erotic attractions: Garbo or Valentino, existing as they do in an androgynous lure. "Human nature was not meant for that strain," Mary Butts writes of the cult of person: "The star-dust at Hollywood is full of dead stars."

In "Two Americans" (1930), the presence of the great negro star Saul Howard awakens in Raymonde some other identification with him as an artist or an American that exorcises the hold Daniel had had. "'No, it's altogether this way. You see,' she was surprised to hear what she said, 'he's removed a silver thorn out of my side, called Daniel.'"

Outside the charged circle of this "incandescence"—as outside the circle of the Imagist poets—there is a "they," those who do not understand, who misjudge: the general's wife, the pro-consul's widow of the poem "Halcyon." H.D. must have been aware of how little sympathy the middle-class, more importantly, how little sympathy the professional class had for this disestablished, self-centered life of the rich. Her discomfort can show itself in the sense of vulgarity about her. But there is also the sense of being hated by the vulgar that she had known in another way as a member of the pre-War circle of poets. The "they" now are the economically responsible, the solid and moral middle-class, and Gareth, having her solid upper middle-class attitudes—having after all the "reality" of the hard cash—can seem to belong at times to "them." In "Halcyon" we find:

> 'tinsel' they said the other lives were,
> all those I loved,
> I was forgot;

and later:

> I never had an illusion,
> they hate me,
> every one, every one,
> but it's worse for you,
>
> you're a baby, a lost star,

"Halcyon" is a dramatic monologue, of a poor relation dependent upon "my late cousin, the wool merchant's wife," isolated from those who understand her, in exile in a commercial port. But H.D. too, during this period of the late twenties and the thirties was "forgot," and where she was remembered, her critics were not sympathetic with this work. All the prejudices of the new educated class were to be against just such irresponsibility. Thomas Burnett Swann in 1963, forgetting her, can note his dissympathy with Raymonde Ransome in summing up the prose of H.D.:

> Most of the characters—poets, temptresses, hostesses—are either precious or tedious, and so, too often, is the heroine, although she seems to be intended as a contrast to her superficial friends.

[Dream, April 5, 1963: "There were things I wanted to ask you," I said. Her attention wavered, yet she was intensely there. There was some impatience with the moment, along with her having all the time in the world. "Did you ever read Blackwood?" I asked, "You must have—" Was her answer there or not? Was she evasive or had it seemed so unimportant that her interest could not recall whether she had or not.

"But I shiver at the thought of you reading the old prose & poems," she had written in 1960 when she was still alive: "To use Yeats' phrase, I am 'dreaming back' but the intermediate writing now seems an obstruction—of course it was a way of life, of living. Don't take it too seriously—"

And wasn't I in asking impatient of her answering now. "I've been finding out the—" did I say "split" or "fault"? "—two H.D.'s." Hilda Doolittle—H.D., Raymonde—Ray Bart.

She looked disappointed in me. But then a flash of fellow feeling was there, a conspiracy of writers. She knew that one used everything to make up one's work. But didn't I pose use as if it were less than or opposed to transformation?

"Yes, yes, I think we did," she said, tentatively, gazing off into space or back into time to see her answer. In the hotel room in New York she had looked past me or beyond me that way, as if clairvoyant, searching some Akashic blank for a sign. I almost caught the titles of books as she searched for them. But I was talking—would I ever hear what *she* had to say? I had to tell her how much I knew as if that could make the bond, awaken the full force of sympathy I wanted.

"Did you ever think how much in this outdoors thing,"—I was thinking of the early poems, the woodlands of "Pursuit," the sea of "The Shrine" "where rollers shot with blue / cut under deeper blue"—

"this back to the elements, back to nature"—I was recalling that story Williams told in his autobiography:

> There had been a storm and the breakers were heavy, pounding in with overpowering force. But Hilda was entranced. I suppose she wasn't used to the ocean anyhow and didn't realize what she was about. For without thought or caution she went to meet the waves, walked right into them. I suppose she could swim, I don't know, but in she went and the first wave knocked her flat, the second rolled her into the undertow, and if Bob Lamberton hadn't been powerful and there, it might have been worse. They dragged her out unconscious, resuscitated her, and had just taken her up to the house.

"Did you ever think how much in this back to nature thing you were at one with the common view?"—with all those free thinkers of the working class and lower middle class, I was thinking, sun-tanned, sun-burnt—Nudists?—followers of a popular theosophy and nature-worship. "'Bright Messenger'—did you read that?" I wanted to tell her how close at first H.D. was to the world of "The Centaur" or "The Education of Uncle Paul." Vaud, *her* Vaud, had been the place too of Algernon Blackwood's revelations of wind and fire gods. But now I was going to lose it again. There may have been a wave of not wanting to lose her.

We sat out-of-doors in an arbor under grape-vines, it was another time now, some revenant-time of my adolescence in the San Joaquin. "Fletcher talked in his review of your poetry about Plotinus, Proclus, Boehme," I went on, trying to recall the conspiracy between H.D., and the old H.D. with her love for theosophy, and my own goings-on, going-too-far: "Didn't you talk way back then in London about the great image, the eidolon?"

"There was a book . . . " she said, and now I was going to lose her I felt again, she was so near, there was a smile with it: "There was a book we all read," she smiled, and I saw again the glint of her playful, affectionate conspiracy. There were times in our interview when I'd been painfully aware of how mistaken I was, how little she liked my digging, digging, digging at Raymonde Ransome. Wasn't she tired, barely tolerant of my book. "Why don't you write a book about your own affairs?" she had asked me at one point; there could have been a barbed impatience in that. But we did talk about writing then and I did not take up the barb if it was there. "I've had a book on my mind—" I said, looking off into the distant possibility myself but just missing it, "But it's lost." Had her question been almost an angry reproof, a rebuff? She meant, that's what I saw when she asked, a book of my own sexual engagements, a series of those I had fallen in love with. *Back to nature*.

"There was a book we all read . . . " she had disclosed. As I woke the name of the author was there and her last curious smile—"taunt" the word came to me yesterday as I was walking back from the mailbox at the corner; I have to work in "the furies' *taunt*" I had thought.—Was that in Helen?

"E. Nesbit Trilby was the author's name," she had said, and then: "It was a silly novel of high society, I'm afraid."]

II.

All given things have a command over the artist; thoughts come to the poet, images are presented not invented; and where there is poetry we see chance as a donation, the universe as a donor. Chosen most gifted, inspired. In French, *La donnée* is the *idée fondamentale d'un ouvrage d'esprit*. The poem itself is a gift in exchange. In these stories and poems of the middle period, H.D. seeks to give herself, a feudal token for a holding, the inner even confused, even painful, account to overlords of love and loyalty. Not only Gareth but Daniel is donor; his the narthex, the initiatory love-death. Not only Gareth and Daniel but the persona Ray Bart and the descending triangle with Katherine and Mordant give the star.

To pay back, to get even, here is transmuted in the return of truth; for the scales of the artist are not only a balance that Thoth holds but they are also the scales of a music, the series of proportions in a drawing from life. In the language we are given there is the Old Norse donation, *skál*, a bowl, the bowls of the scale; there is the Latin donation *scāla*, a ladder, the ladder of ascending or descending tones, the graduations that give measure; the Jacob's Ladder as Denise Levertov evokes it in that poem:

The stairway is not
a thing of gleaming strands
a radiant evanescence
for angels' feet that only glance in their tread, and need not
touch the stone.

It is of stone.

Given, these ascents and descents of spirit, even the rosy glow of the
stone:

only because behind it the sky is a doubtful, a doubting
night gray,

by the actual so that "a man climbing"

must scrape his knees, and bring
the grip of his hands into play. The cut stone
consoles his groping feet.

It is the cut of the stone, the scrape of reality that verifies the spirit.
The night gray, the roughness of the way gives verity, and the artist
seeks it out, for his work is not only a gift for like-souls, for the human
donors before and after, but a gift for the sky, a gift for the very hazard
in which experience has had its keen edge.

"When a man dreams his own dream, he is the sport of his dream";
George MacDonald writes in *Lilith:* "when Another gives it him, that
Other is able to fulfill it."

Where we see certain things in the poem that "appear there" as
Donna Anna who is also something else ("Naturally, I have sung you.
I am your melodies") appears in Hoffmann's *Don Juan;* as the Lamb
appears in Van Eyck's great altarpiece, but also in the rites of the Fleece,
so that He is not only Christ the Lamb or the God-Fleece that the
Argonauts sought, but also the artist's theme, we are aware not only
of the artist but of another. The work of art itself appears as a gift for
another but also as a means for another to be there. Self expression may
be an urgency of art, but the self has no expression except in this other.

In *Tribute to the Angels:* "it was an ordinary tree / in an old garden-square." It is only a half-burnt-out-tree, a survivor of the war; it is also the other half the tree in its flowering; the whole recalling then the Solomon's seal of "Narthex": the half-burnt-out triangle of those before the War and the bright triangle of those after the War—the two are needed to make the design. A *donnée* of the poem: "we saw the tree flowering," in order to see. The tree itself bestows the fundamental idea of *Tribute to the Angels,* but in turn it comes as an answer to a prayer or a question, the "is this union at last?" of *The Walls Do Not Fall,* that may ask union with God or the universe or the union of all the gifts of the poet in her opus. In the creation of a melody there is a given passage of tones that lead towards another phrase or phase to which they belong. Melody arises in the union of otherwise diverse feelings.

Invoking angelic powers in the opening pages of her *Tribute,* H.D. establishes a scale or rather a series of scales: the Judaic and the Greek divine orders are two that in the Christian scale become one; the Christian, the New Dispensation, and the Egyptian, the old Heretical Tradition, are two that in turn in the psychoanalytic and theosophical interpretation become one. What is involved here is a polyphony, proceeding from the choral mode of her earliest work out of Euripides, a formal counterpart of the polyvalence of elements in H.D.'s life-feeling. The poem must find its mode in dimensions that allow for angels to occur as they allow for the worm on the leaf and the star, for shapers and donors outside the person of the poet herself to come into the work. For she, like E.T.A. Hoffmann, yearned for some signal from the unknown. A presentation from the unconscious? But these presents come from outside the signature of H.D.; the leaf, the sea, the shell, the tree in flower come from the actual, natural world; Thoth, *Amen,* Raphael, Annael, Christos, and the Lady come from the lore-world of other men; and the poem itself unfolds before the poet from the rhymes and developments given in the words from the increment of human experience the poet comes to know in the language, from other experience in which her experience comes true. It is in consciousness that the exchange is made; the gift comes into our own consciousness from an other consciousness. The sky, the wave, the blade of grass are elements of writing because they are elements of our conscious life.

The War itself gave proportion to personal feelings of being lost, of surviving, and yet of braving circumstance, of holding to the ideal. The "I do not know why," "we are powerless," "our bodies blunder," "we know no rule / of procedure," "we have no map" reiterates the old Alexandrian mood H.D. knew in her first phase—the Failure of Nerves Gilbert Murray had called the Alexandrian phase in history—but it also is a realistic sense of the human lot at large in the Second World War and after. It is also the statement of the artist's working terms. Form for H.D. "hewn from within by that craftsman" is the shell of organic experience; the work is a territory between the master-mason, her entity, and the oceanic life in which it takes its life. Defined by the tide-flow.

Did *The Walls Do Not Fall* at first seem to her to be complete in itself? The scholar may someday find that:

> His, the track in the sand
> from a plum-tree in flower
>
> to a half-open hut-door,

is a track that leads to some image in the old lore; it may be an actual track seen in Egypt, in "*Karnak 1923.*" The scholar may never find the track, "or track would have been" H.D. calls it:

> but wind blows sand-prints from the sand,
> whether seen or unseen):

but when it comes in *Tribute to the Angels* there is no "half-open hut-door":

> we crossed the charred portico,
> passed through a frame—doorless—

and the tree is an apple tree not a plum.

Tribute to the Angels is placed and dated: *London, May 17–31, 1944;* and *The Flowering of the Rod: London, December 18–31, 1944. The Walls Do Not Fall,* published in 1944, has only the "*from London 1942*" of the dedication to indicate when it was written. There must have been a time in which *The Walls Do Not Fall* stood alone.

These three books were never given a common title by H.D. "The War Trilogy" I call it, and I find now others too came to use that designation. Yet they are three panels of a triptych, related when they are complete to the three panels of an altarpiece: on the left the desolation of the war, center the revelation of the angels and the flowering tree in the midst of a last judgment, and on the right the three kings, the poet herself as Magdalene, and the Child Redeemer. The otherwise incidental image of the flowering tree and the lore of:

> His, the Genius in the jar
> which the Fisherman finds,

from Lang's collections of fairy tales which H.D. read again in the War years, and the:

> He is Mage,
> bringing myrrh.

appear to be enrichments in detail in the *Walls,* are taken up into the center of the design in *Tribute to the Angels* and *The Flowering of the Rod,* as the possibility of his name Amadeus gives Hoffmann the thread of his identity in his story *Don Juan.* What seemed incidental proves to be the key to the realization of a larger picture.

"Invention presupposed imagination," Stravinsky says in his *Poetics of Music,* "but should not be confused with it. For the act of invention implies the necessity of a lucky find and of achieving full realization of this find. What we imagine does not necessarily take on a concrete form and may remain in a state of virtuality, whereas invention is not conceivable apart from its actual being worked out. Thus, what concerns us here is not imagination in itself, but rather creative imagination: the faculty that helps us to pass from the level of conception to the level of realization."

I must have come across the definition before, that poetry, from the verb *poiein,* meant *to make,* but it was in Stravinsky's book that the statement got across, and that poetics is "the study of work to be done." To make things happen. And my idea of melody I found most clearly expressed there too in 1948, that "Melody, *Mélôdia* in Greek, is the intonation of the *melos,* which signifies a fragment, a part of a phrase," for that year, working on "The Venice Poem," I had begun to follow the lead of the immediate particular towards an open invention. "Watch the duration of syllables, the tone leading of vowels," Pound had instructed. Later, in 1950, in Olson's "Projective Verse" this importance of the *melos,* the immediate factor, was reiterated: "Let's start from the smallest particle of all, the syllable," he proposed—let the syllable "lead the harmony on." "To step back here to this place of the elements and minims of language, is to engage speech where it is least careless—and least logical. For from the root out, from all over the place, the syllable comes, the figures of, the dance."

We made in a poem a place for the syllable to occur as it did not occur in the careless rush of speech. The damnation of systematic rime was like the damnation of systematic thought for it was careless of the variety of what was actually going on, the lead one sensed in incident, in factors so immediate they seemed chance or accident to all but the formal eye.

A place was made in the midst of the war for an epiphany to occur. The art in poetry is this art. She made up her mind to see the tree. She made a place for the tree. For this tree that was suddenly there, to be no mere tree but more, to be an occasion of *the* tree, to be just the incidental half-burnt-out apple tree it was.

Prayer, rite, taking thought—these prepare a place for a happening. "Listening for the syllables must be so constant and so scrupulous," Olson writes, "the exaction must be so complete, that the assurance of the ear is purchased at the highest—40 hour a day—price." Atheists and skeptics are right when they say that God is only an occurrence along the line of some human projection; that, otherwise, reasonably, there are no gods, is no God. Rhyme too is a creature of our constant practice and attention. That it was "made-up" meant, so we were told when we were children, that it was a lie in some way. Then there was: if you make up your mind, you can do it. It will come true.

In Cocteau's film *Orpheus* the guardian angel Heurtebise tells Orpheus not to try to understand but to follow. It is a law in the reading of poetry that is a law too in the writing. Unless we follow, unless we follow thru the work to be done, there is no other way of understanding. Participation is all.

Heurtebise is not only guardian but guide. And Orpheus, who brought the poet's lyre into Greece, must follow his lead.

"Hermes," H.D. addresses him in the opening of *Tribute to the Angels*. Hermes, psychopompos, who gives us the lead. It is a matter both of being inspired, a breath, a being given the line, and of being led on, of foot:

> Thoth, Hermes, the stylus,
> the palette, the pen, the quill endure,

Here, first, in *The Walls Do Not Fall,* the God, patron of writers, appears by name, the weigher and measurer of truth, the lord of the scales. We see now the "Hermes of the Ways," the Herm of the early *Sea Garden,* "facing three ways," "of the triple path-ways"—the many-foamed ways of the sea, the sheltered orchard, and the dunes and grass of the open shore—we see that he was a first instance of this other Hermes:

> beyond death; Mercury, Hermes, Thoth
> invented the script, letters, palette;
>
> the indicated flute or lyre-notes
> on papyrus or parchment
>
> are magic, indelibly stamped
> on the atmosphere somewhere,

In the poem we as poets are or aspire to be makers of some immortality, that an instant, a syllable, a least thing pass "beyond death" into song. Whatever love claims and care works may have its name, that once only kings had. "I say the syllable, king, and that it is spontaneous, this way:" Olson writes:

> the ear, the ear which has collected, which has listened, the ear, which
> is so close to the mind that it is the mind's, that it has the mind's speed . . .
> it is close, another way: the mind is brother to this sister and is, because it
> is so close, is the drying force, the incest, the sharpener . . . it is from the
> union of the mind and the ear that the syllable is born.

Mercury is mercurial—evasive, sleight-of-hand, tricky, a
    thief. Quick-silver. Back-of-the-mirror.
Hermes is hermetic—hidden, sealed, occult, a messenger.
    A glass vessel closed by fusion, soldering or welding. Alembic

There was "the meaning that words hide" she had felt in *The Walls
Do Not Fall:*

they are anagrams, cryptograms,
little boxes, conditioned

to hatch butterflies . . .

In the revelation of psychoanalysis there had been a trick between the
mind and the ear, an incest or insect of that brother to this sister, the
syllable that hid the pun within the word. Care, attention, had opened
doors for souls in what they were saying, doors of other things they
were saying.

III.

Ibis of Egypt, *Ibex* of Switzerland, come. *Karnak* 1923, where H.D.
sought in the banquet chamber of Thothmes for a wish or a key, to read
hieroglyph—the Luxor bee, chick, and hare still haunt her in London
1942. I was four in 1923 and learning "I" is for *Ibis*. "I" is for *Ibex.*
Switzerland, Zurich, where H.D. wrote her letters in 1959, 1960, 1961,
until in a stroke the letters were gone, the sequence of syllables was
broken.

Ibis and *Ibex* were, before I could read, bird and animal of the alpha-
bet "I." Not of that other "I," my own person "I." In time, as inci-
dents of "bear" and "owl" occurred in life and then in the course of
poems, my bird and animal were to be owl and bear. They came to me,
but also, by afterthought, by fascination, by saving the words and the
images towards a design, by noticing how things referred to them, how
news or gospel kept coming in of bear and owl, what was occurring in
life and in poems was recognized in them—signs of event.

I accepted the owl, as I remember, during a seminar on Marx which

I attended in 1948. The professor had just said that perhaps man's great insights always came at the wrong time—"like the owl of Minerva," he said, "that flew by night." The message of the light, of mankind's commune in life thru work, came in the dark—too late, after its day; came, looking forward, too early, before its time. And hadn't I, as a young poet, to fly blind for ten years—not until *Medieval Scenes* did I know what I was doing; not until "The Venice Poem" in 1948, ten years after I began, did I know how to do it.

I had not accepted it before, when I was little, with my crossed eyes squinting to focus, with my round-eye glasses, when they said I was owl-eyed.

A word game. *Ibex* was the king of the mountain crags, native of the land of Hans Christian Andersen's story "Little Rudy," a lure of the heights. In the tale there were two maidens: one, Babette, his betrothed, is human, but "she is far above you," her angry father says to Little Rudy; the other, the Ice-Maiden, is a spirit of the Alps. The "heights," I find again, looking up the derivation of "Alps" in the O.E.D.; or, from the Latin, *albus*, "white." For the Ice-Maiden is also an "alp"—a night-mare or demon of the dream. In "Little Rudy," "Alps" and "alp" are one in the lure of the heights.

There is in the height of my fantasy, not an obsession but a thought that persists, a fancy that psychoanalysis has found entertained by many children, of an other more real mother than my mother. In the play of dates, my birth year 1919 and the death of my first mother in the complications of child-birth and the flu echoes in my mind the birth of H.D.'s child in the complications of the London flu epidemic. In the play of the initials H.D., my birth name Edward Howard Duncan— E. Howard Duncan echoes her signature; and in the increased risk of the play, the name of the author in my dream, E. Nesbit Trilby may conceal—between the childhood charm of E. Nesbit's world and the fatal delusive career of Trilby where charm is sinister—its warning.

In H.D.'s *The Hedgehog*, searching for the meaning of a word *herisson*, the little girl Madge climbs "like a bird or a mountain goat or wild sheep," like an ibex then, up where "The steep side of the hill was a very Swiss side of the hill," where "A cloud was nosing its way up over the edge of the rock wall like the nose of a very white and very woolly big sheep," where "The blinding silver across the white cloud a little dazed her."

H.D. is writing at Vaud in 1925 this story of what life is like told for her daughter who is six. Just here, in the heights, Madge, daughter of the story, comes into this "dizziness on hill-paths." "'Who-eee.' A voice up above Madge made Madge pause a moment, one foot fitted in a boulder, the other carefully planted on a space of dried grass . . . "

But the poet, too, may have known how such a call can interrupt, in the heights of writing, suddenly, some voice that recalls an inner voice, that brings one down to earth, as we say. In a moment of panic we remember who and what we are. There is a way in the rising, climbing melodic airs of poetry that those other feet, of the poem's climbing, are in the imagination "like a bird or a mountain goat or wild sheep." Here we must follow, as if we could trust it. Or find ourselves suddenly having those other, unimaginative, feet that make the way, as it is for Madge in the story once she comes to herself, "steeper than she had thought."

"Madge found"—but it is something the poet found too—"that it's better never to stop and think in the middle of a path that goes up the side of a hill or down the side of a hill like a snail-track on a house wall."

For where our feet are on the ground, how unreal it seems that heads are in the clouds.

The other, as early as the alphabet animal I-is-for-Ibex, was there in the nursery. The figure of an Ibis, of the Ibis-headed wisdom. Not on my building block, but on the page in my grandmother's book. It was an emblem of my parent's world. There was then in the beginning the sense that this bird brought with it, him, a reminder of how I did not understand what was going on around me. In the adult world there were always hermetic, sealed, meanings. Beyond my ken. The marsh or river bird, with its long stalk-legs and its fantastic long curved beak, was holy, was adult, was a word in a language we would not read, hieroglyph.

Was there, in old Mrs. Rogers's anteroom, in the room of the Elder Brother as they called her, or Teacher, where I waited while my mother went thru to the other room . . . was there a stuffed ibis? or heron? Or a screen with an ibis—no—a heron on it?

"Now Madame Beaupère said *hérisson,* which is the French and the Swiss-French for hedgehog. Madge, who understood most anybody's French, somehow for the moment couldn't remember just what was a *hérisson.* Some kind of heron, perhaps, she thought."

It was a screen. The shadowy little scene has stayed with me since I was six or seven, because I was guilty of something that I can't recall clearly. I looked behind the screen and saw—was it a wash-basin and pitcher on a table, a lavatory? the laver and kettle of Van Eyck's altarpiece at Ghent? I thought later I had seen a chamber-pot, and that this was what was *unmentionable.* One didn't mention going to the bathroom, I had been taught.

The door to the inner chamber had a double or triple bead curtain which obscured the opening. When they had meetings, I think my mother explained, this was the Veil of Isis. "Iris; I don't really think of iris here," Helen Fairwood says in "Secret Name": "It's so essentially a Greek flower. But *Isis,* it's almost the same thing." However, it was really of the birds she thought.

In Cocteau's *Orpheus* the poet and his angel Heurtebise and his death go thru a mirror as if thru water. Into glory and terror. When Orpheus is returned to life, separated from his angel and his death, he is, in the movie, an ordinary man writing poetry, a facteur of literature. The other, the beyond, has left him. "Let him return to his mire," Heurtebise says.

These others—my parents, my grandmother, and the Elder Brother, old Mrs. Rogers, were not poets. They were—what everybody laughs at California for breeding—middle-class occultists. Grief in the loss of her first two children had brought my grandmother to the spiritualists' tables of the seventies. In the twenties of our century, forty years later, passions, wishes, thoughtfulness, vanity, wisdom, hopes and despairs in my family were colored in terms of this despised way—in terms of reincarnation, astrology, and initiation. It was a muddling of an other world and this world, the mirror, and the mire.

Their master was the magnetic old lady who lived in this stuffy little apartment that they called—no, I don't know that, but I suspect—that just this little suite of rooms, this plan of inner chamber and outer chamber, was also the temple of that god Thoth, the Ibis-headed man, of Osiris and Isis. I was in the waiting room.

As I write now, I am in the waiting room again. I do not see any more than my eyes saw. My eyes have seen the veil, the double or triple moving depths of bead curtain, that in my work may still be my fascination with the movement of meaning beyond or behind meaning, of shifting vowels and consonants—beads of sound, of separate strands that convey the feeling of one weave. Of words games then. Of *Ibex, Ibis, Isis.*

In Charles Olson's warning to me in 1954, *Against Wisdom as Such*, he writes: "I wanted even to say that San Francisco seems to have become an école des Sages ou Mages as ominous as Ojai, L.A."

There is something about looking behind things. There is the fact that I am not an occultist or a mystic but a poet, a maker-up-of things.

Chapter 3

[MARCH 12, Sunday. 1961.]

It is time now for the projected configuration, the visual projection of
The War Trilogy. Not only the images of the poem arise from vision
but the formal concept relates primarily to illumination, painting, or
tapestry, in contrast, for instance, with the musical concept of Eliot's
Four Quartets or Pound's *Cantos*. Music enters in—the "O, What I
meant / by music when I said music" of *Tribute to the Angels* XXII comes
as a poignant yearning:

> music sets up ladders,
> it makes us invisible,
>
> it sets us apart,
> it lets us escape;

"but from the visible," she continues: "there is no escape." What is
seen and in the poem the matter is always the seen, is what cannot be
escaped, the ground of responsibility. For H.D. the eye in seeing is
involved:

> but from the visible
> there is no escape;
>
> there is no escape from the spear
> that pierces the heart.

Vision itself may be the spear; the eye being struck, the necessary vulnerable spot, where reality can get at the hero-poet. Yet this reality in what is seen is just that web of appearance that we also mistrust as the phantasmal, the Celtic glamour or faerie. H.D.'s intensity of image arises in her stricture of the eye to see in the clear, to penetrate the elf-skin or shimmer of excited vision and to locate the object. She holds a limit in poetry against the riot of the imagination, for she seeks a conscious recognition of what is going on. The very tenseness of her line is an attention that functions to hold back from the potency poetry has to produce its own luxe of the unreal, the world seen thru a glass darkly, the shadow of the dome of pleasure, the strange thunders from the potency of song, and the magic casements that open upon fairy seas. This reverie or "escape" in ascent or descent beyond the scale of the consciously analyzed is the medium of what she calls music that she resists. Dream and day-dream are a source of image, as ecstatic states in her waking life are a source, but in the poem she does not dream or day-dream but strives to render an exact account of what she has seen.

In the first panel, *The Walls Do Not Fall,* there is the war, the City (London) drawn under the rain or reign of fire, that in late Medieval Christian painting would have been Sodom and Gomorrah. In classical history, it is "Pompeii has nothing to teach us." In my family's theosophical fantasy this City in its last days was Atlantis:

> over us, Apocryphal fire,
> under us, the earth sway, dip of a floor,
> slope of a pavement . . .

The ruins, the pressure, the fire, where:

> the bone-frame was made for
> no such shock knit within terror,
> yet the skeleton stood up to it:

revivifies the image she had known twenty years before of that burnt-out triangle of iron: the inner psychic state finds its fulfillment in the conditions of the bombardment. Reality for H.D. is an identity between the self and the event.

The tapestry itself weaves the theme of the City under fire to haunt all other areas of the poem. It is not only a figure but a thread. In the foreground are woven, recalling the ground of flowers and small animals of Medieval tapestry, the first forms of our life, shell-fish, worm on the leaf, serpent. In verse XXXVIII the analogy with tapestry is openly drawn in answer to the counter questioning of her own thought. The antagonist of the poem argues:

This search for historical parallels,
research into psychic affinities,

has been done to death before,
will be done again;

and the protagonist of the poem defines clearly that search and research, parallels and affinities here are not operations toward a philosophy but operations of a fabrication, open possibilities of design. History, psyche, biology, the physics of the universe are elements of the artist's creation. The poet and her reader, the animal and plant worlds, the stars and events are revealed in a fabric the poem weaves.

my mind (yours),
your way of thought (mine),

each has its peculiar intricate map,
threads weave over and under

the jungle-growth
of biological aptitudes,

inherited tendencies,

This sense of the interrelation of figures, each particular "map" having its "inherited tendencies" and in turn its "aptitudes," is on the one hand a sense of life in terms of correspondences and evolutions of form, Darwinian and ecological; on the other hand the artist's sense of the work itself in which each part derives from and is source of the design of the whole.

Randall Jarrell is snide and means to dismiss H.D.'s work from serious consideration when in *Partisan Review* he comments glibly: "H.D.

is History, and misunderstands a later stage of herself so spectacularly that her poem exists primarily as an anachronism." Yet the statement "H.D. is History" is curiously right; for she takes her identity in her vision of history.

I make all things new.
I John saw. I testify,

So, in *Tribute to the Angels* she reminds us of another text where John at Patmos "misunderstands" a stage of history—for it is a puzzle of the Christian apocalypse that it mistakes history in order to create a history that had not been there before. So too, Bosch, seeing the conflict of rising nations and warring churches in the light of his Adamite heresy as an Armageddon, misunderstands the "history" of his times. But to speak of misunderstanding thus is to misunderstand History itself, for historians, no less than artists, are creative and *make all their things new*. Gibbon and Spengler have their fire in their "misunderstanding." Thoth, Mercury, is patron of thought itself, mercurial where it informs.

·

"To show how the worm turns" means something mercurial about the psyche, about the worm turning into its butterfly; means too something hermetic about the evolution of the psyche—the worm or dragon, the old serpent, that turns to betray us in ourselves. Following the tradition of the tapestry, the worm on the leaf is just such a detail of the flowering ground as we have seen in medieval work; and turns or leads into other figures of the scene:

Gods, goddesses
wear the winged head-dress

or horns, as the butterfly
antennae

to reappear in "the erect king-cobra crest," the *uraeus* of the god-crown of Egypt.

·

From *The Book of the Dead* I find: "Understanding said of him, 'He is like that which he creates'."

March 12, Sunday
In *The Walls Do Not Fall,* the quick-changing mercurial and the conspiring hermetic appear in the experience of the War itself.

> We have seen how the most amiable,
> under physical stress,
>
> become wolves, jackals,
> mongrel curs;

"Let us, therefore," H.D. turns: "entreat Hest"

> in her attribute of Serqet,
>
> the original great-mother,
> who drove
>
> harnessed scorpions
> before her.

I.

In the background—a scene resembling the City under Fire in *Lot's Daughters,* a painting attributed to Lucas of Leyden, reproduced in *Verve,* January–March 1939. For H.D., it is not a City of the Plain but does recall Pompeii, Nineveh, and Babel. In *Tribute to the Angels,* in the central panel, it is compared to Rome, Jerusalem, Thebes. Above, there is the night sky with stars—Sirius, Vega, Arcturus; the constellations—Scorpion, Archer, Goat, Waterman, Aries—"the wandering stars" and "the lordly fixed ones." Over the world-city, over actual London, the skies open up and pour out their flames. It is the old wrath of god; it is the actual new incendiary attack. Fallen walls and blackened dwellings stand out, silhouetted in the raging light.

So, when in the poem, the poet says:

> O, do not look up
> into the air,
>
> you who are occupied
> in the bewildering
>
> sand-heap maze
> of present-day endeavour;

it is a reference to the incendiary bombardment that has cast a confusing light upon the common-sense business of men. But it is also, we begin to realize, a reference to the stars:

> You will be, not so much frightened
> as paralyzed with inaction,

refers then both to heeding the war and to heeding the stars.

The worship of nature is H.D.'s first heresy; and then, in that worship there is further the willing evocation of and participation in the enchantment of nature. Woodland and sea shrine are primaries of the poet. Helios is a spiritual light but he is always the Sun. But in the first poems the stars do not have the place they are to have later in her feeling of ratios. Hermes is a garden herm; he is not yet Hermes-Mercury having the light of a star. In "The Shrine," She-Who-Watches-Over-The-Sea is not yet thought of as the star Venus, the dual identity with Lucifer:

> Phosphorus at sun-rise
> Hesperus at sun-set

so important in the concept of the later work. In the great ratio that morning-evening star will be for H.D. as for T.S. Eliot in the *Four Quartets* the star of Mary. Eliot's "Lady, whose shrine stands on the promontory," protectress of ships, is the benign persona of that same power, the ancient sea-borne goddess, who in "The Shrine" appears as the wrecker of ships.

The Orion of "Orion Dead" is the titanic Orion, child of earth, as Apollodorus drew him, ravener of the woodlands. Heat of the sun, light of the torch—what touch knows and can know defines the limits of vision. Her early ratios are all within the reality established concert of sensory-sensual data. "Bid the stars shine forever" I find in "Centaur Song":

> O I am eager for you!
> as the Pleiads shake
> white light in whiter water
> so shall I take you?

in "Fragment Thirty-Six" (from Sappho's "I know not what to do: my mind is divided") and in "Fragment Forty" ("Love . . . bittersweet"):

> (such fire rent me with Hesperus,)
> then the day broke.

What is beyond reach enters into *Collected Poems* (1925) only as it appears in earthly mortal experience, a reflection in water, at most an attendant of dawn. And in *The Hedgehog* where H.D. unfolds adventure by adventure her sense of the divine world, though Zeus is translated into "the father of everyone . . . like the other God our Father which art in Heaven" and His messengers are listed, the stars are not among them. This God remains the Weltgeist.

It seems to Madge, questioning the learned Doctor Blum in her search for the meaning of *hérisson*, that it might be a messenger. "'A messenger?' Doctor Blum inquired, having, it appeared, forgotten about the eagle. 'Oh, a messenger'—he remembered—'like—like what, exactly, Roselein?' 'I mean a sort of thing that—that helps people. I mean, like the eagle was a messenger of God, and the cuckoo was God, and the swan was God too, when he was most white and beautiful and had Helen and Cassandra, who made the war of Troy, and the messengers who are called Oreads . . . '" The angels or people of the heaven are birds, but they are not yet stars.

Up to 1925, anyway, for all of H.D.'s early identification of her time with Alexandrian times, her imagination keeps the bounds of the pre-Alexandrian Greek mind. Like Xenophanes of Colophon, she holds to the reality of earth. "For everything comes from earth," Xenophanes maintained: "and everything goes back to earth at last. This is the upper limit of the earth that we see at our feet, in contact with the air; but the part beneath goes down to infinity." This is the chthonian good sense of the Greeks; and the sensory directive of the Imagists in poetry, disciplining the imagination to the concrete and away from aerial fancy, is close in spirit. "She whom they call Iris," Xenophanes wrote: "she too is actually a cloud, purple and flame-red and yellow to behold." "The intelligence of Man grows towards the material that is present," Empedocles taught. Even in Orphism this strong prejudice or practical wisdom insists upon its elements of earth, air, fire, and water; *pneuma* is breath, and the *Anima Mundi* is the element air in which we take our living breath.

The tradition of the substantial resisted the sidereal theology of the Chaldeans "as long as Greece remained Greece," as Cumont puts it. Plato's "great visible gods," divine intangible ultimate realities or essences, were the wedge; but for the imagination to entertain the lords of light or the star of Bethlehem, a conversion of mind had to take place. Vision in and of itself became a highest criterion of the real. Things got out of hand, man saw and took self in what he could not grasp. To have a star then, to take life in the remotest possibility of the real and even in the risk of what was not realized—the unreal—was at the root of the new understanding or misunderstanding of the divine. What we see is Man's deep and transforming engagement with an "other" world of nonsense, and nonsense, the troubling of reality that we know as Christendom, not only the City of God but also Alice's "Wonderland."

The early determination of known limits remains in The War Trilogy working side by side in the fabric of consciousness with the later cosmic ratios. There is not only the stellar phantasm of:

The Presence was spectrum-blue,
ultimate blue ray,

like the blue aura of popular theosophy or the blue flame or light that Wilhelm Reich, heretical psychoanalyst, tells us he saw in the living cell, but there is also the strong counter-feeling of necessary bounds, that the hermit within

> like the planet
>
> senses the finite,
> it limits its orbit

What she has sensed, what she has dreamt, what words suggest are distinguished even as they are interwoven in one experience. "I sense my own limit" remains a primary term of her art. And the dual proportions—the apprehension of the great stars and the humanistic concept of self—give an ironic charm to her admission that follows the "O, do not look up / into the air," address to those others who are occupied in "present-day endeavour":

> and anyhow,
> we have not crawled so very far
>
> up our individual grass-blade
> toward our individual star.

II.

The figures of the foreground must be, and their world, seen as under a microscope's lens, enlarged. To the left we find the world of tidal life, a margin; and the under-water. Her sense here is evolutionary, that given in the earliest life forms we will find "the craftsman," "the hermit" or "self-out-of-self, / selfless, that pearl-of-great-price." In *The Flowering of the Rod,* she will insist again:

> No poetic fantasy
> but a biological reality,
>
> a fact: I am an entity
> like bird, insect, plant
>
> or sea-plant cell;
> I live; I am alive;

To the right: the field where the worm clings to the grass-blade, explores the rose-thorn (that here, in the transformation of the tapestry becomes a forest), eats at the leaf, devours the ear-of-wheat:

for I know how the Lord God
is about to manifest, when I

the industrious worm,
spin my own shroud.

This same insect perspective of the psyche appears in Pound's vision of *The Pisan Cantos,* in the "nor is it for nothing that the chrysalids mate in the air" of Canto LXXIV that colors the meaning of the Confucian "To study with the white wings of time passing" that occurs later in the same Canto. In Canto LXXX:

if calm be after tempest
that the ants seem to wobble
as the morning sun catches their shadows

leads towards the "The ant's a centaur in his dragon world" of the close of LXXXI. These reflections which Pound draws from seeing the actual small world about him enormous are like the mirages or loomings in which ships and the Farallon Islands upon the horizon appear giants reflected from layers of air beyond Stinson Beach.

In *The Walls Do Not Fall,* the worm is an identity of the poet. The identification may be taken as metaphorical, illustrative of the poet's persistence:

In me (the worm) clearly
is no righteousness, but this—

persistence; I escaped spider-snare,
bird-claw, scavenger bird-beak,

clung to grass-blade,
the back of a leaf . . .

But the I that was shell-fish and that was also worm recalls the incantations of the Taliesin wherever life has been or is:

I have been teacher to all Christendom
I shall be on the face of the earth until Doom,
And it is not known what my flesh is, whether flesh or fish.

The Book of Taliesin, Alwyn and Brinley Rees tell us in *Celtic Heritage,* is replete with utterances beginning with "I have been," "and the things he has been include inanimate objects—stock, axe, chisel, coracle, sword, shield, harp-string, raindrop, foam; animals such as bull, stallion, stag, dog, cock, salmon, eagle—and a grain which grew on a hill." These identifications may be also the impersonations of the actor—the animal dancer in the caves of pre-history or the twentieth century student of Stanislavsky.

There were often times in childhood when, lying in the tall grass, the perspective of the world shifted so that this little scope became the eye's universe and an ant or worm was hero or protagonist of that world; his journey along a leaf, over a stem, around a stone, became momentous. So that I would forget myself in the ant's purposes or in the worm's intent. That was one instance where one's consciousness was transported to another world that was still this world.

The other, related perspective, was the one of H.D.'s poem, as the identity would come in dreams, where one *was* an ant or worm, living a life within a life, in a perspective of the ant's "dragon world" within one's own sensible human world. Though I am persuaded to the truth of Freud's sexual analysis of the language of dreams and of our daily lives, as a poet I know that language has many such realms for the wave of life itself strives to speak in us, and from some parent cell drifting in the first seas, child of Ocean and of radiations from Sun or even from the stars beyond, a germ of animal sympathy has survived to find its life in me as a man. In some protomammal—mutation or conversion of a germinal form—all the yet-to-evolve possibilities of wolf, rabbit, elephant, or man lay hidden; we are co-expressions of the idea of the mammal, members of a "kingdom" as the biologists recognize. There may be then in the differentiated members an intuition of the undifferentiated potency in which we belong to a tree of living forms, and may dream in the tree of being not only ancestral entities but collateral entities.

There is the curious poetic tradition that Denis Saurat traces in *Gods of the People* not only of other worlds but of other lives, not only of a divided mind but of a divided existence. What idea of reality lay back of Blake's:

> The Caterpillar on the Leaf
> Repeats to thee thy Mother is grief,

Not only trance mediums made trips to other planets and stars but poets too practiced mental traveling "to the other side" of the waters as in Blake or to the other side of the interstellar abyss as in Victor Hugo's *Contemplations*. Here Saurat traces a cosmos in which every being has many personalities—"each has other parts, elsewhere in space, elsewhere in time." "A frowning thistle implores my stay," Blake writes:

> What to others a trifle appears
> Fills me full of smiles or tears;
> For double the vision my eyes do see,
> And a double vision is always with me
> With my inward Eye 'tis an old Man grey;
> With my outward a thistle across my way—

The great *Maya* of Indian thought seems to invade the West. But if *poiein* means to make, and poet is maker; *Maya,* Zimmer tells us, means to measure, to form, to build; the *maya* or illusion of the real is itself in Indian thought a great poetry. It is not out of order that in the poetic tradition of other cultures, even in England or France or in America, like concepts should appear. Victor Hugo in "Pleurs dans la nuit" hears a stone that he has kicked out of his way cry out:

> I took Thebes in its ruin,
> I saw Susa on its knees
> I was Baal at Tyre! I was Scylla in Rome!

"So each man," Saurat, gathering the idea from fairy tradition and poetic lights and also from folk-lore of unorthodox twentieth century Christianity, finds "is spread out in time and space, has parts of his being in the past, parts in the future, parts somewhere on earth, parts in the stars and in spiritual worlds parallel to this physical world."

The ratio between the worm and the star, the identity taken in the mollusk or the wild-goose, may isolate H.D. from her contemporaries. Deeply as Ezra Pound drank at the fountain of Yeats's occult lore, though in *The Cantos,* as in The War Trilogy, angelic powers appear and parts of the poet's being are in the past, though the ant looms large in reflection, the poet's identity does not become confused in the web of many incarnations. But this same confusion that isolates H.D. from her contemporaries unites her with the imagination of Blake and Victor Hugo.

As early as "Narthex" in 1928 we find a conversion in H.D.'s concept from the Greek one-dimension to the Venetian—"renaissance" Raymonde calls it. She practises a magic of warming and drifting identifications. "The sun would soon go suddenly but mites still swarmed within it . . . people . . . people . . . in the porches of the piazetta, in and out of the cathedral doorways. People swarmed and people drifted . . . " "I want to be a great bee," Raymonde thinks: "I want to crawl in and forget everything in this thing." She sees Saint Mark's Cathedral as a great flower.

Raymonde's mind, it seems to her, rises out of confusion, out of hysteria, "a lily, rising on tall stem." "Loss of identity is the gift of Venice," she continues: "power to crawl, snail self up the surface of high window and creep half-hatched moth in among tenuous rootlets and dynamic deep earth feelers." It is this experience that Raymonde cannot share with Gareth.

"I am the child of Gaia (Earth) and of starry Ouranos (Heaven)," so the Orphic initiate testified in the Underworld. H.D.'s "Earth" or mother was named Helen, was Helena or Greece then. And her father, the astronomer, was a master or keeper of the stars, Ouranos then. The stars had been there in the beginning for her, as her father's study or property—her paternal inheritance. In the prose works of the middle period, 1925 to 1935, there is the Solomon's Seal star of "Narthex" and the movie star of *The Usual Star,* but the stars of Heaven do not appear. In the poems the stars begin to come out—Narcissus in "Myrtle Bough" turns from his "chrysalis of steel and silver" and "who cast my silver-self afar" sees his own image in Hesperus:

for one star
rises above the sand-dunes,

one star lights
the pool above the marshes,

"Yourself in myself, / mirror for a star, / star for a mirror." In "Myrtle
Bough" the Greek theme is mixed with "the contents / of Assyrian phi-
als," with "dreams of Medes and Grecians." The star cult enters H.D.'s
poetry as it entered Greek culture, an invasion of Assyrian-Chaldean-
Persian influences—"*the Median rites.*" In the "Stars wheel in purple"
of "Let Zeus Record," Hesperus, Aldebaran, Sirius, the Pleiades, and
"Orion's sapphires, luminous" appear; they are, we know, also actual
lovers. "Take me home," H.D. will sing in *The Walls Do Not Fall:*

> where we may greet individually
> Sirius, Vega, Arcturus,
>
> where these separate entities
> are intimately concerned with us,

These now seem most surely to be the stars of an astrological cult,
but we must remember too that "take me home" is "take me back."
That "anywhere / where stars blaze through clear air" can be London
before the War, when that brilliant new constellation of poets appeared
together briefly: Pound, Eliot, Lawrence, Williams, Marianne Moore;
each separate entity intimately concerned with H.D. as none of them
were so concerned later. And back of that "home," the first home
appears: it is the study of the father. In *Tribute to Freud* H.D. makes it
clear that the study, the father's room, of Professor Freud leads back to
the study of Professor Doolittle. These great astral forces then of The
War Trilogy:

> where great stars pour down
> their generating strength, Arcturus
>
> or the sapphires of the Northern Crown;

are charged with the powers of living men.

[April 24th, 1963: In the dream I had gone to meet Jess at the coun-
try house or retreat of Muriel Rukeyser, but this Muriel Rukeyser was

another. Even in the dream I was troubled by the fact that I could not identify the woman, and now it seems to me, for Muriel Rukeyser in my mind has always impersonated the poetess, that the house in the dream may have been the retreat of the Poetess Herself. It was in a village on the Pennsylvania Turnpike, a very English village with great trees, that had not changed since the earliest days of colonial America. This Pennsylvania home may have been H.D.'s Bethlehem, and then, because the stars come into the picture, it may be *the* Bethlehem too, for just before sleep I had been rereading her account of her father and mother in *Tribute to Freud*. Her mother, she tells us there, was a descendant of one of the original groups of the Unitas Fratrum, the Moravian Brotherhood, of Count Zinzendorf. The Moravians had settled in the New World, in the earliest days of colonial Pennsylvania.]

What returned to my thought as I began work this morning was the revelation of the stars. For the dream Muriel Rukeyser, the Poetess of the major arcana of my own dream-tarot, took us out to see the night sky. All the stars of the cosmos had come forth from the remotest regions into the visible. At first I was struck by the brilliance of Orion, but as I looked the field was crowded with stars, dense cells of images and then almost animal constellations of the night sky. It was as if we saw the whole over-populated species of Man, and in that congregation of the living and dead, the visible and the invisible members of the whole, we began to make out patterns of men, animal entities whose cells were living souls.

"We see these skies here," the Poetess said, "because we are very close to the destruction of the world."

III.

In the middle ground of the panel, where men and gods mingle, under the stars and the fire, under fire (light and flame), what we see in the Heavens and what we see in terms of our evolutionary life (above and below) are dimensions now of something happening in a multiple image, like those revelations of one thing in another or mingling of images in Salvador Dalí's dream paintings.

Where in the foreground of our Nature the life of the worm is enacted, suggesting in his cocoon a shroud, and in his metamorphosis a resurrection; in the middle-ground of our human Person, we are reminded that men, gods, wear winged and horned head-dresses:

> as the butterfly
> antennae,
>
> or the erect king-cobra crest
> to show how the worm turns.

These images are rhymes and recall previous occurrences of the poem to the mind as echoes of sound do. There is, as there is a highly developed melody of syllables, a melody of figures in H.D.'s work. Neither rime nor image occurs as a device, to punctuate line-end or to enliven some convention in its keeping; but they are cells of the tissue of meaning and feeling itself. Blake's Worm on the Leaf is now not only "thy Mother's grief" but Pharaoh, Lord of Upper and Lower Egypt—two kingdoms or two natures or two minds, and will be, in verse XXXV of *The Walls Do Not Fall:*

> in the light of what went before,

"be ye wise . . . as serpents," woven into one figure, a felt design in the poem that in turn transforms our sense of design in history where Blake, Pharaoh, and the cunning of the serpent that *The Zohar* tells us Jacob stole from Laban, enter in to a new continuum.

"Transformation aims at the continuum of all perceptions," Robert Kelly writes in his "Notes on the Poetry of Images" (1960). "Percepts are from dreams or from waking, rise from the unconscious or from the retina of the awakened eye. Poetry, like dream reality, is the juncture of the experienced with the never experienced. Poetry, like waking reality, is the fulfillment of the imagined and the unimagined." Then: "Poetry is not the art of relating word to word, but the ACT of relating word to percept, percept to percept, image to image until the continuum is achieved." And: "The progression of images constitutes the fundamental rhythm of the poem."

There is always reference to tapestry and painting—these images in

H.D.'s work are interwoven; the movement of the poem in time is parallel to an imagined movement of the eye over the surface of the larger picture in time. But the fusion of voice heard and image seen along the track of a moving, changing picture is more immediately related to the sound-track and the film of the newest "visual" art, the movie. The sequence of the poem in which in the opening "shots" we see first "rails" then "rails gone" then "guns" then the old town square, in fog, for there is "mist and mist-grey, no colour," and the frame changes to reveal "Luxor bee, chick and hare" carved in stone writing. The transitions, the flash-backs, the movement of the eye from object to object to tell its story, the projection—all these aspects of H.D.'s art relate not only to the stream of consciousness or the free associations of her analysis with Freud in 1933 and 1934 but to the techniques of the cinema.

Answering *The Little Review*'s valedictory questionnaire in May 1929, H.D. wrote: "Just at the moment I am involved with pictures. We have almost finished a slight lyrical four reel little drama, done in and about the villages here, some of the village people and English friends. The work has been enchanting, never anything such fun and I myself have learned to use the small projector and spend literally hours alone here in my apartment, making the mountains and village streets and my own acquaintances reel past me in light and light and light. All the light within light fascinates me, 'satisfies' me, I feel like a cat playing with webs and webs of silver." In this new art, contemporaneous with H.D.'s own lifetime, painting and tapestry could be recalled. H.D. sees the projection of the image as a web of silver, or is it the thread of film that she means? But "web" occurs again—it is not only what she most wants to do or know or be, it is also what she most fears: "I fear the being caught in any one set formula or set of circumstances, I fear poverty in that it might catch me up in some ugly web of the wrong sort of things and the wrong sort of attitudes. I fear people from the future who may 'trap' me."

Between 1928 and 1930, Kenneth Macpherson, Bryher's second husband, edited and published *Close Up*, "The Only Magazine Devoted to Films as an Art," with Bryher as assistant editor. Old associates appear from the literary nexus of the early twenties—Gertrude Stein is there to contribute her avant-garde note, and Dorothy Richardson writes an elegiac to the silent film. But the writers in *Close Up* seem not to be associated, as writers in *Des Imagistes, The Little Review, transition,* or *Exile,* were, with a common cause in a new art in writing; they suggest often the intimate amateur correspondence of a social "in-group." "(Dear H.D. Pardon the theft)" Hay Chowl can write in quoting an article of H.D.'s. The "We have finished a slight lyrical four reel little drama" of H.D.'s reply to *The Little Review,* with "some of the village people and English friends" came as an account of how far she was from her old literary associations. The thought of Pound, Williams, or Lawrence is remote now; even the profession of poetry will not do when she is asked "What should you most like to do, to know, to be?" In this "Bryher" milieu new associations were forming however that will play their part in H.D.'s return in full to the profession of poetry in her last phase. When the London correspondent of *Close Up,* Robert Herring, later becomes editor of *Life and Letters Today* a new literary context appears. Gertrude Stein, Dorothy Richardson, and H.D. will be a familiar expectation; Bryher is an even more constant contributor; Edith Sitwell enters the picture (and there may be a common ground of magic and visionary prophetic mode between the later poetry of Edith Sitwell and H.D.'s War Trilogy); carried over from the impetus of *Close Up,* the art of film becomes a new department of *Life and Letters Today,* and more important, the genius of Eisenstein is brought into the new ground.

The history of "in-groups"—Bloomsbury, Villefranche, or Basel— has yet to be studied out. Literary historians are shy, even unhappy, of accounting for the way purely social factors enter in to the picture of the development of the art. We are attracted, moth-mind to the flame, by the brilliance of the company. Within the charmed circle the four reel little drama glows, we are drawn in. To have been included! But just here I falter. From the outside, the circle is an armed exclusion. Raymonde, Gareth, Daniel in H.D.'s novels test each other as if they tested the defenses of a citadel. One could never be certain that circumstances, surroundings—for a moment these walls suggest the other walls of The War Trilogy—would not set one apart among "the wrong sort of things and the wrong sort of attitudes." Here, as in the web that satisfies and the web that she fears of H.D.'s reply, the attractive social circle is forbidding; fearful within, and fearful without.

The group of Bryher's friends is involved now, as she is, in films. In film-talk and film study, and also in the making of a film. For Kenneth Macpherson in 1929 worked on a film with H.D. as star. Somewhere within the charmed circle copies may still exist. The "silver-self" "cast" as a "star" by Narcissus in the poem "Myrtle Bough" takes on a new meaning. And the medium of film is ultimately in the image projected in terms of light, cast upon the screen. Back and forth the puns of being cast in a star-role, being cast on the screen, being cast in a new light dance in bewildering webs of exchange. "The light within light fascinates me," H.D. wrote. It's a risky reading that for a moment again another impulse arises linking the flood of light streaming out from the movie projector with "the rain of beauty" of *The Flowering of the Rod* and just beyond with "where great stars pour down / their generating strength." "The sky is skyey apparition," Dorothy Richardson writes in *Close Up:* "white searchlight. The book remains the intimate, domestic friend, the golden lamp at the elbow."

In the book tapestry, painting, film may be evoked as one vision where the mind is weaver, painter, projector. Here images are not seen in locus of the subconscious or locus of the eye's retina, but they are *visualized,* created in the mind's light that men have always puzzled over. In the midst of the City under Fire in *The Walls Do Not Fall* there is a light in which the artist works "circled with what they call the *cartouche.*" The *cartouche* in French is an escutcheon upon which or within which figures that are emblematic appear; it is also a cartridge. In Webster's it says: "2. An oval or oblong figure, especially one on an Egyptian monument containing a sovereign's name. 3. In some fire-works, the case containing the inflammable materials." H.D. makes a passing joke about it, a play of words between her art and the rival war: "folio, manuscript, old parchment / will do for cartridge cases"; and then that "Hatshepsut's name"

> is still circled
> with what they call the *cartouche.*

Like the surrealists after Freud, she sets up new movements in the mind by the evocation of puns. Or like Eisenstein in his new language of cinematography where montage, rapid sequences and juxtapositions of images extend the vocabulary of the film. "The technical possibility," he writes in *Close Up,* "foolishly called a 'trick,' is undoubtedly just as important a factor in the construction of the new cinematography as is the new conception of staging from which it is sprung." Where it is not their pointedness or cleverness but their power to disturb our set idea, our sense of outline, that counts.

Here the content of the *cartouche,* the Queen's name, and then the thought of her, so that even in reference she appears to the mind's eye, is something that threatens the cherished reality of the tangible; as the immediacy of God in evocation or invocation, beyond the sensory or outside the sensory, is something we resist the thought of. Stars, immortals, gods, contained in their cartouche or cartridge, the poem, if they invade our sense of the actual, disturb, are "inflammable materials."

And The War Trilogy itself in the mode of the apocalyptic revelation contains within the circle of its ecstatic longing and belonging the light of joy that is also the flame-heat of a stored-up wrath. The rain of fire is God's wrath, and in a curious emanation the "sword" emerges from the "word." Were it not for men's thoughts and dreams, we realize, there would have been no war. The realization, once it is there, never ceases to trouble H.D. The terror and evil of the war give power and beauty to the poem.

> Never in Rome
> so many martyrs fell;
>
> not in Jerusalem,
> never in Thebes,
>
> so many stood and watched
> chariot-wheels turning,

from the fearful scene a proud music takes over, and the poet's voice takes on strength and resonance. The poem evoking, summoning forth from where it was hidden, this meaning of war, wrath, and the fulfillment of prophecy—is apocalyptic. Ammunition. A cartouche.

Within the circle of initiates—the "we" that in H.D.'s life had been a group of poets and then an exclusive social group, and now, in wartime London, was a group of occultists—the encircling containment of an art, a knowledge in which figures become emblematic—we see the double image of a group and their patron or leader. One, among whom H.D. as writer belongs, children of Hermes,

> wistful, ironical, willful
> who have no part in
> new-world reconstruction

take on from the cartouche an Egyptian character. But the cartouche that contains or surrounds the group is also "a spacious bare meeting-house" where, within the congregation of the dream, a man appears, "upright, slender." Once, long ago, she had been in love with Him in Daniel. There is no time for that. The whole scene exists in a split-second. The poet was dozing, perhaps . . . anyway: "then I woke with a start / of wonder and asked myself" she says. He is, or might have been, Ra, Osiris, Amen. In the projection, between his circle and the stars, he appears in another avatar as the zodiacal Aries painted in His Zeus glory—the Golden Fleece and the Lamb, as in the late middle ages He had indeed been worshipped at the Court of Burgundy. It is the Christ who impends, and His advent is created in the poem as it was created in history in the alembic of troubled boundaries, superimposed and adul-terated civilizations, dissolved religions—a "trick" montage of Greek, Persian, Hindu, Egyptian, Syrian gods in one unorthodox Jewish god, a synthetic realization scandalous to the orthodox, in His incarnation an heretical affront, as H.D.'s realization in The War Trilogy was scandal-ous to the literary orthodoxy of the day. It was "silly," "irresponsible," "compounded of primitive elements yet rather appealing to a sensibility both modern and confused," to present the world of the poet's imagina-tion in the old sense of the dream-vision; to be aware thruout that this dream-vision was still the very human mode of thought that Freud had studied; and in it all to insist upon the divine inspiration. Not only the thought of the Master in the dream but His Presence:

In the meeting house, we see who the new Master over Love is, whom the star from the beginning announced:

> He might even be the authentic Jew
> stepped out from Velasquez;

As long ago the sculptor appeared at work between the stone and the light in the poem "Pygmalion," creating a medium at once for his art and for the god, and H.D. herself pictured her part as poet in terms of the chiseled line, the tempered and hammered image, now the painter appears at work between the dream and the realization or incarnation, and H.D. names the palette as one with script and letters that:

> are magic, indelibly stamped
> on the atmosphere somewhere.

The magic charges the Christ of Velasquez with living Presence; a confusion between what the painter has made and what has inspired the painter in which the work of art has a life of its own. So that the poet recalling the eyes in the painting lowered know that open they "would daze, bewilder," and in that bewilderment then testifies:

> I assure you that the eyes
> of Velasquez' crucified
>
> now look straight at you,
> and they are amber and they are fire.

IV.

"An *image,* in our sense," Pound writes in his 1916 memoir of Gaudier-Brzeska, "is real because we know it directly. If it have an age-old traditional meaning this may serve as proof to the professional student of symbology that we have stood in the deathless light, or that we have walked in some particular arbour of his traditional paradiso, but that is not our affair. It is our affair to render the *image* as we have perceived or conceived it." In "The Serious Artist" (1913), he saw that the responsibility of the arts was to "bear witness and define for us the inner nature and conditions of man." "Even this pother about gods reminds one that something is worthwhile," he went on. And in "Religio" from the same pre-war period, Pound presents the Renaissance neo-paganism of Gemistos Plethon, Ficino, or Pico della Mirandola, the higher humanism in which gods are "eternal states of mind" manifest "when the states of mind take form" that may appear to the sense of vision or to the sense of knowledge. Gnostic then as well as imagist, but not Christian. "What are the gods of this rite?" Pound asks, and answers: "Apollo, and in some sense Nelios, Diana in some of her phases, also the Cytherean goddess." "To what other gods is it fitting, in harmony or in adjunction with these rites, to give incense?" "To Kore and to Demeter, also to lares and to oreiads and to certain elemental creatures."

Form and rite here are not associated by Pound with the image and practice of the poet, though, as in "Religio" it is by beauty that we know the divine forms, in another early essay "The Tradition" (1913) the tradition in poetry is "a beauty which we preserve," and in passing, Pound tells us "We know that men worshipped Mithra with an arrangement of pure vowel-sounds." This is as far as Pound goes toward a suggestion of the poet's creative involvement with the divine world. Listing the reports that the artist must not falsify, Pound in "The Serious Artist" includes that he must not falsify his report "as to the nature of his ideal of this, that or the other, of god"—where Pound has all but put god aside among the random fancies of some men, with "this, that or the other," as if he wanted to be sure he would not be taken for a Christian sentimentalist or enthusiast. "If god exist," he adds. And not an "ideal" but a fact: there is no qualification here of "if the life force exist." "We might come to believe that the thing that matters in art is a sort of energy," Pound argues: "something more or less like electricity or radio-activity, a force transfusing, welding, and unifying. A force rather like water when it spurts up through very bright sand and sets it in swift motion."

In "Cavalcanti" Pound speaks directly of the god in the work of art: "The best Egyptian sculpture is magnificent plastic; but its force comes from a non-plastic idea, i.e., the god is inside the statue. . . . The force is arrested, but there is never any question about its latency, about the force being the essential, and the rest 'accidental' in the philosophic technical sense. The shape occurs." We recognize here as we recognize in H.D.'s "Pygmalion" the informing genius of Gaudier-Brzeska. For this driven youth sculpted, wrote, or talked late at night to H.D. and Richard Aldington as he talked to Pound or Hulme—to create again and again in talk his vision of the artist-demiurgos at work in a spiritual vortex. In his essays and letters the language is charged with the character of his nature and art: "the driving power," "life in the absolute," "the intensity of existence." In H.D.'s early idea of her art, in images of fire and cut stone, the ghost of Gaudier does enter in; as it enters in in Pound's idea of her art in motives of force and form.

Does Bergson's *élan vital* enter in here? For Ezra Pound in his first London years the *élan vital* was very much in the air—in the theosophical environs of Yeats, Mead, and *The Quest* lectures, and then again in an entirely other circle, in the philosophical environs of the Bergsonian T. E. Hulme. In his "Prolegomena" and "Credo" of 1912, Pound sees his own turning to the Melic poets and to the Medieval romance-tradition in poetry as vital, not literary: "a man feeling the divorce of life and his art may naturally try to resurrect a forgotten mode if he find in that mode some leaven, or if he think he sees in it some element lacking in contemporary art which might unite that art again to its sustenance, life."

When Wyndham Lewis's scorn for the romantic takes over—ranting against what he sees as the cult of Time, the Primitive, and the Child—Bergson will be out of bounds. When Eliot's pervading concern for respectability introduces its criterion with the rhetoric of a new literary orthodoxy—though Pound's *élan* will win thru in *The Cantos,* flooding passages with image and presence of light and divine energy—in Pound's theory kulchur will replace life as the sustenance of art.

But in his first development—pre-war, pre-Eliot and Lewis, Pound's premises are not ideological but psychological. He insists upon the intellectual and emotional complex where "ideas, or fragments of ideas, the emotion and concomitant emotions, must be in harmony must form an organism." In poetry "the mind is upborne upon the emotional surge." This relation of the poem to a wave of life expression is as far as Pound is to go to relate the art to an organic creativity; and in his later criticism even these ideas of emotion and surge become diffident. The Aphrodite of *The Cantos* does not rise as Hesiod would have her from a bloody wave; she is not the goddess of sexual love and life renewal Pound addressed in *The Spirit of Romance* but the Aphrodite of the higher intellect in which Beauty has become a pure essence. The spirit of romance is supplanted by the spirit of the schools. Philosophers, not poets, form the great tradition; and among philosophers, those who seek the victory of the mind over the passions are now Pound's masters. So, in *The Pisan Cantos,* Anchises lays hold of the goddess's "flanks of air / drawing her to him / Cythera potens"; yet even this phantasm of the air is not the very Aphrodite, who is "no cloud, but the crystal body." In Canto XCI, *Section: Rock-Drill,* she appears again as "the GREAT CRYSTAL"—in its capitalization the insistence is clear. "Right reason" takes the place of the earlier "intellectual and emotional complex in an instant of time"; and "from fire to crystal / via the body of light" the Princess Ra-Set "enters protection,"

> the great cloud is about her,
> She has entered the protection of crystal.

Here the "river of crystal" appears, carrying the soul-boat up out of the carnal and psychic mire into "the body of light come forth from the body of fire," a sublimation that contrasts sharply with H.D.'s impassioned evocation in *Tribute to the Angels,* "re-light the flame," where venery and the venereous (the body of *heat*) are called forth from the body of fire and re-related to venerate, venerator in the name of Venus-Aphrodite.

·

H.D. sees the gods not only as eternal states of mind, higher beings, or great images cast in a phanopoeia, but as expressive entities of the worshipper's own creative life:

> Shall I let myself be caught
> in my own light?

Later, her Freudian persuasion will reinforce this view, but as early as "Pygmalion," the worked image (each particular intellectual and emotional instance that becomes experience then) is thought of not only as being realized in itself, an expression, but as an entity in a psychological process, a projection. She has passed from the idea of the artist's work as having its end in the object, the image, as if captured in stone, the closed system of beauty, to the dramatic perspective in which the art is a magic ground in which thought and feeling come into being and meaning returns from the object to inform the artist as he works—a way of participation thru the created object in a self-creating life; from:

I made image upon image for my use,
I made image upon image, for the grace
of Pallas was my flint

to the more involved recognition of poetry as a creative process, as in 1917 she had concentrated in a stanza:

Now am I the power
that has made this fire
start from the rocks?
am I the god?
or does this fire carve me
for its use?

the questions that in the 1930s will lead Malraux to his massive *Psychology of Art*. In turn, the creative process is recognized as a life quest or romance—Psyche's quest for Eros, the soul's quest for salvation, a new Master. She had passed from the persona or mask worn in the play to the psyche, the soul of the play that comes into being thru its masks. When, in *The Walls Do Not Fall*, Christ appears in the Image "stepped out from Velasquez," her sight of the painting, as with the statue of Pygmalion, has broken the boundaries of the aesthetic into meaning. The work is not self-contained but serves another purpose, that eyes "look straight at you"—a magic efficacy, the very presence of Christ.

In such a transformation, paint or stone take on body, as in the Christian mystery the word is incarnate; there is a charged carnality in amber eyes that would shine so in the poem, as if they could shine so in the painting. Here H.D.'s insistence that she is, we are, involved in the poem as if it were a field of associations brings us up against such a bias in aesthetic as Dewey has in *Art as Experience:* "If the perception is then eked out by reminiscence or by sentimental associations derived from literature—as is usually the case in paintings popularly regarded as poetic—a simulated aesthetic experience occurs." The criticism would seem to apply to my own appreciations as I go, where the poem and the painting are not objects but operations in a field of reminiscences, the perception eked out everywhere by associations that are sentimental, these senses of life and the mentality so identical for me. There can be no accident that along with my changing sense of poetry in my reading of H.D.'s work, and in my own writing the flooding out into literary derivations, has come a breakthru or breakdown of aesthetic evaluation of painting to include literary qualities in early Cézanne, Moreau, Böcklin, or the Pre-Raphaelites Burne-Jones and Rossetti, painters long exiled from the dominant taste of my day because of their false poetics. H.D. has been dismissed by adverse critics with slurring references to William Morris; as Pound has been put down with hints of Swinburnism; Joyce with aspersions of Pater. "There are works of art that merely excite," Dewey warns: "in which activity is aroused without the composure of satisfaction, without fulfillment within the terms of the medium. Energy is left without organization. Dramas are then melodramatic; paintings of nudes are pornographic; the fiction that is read leaves us discontented with the world in which we are, alas, compelled to live without the opportunity for the romantic adventure and high heroism suggested by the story-book."

For Ezra Pound, the operation of the work outside the spirit of its art, the excess in which what might have been aesthetic, beautiful, or later, in Vorticism, energetic, becomes psychological—sensually, sexually, or religiously sentimentalized—the psychic chiaroscuro of and in any thing—is distasteful, even abhorrent. After *The Spirit of Romance* in 1910, Pound goes no further in the matter of Dante, though he pays homage to Dante's mastery as a poet, for Pound would put aside the heart of the matter, the imagination of a Christian synthesis; as in *The Cantos* he can include the Greek gods in his history but must dismiss those unchaste aspects that the Cambridge classicists and the Vienna psychoanalysts had begun to suggest; he must exclude too the mire and the star in which Christ is born. There is a threatened chastity of mind in Pound that would put away, not face, the thought of hellish things, here in considering the Divine World, as later in considering fascism, where also he cannot allow that the sublime is complicit, involved in a total structure, with the obscene—what goes on backstage. Spirit in *The Cantos* will move as a crystal, clean and clear of the muddle, even the filth, of the world and its tasks thru which Psyche works in suffering towards Eros.

"The conception of the body as perfect instrument of the increasing intelligence pervades," he writes of Cavalcanti. He is naturally repelled when in Rubens he sees the flesh portrayed as meat. He rages like a Puritan bigot faced with the Whore of Babylon at the adulterous— latinizing—syntax of Milton, who "shows a complete ignorance of the things of the spirit." Usury brings "whores for Eleusis," corrupts the sacred orgy; the art too, under usury, becomes whorish and profane.

Healthy mindedness is an important virtue for Pound's art—the clean line. Clean mindedness, then. "The old cults were sane in their careful inquisition or novitiate," he insists in *The Spirit of Romance*. Here and in the Cavalcanti essay Pound insists upon the "well-balanced," the "*mens sana in corpore sano*" base. "All these are clean, all without hell-obsession," he writes of Ventadour, Guido, Botticelli, Ambrogio Praedis; and then, it does not occur to him that we must turn to others if we seek information concerning the nature of darker matters. To think at all, to imagine or to be concerned with, that state of human psyche whose light is Luciferian and whose adversity is Satanic—much less to admit that in our common humanity we are ourselves somehow involved in that state is, for Pound, to go wrong, to darken reason, a morbidity of mind. "We seem to have lost the radiant world where one thought cuts through another with clean edge," Pound writes of the change from Cavalcanti to Petrarch, and he relates the change in poetry to a change in world view, the loss of "a world of moving energies '*mezzo oscuro rade*,' '*risplende in se perpetuale effecto*,' magnetisms that take form, that are seen, or that border the visible, the matter of Dante's *paradiso*, the glass under water"; "untouched," he concludes, "by the two maladies, the Hebrew disease, the Hindoo disease." In reviewing *Love Poems and Others* by D. H. Lawrence in 1913, Pound, who praises Lawrence's narrative verse, finds "the middling-sensual erotic verses in this collection . . . a sort of pre-raphaelitish slush, disgusting or very nearly so." In writing on the work of Henry James, he tells us: "The obscenity of *The Turn of the Screw* has given it undue prominence. People now 'drawn' by the obscene as were people of Milton's period by an equally disgusting bigotry; one unconscious on author's part; the other, a surgical treatment of a disease." Where we begin to see that Pound's aesthetic disgust is not unmixed with psychological factors that he would like to disown.

Virgil was O.K. for Dante, it seems to Pound, for Dante knew no better. It is not the poet-portrayer of the Underworld and prophet of the coming Christos, but the high-minded master of the Superworld, Plotinus, who leads Pound up out of the mire of mud, bog-suck, and whirl-pool that is Pound's Hell. Holding the Medusa-head downward, Plotinus petrifies the evil; and perhaps Pound sees Plotinus in history as having petrified into the clear crystal of neo-Platonism the murk of the Alexandrian period, the chiaroscuro in which Christ was synthesized. "You advertise 'new Hellenism'," Pound writes to Margaret Anderson of *The Little Review:* "It's all right if you mean humanism, Pico's *De Dignitate,* the *Odyssey,* the *Moscophoros.* Not so good if you mean Alexandria. . . . "

It is to the art of music that Pound looks, to the time "when each thing done by the poet had some definite musical urge or necessity bound up within it." There is an echo of Carlyle's concept of poetry as musical thought here, but it is important too that in music the material of the artist seems most to have transcended the "slush" of flesh and earth, to be furthest from "the metamorphosis into carnal tissue" that represented the decay of values in Rubens. The avoidance of Christ in *The Cantos.* A poem that is after all primarily an epic of the gods and of the divine reality, is complex; but even with those gods who do appear in *The Cantos,* Pound avoids all knowledge of their aspects of embodying our carnal experience of suffering and mortality as a value in life. Aphrodite appears in Her light body, having no association with whorish simulacra men have made of her. There can be no compassion whereby the high suffers in the low. In the highest vision there are not then the eyes of the crucified, with their secret that life's victory lies in the passion of the love-death, but there is the love-light of "the stone eyes again looking seaward" and the Sphinx's riddle in Canto CXV "of man seeking good, / doing evil."

"Unless a term is left meaning one particular thing, and unless all attempt to unify different things, however small the difference, is clearly abandoned, all metaphysical thought degenerates into a soup,"—

so the art for Pound must strive for the dissociation of ideas; in *The Cantos* he strives for the clear entity of things and beings in themselves. For H.D. terms are either duplicit or complicit, the warp and woof of a loom. As in *Paterson,* William Carlos Williams pictures poetry, like a city, "a second body for the human mind," he quotes from Santayana's *The Last Puritan,* having all the complication of one thing in another a city has. Neither H.D. nor Williams is concerned with metaphysical thought. Pound's soup into which metaphysical thought must fall when associations are allowed may be the dream. "*Paterson* is a man (since I am a man) who dives from cliffs and the edges of waterfalls . . . But for all that he is a woman (since I am not a woman) who *is* the cliff and the waterfall." In such a poem or such a dream no entity is unmixed, there is no form that can be satisfied in itself or fulfilled in its own terms.

Since 1938, when at nineteen I began to read *The Cantos* and then in the library the files of *The Little Review,* I have had a strong sense of this quality of a thing in itself, the intensely realized form of Brancusi's columns and heads, the deliberate design of syntax in Joyce's *Ulysses,* the absolute sense of language in context in *The Cantos,* the changes in energy—movement and tone—so exactly made. Here it is the composition, not the exposition, of content that counts, and this count is a mathematic of numbers and the ratios that have been learned in the working hand and in the ear, having to do not only with soundings but with equilibriums, beyond the calculation of the brain alone. I have still this excitement about the masterpiece, the mastery of weights that lie at the edges of intuition, the informed impulse of each nerve in training, the skill that extends our apprehension of what is going on. In my mind H.D.'s War Trilogy and *Helen in Egypt* have been placed, "weighed," with such works of art, realized forms having, as Pound writes of Brancusi, "a mathematical exactitude of proportion." Our awareness of life itself springs from such an aptitude for intricate formulae, keeping the numbers dancing in proportions, the living mechanism of the body and the brain in its analyses and syntheses performing, to be alive to things at all demanding, a high cybernetics. The lasting thrill of the artist's work is that it fits, as our actions fit, when we feel them to be most alive, more than we imagined or longed for, so that we gain a heightened expectation of proportion.

I am sure that these apprehensions do not come from the unknown but are the very beginning terms of consciousness, the first factors of our human communication. The rumor remains of the unconscious, the incommunicable below, and of the super essential, the incommunicable above. But where numbers or images or persona occur we are in the realm of consciousness, for to figure and to sense is the mode of awareness. Even the rumors of psychoanalysts and metaphysicians are, like all rumors, elements arising in consciousness. The unconscious is, to apply the formula of theology, the uncreating; the super-essential, the uncreated. Myths and archetypes, like the structures Plotinus or Jung pursue in thought, are the stories and pictures we know as creation, the ground the collective conscious makes for experience. It is our consciousness not our unconscious that strives to imagine the real and the unreal, that would make a body even in the unrealized, so that the toil of creation is never done. Even these haunting rumors of the beyond consciousness, of the unknowable, appear as creatures of conscious language. Words propose "a Word beyond utterance, eluding Discourse, Intuition, Name, and every kind of being."

After the excitement in the authenticity of masterpieces, having resistant individuality and a demanding skill, I have come to see such works not as the achievement of inventors or masters or diluters or starters of crazes, as Pound would have us classify writers in his *ABC of Reading,* not as objects of a culture, embodying original sensibilities, but as events in another dimension, a field of meanings in which consciousness was in process; where I saw psyche and spirit, as I had come thru Darwin to see the animal organism, arising in an evolution of possible forms, surviving, perishing, derived always from an inheritance in which the formal persisted, arriving always as a trial or essay in which the formal had to live the last of a species, the first of a species, and yet having only its own terms, its own life, in which to make it. Every manifestation of spirit is the matter from which spirit must derive itself.

What is intent here? "Does '*intenzion*' mean intention (a matter of will)?" Pound asks, seeking the sense of certain terms of Cavalcanti, "as understood at that particular epoch," he stresses: "does it mean intuition, intuitive perception . . . ?" The psyche strives to realize; the spirit . . . to render clear? to rarify?—but I would take spirit in a rock, who am yet obsessed with light. Intent is ours for we are at work; and may change its aspect where form is not a container or an object but "an extension of content."

It is the ground art makes for the experience and the dream to become communal that I most value. Our own dreams, like our own lives, are fleeting and insubstantial, unless they are delivered over from the personal into the commons of man's dream. The man I am would stake my person from him, if it would not give itself to his intent. In works of art what was a passing fancy labors to become a lasting fantasy, the "Dream, Vision" of H.D.'s later poetic, personality to become manhood; for our manhood to be a ground of reality, for the gods to flourish, "stepped out from Velasquez."

•

The germ of this sense of art and life as the creation of a community of feeling may have been quickened even as I began to read in Pound's *Cantos* and to have my sense there of art as a personal achievement of form, for in December of 1937, in the first issue of *Verve,* passages of Malraux's *Psychology of Art* appeared. Along with the aesthetic—the concern with the beauty achieved—there was then the psychological—the concern for the meaning that labored to come into existence in art. Going back now I find evidence certainly of what must have encouraged me, under pain of being rhetorical, to search for what would declare itself, however it could in words: where Malraux speaks of "the metabolism of destiny into consciousness," "across particular modes of expression, a plane of communion amongst men," meaning seems to try itself for survival with a risk. And when Malraux tells us "That Jonah in the belly of the whale and Joseph in the pit prefigure Christ in the tomb, that the visit of the Queen of Sheba foreshadows the coming of the Magi—such beliefs quickened in the sculptors an emotion that, in due time, infused their representations of Jonah, Joseph and the Queen of Sheba with the very breath of life . . . ," he seems to speak for me as I would make it clear that not only is the work of the artist to realize a form in itself, but that form is in turn a womb of unrealized feeling and thought that must seek birth in form, in a man's work.

These passages of Malraux, read when I was nineteen, converted my mind so that H.D.'s later work was bound, as by a spell, to seem a break-thru in poetry of a new gain in consciousness. Or the poem had ripened, having in it now more of the permission to live. There was too, I am sure, the redemption that the religion of my parents, the Hermetic teachings in which my own mind had been nursed, would come into its own, having meaning in this new psychological light. Yet these things converted or redeemed because my spirit had taken hold in them, finding life here and not elsewhere, discovering a self and a story in the threads and images with which it worked its self and story, a—

                    •

—TAPESTRY. The visual projection of the poem comes to me in terms of a narrative and emblematic tapestry. To spin a yarn; to weave a tale—so we speak in our common use today long after looms have disappeared from our daily lives. There is back of that sense a scene in which the poem and the tapestry, going on at the same time in the same room, belong together. Where Homer sings of the wrath of Achilles and of Odysseus (as in our day, the song appears in Zukofsky's *"A"*-12, addressed to Celia Zukofsky—and in her, to Bach—*Blest, Ardent, Celia, Happy*:

> Tell me of that man who got around
> After sacred Troy fell,
> He knew men and cities
> His heart riled in the sea
> As he strove for himself and friends:
> He did not save them.
> Tell us about it, my Light,
> Start where you please.

where the poet sings, the women spin and weave, as the poet in turn spins out the thread of his narrative and weaves at the loom of his rhymes and stressed tones towards the workings, the close interrelations of his story.

                    •

There might have been some "joke," a knot or pun of the interchange in the development of the two arts—the two weavings where the story refers to a hero hidden among the women at the loom, or to a Penelope who like Shahrazad in the *Arabian Nights* must contrive to make her weaving or story begin again each day. To avoid something happening, to keep something happening. The exile in which the Odyssey can take place.

·

It is one of the recurrent images of H.D.'s writing of the process itself. "Threads weave over and under" in XXXVIII of *The Walls Do Not Fall;* and it is in the tradition of the tapestry-maker's art that we see the foreground of grass and leaves and enlarged insect life in the poem, a decorative area as well as an area of meaning in the story where each part of the work:

> differs from every other
> in minute particulars,
>
> as the vein-paths on any leaf
> differ from those of every other leaf
>
> in the forest . . .

·

As H.D.'s signature could bring to mind the insignia woven in the design of a palace tapestry, and did, as I was working on *Medieval Scenes* in 1947, so that when the lines came in "The Banners":

> Above their heads the signet of the Prince
> is woven, elaborate blood-red signature.

in the vision of those initials, and in the conjunction of Poet and Sovereign Power as one, the dreamer of the dream or the maker of the poem, I recalled, not my own "R.D.," but a passage in *Tribute to Freud,* which I had read two years before, in which H.D. tells us: "(I have used my initials H.D. consistently as my writing signet or sign-manual, though it is only, at this very moment, as I check upon the word 'signet' in my Chambers English Dictionary that I realize that my writing signature has anything remotely suggesting sovereignty or the royal manner.)"

Chapter 4

Pound in *How To Read* (1927) and again in *ABC of Reading* (1934) lists three practices or faculties of poetry: (1) *phanopoeia* "throwing the object (fixed or moving) on to the visual imagination," where language operates somehow like a magic lantern or a motion-picture projector in relation to the receiving mind that is a screen. The early definition of the image as "that which presents an intellectual and emotional complex in an instant of time" is appropriate for the stationary, almost hallucinatory, presentations of early imagist poems—Pound's "apparition" of faces as petals on a black bough, seen in the blink of an eye or of a camera shutter, or H.D.'s rose, "cut in rock," that exists in a garden as if frozen in time, as if time had come to a stop in the photograph. H.D.'s reiterated hardness and cut-edges may have been in part a critical reaction to the great salon photography of the first decade of the century, to the blurred and softened atmospheric images of Steichen, Stieglitz, or Coburn.

But these stills are few in number. After a handful of imagist poems, the poets were interested in movement. The sequence of images is what tells in *The Cantos,* and, scene juxtaposed to scene, line juxtaposed to line, the poem is built up like an Eisenstein film in the cutting room. In the passing of image into image, person into person, in H.D.'s War Trilogy too we are reminded of the transitions and montage that developed in the moving picture.

The other two ways "to charge the language with meaning to the utmost possible degree" were (2) *melopoeia* and (3) *logopoeia:* "inducing emotional correlations by the sound and rhythm of the speech" and "inducing both of the effects by stimulating the associations (intellectual or emotional) that have remained in the receiver's consciousness in relation to the actual words or word groups employed."

"Imagism" divorced from this concern "to charge the language with meaning" is not the Imagism of Pound, H.D., and Aldington, proposed in the Credo of 1912. The image that would charge language with sensory impression, "Amygism," Pound called it, and the image that would charge language with an interesting effect, Hulme's

And saw the ruddy moon lean over a hedge
Like a red-faced farmer

or Eliot's

When the evening is spread out against the sky
Like a patient etherised upon a table

—these are generically different from the image that would charge language with meaning. Perception and expression are paramount where man's emotions and intellections give value to an otherwise valueless language and world. But, for Pound and H.D., as for Williams and D.H. Lawrence, things and events strive to speak. To evoke an image is to receive a sign, to bring into human language a word or a phrase (in Pound's later poetics, the ideogram; in H.D.'s, the hieroglyph) of the great language in which the universe itself is written.

Here, to experience is to read; to be aware involves at once the senses and the translation into language of our own. It is the belief that meaning is not given to the world about us but derived from the world about us, that our human language is a ground in which we participate in the cosmic language. Living is reading the message or poem that creation is about. Such a sense of the universe as a meaningful creation and of experience as coming to apprehend that meaning determines the change from the feeling that poetic form is given to or imposed upon experience—transforming matter into content—to the feeling that poetic form is found in experience—that content is discovered in matter. The line of such poetry is not free in the sense of being arbitrary but free in its search and self-creation, having the care and tension (attention) almost of the ominous, for a world that would speak is itself a language of omens. Eliot's images are often theatrical devices; but his garden, the drained pool, river, sea, and flowers of *Four Quartets* are images of charged meaning, having their origins in a more than personal phantasy—they are signs of Self that have come to in-form the poet's true self, epiphanies of what is happening, not symbols but *ideas,* seeings of the truth of things. Williams's resolve in the opening passage of *Paterson* does not read "not in ideas but in things"; what he writes is "no ideas but in things." As we enter the poem we are to strive, in order to live, to read such a language of things—river, falls, fire, detritus, words. For words are not thoughts we have but ideas in things, and the poet must attend not to what he means to say but to what what he says means.

.

This is the charge of the mystery cult, the showing forth of a meaning which is a thing seen, where Image and Logos are revealed in the gift of the Idea. We may see what it means or, sensing the meaning, search for what it means; or we may dismiss whatever presentation abruptly with "I don't see any meaning in that." The mythos and dromenon of the Dionysia were a way of participating in the meaningful; the singers and dancers coming into the community of meanings, as the poet comes into such a community when he sings or recites as if our daily words were a language of poetry, having the power in themselves to mean, and our role in speaking were to evoke not to impose meanings. The things of the poem, the words in their musical phrasings, here, are *sacra,* charged with divine power, and give birth to poems as the poet sings, as the powers of stones, waters, winds, in men's rites give birth to gods. In the process itself a magic begins, so that gods and poetry enthrall. "*Le sacré c'est le père du dieu,*" Jane Harrison quotes from Durkheim. "*Le désir c'est le père de la sorcellerie.*" The intent of the poet is to arouse the content and form of the poem as the ritual devotee seeks to arouse the content and form of the god.

The religious image and the poetic image are close in turn to the psychological archetype of Jungian analysis, which seeks to arouse the content and form of the individual life from the collective unconscious. Certainly, we can recognize in Whitman's "eidólon yacht of me," in Lawrence's "ship of death," in the "Ra-Set boat" of Pound's *Rock-Drill Cantos,* and in H.D.'s "Ship to hold all" in *Helen in Egypt,* not only the intensity of a personal expression, but also the depth of a community of meaning. The language is not American or English or Greek or Egyptian but the language of Poetry, in which this image of a soul-boat upon a sea in the poetic imagination comes to speak.

.

Pound's *phanopoeia, melopoeia,* and *logopoeia* are not reasonable literary terms but such magics, the glamour of wizards being to cast spells, "throwing the object (fixed or moving) on the visual imagination"; the incantations and incenses of Hermeticists being to induce "emotional correlations by the sound and rhythm of speech." The "inducing both of the effects by stimulating the associations (intellectual or emotional) that have remained in the receiver's consciousness in relation to the actual words or word groups employed" suggests that the poet has powers to induce, to stimulate; but we see, barely disguised, that it is "the actual words or word groups employed" that have such power. The imagination is not the primary imagination that Coleridge defines as "the living Power and prime Agent of all human perception . . . a repetition in the finite mind of the eternal act of creation," but a screen upon which a higher power that Pound calls *phanopoeia* projects. This image-making or image-casting magic may be Coleridge's secondary imagination, an "echo" of the primary: "co-existing with the conscious will, yet still as identical with the primary in the *kind* of its agency, and differing only in *degree,* and in the *mode* of its operation. It dissolves, diffuses, dissipates, in order to re-create; or where this process is rendered impossible, yet still at all events it struggles to idealize and to unify. It is essentially *vital;* even as all objects (*as* objects) are essentially fixed and dead."

.

Coleridge and Pound alike have a common source in their reading of the Renaissance Hermeticist Marsilio Ficino's version of Iamblichus' *De Mysteriis.* "In most psychologies employing the concept of spirit, and often in Ficino's," D. P. Walker tells us in his *Spiritual and Demonic Magic from Ficino to Campanella,* "*all* sensation is by means of the spirit, and the media of all sense-data are some kind of spirit," and he quotes a passage from a letter of Ficino's that bears upon this matter of the music of poetry and the vision of poetry, *melopoeia* and *phanopoeia,* as a magic to arouse the mind to form and content, of the casting of the image or echo of creation by some affinity of body, soul, and spirit for the manifestation of song:

> Nor is this surprising; for, since song and sound arise from the cogitation of the mind, the impetus of the phantasy, and the feeling of the heart, and together with the air they have broken up and tempered, strike the aerial spirit of the hearer, which is the junction of the soul and body, they easily move the phantasy, affect the heart and penetrate into the deep recesses of the mind.

•

Our consciousness or idea of having heart and mind, as well as of having soul and spirit, being aroused by such a poetry.

•

"The impetus of the phantasy," Walker tells us, "when distinguished from imagination, is a higher faculty, which forms 'intentions'." I would recall Pound's questioning in the Cavalcanti essay: "Does *'intenzion'* mean intention (a matter of will)? does it mean intuition, intuitive perception . . . ?" In working upon his translation of Cavalcanti's "Donna mi prega," which was to be reworked in Canto XXXVI, Pound takes care to distinguish between the concept of "*intellect passif,*" which he finds in Renan's *Averroès et Averroïsme* defined as "la faculté de reçevoir les phantasmata," and the "*possible intelletto,*" which Pound translates as "latent intellect."

•

"Form, Gestalt," Pound notes: "Every spiritual form sets in movement the bodies in which (or among which) it finds itself." Love starts from form seen and takes His place, as subject not object, as mover, in the idea of the possible.

·

> Who will, may hear Sordello's story told:
> His story? Who believes me shall behold
> The man, pursue his fortunes to the end . . .

so Robert Browning opens *Sordello,* calling upon will and belief, where the imagination appears as a theatrical magic, a cooperation between the writing and the reading, between the speaker and the hearer, to participate in the reality of a world evoked by words given the magic of belief. *"Appears Verona,"* the Faustian poet directs, and then, again, as if calling up a spirit—"Then, appear, Verona!" Here the beginning of his *Cantos* in its first version:

> Hang it all, there can be but the one 'Sordello,'
> But say I want to, say I take your whole bag of tricks. . . .

"Has it a place in music?" he asks. The answer may lie in our passage from Ficino, for later Pound proposes in this first draft of Canto I: "We let Ficino / Start us our progress . . . "

> And your: 'Appear Verona!'?
> I walk the airy street,
> See the small cobbles flare with poppy spoil.

"Lo, the past is hurled / In twain," Browning shows us in *Sordello:*

> up-thrust, out-staggering on the world,
> Subsiding into shape, a darkness rears
> Its outline, kindles at the core, appears
> Verona.

The evocation is Shakespearean. But this Verona has no stage but a place in the believing mind—a stage belief makes in the mind (as Shakespeare too has but one place where his world is most real). The scene itself then is a spirit. Both Sordello and Verona are shadows in which the form of the poet itself quickens, setting into motion the body in which it finds itself, the body of a belief.

•

In the same years that Pound worked on *The Spirit of Romance* and "Cavalcanti," studying Avicenna and Ficino, the London years before the War when he was in the excitement of understudying Yeats, gathering the lore of light and forms that continues to work in *The Cantos* half a century later; in the same years that he attended the Quest lectures of G. R. S. Mead on Simon Magus and Helen of Tyre, on Hierotheos's *Book of the Hidden Mysteries,* on the *augoeides* and Origen's "primal paradisiacal body of light as the *seminarium* from which all bodily forms, both subtle and gross, can arise"; in the very years that defined the lifetime of Imagism proper—from the Credo of 1912 to H.D.'s resignation as literary editor of *The Egoist* and her replacement by Eliot in 1917—Pound, as a messenger, angel or Hermes, of Poetry, moved between the generation of Yeats, initiate of the esoteric tradition, and the generation of Gaudier-Brzeska, prophet of the spirit or genius of forms which Gaudier called "sculptural energy" and "the vortex," and of the little group of fellow poets, "Imagists," among whom H.D. was central. The "movement" was not an isolated literary affectation or strategic front but the first phase of certain generative ideas in poetry that were to reach their fruition, after the modernism of the twenties and the critical reaction of the thirties (when Pound, Williams, and H.D. were far apart in their work), three decades later in the period of the Second World War with the great poems of Pound's, Williams's and H.D.'s old age that begin with H.D.'s War Trilogy, with *The Walls Do Not Fall,* published in 1944.

In turn, the germ-idea of the "image" in its beginning phase was a fruition of a general renaissance of theosophy and psychology in the first decade of the century which, like the Hellenistic and the Florentine renaissances, brought back the matter of old mystery cults, "reawakened" the gods and revived speculations concerning the nature of the imagination. Pound's "See, they return," Williams's "Now—they are coming into bloom again!" from the poem "March," H.D.'s cry—

"O gold, stray but alive / on the dead ash of our hearth"—from "The Tribute," these convey the yearning for the revival of the past in the present, the leaven of dormant powers awakened again. Not only poets but intellectuals in the wake of Frazer's *Golden Bough* and Bergson's *Evolution Créatrice* were involved. So, we find Dora Marsden, the editor of *The Egoist,* writing on the image as a factor of knowledge:

> The animal which thinks must have two worlds to think with . . . intellection is nothing other than the interweaving of two worlds. He must have become so well acquainted with his inner images that, when he cognizes (experiences) the outer image, the inner relative springs into effect alongside it. Precisely the superimposition of the external thing by its wraith-like indwelling double constitutes re-cognition.

Or, again, John Gould Fletcher's review of H.D.'s *Sea Garden* in 1917, with its reference to "Plotinus, or Dionysius the Areopagite, or Paracelsus, or Behmen, or Swedenborg, or Blake," may suggest the ambiance of intellectual conversation in which the "image" of Imagism arose.

•

The landscape of *The Pisan Cantos* or of *Paterson,* like the landscape of The War Trilogy, is a multiple image, in which the historical and the personal past, along with the divine world, the world of theosophical and of poetic imagination, may participate in the immediate scene. H.D. had seen this in the 1920s as a palimpsest. In literature, Pound had written, "the real time is independent of the apparent." So, Henry James mingles with lynxes and with the divine powers Manitou and Kuthera attending, and Mt. Taishan appears in the Pisan atmosphere. From a photo in *National Geographic,* the wives of an African chief come into the landscape of *Paterson,* and a dwarf living under the falls is also the genius of the language. So, in the initial dedication of *The Walls Do Not Fall* (recalling the Rome/London/Egypt sequence of *Palimpsest* in 1926), H.D. proposes an image between two worlds: Egypt 1923 and London 1942, which opens into a reality whose time will take a center in the Nativity.

•

Pound had observed that Dante in the *Commedia* had not only given an account of the soul's journey (or "trip," as it is called by the devotees of the psychedelic experience) but had also created an "image" of the divine world: the total presentation of the poem was itself an image. The "idea" of the poem is this concretion of three worlds in one—a unity of real time in which many apparent times participate, a central intention whose meaning appears on many levels, an architecture of reality with its ascending and descending spirits—the whole a vision or seeing of a thing directly treated. The particular images of the poem then are seen to be notes in a melody that is in turn part of a larger movement, and these images belong to movements, in turn forming the "world" of the whole, a single great image. This imagination of the "world" to which the intent of the poem belongs is Coleridge's "primary imagination," and for Ficino the phantasy that is informed by the intention of the whole, the Image of images.

.

"Now at last he explains that it will, when the hundredth canto is finished," Yeats writes of Pound in 1928, "display a structure like a Bach Fugue. There will be no plot, no chronicle of events, no logic of discourse, but two themes . . . and, mixing with these, medieval or modern historical characters." Then: "He has shown me upon the wall a photograph of a Cosimo Tura decoration in three compartments, in the upper the Triumph of Love and the Triumph of Chastity, in the middle Zodiacal signs, and in the lower certain events in Cosimo Tura's day." The whole, Yeats saw as a prescribed composition, or an architectural plan, having sets, archetypal events, even as he himself was forcing his *Vision* into prescribed wheel and gyre, to get the times right, imposing a diagrammatic order of such archetypes upon history.

"God damn Yeats' bloody paragraph," Pound writes in 1939: "Done more to prevent people reading *Cantos* for what is *on the page* than any other one smoke screen." "HEAR Janequin's intervals, his melodic conjunctions from the violin solo," he writes in *Kulchur:* "The *forma,* the immortal *concetto,* the concept, the dynamic form which is like the rose pattern driven into the dead iron-filings by the magnet." Yeats saw structure like Bach's; but Pound contrasts the music of structure, "as J. S. Bach

in fugue or keyboard toccata," with the "music of representative out-
line," which he finds in Janequin's intervals and conjunctions, and which
he would seek himself, as "from the floral background in Pisanello's Este
portrait, from the representation of visible things in Pietro di Borgo, there
is a change to pattern and arabesque, there is an end to the Mediaeval
Anschauung, the mediaeval predisposition." The poem, like music, tak-
ing shape upon the air. In *The Cantos,* Aphrodite appearing to her son
Anchises at Cythera takes form upon the air—that is, upon the element,
"the air they have broken up and tempered," and also upon the air or
melody the violin plays, having the voices of birds as Pisanello has the
pattern of flowers in his art. Pound works to incorporate the voices of
men and even, in the Adams Cantos, the epistolary styles as musical enti-
ties leading into pattern and arabesque, to bring forward phrasings and
syncopations of vowel-tones and consonants. Yet what he had achieved
in *The Cantos,* Pound came to feel by the time he was writing *Kulchur,*
was not the clear line of Janequin, who had transmuted the sounds of
birds into a musical reality, nor the architectural mastery of Bach, but an
art—like the music of Beethoven or like Bartók's Fifth Quartet, Pound
says—having "the defects inherent in a record of struggle." The real time
of *The Cantos* was not to be independent of the apparent time.

.

It is the form of the poet's experience itself that we see in the form of his
work; in *The Cantos,* of struggle and conflict as well as of independent
and sublime vision, of stubborn predispositions as well as of taking
form from the air. "What is a god?" Pound had asked in his "Religio."
"A god is an eternal state of mind," he had answered. "When is a god
manifest? When the states of mind take form." The *religio* was also a
poetics in which the imagination was the eternal state of mind, taking
form in the things of the poem. But Pound in the twenties and thirties
came more and more to depreciate the imagination. Poetic belief, the
belief that is volunteered in what is but imagined to be real, contends
with the authoritative belief, the belief that is commanded and that
must be defended against heresy. Where in the essays of the London
period Pound is exploring ideas of imagination and poetry, in the essays
of Rapallo he speaks not as a visionary but as pedagogue, a culture

commissar, an economic realist, a political authority, and, in each of these roles, he feels that imagination and vision are unsound. Aesthetics has a ground in reality that inspiration does not: "the Whistler show in 1910 contained more real wisdom than that of Blake's fanatic designs." Perhaps he suffered from a blind reaction to Yeats's values, but *The Cantos* would move Pound again and again to ecstatic imagination beginning with *The Pisan Cantos*. Leucothea would be invoked throwing her girdle to rescue the Odysseus-poet of *The Cantos* from the sea of time and space as Blake shows her in his *The Cycle of Life of Man* [reading Kathleen Raine's *Blake and Tradition*, 1969: R.D.], as the neo-Platonists return to inspire the late Cantos. The chapter "Neo-Platonicks, Etc." in *Kulchur* does not disown, but it dissembles: "This kind of thing from the Phaedrus, or wherever it comes from, undoubtedly excites certain temperaments, or perhaps almost anyone if caught at the right state of adolescence or in certain humours." Like the exile of Odysseus, Pound's exile can be read as the initiation of the heroic soul (the hero of a Poetry) descending deep into hubris, offending and disobeying orders of the imagination, and returning at last after trials "home." Odysseus offends Poseidon and is shipwrecked; Pound offends the Primary Imagination and comes at last to trials of old age and despair.

•

In H.D.'s War Trilogy the form emerges along the path of a weaving that, like *The Cantos*, may follow pattern and arabesque in immediate areas, flowers and birds leading on to a world beyond the medieval predisposition ("its art-craft junk-shop / paint-and-plaster medieval jumble / of pain-worship and death-symbol," H.D. writes in *The Walls Do Not Fall*) towards the figures of ultimately real things, intuitions of the truth of things. But like *The Cantos*, The War Trilogy is colored at times by stubborn predispositions. But it is H.D.'s poetics that interprets and transmutes her psychoanalytic and occultist preconceptions (though in "Sagesse" and in *Hermetic Definitions*, occultist systematic interpretations seek to take over the authority of the real). Freud, and later the theurgist Robert Ambelain, come to lead H.D., as Mussolini and Major Douglas lead Pound.

•

The War Trilogy does not evoke comparison for H.D. with the quartets of Beethoven or Bartók. Music as it appears in the Trilogy is transcendental, and the art of the poem has its counterpart in the arts of painting or tapestry, a triptych portraying the soul's journey in an evolution from the shell fish of *The Walls Do Not Fall,* iv, that is "master-mason planning/ the stone marvel," to the woman with her child, her Christ-child, at the close of *The Flowering of the Rod.* Yet the tapestry must incorporate, even as Pound's *Cantos* must, "the defects inherent in a record of struggle." Later in *Helen in Egypt,* H.D. will refer to the tradition of the palinodia of Stesichorus, of the poet's restoring to Poetry the truth about Helen, but in The War Trilogy she strikes out, alone of the Imagists, to restore the truth of the Father and the Son and the Holy Ghost to Poetry. Not a conversion to Christianity, but a conversion of Christianity to Poetry.

.

There is an evolution of life-forms, experiences, yet they exist one in another; the work of art itself contains in its processes the beauty of the shell and the beauty of the Christos or Logos that in the human world has specific manhood. The image of the whole poem is so thrown upon the imagination or aroused in the imagination, "fixed or moving," that "fixed" it appears as a tapestry; "moving" it is the path of something happening on different levels in time, it has plot or mythos. Co-existence in the configuration of the poem and evolution in the history or course of the poem's creation give the dynamics. From the earliest tidal waters of our life, from:

> There is a spell, for instance,
> in every sea-shell:

to the evolution of the old divine orders into the Christos, not only Osiris but Venus and Astarte are also contained in the "jar" or alembic of the Christian mysteries. These mysteries have their authority now not in a church but in a poem. "Over Love, a new Master": the announcement of the Christ may mean also that there is a new genius of forms over the poem.

.

We too must return in our weaving upon the air, following the theme of image and meaning. To look into The War Trilogy again, the "tapestry" disclosing the "world"; and, as we regard once more the little company of poets or of heretics (H.D. herself working now in a belief disowned by her companions of Imagist days) or of disciples in a mystery, in the Presence that is "spectrum-blue / ultimate blue ray," that is "a spacious, bare meeting-house," that is a cartouche enclosing a name, an idea comes into sight—the haunting suggestion of another dimension of the content or form.

As in canvasses of Salvador Dalí we see not a symbol, one thing standing for another, but what he calls a paranoiac image, where one thing coexists in another—a man's head that is also a lion that is also a hairy egg, so, here, the meeting house is also a *heart:*

> We are at the cross-roads,
> the tide is turning . . .

in the turn of a heart-beat.

I.

At heart, we are individual, complete. "The heart of animals is the foundation of their life, the sovereign of everything within them," William Harvey begins the dedication to his *Anatomical Disquisition on the Motion of the Heart and Blood in Animals,* "the sun of their microcosm, that upon which all growth depends, from which all power proceeds." I would recall here Helen Fairwood and Captain Rafton in H.D.'s story "Secret Name," riding back in the dark from Karnak, having seen there the apparition of the "temple or tomb or birth-house," the thud-thud of the hoofs answering the beat of their hearts, arousing another image of their lying beneath the heart of the mother: "As if they in some strange exact and precious period of pre-birth, twins, lovers, were held, sheltered beneath some throbbing heart." "First, before anything else," Harvey writes:

> a drop of blood appears, which throbs, as Aristotle had noted. From this, with increasing growth and formation of the chick, the auricles of the

heart are made, in the pulsations of which there is continual evidence of life. After a few more days, when the body is outlined, the rest of the heart is made, but for some time it remains pale and bloodless like the rest of the body, and does not throb.

•

Then:

Whoever examined this matter closely will not say that the heart entirely is the first to live and the last to die, but rather the auricles (or that part corresponding to the auricles in serpents, fishes, and such animals) which live before the rest of the heart, and die after it.

•

The poem too begins with a pulse, a melodic impulse (a "beat" which belongs to a unique pattern in time), and the melodic impulse contains a form (as that beat of blood in the egg contains the form of the chick at work). There is then an image that is also ("the first to live and the last to die") a rhythm.

•

Genetics teaches us that unseen coordinates, the genes, lie back of this pattern in time, this rhythm of being, that is also a pattern in space, this form or image—of a man, of a chick, of a poem, then—if it be thought of as a part of the process of life. The "free verse" of high poetry was not abstractly free, but free, specifically, from the concept of a poem's form as a paradigm, an imposed plan to which the poet conformed. The form was germinal, the germ being the cadence that began in language ("a new cadence means a new idea," H.D. and Aldington had argued in their 1916 Preface), arousing a life of its own, a poem.

•

Erwin Schrödinger tells us in *What Is Life?* that "we believe a gene—or perhaps the whole chromosome fibre—to be an aperiodic solid." "A small molecule," he writes: "might be called the germ of a solid."

•

So too we may think of an idea, a novel or a poem, as beginning at some point or germ, growing, finding its being and necessary form, rhythm, and life, as the germ evolves in relation to its environment of language and experience. This is an art that rises from a belief in the universe as a medium of forms, in man's quest for form as a spiritual evolution, each realized experience of form in turn the germ of a new necessity for form or affinity for form.

·

In contrast, conventional art, with its conviction that form means adherence to a prescribed order where metric and rime arise in conformation to a regular pattern, has its ground in a belief that man by artifice must win his forms as models, reproductions, or paradigms against his nature, in a universe that is a matter of chaos or that has fallen into disorder.

·

Schrödinger, contrasting organic and inorganic forms in nature, says:

> Starting from such a small solid germ, there seem to be two different ways of building up larger and larger associations. One is the comparatively dull way of repeating the same structure in three directions again and again. That is the way followed in a growing crystal. Once the periodicity is established, there is no definite limit to the size of the aggregate.
>
> The other way is that of building up a more and more extended aggregate without the dull device of repetition. That is the case of the more and more complicated organic molecule in which every atom, and every group of atoms, plays an individual role, not entirely equivalent to that of many others (as in the case of a periodic structure). We might quite properly call that an aperiodic crystal or solid and express our hypothesis by saying: We believe a gene—or perhaps the whole chromosome fibre—to be an aperiodic solid.

·

Genetic thought along these lines is akin to poetic thought that pictures the poem as an organic crystallization, its germ or law or form being immanent in the immediate life—what is happening—in the work of the poem. "I believe in technique as the test of a man's sincerity; in law when it is ascertainable," Pound writes in 1912: "in the trampling down of every convention that impedes or obscures the determination of the law, or the precise rendering of the impulse." Free verse, later projective verse as expounded by Charles Olson, developed a new sense of metric and rime deriving from an inner aperiodic formal intuition. Here, structure is not satisfied in the molecule, is not additive, but is fulfilled only in the whole work, the apprehension of the work's "life" springing anew in each realization, each immediate cell.

•

Marianne Moore is a master of poetry that is periodic in its concept— as if art were a convention—which has its counterpart in her concern for social conformities, in her admiration for rigor, for the survival of vitality where character-armor takes over to resist areas of experience that cannot be included in the imagined social contract of poetry. Schrödinger in his bias for the form he sees in living matter finds inorganic crystals "comparatively dull" in structure; but Marianne Moore's poem "He 'Digesteth Harde Yron'," which is built of periodic units, is not "comparatively dull," for her zest for language as a vitality in itself contends thruout with the use of metric to make a conforming pattern. Words are not yet reduced to the conventional trivial units of New Yorkerese that they become in her later verse. Yet, in the larger units of structure, the structures are already inorganic. Once the stanza is set, there is no further form, no further "experience," realized in its extension. The number of stanzas is arbitrary. The poem presents examples of itself, a series that may be "complete" at any point because, otherwise, it is extensible as long as the poet's rationalizations continue. The form of the whole in conventional verse does not rest in the fulfillment of or growth of its parts toward the revelation of their "life" but in the illustration of the taste and arbitration of the poet. Between the poem's appearance in *What Are Years* (1941) and its appearance in *Selected Poems* (1951) Marianne Moore eliminated three lines of stanza six in "He 'Digesteth Harde Yron'," and all of stanzas seven and eight, without altering the "form" of the whole. The uncertainty she has often shown about the total form of a poem is a corollary of a periodic or imitative structure where, as Schrödinger observes of mineral structures, "there are no definite limits to the size of the whole." In its inception Marianne Moore's verse follows the line of a growth out of a germinal nucleus, and in this it was, especially in the twenties and thirties, akin to that of her peers, H.D., Williams, or Pound. The thoroughly conventional poem projects a prescription of the line-to-line conformity. But Marianne Moore's growth, being periodic, inorganic, has no internal law of the whole. The history of the poem, for Marianne Moore, consists of instances of itself, as natural history for her is, after Linnaeus and pre-Darwin, a collection of types or models of species. In her technical brilliance (as late as the poem "Style" circa 1956), she excels. The very crux of the poem is its mechanical expertness. But in her poetics, in her thought and feeling of the poem then, she does not evolve as life does but repeats; her verse is not *creative* but *exemplary* in form. So there is no process of rebirth, of an evolving apprehension of form in her work, of impending experience, that might make for a major impetus in the later years of her life, such as we find in *The Pisan Cantos,* in *Paterson,* and in The War Trilogy, in the work of poets whose poetry had come to be a "life" work.

•

It is not in their exemplary character-structure but in their passion, in their ripeness, the fullness in process of what they are, that I am moved by H.D., Pound, and Williams. They move in their work thru phases of growth towards a poetry that spreads in scope as an aged tree spreads its roots and branches, as a man's experience spreads; their art in language conveying scars and informations of age without armor as a man may gather in his face and his form acknowledged accumulations of what he is in his life, in his cooperation with the world about him.

•

Thus, in *The Walls Do Not Fall,* it is the cooperation of the elements of the poem that informs. Not imitating but arising from the beat of the heart and from the breath, yes. . . . As in his "Projective Verse" essay of 1950, Charles Olson was to see the impetus of a new poetry: "from the union of the mind and the ear that the syllable is born," the *hearing* of the poem, and from "the HEART, by way of the BREATH, to the LINE," the inspiration and feeling of the poem. Recalling again what H.D. in "Secret Name" sees, where the poet (the H.D. we recognize in the Helen Fairwood of the story) and the god (the Bear Zeus that Helen Fairwood recognizes in Captain Rafton) have their apotheosis in the apparition of the birth-house or germinal cell, as the woman and man "in love," heart-beat to heart-beat, are carried, "brother" and "sister" now, "twins, lovers" in one matrix.

"The mind is brother to this sister (the heart) and is, because it is so close, the driving force," Olson writes, "the incest, the sharpener." I see his meaning superimposed upon H.D.'s image in "Secret Name." Syllable and line, Olson has it, are born "of the incest of verse (always, that Egyptian thing, it produces twins!)." If, as we have been persuaded by Freudian psychoanalysis, we may read in everyday events and speech as in dreams a language that tells of our genital life, that language tells too of our breathing and of the circulation of our blood. Our consciousness of life, our "speech" then, arising from these.

•

H.D. cannot arbitrate but must follow the inspiration (the in-breathing) and the beat, as she follows the feel and balance of the poem, for she works, having all the predisposition of her previous thought, towards the discovery of the whole. She works, as in analysis, to bring the content from latency into awareness. History here consists of "incidents" or parts of something in process, and the work of the poet is to find or render what is happening. Natural history is an evolution. The design unfolds, self-creative. Her sense of affinity with the shell-fish as "master-mason" (pathetic fallacy to the critic who does not believe there is a continuity of spirit in the universe) is morphological. She is concerned with a correspondence that is also, if we believe in evolution as life creating itself, where self is spirit, a sense of psychic origin.

•

In xxxviii of *The Walls Do Not Fall,* the poet's mind operates in a field of human mind, again as a thread weaves in a tapestry:

your way of thought (mine),

each has its peculiar intricate map,
threads weave over and under

the jungle-growth
of biological aptitudes,

inherited tendencies,
the intellectual effort

of the whole race . . .

Each mind has its "peculiar ego-centric / personal approach / to the
eternal realities" and "differs from every other / in minute particu-
lars," "as the vein-paths on any leaf," as each line in the poem has its
"approach" and must be perfected there, having that imperfection that
it is perfected only in the field of its existence, which it experiences as
"approach" or "intention." H.D.'s "eternal realities" I would see here as
figures in a design to which any individual life contributes. The germi-
nal form of Man in which we individuate and out of which we are each
the immediate occasion of our species is such a figure, "of the whole
race." Here she draws upon the biological identity, as in *The Flowering
of the Rod,* ix, she affirms:

No poetic fantasy
but a biological reality,

a fact: I am an entity
like bird, insect, plant

or sea-plant cell . . .

where "poetic fantasy," with its connotation of being made up for
fancy's sake, is not the poet's term but her interior adversary's, not
then that poetic phantasy in Ficino's terms identified with the creative
imagination, for the tenor of The War Trilogy is that Dream and Life
are one—the "spiritual realities" and "eternal realities" are "biological."
It is not only the figure of Man then out of which and to which the
individual thread has its weaving of intention, but, beyond Man, in the
larger field of Life itself, so that the poet strives for organic form as Life

form. This is not a humanist art. The "whole race" is ultimately not the species Man but the race of the living.

                              •

With Olson's "Projective Verse" the field of the imagination was extended to a form that took its imperative in the atomic particular or the cell. The energy of the poem he saw had its spring in the immediate event: "Let's start from the smallest particle of all, the syllable." There is a change then possible that haunts our minds since Olson's charge—that the formal imperative or intent has its spring back of the word or phrase (back of that civilization of meanings agreed upon that the dictionary represents) in the minim of our speech, the immediate sounding event.

In this minim, in our articulation of vowels, lies the crucial evolutionary fact underlying the word. Speech, our specifically human instrument, is a possibility that arose with the separation of larynx and soft palate. "Specialization, semanticity, arbitrariness," these functions of language we share with all primates; "discreteness," "traditional transmission," with our fellow anthropoids; but with the play of vowel color, we have our own music, giving rise to new qualities in speech: "displacement," "productivity," "duality of patterning," the operations of our natural imagination in which sound makes sense. (See Charles D. Hockett, "The Origins of Speech," *Scientific American,* September 1960.)

                              •

So, I see *The Walls Do Not Fall* develop along lines of an intuited "reality" that is also a melody of vowel tone and rime giving rise to image and mythos and, out of the community of meanings, returning to themes towards its individual close. In her work she consciously follows the lead of image to image, of line to line, or of word to word, which takes her to the brink (as "gone" leads to "guns" in the opening of the poem) of meaning, the poet establishing lines of free (i.e., individual) association within the society of conventional meanings. The form of the poem, of the whole, is an entity or life-time—a "biological reality"—having life as her own body has life.

II.

The "Heart" in our projection of the tapestry of the poem appears as the brotherhood of scribes or initiates of Thoth. They belong to, have given their allegiance to, the truth or the heart of things. In the City Under Fire of parts i, ii, ix, x, xi, xii, xiv, xxiv, xxix, xxxiv, and the closing xliii of *The Walls Do Not Fall,* the heart is on trial. As in the code-script involving all the future development of the poem, there appears the accusation that the City makes against the poet:

> your heart, moreover
> is a dead canker,
>
> they continue, and
> your rhythm is the devil's hymn,

It is "Isis, Aset or Astarte" who is accused here; the sexual lure and seductiveness of the poet in her service or her cult—the cult of the love affair, the affair of the heart, the cultivation of heart-ache, heart-consciousness, or passion over mind-consciousness or reason. The theme in *The Walls Do Not Fall* of giving thanks for recovery or survival in a time of war (on this level, a prayer during an air raid) is in turn a thanks for recovery, as in *Tribute to the Angels:*

> *where, Zadkiel, we pause to give*
> *thanks that we rise again from death and live.*

from a heart-attack, consciously or unconsciously included in the statement. In "Narthex" the sign—"triangle set on triangle that makes a star, the seal of Solomon"—is the heart, where the triangle of an old affair—"Katherine-Mordant-Raymonde"—is "burnt out," "residue of suffering" kept or learned by heart, we say. The "half-burnt-out apple-tree / blossoming," the epiphany of *Tribute to the Angels,* may be the heart (the "tree" of arteries and veins) recovering. It was, she tells us, "the spear / that pierces the heart."

•

The attack, the being under fire, is an old theme of H.D.'s. In "Halcyon" from *Red Roses for Bronze* of 1931:

"tinsel" they said the other lives were,
all those I loved,
I was forgot;

what is most the heart of the matter for the "I" comes under the attack of others as irrelevant. In "The Tribute" of 1916: "till our heart's shell was reft/with the shrill notes," Beauty and love are the causes of an exile. In The War Trilogy thirty years later, the "we" who are under attack are devotees of beauty and of a heresy of love; the art of writing, the "script, letters, palette," is itself under attack as tinsel. The actual war, the incendiary attacks, the deprivations, come to illustrate or manifest another war the lover and poet knew under attack, to reactivate the violence felt in the critical and social rejection of her person and her art that H.D. had known. But these voices that accuse have been brought over into the authority of the poem; they are voices of the poetic consciousness itself. The adversary is heart-felt.

.

Returning to the City or Heart under "Apocryphal fire," in *The Walls Do Not Fall,* i, we see it clearly: "the heart burnt out, dead ember,/tendons, muscles shattered, outer husk dismembered,/yet the frame held." This "death" of the physical heart and its "resurrection" in the opening poem lead forward to the poet's taking heart in the Christos or taking love in the Lover, as, in turn, we recognize her "New Master over Love" in the blossoming of the tree, in which the flowering of the rood returns, itself the news of a Vita Nuova from the Cross. So, too, the City burning gives us leads: we see Sodom, or Pompeii with its House of the Dionysian Mysteries, some city of Astarte, Carthage the burned and salted ground (or, as in *Helen in Egypt,* Troy thrown down, the City, like the Woman, "hated of all Greece"). It is a scene like that shown in the *Lot and His Daughters,* attributed to Lucas van Leyden, or in the visionary canvasses of Bosch or Brueghel, where the City is inflamed, from the crusade against the Cathars of Provence, where at

Béziers the Pope's armies turned the cathedral of Saint-Nazaire into a great oven in which the faithful were burned, to the raging wars that swept Christendom in the seventeenth century where Protestant and Catholic sought to exterminate each other, the heart of the Christian reality—the City of God—was inflamed and burned out.

Or the scene is from Bosch's *Garden of Delights* (or, as Wilhelm Fränger argues it should be titled—*The Millennium*), where in the right-hand panel we see those who dwell in the wrath of God, in the volcano of His inner agony. It is Jehovah's realm, before Christ, the intestines of the Burning Mountain. The "we" of H.D.'s poem, who cry:

> Dev-ill was after us,
> tricked up like Jehovah;

have seen the Bad Father, and live in the world as if in the wrath of the last days. Where we cannot identify with the will of powerful groups in the society we live in, we feel their power over us as an *evil*. The word evil, as the O.E.D. suggests, "usually referred to the root of *up, over,*" may then be whatever power over us of outer or inner compulsion. As the power and presumption of authority by the State has increased in every nation, we are ill with it, for it surrounds us and, where it does not openly conscript, seeks by advertising, by education, by dogma, or by terror, to seduce, enthrall, mould, command, or coerce our inner will or conscience or inspiration to its own uses. Like the pious Essenes alienated from Romanizing priests and civilizing Empire alike, like the Adamite cult to which Bosch may have belonged—the Brothers and Sisters of the Free Spirit—alienated from the spiritual authoritarianism of the Church and from the laws of warring feudal lords and principalities, we too may find ourselves, at odds with the powers that be, members of a hidden community, surviving not in history but in the imagination or faith. Like Jews paying taxes to Caesar or like little children suffering under the tyranny of powerful adults, we then live in a world that is "theirs," in "their" power, in which a deeper reality, our own, is imprisoned. Our life is hidden in our hearts, a secret allegiance, at odds with the World, the Flesh, and the Devil, and the true kingdom is "not of this World." The artist—the poet as well as the painter or musician—

striving to keep alive the reality of his art as revelation and inspiration of Truth or Beauty finds himself so at odds with the dominant motives of profit and industry embodied in the society. For Communist and Capitalist alike the work of art is taken to be a commodity of social exchange. Not only gnostics and pacifists but artists and poets, those who live by an inner reality or world, having a prior adherence to the heart's truth or wish, appear as heretics or traitors to those who lead or conform to the dominations of the day.

•

In "The Tribute," the City, stricken by war, has already been betrayed "for a thrust of a sword, / for a piece of thin money" and the gods have been driven out, except for War, and this Mars has "treacherous feet." In "Cities" of 1914, H.D. had seen, "hideous first, hideous now," the hive of a "new" or false city crowd out all vestige of the old beauty, with only a few left to cherish what once was and to await the coming of beauty again, like a heart that has lost love and waits, alienated, for its return.

As the poet Rilke saw the poets as bees storing the honey of the invisible in a time when, from the center of the commodity-culture, "there come crowding over from America empty, indifferent things, pseudo-things, *Dummy-life*," so H.D. sees the City as a hive where the few remnants keep "grains of honey" and there appears a mass-people of the new age, larvae spreading "not honey but seething life." "We are perhaps the last to have still known such things," Rilke writes to von Hulewicz in 1925. "We would feed forever / on the amber honeycomb / of your remembered greeting," H.D. reiterates in *The Walls Do Not Fall* in 1942:

> but the old-self,
>
> still half at-home in the world,
> cries out in anger . . .

•

The surrender of this-worldly purposes so important in religious conversion, and the separation of desire from passion into its own pure kingdom, so important in the conversion of lovers to love: these are like the conversion of outer and inner reality to form a poetic real. Outer and inner conflicts enter into and surcharge the poetic. At odds with powerful influences, whether they be his own impulses or the opposing will of other men, the poet holds the new reality only by a heightened intensity. Realizations come not as charming experiences but as rare gains in reality, as raptures. The "honey" Rilke and H.D. speak of is such "rapture," the secretion of the life experience of a besieged spirit, part then of a complex that includes the other features we find in apocalyptic statement—anger, outrage, despair, fear, judgment. The flaming cities are not only representations of persecutions suffered or punishments anticipated in heresy, they are also representations of a revenging wrath projected by the heretic, the stored-up sense of injustice and of evil dominations raging outward. Within the picture painted or raised in the poem, as in the individual psyche and in the society at large, we see the same symptoms. Everywhere, we find at every level the content felt as psychic is manifest. The individual psyche lives in the psychic society, as the individual physical body lives in the physical City. The artist then is not only psychically at odds but physically at odds. His art is a physical contradiction of the pseudo-things and advertisements about him, as his spirit is a psychic contradiction. The manifest ugliness of things made in the spirit of investment and profit is physically oppressive.

The triumph of utility over beauty in the square unornamented functional architecture of the "International" style is the dominant idea in our contemporary utilitarian City, appropriate expression of the will-to-power of large corporations over all individual variation; as, in turn, the dominant idea in international affairs—the Atomic War—hints at the anger, outrage, despair, fear suffered by corporation-men themselves living in their own system.

•

H.D.'s apocalyptic vision in The War Trilogy, like her identification with Hellenistic decadence in the period between the first two World Wars, provides an historical perspective in which the experience of London under attack in the Second World War becomes meaningful in relation to depths and heights of personal reality—depths she had come to know in her psychoanalysis with Freud and then in new terms with the study of occult and hermetic lore, heights she had known in aesthetic and erotic ideals earlier inherited from Pre-Raphaelite sources and developed in Imagism. To be a poet appeared as a challenge of existing things, and poets seemed to form a heretical group. Among poets, "Imagists" in turn were viewed as heretical by conventional versifiers. "She is fighting in her country," H.D. wrote of Marianne Moore in 1916 in *The Egoist*, "against squalor and commercialism. We are all fighting the same battle."

She had known too in the war years the persecution that dogged the little pacifist group around D.H. Lawrence, for Frieda and Lawrence had taken refuge in the house where H.D. lived. "Victims, victimised and victimising," she writes in *Bid Me to Live:* "Perhaps the victims came out, by a long shot, ahead of the steady self-determined victimisers." They were, she and Lawrence and Pound, not of the lost generation but "they had roots (being in their mid-twenties and their very early thirties) still in that past. They reacted against a sound-board, their words echoed . . . What was left of them was the war generation, not the lost generation."

·

Beauty under attack, *Imagism* under attack, pacifism under attack, and, as the Wars like great Dreams began to make it clear, life itself under attack—H.D. had an affinity for heretical causes. In psychoanalysis again she found a cult under attack. "Upon my suggestion to H.D. that psychoanalysis seemed to affect some people as does Christian Science," Robert McAlmon argues with the contempt commonsense has for such things, "she took me seriously and said yes, it was a religion." It was, Freud felt, to take the place of religion, and he thought always of psychoanalysis under attack as Truth under attack, for the civilization itself—indeed, civilization itself—was at war against knowing anything about, much less recognizing within, the contents of the unconscious. "My discoveries are a basis for a very grave philosophy," Freud tells H.D.: "There are very few who understand this, *there are very few who are capable of understanding this.*"

·

To be analysed was not only an initiation, a learning to read the meaning of dreams, of daily life, of the poem; it was also a trial. "'I am asking only one thing of you,' he said," H.D. tells us in *Tribute to Freud;* then: "Even as I write the words, I have the same sense of anxiety, of tension, of imminent responsibility that I had at that moment."

What he asks is that she not defend his philosophy. (Is it in some way like Augustine's perception that while Rome falls to the barbarians, the Christians, seeking out the meaning of Rome, must not defend the city or truth against the enemy but convert the enemy to the city—a "City of God" that Rome may be but that is not Rome.) "At the least suggestion that you may be about to begin a counter-argument in my defense, the anger or the frustration of the assailant will be driven deeper. You will drive the hatred or the fear or the prejudice in deeper . . . The only way to extract the fear or prejudice would be from within, from below."

•

The apocalyptic picture of the world that is also the heart under attack is a complex image of correspondences between what is felt as inflicted and what is felt in projection, of wishes for vengeance that are also fears of punishment seen fulfilled in actual events. "Pompeii has nothing to teach us," H.D. begins the Trilogy:

we know crack of volcanic fissure,
slow flow of terrible lava,

pressure on heart, lungs, the brain . . .

The events of the London blitz illustrate the wrath of the Father, and the arguments of the pro-war forces in English society demanding the adherence of all wills to the war effort reappear as voices of the Protestant Ethic, the very spirit of industrial and commercial capitalism, in attack upon art, sexuality and Woman. Behind the war is an old war against Tiamat. On a psychological level, an analytical level, the war is sensed in pressures of inner wrath—of the "Jehovah" within— upon living organs. Such a condition demands of the imagination a new heart and a new reality in which there is the germ of survival.

III.

So the Trilogy is the story of survival, the evolution of forms in which
life survives. In the tides of oceanic life-force, the *élan vitale*, the indi-
vidual heart appears as the shell-fish. "That flabby, amorphous hermit /
within" is the brain in its skull-shell, and its limit the limit of thought
in the overwhelming element of what is. But it is also the heart, holding
against too much feeling:

> it unlocks the portals
> at stated intervals:
>
> prompted by hunger,
> it opens to the tide-flow:

A correspondence is felt between the tide of the sea and the tide of the
blood, between ebb and flow and the systole and diastole, between the
valves of the heart and the valves of the shell-fish who lives in the tidal
rhythm, as the brain lives in the tidal flow of the heart, fed by charges
of blood in the capillaries.

.

Here (*The Walls Do Not Fall*, iv) the individual life begets itself from
and must also hold itself against the enormous resources of life, against
the too-much, "beget self-out-of-self," take heart in what would take
over the heart in its greater power. The theme recurs: in xvii: "the tide
is turning"; in xxv: "my heart-shell / breaks open." It leads forward in
Tribute to the Angels to Gabriel, the Moon-Regent, Lord of Spiritual
Tides, and, in *The Flowering of the Rod,* to the echo of the sea and of her
Tiamat-identity that Woman brings with her to the Christ.

.

The "indigestible, hard, ungiving" thing, of iv, that "living within"
begets "that pearl-of-great-price," may be a coal, in xvii, "for the
world's burning"; for, in xxv, we learn that the phoenix dropped "a
grain, / as of scalding wax" from its burning, that "lodged in the heart-
core, / has taken its nourishment" and, in xxviii, that the grain fell

"between a heart-beat of pleasure / and a heart-beat of pain." We see readily the statement that the nucleus of the poem itself as a pearl may grow from a painful "indigestible" thing. Underlying it we may sense the statement that the poet has taken heart in a long-forgotten burning event.

•

As, in the systole-diastole reference, the *consecration / affirmation* of xxxix is charged with biological meaning:

> We have had too much consecration,
> too little affirmation,
>
> too much: but this, this, this
> has been proved heretical,
>
> too little: I know, I feel
> the meaning that words hide . . .

The presentation of intellectual alternates—the orthodoxy arising from convention and the consensus of authority versus the heresy of the individual experience—would seem farthest from referring to the physical image of the heart, but in its form of alternating beats, of a flux between too much and too little, it proposes not the image of opposites but the image of a circulation, the returning flood from the ventricle of the heart into the arterial circuit, where the sense of the more-than-enough in the word "too" may refer to the crisis or strain. The "hermit / within" who would survive and create "self-out-of-self" in the tide flow of oceanic feeling must keep his limits, "of nothing-too-much."

In the opening poems of *The Flowering of the Rod,* this theme of crisis or heart-beat in a duality flowers in full song, beginning with the "I go where I love and where I am loved," (ii) and continuing thru viii—a song of assent and affirmation in the alternating current of human will. Here, beyond the of-nothing-too-much, she acclaims "the insatiable longing," "the eternal urge," "the despair," then the desire itself "to equilibrate the eternal variant."

•

"To charge with meaning to the utmost possible degree," Pound had commanded the poet. To the heart's limit? "Meaning" may be then H.D.'s new Master over Love, that is also a new heart taken in poetry and appears as the key from which the new feeling of history distributes its rhythm. The "but gods always face two-ways" of *The Walls Do Not Fall,* ii, charged with meaning to the utmost possible degree, means that times too always face two ways. "Every hour, every moment," H.D. tells us in *Tribute to the Angels,* "has its specific attendant Spirit"; there is no time that is not a god, the dying and rebirth of self. "The tide is turning," of *The Walls Do Not Fall,* xvii, where "we" are "coals for the world's burning," refers not only to a turning-point in the orders of human history but to a turning-point in the body's history, the diagnosis of a crisis; and, back of these, to a turning-point in which we know the intent of life itself manifest.

.

"When I first tried animal experimentation for the purpose of discovering the motions and functions of the heart by actual inspection and not by other people's books," Harvey writes: "I found it so truly difficult that I almost believed, with Fracastorius, that the motion of the heart was to be understood by God alone. I could not really tell when systole or diastole took place, or when dilation or construction occurred, because of the quickness of the movement."

.

It is in the "I could not really tell when" that only the imagination pleads us on—the *affirmation,* H.D. calls it. The vision of history in *The Walls Do Not Fall* grows from a seed of light or pulse—it is an old occult tradition. A heart-beat, a seed of time, a mustard seed, so immediate that it precedes our sense of it:

then I woke with a start
of wonder and asked myself,

but whose eyes are those eyes?

"All that we can observe," Whitehead argues in *Adventures of Ideas,* "consists of conceptual persuasions in the present . . . Literature preserves the wisdom of the human race; but in this way it enfeebles the emphasis of first-hand intuition. In considering our direct observation of past, or of future, we should confine ourselves to time-spans of the order of magnitude of a second, or even of fractions of a second."

IV.

[July 31st, 1964.] Conceived first in the Spring of 1961 as a daybook—allowing for sketches of thought, digressive followings of impulse, and searchings for content, for design within design, a demonstration of what occurs as I take H.D.'s War Trilogy as the ground of interpretation, days haunted by passages of her poem, introducing new elements, rendering new possibilities—three years later in the Summer of 1964, as in those drawings at the cave-temple of Pech-Merle in the Hall of Hieroglyphics "superimposed, drawn by fingers in the soft clay (soft and pliable even now), with no dominant direction, crossing and interpenetrating one another," where, Giedion tells us in *The Eternal Present: The Beginnings of Art,* "Aurignacian man gained magic possession of coveted animals by drawing their outlines in the darkness of the caverns, illuminated only by a flickering torch," or, as in Marie and Pierre Curie's working the pitchblende, following the lure of an unseen-as-yet element, who appear in *Paterson* Four as personae of the poet himself working the language where "A dissonance / in the valence of Uranium / led to the discovery":

> to get, after months of labor .
>
> a stain at the bottom of the retort
> without weight, a failure, a
> nothing. And then, returning in the
> night, to find it   .
>
> LUMINOUS!

the book returns again and again to this material in which the lure of a seed or a heart-beat or a minimal nucleus of consciousness lingers. Thought here, not expository but experimental, trying the materials, and operative, the matter itself changing in experiment, the immediate work in its working creating itself anew as gold or goal. In places I am thinking-thru lines twice thought thru before, not to come to the conclusion of a thought but to return to its movement, to old traces, drawn by the idea that is a generative force, inhabiting these lines, along these lines, to find out what draws me, in the dark by the light of what I have known towards the light of what I do not yet know, am about to know as I draw; the drawing, a dramatic rehearsal.

A finding then, a finding out of a way in going, of the poet in the figure of the poet traced from lines where H.D. before me worked along these lines. Life of poet crossing and interpenetrating life of poet in the imagination of something "to gain magic-possession" of that most coveted animal power, the lion-voice, the serpent-wisdom, the nightingale-song, the antlered crown—to commune with the animal force felt in the poem return to the working of the poem. So, the rehearsals of self as "that craftsman, / the shell-fish," or, "when I, / the industrious worm, / spin my own shroud," or "erect serpent" in *The Walls Do Not Fall;* so, the ecstatic flight as "the first wild goose," having the migratory bird's instinctual drive to "hover / over the lost island, Atlantis."

For I am not a literary scholar nor an historian, not a psychologist, a professor of comparative religions nor an occultist. I am a student of, I am searching out, a poetics. There are times when my primary work here, my initiation of self as poet in the ground of the poet H.D.—and also my working of what is now a "matter of Poetry" (as the Arthurian lore is called the matter of Britain) and in turn an element in the great matter of the Creation of Man—there are times when my work has given way to literary persuasions and arguments, as if I might plead the cause of my life experience before the authorities at Nicaea and have my way, no longer heretical, taken over by those good bishops who control appointments and advancements as established dogma, a place won for H.D. in the orthodox taste and opinion of literary conventions.

But just here I would admit those crossed lines, mixed purposes, almost of a literary scholar, an historian, a psychologist, a professor of comparative religions, overwriting the poet and the figure before us that we are striving to realize.

We have only this one way to go, to the knotting and the untying of knots, moving along the line of our moving, the sometimes multiphasic sentence, we follow, trace of this coveted animal or animating power we address, crossing and recrossing and re-recrossing its charm as if we could so bring over into our human lot the form it is of a book we are writing or of a life we are leading, is the nucleus itself of our work which we feel as an impending lure, the turning point where we are, leading us on.

•

We are—where a work of art is thought of as organic, related to a concept of life itself as a process of form in creation—always where "the tide is turning." In the opening of *The Walls Do Not Fall:*

> unaware, Spirit announces the Presence;
> shivering overtakes us,

The Presence in which we shiver is the entity of the poem itself in which the poet shivers, the immanence of the design of the tapestry in the weaver's held breath as he works.

•

The heart, felt in the very beat of the verse, expressed in the insistent figure of alternating ebb and flow, consecration and affirmation, "hot noon-sun" and "the grey / opalescent winter-dawn," appears in the foreground of the design as a jar carried by the Mage Kaspar to a new Master over Love (over the heart then). And Life appears as genius, an odor of myrrh, where the seal of the jar or heart was unbroken, that comes from the Christ-Child as if from one's own heart. Life is the Presence, "spectrum-blue, / ultimate blue ray," H.D. addresses it in *The Walls Do Not Fall*, xiii: "rare as radium, as healing," toward which or from which the memory of the Curies from William Carlos Williams's *Paterson* may have come. So, too, Wilhelm Reich saw Life in each cell, as he tells us in *The Function of the Orgasm,* as a blue flame. In poetry, perhaps, we can allow the vision, though H.D.'s critics were suspicious of poetic fraud; in psychiatry, it brought disgrace for Reich and, ultimately, actual imprisonment for medical fraud upon the seer.

.

We can allow the blue light? But once H.D. presents it, the "ultimate blue ray," what we could not really tell then, is not a passing fantasy but some ultimate term of the reality of the poem. The empire of her thought and feeling is always precarious, in excess of critical permission, and now to bring in this remnant of theosophical color-theory? of romantic dream-key? the blue flower of Novalis's *Heinrich von Ofterdingen?* The very names *Theosophical* and *Romantic* are pejoratives in the great court of that Nicaea I am tempted to address.

.

So, we are lost, we have lost our argument and must go on deeper to follow the lead of this Heart, as if the heart were itself an organ of intelligence and we would find more than a figure of speech in the intuition of "to know by heart" or "to know in one's heart." But now it is a jar that we follow in the poem, and the blue light is an odor. . . .

.

When the first announcement comes in *The Walls Do Not Fall* of the Christos, we are told:

> His, the Genius in the jar
> which the Fisherman finds,
>
> He is Mage,
> bringing myrrh.

The "stone-marvel" of the sea-shell, the "egg-shell," are little alabaster jars. Stars, too, are "little jars of that indisputable / and absolute Healer, Apothecary," and contain something; as words and then poems are containers, where meaning and presence are myrrh and the odor of myrrh.

.

O heart, small urn
of porphyry, agate or cornelian,

how imperceptibly the grain fell
between a heart-beat of pleasure

and a heart-beat of pain;
I do not know how it came.

As in Kaspar's vision of the unfolding of the seed or pearl as a nucleus of
light in the world is contained and revealed: "no one will ever know /
whether the picture he saw clearly / as in a mirror was predetermined"
or "no one will ever know how it happened / that in a second or a sec-
ond and half a second" there is a gnosis beyond knowing. "Of the order
of magnitude of a second, or even of fractions of a second," Whitehead
says. "I could not really tell," Harvey testifies. "A small molecule,"
Schrödinger tells us, "might be called 'the germ of a solid'."

            •

It is not abstract, a separate mental conception, apart from the mate-
rial instance; but ineffable, elusive to definition. "The sense of having
lived," Henry James writes in his Preface to *The Wings of the Dove,*
trying to recapture the germ of that work—the idea of Milly Theale
desiring "to achieve, however briefly and brokenly, the sense of having
lived."

            •

So, "the hidden seed, the myrrh or meaning, the heart's rapture" may
also be such a sense of having lived, for it is to live that I find myself
returning to the poem.

            •

As it was the title *What Is Life?* that drew me to Schrödinger's work,
and the sense of life, the excitement or immediacy in the writing of
Schrödinger that leads me on to read. To bring forward into fullness of
consciousness and involvement "the sense of having lived." That must
then spring from the immediate presence of one's having lived in the
only area the sense of anything can take place or time in—in the present

intuition. The writer's having lived in the writing the reader in turn lives in.

"The image so figured would be, at best, but half the matter," James writes: "the rest would be all the picture of the struggle involved, the adventure brought about, the gain recorded or the loss incurred, the precious experience somehow compassed."

.

The image and the tissue of the image, the weaving and the woven tapestry, contain something, the sense of having lived, so that where we respond to books or to works of art intensely we think of them as living, we have the sense of having lived in the world of our reading. In *Tribute to the Angels,* the Lady, Mother of God, appears to H.D. bearing not the Christ but a book, as if Life or Love were also Poem or Work of Art—"her book is our book; written," H.D. confides in xxxix:

or unwritten, its pages will reveal

a tale of a Fisherman,
a tale of a jar or jars,

.

"I have trouble following," my friend Thomas Parkinson had noted in reading the first draft of the Day Book at this transition from James's evocation of the picture or image, the adventure, the gain or loss, and the precious experience somehow compassed, to H.D.'s "her book is our book." The passage from James had come abruptly to my mind as I wrote, and I, following, also had trouble. Certainly, the intensity of James's living in the writing itself, life in turn the germ of the book, comes near to the sense I have of H.D.'s cult within the poem. Now, going back to the passages in which the Lady appears, from the xxiv with its beginning lines I have quoted more than once in this work: "Every hour, every moment/has its specific attendant Spirit" thru xli with its return of the Angels as bells tolling the Hour—"our purpose, a tribute to the Angels," the lines leap up from xxxvi: "she brings the Book of Life, obviously."

.

This is the religion of the Book. The People of the Book, so Islam denoted the Jews, Christians, and themselves. And we who take our lives in the afterlife of Christendom in writing and in reading must come across hints of the Word as we follow the word and of the Presence as we find a book lively. The Lady in *Tribute to the Angels* may be the Mother of the Word—the writer herself:

> She carried a book, either to imply
> she was one of us, with us,

or she may have been the Bride of the Word, the reader:

> or to suggest she was satisfied
> with our purpose, a tribute to the Angels;

At the close of the work itself, in *The Flowering of the Rod,* we see Her again, here Kaspar brings forward the jar in which the old lore or sacred orthodox but esoteric story has been stored. But the bearer of the gift has met a woman along the way, the myrrh has become mixed perhaps, the story even as the woman tells it passes into another lore belonging to the world of Woman, the Mara of bitter experience to become "Mary-myrrh." Receiving the gift for the Child, the Mother may be the Muse receiving the poem on behalf of the Poem or Poetry. "Sir, it is a most beautiful fragrance, / as of all flowering things together." As, we realize, in the presentation of the poem itself H.D. as bearer of the content of the poem is like Kaspar for she is not sure the content has not been "changed," mixed, and yet she comes to know the gift—for the poem comes as a gift to the poet writing—is one of having lived in the pleasure of "a most beautiful fragrance," the music of the poem.

•

The ambivalence of the heart ("facing two ways"), the secretiveness of the heart, these are to be brought before the Christ Child; He Himself a sealed jar, yet a-jar somehow, for the essence escapes everywhere—mercurial, hermetic. He had been declared King, heir of the Fathers, even as the myrrh had been the secret or secretion of the Fathers, yet the suspicion lingers that another intention, a Woman's, has interfered.

The hardness of the heart is brought before the Child in the gift, for it is contained in the "small urn" of alabaster. As in "Narthex" almost two decades earlier, where H.D.'s seeing-in-depth first appears, she must bring the burnt-out triangle of painful experience into the hieroglyph of Solomon's seal, a woman's message worked into the sign of the Mage, so here, the odor of a woman's bitterness, of brine, "a Siren-song" is brought into the myrrh: "in recognition," she tells us in *The Flowering of the Rod,* xx, it might be "of an old burnt-out / yet somehow suddenly renewed infatuation . . . " Alabaster and salt of the sea had been terms of her first poems.

But then, as if love everywhere, even bitter love, burnt-out and lost love, were Love, it is not from the jar, whatever became of its myrrh, but from the Jar, the heart of the matter:

> the fragrance came from the bundle of myrrh
> she held in her arms.

"I am the Way," this God had said. And the way as we write may be the Christ; its music, the fragrance. "I am the Life," the sense of having lived, of its living, the closeness to essential Life in which our recognition of any work of art is involved may be our sense of its Mastery. He is the book she carries as she appears to the poet, and in the close of the book the poet writes, as at the close of The War Trilogy, He appears as the Child. "The Kingdom is within," He also said, where the Way, Word, Life, Master, World are one, in the Heart.

Chapter 5

I.

Without thought, invention
you would not have been, O Sword.

"Rails gone (for guns)," the poem begins, with the officers of the State, in the name of the War Effort, taking over all the conditions of personal reality into their own use, "from your (and my) old town square." With the declaration of war in the modern state, which claims to represent the authority of the people, the means and ends of the war become the ultimate reality (as in the interim between wars, which we call "Peace," to face reality means to accept and work with the terms of the dominant mercantile capitalistic and usurious system). The critical contempt that met H.D.'s War Trilogy was in part the contempt of the Protestant ethic for womanish ways, and back of that the old war between the Father and his hero-sons and the heathen realm of the Mothers, anticipated by H.D. in the "they snatched off our amulets, / charms are not, they said, grace" theme introduced in *The Walls Do Not Fall,* ii. But there was also the contempt of those concerned with the War Effort for H.D.'s sense that ultimately the War was to be subject to Writing itself as a higher prime of reality. To bring up the old gods of Egypt, already proved false and declared out-of-bounds by the historical victory of the Bible, was anachronistic in the face of the air attacks on London. The critics of the day—Dudley Fitts and Randall Jarrell—found her concept of history silly, if not dangerous, an offense to any common sense. The "still the Luxor bee, chick and hare / pursue unalterable purpose" and the "eternity endures" of the opening passage of the poem was the declaration of a personal real equal in its terms to the real terms of the war, i.e., political and national contentions, and H.D. had known from her experience of the pillory undergone by the Lawrences and other friends in the First World War that the cost of such a declaration was to suffer an all but overwhelming rejection. Here too the criticism is anticipated in the poem, where, in xxxi, the main statement of the voices of the adversary begins, accusing the poet of "intrusion of strained / inappropriate allusion, / illusion of lost-gods, daemons; / gambler with eternity . . . "

Robert Lowell's *Land of Unlikeness,* published the same year as *The Walls Do Not Fall,* with its "Tonight the venery of capital / Hangs the bare Christ-child on a tree of gold," was acceptable, for it recognized the victory of the industrial order over Christendom as ultimately real; Lowell held no unreal confidence in a higher reality of Christ. He was appropriately despairing in his opposition to the facts of the war. He acknowledged what Tate calls in his introduction to Lowell's first book "the disappearance of the Christian experience from the modern world." The young poet in despairing anger refers to Christ thruout with the realistic recognition that He is a lost cause or an absent spirit, like a Hamlet crying "Looke heere upon this Picture, and on this." "The ghost of risen Jesus," "my carrion king, Jesus," "the Hanging Jesus"—the Jesus that history crucifies haunts his mind. At one time only, in "Cistercians in Germany," does the ahistorical, anachronistic, or eternal image of Christ appear: "To Bernard gathering his canticle of flowers, / His soul a bridal chamber fresh with flowers, / And all his body one extatic womb, / And through the trellis peers the sudden Bridegroom." The poet is upon the verge of an epiphany, but he remains intellectually discrete and clearly takes this near appearance of Christ not as an Image but as a description of Bernard's scene. Perhaps upon later consideration Lowell felt even this spiritual pretension false; he does not include it in the canon of *Lord Weary's Castle*.

In contrast, H.D.'s insistence upon the Living Christ, her sense that not only the Christian experience but the Greek and even the Egyptian experiences have not disappeared from the modern world but gather immediate to our own experience, does not recognize what the consensus of opinion of reasonable men has determined is the true nature of history. For all of human history appears to H.D. as if it were a Creation or fiction of reality, involving wish as well as world in its works—and here, the war as much as the writing is wish, but the writing triumphs, for it most approximates the total configuration. It is the "unalterable purpose" of the poem to convert the War to its own uses; the bombings of London are read as signs in the Poem Effort which claims priority over the War Effort. "Eternity endures" means not only that the eternal themes of the poem, the images—the cartouche or the sword—last beyond the war, but that they, like the poet, endure, as one endures the insolence of those who cannot understand, the War's usurpation of human life from its most real purposes. There is the sense too that—as in the *Gospel of Saint Luke,* Jesus' "Father, forgive them; for they know not what they do," or His "He who joins not in the dance mistakes the event" in *The Acts of Saint John*—the War is not to be taken for granted as simply an economic or political opportunity or as a disorder, but it is also a Mystery play or dream projection to be witnessed and interpreted, to be endured in order to be understood. The War rises from the dramatic necessity and informs: "Pompeii has nothing to teach us, / we know crack of volcanic fissure," H.D. testifies. So, there were gnostics who taught that the human soul must come to know the depths of hell and sin as well as the heights of heaven and the good before it completes its human self or experience. In Freudian terms, the War is a manifestation of the latent content of the civilization and its discontents, a projection of the collective unconscious. "And beyond thought and idea," H.D. continues: "their begetter . . . "

Dream,
Vision.

•

"The total world of which the philosophers must take account," William James writes in his *Principles of Psychology* in 1890, "is thus composed of the realities *plus* the fancies and illusions." What we must deal with in such a totality of the human experience demands in poetry, as James saw it demanded in philosophy, a new structure of thought and imagination. "For there are various categories both of illusion and of reality, and alongside of the world of absolute error (i.e., error confined to single individuals) but still within the world of absolute reality (i.e., reality believed by the complete philosopher) there is the world of collective error, there are the worlds of abstract reality, of relative or practical reality, of ideal relations, and there is the supernatural world."

·

It is "the total world which *is*" that concerns James; and in his sense that What Is is multifarious, in his insistence upon the many strands we must come to see before consciousness have something like the fullness demanded by What Is, James is kin to Emerson before him and to Dewey and Whitehead after. The quest he projects is not only that of the philosopher who would approach the nature of human experience in its complexity but also that of the poet who seeks a poetics adequate to convey various levels of feeling and thought toward the complete. Whitman's "Self," expanded to include the variety of human existence, is such a concept. The at-homeness in many persons, times, and places, that characterizes *The Cantos*, The War Trilogy, or *Paterson,* represents the tendency to think of completeness in terms of the variety of human life, even of life itself, beyond the less-than-total individual sub-world: "to determine the relation of each sub-world to the others in the total world which *is*."

·

In the world of the imagination, of fiction and fable—the world of creation—James includes "the various supernatural worlds, the Christian heaven and hell, the world of the Hindoo mythology" with "the world of the *Iliad,* that of *King Lear,* of the *Pickwick Papers.*"

·

Money and war are also fictional entities, for men believe in them, as they believe in elves and gods, to make real their lives. Swords, spades, hearts, diamonds, and the drawings upon the walls, poems keeping their time, too, are conditions of the real, of What Is, man-made. All makers are at work between thought and the actual, feeling their way. It is what we call Poetry of The Making that articulates the feeling in language—the wish manifest in the image, Sword or new Master over Love—toward the fullness of experience. We see our Way and create our Thing in the world about us as desire illumines. "The 'larger universe,' here," James writes, "which helps us to believe both in the dream and in the waking reality which is its immediate reductive, is the *total* universe, of Nature *plus* the Supernatural."

.

Conventional poetics, which belongs to the Age of Reason that sought to reduce even religion to a consensus of the opinion of reasonable men, had reduced the frame of mind to exclude the supernatural from individual experience, to rationalize genius and make a metaphor of inspiration, to confine reality to what, as Dryden has it in his Preface to *All For Love,* "all reasonable men have long since concluded." In philosophy, in poetics, in science, and in politics, men strove to make and to hold a world of sense, practical knowledge, ideal relations, logical conclusions, around which what Freud calls the Super-Ego, grown enormous, built its authority, against an enemy world of the irrational—fearful, to be avoided or rendered harmless—the world of fictions (romance, supernatural, vision, and dream), of "sheer madness and vagary." Howling hairy madmen and shrieking desolate virgins appeared in the imaginations of Fuseli, Blake, Goya, Hoffman, Potocki, the Marquis de Sade.

.

James's world of fictions is the real of the creative imagination. It is in the work of realizing, composing or bringing into cooperation the various worlds of senses, sciences, fictions, opinions, ideals, ideas, and "sheer madness and vagary," held as one creation or poetics, that the artist develops the imagination "to charge with meaning to the utmost possible degree."

•

To recognize madness as a term of the real extends our life in What Is. This is the revelation of Goya's *Caprichos* or of Gérard de Nerval's *Chimeras,* that what otherwise had been isolated obsession and hallucination is brought into the communal imagination to become mystery and mystic vision. As, again, in the ritual of the Christian Mass, "madness and vagary" have been brought over into the order of the communal reality—a play enacted in which the body of Christ is eaten and His blood drunk, that must be held by the communicant as a mystery, an idea, but also an actual happening within a world of its own; that must also be not a play but a greater reality. The power of the Mass, its numinous force, its real, is that of a fiction where ideal and madness become contrasting elements of one structure. Conflicting elements, love and devouring cannibalistic hunger, are sublimated or condensed, held in a third element of devotion, the intensity of the created feeling arising from the incorporate disturbance.

•

"Dichten = condensare," Pound notes in his *ABC of Reading:* "Basil Bunting, fumbling about with a German-Italian dictionary, found that this idea of poetry as concentration is as old almost as the German language. 'Dichten' is the German verb corresponding to the noun 'Dichtung' meaning poetry, and the lexicographer has rendered it by the Italian verb meaning 'to condense'."

•

"The first thing that becomes clear to anyone who compares the dream-content with the dream-thoughts," Freud writes in *The Interpretation of Dreams* (1896), "is that a work of *condensation* on a large scale has been carried out."

•

Ezra Pound has the daemon of a poet and has described the genius of a poem not as a descending spirit or inspiration but as a welling-up of a spring or emotion. So, in his "Retrospect" of 1918 he inscribes: "Only emotion endures." "We might come to believe that the thing that matters in art," he writes in "The Serious Artist" (1913), "is a sort of energy, something more or less like electricity . . . transfusing, welding, and unifying. . . . " Then: "A force rather like water when it spurts up through very bright sand and sets it into swift motion." But Pound is a man of divided mind, and a mind, further, impressed during his years as a would-be candidate for his doctorate with the concerns and ambitions of a would-be professor of literature. The poetic emotion which Pound experiences as being a truth of his own nature is complicated by considerations of a different order, the concern for literary opinion, for changing established standards and reading lists. In "The Serious Artist," the arts "bear witness and define for us the inner nature and conditions of man" and are falsified if they be altered to "conform to the taste of the time, to the proprieties of a sovereign, to the conveniences of a preconceived code of ethics." In *Guide to Kulchur,* as in *The Cantos* of the 1930s, the ideogram which presented in configuration the inner responses of the man became confused with the ideogram of a proper sovereignty. Ideas in action became *idées fixes* acting upon a recalcitrant world. "As the man, as his mind, becomes a heavier and heavier machine, a constantly more complicated structure," Pound observes in "The Serious Artist," "it requires a constantly greater voltage of emotional energy to set it into harmonious motion." Only with the upsurge of emotional crisis that came at Pisa, where in the death-camp Pound came at last into the destiny of his poetic identity, did the conglomerate that had gathered in *The Cantos* begin to move again, and then it was to be a breaking up of fixed ideas into drifts and debris in the creative currents.

•

In certain works of his pre-War London period, in *The Spirit of Romance,* "Religio," "Aux Étuves de Wiesbaden," "Genesis (after Voltaire)," and

"Cavalcanti," Pound derives from the neo-Platonic cult of Helios, from the Provençal cult of Amor, from the Renaissance revival of pagan mysteries after Gemistos Plethon, and from the immediate influence of the theosophical revival in which Yeats was immersed, an analogous tradition of poetry as a vehicle for heterodox belief, a ground in which the divine world may appear (with the exception of the Judaeo-Christian orders). At the thought of Jesus, Pound has all the furious fanaticism of the Emperor Julian; he is a pagan fundamentalist. Aphrodite may appear to the poet, and even Kuanon, but not Mary; Helios and even Ra-Set may come into the poem, but not Christ. Yet these gods of the old world are not only illustrations of a living tradition; they are, Pound testifies thruout *The Cantos,* presences of a living experience. Does the poet cast them as images upon our minds or do they use the medium of the poem to present themselves? They come to the poet or he calls them up. So, in the first draft of *Canto* I: "Gods float in the azure air . . . "

    'It is not gone.' Metastasio
  Is right, we have that world about us.

        •

Even as H.D. testifies in *The Walls Do Not Fall* in 1942 to the attendance or Presence of Ammon-Ra-Christos and of Mary in London, so in *The Pisan Cantos* Pound in 1945 testifies he was attended in his tent by his familiar gods—Helios, Hermes, Aphrodite, and the Lady of the Pomegranate. It was a heterodox religion to hold, and Pound in other works of the pre-War London period, particularly in "The Serious Artist," strove to rationalize or make respectable the content of this tradition in terms of a natural philosophy of poetry, after the models of Remy de Gourmont's *Natural Philosophy of Love* or of Allen Upward's *The Divine Mystery,* appealing to the authority of Fabre and Frazer, to give his adherence a biological and anthropological reality, but also to uphold the poetic intuition itself against the attack of what he knows cultural and religious orthodoxy to be. To hold the poetic intuition in the face of his own professorial or professional righteousness, the rationalizing authority, Pound often writes to cover for the shamanistic poet he is at heart. But this Super-Ego could disapprove too of Pound's delite in pedantry. This is the poetic pathos in *Thrones* where, pursuing lexicographical speculations, Pound breaks with impatience to answer the impending voice of an inner adversary:

> *If we never write anything save what is already understood, the field of understanding will never be extended. One demands the right, now and again, to write for a few people with special interests and whose curiosity reaches into greater detail.*

Not only must the poet cover for the devotional character of the poem but he must defend the scholarly character too against some shadowy critical authority.

•

Only by interrupting the imagination can Pound incorporate certain "worlds" of his individual reality. The texture of the poem must allow for the contention of the mind. Abrupt interjections appear, dramatizing the conflict between two drives: one, akin to that of William James or William Carlos Williams or H.D.—"to extend the field of understanding"; the other, after Dryden, akin to Eliot, to appeal to "what all reasonable men have long since concluded." The problem thruout is one of translation between the individual experience, which is repressed in the official culture or banished to the realm of madness, and the body of what is taken as authoritative. Fenollosa's Chinese written character, Gaudier-Brzeska's vortex of energy in sculpture, Frobenius's culture-morphology, Gesell's justice and freedom in the exchange of goods—all these correspond to the poet's inspiration to extend the field of understanding in a new poetics. Ideogram, vortex of energies, form as meaningful and organic, and equilibrium in the circulation of goods (feelings and thoughts) are basic terms of what happens in *The Cantos.* Just as, significantly, they, like *The Cantos,* are rejected by the taste and opinion of reasonable men or relegated to the peripheries of the culture where harmless fantasies, or worse, madness and vagary begin to appear. The form of *The Cantos,* like the ideal form of a democratic government, must allow for the authority of the individual—here the authority of the individual response or impulse—within a community of differing responses. Of all contemporary poetries it has the greatest inner tolerance for even conflicting tones, certainties, doubts—the texture of a widely, even wildly, multiphasic personality.

•

For there is another voice, corresponding perhaps to the regular-guy voice of Williams, that breaks thru, as in the transitions of puberty the voice breaks between boyhood and manhood, and the personality breaks too, between the familial and the communal consciousness, making dramatic the conflict between the new sexual nature and the forces of authority in custom and government that forbid its expression and would compel its expression. The bold-face emphatic, the rant, the caricature of voice, the contentious mode appears, where another Pound roars and pounds on the table to bring Fenollosa or Frobenius, Gaudier-Brzeska or Gesell, whatever had opened the way for new inspiration and life-sense for the poet, to the consideration of government officials and university professors of literature, or reasonable men, to become part of the authoritative. There is hysteria, but we see too that it rises, most markedly in the irritations of Pound and D. H. Lawrence, men who, like H.D., testify to elements in experience that are not accepted in the social norms, just where the man strives to bring his individual awareness and the communal awareness into one.

•

The voices of Eliot or of Wallace Stevens do not present us with such disturbances of mode. They preserve thruout a melodious poetic respectability, eminently sane in their restriction of poetic meaning to the bounds of the literary, of symbol and metaphor, but at the cost of avoiding facts and ideas that might disturb. Both the individual and the communal awareness are constricted to fit or adapted to the convenience of an accepted culture. Writing in *The Dial,* January 1928, Eliot finds that Pound might actually believe what is suspect or outside the terms of proper English belief simply unbelievable:

He retains some mediaeval mysticism without belief, this is mixed up with Mr. Yeats' spooks (excellent creatures in their native bogs); and involved with Dr. Berman's hormones; and a steam-roller of Confucian rationalism (the Religion of a Gentleman, and therefore an Inferior Religion) has flattened over the whole. So we are left with the question (which the unfinished *Cantos* make more pointed) what does Mr. Pound believe?

Pound, as well as D. H. Lawrence, belonged to the side of those who hankered after strange gods. In the ranks of Poetry itself, and in those ranks among poets who were surely their peers, Pound and Lawrence were heterodox in their cult of the daemonic both in terms of the old orthodoxy of the consensus of religious beliefs within the society and in terms of the new orthodoxy of the consensus of rationalist scientism. From the beginning H.D. had been of the pagan party, and with The War Trilogy she moved as a poet to the battlefront. The full roster of Mr. Eliot's accusations against Pound, carefully loaded to excite the prejudices of right-thinking critics, was to be applied against her by her critics. Mysticism without the sanction of any church, daemonic and ghostly personae, biological and sexual coordinations, and, in H.D.'s case, Freudian in place of Confucian rationalism.

•

It is just the discordant note—the rant of Pound, the male bravado of Williams, the bitter anger of Lawrence, the feverish exaltation and heightened concern with adverse arguments—it is this not only being aware of the loss of community but being involved in the heart of the trouble, undertaking the trouble, that gives to the heterodox their vital meaning, beyond the special culture of the times, in the process of our own art, for they challenge what we would take for granted. The rant, the bravado, the sarcasm, the exaltation are purposeful overcharges that touch again and again to keep our sense alive to the disorder, the demand of experience for a higher order of form. The discord of their modes to the social norm is a therapeutic art.

•

Where the individual protest is vehement and then, as with Pound and Lawrence, out raging against the "democratic" norms that oppose and confine the development of man's inner nature, there is the seed of the totalitarian reaction. Where the individual despairs of his living his own life or finding his own life within the society under the domination of established proprieties, he may give over the struggle for liberation and seek a design for privilege within conformation or strike out for the domination of his own will. A Hitler or a Mussolini, a Lenin or a Stalin, successfully find the way to dominion; surrendering all inner freedom they become possessed and impersonate the absolute authority of the state that was once the enemy. Where a democracy is composed of a people in which the individual conscience and nature is not liberated, so that a common standard or consensus of the majority rules and not the union of each in free volition, the state is already totalitarian.

Pound must protest his right to write "for a few people with special interests." The hostility of a popularist democracy for "special interests" may be politically directed towards the overweening powers of industrial tycoons, Papist plots, and military lobbies, but it extends too to any sensibility, science, or art, that is not readily available as a commodity to all interests and uses. It is the unpopular sensitivity of the poet, for one thing, that is under attack. Complex or obscure considerations threaten the security and self-esteem of men who take pride in their common sense against any uncommon concern. "They claimed, or rather jeered in Provence, remonstrated in Tuscany, wrangle today, and will wrangle tomorrow—and not without some show of reason—that poetry must be simple." That's part of it. The popular mind resists and resents any extension of awareness beyond the use of public polity, for thought and feeling must cope there with new complexities and obscurities.

·

"Could beauty be done to death," H.D. cries in 1916, during the First World War, in "The Tribute":

Could beauty be caught and hurt
they had done her to death with their sneers . . .

That, too, is part of it. The beauty of the poem, the poet's sense of beauty, in itself, that cannot be bought and sold. Beauty, in a society based upon commodity-profit is ambivalently praised and despised. The popular mistrust, the industrial and commercial mistrust, opposes and destroys where it can individual sensitivity, as out of place in the "democracy" of big party politics or in the "community" of the modern city as individualist architecture with its romantic and expressive form, even ornament, is in the plans of the new functionalism.

But the mistrust is within too. The poets turn upon each other and themselves in accusation and guilt—Lawrence accuses Joyce of obscenity; Pound finds Lawrence's erotic poems "disgusting or very nearly so"; H.D. strikes out against the bravado of Williams; Williams hits back with exacerbated sensitivity against H.D.'s exaltation of the "sacred" ("her real beauty is a rare and sacred thing in this generation").

.

"So what good are your scribblings?" the partisans of the Sword demand in *The Walls Do Not Fall*. The immediate contention means "of what good for the War Effort?," but the accusation gives rise to answers in the poem that it is her very way of life, her ultimate individuality that is under question. Not only in wartime conditions but thruout the society living for love or living for experience is heretical, so contradictory to the common persuasion of the use of life—to career, to comfort, to security—that it gives rise to defensive affirmations where we feel the "I know, I feel" transcends the question, pushed, in order to survive as a life-purpose, to the ultimate. But the voices of disapproval remain, for they are part of what the poet knows and feels. Deeper, they have been incorporated in the poet's psyche, taken-to-heart. The old arguments against the cult of beauty, against Imagism, against the ecstatic, against the occult and mytho-poeic, crowd in to impersonate the poet's own duality between doubt and conviction in writing.

.

What I am getting at here is that the man individualizes himself, deriving his individuality from the ideas and possibilities at large of manhood in a community that includes all that we know of what man is ("Grandeur, horror!" Victor Hugo cries out in his vision of that Leviathan). And the desire to know more of what man is, extending the idea of man beyond the limitations of particular nationalities, races, civilizations, the taking of self in the species, or in the life force, or in the cosmos, is the need for self beyond what can be granted by whatever known community, the need for a manhood big enough to live freely in. The poetic urge, to make a poetry out of the common language, is to make room for the existence of the poet, the artist of free speech. As in the beginning, the sky was divided from the earth below, or Heaven from Hell, to give space, a height and a depth, in human life. He differentiates the area of existence, creating his "own" area, deriving the individuality as much from dissociation as from identification, disowning as well as owning possibilities of his being, making a place for self in the community of his total consciousness which is an inner counterpart of his awareness of the outer community in which he lives. He recognizes in the world about him those contentions he feels within.

•

Pound in *Canto* XIV not only attacks in society at large but attacks in his own mind "the betrayers of language . . . those who had lied for hire . . . the perverters of language," disowning the corrupt language of the press even as he strikes out in the very excesses of that language, having the bigotry to damn "bigots, Calvin and St. Clement of Alexandria," allowing them no more understanding than they allowed their enemies, inflamed against inflammatory words. In contrast, the famous Usura Canto (XLV) has a grandeur of tone that would seem to indicate that the poet has no such secret temptation to use his art for profit as he has to use his art for public persuasion and attack, for defamation of character. In the troubled flux of the late *Cantos* "the temple is not for sale" stands with equanimity.

•

In *The Walls Do Not Fall*, H.D. gives some assent to the "we fight for life" terms of the Sword's claim, for she answers here only that Writing too is part of the fight for life. But the communal pronoun "we" proper is used thruout the poem to refer to the community of a mystery within the larger society: "we know not nor are known," "we passed the flame," "they were angry when we were so hungry," "we reveal our status / with twin-horns, disk, erect serpent," "we, authentic relic / bearers of the secret wisdom," "we take them with us [our writings] / beyond death," "we are proud, / aloof, indifferent to your good and evil," "we know each other / by secret symbols," "we know our Name / we nameless initiates"—this is the language of the Holy Spirit cults of the sixteenth and seventeenth century Reformation, where community as well as self has been dissociated from the society at large and created anew in order to survive as a living reality in the consciousness. H.D. would create not only a life of her own but she would fuse elements of the community of poets, the community of the psychoanalyzed, and the community of Christ, to have a community of her own. In the light of what that community means by Life, the War is not all, mostly is not at all, a fight for life. "I am hungry, the children cry for food / and flaming stones fall on them," she returns in answer to the Sword's claim: "our awareness leaves us defenseless." In *Tribute to the Angels,* those who suffer in the bombings of London are not victims of a fight for their life but of a contention that is not theirs. "Never in Rome / so many martyrs fell," yes, but the war in the sky is "the battle of the Titans." In *The Flowering of the Rod,* her dissociation from the purposes of the war, like Pound's from the purposes of the peace in the Usura Canto, is clear:

> the harvester sharpens his steel on the stone;
> but this is not our field,
>
> we have not sown this;
> pitiless, pitiless, let us leave
>
> The-place-of-a-skull
> to those who have fashioned it.

In section x, she declares again: "It is no madness to say / you will fall, you great cities . . . it is simple reckoning."

•

This putting away of allegiance that obstructs the poetic or religious reality is an inner psychic as well as an outer social struggle for life-space, for the identity of the poet and the way of poetry to create itself and find its true community, that is, its freedom, within the mass of a populace where forces rule that care nothing for or are hostile to its existence.

.

Even as these poets strove to make a place for their poetry, they had a strong drive to disown those aspects of poetry that might be held up to the derision of the rigorous minded. In a letter to Williams in 1908, Pound writes: "Here is a list of facts on which I and 9,000,000 other poets have spieled endlessly." *He* at least is not to be taken in by the pretensions of the *poetic*. There follows a list of themes:

1. Spring is a pleasant season. The flowers, etc. etc. sprout bloom etc. etc.
2. Young man's fancy. Lightly, heavily, gaily etc. etc.
3. Love, a delightsome tickling. Indefinable etc. A) By day, etc. etc. etc. B) By night, etc. etc. etc.
4. Trees, hills etc. are by a provident nature arranged diversely, in diverse places.
5. Winds, clouds, rains, etc. flop thru and over 'em.

So. Pound continues. The tone is not simply vernacular, but a sophisticated putting-on of common sense—it protests its being wise to some shame incurred in poetic themes that might be betrayed in its own voice. "Delightsome tickling" covers with male bravado any suspicion of being taken-in by sexual excitement or love, lest the poet be caught in some "unmanly" emotion. Pound, deeply pre-Raphaelite in his affinities, will protest as a modernist in 1913 against Lawrence's "middling-sensual erotic verses" as "a sort of pre-raphaelitish slush, disgusting or very nearly so." Behind his "jesting," as he calls it, is Pound's native Puritanical mind in its distaste for the sensual. But deeper going, there is the intellectual disclaimer.

.

Compare Dante in *De Vulgari Eloquentia,* speaking also to his peers on the themes of poetry:

> These we call the worthiest of those subjects which can be handled; and now let us hunt out what they are. And, in order to make this clear, it must be observed that, as man has been endowed with a threefold life, namely, vegetable, animal, and rational, he journeys along a threefold road. . . . Wherefore these three things, namely, safety, love, and virtue, appear to be those capital matters which ought to be treated supremely, I mean the things which are most important in respect of them, as prowess in arms, the fire of love, and the direction of the will.

The direction of the will in the course of the twentieth century is deeply disturbed. The main drive of the Imagists away from the specially "poetic" dictions of the nineteenth century toward the syntax and rhythms of common daily speech was that of Dante in his *De Vulgari Eloquentia,* who argued that the vernacular "because it was the first employed by the human race, as because the whole world makes use of it" was "nobler than learned speech—" and "It is also nobler as being natural to us, where as the other is rather of an artificial kind." Pound's *Cathay,* meant as Hugh Kenner has pointed out to be carried in the soldier's pocket, in 1914 had the eloquence of a new poetic vernacular, the force of a common nobility; but in the *Confucian Odes,* following the Second World War, the voices of his translation grow disparate; a jazzy and folksy dialect takes the place of common speech— the low-life specialty that operates even as the learned grammatical speech of upper classes to convey a class consciousness set apart from our common humanity. In his version of *The Women of Trachis* Pound runs the gamut between the Shelleyan sublime of the choruses and the stereotyped vulgarity of the Cockney waiting-woman or nurse. Her speech has just that artificiality that Dante felt robbed learned speech of nobility—it is furthest in Pound's mind from the vernacular. Yet Dante sees this true or natural speech "as that which we acquire without any rule, by imitating our nurses." Herakles has the voice of Pound's own nature as he cries: "Splendor. It all coheres"—a cry that has tragic pathos in this translated play that incorporates the play of the poet's own poetic tragedy, where Pound had been heroic in his life to restore the word "common" to its coherence from the meaning of the word "common" as used by the middle-class of "lower classes." But the hubris of self-improvement and advancement in status goes deep in our American world, of rescuing ourselves from the common lot, and, profoundly American, Pound inherits in full the class and racial antagonisms in which our American culture has developed, even as he struggles to transform that culture. The Nessus shirt in which Heracles burns is the shirt of a consciousness of what is going on, where Heracles is heroic, as Pound is, by his strength of character in adverse fate, by his taking on in full the way it is.

•

"We are alone . . . " Freud writes in "The Dream-Work," an essay of that last year of the nineteenth century: "We are alone in taking something else into account."

"We have introduced a new class of psychical material between the manifest content of dreams and the conclusion of our enquiry." It is this area between the manifest and the conclusion of his enquiry, between the manifest content of the poem and the enquiry into that content, that Pound cannot introduce as a conscious artist. The poetic genius "rescues" the content. This is the authenticity of *The Cantos:* the poet's sensitivity, his feel for the material he admits. In his essays before the First World War his conscious mind allies itself with his genius; but, for the author of *Kulchur,* major themes of his poetic inspiration, indeed, inspiration itself, is suspect. The content of his great poem begins to seem to have "the defects of a time of struggle." His conscious aesthetic contradicts the work of his creative aesthetic which must then come more and more as an unconscious directive—to the consciousness a matter of defect and struggle.

Because the poem-work then, like the dream-work, is a composition that takes place in the unconscious that the consciousness feels as an imperative towards form, in *The Cantos* we read, as Freud saw the dream was to be read, "as it were a pictographic script, the characters of which have to be transposed individually into the language of the dream-thoughts." In the ideogrammic method, Pound finds a configuration that returns, beyond his rationalizations and predispositions, to the feel of things; he has faith in the truth of the instinctive synthesis, where he must exceed his own conscious reading analysis.

Where intelligence is consciousness, Pound is a marred intelligence. Not in the complex of heterodox material he has admitted into his ideogram, but in repressed contents of his experience that he does not and can not admit. Good or evil, Will moves in *The Cantos* separated from any psychological insight until the crisis of the Pisan Death Camp. But since intelligence is something larger than what consciousness can admit, an awareness that may lie in the feel of things' fitting imperatively as they lead toward the form of the poem, even when the consciousness cannot think of what is at work there, at the fingertip's sensitivity, at the ear's equilibrium, and in the secret mind's sense of undercurrents, *The Cantos* are a major breakthru. Pound is a great Dreamer, and it was a condition of his Dream that he vehemently and even violently reject the Freudian breakthru that began the translation of the language of dreams into our daily consciousness.

We may see the deeper significance the role of translation has had for Pound as a poetic task, when we think of how in psychoanalytic translation dreams and daily life have begun to appear as a language we must learn to read in order to translate something we have always to say that we do not know yet to hear. "The dream-thoughts," Freud writes, "and the dream-content are presented to us like two versions of the same subject-matter in two different languages." So, too, we see the importance of the ideogram for Pound for it is his route towards—"as it were a pictographic script"—the *condensare* of the dream.

2.

I

Poems are events of Poetry, of our consciousness of *making* a universe of feeling and thought in language. Celebrating, is it? or praying for? Of singing, of dancing, What Is.

•

As our concept of What Is changes, our concept of form changes, for our experience of form *is* our experience of What Is. As I begin to see in terms of William James's pluralistic reality, a sense of the total world emerging from many kinds of apprehension, and, in terms of Freud's exploration of one kind of psychosexual reality with its sense of the divine will as Eros and Thanatos, the three things Dante named as worthiest concerns in the poem—*safety, love,* and *virtue*—and their three appropriate means—*prowess in arms, the fire of love,* and *the direction of the will*—whatever their meaning in the thirteenth century and in Dante's universe, take on new and troubled meanings when they are taken as primaries in the creation of our own world. Dante understood *safety* as having to do not with the interests of his city Florence primarily but with the good of humanity as a whole, and so he took the cause of the Emperor and the government of the Empire as even against the party of the city, and he was condemned to death, a traitor, in Florence. As today, for the sake of safety of humanity our own prowess of arms would have to be given, were we to take Dante's sense of true government, to the union of all nations, against the contention of those who direct the United States in the name of private enterprise against communal goods and who are engaged in a disastrous struggle for domination against their counterparts in Russia and China. We live today, as Dante lived in the thirteenth century and in Florence, in a crisis of just these three worthiest subjects of the poem that must have their definitions not in our personal interests, or we find ourselves at war with our human commonality, not in our national interests, or we find ourselves at war with other nations, but in our human interests, our understanding of the universal term that is Man, the term not of a given reality but of a creation in process. "Of all civilizations," Dante argues in *De Monarchia,* not of the city of Florence, not of Rome, nor even Christendom alone. The goal of the governing art he discerns is "the realizing of all the potentialities of the human mind." "And this demands the harmonious development and co-operation of the several members of the universal body politic." It is a body that extends not only thruout the global space of Man but thruout the time of Man.

•

All thru the body of our nation, where men are fighting for the real-
ization of all the potentialities of the human mind, against exploita-
tion and discrimination, for the potentialities that have been denied
blacks, women, xicanos, and for our own potentialities of community,
of brotherhood, companionship in work, and marriage, that have been
denied, they are fighting, we are fighting, for our true "safety" and
have that "prowess of arms" that poets would praise. "I too," Whitman
answers the Phantom, genius of poets of old, who challenges him that
he does not sing the theme of War:

> I too haughty Shade also sing war, and a longer and greater one than
>   any,
> Waged in my book with varying fortune, with flight, advance and
>   retreat, victory deferr'd and wavering,
>
>   . . . the field the world,
> For life and death, for the Body and for the eternal Soul

                    •

Living in the warp of a capitalistic oligarchy, we begin to realize that
the potentialities of human mind lie hidden in what Pound calls "the
increment of association," our individual realization is curbed wher-
ever there is private interest, our own or another's. We must struggle
for the extension of communal property in order to provide for the
safety of our individual potentialities. As, we can see too, in Russia, the
safety of the communal potentiality lies in the struggle for individual
freedom.

                    •

James and Freud in the eighteen-nineties were drawn to study hal-
lucination, hysteria, and neurosis, where feelings of safety, love, and
virtue were confused and even lost. James saw that man must cope
with a more and more complicated picture of the real—the communal
composite—if he desire fullness. Freud saw that the unconscious cre-
ativity of man—where arts, wars, rituals of flower worship and death
orgy, forbidden sexual cravings, and the highest ideals swarmed—must
become part of man's conscious life, his responsibility, or else, if it does

not have to do with the nature of his individual potentialities, there was the hubris incurred. Safety, love, and virtue were under threat.

·

For men at the beginning of the century aware of the gap between the ideals men sounded and the motives of their actions, cynicism and embarrassment, seeing thru or dismissing, was an alternative to taking things too seriously. Thus Pound and Williams, not to be taken in by things that are "poetic"—Spring, Love, Trees, Wind, are embarrassed before their inspiration. And then, as if to disavow their manliness, their sincerity, in writing to each other they cultivate this special Man-Talk. It had its counterpart in the girlish-idiotic manner cultivated by some women; and it seemed to provide a striking method for achieving style in a period obsessed with style. Not only Anita Loos, where the effect was for a comic chic, but Stein, Hemingway, McAlmon, Cummings, became sophisticated in language as a jargon. It was the crux of H.D.'s objection in the letter Williams was to quote in the Prologue to *Kora in Hell* concerning the "hey-ding-ding touch," the "flippancies": "It is as if you were *ashamed* of your Spirit, ashamed of your inspiration!—as if you mocked at your own song."

·

In Williams's reply we see that back of the challenged "hey-ding-ding touch" that Williams said "filled a gap that I did not know how better to fill at the time" lay something else, a felt need of the man in his struggle for individual feeling against the popularly-debased meanings. "The true value," he goes on to say, "is that peculiarity which gives an object a character by itself. The associational or sentimental value is the false."

·

But turning to the poem "March," as it stands in *The Collected Poems* of Williams, I cannot find anything to substantiate H.D.'s sense of flippancy. I find:

I deride with all the ridicule
of misery—

and the realization that follows, where the image has meaning in a series of realities—poetic, politic, physical, and erotic:

Counter-cutting winds strike against me
refreshing their fury!

William Carlos Williams and Ezra Pound had this prowess in arms, anyway, to take their stand, winning a high place for the art of poetry again in men's minds. If Williams takes on the regular-guy voice, or Pound his cracker-barrel Alfred Venison or Uncle Ez voice, it is defensive strategy in a society that demanded the manner and condemned the nature. He-man bravado or working-class lingo was their affectation of the vernacular, meant to cut thru the genteel affectation of devotion or culture with which the middle-class poetry-lover read.

•

It was the false currency of middle-class associations and stereotyped sentiments that had converted safety, love, and virtue into mistrusted words. He-man bravado was popular; but manliness was a threat to the values of the marketplace. The anti-poetic voice was not only a defense but an attack, a show of sophistication to the pretension of the cultured. Associations and sentiments in themselves had come to seem false to the modern sensibility, and Williams took up his crusade for what he called "that peculiarity which gives an object a character by itself," for the "no ideas but in things." Pound, H.D., and Aldington in 1912 agreed to "direct treatment of the thing." To regain the feeling of the thing itself was a battle against its conversion into use and commodity values.

But this idea of the image in itself, of a character by itself, does not last long as a primary. By 1914 Pound is concerned with the vortex of energies. By 1916, H.D., reviewing John Gould Fletcher's *Goblins and Pagodas,* speaks of "a more difficult and, when successfully handled, richer form of art: not that of direct presentation, but that of suggestion." Only Williams remained as protagonist for the theory of the thing in itself, which culminated in the Objectivist movement of the thirties, where the poem was thought of as a *thing*.

•

Yet, with *The Wedge* in 1944, Williams projects a new definition of poetry. No longer the peculiar but now the total experience defines the art. "The war is the first and only thing in the world today," he begins his Introduction, where *the war* is a matter of stirring up the most general and active associations and sentiments. Then, "The making of poetry . . . is the war, the driving forward of desire to a complex end." "It is the war," he insists, "or part of it, merely a different sector of the field." With *Paterson* I in 1946, the later poetry of Williams begins, and the turn from the concept of the poem as a thing in itself to the concept of the poem as a thing in process is clear. Poems now appear as different sectors of a poetry going on, and we begin to read not only to recognize a thing well-made, its fittings and composition, but more and more to recognize "the driving forward of desire to a complex end." Themes and images reverberate. Williams, like Pound and H.D., begins to compose in relation to a field of poetry. "Until we have reorganized the basis of our thinking in any category we cannot understand our errors," Williams writes in his *Autobiography:* "An advance of estimable proportions is made by looking at the poems as a field rather than an assembly of more or less ankylosed lines." Following *The Pisan Cantos* and *Paterson,* Charles Olson in his "Projective Verse" essay of 1950 had opened his reconsideration of the nature of poetry, to see form not as solidification or codification but as the directive of energies in process, and to see image as vector. With the chapter "Projective Verse," introducing a part of Olson's essay, Williams indicates in his *Autobiography* the leap forward in a direction he too worked in, and, placing "Projective Verse" in the immediate context of chapters on Ezra Pound, conveys its relevance to Pound's poetics.

•

"To make clear the complexity of his perception in the medium given to him by inheritance, chance, accident or what-ever it may be," Williams writes in *The Wedge:* "to work with according to his talents and the will that drives them." The change in Williams as a poet is toward a conscious art, to be aware of the will that drives. In the "Projective Verse" chapter, Williams sees the poem as "a cell, a seed of intelligent and feeling security. It is ourselves we organize in this way not against the past or for the future or even for survival but for integrity of understanding to insure persistence, to give the mind its stay."

.

It was to give the mind its stay that H.D. came to Freud as a patient, for she was sick of soul, but also she came as a student, for she followed the sense she had that he had opened a way toward the integrity of understanding in language; he had found a means of translation. "Safety, love, and virtue," those old themes of the poem that had come so into question in the modern attitude, disillusioned by the misuse of "safety" in the interests of selling the war, by the misuse of "love" in the interests of sexual affairs, by the misuse of "virtue" in the interests of moralistic Christianity, and now it was argued that one must read Dante in the suspension of belief, and even, finally, poetry in the suspension of belief. In *Ion,* in her notes to the close of the play, H.D. recalls her theme of the fall of the city in time of war, the fall of Athens in whose art "the conscious mind of man had achieved kinship with unconscious forces of most subtle definition." And she tells here the story of an Athenian youth discovering where he thought the tree of the mind, the olive planted by Athené, "the charred stump of the old": "Close to the root of the blackened, ancient stump, a frail silver shoot"—not only that Athens, like those cities, the Wagadu of the Sahel or the Ecbatan of the Medes, recalled in *The Pisan Cantos,* is immortal, but that the mind itself and the language, charred, burnt-out, revives.

.

"Intelligent and feeling security," Williams says; a poem, "a seed of intelligent and feeling security"—a cell, a seed, then, of Dante's safety restored in meaning. Is there a common ground in *The Walls Do Not Fall* where Sirius may be the hidden source of true security?

Sirius:
what mystery is this?

you are seed,
corn near the sand . . .

.

Where the events of the poem are not viewed as peculiar but as events in a field, having their identity in areas that extend beyond the knowledge of the individual consciousness, Dante and Williams may inform a continuous—but we see it too as an eternal—great field of poetry. H.D. never mentions Williams in her writing after *The Egoist* days, and Williams recalls her only in rancor; but as poets, in the midst of the personal aversion, they come along separate ways to a common ground of language charged with old meanings revived, of form and content as immanent in the universe, where the responsibility of the poet is to recognize what is happening. In *Paterson* as well as in The War Trilogy— it is in this that they differ from *The Cantos*—there is the conviction that meaning everywhere is complex. "You're listening to the sense," Williams writes in *Paterson* Five, "the common sense of what it says. But it says more. That is the difficulty." For H.D., as for Williams, there was the recognition of subconscious directives that Freud had introduced. "I feel / the meaning that words hide;" she writes in *The Walls Do Not Fall,* "they are anagrams, cryptograms, / little boxes, conditioned / to hatch butterflies . . . "

II

Ion, begun in the Spring of 1920, continued in the Spring of 1922, was taken up again and completed in the Spring of 1932. With its peroration in praise of the intellect's work with the unconscious, *Ion* is not only a translation of Euripides but a translation of Freudian thought. It stands as a statement opening toward her analysis with Freud, a preparation, an expectation. "True, the late war-intellectuals gabbled of Oedipus across tea-cups or Soho cafe tables," she tells us in *Bid Me to Live.* That Freud had brought forward out of classical Greek poetry a central figure in the Greek mystery drama as a key to the new psychology and, more, that psychoanalytic thought drew upon and drew near mythopoeic thought must have attracted H.D., for whom a Greek name in itself had often excited poetic voice. *Psyche, Eros, Thanatos*—the cast of the Freudian metapsychology were members of a new mystery cult, a revival of the Greek spirit in psychoanalysis as it had revived before in the humanism of the fifteenth century and in the Hellenism of Alexandria. The Oedipus complex itself does not preoccupy H.D. She never pursues the sexual aetiology of neurosis or the sexual reference of symbolic charge. In the "Electra-Orestes" sequence which appeared in 1932, a year before her sessions with Freud, Electra speaks as if she were a mystagogue: "To love, one must slay, / how could I stay; / to love, one must be slain . . . "—recalling not the Viennese mysteries of the Elektra complex nor the theater of Euripides but the epiphanic intent of Orphic or Eleusinian mystery-play. "No one knows what I myself did not," Electra tells us: "how the soul grows / how it wakes / and breaks / walls,"—there may be a hint here of psychoanalytic waking and breaking of repressions, and in her refrain "that the soul grows in the dark" a hint of the Freudian unconscious; but neither in this sequence published in *Pagany* nor in the "Orestes Theme" published five years later in *Life & Letters Today* are we confronted with the Freudian concept of the violent sexual love and hate for father and mother as the primary content of the drama. What was important for her in Freud was that "he had brought the past into the present"; "he had opened up, among others, that particular field of the unconscious mind that went to prove that the traits and tendencies of obscure aboriginal tribes, as well as the shape and substance of the rituals of vanished civilizations, were still inherent in the human mind" (as what she had found in the Electra-Orestes sequence was a ritual of a vanished civilization); and that "according to his theories the soul existed explicitly, or showed its form and shape in and through the medium of the mind, and the body, as affected by the mind's ecstasies or disorders." Thruout the *Tribute to Freud,* it is clear that H.D. saw him not as the psychosexual theorist but as a guide of the soul, psychopompos—"Thoth . . . the original measurer, the Egyptian prototype of the later Greek Hermes" or "Asklepios of the Greeks, who was called the *blameless physician.*" If she displaces Freud, the displacement is not downward but upward. In 1944, writing a decade after her last sessions, she sees him in the light of occultist preoccupations that were already evident two years earlier in *The Walls Do Not Fall.* The Doctor who stands at the door of the unconscious also stands at the door of the other world, and his once-patient or student now works to bring him from the past into her present terms. Yet ten years before, in going to Freud, she had been in search of hidden content, of "the occult"; predetermined to find in her analytic sessions a way in her writing that would lead eventually from the Greece of the Oedipus of the tragic theater and of her own early translations from Sappho and Euripides, and from the Greece of the Viennese Oedipus and of her own stream-of-consciousness novels and stories, of "Murex" and "Narthex," to the Renaissance Hermeticism of the *Œdipus Ægyptiacus,* which she follows in 1957 in the poetic sequence "Sagesse." Her sessions with Freud were initiations.

•

"The first series began in March, 1933, and lasted between three and four months," she tells us. The second series began at the end of October 1934 and lasted for five weeks—until December 1, 1934. "I had a small calendar on my table. I counted the days and marked them off, calculating the weeks. My sessions were limited, time went so quickly."

•

In 1944, Dr. W. B. Crow's *Mysteries of the Ancients* calendar has replaced her calendar of analytic sessions, and the schedule of hours with Freud has been replaced by another schedule in which "Every hour . . . has its specific attendant Spirit," the angelology of the 1944 *Tribute to the Angels.* The appointment of hours itself gives pattern. Back of the later occultism, as back of the Freudianism of her middle period, her primary concern in life is for poetic life, and she converts subject matter and design into the working form of her poetry.

•

The secret of the poetic art lies in the keeping of time, to keep time designing or discovering lines of melodic coherence. Counting the measures, marking them off, calculating the sequences; the whole intensified in the poet's sense of its limitation. "My sessions were limited, time went so quickly," defines the span of the poetic sequence as well as the span of the analytic sequence.

"Here," "there," what once was, what is now—this return in a new structure is the essence of rhyme; the return of a vowel tone, of a consonant formation, of a theme, of a contour, where rhyme is meaningful, corresponding to the poet's intuition of the real. "The heart of Nature being everywhere music," Carlyle writes in *The Hero as Poet,* "if you only reach it." The poet would go to the heart of things because he believes he will find Poetry there; to the heart of his self, not only for his case history, but also for the key to poetic form that he is convinced is there.

H.D. in her work with Freud followed, she tells us: "my own intense, dynamic interest in the unfolding of the unconscious or the subconscious pattern." The unfolding pattern of the psyche is not primary for her, but the unfolding pattern of a poem the psyche enacts. The poet, like the scientist, works to feel or know the inner order of things, but for the poet the order is poetic, measures that renew his own feelings of measure in his art. The form in process of the poem, the form in process of the psyche, correspond in turn to the form in process of What Is. "The world ever was, and is, and shall be," Heraklitus says: "a Fire, kindled in measure, quenched in measure."

•

Where? When did it happen? these are terms of a felt form. A map or a calendar. "Isles of Greece, Spring, 1920" of *Hippolytus Temporizes* or the "War and post-war London (circa 1916–1926 A.D.)" that parallels or sets up a reincarnation of the "War Rome (circa 75 B.C.)" in *Palimpsest* are intensifications of pattern in history. The extension of historical timing becomes a compositional pattern in writing. Metric, ratio, is at the heart of the matter.

•

The artist seeks to render articulate a figure in process. In conventional forms, the poet refers to the literary set pattern before him. But the poet may derive his formal feeling from patterns that he has experienced in nature—from the tidal flow of the sea, from the procession of seasons, or from the growth of organisms. The map of a city, the flow of its traffic, or the daily change of its moods may give formal feeling. So, following the series of analytic hours with Freud that in 1933 and 1934 had been her initiation into the mysteries of the subconscious or underworld, H.D. carries over the "Freudian" presence of the past in the content of the present and derives form from the appointments themselves in a sequence of poems that are "sessions" of the narrative to which they belong.

The "for Karnak 1923 / from London 1942" of *The Walls Do Not Fall* continues the "there, as here" dimension that she had worked with in *Palimpsest* but now, beyond the earlier hint of reincarnation-time of the palimpsest-time of life written over life in one ground, she may refer too to the Freudian-time in which the experience of the species is the ground of the individual experience. The important thing here is the presence of one time in another, of one work in another, giving rise to possible reverberations—depth the form demands—and information—complexity of structure the form demands; as in rhyme there is a structure of message within message in which sound and meaning in pattern cooperate to give qualities of portent and fulfillment.

With *Tribute to the Angels* a new notation of time is incorporated in the work at its close: "London / May 17–31, 1944." We not only know when it was written, but we are led, if we follow the notation to what it implies, to apprehend the order of experience from which the order of the poem arises in which the specific days "count."

.

The calendar kept in those psychoanalytic sessions becomes now the calendar in poetic sessions. Freud had asked of everything, What does it mean? What is back of *that?* "When?" "Where?" Now, in the realization of the poem, as it had in the first series at Berggasse 19, Wien IX, or at Döbling, place and time begin to tell. It had been Freud's great "discovery" to bring back into our consciousness how names and numbers as well as images build up references in our feeling of things. It was not new, it was the return of an old Jewish way of the mysteries. Names, numbers, images, events in *The Zohar* of Moses of Leon in the thirteenth century co-operate as puns and hidden meanings to reveal the inner Nature of What Is.

.

"The arrangement for receiving us (at Döbling)," H.D. writes, "was more informal, and one did not have quite the same sense of authenticity or *reality* as in the Professor's own home." Here, the formality of the Professor's own home is also the specific genius of place and time—the potential *form* the artist feels in the occasion. Authenticity and reality tend to be identified with the appropriate and significant; the artist is searching for compositional openings in a complex experience.

III

The "Ion" of Euripides, Translated with Notes, was sent to Freud when it was published early in 1937. The translation begun in 1920 had been finished in 1932, but the notes extend the play as if it had been seen anew, after not before the Freudian illumination. In the passage I had taken the dating of the work from: "numerically 1920, 1922 and again (each time, spring) 1932, we touched the stem of a frail sapling, an olive-tree" the notes would seem to be recalling at a later date the work of the translation.

"Deeply moved by the play (which I had not known before)," Freud wrote in thanking her for the gift: "and no less by your comments, especially those referring to the end, where you extol the victory of reason over passions. . . . " In the play itself lines 1334–5, translated by Ronald Frederick Willetts in *The Complete Greek Tragedies,* edited by David Grene and Richmond Lattimore, as follows:

Ion: All men are pure who kill their enemies.
Priestess: No more of that—hear what I have to say.

have been given an import Freud would appreciate in H.D.'s translation:

Ion: to strike at evil, is pure:
Pythia: you must know why you strike:

•

In the "Translator's Note" at the beginning of *Ion* we can see a gain, from the earlier intuitive form, toward a conscious speculation and projection of form. Not only has H.D. articulated the play into felt sections, but she is concerned with the interpretation of her aesthetic feeling. Once the psyche of the person has been analyzed, a new sense of the psyche of the poet arises along analytic lines as well as the pure stroke of the original inspiration. You must begin to know why the impulse is appropriate.

•

H.D. had found her poetic style in the beginning in the process of rendering choruses from Euripides. She did not exactly find it in the text alone but also in her own critical reaction to the text. Writing in *The Egoist* in 1915, she observed: "It seemed that the rhymeless hard rhythms used in the present version would be most likely to keep the sharp edges and irregular cadence of the original." But there was also "the repetition of useless ornamental adjectives . . . where the Homeric Epithet degenerates into what the French poets call a *remplissage*—an expression to fill up a line. Such phrases have been paraphrased or omitted." It was style, the cut-line and facet, the tensions that the modern movement in music and painting as well as poetry demanded, that H.D. was searching out of Euripides in 1915.

Now she returns, after Freud, to search out that workable stuff of Euripides' text, not the manner that made for a new style in poetry, but deeper, back of that, for the level at which manner and style are seen as form and meaning. She makes much then of Hermes' entrance to give the Prologue: working now beyond the line-edge for depth. "He might bear a lighted torch," she notes; there is no stage property specified, but "the torch is symbolical as well as practical. This is Delphi, still night, the sun has not yet risen."

She wants the opening read from a script, almost chanted. "This would give a rhythmic, hypnotic effect and heighten mystery, in the manner of cathedral litany, heard at the far end of a great vault; our vault, here, is the dome of heaven." And *Ion* we read is a mystery play; its great god—Apollo, the Sun. And the nineteen divisions into which she has articulated the play are not only then practical, where "Each one represents an entrance, an exit, a change in inner mood and external grouping of the characters," but in her description of the proportioning of scenes, we read suggestions of an initiatory sequence: "two gods who comment on the beginning and the end; a messenger; in this case, a servant who is also an outside observer, half-way as it were, between the gods and men; a trinity of father, mother and son; the father, in this instance, being a divinity, has a double in the earthly manifestation of the king of Athens; an old man, a stock figure, and the Pythian priest-ess who, in the hands of this fifth-century 'modern' genius, is freed from all taint of necromancy and seems almost to predict a type made famous by Sienna and Assisi," then: "The choros in a Greek play is, in a sense, a manifestation of its inner mood, expression, as it were, of group-consciousness; subconscious or superconscious comment on the whole." Here the formal elements of the play, even the numbers, the twos, the threes, and the many of the chorus, have been extended into meaning.

.

"The word ION has a double meaning," we noted. We were thinking then of the opening of levels of meaning; but here, tracing the develop-ment from the first and second series of analytic sessions to the narrative poems written in series, we note too that to have a double meaning is to open up a new sense not only of possible depth in the work but of the work's possible existence in depth. ION extends in two directions or opens up counterpoints in the composition of the whole. Order ("proportion" H.D. calls it) and significance appear as properties of the work itself, not only as acknowledged content, but, just in that, as the feeling for form. Where the Pythian priestess "predicts" St. Catherine or St. Francis, form also is not self-contained but predicts and inherits, is process.

.

The two gods are two points, but also two directives. There is "begin-ning and end"; there is "half-way as it were." Geometrical figures begin to appear, for the sense of the when-where map of the diagram is oper-ating—a trinity of counterparts, father above and below, mother and priestess, son who is also our source. Personae have roles in a drama that is a graph: fate = form. Hadn't Aristotle come close to our sense here? The *mythos* he saw as the plot. To draw, draw out, figure out. To plot the movements and positions of the stars that are points in time.

.

In the beginning H.D. had been an initiate in Poetry, taking Euripides as her Master, as later she was to take Freud. She had found out the imagist manner that was to be her own in translating—"to keep the sharp edges and irregular cadence." But—there was also in Euripides, disagreeable to the modernist taste, "the repetition of useless ornamental adjectives." There was *remplissage*—fillings in to make up the measures of the line set by convention. The new temper of the 1920s strove to prune away and to attack ornament, *remplissage,* or sentiment, association, toward a clean, energetic and ascetic beauty. We see it in the austerities of Juan Gris or Brancusi. William Carlos Williams could call it in H.D. "the desolation of a flat Hellenic perfection of style"; but he himself, at the inception of his late period, still speaks in *The Wedge* of a "machine made of words." "When I say there's nothing sentimental about a poem," he writes in 1944: "I mean that there can be no part, as in any other machine, that is redundant."

.

It was Freud's role in H.D.'s second initiation to bring her from the formative prohibitions that had given rise to the modern style, from the stage which Pound's "A Few Don'ts" represents, into a work which involved exactly those prohibited areas—repetition, *remplissage,* or sentiment. Associations must here not be cut away, dismissed, paraphrased or omitted, but dealt with, searched out until they yielded under new orders their meanings. Where the modern artist had sought a clean, vital, energetic, ascetic form—repression and compression—Freud sought the profound, delving in unclean thoughts, depressions, neuroses, voluptuous dreams. The Freudian permission or command saw form as a swarming ground.

.

Command, suggestion or permission—Freud helped H.D. to come in her art from a compressed style into an open exploratory form; from the cut-edges of *Sea Garden* to the woven tissue of The War Trilogy. The diagram comes in then, the map, for Freud led the consciousness into territories the mind had forbidden itself. One of the determinants of an art, of our existence as artists, is where the permission is given.

It was not only sexual and erotic knowledge that had been prohibited. For sentiment, association, like repetition and ornament, were distasteful—fearful then, in Freudian terms—to the mind of the twenties. "The impact of a language," H.D. writes "as well as the impact of an impression may become 'correct,' become 'stylized,' lose its living qualities." It was, in this sense, away from style itself toward the act of writing itself that Freud helped H.D.

IV

The Permission is the Grace. God's Grace, yes; and likewise, the grace of a line or of a melody, a grace note or note of grace. Where, too, there is an art the poet has by the reader's grace. The style of the artist, his signature or control, is something different, analogous to his character, the operation of energies in repression, of challenge and attack upon the world about him then. The grace of the artist is analogous to his nature, a given thing, the operation of energies in freedom, of response and self derivation from the world. Style, being wrested from Nature, is mastery; Grace, being given, is the service. The Art here being to keep alive in one process mastery in service, service in mastery.

·

H.D. was brought in the Freudian dispensation into a larger permission in writing. Her earlier "pure" style—even among those literary puritans the Imagists, the most "frozen," "crystallized," "controlled"—and the fervent, even fevered, voice of the *Red Roses for Bronze* period are followed now by a writing that opens to influences. The early Imagist style is not gone but has awakened; it is the sea-shell of *The Walls Do Not Fall* iv, "bone, stone, marble" as she had often imagined her verse in Imagist days, but now the image is larger, to include "that flabby, amorphous hermit / within," who "prompted by hunger" "opens to the tide-flow." The catalogue of adverse criticisms that begins with the "charms are not, they said, grace" announcement in *The Walls Do Not Fall* ii and takes over in xxxi, xxxii, and xxxviii, has been admitted, let into the creative activity of the poetic consciousness itself as a force toward its own structure.

·

We speak of the poet as "gifted," as having the gift of song or imagina-
tion, and we obscure in this the fact that the willingness of the poet to
receive, his acceptance of what is given is initial to the gift. The poet
must be a host to Poetry, "open to the tide flow," even as he with-
holds that area in which experience becomes peculiarly *his*. The uncon-
scious—like God, in George MacDonald's *Lilith,* Who gives always,
everywhere, unconditionally, forgiveness and love—gives ground for
the experience of manhood, as words give everywhere their sound and
meaning, the open secret of their magic. It is something in us: "Lilith,"
MacDonald names Her; the neurotic, Freud describes it—that cannot
and will not receive; but it is as important in the etiology of the artist as
that which receives: the will to distinction, toward the self-containment
of the work of art. The "I sense my own limit" in *The Walls Do Not Fall*
ii is humility and leads to the close of xiv:

> we have not crawled so very far
>
> up our individual grass-blade
> toward our individual star.

but it is also the pride of the artist in his originality, the line of his
signature drawn that can be no other, and leads to H.D.'s claim as in
xii: "we are proud and chary / of companionship with you others, / our
betters. . . . "

•

Self acceptance may mean then not self defense but the acceptance of a
permission recognized, the acceptance of self beyond self. In the pro-
cess there is an interchange of gifts, for one gives oneself to the experi-
ence, to love, to the poem, in being given love or the poem. So too,
the visible world always and everywhere would fill the imagination in
that interchange in which the imagination would fill the world. Here
one has one's origin in another. "I will be myself and not another!"
Lilith, in George MacDonald's novel determines. "My own thought
makes me me; my own thought of myself is me. Another shall not make
me!" Unawakened, she would dwell in her own shadow, refusing sleep

and dreams, for in Dream (and here that Life is a Dream takes on new meaning) an other makes us.

•

The new dispensation is not only a new permission but, in that, a new communion. As early as 1928, in the story "Narthex" H.D. had raised an alternative to the purity of Athens (as in *Ion:* "While one Ionic column stands, stark white and pure on the earth, that name shall live") the impurity of Byzantine Venice, the complex fascination and involvement of the facade of Saint Mark's. "Loss of identity is the gift of Venice," it seems to her then: "'Crystallized and over static identity . . . ' she stumbled. Words when Greek meets Greek mean nothing. 'You crystallize identity.'" But beyond this loss of identity, of self, there is the giving up of self to "this new protection, this going into all things," into the narthex of Saint Mark's, into the "power to crawl, snail self up the surface of high window and creep half-hatched moth in among tenuous rootless and dynamic deep earth feelers," the hard line, the boundary is lost, and from the depth of the confusion of associations and montage the name, the figure, and the words of Christ begin to appear, as in The War Trilogy, some fifteen years later. He will be central; the "new protection" leading to the "new Master" over Love.

•

In *The Flowering of the Rod,* Mary Magdalene passing from her life as a whore into her new life, even as H.D. had passed from her period of passionate love affairs, the emotionalism of *Red Roses for Bronze,* into a new phase, has seven devils cast out of her by the Master, but these are also brought forward into the new self: "these very devils or *daemons,* / as Kaspar would have called them, / were now unalterably part of the picture." Acceptance of the new self means also acceptance of the old, forgiven, redeemed, loved. *"Lilith born before Eve / and one born before Lilith, / and Eve; we three are forgiven. . . . "* The first persona of H.D., the stark white and pure, cold, Ionic perfectionist *daemon* is there then too.

•

She had gone whoring after strange gods, among whom the new god Christ appears, or was He Helios? In The War Trilogy His identity multiplies: Ra, Osiris, Amen, Christos, the authentic Jew stepped out from Velasquez. Her identity multiplies: Isis, Aset, Astarte are among the seven daemons who are now unalterably part of the picture of Mara, Mary, Mary Magdalene. Not only the old gods return in this return of the repressed, but the old themes—Spring, Love, Trees, Winds—threaten to come back without the sophistication that modern taste had demanded. "*Kennst du das Land, wo die Zitronen blühn?*" "The words return with singular freshness and poignancy," H.D. writes in *Tribute to Freud,* as Goethe's song, sung long ago in childhood, comes forward to be part of the picture. Greek aesthetic—white marble—changes now to Greek mystery cult, as Renaissance Hermeticism and the Romantic Revival enter in. The very tradition in which H.D. conceives her work becomes complicated. In *Helen in Egypt,* she will move in a Greek world that is of shadow and astral light, not only the Helen in Egypt, but also the phantom Helen Euripides tells us walked the walls of Troy but also the Helena of Goethe's "Classico-romantic Phantasmagoria" in *Faust,* who is the lure of Beauty the poet follows. "It is for him a necessity of nature to live in the very fact of things," Carlyle writes of the Poet in the spirit of Goethe; the very fact of things being the total world of which the philosophers must take account, the *open secret* Goethe had called it: "He is a *Vates,* first of all, in virtue of being sincere. So far Poet and Prophet, participators in the 'open secret,' are one."

·

"What you gave me, was not praise," Freud wrote to H.D.: "was affection and I need not be ashamed of my satisfaction."

"Life at my age is not easy, but spring is beautiful and so is love." To admit affection, sentiment and association, and to need not be ashamed would strike at the repression of sincerity in the modern as his admission of the very fact of sexuality hit at the repressions of the nineteenth century.

·

Going back to the poem "March" of William Carlos Williams, I find its voice is everywhere sincere not sophisticated. He admits winter, spring, bitterness of wind, as immediate to the very fact of things, without the self-consciousness that will come later. I cannot find what H.D. in that letter so long ago had accused. What she accused, the lack of grace, does flare up in Williams's answer: "I'll write whatever I damn please, whenever I damn please and as I damn please." The "I" throws up its defiance to hold its own in writing against being taken over by what is not its own, the grace of men's associations, and the grace of What Is. We sense a mind at war with prohibitions it is making for itself. There was a block in view, an intensification of style that was a necessity for correctness, for modernity. It makes for fits of temper and outrage in both Pound and Williams. The romantic vision was outlawed: "And you do NOT get out of such slumps by a Tennyson or a Rilke," Pound writes in *Kulchur,* or in the London pre-war period of the Imagist movement, in the essay "The Renaissance," I find, of Goethe: "but outside his lyrics he never comes off his perch. We are tired of men upon perches." But this is the very perch of the time. Out-of-Bounds signs proliferate. The nineteenth century appeared as a forbidden territory, like the barbarian world outside of Athens, or the savage world outside the Puritan stockade. Giving a figurative account of her turning to Freud, H.D. instinctively uses terms out of Fenimore Cooper: "Say it was a birch-bark canoe. The great forest of the unknown, the supernormal or supernatural, was all around and about us. With the current gathering force, I could at least pull in to the shallows before it was too late, take stock of my very modest possessions of mind and body, and ask the old Hermit who lived on the edge of this vast domain to talk to me, to tell me, if he would, how best to steer my course." Or now it seems to glide into a passage from one of William Morris's great romances, *The Wood Beyond The World* or *The Water of the Wondrous Isles*—"those prose romances that became after his death," Yeats writes in *The Trembling of the Veil,* "so great a joy that they were the only books I was ever to read slowly that I might not come too quickly to the end." The aestheticism of Pound and of H.D. had taken seed in pre-Raphaelite soil, their sense of Beauty haunted by the slim forms of Burne-Jones and the sylvan lovers of Morris, but the spirit of the modern formed itself in reaction against—"pre-Raphaelite slush disgusting or very nearly so" as Pound was to call it—the erotically enriched, fused, or sentimentalized forms, toward hardness. For the time *The Wood beyond the World* was to be put away with shame.

·

"*Per una selva oscura,*" Dante had called it, referring to finding himself in some darkness, lost in a wood. Pound, inheriting Dante from pre-Raphaelite sources, kept that *ben dello intelletto* that he would relate to the crystallizing thought of Plotinus or Erigena, shedding the spirit of romance, and would avoid "the great forest of the unknown, the supernormal or supernatural" that carries H.D. from some memory out of Cooper's American wilderness into another romantic forest with its Hermit, close upon the marges of Morris or even the forbidden Tennyson. In the modern sensibility romance is divided against itself. In *The Cantos* Pound worries again and again hints of Manichaeism, the good infected by evil. So, too, contemporary studies of the Romance tradition by Charles Williams, C. S. Lewis, or Denis de Rougemont are alive to the duality of their material, the ambivalence of love. In our own time, after the Second World War, there appears in the works of Burroughs, Beckett, a black romance, in which the ambivalence has disappeared and hate alone is real.

·

"*Tanto è amara, che poco è più morte,* So bitter is it, that scarcely more is death," Dante says in the opening of *The Inferno;* he is talking not of hell but of the dark wood. Eastertide of the year 1300; Dante was 35. "*Nel mezzo del cammin di nostra vita,*" he begins.

·

H.D. was 47 when she began her analysis with Freud, and the figure read in passing of finding the Hermit in the forest may refer to finding Freud in the increasingly dark woods of the middle years. She will take Freud then as Dante takes Virgil as a guide into the darkness itself. "That fountain which pours abroad so rich a stream of speech" Dante addresses Virgil, and for H.D. too Freud may have been water-witch, a finder and releaser of speech once more. Something was blocked in her and she sought a new course.

Words can become correct, stylized, she tells us. She had been the perfect stylist—*the* Imagist, May Sinclair had said in the *Egoist* days. The thrust of the soul's life, of energetic imperfections, was keen against the resistance of her perfectionist style. The writing of H.D. gives way first in the prose of the late 1920s, stemming from May Sinclair perhaps, ultimately then from Henry James, and openly taking up from Joyce—a prose that strives to carry in the stream-of-consciousness mode the burden of a tangling experience.

•

We are in the dark thicket itself in the "Murex" section of *Palimpsest,* that grows more confused and lost (*che poco è più morte*) in stories like "Narthex." It was the time for a call to order, for the Work to begin or all to be lost. The stories are peopled with victims of the modern sophistication—we see them also in the novels and stories of Lawrence and Mary Butts, in the paintings of Marie Laurencin and Kees Van Dongen. Abysses of psychic life, where identity wavers or goes void, open. The mind goes back, back, back, to certain scenes of agony or loss. The present falls into the past tense. In one of her most beautiful later passages, in *The Flowering of the Rod,* H.D. recalls with affirmation this lure of the insistent past event:

for they remember, they remember, as they sway and hover,
what once was—they remember, they remember—

It is the intoxication here of the reiterated yearning. "For theirs is the hunger / for Paradise," she writes. Where we realize that this Paradise or first Eden survives in its never having yielded satisfaction. A rapture that leaves the poet hungry for rapture.

•

"He had brought the past into the present," H.D. wrote of her teacher or doctor, Freud. The modernity, the up-to-dateness, the sophistication of the twenties had sought to avoid the consequence of Spirit by living in a time of its own as if there were no current in men's lives. The Spirit of the Nineteen-Twenties could be defined, given distinction; it would not sweep one up into larger or more complex involvement in human experience. *The Golden Bough, The Varieties of Religious Experience,* and *The Interpretation of Dreams* to the sophisticated reader lead not toward an increased sense of the immanent and numinous in daily life but toward a mythological know-all in which the immanent and numinous was seen-thru. For Yeats or Hardy, fatefulness and the supernatural strengthened the substance of their feeling; at the very threshold of the modern period the fascination of the depths seems to rise to a pitch of intensity. "The Trembling of the Veil" Yeats called his portrait of the nineties: "I found in an old diary a saying from Stéphane Mallarmé that his epoch was troubled by the trembling of the veil of the Temple. As those words were still true, during the years of my life described in this book, I have chosen *The Trembling of the Veil* for its title."

·

For the next epoch, announced by the works of Darwin early in the century, and then by Frazer, Freud, and James, it is the comparison of all things or the Mixing of the Waters—but this is the thicket. Bushman, shaman of the Lapland wastes, the child at his watercolors, and Michelangelo are brought into one complex concept of Art. In the new Jungian religious psychology, Attis mixes with Christ; Christ mixes with the dream figures of school-teachers in Iowa; the Serpent in the apple tree mixes with Attis and the beneficent Damballah of the Gold Coast.

As peoples mix—toward the Cosmic Man, Wyndham Lewis calls him—so in the new poetry, appearing first it seems in Whitman's *Leaves of Grass,* the song of the populated Self, French, German, Italian, Latin, Greek enter in to form a cosmopolitan language. Voices, images, times mingle and become transposed in a poetry in which a crowded traffic of ideas moves. It is the obscure medium, the thicket of impressions, of experience suffered without rest. "Ezra is a crowd; a little crowd," Lewis writes in *Time and Western Man,* attacking this new breakdown of boundaries in time and space in which the individualization of the man is threatened. As in H.D.'s "Murex" or "Narthex" impressions crowd in to take over the person of the poet; or in "Cities" "packed street after street, / souls live, hideous yet—" the psyche identifying with the cosmopolis finds itself infected by antagonistic elements of the city's population.

.

Williams in that reply of 1920 reveals the internal conflict of the modern sensibility that would use, somehow, anyhow, the terms of the times, even when this public spiritedness hits against the sacred: "*sacred* has lately been discovered to apply to a point of arrest where stabilization has gone on past the time," he writes, and then: "it'll be good if the authentic spirit of change is on it."

.

H.D. tells us in *Tribute to Freud:* "I wanted to free myself of repetitive thoughts and experiences—my own and those of many of my contemporaries." In trying to perfect a form or perfect an experience that has left us dissatisfied we find ourselves coming back to it again and again. In H.D.'s early "Ionic" style, the lines have the polish of their being tried in the ear again and again, the phrases turned as stones are turned in a mill to bring out their high surface, to wear away "imperfection." The poetry of Williams and of Pound in *The Cantos* attempts to incorporate imperfection even to the accretion of voices antithetical to the poetic voice. "It filled a gap that I did not know how better to fill at the time," Williams replied to H.D.'s objections to such elements; but these elements were not stop-gap, they had entered the primary matter of our poetry. Or the realm of the poetic consciousness had extended to demand them. The gap too was becoming a primary of the American consciousness. The very elements that Williams, Pound, H.D., and Wallace Stevens find most questionable in each other's work become in turn generative terms of my generation in poetry. Our admission in consciousness of what must be included in our humanity, in our poetic art, in our history is not only vastly extended and complicated but intensified. The experience of men today is one of overwhelming increase, expansion, and density, of over-population in consciousness as well as in social space, of pollution in culture as well as in industrial production—it is the dramatic force of the creative identity, charged and overcharged in the abundance of resources, exploitative, glutted, driven on to lay waste or to conserve but to work with the terms of a world mind which has succeeded the nation mind or the city mind or the tribal mind, driven by the command that no individual, no idea, no impression be suffered to die or to be lost.

The exaltation of H.D.'s early art and her feeling for the perfect, her "real beauty is a rare and sacred thing in this generation" in that letter to Williams, was not integral in itself, but reactive, a front held against the tides of the time, the agoraphobia of a temper that strives to preserve its fine edge in a mêlée, but the temper itself an element of that mêlée. She was not "Greek" but ultimately, as Sapir saw, American. Her intensity was the intensity of her feeling of the war-time society and its claims not only upon her but within her. She was at war with war.

·

"Counter-cutting winds strike against me," Williams had sung in "March": "refreshing their fury!"

·

In every area the process of mixing, of adultery, breaking down the inner reserve and private claim of the individual, toward public uses, goes on. Look at the process again, and it leads to a higher integration. Beyond the terms of the private and public, in the great terms of Self and Mankind, there is the vision of a larger and freer cooperation. The reality of both views remains.

For the modern artist the mixing of classes, the mixing of races and cultures, the mixing of gods, the mixing of economies and industries, has provided an open material, but it has also demanded almost cultish gestures for the artist's purposes to survive. "We," "They"—the intensity of opposition grows as we all but despair of any equilibrium to be worked out in the mass. Something public-minded resists as overly sensitive, histrionic, even hysterical, the private and unpopular tone of H.D.'s review of Marianne Moore in *The Egoist*. Doesn't she lack a sense of proportion, in the midst of a World War with its very real battles, to speak of "a battle against squalor and commercialism." The claim of the mass of men, projected by the manufacturers, the politicians, and the military caste, who work in terms of that mass, would seem to have ultimate reality, before which all other terms of individual human reality are declared unrealistic—pretentious then, defensive, or vainly idealistic. H.D.'s "We are all fighting the same battle," can ring with a valor that the very profit and wage-centered world it faces has persuaded us to scorn or to be ashamed of in ourselves, for it has been rung false in the familiar atmosphere of public rhetoric and private contempt, of mean men protesting noble virtues. When H.D. continues: "we must strengthen each other in this one absolute bond, our devotion to the beautiful English language," her resolve sounds high, even isolated and shrill, pathetic then, above the uses of practical speech. Pound and Williams were quick to hear in such declarations tones of a poetic earnestness that seemed unmanly or female, before which they bridle, protesting their not being taken in by such sensitivities. "Alexandrine Greek bunk," Pound calls it in a letter to Williams: "to conform to the ideas of that refined, charming, and utterly narrow minded she-bard 'H.D.,'" as in the same letter he refers to "the spinsterly aversion" of Marianne Moore's "I will not touch or have to do with things which I detest" and to the "perfumed shit" of Amy Lowell's sensitivities. The male poets are most concerned to disown refinement, fastidiousness, sensitivity—whatever has been identified as poetic and effeminate among men of sound business sense.

But this high or beautiful English language to which H.D. refers is not the language of the genteel or elite or of grammarians and the literary academy; it is the noble vernacular of Dante's *De Vulgari Eloquentia,* "which we acquire without any rule, by imitating our nurses." It is the language we found beautiful when first we began to distinguish words. Nobler, Dante argued, "as being natural to us" than the secondary speech, "which the Romans called grammar." And these our nurses, in turn, were not, it should be clear in Dante, the hired help of a middle-class well-to-do household, but they were women having a vernacular nobility, the nobility of man's common nature. True vulgar eloquence was speaking one's own language, beyond class, beyond nationality, without affect, as if it were the common language of all men in their humanity.

.

In Williams and in Pound, often self-conscious of poetic voice as if it were not natural but were a putting on of airs, another kind of vulgarity appears, not a dialect of the language of humanity but, in reaction to the felt accusation of having high-flown speech, a jargon of the "low." "It filled a gap I did not know how better to fill at the time," Williams said in 1920. A gap in language, but it was also a gap in humanity itself, a gap in consciousness. In *Paterson,* almost three decades after the poem "March" in which H.D. had found that tendency which she felt was not Williams's "very self," Williams faces that gap still, now as a divorce between man and woman, now as a divorce in the language—a divorce:

> Some say
> it is the decay of the middle class
> making an impossible moat between the high
> and the low where
> the life once flourished .

In a letter to Robert Lowell in 1952, he sees the division of high and low in the artistic consciousness itself, speaking of Eliot and Pound: "They both belonged to an alien world, a world perhaps more elevated than mine, more removed from my rigors. I have always felt as if I were sweating it out somewhere low, among the reptiles, hidden in the underbrush, hearing the monkeys overhead. Their defeats were my defeats. . . . "

> •

This conflict of high and low is an inner conflict, felt as a gap, or felt as a war of ideas in the poet's mind; as in "Narthex," the earlier one-dimensional Ionic purity contests for place with the post-war modern complicity. But as early as 1917, Pound had warned against the possibility of such a muddle in H.D.'s work: "(under I suppose the flow-contamination of Amy and Fletcher)," he advised the editor of *The Little Review,* "she has . . . let loose dilutions and repetitions, so that she has spoiled the 'few but perfect' position which she might have held on to." Was he thinking of the poem "The Tribute," which had appeared in November 1916 in *The Egoist,* with its litany, repeating the beginning line of stanza after stanza: "Squalor spreads its hideous length,"

"Squalor blights and makes hideous / our lives," "Squalor spreads its hideous length" and at the close the choruses of "Could beauty be done to death," "Could beauty be caught and hurt?" But as early as July of 1914, along with the first Imagist poems, the poem "Cities" had been published, anticipating the type of "The Tribute." What Pound disliked may have been the beginnings of H.D.'s thought in poetry, for in "Cities" and in "The Tribute," beyond the pure sensation of a poem like "Oread," the poem moves toward a concept of City, artist, war. "H.D. is all right," Pound writes to Margaret Anderson in an earlier letter in 1917: "but shouldn't write criticism."

In that literary eminence she might have held, had she kept to poems of the type approved by Pound and still favored by anthologies at large—"Oread," "The Pool," or "Hermes of the Ways"—perfection had arisen along lines of resistance to the surrounding elements, as later in "Narthex" she was to describe the would-be single image of a lily rising in the midst of an agonized flood of images and impressions, where "Her own brain now was static, cloud of outward circumstance had so contrived it. Her own mind rising, a lily on tall stem out of hysteria," and there is the felt divorce between contending aspects of experience finally: "Dream is the reaching out feelers like a snail's horns. Reality is the shell or the thing of crystal boxes. We must have the two together."

In her "few but perfect" type of poem, image had been worn against image, as lines were perfected against lines, toward only what resisted erosion, what met the test and survived. The harsh flower of "Sea Rose," "sparse of leaf," surviving surf and wind-driven sand, that is then "more precious / than a wet rose / single on a stem" is at once the image of the emotion that survives after passionate confusion and of the poem itself, sparse of line. Brought toward the exceptional luster of the ecstatic moment, in the rubble of tumbling stones, the poem is refined; but this perfect moment is an agony in consciousness, held in contest with the rest of the field of experience from which it has been won.

•

Racing, as in "Pursuit," "Huntress," or unable to move, as in "Mid-Day," "Sheltered Garden," "Heat"; the swirling tides of "The Shrine" or the other sea "unmoving, quiet" of "The Gift"—these alternates or opposites are stated over and over again in the early poems, repetitions but also insistences of a note demanding melodic satisfaction. "I endure from moment to moment—" she says in "The Gift":

days pass all alike,
tortured, intense.

Perhaps, as Pound argued, to have isolated the ecstatic and kept its almost hallucinatory intensity would have insured her poetic repute, but poems do not rise from nor toward poetic repute. The stillness in her poetry is charged with the energy of an impending movement, the exactness of tone does not exist out of place but in relation to an expected rime. Not only the philosophers but the poets too faced a total world of which their art must take account, and the alternates or opposites, the kinds of poems of a poet, represent approaches to totality that require a pluralistic statement if it not be circumscribed. If dilution and repetition appear as routes toward the felt totality, the poet will dilute and repeat, or, like Williams, work in the hey-ding-ding touch, "derivative," to give content to the gap in composition. It's just here, in what is most unsatisfactory, that the urgency of life to be satisfied, to find melody and rhyme is strongest. The perfection, the shell or crystal, is incidental, a product of the life that springs from the unsatisfied imperfection, the poet's necessity to struggle with language driven by wish, "Dream . . . the reaching out feelers like a snail's horns" H.D. calls it in "Narthex," hunger or the gap in feeling that all imagination and invention strives to transform into the totality of feeling required. The poet strives to know the terms of his defeat, not to escape from them or to be cured of them—but to work with them. Here H.D. was a student or disciple not a patient of Freud's. In the rhapsodic passages of The War Trilogy, she is exalted, as if in love, in the very split in feeling that had been traumatic before, in "this duality, this double nostalgia," "the insatiable longing" and the pattern of alternating moods.

•

There is a decisive change but there is also a continuity, for it is a change in patterning not in content, between the early work with its alternates of static image and turbulent feeling, and the later work, where the duality has been brought into the continuity of a single poem. Analysis has shown no image to be static; this was the contribution of Freud that any image was the key to meanings in associational depth, back of what was seen, and again the link to meanings in an historical drama, a hieroglyph in a sentence unfolding. So, in The War Trilogy figure discloses figure: "ruin opens," "the shrine lies open to the sky," "the fallen roof / leaves the sealed room / open to the air"—these images at the beginning of *The Walls Do Not Fall* are initial proposals of a world in which even sealed moments are not perfect in themselves only but imperfect to give way into all areas of life, where even desolation and despair are not closings of feeling but doors to something beyond, where defeat prepares. The earlier image of the gem as sculpture, the stone of the poet's emotion shaped in resistance under the attack of his passion—Pound's "only emotion endures" proposition—that gave rise to the questions of "Pygmalion" in 1917:

> Shall I let myself be caught
> in my own light?
> shall I let myself be broken
> in my own heat?
> or shall I cleft the rock as of old
> and break my own fire
> with its surface?

the questions that relate to H.D.'s transition in concept from Imagism to an art related to the Vorticism of Gaudier-Brzeska: working in language as if in stone, striking sparks of feeling in the hardness of words, is replaced in the work of *Ion* and after by the concept of the poem as being analogous to weaving, those sparks or intense images, the ecstatic moments, now knots in the fabric of experience and medium in one. The work of art no longer stands apart, clear in being separated from its material, but comes into existence in a process of involvement, information—revealed in the depths of the material.

·

The image of the living animal "reaching out feelers like a snail's horns"—the life-dream—and of the shell it makes reappears in *Ion* where the way "in which shell-fish may work outward to patterns of exquisite variety and unity," is compared to Ionic art in which: "The conscious mind of man had achieved kinship with unconscious forces of most subtle definition." Now she sees the forms of high art "no matter how dissimilar, had yet one fundamental inner force that framed them, projected them . . . as a certain genus of deep-sea fish may project its shell." There is the hint ("The human mind dehumanized itself," she says) that the imperative to form belongs to the life force, beyond humanity as it is beyond personality—it will operate at the cost of humanity or personality, an instinct for mathematical ratios and equations, for sequences and continuities of disequilibrium so that the requirements of number—the gestalt—supersede the psychological forces. Here, she seems to anticipate the primacy Charles Olson will give in his concept of a *projective verse* to the cosmic imperative of form over the psychic need for fulfillment or story. But in The War Trilogy, the cosmos itself is humanized, as returning to the concept of planetary regents, she personalizes the immediate solar system; and returning to the concept of the Christos as the incarnation of Helios, most real or only real in His manhood, she gives primacy to the quest of the Psyche, to "wish fulfillment" over the beauty or perfection of the mathematical imperative. In *Helen in Egypt* finally the entire universe of the poem will be the psychic reality, that realm of the primacy of fear and wish that the theosophists call the Astral World.

•

Beginning with The War Trilogy, H.D.'s works in poetry project part, I think, of a pluralistic concept of the total world, where statement supplements—not contradicts or corrects—statement. And if we take into this composite account "thus composed of the realities plus the fancies and illusions," to recall William James's requirement for our sense of the total world, the suggestion of an inner fundamental force toward perfection from her notes to *Ion*, we have a brief statement of the physical reality of our existence, with its primary imperative toward the perfection of order and inertia; then in The War Trilogy the statement of individuation as a biological reality, where the forces of hunger and creation of identity are primary. The shell as work of art is seen now not as a battle of the artist against the squalor about him to create beauty, but as part of the process of the artist deriving his inner life from the outside world. At once a wall that does not fall:

There is a spell, for instance,
in every sea-shell:

continuous, the sea-thrust
is powerless against coral,

bone, stone, marble
hewn from within by that craftsman,

the shell-fish:

and that at the same time sustains "that flabby, amorphous hermit/ within"—the possibility for the living organism to keep its tenderness to experience, its vital weakness—and is so designed "the stone marvel" to obey:

prompted by hunger,
it opens to the tide-flow:

Is the command of Pallas Athena in *Ion,* the "of nothing too much" imperative of strongly felt ratios and proportions, ultimately mathematical not psychological, reiterated in the "of nothing-too-much" in the song of the mollusc, master-mason, of *The Walls Do Not Fall?* As too, it is the injunction of the rational genius, the gift or grace or command of ratio, that quickens with the first motif of the poem, the "here / there," giving a sense of proportions in time. The individuation process, to know limits in knowing the beyond, to feed and to convert to one's own body-chemistry, may belong then beyond the biological to the physical, mathematical reality whose laws we sense as formal imperatives.

•

So, in the fabric of The War Trilogy, life-centered as it is, ultimately humanized, where we read "Splintered the crystal of identity," we may not be wrong to read into this that identity is thought of here as a crystallization process contrasted with personality which is animal. Then loosely evoked, in passing, there are other hints of extrahuman forces at work. There is "this is the age of the new dimension,"—changing from the suggestion of physics to that of magic and of depth psychology to mean "occult lore" and then "sub-conscious ocean"; for in this passage of *The Walls Do Not Fall*, the voice of the adversary of the poem is beginning to take over, the poem incorporating its own antibody. Where we find incorporated accusations that H.D. is "stumbling toward / vague cosmic expression," . . . "jottings of psychic numerical equations," and in the close of *The Walls Do Not Fall*: "*lightning in a not-known,* / unregistered dimension," hints of an idea that the poem may have to do, our identity may have ultimately to do then, with our consciousness of our atomic physical reality as an event in process. An identity felt not in personality or psyche but in the very chemical nature in which we have our being. That briefly, H.D. had addressed in her "Hellenic perfection of style," an art directed not by psychological formations but by the higher claim of physical impulses, the formal drive of the cosmos. "For this new culture was content," H.D. writes of the Ionic spirit, "as no culture had been before, or has since been, frankly with one and but one supreme quality, perfection."

Chapter 6

In the current issue of the poets' journal *Open Space,* I find in an untitled poem by Harold Dull upon listening to the opera *Orfeo* the concept that in each step of the life drama of Orpheus he gains a question: "and by the time / he goes into the dark / to lose her the second time":

> he has as many apparently forever to be unanswered questions
> as there are strings on his lyre.

striking a chord with those passages of H.D.'s *Helen in Egypt* where in Book Two of the "Eidolon" section it seems that Helen in her living has gained "a rhythm as yet unheard," and that history—the war at Troy and Troy's fall are "Apollo's snare / so that poets forever, / should be caught in the maze of the Walls / of a Troy that never fell."

"Was it a question asked / to which there was no answer?" H.D. asks, and then:

> who lured the players from home
> or imprisoned them in the Walls,
>
> to inspire us with endless,
> intricate questioning?

So the proposition of the last poem in "Eidolon," Book Two, states: "*There is only a song now and rhetorical questions that have been already answered.*" But the rhetorical question, it has already been answered in the poem, is meant not to find its answer but to incite the movement of the poem, leads on, opening a way for the flow of the poetic feeling to go, question and answer for the sake of a rhythm; as the questions of high and low, of the gap in society or consciousness or concept, of the proposition taken up from William James's *Principles of Psychology* of many realities entering into the picture of the total world of man's experience, or the idea of a Permission or Grace given, are instrumental and will be seen at last to be as many as the strings of the lyre to which they belong upon which I play. The lyre in turn existing for the sake of the book I am making here, drawing from the faces of Pound, Williams, H.D., the faces of the book's Pound, Williams, H.D., or from the face of the Permission Itself, the face that appears in the drawing, belonging to the work we are about, you with me, if you follow. "There is a spell, for instance," the Poet has told us in the beginning, "in every sea-shell," that given life we make it a life of our own, and that that lasts—the potsherd, the ghostly outlines of Mohenjodaro's city plan, the song of Troy—when the life and the men are lost. Back, back, back we must go to find sufficient self to live in to these beings, taking being.

For I needed this book for a place for her to exist in me. "The fate of modern poetry as a whole," Burkhardt wrote a century ago in *The Three Powers,* "is the consciousness, born of the history of literature, of its relationship to the poetry of all times and peoples. On that background, it appears as an imitation or echo." By imitation or echo alone then, if they alone are possible. Searching whatever text mind or heart recalled, argument or the beginning of a rhythm, to find out an H.D., the H.D. this book means to unfold. A rhetorical question, to give rise, as the pencil draws, as the brush paints, to a figure of many faces known and yet to be known. The lady has her own life. She is not now Hilda Doolittle, and only in her special sense is she the poetess H.D.—she is the person who narrates her story in The War Trilogy and she has just that one poem in which to exist; as Claribel of H.D.'s poem "Good Frend" is given the poem in which to have a life, to be a person of the drama. She is not in the *Dramatis Personae* of Shakespeare's *The Tempest,* where she is named only in passing *"the king's fair daughter Claribel"*:

And we read later, *in one voyage*
Did Claribel her husband find at Tunis:

Claribel was outside all of this,
The Tempest came after they left her;
Read for yourself, *Dramatis Personae.*
. . . .
Read through again, *Dramatis Personae;*
She is not there at all, but Claribel,
Claribel, the birds shrill, Claribel,
Claribel echoes from this rainbow-shell,
I stooped just now to gather from the sand;

has just that poem "Good Frend" in which to exist in the heart of H.D., taken over from Shakespeare. Go read thru The War Trilogy; you will see how I have taken up what would furnish my even blind will as I work with its substance. As if I were a gap, making up my self. A critical study? There may be times when the painter sees his own insight in a passage of his painting and he had then to look deeper until he saw what otherwise might have been his insight as the work's factor. And passages of fine writing, bravura, might come in, only to be obliterated in the trying, painstaking drawing out of a task he knew no other way to do, or kept once he had taken that way, like the under drawing showing thru in Picasso's *Guernica* that reminds us it is to participate in the idea that we work, line over line as in the first drawings we recall in the cave's depths, and so in faith—his one faith—in the saving grace of his being involved in the Work itself, and having this work given—as if in love giving himself over to the Work—in the (unknown) creative will that drives all speech, all writing, all language he believes. . . .

You know the poem, you have read it well. I do not feel you do justice to The War Trilogy yet, you write; for you as a friend (a reader) of the original know it is so much more, so much other than the likeness I have drawn. Or you, who have never loved (read) the original, tell me that I make too much of a poor matter, the passages of the poem that appear never come up to the poem I am imagining. The lady smiles at us, for this figure I am drawing from of the Lady with a Book may be the very lady who appears in her *Tribute to the Angels,* her author in my author:

> which is no easy trick, difficult
> even for the experienced stranger,

H.D. tells us. Is she talking about this Person's relating Herself to time here, in the rhythm of the clock's ticking, to appear to the poet in her dream? But it is a double image, for the Lady appears to the reader as She appeared to the writer in the medium of the poem, another trick, in the hypnotic measure, the evocative tick of syllables in procession. She is so communicated.

My other reader who is not H.D.'s reader, who does not get what I draw from or, unsympathetic, sees only in a bad light or a poor light— what can be known of my own sense in working of how little I get it, how blurred often the work is, yet, for I have been working here over four years, having always the source of the original that does not go dead on me, that gives again and again, of what a life there is in this for me, keeping the nexus of what she means to me working in the imagination.

> I see her as you project her
> not out of place

the reader or critic with goodwill addresses the artist in *Tribute to the Angels:*

> you have done very well by her
> (to repeat your own phrase),

> you have carved her tall and unmistakable,
> a hieratic figure, the veiled Goddess,

"O yes—you understand," the poet replies:

> but she wasn't hieratic, she wasn't frozen,
> she wasn't very tall . . .

.

She was demented surely. Though analysis may read unconscious sexual content in poems, only in the early erotic masque *Hymen* with its "dark purple" color have I found overt reference to sexuality, heat and snow of maiden chastity, and then in the tradition of the true nuptial rite a recounting of what happens in the taking of the flower of the bride's vagina:

> There with his honey-seeking lips
> The bee clings close and warmly sips,
> And seeks with honey-thighs to sway
> And drink the very flower away.
>
> (Ah, stern the petals drawing back;
> Ah, rare, ah virginal her breath!)
>
> Crimson, with honey-seeking lips
> The sun lies hot across his back,
> The gold is flecked across his wings.
> Quivering he sways and quivering clings
> (Ah, rare her shoulders drawing back!)
> One moment, then the plunderer slips
> Between the purple flower-lips.

These images clothe but to enhance the sexual lure. But thruout her work she bears testimony to a fever that is not localized, the heat of "Mid-Day" and a fierce yearning that can be avid, a sensuality that can declare, as in "Red Roses for Bronze":

> sensing underneath the garment seam
> ripple and flash and gleam
> of indrawn muscle
> and of those more taut,
> I feel that I must turn and tear and rip
> the fine cloth
> from this moulded thigh and hip,
> force you to grasp my soul's sincerity,

The clothing postpones, incites, and increases the craving the sexual organ itself will exorcise. The question that calls up not an answer but an increased rhetoric or current, the freefloating desire, takes over. In the prose work *Nights,* written in the 1930s, Natalia Saunderson seeks this excitement in itself in making love; as a poet might seek the excitement of inspiration in itself in writing poetry:

> Her deity was impartial; as the radium gathered electric current under her left knee, she knew her high-powered deity was waiting. He would sting her knee and she would hold muscles tense, herself only a sexless wire that was one fire for the fulfillment. She was sexless, being one chord, drawn out, waiting the high-powered rush of the electric fervor. It crept up the left side, she held it, timed it, let it gather momentum, let it gather force; it escaped her above the hip-bone, spread, slightly weakened, up the backbone; at the nape, it broke, distilled radium into the head but did not burst out of the hair. She wanted the electric power to run on through her, then out, unimpeded by her mind.

·

The rhymes, the repetitions of the incantation, would hold the serpent power mounting in the work, to time it, "let it gather momentum, let it gather force." In shaman rite and yoga rite men have come into heavens or crowns or nirvanas of a thought beyond thought, like the poet inspired, carried away by words until vision arises, as of the whole.

But this blowing one's top or the Taoist ecstatic's churning the milky way with his lion tongue is fearful. The snake in the spinal tree of life has made a nightmare of impending revelation for me, for he wears still the baleful head of the diamondback rattler, the hooded fascination of the king cobra. The Nagas that sway above the Buddha's dreaming form keep my thought away from him.

For a moment this power, this would-be autistic force of the poem, glints forth in *The Walls Do Not Fall:* "or the erect king-cobra crest / to show how the worm turns" and then, where "we" refers to the poet-initiates:

> So we reveal our status
> with twin-horns, disk, erect serpent,

"Walk carefully, speak politely," she warns, for words conceal meanings, "in man's very speech"—as in the world, "insignia":

in the heron's crest,
the asp's back,

Is it to hide the serpent power that Helen, evoking Isis, in *Helen in Egypt*
would "blacken her face like the prophetic *femme noire* of antiquity"?

How could I hide my eyes?

how could I veil my face?
with ash or charcoal from the embers?

Helen thinks, but Achilles already sees something in her and turns
upon her in horror:

What sort of enchantment is this?
what art will you yield with a fagot?
are you Hecate? are you a witch?

a vulture? a hieroglyph?

Vulture crown but also serpent crown. The eyes of the woman in
Stuck's painting *Die Sünde* watch with the eyes of the anaconda or
boa constrictor who is coiled about her, its head flattened in the nape
of her seductive neck. Lying in wait. In the depths of intimacy, the
hidden will show itself to strike. In such flashes of hate, the Great
Mother shows her Hecate face. The jeweled and painted fan upon
the floor of the dream was I had to remember the spread hood of a
cobra treacherously disguised. "Hated of all Greece!" the cry rings
as a refrain in *Helen in Egypt,* an echo or imitation of "Desired of all
Greece." And now with naked feet I walked among snakes. In the
Hindoo story a wife walking so at night in the dark wood among
snakes proves the strength of her faith and devotion to a new Master
over Love.

But the Pythian oracles, shamanesses of Attic snake cult, the bird
priestesses in winged and feathered robes of owl or sea-hawk, the car-
rion Lilith or Eve with her familiar, must have turned fanatical eyes,
painted eyes of peacock blue and red and gold, cobra eyes. Angry hurt

and hurting eyes. Fearful eyes. The gorgoneion mask whose snaky locks writhe with power.

·

September 3, 1964

"An art is vital only so long as it is interpretive," Pound proposes in "Psychology and Troubadours": "so long, that is, as it manifests something which the artist perceives at greater intensity, and more intimately, than his public."

"We have about us the universe of fluid force, and below us the germinal universe of wood alive, of stone alive," he continues: "When we do get into the contemplation of the flowing we find sex, or some correspondence to it, 'positive and negative,' 'North and South,' 'sun and moon'":

> For the particular parallel I wish to indicate, our handiest illustrations are drawn from physics: 1st, the common electric machine, the glass disc and rotary brushes; 2nd, the wireless telegraph receiver. In the first we generate a current, or if you like, split up a static condition of things and produce a tension. This is focused on two brass knobs or 'poles.' These are first in contact, and after the current is generated we can gradually widen the distance between them, and a spark will leap across it, the wider the stronger, until with the ordinary sized laboratory appliance it will leap over or around a large obstacle or pierce a heavy book cover. In the telegraph we have a charged surface—produced in a cognate manner— attracting to it, or registering movements in the invisible aether.

The *trobar clus,* the cult of love in Provence that was also a cult of poetry, was "an art, that is to say, a religion," Pound suggests, of a way to the experience of "our kinship with the vital universe." "Did this 'close ring,' this aristocracy of emotion, evolve, out of its half memories of Hellenistic mysteries, a cult—a cult stricter, or more subtle, than that of the celibate ascetics, a cult for the purgation of the soul by the refinement of, and lordship over, the senses?" Does the Lady stand to the lover, as his Muse to the Poet, to inspire and cooperate in the art, to demand and command in the name of Amor or of Poetry—a new

Master over the Art, so that the poet gives his will, his hunger and the satisfaction of his hunger over to a higher authority—*donna della mia mente*—that appears to him in the art. In faith he writes in the dark upon a ground that may writhe with the thrill in which he walks, but, devoted to the rule of the art, he is saved in the increase of his phantasy.

In the heightened state, exceeding immediate satisfaction, the goal of genital release is increased from a physical to a spiritual tension, and the original object becomes an instrument towards a sublimation. "The Greek aesthetic would seem to consist wholly in plastic, or in plastic moving towards coitus, and limited by incest, which is the sole Greek taboo," Pound observes in the Cavalcanti essay. In the aesthetic of Provence "the conception of the body as a perfect instrument of the increasing intelligence pervades"; beyond the sensory reality, "the impact of light on the eye," and its ideal forms, in the spirit of Romance, the poets sought "an interactive force: the *virtu*." A magic begins, and the poem as an operation of the new theurgy—love, sexual intercourse, as operations of the new theurgy—becomes other-worldly centered. Beatrice and Virgil, spiritual beings, are the true inspirations and hence critics of *The Divine Comedy*. In the high humor of the tradition, Blake will truly declare that he writes not for this world but for his true muses or lovers or readers in the spirit.

"Sex is, that is to say, of a double function and purpose, reproductive and educational; or," Pound continues in "Psychology and Troubadours": "as we see in the realm of the fluid force, one sort of vibration produces at different intensities, heat and light." Then:

> The problem, in so far as it concerns Provence, is simply this: Did this 'chivalric love,' this exotic, take on mediumistic properties? Stimulated by the color or quality of emotion, did that 'color' take on forms interpretive of the divine order? Did it lead to an 'exteriorization of the sensibility,' and interpretation of the cosmos by feeling?

"Thirteen years ago I lost a brother," Blake writes to his patron Hayley, upon the death of Hayley's son in May of 1800: "and with his spirit I converse daily and hourly in the Spirit, See him in my remembrance in the regions of my Imagination. I hear his advice and even now write from his Dictate." And in a letter to Flaxman in September that same year, he writes:

> And Now Begins a New life, because another covering of Earth is shaken off. I am more famed in Heaven for my works than I could well conceive. In my Brain are studies & Chambers filled with books & pictures of old, which I wrote & painted in ages of Eternity before my mortal life; & those works are the delight & Study of Archangels. . . . I see our houses of Eternity, which can never be separated, tho' our Mortal vehicles should stand at the remotest corners of heaven from each other.

In his excited state—"my Enthusiasm," he calls it in his letter to Hayley, "which I wish all to partake of, Since it is to me a Source of Immortal joy . . . by it I am the companion of Angels"—Blake sees in terms of his Divine World, radiated with Love, a feeling as in Heaven above earthly feeling. This "Above" in Blake contrasts sharply with a "Below"—there seems to be a gap in feeling; for Hayley in Blake's earthy moods is "Pick Thank" and Flaxman, "Sculptor of Eternity," is "Blockhead." Between 1808 and 1811, feeling mocked by Flaxman who had been his teacher and driven by Hayley who all Blake's life was his patron or "angel," Blake reviled them in epigrams and verses:

> Anger & Wrath my bosom rends:
> I thought them the Errors of friends.
> But all my limbs with warmth glow:
> I find them the Errors of the foe.

He had come to suspect that Hayley was patronizing and that Flaxman put him down as a madman. Hayley's commissions for prints that had not been done yet pressed him and then depressed him. "I curse & bless Engravings alternately, because it takes so much time & is so untractable, tho' capable of such beauty & perfection," he writes Hayley or, again: "Your eager expectation of hearing from me compels me to write immediately," Hayley's very "generous & tender solicitude," Blake calls it when Hayley paid his bail and court costs in Blake's sedition trial, leave the artist feeling indebted and driven. "I received your kind letter with the note to Mr. Payne, and have had the cash from him."

> . . . Mr. Flaxman advises that the drawing of Mr. Romney's which shall be chosen instead of the Witch (if that cannot be recovered), be 'Hecate,' the figure with the torch and snake, which he thinks one of the finest drawings.

September 4 [10], 1964

Joey, the "Mechanical Boy" of Bruno Bettelheim's study in the *Scientific American,* March 1959 ("A case history of a schizophrenic child who converted himself into a 'machine' because he did not dare be human"), lives as a creature in a world created by an inaccessible creator, as a machine charged by invisible "pretend" electricity. "He functioned as if by remote control, run by machines of his own powerfully creative fantasy. Not only did he himself believe that he was a machine but, more remarkably, he created this impression in others," Bettelheim tells us. "Entering the dining room, for example, he would string an imaginary wire from his 'energy source'—an imaginary outlet—to the table. There he 'insulated' himself with paper napkins and finally plugged himself in. . . . So skillful was the pantomime that one had to look twice to be sure there was neither wire nor outlet nor plug. Children and members of our staff spontaneously avoided stepping on the 'wires' for fear of interrupting what seemed the source of his very life."

The higher claim to reality of Joey's created world over the uncreated world is a counterpart of the higher reality the world of his creation has for the artist over the world as material from which it is drawn. The "charge" we feel in the recognition of high art, the breaking thru into special truths or keys of existence, is a power the artist has evoked in transforming a content from a private into a communal fantasy. At certain conjunctions, where form and content are suddenly revealed in full, waves of excitement, as if a current had been turned on, pass over the brain and thru the nervous systems, and the body seems tuned up in apprehension of what is happening in the work of art. "Many times a day," Bettelheim tells us, Joey "would turn himself on until he 'exploded,' screaming 'Crash, crash!' and hurling items from his ever present apparatus—radio tubes, light bulbs, even motors. . . . " It is as if he were seized by the reality of his conception. It is not Joey's retreat into a private world that we experience, but rather the intensity of his communication, the obliterating power of the language he has made, that takes over not only his reality but also that of those about him. Even at night he is governed by his work, fixing apparatus to his bed to "live him" during his sleep, "contrived from masking tape, cardboard, wire and other paraphernalia." With such an intensity, Orpheus in Harold Dull's poem transforms the actual events of his life into fantastic events—questions that refuse their answers—that are really strings upon a lyre that is a triumph of the imagination. The poet would give himself over to the charge of song, or, beyond poetry, the seer Blake would give himself over to the charge of vision, as Joey gives himself over to the charge of his made-up machine.

Certainly at times we confront in Joey's work the operations of metaphor, correspondence, persona, and word play that govern the poem, and like the poet, Joey must be obedient to laws that appear in the structure he makes. "He was unable to designate by its true name anything to which he attached feelings. Nor could he name his anxieties except through neologisms or word contaminations." But the artist too must find new names and knows that the true name is hidden in the work he must do, as Isis knows that Ra's Secret Name is not the name that all men know but is hidden in his breast. ("They are anagrams, cryptograms, / little boxes, conditioned / to hatch butterflies," we remember from *The Walls Do Not Fall*.)

"For a long time he spoke about 'master paintings' and 'a master painting room,'" Bettelheim continues, and translates "(i.e. masturbating and masturbating room)." But now it is as if "masturbating" were not the true word until we also understand it is "master painting," an ideogram is forming that when complete may reveal the hidden, as yet unexperienced, term; something that masturbating and master painting are but instances of. As here, from Orpheus transforming his life into an instrument of music, or Natalia Saunderson transforming her sexual seizure into an electricity, or Pound's concept of a universe of fluid force, Joey's idea of being lived by an electric current, I would gather a picture of a power the artist knows in which the fictional real becomes most veridical, in which art comes closest to religion—as in Blake's world, in which man appears as a creature of his own creative force.

Like the poet, Joey must face his adversary in his work. "One of his machines, the 'criticizer,' prevented him from 'saying words which have unpleasant feelings.' Yet he gave personal names to the tubes and motors in his collection of machinery. Moreover," Bettelheim tells us, "these dead things had feelings; the tubes bled when hurt and sometimes got sick." The excitement and the discharge of excitement in the work of art, "master painting," and the aesthetic requirement, the inbuilt 'criticizer' of the artist that determines appropriate material, appear in a grotesque guise in Joey's universe. His tubes and motors are personae of his poem that has overcome all terms of identity outside of its own operation; as in "Good Frend," Claribel, no more than a name, is so a person. Joey's tubes and motors are not dead things, for they are words in a language that would be living. Deprived of communication, for the adults about him would not listen, "When he began to master speech, he talked only to himself." We gather that his parents cut off that current of questioning by which a child participates in first communications, taking apart and putting together the machinery of language which before he had known only as a vehicle of electric emotions and persuasions. But Joey turns to another mute or frozen language embodied in man-made objects about him. "At an early date he became preoccupied with machinery, including an old electric fan which he could take apart and put together again with surprising deftness."

Bettelheim is concerned with the loss of the flow of feeling, represented in the universe of Joey by the need to be turned on or charged; but we are concerned here with how Joey's powerful creative fantasy is like the poet's creative fantasy, the poetic imagination that must have a higher claim to reality than immediate "distractions," in order for the poem to come into being, and how much Joey, run by his own fantastic machinery, is like the inspired poet in his divine madness. Pound, Williams, and H.D. do not make that romantic claim, but all three are disturbed by the power of words over them. Memory (the past), awareness (the immediate), wish (the future) are all heightened and demand satisfaction in the excitement of the work; and more, in that nexus of three, a creativity is at work to change the nature of truth. Blake gave the Imagination highest authority and sought to live in Creation. He could call up the shades of Moses and the Prophets, Homer, Dante, Milton—"majestic shadows, grey but luminous, and superior to the common height of men" and converse with them by the seashore. In his marginalia to Lavater's *Aphorisms* Blake writes:

> As we cannot experience pleasure but by means of others who experience either pleasure or pain thro' us, And as all of us on earth are united in thought, for it is impossible to think without images of somewhat on earth—So it is impossible to know God or heavenly things without conjunction with those who know God & heavenly things; therefore all who converse in the spirit, converse with spirits . . .

> Such tricks hath strong imagination
> That if it would but apprehend some joy
> It comprehends some bringer of that joy.

There is a story that when Blake was making a drawing of "The Ghost of a Flea" the sitter inconsiderately opened his mouth. The artist, "prevented from proceeding with the first sketch," listened to the Flea's conversation and made a separate study of the open mouth.

•

Joey lives in the Imagination deprived of the current of human friendship except for the love and care invested in the machines about him. He does not retreat to become a 'mechanical boy' ("because he did not dare to be human," Bettelheim sees it)—but he advances in the one initiation into human spirit opened to him, the area of achievement and wish embodied in the operations of electrical and plumbing systems, even as in words it is the human work embodied that makes possible the formation of consciousness. The shapes of Homer, Dante, Milton gathered in the mind in the magic of Blake's intense reading, as a person of the electric fan—the human invention—gathered in Joey's mind in the magic of his intense taking apart and putting together again, cast shadows "superior to the common height of men," as Joey was convinced, Bettelheim tells us, that machines were superior to people, or Plato that ideas were superior to things. "If madness and absurdity be synonyms, which they are not, then Blake would be as 'mad as a March hare'," Samuel Palmer wrote to Mrs. Gilchrist in 1862: "for his love of art was so great that he would see nothing *but art* in anything he loved." So Joey in his love for mechanism saw nothing but mechanism in what he loved. Language may mean all to me, more than art, for the universe seems striving to speak and the burden of life to be to understand what is being said in words that are things and persons and events about us.

"Not every child who possesses a fantasy world is possessed by it," Bettelheim observes: "Normal children may retreat into realms of imaginary glory or magic powers, but they are easily recalled from these excursions. Disturbed children are not always able to make the return trip." And those who know no disturbance of reality, we would add, cannot make the trip out at all.

The shaman's trip to the Other World, the medium's trip to the Astral field, the poet's trip to Hell, Purgatory, and Heaven, is a counterpart of the dreamer's trip to the dream or the child's trip to the land he plays. In the process of realization, the Creator must so go into the whole of His Creation in order to create it that it becomes the most real and He becomes most real in it. In the full power of the Imagination, Creation is all, and Who had been Creator is now Creature. God is immanent in the Universe, and incarnate in a person. This is one of the mysteries of the human Christos. Here too there must be a round-trip, the return to God, but it must also be not easy but the least easy of all recallings, for Christ's apotheosis in hubris must be fulfilled in crucifixion. In the full Christian persuasion—most high divine madness—there is a triumph of creativity: the Eternal insists that He has had a life-time and death in history; the Supreme Fiction insists that It has had a personality in the nonfictional Jesus.

October 1, 1964
To be easily recalled from these excursions, to possess a fantasy world and not to be possessed by it—the way of normal children—is achieved by keeping in mind that the imaginary is not real, that such areas of the psyche's life are no more than child's play, that it is no more than

a story. Here, in the fairy tale, taking place in whatever far country and having that time between once upon a time and forever after, stored away for children in the minds of their old nurses and, since the seventeenth century, in a new literary form initiated by the *Contes de ma mère l'oie* of Charles Perrault, the nursery romance, the subversive force of man's creativity hides in an amusement. *"In den alten Zeiten, wo das Wünschen noch geholfen hat"*—in the old times, when Wishing still could help—the German folk *Märchen* begins, and in the guise of entertainment, the old woman imparts to her infant audience news of the underworld of man's nature, of betrayals and cheats, of ogres and murderers, thieves and shape-changers. They learn to mistrust the real, but they learn also the wishes and powers of old religions and states that have fallen away. The fairy tale is the immortal residue of the spirit that seeks to find its place in the hearts of each generation. As in the twelfth century, religious mysteries and erotic formulations found immortal life in the high romances of the Arthurian cycles, so the folk world perpetuated itself in the yarns spun at the hearthside, and even now, when the spinning wheel has gone from the household way and the fireplace has lost its central function there, the *märchen* has survived in book form, rescued by the devoted Brothers Grimm. As, again, in the court nurseries of *le Roi Soleil*, like bees secreting the royal jelly to feed the possibility of a queen, imparting style and sentiment, plot and wish, to life, a group of courtiers, after the revocation of the Edict of Nantes, as if apprehending the death of their way—Perrault, then the Countesses de Murat, d'Aulnoy, d'Auneuil, and the Count de Caylus—write their *Cabinets des Fées*. When the dust of the revolutionary tumbrels and the blood of the guillotine have come and gone, and the bourgeoisie, the merchants, industrialists, and managers of our age have taken over, Perrault's Cinderella, like the Queen of Elfland who carried away Thomas of Erceldoune, would carry away the young from the common sense and capitalist reality into her irresponsible romance, the unreal of falling in love and being loved. Early in the process of the Christian era, Augustine, inspired by a most Puritanical demon of righteousness, had warned against such a corporeal light that "seasoneth the life of this world for her blind lovers, with an enticing and dangerous sweetness" and deplored the lot of those who are misled by requited love. Yet the ghosts of the dead, of defeated forces in history, survive in the fascination of the living. When the last nobility had died out in the nobility and the rule of public utilities succeeded, Beauty and The Beast from Madame Leprince de Beaumont's eighteenth century tale, as well as Oedipus from the drama of Sophocles, revive in the art of Cocteau.

March 15, Wednesday. 1961
"Hellenic perfection of style . . . "

.

In the book *The Hedgehog,* written at Vaud, 1925, the Greek gods belong to the story-world, and, in turn, the little girl Madge, who may be, as H.D.'s daughter Perdita was that year, six, who lives then in an age previous to reading, figures out the actual world with information from stories her mother has told her so that her own experience becomes a story. "The stories weren't just stories," Madge's mother tells her, "but there was something in them like the light in the lamp that isn't the lamp." She sees things in story-light, and in this light Pan, Weltgeist, Our-Father-Which-Art, are lights in turn in the world about her which is a lamp to see by.

.

Madge in her story is searching for a secret word. It is a matter of the open secret of Goethe, there, everywhere, a word everyone uses, but only experience unlocks the meaning *"Hérisson."* Don't find the word too quickly; mistake it in order to look for it. The girl Madge knows French, but she does not know what this word *hérisson* is. "Vipers!" Madame Beaupère exclaims, "you should have a hedgehog"—but she is French—*"Hérisson"* she says. Madge "somehow for the moment couldn't remember just what was a *hérisson.*" "'Ah,' said Madge knowingly, 'but yes, the very thing, a hedgehog.' She said hedgehog in French, not knowing what it meant." She must set out in quest of the word in the world.

.

In *Tribute to the Angels,* twenty years later, we find just such a riddle or search for a name again:

> it lives, it breathes,
> it gives off—fragrance?
>
> I do not know what it gives,
> a vibration that we can not name
>
> for there is no name for it;
> my patron said, 'name it';
>
> I said, I can not name it,
> there is no name;
>
> he said,
> 'invent it.'

·

So in 1912 Pound had given a name "Imagism" to something required in poetry, and returning to the propositions of the 1912 Credo we can see in "Direct treatment of the 'thing'" and in "To use absolutely no word that does not contribute to the presentation" the directive towards an art that strives to find in the image a secret name or pass-word in which "thing" and "word" will become presentation. But this name "Imagism" bound. There was an excitement of introducing the new Imagist poets in *The Egoist* and the excitement too of not knowing what it meant. May Sinclair said that H.D. was *the* Imagist, an epitome. Had she achieved the definitive Imagist poem? But then, Pound had said that he launched the word to define the poetry of H.D. And he had meant too to confine her work to what he had admired.

·

The idea of H.D.'s cut-stone, pure, terse line was her own version in part, a demand of her temperament that fitted the Credo's demand for a literary functionalism, a clean line against ornament. In her note to the Euripides translations that appear in *The Egoist* in 1915 she writes that she sought "rhymeless hard rhythms" to capture "the sharp edges and irregular cadence of the original." But these hard rhythms, sharp edges, and irregular cadences are not only of the original but of a modernist aesthetic in painting, music, and architecture, where ornament, as in poetry rhetoric, was coming to be a term of derogation.

•

Early poems like "The Contest" with its "you are chiselled like rocks / that are eaten into by the sea" or "Sea Lily," where the flower petal is "with hard edge, / like flint / on a bright stone" operate to define the meaning of the Imagist poem as well as the quality of the immediate image; as early titles "Hymen" or "Heliodora" contributed to the idea of a new Hellenism. Idea and ideal are as essential to the image as the immediate sensory presentation. To dig the poem we must be receptive, back of these images of free wild elements in nature, and of sheltered gardens, of delicate stony flowers, and of flowers torn and trampled under foot, of unruly surfs, not only to presences of gods and daemons, the elementary idols of the poem, but to the temper of the verse itself, the ideal of human spirit presented. "Posing," the unkind were likely to judge it, but for her kind H.D.'s tone presented a key in which to live. This ideal is what in my generation Charles Olson has called a stance. Poetic will is involved, awkwardly at first, trying, in what we call style or tone, but it would go beyond manner, to take over and make its own definition of poetry, where we strive to exemplify something we desire in our nature. "There was about her," Williams writes of H.D. in his *Autobiography:* "that which is found in wild animals at times, a breathless impatience, almost a silly unwillingness to come to the point." But now, seeing past Williams's meaning to convince us that he was not taken in by H.D. and even, we are aware, to stir up our disaffections—seeing, past that, the content here with the role in mind that idea and ideal have in the artist's search for a definition of what he is to be, Williams does give us telling details. "She said that when she wrote it was a great help, she'd splash ink on her clothes to give her a feeling of freedom and indifference toward the mere means of the writing."

•

If in Imagist poems like "Heat" there had been, as well as the perfectionism, the intense realization of an instant in time, the prayer for life beyond perfection and realization, in *The Hedgehog,* having "almost a silly unwillingness to come to the point," the mode of story exorcizing the mode of image, there is a first statement as early as 1925 of the sense of life as an intellectual and spiritual adventure that is to become the dominant mode of H.D.'s imagination in the major phase that begins with The War Trilogy. We have taken *Ion* as a turning point, with its commentary that incorporates poetic experience and psychoanalytic experience to give depth and complexity of meaning to form and content: now, not only an intensity of image, not only a style, but also a perception in organization, a way, is to be essential in the creative force of her work. We may take *The Hedgehog* as an announcement. It seems isolated, her only children's book; the Greek world in story is so different from the Greek world in the "intellectual and emotional complex in an instant of time" that the Imagist Credo demanded. And it is different too from the exalted, enthralled, or ecstatic voice of the personae of H.D., whether of the poems of the Lawrencian period—"Adonis," "Pygmalion," or "Eurydice"—or of the Sapphic fragments, or of the prose of *Palimpsest;* for a new voice, the common sense of the wise nurse telling what life is like to the child, or the questing sense of the child seeking in a story to find out what is going on, enters in. H.D. will all her life be concerned in her work with conveying to our sympathy the fact that agony seems to be in the very nature of deep experience, that in every instant there is a painful—painful in its intensity—revelation. In *Palimpsest,* Hipparchia, Raymonde, and Helen Fairwood agonize; the interior monologue means to communicate the impact of ineffable experience. But in *The Hedgehog,* Madge's interior monologue is talking to herself in search of a language. The meaning of *hérisson* is not beyond finding out, but it is postponed until Madge can gather, asking from everyone and from everything, the most common sense—the communality—of what it is. In the very opening of the book, the lead is given. *Quoi donc?* And then: "Which means," Madge recognizes: "well what do you mean by trying to tell me that anything like that means what you seem to think it means." The adventure is the old guessing game *I am thinking of a word; What is it?* and Madge seeks to find out a definition that does not confine.

.

She seeks too to find a definition of her self that does not confine, as H.D. was seeking to do in her own life. And Madge trying out her style can miss. In talking with Madame Beaupère, she speaks "in such a funny unnatural affected little way" at one point that Madame Beaupère is put off, and Madge perceives "that her grown-up manner had not quite worked." But the ideal is rightly a matter of trial for it is part of the searching out of means towards feeling: "she thought and practiced it, in order to give her a feeling of freedom and indifference," as later, H.D.'s ideal of the Hellenic tries to reach the feeling of hardness and perfection. And does, for what changes in H.D.'s concept is not that the feeling of hardness and perfection ceases to be desired but that other feelings enter in to the picture. "Echo is easy to find," Madge knows, "and the boy Narcissus," but "Some of the light-in-lamp people you look for and never find."

.

In Homer we know it is all a story told, as Shakespeare would remind us, even while we are entranced, that this "life" is a stage upon which actors play. This is their nurse voice, when even the greatest poets amuse us as if they were giant maids and we were children. So Cocteau and Bergman would involve us beyond the being moved in the moving pictures in the knowledge thruout that we entertain their entertainment. It is in the mystery of the Muses that we transcend belief and disbelief and follow the story, for the story-teller has as part of his art not only that he leads us into the magic realms but that he can recall us from the excursion. Where there is no story magic, blood will be blood and pain pain so that misled, carried away, the child is hurt and cries out or is afraid. In Flaherty's film of Samoan life, I fainted during the tattooing ritual, flooded with the apprehension of pain. But in story, in the self-mutilation of Oedipus or the immolation of Christ, the pain is not a thing in itself but belongs to a configuration of action, fulfills and leads on. My mother would lean over in the dark of the movie house to recall me: "it is only a movie, it is just a movie," she would whisper. Shakespeare's actors reminding us that it is but a stage seem finally to be saying that our actual life is only a stage from which we may be recalled at death. And Christ in the testimony of St. John at Ephesus told his beloved disciple that the death upon the cross was but a figure in a dance—"and if you have not entered the dance, you mistake the event." "Growing up and last year's shoes that didn't fit this year—these were things that were part of a dream, not part of reality," Madge thinks: "Reality was the Erlking and the moonlight on Bett's room wall."

·

The story-telling voice of *The Hedgehog* enters into the commentary of "Ion" in whose voice the Greek drama appears in the guise of fairy tale. And the address of the opening of *The Walls Do Not Fall* establishes such a voice in which we are aware of the story-teller and his following, the *I* and a *you* in which the individual reader is but one; "from your (and my) old town square," belongs to the nurse's art, drawing us into the realm of her telling. The "we" and the "they" are people of the story, as the "I" is at one time a person of the story—"I sense my own limit" is part of what she has to tell—and the poet who may address her audience as well as the "they" of the poem: "but if you do not even understand what words say, / how can you expect to pass judgment / on what words conceal?" Those of the audience who are with her will think of themselves as "we," those who are not in it and would interrupt will think of themselves as "they." And the story-teller anticipates their doubts of the story and exhorts them to surrender: "Let us substitute / enchantment for sentiment." Yes, she continues: "re-dedicate our gifts / to spiritual realism"; but it is all to be "a Tale told of a Jar or jars," having the truth of what "we are told." In *Helen in Egypt,* which H.D. saw as her culminating master work, Helen is entirely a creature of story, having her life in all that has been told of her.

·

There remains the actual feeling, a Greece that is all H.D.'s. She evokes a realm of pagan things—hinterlands of the psyche—but also inner qualities of places and times, woodlands, sea-coasts, gardens, mountain ledges. In *Hedylus* the stranger-father-critic says to the young poet: "Your idea of the rock-ridge becoming re-divided into separate efflorescence, according to the altitude, implying, as I judge, a spiritual comparison as well as a mere natural one, is unique, differing in all particulars from anything I have yet met with."

.

It was not pure beauty, or it was something besides pure beauty, that even the poems that gave rise to H.D.'s repute for the rare and pure strove to capture, but beauty or perfection as it was a key somewhere to the nature of event, and finally, as it played its part in the development of the story.

Yes, but this striving was not only to capture a quality in what she had known, but was to challenge experience itself in turn to yield a quality. "Beauty" was from the first, as in the review of Marianne Moore's work or in the poem "The Tribute" she makes clear, a battle-cry, a cause. The Image too was a demand as well as a response.

.

In December 1916, reviewing Fletcher's *Goblins and Pagodas* in *The Egoist,* she criticizes or challenges "certain current opinions concerning the so-called new poetry," and against the proposition of the images upon a Greek vase as things of art, self-contained images, she proposes: "How much more than the direct image to him are the images by shadow and light, the flicker of the purple wine, the glint across the yellow, the depth of the crimson and red. . . . When the wine itself within the great jar stands waiting for him." Then: "He uses the image, direct it is true, but he seems to use it as a means of evoking other and vaguer images—a pebble, as it were, dropped into a quiet pool, in order to start across the silent water, wave on wave of light, of color, of sound."

There is at least the possibility that whatever battle-cry of "Beauty" or idea of the fine-wrought image, there was also another thing a poem was—"a pebble . . . dropped into a quiet pool" to set up reverberations in life so that "Here," "there," Greece and its things, old gods and pagan places or the mode of story, enlivened consciousness in living, made it moving with "wave on wave of light, of color, of sound." Story, like perspective in painting, may be an invention to satisfy a need in experience for design, to build a house for feeling in time or space. Does story stand within the actual life or the actual life experience stand within the story as the wine itself is stored in the great jar upon whose surfaces the artist has painted his image of the wine and the jar?

.

The threads interweaving create a close intricate field of feeling; and we admire the work in which there is no ornament dismissed but where light flows from what we took to be ornament and proves to be essential. In the shuttle flying under the swift sense of the work, the "incident here and there" gathers so many instances from themselves into a moving significance, unfolding or discovering a design, that we see now the art was to set things into movement, was not only the weaving of a work of art but as if each knot that bound the whole into the quiet of a unity were also the pebble that dropped into that quiet as a pool broke up, was knot but also slipping-of-the-knot, to set up an activity thruout in the work of time and space within time and space.

.

The sense that "we are at the cross-roads" then has structural as well as historical and psychological meaning in The War Trilogy. Given the name *Imagiste,* H.D. was never satisfied that it meant what she seemed to think it meant, and even after her analysis with Freud, she did not rest with the Freudian image but went on to the *eidola* of *Helen in Egypt.* What was required was that there be the full power of a double meaning, that the real refuse to be defined. In word and image and then in story her sense was always that "the tide is turning."

Chapter 7

October 8, 1964 [*i.e.,* March 20, 1961. Monday.]

I seek now in working upon the later draft of the book not to correct the original but to live again in its form and content, leaving in successive layers record of reformations and digressions as they come to me. The form realized then is not to be a design immediately striking, like those housing developments and landscapings that rise where disorderly areas of a city have been cleared away, but it may be like an old city—Freud's picture of Rome upon Rome—in which in the earliest remains, in the diary of March 10th to March 15th, March 20th to March 29th, then May 25th of 1961: later additions may appear, anachronistically like the Gaudi restorations in the gothic cathedral of Palma or the Casa Guell's art-nouveau romanticism in the midst of old buildings, where we are aware of periods of creative activity and conservative inertia. Altering and using old streets, laying out new districts, surrounding old barrios, willing to carry out the project of a Frank Lloyd Wright palace upon the Grand Canal of my Venice, having most in mind to convey the life of the idea of the city, a book of continuations not of conclusions, I build even as I prepare the book for the publisher at last, living once more as I copy, and take over wherever I see a new possibility in the work.

4:20 A.M. March 20, 1961. Monday.
A first vigil? I had wanted, after Hoffmann's *The Golden Pot,* to bring forward the likeness between Hoffmann's method in that Hermetic

romance of telling the story by "vigils" and H.D.'s keeping her appointment with the sequences of her later work. The ancient time-cult of the gods in which the time of the work had its appointed spirit or genius and the modern appointment of the psychoanalytic hour, each day taking up the work anew and continuing, contribute to the method I would follow here having the continuity of a daily return, having the commitment in each session to whatever may arise there, so that the conscious concern may be immediate to impulse and those felt but not yet articulated senses of what is involved that we call intuition, risking the coherence of the whole in the attention at hand. Going in faith that all such attentions are creative of the whole I seek. Open to impulse, so that I must trust peripheries and undercurrents to lead me.

·

Wherever I work the directive increases.

·

In this method, the break of four days—from March 15th to today—is not a day of rest but a withdrawal from, and then perhaps a withdrawal of, direction.

I.

THE DREAM: A manufacturer had commissioned me to do a rug. The rug it turns out is the rug that I began in 1954 for Jess and finished in Mallorca in 1956, having no cartoon previous to the work but in each phase of the work the form being conceived. Writing the date for this chapter or vigil, I had started "4:20 A.M. March 20, 195–" I had put down the 5 of 1954, but recalled that it was 1961, going on, but knowing that now in the course of the work I would have to account for that 1954.

In the dream scene, going to the factory to see the reproduction of my work I found a mint reproduction. Yes. That was the disturbing thing in the dream: that they had arrived at their copy by some translation from my concept, as if it were mint, so unlike the rug I knew that

I could not account for what had happened. Was it for what had happened to the rug since the 1954? Had there been then an alternate rug, a form from which not towards which I had worked?

The copy was mostly lavender, a color which is minor in the original (here it may have been changed by the painting by Tom Field that I had during the spring and summer of 1956 at Black Mountain), but it had the inconclusive asymmetrical order that I work towards. Yet it had not been built up of intricate color localities—"when/wheres" I've called them in this study; "orchestrations" they seemed to me when I was working on "The Venice Poem" in 1948, for I was following impulses towards design that haunted me in listening to the *Danses Concertantes* and the *Symphony in Three Movements* of Stravinsky where it seemed to me that form impended thruout, that every particular of the structure was charged by the numen of the whole. Having no musical literacy, certainly having only an analogical understanding, I derived certainties of my own aesthetic, and then of a poetic, of a theory of forms and of the nature of making itself, as I have derived understandings from sciences I do not "really understand."

•

I had wanted to describe the "orchestration" of H.D.'s work, the intricate resonances of particulars that contribute to the symphonic whole.

•

The manufacturer had, anyway, "lied" about the model. And the rug that must stand for the original work, that must do to represent what I had done, when I tried to find grounds for acceptance, bewildered. They had "missed" thruout. Maybe they had evaded.

•

"You will want to take credit," the official of the company said. Representative? There were two officials, anyway: a foreman who was an efficient woman explaining to me as I stood, undone as I was by what they had done, that the rug still needed cutting, was first. Here it seemed to me she meant they had taken some aspect of my total concept as if it were only a texture and had used it for long runners of weaving that were trimmed to fit the original. There had been, hadn't there? I remembered in my dream, or now writing, remember, such complexly textured rag-rugs in halls long ago at home. She explained too that there had been some of my colors they hadn't been able to get.

.

I could not visualize in these terms what their reproduction would be like.

.

The other official, the business manager, was discussing with me my agreement with the company to accept the reproduction. Yes, that was unavoidable. There was no way, I felt, to account for my disagreement which was actually the disagreement between the image (my rug) and the copy. But the manager was discussing our terms. I would want to take credit, he was saying. "Oh yes," I replied, "as I always do on books and records." But even as I said it I was puzzled or uneasy about what I assumed when I said "records" and was substantiating the claim in my mind with credit I did not mean as true. I wanted to be paid, I said, as I always do want, on the basis of royalties. "That way," I said, "if the work is disliked or liked, I have not been underpaid or overpaid."

.

But the impossible thing thruout was my claim in relation to the rug they were releasing as mine. In no way could I see it even looked like my work.

.

Earlier in the dream, just back of this manufacturing scene, had been another scene of Landis and his friend stealing from the corner grocery, which I read upon waking as relating to stealing in writing. There may have been some translation between taking food without paying, without crediting it? and the credit-payment theme of the manufacturer's episode. The product the company offered somehow copied my work without the stealing, the installment and credit planning, that had been essential in its conception.

II.

Recording the dream, I find myself repeating the perplexity of the dream-situation. I cannot reproduce it, as the manufacturers in the dream could not reproduce the rug, because I cannot or will not supply the particulars. Now, I have lost, perhaps, the "message" that lingered in my mind when I woke at four. It had to do with the key to H.D.'s poetics that was my own.

•

That in working this book, it must be built up, risking the composition of the whole (where I incur some critical failure in the book's not resembling what literary criticism calls for today) in order to, but also because I must, take the directive of the immediate sense, as in Charles Olson's "instanter" movement that projective verse demands.

•

"Overlook."
    As one oversees and then naturally overlooks the "when/where" if one follows a plan. Overlook is what the director (both the forewoman and the manager) does in the dream.

•

Supplying the particulars. That may be in the "they wrote parts of color," as I remember the line in my longer invention on the Adam. As hooking in each tuft of colored wool to become a new term of my vision of the whole design, I came to think of life itself being so worked: if one determined to take up one's vision of life from each immediate happening.

•

Between the chapter of March 15th and this chapter there is the break that I must work with then. In the midst of the first series of days, on the 10th, Saturday, hitch-hiking to the other side of Tamalpais to see my cousin Carol as Sabine in Wilder's *Skin of Our Teeth,* getting out of a foreign car, a Renault, I smashed the little finger on my writing hand.

By Wednesday it was infected, by Thursday the swelling, the swelling pain had taken over. It had to be lanced. To drain away the intolerable accumulation. And last night, again, the finger was lanced to clear up the foreign matter.

•

Is everything of account? There is in the poetic of H.D.'s later work an aesthetic of accounting, of keeping record? A vision in terms of what–is that is built up into a poetry of what counts? Where everything counts—impossible to reproduce. The atomic in writing is, as Olson gives it in "Projective Verse," the immediate sound particle. But for me the resonance of the particle infects everything.

•

The rug was hooked-work ("Stolen" then), the whole vision emerging from individual determinate after individual determinate as I put in bits of color.

•

And in that work too there would be periods, even long periods, of waiting on the work. I would wonder about the total design, trying out in my mind various paths. How the whole thing looked if I were to make a large yellow area "there" or carry out a continuous flowing line "here."

•

Or I would desert the work, lose track of it. There were times when there was nothing I could do. Or nothing I would do.

•

In the work itself the multiplicity of wonderings makes for impulse after impulse towards larger form, broken by other apprehended forms. It is in the departures from what is forming that the poetic of the rug appears—a form disturbed thruout by the directive of many forms. It was in the process of coming to know what I was doing and just there letting go, breaking, even rebelling, so that I might come to what I did not know I was doing. The making of the rug seems now to relate to the concept of a universe of many realities I have drawn from William James.

•

In any immediate area, if the articulation be made, an almost single directive might be kept (a rendering then, a clarification of issues, to make a definition of what is) with minimum confusion (mixing of one sense of the real with another). But the challenge for the artist is to find his equilibriums in the mixed matter.

III.

What I rose to write here I lost. But as I got just here to the word "rose," I remembered the idea or key I had gotten out of bed in the early morning dark, searched out the notebook in the study, to start with:

It was "aroused"; and then, hadn't I been thinking of the word "excited" just before that? "Excited" was the feeling of being a terrier on the track of something, of sensing, of sniffing, getting the scent, being sent. "Aroused" was this too but was also that I was aroused from sleep by the dream and then the beginnings of ideas, was also that I was angry. Curiosity and anger certainly are part of what I have had to deal with in this approach to reality. The line of my prose sought sentences that would hunt down, track out another line of something I wanted to find. There was also impatience then, how often I wanted to win something before I won thru. That was an element in the crisis of anger.

•

This is an age of criticism, so the critics tell us. An age that has sought to denature and exhaust its time of crisis in bringing philosophy, the arts, human psyche, historical spirit, and the inspiration of the divine world into the terms acceptable to academic aspirations. To undertake this study I must go against the grain of values and rationalities established in my lifetime by a new official literary world. Finding their livelihood in American universities, a new class of schoolteachers has arisen, setting up critical standards and grading responses to fit the anxieties and self-satisfactions of their professional roles and writing verses to exemplify these ideals. In *Hound & Horn* they begin to appear. In *The Southern Review, Partisan Review,* and *Kenyon Review* they take over. An age of criticism does not mean Pound's Cavalcanti essay, Cocteau's "Call to Order," Dame Edith Sitwell's notebooks or H.D.'s "The Guest," Charles Olson's "Projective Verse," or Louis Zukofsky's *Bottom: On Shakespeare,* for these are concerned with the inner nature and process of poetry itself. The university versifiers mistrust or despise equally the ardor of the scholar where it appears, Lowes's *Road to Xanadu* or Pater's Renaissance studies. What they seek is not the course of some passionate intuition that men have called inspiration or divine fire or the inner melody of things; these very words are signals for critical contempt. We may recognize or feel what men call the divine fire but we cannot grade or weigh it. We cannot make it count or assign it its place in literary affairs.

•

My vision of poetry has been drawn from Carlyle as well as from Whitman, from Dante, from Burckhardt, from Pater and Symonds as well as from Pound or Olson—wherever another man's vision leads my spirit towards a larger feeling. And there has been a fire, a fire of anger that rose, as I found the Romantic spirit and back of that the Spirit of Romance and back of that the cult of life as a romance of the spirit belonged to an order that was under attack or was under boycott. There was another, an official, an authoritative order of "poets": Allen Tate, John Crowe Ransom, Yvor Winters, Louise Bogan for whom poetry was not a process or nature of life but a disciplining. And after them, Randall Jarrell, Brooks, and Warren. Their name is legion; they swarmed and swarm in competition with one another to establish an idea cut each to his own limitation for the poet.

•

It is an anger that pressed up to take over the direction of my writing on H.D. against slights and insults to her work. The polemic urge was there, to take offense wherever it was found in the context of old abuses, neglects, and mistakings of the poetry. Randall Jarrell's "H.D. is silly in the head" response to *The Walls Do Not Fall* or Louise Bogan's revelatory contempt for the Notes to *Ion*—these are telling efforts on their part. In Untermeyer's anthology with Wilbur and Jarrell as editors H.D.'s work no longer appears.

.

Yet how mistaken the anger seems. The War Trilogy was not written, any more than *Paterson* or *The Pisan Cantos* were, for classrooms, anthologies, or the new reviews. Jarrell and Louise Bogan were most right in their recognition that H.D. was not for them.

.

What remains is the first thought on waking. The word "aroused," and back of that "excited," may lead too to the word "inspired"—a key to how the body built up its tone or mode (mood) for writing. Here, on the physical level, the cooperation of different systems is demanded. "Aroused"—our visceral participation. "Excited"—our nervous participation. "Inspired"—our respiratory participation (heart and lungs). Then—But what is the word that applies to the circulatory (heart and brain)? I cannot find the word—a word in the series "aroused," "excited," "inspired." Is "ardent" the word? "Fired"? There was the ardor of Lowes or of Pater that gave their prose the heat of high art. Was *anger, angry* the pain of something burning one, part of it? The ardor for *The Cantos,* for *Journey to Love,* for H.D.'s work, being a fire that burned in another way when I came into contact with derogatory critics.

IV.

In his commission, the germ of this book, Norman Holmes Pearson started in my mind an "original" of this book that I thought of as a task, to ride out on quest or trial, for the Lady. He did not ask for that. We had discussed her work in correspondence, and then, he had asked— would I try a book, a tribute on the occasion of H.D.'s seventy-fifth birthday, October 24, 1961. I did not mistake what he hoped for, a small book, a critical appreciation, but I knew too, I warned him, that I must be involved, if I get at what H.D.'s work meant to me, in the unresolved matter of my own poetics. I must increase the risk of her reputation in grounds of my own reading, drawn as I was to just those elements of Alexandrian, Renaissance, and twentieth century theosophy and of Romanticism that among orthodox theologians and literary critics are held most disreputable.

I must make up for the critical disregard, I thought. To take up arms for her honor? There was, is, anyway this being aroused to defense, to offense, to fight for her cause that I saw as my own. To wear this challenge on my sleeve.

.

Nor could there ever have been a small, a proper book. H.D. did not stand alone, but her work, like that of Pound and Williams, belonged to a nucleus of the poetics in which I had my own beginnings; as also I saw Lawrence and H.D. forming another nucleus. In the inheritance of the art, each poet released complex chromosomes, forces that entered into new syntheses of poetic individuality. There were agreements, reinforcements of one poet's imagination in another's. But also, I found their disagreements were crises in the formation as I worked, contending with Pound and Williams where they took issue with her or with each other, searching out the issue to be my own.

.

Then I began to see the book as being not only the story of a poetics but of the role of women as muses and even, as Robert Graves does, as deities over Poetry, but the term *poetess* was derogatory. The relation of a man to the idea of mother or sister or wife raised the specter of the female will to trouble his idea of woman's genius. So, Marianne Moore in her modesty claiming no more than an honest craft was commended and even admired, but H.D. or Dame Edith Sitwell, writing in the personae of the inspired seer, pretenders to the throne of Poetry that gives voice to divine will in an age which mistrusts even the metaphor, excited contempt. I had heard Randall Jarrell and Richard Wilbur give

voice to their outrage at the pretension of Edith Sitwell or had read
Hugh Kenner who placed her among the starters of crazes, the moun-
tebanks of literature. As, in *The Flowering of the Rod,* Simon thinks:

> we must draw the line somewhere;
>
> he had seen something like this
> in a heathen picture . . .

harkening back to a prehistory in which there was mother rule. In our
diagram of the orders of Poetry, the Poetess appears, as the Empress
appears in the configuration of the Empire, or the Priestess or Pope
Joan in the orders of the Church, having the majesty of a first power.

Emily Dickinson and Walt Whitman might form in my mind a gen-
erative figure of American poetry in the nineteenth century.

·

"H.D. / Ezra Pound?" In her accounting of her personal life she goes
back again and again to her marriage with Aldington and his leaving
her; in her old age she will still try to tell the story, keeping alive a hurt,
a being betrayed that can surround her sense of having lost. But for
H.D. too there was a sense of herself in relation to Pound, to Lawrence,
and in her *Hermetic Definitions,* written in 1960, to St.-John Perse as
poetess or seeress in a mystical marriage with a poet or seer, Mary
Magdalene in *The Flowering of the Rod* who, in going over to the Christ,
brings her seven demonic powers into His power, or Helen of *Helen in
Egypt* in her encounters with Achilles, Paris, Theseus. Nowhere does
H.D. refer to Williams, but in his own record from the initial letter of
1905 until the bitter recounting of that meeting in his *Autobiography* in
1951 Williams's thought goes back to his encounter with her.

·

Mother and father of our poetry I keep trying to project. Reproduction,
"that was the disturbing thing in the dream," I wrote. And then later,
"Where everything counts—impossible to reproduce." The fact is that
Emily Dickinson, Walt Whitman, H.D., Ezra Pound, William Carlos
Williams, are not mothers and fathers to us but lonely isolate spir-

its, akin only as we read. The fact is that our contemporary diagram demands these three, H.D., Pound, and William Carlos Williams, only as The War Trilogy, *The Pisan Cantos,* and *Paterson* were battlegrounds in our own struggle towards the realization of a poetry that was to appear in the early fifties. "Aroused," "excited," "inspired," "fired," we found ourselves contending for these masterpieces against those for whom our own work was never to have a place.

•

When, as following the method of H.D.'s later work, of a day by day account, I began this section, I have imagined another intent in which the matter of H.D. is taken as a *mantra,* my thought ever returning thereto and taking its way anew. And the book becomes, not some challenge to the literary lists—as if I might win a place for her honor in establishing (by my authority, by being an author in that sense) a place in men's minds of active concern—but another original, in my thought (for Norman Pearson had suggested a gift for her herself), the gift of itself love seeks to make.

•

A rose. He arose or rose early in the morning. Aroused to the book.

•

To be aroused, *angry,* I said. It is certainly too to be sexually aroused, where we follow the Freudian persuasion. To rise to the occasion. An aroused content is a disturbed content, as now, bringing the Freudian reading in at all, a shadowy suspicion begins. In following Freud, I am concerned not with what might be my own psyche but with whatever news of Man's psyche, in which I have my share—Psyche, then, of the story that Apuleius tells. She was a searcher in the story, as a consequence of her looking where looking was forbidden. And now, in the conjunction of the hour, 4:20 A.M., the dream of the rug that may be a rug in a hall, or a cover of a bed, or an original design, and the ghost of the word "aroused," another searcher, a figure of myself as a child comes to form a link. There was, before I could read, another event in which what I was to be took root. The little figure aroused, in the cunning of sleep, walking, goes to see what he heard. Was it at the same hour? 4:20 A.M. To rise early and following a scent . . .

What I remember is searching for and finding the hiding places of the Easter eggs before Easter morning. In the dream there was a reminder of those rag-rugs in the hall between the nursery and the parents' bedroom.

•

Aroused then is, as the Freudian thought would have it, the penis aroused; the ghost of the word "aroused" the ghost of the Freudian idea. With the sense that the pen is ready to write.

•

In this book where my purpose is to give my soul into the work, the cause appears in a new light. For I have taken psychic being, taken fire, from these works. Over years, I have confused my self with them—the open secret in the Freudian primal scene is only a ground floor—used The War Trilogy in creating the poet I am. We are concerned with the architecture of a man, but building with words, with the breath or spirit forms, morphemes in inventions of time, we build structures of air, rising one within another without displacement. "Forged" myself, remembering Joyce's word. And may have evoked that primal scene to create the scene where we are, as the magician enacts the spying upon the naked body of Noah, repeated in the spying upon Jacob in intercourse, to incite in the mind a mystery of curiosity that would see the secrets of Creation Itself, of discovery and hubris.

•

Where is the original? I took thought from her thought; I took heart in her heart.

•

In working on "The Venice Poem" in 1948 I first realized that I was not original but derived my spirit in poetry. Taking my cues from adopted parents, I found my speech and play ready, as from the sounding of the bells "a tribute to the Angels;"

yet though the campanili spoke,
Gabriel, Azrael,

though the campanili answered,
Raphael, Uriel,

with other bells of the campus campanili actually sounding in my ear, studying the architecture of St. Mark's, I began the poem, evoking attendant spirits as I had seen H.D. in *Tribute to the Angels* evoke lords of the poem. Archangels, for archangels, Ficino tells us, "direct the divine cult and look after sacred things." I meant to derive a poet and to take my origin in him, having no genius of my own to take the genius of the language, as H.D. had dared to take the great genii of the hours to direct the poem. [But I was "adopted"; I would never really look like my adopted parents or my representatives of the parents.]

The Cantos had shown a way to take ancestors in time, as Homer, and then the Renaissance translator Andreas Divus "In officina Wecheli, 1538, out of Homer," are ancestors of Pound as he translates the eleventh book of the *Odyssey* and brings it into his own *Cantos*—adopted fathers or authors of the original (Pound's actual father's name being Homer, as we remember H.D.'s mother's name was Helen); and in the "*Et omniformis omnis intellectus est*" of Psellos that opens Canto XXIII I had found a lead towards that magic in which the mind becomes whatever and all that it will. Jane Harrison in *Themis* had supplied another lead with her observation that the dithyramb was Δι-θορ-αμβος, "Zeus-leap-song, the song that makes Zeus leap or beget," a mimesis in which the Zeus-Child, Zagreus, was brought to birth. But it was in The War Trilogy that begins with its declaration of a new Master over Love and closes with the presentation of the Child, with its early proposition—

so that, living within,
you beget, self-out-of-self

—that prepared my thought for "The Venice Poem," the first poem where I not only knew what must be done—in *Medieval Scenes* I knew what the poem wanted—but also how to do it. In *Medieval Scenes* I had thought of myself as artisan and medium of the poem in one, receiving certain scenes and working them in language. In "The Venice Poem," the world of the poem was not a scene received and rendered but a matrix, within which and thru which I lived, into which I brought my actual life, the unfortunate course of love and betrayal which I suffered during the time of writing, not in order to express what I experienced but in order to take what I experienced as a passion, to in-form myself with the content of the poem, to form a womb or to adopt a womb in the matter of the poem, in order to beget in a Zeus-leap-song a Child out of myself that was to be my poet.

Chapter 8

I.

I woke again this morning before dawn. But there is only what I rejected of the dream to work with, and back of that—not even an image but a name that seems out of order, disorderly,—"SALLY RAND." Once I bring the name up, back of the name I glimpse the fragment of a dream image I must recover now. I had, I gather, in a scene that must form part of our pictograph, been caressing H.D.'s naked back. One member of the dream-work or of the "Chinese written character as a medium for poetry" I have to do with, was my hand moving over the bare shoulders and back of a woman who in the dream was H.D. But she was also the fore-woman, the last element in sequence was—well, I have no more than the name, the popularity, the vulgarity, the *De Vulgari Eloquentia,* of "SALLY RAND" to work with. Must I bring this matter up? In the transgression of boundaries, even here where I have meant to keep boundaries fluid and self-creative so that no content would be out-of-bounds, I feel uneasy. [One of my readers writes in the margin: "I find these pages a little querulous and oddly defensive in an almost petulant manner."]

•

"We can see," Fenollosa writes in his essay *The Chinese Written Character as a Medium for Poetry,* which coming into Pound's hands in 1916 opens the way in modern poetry for ideogram and projective verse, "not only the forms of sentences, but literally the parts of speech growing up, budding forth one from another"—as the scene of the naked back and the name of Sally Rand are for us parts of speech. "All that poetic form requires is a regular and flexible sequence, as plastic as thought itself. . . . Perhaps we do not always sufficiently consider that thought is successive, not through some accident but because the operations of nature are successive. The transferences of forces from agent to object constitute natural phenomena, occupy time. Therefore, a reproduction of them in imagination requires the same temporal order."

•

But some "accident or weakness" in or of my subjective operation did break away from the pictograph. The hand caressing the bare back of the woman who represented H.D. was changed or the scene was disturbed, the surface of the pool stirred and the scene dissolved into . . . into—what? There was the name foremost in my mind as I woke up: Sally Rand.

•

My father and mother went to the Chicago World's Fair that year. Was it 1933? It would then have been the year when H.D. began her analysis with Freud. Yesterday as I was writing down the previous dream, and then as I came to picture the various books to which this study refers as if the work of art were itself a cover-image of some original, that title of Baudelaire's *Mon Coeur Mis à Nu* kept coming to mind. *My Heart Stript Bare.* Was that one of the requirements or realizations the book demanded? The title kept insisting to be admitted.

But Baudelaire's *Mon Coeur Mis à Nu* is only a title for me. Of a book that has been on my shelves since 1946 with pages uncut. Henry Miller had had in his *Tropics* and in *Black Spring* this *coeur mis à nu* directive. I had picked up the Baudelaire to have near at hand one of the key books of the nineteenth century, but I never read it. I didn't really like this idea of trying to expose the heart. It stood in critical reproof of my wanting a fiction within which the heart hidden might reveal itself as it would in the working.

•

For those of us who are weavers of the veil, spinning the thread that changes life into its story, Mon coeur mis à nu, if it must be there, appears as a clothing of the heart, a figure in the cloth—but the cloth is itself the tissue of the heart. As the heart in H.D.'s *The Flowering of the Rod* we saw brought forward by the mage Kaspar as a gift for the Child—a sealed jar. But unbroken, it has also been broken. It is an open secret. Everyone has heard the story.

•

Seven seals upon the book. Seven veils of Ishtar. In reading, in penetrating the secrets of the author—so in arts and in sciences—Freud tells us, an anxiety can grow as "budding forth one from another" a sexual curiosity works behind a scientific quest. And, doctor and scientist of the soul, Freud advanced another idea—that behind analysis itself was another anxiety, *anal,* he called it. Prying into, cutting up, laying bare the heart was, is, a surgical operation and also something more distressing, a destructive intent. There were transformations or "transferences of force from agent to object" in critical curiosity of cruel and bloody impulses.

•

Mon coeur mis à nu, this work of Baudelaire's that is in my mind entirely an imaginary work, an emanation from some hidden book, is then an operation, takes on the hubris, the transgression, of my own "scientific curiosity." There is a work that I have read many times that comes to mind now, standing as it has for years (since I first read it at fifteen or sixteen) for this *mis à nu* violation of life, the story of an act that cuts the threads of the story. It is Hawthorne's *The Birthmark.*

•

"No, dearest Georgiana, you came so nearly perfect from the hand of Nature that this slightest possible defect, which we hesitate whether to term a defect or a beauty, shocks me, as being the visible mark of earthly imperfection."

He operates. He is "successful." He removes all trace of the mark of birth; of what Christians called the original sin; of the vulnerable spot where the hero's death will strike. "You know better than to try to improve in poetry," Jack Spicer said, when I was distressed by the failure I felt in working on this book—"Why do you try to correct your prose?" Rewriting, reworking—just over what we are most unsure of, most do not know how to work, "whether to term a defect or a beauty."

•

The story Hawthorne tells in "The Birthmark" has to do with the artist's urge to render the essential free from its contaminations. It is an alchemical tale then. It has something to do with laying the heart bare, to know its secrets of life.

With criticism too, then, with the concept of cleaning up a written sentence, erasing the blemishes of this prose as I write it, removing what seems to mar some possible clear thing.

•

Georgiana then is our book, our inner nature, our own body. And the alchemist or doctor or gnostic or perfectionist, the critic and artist Aylmer at last gazes down upon the perfected image of his wife.

Waking, she perishes. Was it that the life was in the flaw? "That crimson hand which had once blazed forth with such disastrous brilliancy as to scare away all their happiness?"

"Do not repent," she instructs her stricken husband, "that with so high and pure a feeling, you have rejected the best the earth could offer."

•

Waking from the dream, I rejected the best it had to offer. SALLY RAND. "Ecdysiast." A joke. She had been brought up. Hey-ding-ding. Something had risen to the occasion. She was there, and I awoke. An instruction. "I cannot use SALLY RAND in the H.D. Book," I said. "I cannot bring *that* up."

•

But it had been brought up—the dancer with her ostrich-feather fans.

.

As, pursuing the pun, I am a fan of H.D.'s. This cult of the movie-star, of the dance-star, of the sports-star, and then among us in our common selves, of the poet-star, is as much of our daily reality as Sally Rand and her fan dance.

.

And there may have been another transference of force, a pun, that gave Sally her power over the popular imagination. For everyone knew, though they would only subconsciously remember (I do not recall that any of the jokes picked up on that word "ostrich") that the ostrich hides its head in the sand, is afraid to see the facts of life.

.

Sally Rand was surrounded by the vulgar laughter, the knowing smirk. She was the victim of a joke? She had her popularity in a joke, in the "Sally Rand" jokes, and when they died out, what she was died out, leaving only the ghost of her name to haunt the jumping rhymes of children who have no other memory of her—"Sally Rand has a fan," Iona and Peter Opie report in *The Language and Lore of Schoolchildren, 1959*: "If she drops it—oh man!"

.

She was, incarnate, a creature of the hey-ding-ding touch or mark that H.D. had wanted removed from William Carlos Williams's poetry to reveal the real beauty. The H and D, above and below.

.

There was as I recall no more than the gentle joking about did Father go to see Sally Rand and her dancers? In—wasn't it called "Elysium"? In their side-show burlesque or nudist *Elysium*. Did he want to see? It would all turn out to be a joke. They would rag him. The ladies would laugh gently to cover something that I did not understand. Sally Rand was "common," was somehow both alluring and distasteful.

•

In *Bid Me to Live* ("my Madrigal, my *roman à clef*," H.D. called it in her *Newsweek* interview upon the publication of the book), H.D. gives her account of a charade, an evening's game in which Lawrence and Frieda (Fredericks and Elsa, in the novel), Rafe and Julia Ashton, Bella Carter and Vane impersonate God and serpent, Adam and apple-tree, Eve and the angel at the gate. It is not part of their play, or, it is not openly part of their play; but in the original of that charade, in the story of our Ur-Parents in the Garden, they are of the Tree of Knowing and they saw the hey-ding-ding touch. In the lore the Above and the Below separated into two. They saw they were naked.

•

In a collection of memoirs, letters, and biographical sketches presenting a portrait of D.H. Lawrence, I found another account of just that evening: where another charade is presented in which Fredericks, Elsa, Rafe and Julia Ashton, Bella Carter and Vane appear as Lawrence, Frieda, Richard and H.D. Aldington, Bella (who is to be the second Mrs. Aldington), and the British composer Cecil Gray.

•

Was it before or after Lawrence wrote his poem "Elysium" that appears in *Look! We Have Come Through!?*

•

Once the charade is set going in the novel, elements take on new levels of meaning, new circles of meaning ringing out from each pebble. "Somewhere, somehow, a pattern repeated itself, life advances in a spiral." That is it, part of my sense here. For the pattern, the spiraling advance, is in the swirling veil of Ishtar or Isis or of our Nature, not the heart but the charade of the heart. "Every breath she drew was charged with meaning," H.D. writes of Julia. This sense of the meaningful is the charge we have as weavers in the weaving, to bring forward meanings into the work, as creatures ourselves of the tissue of life. Or the *screen*?

.

Sally Rand was, to my Freudian persuasion, a screen-image.

.

"They have to bring forth," Mary Butts writes in 1932 in *Traps for Unbelievers,* "from the eating-houses of Brooklyn, from farmsteads in Kansas, from shepherds' huts in the Puszta in Hungary, flesh that can bear the weight of the world's imaginings about Aphrodite. . . . All the young gods, of sex and war, of art and sport and maidenhood; of drink and the mysteries of excitement and moving about . . . the gods of ourselves, in the order we most want them.

"Only it is men and women now who have to bear the burden of that desire: the movie star and the athlete, the flying man and woman, the speedboat racer and the boxer."

And the artist? the cult of Picasso? and the poet?

.

Certainly T.S. Eliot belonged to this order, standing as an idol of the higher sophistication called culture, as Noel Coward stood for the lower sophistication called show business.

As in our day, Ginsberg and Kerouac are stars, beside whom any flyer or racer dims.

.

There is a priestess, a personality of this cult of ourselves I would make H.D. to be—this too? A bare-back rider of Pegasus of the Circus?

.

It was my hand caressing her bare back, as if it were in touch with fame, with this woman, from which sprang, once the dream was disturbed, the other famous, *popular* name.

.

"Not, it may be observed, the older and soberer incantation," Mary Butts writes: "not the Father or the Grandfather or the Intellect; not Zeus Chronides or Athene; not 'Zeus of the Underworld and dread Persephone'."

•

But, waking this morning, disturbed, I thought . . . the thought kept coming back . . . "Did I ever . . . ?" It was the hand kneading, needing then, the bare back. " . . . stroke my mother's back so?" Or *the* mother's back?

•

Jehovah, I remember now from my reading in the Works of Thomas Vaughan last night, showed Moses His bare backside. How had they ever been able to keep that Rabelaisian detail as part of the story? of the real beauty?

II.

I had gleaned from some reference to a dictionary that the word *verse,* our verse in poetry, like our *prose* in poetry, was *backwards* and *forwards,* as a man ploughing goes along one line and returns. *Prose,* forward in the row or line; then "turning to begin another line" (as now I find in the O.E.D.) *versus.*

As men plough forward and back, did they once write, turning
?enil eht fo dne eht ta

But in verse now, we *return* to begin another line. We do not reach the end or margin.

•

It is a fanciful etymology. To demonstrate that, once words cease to be conventional, customary or taken-for-granted in their meaning, all things begin to move, are set into motion. In the figure of ploughing, we see that prose and verse are two necessary movements in the one operation of writing. That here what we call the ploughing of the field we also call poetry or our own operation in language. Writing that knows in every phase what it is doing.

•

Forward and back, prose and verse, the shuttle flies in the loom.

•

"It means *against* too," Spicer noted in the margin of an article I had written on Ideas of Form, and he asked me to look the word up in the O.E.D. There was *pro* and *versus*. My polemics. Lines of a poem "employed in *Law* to denote an action by one party against another."

•

There is from *vertere* to turn, *version:* "a rendering of some text or work, or of a single word, passage, etc., from one language into another"; and too, "the particular form of a statement, account, report given by one person."

•

aversion

•

There is the *verso* or "the side presented to the eye when the leaf has been turned over." The other side of the fabric, where the colors are more vivid for not having been brought to light. The underside of the weaving.

There is the verso, the world beneath the stone, the underworld. Where not only mystery but misery hides. Where not only occult wonder but obscene infection swarms. Life revealed when the stone is turned over, reversed.

•

For wasn't there, as Freud found, dug out, exposed: anal and oral phantasy—shit and devouring demons everywhere. The witch in the wisewoman?

•

There is in the operation Freud describes as the screen image a standing of one thing in the place of another. "It may indeed be questioned whether we have any memories at all *from* our childhood: memories *relating to* our childhood may be all that we possess," he writes in "Screen Memories" (1899). The fabric of history, of memory, then, must be continually woven in order to exist *because it is not the fabric of the past but the fabric of the present that we weave.*

·

We find meanings and significances to make up the Presence in which we, I, are, am.

·

"Out of a number of childhood memories," Freud had pointed out, "there will be some scenes which, when they are tested (for instance by the recollections of adults), turn out to have been falsified." Fabricated or forged, made-up, worked, to be a scene at all means that facts have been taken over by the restless human creativity. In the terms William James gives of a plurality of reals, we read: "there will be some scenes which turn out to have only a personal, not a conventional, reality."

·

Then, describing this operation—it is the operation of our weaving, the classical operation or pretension of the magician, Freud observes: "They are false in the scene [sense?] that they have shifted an event to a place where it did not occur . . . or that they have merged two people into one or substituted one for another, or the scenes as a whole give signs of being combinations of two separate experiences."

·

As in the charade which the poets and lovers play in War-Time London, the loss of Paradise is brought into the loss of the pre-War world, and in their impersonations the personalities of Lawrence and H.D. become linked to the archaic personae of Jehovah and the Forbidden Tree.

·

"She had the same feeling," H.D. writes in *Bid Me to Live,* "that she had had in Capri, her word would call any Spirit to her, but she must be careful how she spoke. How she thought, even. It would be tempting something, luring something too poignantly near."

•

Screen-images or screen memories Freud calls them, these things too poignantly near. Figures of the veil, we have called them. The heart figured to clothe the heart. He speaks in that essay of "the high degree of sensory intensity shown by the pictures and the efficacy of the function of memory in the young." I have suggested that we are not only creators, but, if and where we are creators, we are creatures of the veil we weave, children out of the whole cloth, charged with the intensity of the transforming work itself.

•

Then Freud warns: "these falsifications of memory are tendentious, that is, they serve the purpose of the repression and replacement of objectionable or disagreeable impressions." But he goes further to question whether we have any memories at all from childhood. He almost raises this picture of everywhere objectionable or disagreeable realities giving rise to the what we are in what is, creatures of our own transformation of what we could not satisfy in life, satisfying realities disappearing into their satisfactions.

"In these periods of revival," Freud continues, "the childhood memories did not, as people are accustomed to say, *emerge;* they were *formed* at that time."

•

What we are involved in now, after the brooding thought, the penetrating analysis, the pervasive suggestion of Freud, is that our recognitions must go two ways. Though, after Freud, enthusiasts have tended to see the underside as the true and the overt statement as a cover, we would see both as present terms of the weave of truth.

•

As what sent me off along this line of *prose, verse; versus; version, aversion, verso,* was that bit out of Vaughan's *Anthroposophia Theomagica:*

> This fire is the vestment of the Divine Majesty, His back-parts which He shewed to Moses; but His naked, royal essence none can see and live. The glory of His presence would swallow up that natural man and make him altogether spiritual. Thus Moses his face—after conference with Him—shines, and from this small tincture we may guess at our future estate in the regeneration.

"But I have touched the veil," Vaughan continues, "and must return to the outer court of the Sanctuary."

"The trembling of the veil of the Temple," Yeats had called the generation of Mallarmé. Between the high-mindedness and the low thought-forms a Void—but it was also a Maelstrom—trembled, shimmered, began to cast forth its old fascination. What is on my mind is that Yeats too, like Freud, poetics as well as psychology, was drawn to find out hidden content, working to bring us into a new consciousness in magic, away from the abstract and absolute, towards the coordination of above and below.

> Those masterful images because complete
> Grew in pure mind, but out of what began?
> A mound of refuse or the sweepings of a street . . .

•

There was a time of the trembling; then a time of the forcing of overt images. We now have our sanctuary only within the open secret in which the tissue of life reverses and restores the face, as Waite in a footnote to Vaughan quotes the Vulgate: *ignis involens.*

•

We no sooner saw the backside that God showed Moses, because the Glory, the face, was forbidden, was *too much,* than we saw the sexual figure with which this image was charged, the other back-side that Freud forced us to admit existed in our thought.

As Satan, the Goat of Mendes, presented in parody, in a charade of the verso, his ass-hole to be kissed by the devout. Where, too, the face of the devotee "shines and from this small tincture. . . . " When Madame Blavatsky tells us that Isis has revealed to her "the secret meaning of her long-lost *secrets*," in the context of a garment that becomes more transparent, the sexual reference of the word contends to take over the tenor of the statement.

.

H.D.'s allegiance, like Freud's, belongs to the high mind. Pound, we remember, called her, long long ago, "that refined charming, and utterly narrow minded she-bard 'H.D.'" and yet, had wanted her to keep the "few but perfect" position in poetry. But in *Ion*, in her apostrophe to Athene, H.D. addresses "this emanation of pure-spirit" with a new sense of what high-mindedness might mean. Reading the passage again, in the context of the Hermetic "above and below" (the "As above, so below" of the Smaragdine tablet) and also of the Freudian idea of displacement above and below, we see that the above must work in the below and the below in the above, there must be a circuit for thought to be creative, for desire to be intelligent: "This most beautiful abstraction [the Athene] pleads for the great force of the undermind . . . that so often, on the point of blazing upwards into the glory of inspirational creative thought, flares, by a sudden law of compensation, down, making for tragedy, disharmony, disruption, disintegration." In our task, we must have "the desire actually to follow all those hidden subterranean forces," if we would come to the reward of thought. "'You flee no enemy in me, but one friendly to you,' says the intellect, standing full armed. . . . "

.

High mind must labor—Williams in *Paterson* calls up the figure of Madame Curie working the pitchblende—in obscure matter. But just where the mind disavows its sexual motivation or where the genital organ disavows its mental imagination, a contention begins in man's nature. What a dark filthy fabric of lies and richness the political figures of our day seem to weave towards their precipitation of "tragedy, disharmony, disruption, disintegration"—as if driven by necessity—the old Judeo-Christian dream of a War to end the trials of Creation in a holocaust of fire. What does it mean? In 1935 and 1936, as Jung began to first publish his studies of Alchemy, that matter of the Second World War was gathering in men's minds everywhere. These falsifications of memory were tendentious. Possessed by the thought of the enemy, in fear and anger, men turned their high minds to the invention of the nuclear explosion in matter, to the cultivation of last diseases, to research in gasses that would cripple the minds of whole populations.

·

In Alchemy, so too in psychoanalysis, the work depended upon some equivalence or ambivalence between the gold (the Good, the life, the essential) and the shit (the waste, the contamination—but it was also that which was returned to the life or richness of the soil). The Tree had been of Good *and* Evil, but in the contention of Man's knowledge it had appeared as the Tree of Good contending against Evil, a universe in agony. For the Christian convert Augustine the very curiosity to know at all could appear as adversary to faith, as the primary evil.

·

It was the work of Freud in psychology to follow an adverse curiosity, to bring to light just those references that had in the old religion or magic been sacred-taboo, hidden in order to be revealed, set aside, filled with awe / awful. Privates or secrets: penis, testicles, vagina, labia, clitoris, intercourse—words hidden in their latin propriety, proper *in their place.* In the doctor's inner offices, in the medical report or in the criminal courts, the words might appear as symptoms or charges: sodomy, unnatural relations, perversions—acts that had once been communal in ritual or initiation. Driven, out of mind, out of the community of men, as the old gods went. In bad taste. Or, in bad smell, bad repute. *Virtu,* that Olson suggested to me once must have meant man-smell. "That smells," we say of some work of art that offends our taste.

·

Freud is a hero in a work that had begun to bring up out of the festering darkness (out of the darkened backrooms, the atmosphere of evil thought and shamed confession, in which the decadents of the nineties found their vices; out of the misery and suffering in which the realists found their doctrine of sexual bondage) into the light of day the vanished goods. The rich store underground was to be restored in the sight of man and god.

·

In the Judeo-Christian mythos, as in the Orphic tradition, God—Jahweh or Phanes—is Maker or Poet of a universe that as a work of His art, is good. Day by day of creation the "and God saw that it was good" is reiterated, the sublime assurance of the artist. But in the Christian myth, Lucifer, light-bearer of the high mind, is adversely critical of What Is and declares matter itself to be bad, the breeding of animal life vile and the image of Man distasteful. Shame in their nakedness is one of the first illuminations knowledge brings to Adam and Eve. Lucifer becomes the Enemy as he becomes the Critic, and in the Below, which now is a Hell where criticized or condemned men are in pain, he appears as Sathanas, the Adversary.

·

But in the work itself, the Creation as a work of art, Lucifer-Satan and Jahweh too, the author, are parts. The reader who is concerned with the structure, with form and content, will exclaim "it is good" at the appropriateness of even adversity in light of the composition. But now, as we begin to see this mythos as having just the truth of its composition, the truth of any story, it itself becomes a part of our own story in which we may try to restore the whole of experience or, rather, within that whole, to bring back the sexuality of man into his common goods.

·

The work was in Joyce's interior monologue, where Bloom's thought works back and forth between the vision of the nymph Gerty MacDowell where "all melted away dewily in the grey air" and the versions of sexual excitement, the screen weavings of "Licking pennies," "that's the Moon," "Mutoscope pictures in Capel street: for men only. Peeping Tom." to romantic phantasies "Dare say she felt I. When you feel like that you often meet what you feel . . . " announcing the sexual urgency: "Well cocks and lions do the same and stags." He is avoiding, his conscious mind is playing over, or above, a below, where "lions do the same." Bloom discharges his excitement. "Mr. Bloom with careful hand recomposed his wet shirt. O Lord, that little limping devil."

.

The mutoscope pictures are "for men only," but *Ulysses* itself in the installments of *The Little Review* took its place immediately in the high mind, and broke down in its directness the double standard that had divided what was proper for men to think of from what was proper for women to hear. When Virginia Woolf speaks of *Ulysses* as "an illiterate underbred book . . . egotistic, insistent, raw, striking, and ultimately nauseating," it is she not the book that fails. The bare, simple words— the sexual words that belong to an inner poetry—begin to appear with the poetic ramblings of Molly Bloom: cunt, cock, fuck, "Let out a few smutty words," Molly Bloom says. But they were let out of their smut into the light of day, having their place with the other nouns of Molly's soliloquy: "that would do your heart good to see rivers and lakes and flowers all sorts of shapes and smells and colors springing up even out of ditches. . . . "

.

Then in Lawrence's *Lady Chatterley's Lover* Mellors must talk the speech of the lower orders too but these lower orders are the country-folk, the dialect of pagany then. "A woman's a lovely thing when 'er's deep ter fuck, and cunt's good," Mellors says echoing the words of the Creator.

It was there, in those pages of a novel, between Mellors and Connie, made up out of some other thing between Lawrence and Frieda that had or hadn't happened. For us, that Mellors and Connie, after arguing and accounting for the tribal lore of sex, as they do; after setting things to rights; make love, and that Lawrence has words for it, is—like the other sexual revelation of Freud's and like Molly Bloom's sexual reveries—a breakthru, a release of withheld words into the common language, a release then of withheld feelings into the possible grace of common understanding.

.

There's "a woman's a lovely thing" and "cunt's good" given as threads of the loom, as themes of working good.

And just this earnest, ardent thing in Lawrence, this assertion and affirmation in the words "lovely" and "good" has called forth, calls forth, the smut-hounds and censors who believe that women and cunt are evils, powers over them, and the smirking sophisticates who believe women and cunt are commodities. "Don't you think all that stuff is *old hat?*" an informant for *Time* magazine asked me when *Lady Chatterley's Lover* was going to be republished. "How *dated* the novel is!"

.

As, in its way, *Sally Rand* was dated and showed up something in me. Mellors and Connie are in a strip-tease for some readers. *Mis à nu* in order to find naked reverences, the old reverences of the earth, Elysium, they are naked, exposed not only to the love of some readers in those pages but naked to the ridicule of others.

.

"He heard the distant hooters of Stacks Gate for seven o'clock. It was Monday morning." We too are reminded of the industrial practical realities of men's lives, of the living that must be worked for. This is the reality James described as utilitarian. Beyond ideal relations, sensual immediacies, imagination and the supernatural, this distant hooting is from a world where reality is fitted to men's uses and productions, the reality of up-to-date. How silly, once we are aware that what we are reading is in the light of other men's opinions, Lawrence's nakedness appears. The hooting is in the background. It is the factory whistle. The conclusions of reasonable men are bearing in upon the scene.

"He shivered a little, and with his face between her breasts pressed her soft breasts up over his ears, to deafen him."

.

In *Tribute to the Angels* H.D. invokes (against the hooters?) by the sound of bells and by the sign of candle, guardian angels to stand with the old daemons or demons.

.

H.D. in her work does not bring the anglo-saxon words, banned by genteel proprieties, into use. In her generation, heirs of the suffragette fight for equal rights, women began to claim an equal share in the right to consciousness, including sexual consciousness. "Bearing in mind that all men conceal the truth in these matters," Freud in 1905 writes of his initial enquiries into the sexual disturbances that underlay neurotic disorders. With *Ulysses* and *Lady Chatterley's Lover* in the 1920s and then, in 1937, Pound's *Canto* XXXIX, where in Circe's ingle:

> Girls talked there of fucking, beasts talked there of eating,
> All heavy with sleep, fucked girls and fat leopards,

as the physical realities of sex, referred to in the language of the Protestant ethic as "privates" or "secrets," begin to be thought of as communal goods, the words for organs and acts begin to appear in works no longer written for private circulation but to be "published." *"James Joyce was right,"* rings as a refrain in the prose of "Murex" which follows the mode of the interior monolog, but, though H.D. is a poet for whom the revelation of inner truth is primary, delineating changes of erotic emotion from tensions of withholding to raptures of release, she does not and perhaps could not refer to the sexual parts of the body openly. Not until Denise Levertov's "Hypocrite Women" and "Our Bodies" in 1963 will the right Joyce had won be claimed by a woman and the words "cunt" and "balls" take their place with "hands," "eyes," "mouth," "feet" in the language of the physical body in a woman's poetry.

But not only sexual names had been banished by the Protestant ethic. Indeed, the names flourished wherever they were used to express scorn or irreverence. Back of the sexual organs and the names, more feared and hated were the sexual mysteries and powers. Calling up Lilith, "and one born before Lilith," and Eve, Isis, Astarte, Cyprus in *The Flowering of the Rod,* H.D. would bring back other banished names in which the daemonic sexual nature of woman is evoked. The Puritanism of Augustine in the 4th century or of Calvin in the sixteenth would censor spiritual as well as physical possibilities. So, Mary Magdalene in *The Flowering of the Rod,* "outcast," "unseemly," is City-goddess of Magdala and also "myrrh-tree of the gentiles" and also a Siren of the sea—a numinous power of the ancient Mother-world—as well as a whore. She returns like the very sacred and taboo divinity of Woman as ruler of sexual mysteries that in the nineteenth century began to be called pornography. Having called up:

> a word most bitter, *marah*
> a word bitterer still, *mar*

H.D., in turn, invokes the star of morning, Lucifier above:

> Phosphorus at sun-rise,
> Hesperus at sun-set.

Then she calls upon the disturbance below, what Boehme called the *Turba:*

> xi
>
> O swiftly, relight the flame
> before the substance cool,
>
> for suddenly we saw your name
> desecrated; knave and fools
>
> have done you impious wrong,
> Venus, for venery stands for impurity
>
> and Venus as desire
> is venereous, lascivious,
>
> while the very root of the word shrieks
> like a mandrake when foul witches pull
>
> its stem at midnight . . .

thru to:

> O holiest one,
> Venus whose name is kin
>
> to venerate,
> venerator.

      •

It is this trouble with names, or this trouble of a name, that is followed by the section we have already considered when I wrote about searching for the name of something, of *hérisson:*

> it lives, it breathes,
> it gives off—fragrance?

but then:

> I do not know what it gives,

The patron who said "name it," who said, "if you cannot, if there is no name, *invent it*," was, if not Freud himself, very like Freud.

      •

A long way round. "Beating about the bush" is our common expression. I gather what I mean as I go. And must write as if I gathered my sense as a man would gather water in a sieve.

      •

Lady Chatterley "had not even heard the hooters. She lay perfectly still, her soul washed transparent."

      •

Yes, it is true. Writing in this book on that Saturday, just after I had smashed my finger, I was out of touch with the pain. The finger, insulted as it was, after all, hooted.

What I was going to write but dissented, but still must go on with, is that in the higher orders they do not hear the hooters? they are not offended? but "perfectly still," "washed transparent"? A realm of ideas that is above the distraction of an injured finger.

•

Dame Edith Sitwell has turned like an outraged falconess from the higher orders swooping down, distracted, clawing and tearing at the self-esteem of petty critics and versifiers, at the journalistic smirk and hoot. Is it—*lady* like?

•

Where the hooting is, there is a division between the upper and the lower; there is a war in the void.

•

Working towards this study, I have found H.D.'s deriders, hooters of the daily press, of the current literary reviews. It is part of the polemic, the store of outrage, my hearing at times not the Michael, Raphael, Gabriel of the angelic orders, not the bell-notes over the waters, over the medium of language where those great rimes sound, but the derisive Monday morning reproofs, denials, and smirks of Randall Jarrell, Louise Bogan, Robert Hillyer, industrious literary businessmen, and back of them, the conspiracy of silence. Into the texture of the poem H.D. has woven their voices, as life does weave into the tissue of our physical bodies memories that make for a lasting resistance against insult, for possibilities of repair.

•

The poem takes as its condition of being its liabilities,

> and fixed indigestible matter
> such as shell, pearl; imagery
>
> done to death; perilous ascent,
> ridiculous descent . . .

where the poet lets the voice of the adversary play and list against her work just those qualities that rescue the work from what is correct and invulnerable.

•

The war, the actual bombing of London, the daily attacks, the lies and ambitions of wartime politics, may have made real and immediate again the experience of attacks and strategies of literary wars the writer had known.

This search for historical parallels,
research into psychic affinities,

has been done to death before . . .

.

"The meaning that words hide" remains. And where—sick, tired, I imagine her, tired of these voices—she came to Freud in 1933, in the exhaustion of her first creative tide that had carried her high in 1916 and the early twenties, in the waning of her critical reputation in which *Red Roses for Bronze* of 1931 and *Ion* of 1937 appeared, there was not only a personal but a creative need for a new Master over Love.

.

"To greet the return of the Gods," she wrote on a card, sending gardenias to Freud upon his arrival in London after the Nazis' taking of Vienna in 1938. One of the high orders, the Princess George of Greece had arranged for Freud's collection of Greek and Egyptian antiquities to follow him to London. "Other people read: Goods," he wrote in reply.

.

They had in common our ardent "high-minded" (as Pound might have called her, as he called her in that letter to Williams "narrow-minded"), our high-minded poetess who sought the return of the gods and our earnest "low-minded" (as Pound would have called him, as Pound called him in the *Rock-Drill Cantos* "a kike") psychoanalyst who sought the return of the goods—not only genius but the derisive voices of critics in their ears. They excited antipathies. Science like art had provided smirks of distaste. Art like science had shown its conspiracy of silence.

.

In the trilogy, in the three panels of the poem, there is a narrative of the old order entering into the new, the despised becoming part of the revered—as the all but forgotten "Red Roses for Bronze" is remembered in H.D.'s last work, *Hermetic Definitions* of 1960. Kaspar, a mage of the old pagany (of the stars), in *The Walls Do Not Fall* no more than a promise of the story:

> His, the Genius in the jar
> which the Fisherman finds,
>
> He is Mage,
> bringing myrrh.

that might also for a moment have been the story of Arabian Nights fame, brings forward a jar (it is the heart, the Word, the Star), stars, hearts, words—containing—"the Genius in the jar," she says; "bringing myrrh," she says. Containing life, meaning, light.

·

Life, meaning, light are in the jar. But then a woman enters the picture; as in the alchemical passage of the alembic or the witchcraft passage of the cauldron—in "the crucible," from marah, bitterness, an operation begins as brine and tears of the sea join:

> and change and alter,
> *mer, mere, mere, mater, Maia, Mary.*

Kaspar, admitting her at all, admits the Siren-seductress, even the pornographic—"disordered, disheveled," "unseemly" and in the disorder, "the light on her hair like moonlight on a lost river" he has a vision of the old orders. There is vision then in the jar, he sees the Islands of Paradise. "I am that myrrh tree of the gentiles," the woman declares, and she shows in her speech a glimmer back of paradise of unseemly sexual rites:

> there are idolators,
>
> even in Phrygia and Cappadocia,
> who kneel before mutilated images
>
> and burn incense to the Mother of Mutilations,

that contain the image to come of Mary weeping bitterly over the mutilated body of the Christ.

.

Seven devils that had been cast out are part of the story, the *marah* itself, perhaps, "were now unalterably part of the picture"

> *Lilith born before Eve*
> *and one born before Lilith,*
> *and Eve; we three are forgiven,*
> *we are three of the seven*
> *daemons cast out of her.*

.

It was in hiding away the daemons, the sexualities, even the armpits and ass-hole of our bodies, in guilt or shame, divorcing them from the goods (for only that is a good that is communal and above-board), taking them away from God into the claim of secret or private property, that they became evils, lords "over" us.

.

In his *Three Contributions to the Theory of Sexual Love* of 1912, Freud tells us that besides the realm of eros, where men and women become lovers, discovering their bodies anew, and come into the drama of their romantic phantasies, he found another falling in love, with pieces and parts, where there was no reciprocity. Beneath the surface, hidden in the heart, repressed from consciousness, he detected perversions, sexual acts and appetites in exile.

"The highest and the lowest in sexuality are everywhere most intimately connected," he observed.

.

Kaspar, who may have been Abraham, the poem tells us, is the old patriarchal order, Mage of the star-world above; as Mary Magdala represents the powers of the matriarchal world. In their meeting, an exchange takes place—he is initiated into the revelation of the sea, as she in turn has prepared for her becoming one of those whom the Son will bring with Him into the new Paradise. But now the persons change and Freud, the image of the sea-world of the unconscious, the initiate of the Libido, takes the place of Kaspar, and the poetess evoking the heavenly powers takes the place of the Sea-priestess. Between the man and the woman a work is begun, to bring up into the light certain banished elements of our being, to bring up the full confession of the heart into joy. "The Wedding of Heaven and Hell" Blake proposed. The mixture of many things in the configuration of the poem, the associational method in the psychoanalysis, bring the above into the below, the below into the above; and in time, we see they bring over the primal Paradise into the new.

·

In the weaving under and over of threads we bring these things from the light of the verso that men call Night into the Light of the face that men call Day.

·

Already, the hooters, who had hooted at Freud because they would keep sexual matters in the dark, use Freudian hoots to cast shame and darkness once more over our nature.

Rand or round? "It's a German word," Jess said, and searched out the dictionary to draw the sorts. "Will you draw the sorts?" "No! I don't want to know!" I replied, and then: "Yes. Give me the German."

: edge, brink / margin (of a book)

Sally Rand was marginal then. aus Rand und Band sein, be out of bounds, out of hand, be unmanageable.

den Rand halten : hold one's tongue, shut up.
bis zum Rande voll : brim-full.

Chapter 9

MARCH 22, 1961. Wednesday.

"Ne pas oublier un grand chapitre sur l'art de la divination par l'eau, les cartes, l'inspection de la main, etc." So Baudelaire writes in *Mon coeur mis à nu*, which now that it has come up, I begin to use in my own divinations. Finding my rhyme in the opening propositions of Baudelaire's essay: *"De la vaporisation et de la centralisation du* Moi." Where he, too, proposes to start *"n'importe où, n'importe comment, et le continuer au jour le jour, suivant l'inspiration du jour et de la circonstance, pourvu que l'inspiration soit vivre."*

•

To bring one thing into another as, primary to art, the painter draws from life until the object or person or scene selected informs his eye and hand, the painting a colloquy entertained. But I have in mind now the great conversation—conversion—of painting within painting: Picasso's bringing up Velasquez's masterpiece *Las Meninas* where the elements of that painting speak at Picasso's talking table, as in the beginning of his work Picasso had spoken in the language of El Greco to draw sentiments of hunger and cold, figures of an agony, from his own life in Montmartre. The martyrs of the religious heresy of art, of Bohemia, in the wake of Baudelaire and the Romantic agon appearing in the very style of those martyrs of the Catholic world that writhe in the canvases of El Greco in the wake of the Renaissance, where the sensuality of the

467

pagan revival and the all but Manichaean spirituality of the Reformation contend. As later, king now over a Spanish empire of painting, Picasso reiterates the splendor of the Prado in the splendor of his own palace *La Californie*. "The dog we see in his study of The Maids of Honor," Jaime Sabartes tells us, "is not the dog painted by Velasquez, but Picasso's dog. . . . Here and there, features of his intimates show up in the face of the Infanta or the faces of other figures. . . . When we look closely at these 'studies,' we have the feeling we are looking over Picasso's shoulder as he works, one day in a dark mood, relaxed on another, but always preoccupied in pursuit of an idea, a fugitive thought. . . . "

•

Picasso would divine his life in the depths of Velasquez's painting—but this life is his own sight in creation as the chiromancer would divine the lines of a life in the hand, following from figures seen towards fugitive ideas, or as any old gypsy reading the cards would call up the cast and numbers of scenes in which a play will begin. "Whenever I examined this painting closely," Sabartes says of the Velasquez in the Prado, "I always had the impression I was looking at a scene from a play. Was this because of the characters represented, their gestures and attitudes, and the court costumes of another epoch? Was it because of Velasquez's way of representing them, some suspicion of his motives in grouping them as he did?" Bringing into play a confusion of immediacies and mirrors of immediacies, Velasquez presents the eyes with a mystery of their point of view: behind the painter's back the figures of Philip IV and his queen appear reflected in a mirror so that we begin to realize that they must stand where we do, facing the painter—outside the canvas in its own representation, for we see in the painting the verso of the painting facing us and the painter's face is towards us as if he worked in a mirror; upon the walls of the room in the picture are copies (mirrors) by Mazo of originals by Rubens now in the hand of Velasquez.

•

Divination is working with things to release the content and form of a future or fate, sometimes bringing up what we choose upon a conscious impulse, sometimes drawing the sorts by chance to bring a foreign element into action. Here sorting and mixing are functions of a higher organization in which, troubled by my thought of Baudelaire's *Mon coeur mis à nu,* I begin to take thought in Baudelaire's thought. *"De la vaporisation et de la centralisation du* Moi," appears reflected almost as if contrived to fit the composition of my own reflections. And as I read Baudelaire the specter of my trouble with his trouble begins to come forward, as if in a mirror behind me as I work. He is a voice set into motion from a deck of fifty-two playing cards or from a tarot deck of seventy-eight, but this deck is another, of playing poets or voices of poetry. He has been brought into play as if by hazard; but in the configuration of the fifty-two cards or seventy-eight names of God, interrelated sequences and sets have been imagined that form such a tradition or interpretation of what Poetry is that every number moves towards order. Kurt Seligmann in *The Mirror of Magic* argues that the Tarot's "entire magic theory rests upon the belief that in nature there is no accident—that every happening in the universe is caused by a pre-established law," but in the poetic theory of our Tarot there is no accident, yet there is no pre-established law, for every happening destroys the law before it, moving as it does towards the creation of a law that will be established only in the composition of the whole.

•

When I spoke of H.D.'s being the Poetess and recalled too the charge of Pound's so-long-ago "refined, charming and utterly narrow-minded she-bard" and of Williams's "Hellenic perfection of style," I had in mind another specter—the genius of a woman that men would propitiate or exorcise. The Poetess was an enormous persona like the hieratic figures of women in the major arcana of the Tarot—*l'Impératrice, la Papesse*—who with the Juggler, the Emperor, the Pope, the Hermit, and the Fool, belong to a series of types brought forward from the later Medieval World (in which *la Papesse* may well be not Pope Joan but the Albigensian Esclarmonde, and the Fool may be the Parsival-Hero of twelfth century romances and fairy tales) into the Renaissance configuration. The Tarot, like the Hermetic charades of Catherine de Medici or the alchemical romances of the seventeenth century, provided the ground for the creative imagination to work in and its figures are projects of that creation. Poetry is another such matrix of surviving, evolving, and changing entities, and the Tarot, like Poetry, has periods and reformations. The Tarot I had in mind is not the Tarot of Marseilles, but the presentation belonging to the London of 1910 and the mysteries of the Order of the Golden Dawn, the Tarot drawn by Pamela Coleman Smith following A. E. Waite's prescriptions. *La Papesse* now is *The High Priestess,* recalling not Esclarmonde, but MacGregor Mathers's wife, Henri Bergson's sister, as Isis. The scenes on the lesser arcana might be from the great prose romances of William Morris, and in the idealization of its women, Birdalone and Elfhild mingle with the cult figures of Art Nouveau. Egyptianized to become the Book of Thoth in the eighteenth century, Hebrewized to become a Cabalistic text in the nineteenth, the cast of the original play survives, however costumed, in Waite's deck, but now the abstract numbers and impersonal face cards give way to illustrations, the cryptogram of numerical symbols becomes directly a romance or fairytale in moving pictures. Even as in poetry the Imagists were beginning to demand a clairvoyant art and to project scenes of enigmatic content—primary vision or insight, as in Pound's "April":

> Three spirits came to me
> And drew me apart
> To where the olive boughs
> Lay stripped upon the ground:
> Pale carnage beneath bright mist.

Slight as the imagist poem might seem to be, it has also the charge of a vision—it is a card predicting a poetry. In that passage from *A Packet for Ezra Pound* in which Yeats speaks of *The Cantos* he sees the sequences of that poem as sequences of cards: "I have often found there," he writes, "brightly printed kings, queens, knaves, but have never discovered why all the suits could not be dealt out in some quite different order," and when he tells us that Pound "has scribbled on the back of an envelope certain sets of letters that represent emotions or archetypal events . . . then each set of letters repeated, and then A B C D inverted and this repeated, and then a new element X Y Z, then certain letters that never recur . . . and all set whirling together," where "the Descent and the Metamorphosis—A B C D and J K L M—his fixed elements, took the place of the Zodiac, the archetypal persons—X Y Z—that of the Triumphs, and certain modern events—his letters that do not recur—that of those events in Cosimo Tura's day," Yeats envisions the order of *The Cantos* as being very much indeed like the laying out of cards in a divination.

∙

Taking the Major Arcana as a set of projected parts for the woman to play in a drama, the Tarot provides us with the two figures in the hierarchical order—the Empress and the Popess, two in the order of virtues or powers—Justice with her scales and sword and the virgin Strength forcing the lion's mouth. In the Marseilles deck the winged figure of *Témperance* is a woman; pouring water from one vessel into another, she may be pouring the Soul or Life from one body into another. In the Waite deck this figure has been re-formed to be "neither male nor female." We see her as a virtue, but she is linked in what we see to one of the two women who appear in the cosmic orders—the World, the figure of a dancing woman ("the rapture of the universe when it understands itself in God," Waite gives us), and the Star, the naked figure of a woman kneeling who pours water from two vessels, like Temperance then, but She returns the water of life or the soul to its elements or sources, from one vessel to the spring and from another to the earth.

∙

How far abroad have we gone, preoccupied in pursuit of this fugitive idea of the Poetess as a card in divination? H.D. is immersed from the period of The War Trilogy on in the lore of occultism, and it is not surprising that in a poetry that means to keep Hellenistic mysteries alive in the imagination, as in Freudian analysis the repressed is brought forward into the present consciousness, the emblems of Renaissance hermeticists, astrologers, and alchemists who mixed pagan and Christian images play their part. In "Nights," published in 1935, after H.D.'s analysis then, the protagonist Natalia Saunderson plays the Tarots with Felice Barton "an overblown queen of hearts or *(Tarots)* queen of cups," and there is a kind of emotional magic going on: "She tapped something in you," David says of Mrs. Barton.

"He understood, in his ridiculous way, everything," it seems to Natalia, "things she herself couldn't cope with." "No, she didn't," she tells him, "I mean, it was talking about those cards." And later, Natalia refers again to the cards: "She lent me those German Tarots. We had such fun, we spread out all the cards and that diluted sort of Burne-Jones English set I have."

.

In The War Trilogy, although alchemical and astrological lore enter into its synthesis, there is no use of Tarot. Thoth is evoked as patron of scribes, and in his Hellenistic identification with Hermes, as in *Tribute to the Angels,* he is patron of thieves and poets, but there is no *Book of Thoth,* that favorite Tarot fantasy of nineteenth century occultists, in H.D.'s poem, for she is relating faithfully a synthesis in which the Hellenistic Christos was born that knew nothing of Tarot. Though the opening scene of the City under Fire could have been related to the Tower; and the Moon, the Sun, Death, Judgment, the Devil, the Wheel of Fortune, the Lovers—all could have been resurrected in the meaning of the poem; though the High Priestess may correspond to the Lady of *Tribute to the Angels,* for she too holds a book ("The same—different—the same attributes, / different yet the same as before"), they do not enter in.

.

Yet the unfolding of the poem is very like a reading of cards. "An incident here and there" like a hint here and there in the first distribution of cards from which the Seeress will read what is happening. The ruin where the fallen roof leaves the room open to the sky, the tide pool, the worm on the leaf, the track in the sand from a tree in flower to a half-open hut-door, the bare early colonial meeting-house: these do not appear as *mise-en-scène* or as images in themselves to be captured but as elements of a language to be deciphered, as the chiromancer divines her meanings from the scenes of that deck Pamela Coleman Smith designed in the manner of Burne-Jones. The major arcana of this divination in H.D.'s trilogy will be the great powers of the Semitic,

Egyptian, Greek, and Magian worlds that mixed in the alembic of the Alexandrian imagination prepare the syntheses from which the powers of the Christian world will emerge.

•

But in this reading the meaning of things, as if conversant in dreams with the Presence or with Our Lady, having some poetic gnosis of the divine world, H.D., like Caedmon, commanded by the angel to sing something, or like the Ploughman, whom Blake saw releasing souls from their seeds to grow into the day, is inspired, reviving in the meaning of poet the spirit of shaman magic and vision. Something of the awesome remove of this order belongs to the imagined card of the Poetess, the title itself having that ambivalence of the sacred in which travesty and honor contend.

•

The Poetess like the Popess is a disturbing persona; like the woman Mary of Magdala, who is "a great tower," she is a demoniac, for her simple humanity is contaminated by genius.

•

The daimones of Mary Magdala are female powers—Lilith, Eve, and one before them, from the Hebraic orders, and the great goddesses of the classical world. The one before Lilith and Eve in the teachings of Jewish Gnosticism may be Sophia, the Daughter of God, whom the Samarian Simon claimed reincarnated in his Helen. But, as for man or woman the Muse remains female, the genius is male. As Maker or Poet the man, like God, creates; and the idea of the Poetess as Creatrix is again like the Popess—Pope Joan—the idea of a woman as a pretender to manhood, a disturbing sex magic. Men live uneasily with or under the threat of genius in women.

•

In the ballad *The Queen O' Crow Castle* the poetess Helen Adam takes over from folklore such a tale of a man winning a possessed queen, where here I would see the drama of sexual love that would conquer a demoniacally inspired woman. The hero has a genius of his own: "He walks wi' an angel baith morning and night" that casts fear of sex, for "Nae lassie daur step 'neath the stir o' those wings." This angel of Callastan's has his counterpart in the *deil* of the Queen O' Crow Castle; both are the solitude, the genius of the poet. To the would-be lover of the Queen her genius appears as a demon-rival:

> Fire,
>> Fire,
>>> Fire fierce and red.
> The gay fires o' danger in the dark o' her bed.

·

"L'eternelle Vénus (caprice, hystérie, fantaisie) est une des formes séduisantes du diable," Baudelaire writes.

·

In Courbet's great canvas *L'atelier du peintre* of 1855, humanity is gathered in its types about the studio of the painter. "The metamorphosis of womanhood," Werner Hofmann tells us in his *The Earthly Paradise,* "is distributed over various parts of the picture. We have the mother, and not far from her the harlot still dressed in her plain country clothes (to the right behind the grave-digger's top-hat); and we have the central figure of 'Truth'." In addition to these Courbet had originally painted in the elemental female figure, the animal-like *femme fatale,* giving her the features of Jeanne Duval, the mistress of Baudelaire.

·

Mon coeur mis à nu was written between 1859 and 1866. In the high romantic fashion of the day there was a cult of the *femme fatale,* and for Baudelaire the fascination of women had a powerful and threatening psychic reality. But thruout the nineteenth century, the Popess changing into the High Priestess, this persona is persistent: Helen, Seraphita, Kundry, Lilith, She. In the formative years of H.D.'s generation, women were fighting to free themselves from the bondage they felt in such stereotypes, to take their places as equals of men; yet these were also the high years of Art Nouveau, when the powers of women to charm, to enthrall, and even to enslave, were portrayed everywhere. In the battle for women's rights, women's powers would seem like powers of darkness, a tyrannical myth, against which the light of reason must strive. With the World War common sense seemed to have won, and the Mom, the Career-Woman, and the Model to have taken the place of the Eternal Female. The flat planes and straight lines, the functionalism, of the modern seemed to have cast into permanent disrepute the devious courses of Art Nouveau. The analytic functionalism of Freud's psychology seemed to have exposed at last to the light of day the shadowy demons of hysteria and dream. A new Oedipus had overthrown the Sphinx—for the answer to her dark riddle was "the Oedipus complex"—and Thebes was freed from the pestilence of neurosis. In the twenties and thirties, the emancipated, shedding the passionate masks of man's ancient dramas, hoped to be cured of tragic fate. So the Old Man in Yeats's last play *The Death of Cuchulain* rants against the modern and spits upon the dancers painted by Degas—"above all upon that chambermaid face"—for the women who could dance Emer are gone. "I am old, I belong to mythology," he says: "I could have got such a dancer once, but she has gone; the tragi-comedian dancer, the tragic dancer, upon the same neck love and loathing, life and death."

•

Not only in art, but with Bachofen's *Das Mutterrecht* in 1861 in the revision of history the nineteenth century image of woman took hold. Back of the caprice, hysteria, fantasy—the psychic entity in men's minds of woman as all powerful—and back of the other figure, the pure, higher, suffering Psyche-woman, in the primal myths Bachofen found hints and certainties of a war in which Mother-rule was overthrown by Father-rule. Before the Father-Gods, Jehovah or Zeus, and their law, Bachofen argued, there had been the Mother-Goddess and her law; before History, there had been Nature.

Digging into her realms, under earth, into the prehistory of caves and middenheaps, men searched to bring up once more long forgotten images of what woman was—at Willendorf, at Lespugue. Scholars and archaeologists making finds at Ur and Minos, at Mycenae and Malta, brought a visual reality to the romantic idea of the Mother of the Gods.

"Delve into the deepest depths to reach them," Mephistopheles says to Faust in Goethe's phantasmagoria when Faust would seek the Mothers— that was in the twenties of the nineteenth century.

So too from old wives' tales and from heretical texts in the swarming ground of Gnostic and hermetic belief from which Jews, Christians, and Moslems had drawn, scholars of Greek and Coptic found, where texts spoke of deep things, teachings concerning a femality in God, a person who was Mother or Wisdom or Glory, a daughter but also a mother of God. It was as if the oldest mysteries had returned to take up their stand in woman just as the new rationalism of modernity promised to free her. As if an ancient image were taking over, even in the citadel of Roman Catholicism where the Mother of God was to be advanced in the dogma of Her Immaculate Conception and Her Assumption. The giant head of Kore was rising again into the identity of woman.

•

With *King Jesus* in 1946 and *The White Goddess* in 1948, Robert Graves, a poet antagonistic to Yeats as to Pound—and I would take it ignorant of H.D.'s War Trilogy—advanced a grammar of myth where Mary Magdalene appears as a Great Queen or Fate ("In *Tom o' Bedlam's Song* she is Tom's Muse—Merry Mad Maud.") and where that refrain "Lilith born before Eve / and one born before Lilith, and Eve; we three" began to be explicated. According to Graves the Semitic goddess Michal of Hebron was Adam's creatrix; but then from gnostic sources he goes on to identify the Virgin Mary with Michal and in turn from the Essene Ebionites with a female Holy Spirit. "We have come to be governed by the unholy triumvirate of Pluto god of wealth, Apollo god of science and Mercury god of thieves," Graves protests. There can be no end to the present miserable condition "until the repressed desire of the Western races, which is for some practical form of Goddess worship, with her love not limited to maternal benevolence and her afterworld not deprived of a Sea, finds satisfaction at last."

•

Horace Gregory tells us in the lore of contemporary poets that Graves and the poetess Laura Riding had inscribed above their bed: "God Is

A Woman." It became the epigraph of my suite of heresies (of gnostic orthodoxies) *Medieval Scenes* before I had read *King Jesus,* indeed, before *The White Goddess* was written. I had found the lore of Morgan le Fay in the Freudian Roheim's *The Riddle of the Sphinx,* but then, as this book must have suggested, I had come to live in the ambience of such meanings and H.D.'s twentieth century Gnostic "Tale of a Jar or Jars" had opened the way.

•

"Woman is not a poet: she is either a Muse or she is nothing," Graves argues and then explains that he does not mean that a woman should not write but that she should "either be a silent Muse and inspire the poets by her womanly presence, as Queen Elizabeth and the Countess of Derby did, or she should be the Muse in a complete sense; she should be in turn Arianrhod, Blodeuwedd and the Old Sow of Maenawr Penarrd who eats her farrow, and should write in each of these capacities with antique authority."

•

Sometime in the Spring of 1942 I chanced upon a copy of Laura Riding's *Progress of Stories* and within the year had come so under the spell of her authority or the authority of her spell—she confounded the two—that I could feel her scorn over my poetic fumblings until I ceased, the poet in me abashed as the force of her seeing thru what poets made of poetry became more persuasive. In the characters of Lilith Outcome, Lady Port-Huntlady, Frances Cat, or the Indescribable Witch, Laura Riding projected masks of herself as their creatrix, a woman self-banished into a female critical mentality to stand opposite the male humanity of God in a creation removed into a humorous existence by or from the Creation. In "Their Last Interview," God is "tired as ever of his uncompletedness," "his ministry of sympathies," and "anxious to fade back into humanity"; Miss Lilith Outcome is delighted by his tolerance of her existence. "Then you quite forgive me for being more correct?" she asks. "I haven't your authoritative touch," He replies.

Miss Riding would have nothing to do with talk of Muses; it was, she argued, a dishonesty that obscured the right reasons of poetry.

"Poets have attributed the compulsion of poetry to forces outside themselves—" she wrote in the Preface to her *Collected Poems* in 1938, "to divinities, muses, and, finally, even to such humanistic muses as Politics . . . The nineteenth-century lament was: 'Where is the Bard?' The twentieth-century version is: 'Where is the Muse?' In America: 'where is the Myth?'"

In her argumenting Laura Riding could play the Old Sow of Maenawr Penarrd very well indeed, devouring the world if need be. She liked playing Witch, Mrs. Story, Dame Death, and Poetry Herself, and talking with men who would be poets like an older and naturally superior sister. In Graves's life between 1927 and the outbreak of the Second World War, she was Queen Tyrant of his thought. "There was thereupon a unity to which you and I pledged our faith," he writes in the "Dedicatory Epilogue to Laura Riding" from the 1930 edition of *Goodbye to All That:* "How we went together to the land where the dead parade the streets and there met demons and returned with demons still treading behind. And how they drove us up and down the land." Before the White Goddess was, Laura Riding was.

•

There was a way of gaining correctness and authority that Laura Riding sought in putting away uncompletedness, humanity, the ministry of sympathies. She became obsessed with the proper use of poetic faculties, the right reasons for poetry, and sometime after her *Collected Poems* in 1938 writing poetry at all came to seem impossible. She set about making a dictionary to free words from their corrupting associations, still driven up and down the land by demons.

I.

There was the trouble with names and bound up with that the trouble with what a man and a woman was. Beyond the democratic man-voice of Williams or the exalted or ecstatic woman-voice of H.D., there was in one direction the possibility Laura Riding exemplifies—the tyranny of style over the matter of life, the poet's removal from the contaminating medium, where eventually the language itself seems an Augean stable of meanings one does not want to mean. Graves too in his grammar of myth strives to restore—"the unimprovable original, not a synthetic substitute"—the true language of poetry from the corruptions of other men's uses. "What ails Christianity is that the old Mother-Goddess religious theme and the new Almighty-God theme are fundamentally irreconcilable. Catholicism is not a religion based squarely on a single myth; it is a complex of juridical decisions, often contradictory, made under political pressure in an age-long law suit between Goddess and God." This fundamentalism, intolerance of contradictions, single-mindedness, sets Laura Riding and Robert Graves at odds with the pluralistic, many-minded poetry of Pound, Williams, or H.D., where there is not one myth alone but a gathering of myths. Here the poet does not see the language as a system but as a community of meanings as deep and as wide as the nature of man has been, and he seeks not rightness but the surrender of style to the feeling of words and associations. To become impure with life, if need be.

•

In the "suddenly we saw your name / desecrated" passage of *Tribute to the Angels* xi-xii in an alchemical alembic of the poem a flame burns between the star Venus and venery or "desire is venereous" to sublimate the name until the word "to venerate, / venerator" is restored. But following the word "venereous" the name passes thru the blackness of its contradiction:

> while the very root of the word shrieks
> like a mandrake when foul witches pull
>
> its stem at midnight,
> and rare mandragora itself
>
> is full, they say, of poison,
> food for the witches' den.

The poet may have meant to rescue the name Venus from its desecrations—"knaves and fools / have done you impious wrong," she protests; but in the actual operation of the poem not only is the name brought to its sublimation but it has been brought thru its *nigredo*. We are meant to remember the lurid scene of witches' sex magic in which the root of the word (Venus) appears as a phallic mandrake full of seminal poison— an image from the underworld of the mind, the more potent because we may remember now also from Hesiod's account of the origin of Aphrodite that she grew from the white foam of the penis of Ouranos which Chronos had cut off and cast in the sea, and that men called her Philomedes "member-loving" "because she sprang from the members."

.

The important thing here is not only the sublimation but the accumulation of experience in that sublimation, the union of opposites, yes, but also the having passed thru the dialectic of these opposites. Here again we are in the tradition of the Gnostic cults that in The War Trilogy has begun to inform H.D.'s mythopoeic thought. Hans Jonas in *The Gnostic Religion* gives us from Irenaeus's report the teaching of Carpocrates that "the souls in their transmigrations through bodies must pass through every kind of life and every kind of action" and, again: "their souls before departing must have made use of every mode of life and must have left no remainder of any sort still to be performed: lest they must again be sent into another body because there is still something lacking to their freedom." We might see in a new light the evolution thru the spiral of animal forms that the Psyche claims in *The Walls Do Not Fall* and the passionate yearning for opposites—"the insatiable longing / in winter, for palm-shadow / and sand and burnt sea-drift"—in *The Flowering of the Rod*. This doctrine of salvation as freedom thru the fulfillment of all servitudes under all powers is at least near the concept of The War Trilogy. Jonas points out that the doctrine of Carpocrates is one of the antecedents of mediaeval Satanism and of the Renaissance Faustian myth. My reading of the mandrake-mandragora passage then not as a protest but as a bringing in of the phallic *nigredo* to the poem has in mind H.D.'s Freudian persuasion and also her Gnostic sympathies. We may read in the light (or darkness) of the Carpocration creed the "parasite, I find nourishment: / when you cry in disgust, / a worm on the leaf" in *The Walls Do Not Fall;* the "I am yet unrepentant" is not a cry of defiance against the Father in a Protestant belief that sin is an act against God, but a resolution of acceptance of experience in a Gnostic belief that all human life is a manifestation of the Father's creative will. Mary Magdalene in *The Flowering of the Rod* does not repent to put away, but the demons cast out of her, the poem tells us, "were now unalterably part of the picture." Lilith, the carrion owl-goddess, the Satanic female, is "forgiven," taken into the new dispensation.

•

The imagination raises images of what a man is or what a woman is again and again in order to come into the shape of our actual life; or it seems in order that we come to live in terms of imagined being where we act not in our own best interest but in order to create fate or beauty or drama. The Christos and the Magdalene-Ishtar of The War Trilogy are persons in whom the divine may become real for H.D.; they are begotten in a matrix of the word's "mediation" where "Dream" and "Vision" are at work. They are begotten in the operation of the poem in which they occur then, thru which they come into our consciousness, and H.D. is very much aware of this. Reality is not only received but also created, a creation in which the poet, the language, the beings who have arisen in man's dreams and vision as far as we know them, all participate as creators of a higher reality.

•

Robert Graves is most consciously concerned in *King Jesus* or in *The White Goddess* with correcting the image of Jesus from its creative flux; the mode of his Muse is argumentative. He protests that his Jesus is not an entity of the imagination—tho for him dream and vision are the sources of authority, and his Jesus is drawn as is H.D.'s from Gnostic and cabbalistic traditions—but an actual entity to be discovered only once righteous reason has rendered him free from imaginative accretions. In Grave's knotted reason, like most Christians he cannot accept the Christos Who belongs entirely to the realm of desire and creative will but he demands the verification of an historical Jesus.

•

The Christos in The War Trilogy and the persona of Mary Magdalene, though they arise from a common ground of lore with Graves's Jesus and Mary Magdalene, are closer to the story entities of D. H. Lawrence's *The Man Who Died,* where we are concerned with the imaginary life of Jesus as "Reborn, he was in the other life, the greater day of the human consciousness." In this new life, the Lawrencian Jesus turns away from his being the Master, putting away "the young, flamy, unphysical exalter," and living in a nausea, awaiting his physical awakening. In Lawrence's Madeleine we see not the aloof lady of *The Flowering of the Rod* but another person of H.D.'s, the "I" of *The Walls Do Not Fall,* who cries in *The Man Who Died,* "Master! . . . Oh, we have wept for you! And will you come back to us?" In the curious turn of Lawrence's vision, the spiritual man—but Lawrence does not say the spiritual man, he says the "unphysical" man—is the old dead self and the physical man, the indwelling in the body's awareness, is the new. For Madeleine, the woman who worships him as the Messiah, he has pity and revulsion, a nausea of disillusion. In the new life a second figure of the woman appears, the priestess of Isis, who attends not his image but the image of the woman's powers. In the first part of *The Man Who Died* the crow of the cock may be the Word, the young cock Master of his hens "tipping his head, listening to the challenge of far-off unseen cocks, in the unknown world. Ghost voices, crowing at him mysteriously out of limbo." When the Lady of Isis presses him to her in the ritual of healing the wounds: "the wailing died out altogether, and there was a stillness, and darkness in his soul, unbroken dark stillness, wholeness."

•

So at last he saw the light of her silk lanthorn swinging, coming intermittent between the trees, yet coming swiftly. She was alone, and near, the light softly swishing on her mantle-hem. And he trembled with fear and with joy, saying to himself: I am almost more afraid of this touch than I was of death. For I am more nakedly exposed to it.

Life, here, is the revelation of Isis thru her priestess: "dimlit, the god-dess-statue stood surging forward, a little fearsome, like a great woman-presence urging." Not in their selves but in the presences of Isis and Osiris they meet.

•

He had been, before, the Messiah, the spirit of the crisis in self, the great Critic or Savior, but now, as he tells Madeleine: "I am glad it is over, and the day of my interference is done." Beyond lies the other, "the greater day of the human consciousness." "My public life is over," he says, "the life of my self-importance."

•

In *The Walls Do Not Fall* the Messiah or the Christ is not the embodiment of a self-importance or Messianic inflation of the ego that Lawrence saw in him. Love, itself, was for D. H. Lawrence mixed with the day of interference. For H.D. He comes as a new Master over Love; but this Christos, like Lawrence's *Man Who Died,* must be freed from "old thought, old convention," the nausea of His false image "of pain-worship and death-symbol"; and, like Lawrence's Christ again, H.D.'s Christ passes thru this stage to be united with the person of Osiris. As, in turn, we can see the Mary Magdala of *The Flowering of the Rod* as the psyche-woman "I" transformed in the magic of the daemons of womanhood—Isis among them—like the Priestess in *The Man Who Died,* belonging to the greater day of the human consciousness.

•

The more correctness, the authoritative touch of Laura Riding's Lilith Outcome, the "mania of cities and societies and hosts, to lay a compulsion upon a man, upon all men" in which Lawrence's *Man Who Died* had had his share—and the concern with what shall and shall not be included in literature, with arbitration and the exemplary, that has made for our Age of Criticism—this critical superego is embodied in H.D.'s Simon, as the Poet may be embodied in Kaspar.

> But Simon the host thought,
> we must draw the line somewhere;

•

It is not fair, H.D. tells us, to compare Simon with Kaspar, for Simon

> was not conditioned to know
> that these very devils or *daemons,*
>
> as Kaspar would have called them,
> were now unalterably part of the picture;

.

We are concerned here with the *daemons* or *genii* of the woman, her powers as a creative artist. Simon, like Kaspar, in the poem is one of the dramatis personae—he, too, is unalterably part of the story. In the conception of the whole fabric there is, unalterably part, a contentious demon, an adversary—the "Dev-ill" of *The Walls Do Not Fall,* "tricked up like Jehovah." We hear his voice in the legion that the poet answers in her passages of apology. He appears in the third person plural *they* of "charms are not, they said, grace" and of "we fight, they say, for breath, / so what good are your scribblings?" Is he then, the Spirit of our New Criticism, the one addressed as "Sword" in *The Walls Do Not Fall?*

> you are the younger brother, the latter-born,
>
> your Triumph, however exultant,
> must one day be over.

.

In *The Flowering of the Rod* Kaspar, who knows the story the stars tell, what is "now unalterably part of the picture," knows:

> the first actually to witness His life-after-death,
> was an unbalanced, neurotic woman,

The myrrh which he carries in the jar is also the genius and the gospel or lore of the poem itself. In *The Walls Do Not Fall* words, we were told, were little boxes that hid or kept meaning; as stars were "little jars of that indisputable / and absolute Healer, Apothecary . . . to hold further / unguent, myrrh." So, now:

though the jars were sealed,
the fragrance got out somehow,

and the rumour was bruited about,

"fragrance" and "rumor" are identified. Kaspar, the Mage, bringing his
gifts in recognition of the birth of the Christ Child brings (fragrance/
rumor) the gospel of the Christ-Life as a present in the beginning:

or another—Kaspar could not remember;

but Kaspar thought, there were always two jars,
the two were always together,

why didn't I bring both?
or should I have chosen the other?

·

The two myrrhs or two genii refer on one level to the two tradi-
tions of Christ—the Christ of the exoteric Church and the Christ of
the esoteric Mysteries. They may refer too to the Law of the Father-
God and to the Realm of the Mothers; for Kaspar brings his essence
from the tradition of patriarchal Zoroastrian shepherd kings, and the
essence which Mary Magdalene comes for, related to "those alabaster
boxes / of the Princesses of the Hyksos Kings," is the odor of her own,
"incense-flower of the incense-tree," and of the sea. The two not at
war but mixed; once separated, but now reunited in the birth of the
Christ-Child.

So Proclus in his Commentaries upon Plato's myth of Atlantis tells
us that it is a myth of two orders in the ancient world: "beginning from
the Gods, of Olympian and Titanic divinities" or

beginning from the intellect, of permanency and motion, or sameness
and difference; or from souls, of the rational and irrational; or from bod-
ies, of heaven and generation; or in whatever other way you may divide
essences, according to all divisions, all the genus of those within the pil-
lars of Hercules will be analogous to the better, but of those without to
the less excellent co-ordination of things.

"It was always maintained / that one jar was better than the other," Kaspar remembers in the poem:

> but he grumbled and shook his head,
>
> no one can tell which is which,
> now your great-grandfather is dead.

For H.D. heralds the mingling of the essences, the confusion of the traditions, in the first century, echoing the neo-Platonic confusions of the fifth century, in the twentieth century. "Hence," Proclus concludes:

> whether you are willing Orphically to arrange the Olympian and Titanic genera in opposition to each other, and to celebrate the former as subduing the latter; or Pythagorically, to perceive the two co-ordinations proceeding from on high, as far as to the last of things, and the better adorning the subordinate rank; or Platonically, to survey much of infinity and much of bound in the universe, as we learn in the Philebus, and the whole of infinity in conjunction with the measures of bound, producing generation, which extends through all mundane natures,—from all these, you may assume one thing, that the whole composition of the world is co-harmonized from this contrariety.

.

Kaspar, like Simon, was disturbed by the thought of a woman, but he cannot exclude her. In the mingling of the myrrhs in one jar there was the mingling of sexes: the Christ uniting not only the contrary orders of history and prehistory, Athens and Atlantis, but as the new Adam uniting again the Eve and Adam. Nowhere does H.D. fuse male and female in one body, except in the implied fusion here in the identity of the Child. Not only Simon, who abhors the female, but Kaspar, who is troubled by her but moved to ecstasy in her presence, remains male; as Mary Magdalene remains ultimately female. Yet "though the jars were sealed, / the fragrance got out somehow / and the rumour was bruited about"—in the most real the two were always at one. H.D. would have found such a tradition in the neo-Platonists, or in the Kabbalistic tradition of the *Adama Kadmon;* she must have come upon it in the period of her psychoanalytic conversion, for the psychic bi-sexuality of man is an axiom of Freud's. There was also, more immediate to our study here, the fact that a woman's genius had come into the genius of the Poet thru her own operations as poet in this work.

•

In *Tribute to Freud,* writing of the signet or "sign-manual—the royal signature, usually only the initials of the sovereign's name," she suddenly sees that her writing signet, her H.D., has something "remotely suggesting sovereignty or the royal manner." The initials H.D. present the suggestion of a hidden identity, something more poetic certainly than the immediate plainness of Hilda Doolittle. But were those initials in the beginning not only this but also to suggest the Poet, without suggesting a woman, to help the reader to overlook or confuse the gender of the writer?

•

"Averse to personal publicity," Charlotte Bronte wrote in her 1850 preface to Emily Bronte's *Wuthering Heights,* "we veiled our own names under those of Currer, Ellis, and Acton Bell; the ambiguous choice being dictated by a sort of conscientious scruple at assuming Christian names positively masculine. We had a vague impression that authoresses are liable to be looked on with prejudice."

•

Aroused to battle by the claims of *genius* wherever they are made—for *genius* is itself of the old titanic order—male guardians of the literary Olympus have been the more aroused when the titaness appears, with the sense that

> it was unseemly that a woman
> appear disordered, dishevelled;
>
> it was unseemly that a woman
> appear at all.

for the dominance of man's rules must be maintained over woman's realm. Woman, identified with the whole Atlantean sequence of disorder, irrationality, change—Dame Mutabilitie herself—may be permitted to operate in her place, if it is clear that hers is the inferior claim. Gertrude Stein, Dorothy Richardson, Dame Edith Sitwell, H.D., Mary Butts, coactive in the avant-garde of the nineteen-twenties with Joyce, Pound, Eliot, Lawrence, and Williams, form in the conventional estimate a second rank, and where their work has exceeded that allotment their presumption has been bitterly attacked and derided. Marianne Moore who established early and definitely the propriety of her claims has escaped the worst censure. Laura Riding who argued the superiority of her reasons in Poetry over the false and distorted reasons of other poets was ridden out of town. With Dame Edith Sitwell her presumption of noble class as well as of sibylline genius and gender added to the fury of status-conscious verse-writing and reviewing professors of English Literature. Even Virginia Woolf, wrapped round as she was by the genteel literary guarantee of the Bloomsbury group and writing as a sensitive and sensible adherent of their high civilization, smarted under the goads that would keep woman in her place.

·

But there is, too, a deeper suspicion, not only that men are prejudiced to keep their dominance in the society but that men find genius itself unwomanly, unmanly. Women too have had that fear and then envy or hostility towards genius in men. Strindberg, Joyce, Lawrence, Williams have given expression of their creative isolation even in marriage, and defend or apologize for the shadowy other daemonic male being.

In sexual love between man and man, where there is creative genius, where the lovers have their daemons, there may be a counterpart to the Isis between the man and the woman in Lawrence's *The Man Who Died* or to the new Master over Love in H.D.'s *Trilogy*—a God, governor of the creative powers in whom they love. Thus, Socrates, who has his daemon, argues that love is most true when addressed in the name of the First Beloved, the One because of Whom we love. He, like Christ, is a Sun, or is the Love the Sun has for us. Apollo Musagêtes, Leader of the Muses, of the female powers, and Director of the Genii, of the male powers. Whitman called him "the President of Regulation."

So too, in sexual love between man and woman Christian magic teaches not falling in love but rising in love to a mutual love in God, where Christ is the First Beloved. To exorcize the daemonic or to compose the daemonic.

·

The narrative of The War Trilogy is the story of the restitution, of the daemonic and of woman, cursed by the Fathers, into the sight of God or among the Goods. It is the story told in George MacDonald's *Lilith* in the nineteenth century. The bringing up into the fullness of the Self of the most disturbing contents, of what the persona most fears.

As poets in the romantic tradition have identified with Lucifer (Milton unconsciously, Blake and Hugo, then, consciously) and sought the wedding of heaven and hell, the poetess H.D. identifies with a Mary Magdalen who brings up all outcast spirit into the new dispensation.

It is the prostitute; it is *venery, venereous, venerate, venerator* in the star Venus, the same light that shines so brilliantly just after the sun has gone down or just before the sun rises, Hesperus at sundown or Phosphorus at dawn, Lucifer-Venus. It is the card of our Tarot reading then—*L'Étoile*. It is Mary of Magdala, where:

through my will and my power,
Mary shall be myrrh;

·

But this will and this power, this Mary and this myrrh is the genius of the poem, the genius of the jar.

It is not only Mary in the presence of the Wise Man, seeing as he does "it was unseemly that a woman / appear at all . . . ," it is the poetic or daemonic creativity of the woman. "Turned towards the world," Jung writes in *The Archetypes and the Collective Unconscious,* "the anima is fickle, capricious, moody, uncontrolled, and emotional, sometimes gifted with daemonic intuitions, ruthless, malicious, untruthful, bitchy, double-faced, and mystical."

·

"*La femme est* naturelle, *c'est-à-dire abominable,*" Baudelaire confesses. "*Aimer les femmes intelligentes est un plaisir de pederaste.*" "*J'ai toujours été étonné qu'on laissât les femmes entrer dans les eglises.*"

•

It is not only the lady, in whom this gospel says were seven daemons forgiven—Isis, Astarte, Cyprus—Lilith, one born before Lilith, and Eve—and back of them Gemeter or Demeter. Earth-mother and Venus. . . . It is not only this *woman* kissing the feet of Him Whom they call Master, but it is the woman H.D. too, this *poetess,* with her presumption—the poem itself—it is, was, will be to some unseemly that she be there at all.

•

We may see then behind or over or included in the scene between the Wise Man Kaspar and the Fallen Woman Mary another scene. Let us not imagine now a critic—the distaste of the fundamentally unsympathetic and then antagonistic Fitts or Jarrell must not stand for the caution, the discretion, that Kaspar with his tradition and profound gender carries. It must be the poet Williams or the poet Pound or the poet Baudelaire then that confronts the poetess:

> he drew aside his robe in a noble manner
> but the un-maidenly woman did not take the hint;
>
> she had seen nobility herself at first hand;
> nothing impressed her, it was easy to see;
>
> she simply didn't care whether he acclaimed
> or snubbed her—or worse; what are insults?

•

"*De la nécessité de battre les femmes,*" Baudelaire writes. He is not writing here his heart stripped bare. He is not writing that fiery book that Poe had proposed. "No man dares write it," Poe had said, "true to its title."

But Baudelaire's own daemon projects the persona of the dandy; he strives for the telling *mot,* the keys of a Baudelairean attitude. He is a *litterateur.* It is a disease of the French literary world that infects Cocteau in his phantasy and Artaud in his madness alike. They hear or sound the currency of their own phrases ringing upon a stage and let their masks speak what they will.

But: "*Quelles conversation peuvent-elles avoir avec Dieu?*" he asks.

•

As Simon in H.D.'s story of the hidden essence, questioning the Master's allowing her to kiss His feet, may question the gift she brings:

this man if he were a prophet, would have known
who and what manner of woman this is.

II.

In "Murex" the poetess Raymonde Ransome has a pen-name Ray Bart. We find ourselves in the story in the mixing ground of two persons, the woman and the poet, of what we are in the actual real and what we are in the real of the imagination. There is the atmosphere of London itself: "an ineffable quality of merging so that one never knew the barrier of day or night" that relates to a state of suspension in the story, the "cocoon-blur of not-thinking that was her fixed and static formula for London."

We are at the inception of a poem. In the stream-of-consciousness two things impend. For Raymonde Ransome there is a recall, the bringing up of an old betrayal with associations involving the loss of a child in birth and with the loss of a lover. For Ray Bart, there is a poem impending, and these losses now are gains in intensity.

•

"Raymonde Ransome had wanted to drift and dream through the obliterating afternoon. Nothing to do but listen, nothing in London to do but wait. Listen to what? Wait for what?"

•

It was, in 1926, a prose prepared to find its way along lines of association. The process we have now in the verb "to dig" had begun. Opening distances back of things, as Proust had, or digging to uncover layers of meaning as Jane Harrison had in her *Prolegomena* and in *Themis,* or searching out psychological levels as Freud had, writers sought a new syntax that could provide shifting perspectives in consciousness.

.

Somewhere, working on *Mrs. Dalloway* or on *The Waves,* Virginia Woolf had the sensation of digging out a space in which her characters had their existence. "Whenever I make a mark," she says of working on *The Waves,* "I have to think of its relation to a dozen others." These are the rudiments of a projective-feeling in writing, of composition by field. August 30th, 1923, she writes of *Mrs. Dalloway* in progress: "*The Hours* and my discovery: how I dig out beautiful caves behind my characters: I think that gives exactly what I want; humanity, humor, depth. The idea is that the caves shall connect and each comes to daylight in the present moment." Monday, October 15th: "It took me a year's groping to discover what I call my tunneling process, by which I tell the past by installments, as I have need of it . . . One feels about in a state of misery—indeed, I made up my mind one night to abandon the book—and then one touches the hidden spring. . . . "

.

It was to touch the hidden spring, "that the caves shall connect and each comes to daylight in the present moment," that I read *Ulysses* or *The Tempest,* the *De Vulgari Eloquentia* of Dante or "The Guest" of H.D.—as I read cards, water, signs in dreams or the tenor of life around me—not to find what art is but thru the art to find what life might be.

.

How Virginia Woolf labors at her art, suffers under the thought of what her writing might be worth as literature. Her journal reveals, if our reflection or common rumor had not told us before, that she labored to bring forth her own life out of a dark place. There is: "I was walking up Bedford Place is it—the straight street with all the boarding houses this afternoon—and I said to myself spontaneously, something like this. How I suffer. And no one knows how I suffer, walking up the street, engaged with my anguish, as I was after Thoby died—alone; fighting something alone. And when I come indoors it is all so silent—" Against which, the elaborate structure must hold. The art draws upon the anguish, brings illuminations that lift the heart up, breaks thru to the light; the art draws the writer up out of the anguish into the writing, setting into motion what had been the matter as if frozen underground.

●

The cards when we read them, anyway, open fearful ways into the light of day: the goat of Mendes, the card of abject grief, the inversions of goods, the cards that show my own soul swollen with vanity or darkened in deceit—these were parts of the ideogram drawn out of the Tarot reading for this book.

●

In every story of the soul there is this anguish of giving birth to one's self. For Virginia Woolf and for James Joyce those cards were dark at the end of life, darkened by the beginning. As in *Between the Acts:* "Isa let her sewing drop. The great hooded chairs had become enormous. And Giles too . . . It was the night before roads were made or houses. It was the night that dwellers in caves had watched from some high place among the rocks." Or in *Finnegans Wake:* "it's old and old it's sad and old it's sad and weary I go back to you, my cold father, my cold mad father . . . One in a thousand of years of the nights?"

●

The content of the dream, that Freud tells us must be read as a pictographic script. Or, as Schrödinger tells us in his essay upon the nature of life: "this tiny speck of material, the nucleus of the fertilized egg . . . contains an elaborate code-script involving all the future development of the organism." The cast of the play or the members of the major arcana of the Tarot, the themes and persons of the poet, the periods and recurrences of dark and light of the artist—likewise in a configuration of events we have our own unique patterns or soul stories. But in the works of man, in the testimony of painting, music, and writing I find an other self as if I belonged to a larger language where minds and spirits awaken sympathies in me, a commune of members in which myself seems everywhere translated. If there are, as Freud argues, no memories from childhood but only memories referring to childhood, it is not surprising that all writing that contributes to one's consciousness in the present belongs to one's own past, or is lost.

•

What I am trying to get across is that just as there are threads weaving H.D.'s trilogy *The Walls Do Not Fall, Tribute to the Angels,* and *The Flowering of the Rod* to form a moving coherence, out of and into the lore of the human past—in art what Schrödinger called in physics "an aperiodic solid"—a ministry of sympathies, so, the three works are in turn one articulated cell of a larger fabric. These almost extraneous sorts I have drawn out of Virginia Woolf and Joyce, out of Baudelaire, out of my dreams—the *Sally Rand* theme then, and the "aroused" being a key, to remember "aroused" as well as "excited" and "inspired"—refer to some larger form or soul-self of which all of H.D. comes to be a part. To which I belong, in which I have my present/presence or womb of myself.

•

Thru time this fabric extends. It is my own creation as I mistake it. I have never found another human being who does not exclude from his fabric some star of first magnitude in mine; who does not include in first magnitude some "blindspot" or "aversion" of mine.

•

Yet just this tissue is the cosmic extension of the aperiodic solid of me. These are the works whereby I have come to know the Work. Thus have I bound Tiamat; in this series, out of these stuffs come into my code-script.

•

There is no such unique net of being, no code-script, that does not dance in the outpouring rays of the stars, no knot of my work that does not tremble between truth and falsity as it touches the human fabric that extends thru time.

This net is not now my creation but my creator. Where the caves or the cold feary mad father of the "earliest" memories of the Fathers reappear in other caves that "come to daylight at the present moment."

.

Freud in "Screen Memories" gives us a vision of men weaving the past as the tissue of the present. That is all a tissue of lies, yes—of the imagination. But then there was "when they are tested (by the recollections of adults)." There are tests or trials in which the communal fabric becomes the over-truth.

.

Heraklitus said of our great imaginary web or fabrication or reality of realities: "God is day and night, winter and summer, war and peace, surfeit and hunger. But he undergoes transformations, just as fire, when it is mixed with spices, is named after the savor of each."

.

The net is not the world; it is the imagination of the world.

.

Of our great net, of our humanity or ministry of sympathies, Heraklitus said: "Immortal mortals, mortal immortals, one living the others' death and dying the others' life."

III.

So, Mary of Magdala may have brought her *marah* into the *myrrh,* brought her genius or her daemon or her seven into the Presence, into the Child—as we, too, bring our selves into what we call our Childhood.

.

If there is some exchange, some rumor of Virginia Woolf in the caves of the ice age, some cold draft of that inner dark in James Joyce; if I too now find these rumors or drafts or odors everywhere that I find what I am as a man; if I too, because I have come into touch with the work of some neurotic woman—it is only the inbinding or sentence a Virginia Woolf makes of words we use all the time, "the great hooded chairs had become enormous," so that a spell is cast—if I too become the ground in which the words of others grow and change my soul; so I understand then the translation of the myrrh in H.D.'s narrative and how

the house was filled with the odour of the ointment;

•

Gospel is rumor or news, a good spell. We have only rumor or news of what is. The real world, Thomas Vaughan tells us, is invisible. And in our contemporary physics too thought must work beyond the visible with ideas of the unseen or not yet seen seeking the nature of the real world.

•

Thomas Vaughan refers then to the mustard seed, the smallest of generative particles in which the esoteric meaning of things hides itself awaiting its season and new ground in those whose hearts are receptive and whose minds are willing. In the Christian mystery given in Matthew, Mark and Luke, "The kingdom of heaven is like to a grain of mustard seed, which a man took, and sowed in his field." Christ telling this parable says that he means to speak of "things which have been kept secret from the foundation of the world." But this seed is, He tells us, the word: "Which indeed is the least of all seeds: but when it is grown, it is the greatest among herbs, and becometh a tree, so that the birds of the air come and lodge in the branches thereof."

It is this passage that H.D. draws upon when, in *The Flowering of the Rod,* Kaspar stoops for the lady's scarf and sees "in that half-second" a fleck of light in a jewel that opens like a flower to disclose the real world—the kingdom of heaven, "the lands of the blest, / the promised lands" H.D. names the kingdom in terms of the Hesperides and Atlantis. In *The Walls Do Not Fall,* the heart portrayed first as a shellfish in the systole and diastole of the tide-flow, then as a psyche or butterfly, "dragging the forlorn / husk of self after us," in xxv is revealed in terms of such a seed, the heart-shell now breaking open like the husk of a grain:

> the Kingdom is a Tree
> whose roots bind the heart-husk
>
> to earth,
> after the ultimate grain,
>
> lodged in the heart-core,
> has taken its nourishment.

The mustard seed of time and the mustard seed of light, invisibilities, in which Kaspar sees, are immediacies of knowledge contrasting with "the old tradition, the old, old legend," expanses of time and space that characterize learning. In *Tribute to the Angels,* H.D. uses the language of spiritual alchemy so rhyming the terms of the word and of *"mer, mere, mere, mater, Maia, Mary"* with the elements in the alembic where the stone is being made, that meaning and odor and the jewel are identified with the *marah,* the sorrow of woman, and with the *myrrh.* The jewel in which the fleck of light comes to Kaspar's vision then is the *Philosopher's Stone.* It seems almost not to happen for its moment of time is a grain in which his spirit dwells but invisible to his mind.

Some ten years before H.D. wrote this passage, Whitehead in *Adventures of Ideas* wrote in a passage we have considered earlier:

> Literature preserves the wisdom of the human race; but in this way it enfeebles the emphasis of first-hand intuition. In considering our direct observation of past, or of future, we should confine ourselves to time-spans of the order of magnitude of a second, or even of fractions of a second.

·

H.D. will see the mustard seed as Thomas Vaughan, the Rosicrucian, does. "So in me," she tells us in *Tribute to Freud,* "2 distinct racial or biological or psychological entities tend to grow nearer or to blend, even, as time heals old breaks in consciousness"—as in the alembic of the alchemists diverse elements are brought into one work. She relates herself here to the esoteric tradition as "a descendant of one of the original groups of the early 18th-century, mystical Protestant order, called the Unitas Fratrum, the Bohemian or Moravian Brotherhood" and she goes on then to associate Count Zinzendorf and Freud: "Count Zinzendorf, the founder of the renewed Bohemian brotherhood, was an Austrian, whose father was exiled or self-exiled to Upper Saxony, because of his Protestant affiliations. The Professor himself was an Austrian, a Moravian actually by birth." It seems part of H.D.'s design to leave no more than this hint that we must search out for ourselves. In The War Trilogy again we can see these two as entities that tend to grow nearer or to blend: the New Master over Love who commands "name it," when, in *Tribute to the Angels,* the poetess cannot name the color of the jewel in which *"venerate"* and *"venereal"*—a break in consciousness—are united, is surely Freud; but when in the dream sequence of *The Walls Do Not Fall* He appears in "a spacious, bare meeting house"—"the Dream / deftly stage-managed the bare, clean / early colonial interior"—the figure of Zinzendorf has replaced Freud. We are no longer in the psychoanalyst's rooms but in the environs of Herrnhut, the Lord's House, where "The Order of the Grain of Mustard Seed," as Zinzendorf named the revived Moravian church, meets. Or in the environs of the first log house at Bethlehem in Pennsylvania which Zinzendorf dedicated himself on Christmas Eve in 1741, for Bethlehem was not only H.D.'s ancestral city but the city of her birth and her first eight years, of her "childhood" then.

•

Was there—I do not know if I read it or dreamed it—a teaching among these believers who kept their Christ as a hidden mustard seed in their hearts that they would recognize Brethren among the professing-Christians about them by the illumination of eyes, by a fleck of light from the jewel that a luminous eye is? In the Moravian scene of the dream it is the look of Christ's eyes that speaks—"as if without pupil / or all pupil, dark / yet very clear with amber / shining . . . " In the centuries of persecution after the Hussite wars of the fifteenth century, driven to live in the forests in hiding like the Albigensians before them and the Waldenses who took part in the new movement, and then taking the way of being a church hidden within other churches, the Brethren had to recognize each other silently, with no more sign than the inner sympathy could read like the exchange of a glance in which a would-be lover reads forbidden response.

•

Count von Zinzendorf not only was patron of the renewed Church but he created rituals and wrote hymns in which a new religious language emerged that brought out the associations of sexual and spiritual images. The spear, the wound, and the flow of blood from Christ's side were deliberately related to the penis, the vagina, and the menstrual flow. Sessler in his study of the Moravian movement tells us: "It is said that a niche covered with red cloth was built into the wall of the church, into which children were placed to symbolize their lying in Christ's Side-Wound, and that Christian Renatus, Zinzendorf's son, built a *Side-Wound* through which the congregation marched"—called "the true Matrix." Zinzendorf, like Freud, worked towards a sense of words in which the *"venerate"* and *"venereal"* were again restored.

•

H.D. does no more than indicate a relationship between the world of her poem and the world of the Zinzendorfian Brethren. We no sooner see the eighteenth-century meeting house than we are told that He, the Christ of the poem, looks with "the eyes / of Velasquez' crucified"; we have passed from the reality of the religious enthusiast to the reality of the painter. All around us in the poem is the atmosphere of religion, numinal suggestion. What, in the terms of the art itself, is this "fleck of light," this "grain" or "flaw or speck" where:

> the speck, fleck, grain or seed
> opened like a flower.

•

The religious serves in the poem to tell us something about the nature of the poetic experience; as we come to recognize shifting depths of myth or of mystic doctrine in the images of the poem we begin to feel the world as H.D. does, as a ground of such depth. Life itself is revealed to the poet as to us in light—the immediate flash—of a particular reality, where metaphor, multiple reference, rhyme and melody, quicken and organize time and the spatial world in which the reality exists.

·

And the flower, thus contained
in the infinitely tiny grain or seed

opened petal by petal . . .
. . . .
and the circle went on widening

and would go on opening,
he knew, to infinity.

·

Do we believe that? the germ of William Harvey? the tiny speck of material containing the code-script of Schrödinger? the universe expanding from its primal atom?

IV.

I do not believe, for I am a poet: I imagine as I make it up. Or my thought goes along lines of imagination here as it will, guided by the feeling of what fits, what informs or what promises form; where it knows only pain and trouble in working where belief is needed. These rumors ring true or are true to a form towards which I move. "I go where I belong, inexorably," H.D. writes in *The Flowering of the Rod:*

In resurrection, there is confusion
if we start to argue; if we stand and stare,

we do not know where to go;
. . . .
does the first wild-goose care
whether the others follow or not?

I don't think so—he is so happy to be off—
he knows where he is going;

so we must be drawn or we must fly . . .

•

The wild-goose flight has the truth of inner impulse, taking thought in the flight itself, true to a wish when we know only its felt imperative. The affirmations of inner nature, of biological instinctual reality—what we call "blind" instinct—in the opening pages of the poem have prepared our recognition here, and then in the spirit of the poem our assent, that in this life-will we are moved by the deepest imperative. The imperative of the poem towards its own order is of this kind for H.D., a feeling she must follow and cannot direct, taking command over her from within the process of its creation as she works. She compares the soul's objectification with "the stone marvel" of the mollusc, "hewn from within," but it may represent a spiritual force of the cosmos beyond the biological. This "life"-will towards objective form is ultimately related to an animal crystallization, and the images of jewel, crystal, "as every snowflake / has its particular star, coral or prism shape" suggest that there is—not an inertia but a calling thruout the universe towards concretion. The poet in the imminence of a poem (what now after Olson we may see as the *projection*) answering such a calling as a saint has his calling or a hero his fate. "Inexorably."

"It is geometry on the wing," H.D. has it in section x of *The Flowering of the Rod;* "not patterned," she adds, where she means that this imperative, the deepest imperative of the poetic-urge then, is not pre-planned but created in a trajectory that will not, must not, be satisfied until it reaches *Paradise*. The ecstasy of the poem, an intimation of—the Hesperides, the Isles of the Dead, heaven, Atlantis: H.D. gives the various names that the hidden promise of Paradise has been given from Homer to the Renaissance syncretists that discarded and even despised by sophisticated modern scientific orthodoxy has been left to be cherished only by occultists and heretical minds. And again, we find this inner impulse is called by H.D. "that smallest grain," the mustard seed invisible to the conscious consideration that moving the consciousness "grows branches / where the birds rest" and "becometh a tree."

•

A wild-goose chase the projective must always seem to men who want prescribed directions and ends and who must fight to put down impulse towards whatever kingdom not of this world as an enemy of conventional or social values.

•

In the nineteenth century the last echoes of such a kingdom not of this world sounded in the call of socialism, communism, and anarchism, as in the eighteenth century it had sounded in the creative fiction of liberty. In the "from each according to his abilities, to each according to his needs" the command of the loving Father in the new dispensation of His Christ; in the communalization of property the individuality held as a little child—the lingering dream of Christendom. But in Russia, Marxian communism gave rise to the specter of the wrathful Father, the old pre-Christian tyranny, in the Bolshevik dictatorship. In America, democracy gave rise to the second diabolic specter—for in the Satanism of industrial capitalism, the large forge of the General Economy days in Zinzendorf's little colony of the Mustard Seed was developed into the present Bethlehem Steel Corporation.

•

H.D.'s War Trilogy came to me in the period after the Second World War as a revelation of truth, true to a life or consciousness sought. As in the war years, I found in Dorothy Richardson's *Pilgrimage* such a work. The outrage of the critics of the day was similar to the outrage of like minds when confronted by The War Trilogy. "I very much dislike this work," Lionel Trilling forthrightly began his put-down in the *Kenyon Review*: "*Pilgrimage*, of all the ambitious works of our time, is the least fruitful and the least charming." It was like Proust without sex, the more abruptly sophisticated *Time* magazine line went. Trilling bridled at Miriam's thought that "By every word they use,

men and women mean different things," mistaking it not as an opera-
tive element in the process of the character's inner reality but as an
article in the author's doctrine of militant feminism. "However close
Miss Richardson may stand to Virginia Woolf," he continued, allowing
that Virginia Woolf, and Jane Austen before her, might be of Dorothy
Richardson's ilk, it was offensive that Miss Richardson felt an affinity
in her work, that she had the presumption to claim in 1938 an affinity
with Joyce, Proust, and James. "There is between her and the work of
these three masculine writers a very real and important difference," he
warns and proceeds to argue and rationalize towards the conclusion
that "speaking from the literary point of view, it [the emotional solip-
sism of Richardson's interior monolog] has produced a literary manner
private without being personal, arbitrary without being original, mak-
ing a demand upon the reader which is not rewarded as demands of
equal difficulty are rewarded by the three men we have spoken of, in
the reader's enhanced sentiment of reality." The distaste that governs
Trilling's reading might be a prototype of the critical distaste for H.D.'s
work as early as *Palimpsest* but especially for the poetry of the major
phase. Was there some link that bound in one syndrome—from our
text we might call it the Simon complex—a religious orthodoxy and
a literary orthodoxy in a guise of criticism that must "draw the line
somewhere" to exclude the female revelation?

.

But from the opening pages of "Pointed Roofs," thru the valors and
shames of Miriam's girlish experience, haunted by some "break in
consciousness" that cast up dark moods and images, into the troubled
depths of Miriam's *selva oscura* in *Deadlock, Revolving Lights,* and *The
Trap,* I had gathered what the outraged critic had so specifically denied
the reader would find—my enhanced sentiment of reality. There was in
Miriam's consciousness the presence ever immanent of an illumination
in experience itself, a grief or agony ready to leap up into reality to add
its color to her impressions, and, bound in with this, an apprehension at
moments in climbing a stair or in the opening of a door of an awaited
ascension into the light. Her mind strained after it; her spirit came to

be sure of it or to be sure in the thought of it. Then there would be moments of epiphany, pure sensations of the light in rooms, that I too had known. I took community in the work of Dorothy Richardson even as in the criticism of men like Trilling I was aware that that community was despised in the world of the great reviews.

•

"There was glory hidden in that old darkness," Miriam thinks coming home late at night from a socialist meeting. "Within the radiance, troops of people marched ahead, with springing footsteps; the sound of song in their ceaselessly talking voices; the forward march of a unanimous, light-hearted humanity along a pathway of white morning light." Like Dante, Dorothy Richardson pre-dates the present of her work (1900) so that she can work with foreshadowings. Miriam's thought grows darker; in their unity she feels her own isolation and now the socialists appear as "*Men*," she capitalizes and italicizes the word, Russian revolutionaries (her suitor Michael Shatov). "Their scornful revolutionary eyes watched her glance about among her hoard of contradictory ideas. . . . " Miriam, like Stephen Dedalus or Proust's hero, is a self recaptured, a creation of the author's youth, and as in Stephen's thought we find germs of something like Joyce's later concepts, so in Miriam's stream-of-consciousness propositions of *Pilgrimage* appear. "She offered them," Miriam thinks, "a comprehensive glimpse of the many pools of thought in which she had plunged, using from each in turn, to recover the bank and repudiate; unless a channel could be driven, that would make all their waters meet. They laughed when she cried out at the helplessness of uniting them. 'All these things are nothing'." There are religious undertones in the uniting of waters, and now Miriam's repressed memories of the break-up of her childhood begin to take over and more ancient or atavistic ways of thought, of *eros* and *thanatos,* take over:

"There was a glory hidden in that old darkness, but they did not know it; though they followed it"—the socialists, but they are now also Miriam's parents in their marriage, working in the darkness of history or of the wedding-bed, appear now as a "they," a hidden order like the "they" of H.D.'s work: "Accepting them, plunging into their darkness, she would never be able to keep from finding the bright devil and wandering wrapped in gloom, but forgetful, perpetually in the bright spaces within the darkness." It is her father's death and the trauma of her mother's death by cancer that give hidden direction to her thought. "But even if factories were abolished and the unpleasant kinds of work shared out so that they pressed upon nobody," she thinks, "how could the kingdom of heaven come upon earth as long as there were childbirth and cancer?"

.

Joyce's *Portrait,* with its closing passages in Stephen's diary where *eros* and *thanatos* again move his thought, had had this quality of a revelation for me earlier. The dark disorder of "I fear him. I fear his redrimmed horny eyes. It is with him I must struggle all through this night . . . " setting off the flame of the close, which Joyce in *Finnegans Wake* playing upon his troubled sense of "*forge*" and "*forgery*" was to darken. But we took Stephen's resurrection as an affirmation of our own youthful intent.

> April 26. Mother is putting my new secondhand clothes in order. She prays now, she says, that I may learn in my own life and away from home and friends what the heart is and what it feels. Amen. So be it. Welcome, O life! I go to encounter for the millionth time the reality of experience and to forge in the smithy of my soul the uncreated conscience of my race.
> April 27. Old father, old artificer, stand me now and ever in good stead.

The figures of the artificer Daedalus and of his unfortunate son, tricked out in wings of wax, haunt with irony the high resolution, but Joyce contrives to be true not only to the later knowledge but to his youthful inspiration as well.

.

Emotionally true? Psychologically true?
In "The Serious Artist," Pound wrote: "The arts give us a great percentage of the lasting and unassailable data regarding the nature of

mankind, of immaterial man, of man considered as a thinking and sentient creature." Then: "By good art I mean art that bears true witness."

•

True witness, where I have found it, to the troubled psyche, the searching, yearning heart and mind, to the instability of opinions, to the grandeur of fate, to the states of another consciousness of being at one, to the solitude that is a condition of communion, to the "is there one who understands me?" cry of a *Finnegans Wake,* to the sense of a melody in experience itself that transcends argument, true witness to the immediacy of life is contrasted with that other aim in writing exemplified by Dryden's correction of Shakespeare to suit "what reasonable men have long since concluded."

•

Truth in Richardson, Joyce, or Proust, as in Pound, Williams, or H.D. arises as the truth of "what the heart is and what it feels." Close to confession then, but the intent is not to unburden the soul. It is to project the wholeness of his experience—in this way close to the psychoanalytic process—as the content of a work that will present the scales, the ratios, chords and discords of the soul's own creative order.

•

"Let us just for the moment feel the pulses of *Ulysses* and of Miss Dorothy Richardson and M. Marcel Proust, on the earnest side of Briareus," D. H. Lawrence wrote in "Surgery for the Novel—Or a Bomb." He loathed their portentous search for self or accounting for their lives:

> Absorbedly, childishly concerned with *what I am.* 'I am this, I am that, I am the other. My reactions are such, and such, and such. And, oh, Lord, if I liked to watch myself closely enough, if I liked to analyze my feelings minutely, as I unbutton my gloves, instead of saying crudely I unbuttoned them, then I could go on to a million pages instead of a thousand. In fact, the more I come to think of it, it is gross, it is uncivilized bluntly to say: I unbuttoned my gloves. After all, the absorbing adventure of it! Which button did I begin with?' etc.
>
> The people in the serious novels are so absorbedly concerned with

themselves and what they feel and don't feel, and how they react to every mortal button; and their audience as frenziedly absorbed in the application of the author's discoveries to their own reactions: 'That's me! That's exactly it! I'm just finding myself in this book!' Why, this is more than death-bed, it is almost post-mortem behaviour.

•

Joyce taking over his Roman Catholic examination of conscience into the operations of the personal imagination, or Dorothy Richardson the Quaker interior voice, write as if they received in the magic of their transmuted experience a book in which revelation was given of a true otherwise hidden life. So, in *Tribute to the Angels* Our Lady carries a book in place of the Lamb. "Her book is our book," H.D. writes: "its pages will reveal / a tale of a Fisherman, / a tale of a jar or jars." And earlier: "she brings the Book of Life, obviously."

In *The Zohar,* Abraham it is said gives account of all his moments, hours, days, years; rendering up his life in the wholeness of its living, as Proust strives to remember the fullness of his time. Freud, here as in many things continuing the Kabbalistic tradition, brings into the modern science of the soul such an accounting for one's world. Not only in the Jewish world but in the Greek world of Orphic mysteries there was such a concept of being responsible for the whole of one's life—for the redeemed souls had to drink not of Lethe but of a fountain of memory.

Beyond confession or remembrance, this dual creation of self and consciousness that Lawrence reacted against—as surely he would have reacted against the "I'm just finding myself in this book," the million pages instead of a thousand, mode of my own writing here—in their being "so absorbedly concerned with themselves and what they feel and don't feel," these writers of the new interior monolog read their lives as the Kabbalists read the Torah, exploring the permutations of meaning in each letter and diacritical mark. As in H.D.'s version of the *Ion* of Euripides where Ion, who might be Lawrence, demands unreflective action: "to strike at evil, is pure:" and the Pythia replies "you must know why you strike," the ordeal of the contemporary psyche was to recreate the meaning of its life.

•

"Their thoughts are in them as the thought of the tree is in the seed," we would recall from Pound writing of the germinal consciousness, as he called it in 1916: "And these minds are the more poetic, and they affect mind about them, and transmute it as the seed the earth. And this latter sort of mind is close on the vital universe; and the strength of Greek beauty rests in this, that it is ever at the interpretation of this vital universe." As in "Religio" he writes: "A god is an eternal state of mind." But that the germinal consciousness, affecting mind about it, was dark as well as light, Pound can never accept. Again and again in *The Cantos,* the question of dualism troubles him. Like a Christian Scientist he wants to say that suffering is a mental error. Yet what Pound called "the two maladies, the Hebrew disease, the Hindoo disease"—the brooding mind correspondent with suffering and corruption, as well as the radiant mind correspondent with joy and purity, rested in its being ever at the interpretation of the vital universe. Pound demanded that the mind take thought only in "the radiant world where one thought cuts through another with clean edge"; wherever he faced muddle, the digestive and excretory functions of the universe or the digestion and excretion involved in transmuting the meanings of experience, he could no longer think, he could only—closing his mind in distaste—react.

.

Wherever Hell appears in earlier *Cantos* it is exterior to Pound. The light is fluid and pours, but Plotinus commands: "Keep your eyes on the mirror."

> Prayed we to the Medusa,
>   petrifying the soil by the shield.

.

Then, after the trauma of the Second World War experience, when in the debacle of the Fascist last days he was forced almost to admit the disorder, the Hell, of Mussolini's reign which he had held as a model of order, the later *Cantos* pour forth the contradictions of the mind no longer removed from its underworld. "Tho my errors and wrecks lie

about me," he will sing in *Canto* CXVI: "I cannot make it cohere."
"But the beauty is not the madness," he confirms.

•

In *The Pisan Cantos,* as the voice of Pound ransacking his broken con-
sciousness begins, like Lear, his testimony of what the heart knows,
outrage as well as tenderness comes. God Himself, Boehme argued in
the sixteenth century, was the fire of Hell as well as the light of Heaven,
wrath as well as love. Ugly flarings up of the *Turba*—the unrest of all
creation—must be there if a man bear witness to what he is and feels,
even though he is aware his thought and feeling are dis-eased. For the
business of the artist is to bring things to light. In Pound's *Canto* XCI,
it is the light that presides:

> *ab lo dolchor qu'al cor mi vai*

entoned, then:

> that the body of the light come forth
> > from the body of fire
> And that your eyes come to the surface
> > from the deep wherein they were sunken . . .

It is in this context of a testimony to the light, evoking the lore and
vision of light:

> Over harm
> Over hate
> > overflooding, light over light
> . . . .
> the light flowing, whelming the stars.

that the harm, the hatred, rises into the light of day. Marx, who would
compel the mind to take up the cause of the oppressed, and Freud, who
would compel the mind to take up the cause of the repressed, appear
as enemies of the high mind. Here, no Athena comes as she comes in
H.D.'s version of *Ion* to declare the alliance between the intellect and

the great forces of the under-mind. The out-raging voice breaks (as in the text, the italics indicate the interjected mode) and the poem shifts abruptly to low-minded rant:

> *Democracies electing their sewage*
> *till there is no clear thought about holiness*
> *a dung flow from 1913*
> *and, in this, their kikery functioned, Marx, Freud*
>   *and the american beaneries*

•

He might have used the high King James tone that he had used in the Usura *Cantos*. But Pound had written: "You can be wholly precise in representing vagueness. You can be wholly a liar in pretending that the particular vagueness was precise in its outline." And here, in this discordant passage, where his hatred of American policies beginning with the First World War, of Jews, and of colleges, in images of sewage and dung flow stands contrasted with his adoration of great women with their lovers, queens of nature and heaven, in images of light and crystal waves, Pound does not pretend to the urbane anti-semitism of Eliot but breaks into the true voice of his feeling—not only what he feels but exactly as he feels it. Because of this, we see, as we are never quite sure in Eliot, the nature of Pound's hatred of Jews.

•

Baudelaire in *Mon coeur mis à nu* had raged not only against women but against Jews:

> *Belle conspirations à organiser pour l'extermination de la race juive.*
> *Les juifs* Bibliothecaires *et temoins de la Rédemption.*

The dis-ease or out-rage is presented in the high tone of his Dandy style; it is incorporated in the Baudelairean attitude. But in Pound, to express these feelings at all breaks the voice. *Sewage, dung flow, kikery, beaneries* are raw words and deliberately low. The contrast may be between the man Baudelaire and the man Pound, or the times; but what we would note here is that the imperative in *The Cantos* is to expose the character of the thought and feeling involved; where the journalistic notes of *Mon coeur mis à nu* are governed by manner.

•

To render it true, then. Not only the truth of outrage in Swift or Baudelaire, in Pound or Céline, that suddenly forces us to recognize the virus (these passages, out-rages, are lesions of feeling and thought) that others would keep hidden or dressed up; but the truth of how consciousness moves, where form has been developed to bear testimony to undercurrent and eddy, shifts, breaks and echoes of content. In a conventional art, the sense of Beauty is a sense of what other men will find beautiful, pleasurable, enhancing, and exemplary in their social terms. Poetry would present models of feeling, and reviewers of this order commend or chastise the poet's being to their taste or exciting their distaste. But there is a higher or larger order of poetry where Beauty is a sense of universal relations, of being brought into intensities of even painful feeling. Here, the virus is life, the hatred is emotion, the breaks in consciousness—that in conventional thought seem inroads of natural chaos or damaged passages that need surgery or correction—are surfs or sun-spots of the deep element.

V.

March 24, 1961. Friday.
If Truth lived in a well, and I do not remember where that was, she appears as a Pre-Raphaelite illustration—perhaps a drawing by H.J. Ford in one of Lang's Fairy Books—a beauty in rags.

•

Diogenes, a man looking for Truth, lived in a barrel. Another figure in rags. And Truth in the Well, in *Les Enfants du Paradis* is presented by Carne and Prévert as a woman in a barrel of water. Garance, the naked truth, a nineteenth century strip-tease.

•

But when I first took a name for that Greek philosopher, I mistook the name. *Demosthenes,* I thought it was, but I knew, too, that I was wrong. That was the name of another, somehow, misfit, learning to speak with pebbles in his mouth. "What was the name of the one who was looking for truth with a lantern, the Greek philosopher?" I asked Jess. "Demosthenes," he answered, reiterating my thought.

•

Old figures, the well of wisdom or the well that reappears in the lives of the Jewish fathers and the maiden drawing water from the well, reappear in low guise: a strip-tease artist in a barrel, a pesty old man with a smoky lantern. "The well is dry," the ravens cry.

•

Keats's "Beauty is truth, truth beauty" strikes another image that is not Keats's but our common speech. When an arrow has been shot to its mark we say, "The aim is true, that's a beauty!"

•

But when I go to Keats's text, as I must, following the path of my associations here, to find the truth of the matter, I see Keats addresses our Truth who lived in a well in the fairy tales: "Thou still unravish'd bride of quietness," he calls her. "Thou foster-child of silence and slow time . . . "

•

The figure of Diogenes as he comes to mind searching for Truth, or rather daring the Truth, is a dismisser of words, accuses our speech everywhere of hiding or disguising the truth, of deceiving then. Here the lie is a mask some truth wears, a false face. Truth speaking tells us a story, the story takes over from the teller. Unmask her!

But Garance in the movie wears only a smile, she does not speak. She wears the curving lure of silent lips and the seductive reflection of eyes dwelling in a woman's "quietness," "silence and slow time," that we have seen before in Leonardo's vision of *La Gioconda.* Just beyond this moment at which she is Keats's "unravish'd," she is, we see, as the poet saw her elsewhere, *La Belle Dame Sans Merci.* "Unravish'd" means not only that she has been had by no man, but that we too are not to have her. Truth, Beauty, here is pure lure. She will be the Sphinx, even the Medusa.

·

The other figure that came to my mind—Demosthenes—is the rhetor. We see him walking by the sea-shore, trying his voice against the waves. Just as Diogenes in his barrel in the Greek world had his counterpart in the Celtic fairy tale of Truth in a well, so Demosthenes has a counterpart in Canute trying his voice, his command, over the waves. In whose defeat, his word is proved false. Here it means powerless against the waves. He has no such command.

Our Demosthenes must work with only that Truth that can persuade the waves. These waves are the people.

·

Both the skeptic and the rhetor bring to light conditions of human concern where poetry does not work. In the hardness of heart where it has gone so hard by a man's heart that he searches after the bitter truth—truth, to expose his mother to the light of day—poetry, that's-just-poetry—means playing it false. Words are not to be trusted. At last, in the last of the world's suffering, all of What Is he will claim to be Maia, the false mother of meaning, the deceit of wish, where the powers of heaven and hell raven in a smile.

·

Looking for Diogenes, I find in Dodds's *The Greeks and the Irrational:* "As Tylor pointed out long ago, 'it is a vicious circle: what the dreamer believes he therefore sees, and what he sees he therefore believes.'" "But what if he nevertheless fails to see?" Dodds asks: "That must often have happened at Epidaurus: as Diogenes said of the votive tablets to another deity, 'there would have been far more of them if those who were *not* rescued had made dedications'."

·

The skeptic voice in the interior dialogue of The War Trilogy that finds the paraphernalia of the mysteries "trivial/intellectual adornment" decries the poet's uselessness in the time of war, seizing the opportunity to put him in his place. But back of the accusation against the Poet we find another accusation, against the psyche of Woman. "They snatched off our amulets," the Poetess tells us: "charms are not, they said, grace."

.

"We have them always with us," Pound wrote in *The Spirit of Romance:* "They claimed, or rather jeered in Provence, remonstrated in Tuscany, wrangle today, and will wrangle tomorrow—and not without some show of reason—that poetry, especially lyric poetry, must be simple; that you must get the meaning while the man sings it." Against the *trobar clus,* against Truth veiled in charm or in a woman's smile. In the tradition of the mystery poem that Pound traces from Apuleius to Dante the figure of a woman is central: Isis, then the Venus of the *Pervigilium Veneris,* the Lady of the troubadours, and Beatrice. They are ancestresses of our Bride of Quietness, Truth at the Well of the fairy tales, and the language of this poetry is the old speech, the *lingua materna,* as Dante called the Provençal.

.

In the lure of Beauty, Truth seems untrue. And wisdom likewise is a lure, so that in Gnostic cults wisdom is a woman. The Brotherhood of Poetry answering the Fellowship of the Sword in *The Walls Do Not Fall* are no better than women, asserting against the realities of work and war, against the claim that crisis makes in truth, a way of alluring promise. Recalling another passage in Dorothy Richardson's *Pilgrimage* where, following upon thoughts of the toiling masses in their struggle for socialism against exploitation, the thought of Yeats comes to Miriam's mind, "the halting, half man's half woman's adoration he gave to the world he saw, his only reality."

.

In the face of what we call reality, the poets in H.D.'s Trilogy claim a prior reality. They are pretenders to a throne in Truth that does not seem real to common sense:

> we are the keepers of the secret,
> the carriers, the spinners
>
> of the rare intangible thread
> that binds all humanity
>
> to ancient wisdom,
> to antiquity;
>
> our joy is unique, to us,
> grape, knife, cup, wheat
>
> are symbols in eternity . . .

•

"A list of facts," Pound had written to Williams of the old themes of poetry, "on which I and 9,000,000 other poets have spieled endlessly." Spring, Love, Trees, Wind. This voice of sound sense putting the merely poetic in its place will often take over in Pound. But in another vein, a rare intangible thread or umbilical cord binding him to the womb of pre-history, to the Mutterrecht, Pound loses the "spiel" of the American businessman who knows that poetry is a commodity among commodities. Then he sings, not with 9,000,000 other poets, but with those few who practise the *trobar clus,* for whom Spring, Trees, Love, Wind have enduring and hidden meaning. As in *The Pisan Cantos* he will recall: "in the hall of the forebears / as from the beginning of wonders. . . . The wind is part of the process." In the Rock-Drill he will present an ideogram of hearts, diamonds, clubs, spades. These things, like the "grape, knife, cup, wheat" of H.D.'s poem, like "the house, the fruit, the grape into which the hope and meditation of our forefathers had entered" of Rilke's letter to Von Hulewicz, are not a list of facts but are "vessels in which they found and stored humanity."

•

This art, Pound writes in *The Spirit of Romance* is good "as the high mass is good art."

Man-to-man the poetic voice had broken with embarrassment in our American self-consciousness. In the generation to which Ezra Pound and William Carlos Williams belonged there was still the break between man-talk, that presented a show of even brutality in defense against any hint of vulnerability—it was the tone required for the competition and profiteering of the capitalist society—and the woman-talk to which all things that required inner feeling and sensitivity had been relegated. Poetry belonged among womanish things, a song Herakles sang while sewing for Omphale.

•

The *trobar clus* was outlawed. The Spirit or the sacred in man's being appeared in the old order as a woman, an angelic presence or Truth in which a man took his being, as Dante took his being in Beatrice. Bound by the rare thread to—"the ancient wisdom," H.D. calls it—some unmanly otherness.

Pound and Williams, whose art belonged to the *trobar clus,* in their dis-ease were often ashamed of their Spirit. In *Paterson* the split, that in H.D.'s War Trilogy comes between the official society of church or army and the secret society of the poet, appears as a divorce within the language itself, a hidden divorce between man and woman. In *The Cantos,* where Pound is concerned with economics or politics, "men's affairs," he will put on the man-in-the-street persona or, as in early Hell *Cantos* or in *Canto* XCI, break into a subliminal voice from some barracks or locker-room—"The petrified terd that was Verres," "fahrting through silk," "frigging a tinpenny whistle," "*sh-t.*"

•

Even for women, areas of poetic feeling must contend with limits that social attitudes would set within the psyche itself against womanish excess. In *The Walls Do Not Fall* H.D.'s accounting of her experience is an accounting for such an excess:

so mind dispersed, dared occult lore

found secret doors unlocked,
floundered, was lost in sea-depth,

We are prepared—Freud and Jung have prepared us—for what "depth" means in the contemporary cult of analysis. It is as real as "hell" once was. And in the depth, where the earliest human time stirs us, we know that wisdom and occult lore are an old wives' tale—"sub-conscious ocean where Fish / move two-ways and devour." Then a self-mocking voice begins, where H.D. anticipates the reproof of the utilitarian realist: "jottings on a margin, / indecipherable palimpsest scribbled over / with too many contradictory emotions."

The accusation of the Poet and another accusation of the Woman fuse in a third accusation of the heterodox tradition. She dramatizes the desecration of the psyche in the definitions of reality set by the Protestant ethic, as later, in *Tribute to the Angels,* she dramatizes the desecration of woman's and the poet's spirit in the *Venus-venery-venereous-venerate-venerator* passage. "Stumbling toward / vague cosmic expression," H.D. continues now in imitation of the mercantile skeptic voice:

obvious sentiment,
folder round a spiritual bank-account,

with credit-loss too starkly indicated,
a riot of unpruned imagination,

•

She was not wrong in so picturing her adverse critic's reaction. "Felt queer, sincere, more than a little silly," Randall Jarrell wrote in *Partisan Review:* "the smashed unenclosing walls jut raggedly from the level debris of her thought (which accepts all that comes from heaven as unquestioningly as the houses of London). H.D. is history and misunderstands a later stage of herself so spectacularly that her poem exists primarily as an anachronism."

•

"Wandering among barbarians, patching what religious scraps she can pick up," he wrote a year later when *Tribute to the Angels* appeared: "Imagism was a *reductio ad absurdum* upon which it is hard to base a later style: H.D.'s new poem is one for those who enjoy any poem by H.D., or for those collectors who enjoy any poem that includes the Virgin, Raphael, Azrael, Uriel, John on Patmos, Hermes Trismegistus and the Bona Dea."

What lies back of Jarrell's advantage here, his taking it for granted that the less said of this kind of thing the better, is not an idiosyncratic stand (though some personal contempt finds occasion for expression), not a special disrespect (though his impressions of the texts in question are glib almost to the point of disrespect), but an orthodoxy of view. Jarrell's great forte was that he successfully impersonated and then genuinely represented the needs and attitudes of the new educated literary class that was making its way in the English Departments of American colleges and universities, an increasingly important and established group of professor-poets concerned with what poetry should be admitted as part of its official culture. His appeal in rejecting even the "felt" and "sincere" where it was "queer" and "more than a little silly" was an appeal to some right proper and respectable range of thought and feeling that any member of a university faculty must keep in order to maintain his position. It is not at all clear in Jarrell's reviews what H.D.'s work is, but it is most clear, if we accept unquestioningly all that comes from his authority, that whatever it is it is "silly," "level debris," "anachronism"—not to be countenanced by reasonable men.

And Jarrell's judgment here as elsewhere stood for that of his class. Dudley Fitts found *The Flowering of the Rod* a play of "pretty, expected and shopworn" counters. He had found *Tribute to the Angels* "compact of brought-down-to-date Pre-Raphaelism: angels and archangels, lutes and cytharists, musks, embroideries, mystical etymologies, and the like," and now, again, in the new work: "the reader is off on an uneasy Dolben-cum-Morris jaunt that starts vaguely from somewhere and ends barely more convincingly, in Bethlehem. I do not wish to be brutal; I should be a fool to pretend that H.D.'s intentions—her conceptions, even—are other than the highest; but it does seem clear to me that her whole method in these poems is false. For one thing, the diction is as pseudo-naive as the imagery is pseudo-medieval." We begin to sense that something more is at stake than the question of what is academically respectable. Where the whole method is false, intention and conception which give rise to method must be false. Fitts would dismiss all the things of the poem as "counters," inferring that they have no more real (true) nature in experience. It may be that the very claim to experience in terms of the heterodox tradition made thruout the poem seems false to him.

·

There are no lutes and cytharists in The War Trilogy. Mr. Fitts was a little carried away in his zeal to portray the distasteful Pre-Raphaelite mode of the poem. In another work under attack in those years, where Pound sang in *The Pisan Cantos* and the hounds of the *Partisan Review* bayed in protest, I find: "Has he curved us the bowl of the lute?" Pound has always been attacked for the medieval and the pseudo-medieval.

But the suspicion that disturbs Fitts is not mistaken; Pre-Raphaelism brought-down-to-date "and the like" does enter in. Back of H.D., as back of Pound or of Yeats, was the cult of romance that Rossetti and then Morris had derived from Dante and his circle, the *Fedeli d'amore,* and revived in the Victorian era. The Christ of H.D.'s trilogy is not the Christ of church prescription but of the imagination, related to the Christ of the mysteries, the Christos-Angelos of Gnostic myth and the Angel Amor of the *Vita Nuova;* and here again, the elder Rossetti and then Dante Gabriel in their revival of Dante had played their part. Beatrice in the Christian mystery cult of Amor may have been herself a presentation of the Christos-Angelos. Gabriel Rossetti tells us in his *Early Italian Poets* that Dante had identified the Lady with Love Himself.

·

"This Figure imposes itself in the imperious manner of a central symbol," Henry Corbin writes in *Avicenna and the Visionary Recital:* "appearing to man's mental vision under the complementary feminine aspect that makes his being a total being." The crisis in angelology came in the Western World in the thirteenth century when William of Auvergne led the attack against the Avicennan notion of natures operating in virtue of an inner necessity and according to the law of their essences and especially against the concept of the soul's finding its inner necessity and the law of its essence in awakening thru love to the presence of its Angel, the Active Intelligence. In the Moslem world as well as in the Christian world this concept of being united with the divine reality by a love union with the Angel who is present in the person of the Beloved becomes a prime heresy. Fitts's "angels and archangels . . . mystical etymologies, and the like" would dismiss any such vision with something like the contempt of medieval theologians—for there were critics in the middle ages who raged in Provence against the lutes and cytharists, troubadours and catharists, against musks and embroideries and the pseudo-medieval. But, as Henry Corbin proposes of Avicenna: "our whole effort was bent to another end than explaining Avicenna as a 'man of his time.' Avicenna's time, *his own time,* has not here been put in the past tense; it has presented itself to us as an immediacy. It originates not in the chronology of a history of philosophy, but in the three-fold ecstasy by which the archangelic Intelligences each give origin to a world and to consciousness of a world, which is the consciousness of a desire, and this desire is hypostatized in the Soul that is the motive energy of that world." Corbin would read Avicenna's recitals not as plays with counters but as visionary experiences. "The union that joins the possible intellect of the human soul with the Active Intelligence as *Dator formarum,* Angel of Knowledge or Wisdom-Sophia, is visualized and experienced as a love union. It is a striking illustration of the relation of personal devotion that we have attempted to bring out here and that shows itself to proceed from an experience so fundamental that it can defy the combined efforts of science and theology against angelology." What the dogma of science with its imagination of the world in terms of use and manipulation for profit and the dogma of theology with its view of reality in terms of authority and system oppose in the cult of angels is the absolute value given to the individual experience that would imagine the universe in terms of love, desire, devotion, and ecstasy, emotions which men who seek practical ends find most disruptive. "In symbolic terms, let us say," Henry Corbin comments: "that the Avicennan champion will always find himself faced by the descendants of William of Auvergne, even, and not a whit the less, when those descendants are perfectly 'laicized.'"

•

The hostile reader will find that all visions start "vaguely from somewhere Biblical" or like Dante's from somewhere Virgilian and end up "barely more convincingly, in Bethlehem" or like Dante's in the high fantasy of the luminous eye of God. Dante and his circle, Corbin makes clear, were deep in this matter of angels "and the like." The whole method, William of Auvergne almost a century before Dante had shown clearly and with telling scorn, was false. But the poets followed the tradition of Provence, not the convincing arguments of the University of Paris. What Dante drew from translated Sufi texts as well as from the songs of Toulouse and Albi where such Images of the First Beloved appeared was the Spirit of Romance. Corbin admits too to an Avicennan romanticism. "Nothing could be clearer then the identity of this 'amorosa Madonna Intelligenza' who has her residence in the soul, and with whose celestial beauty the poet has fallen in love. Here is perhaps one of the most beautiful chapters in the very long 'history' of the Active Intelligence, which still remains to be written, and which is certainly not a 'history' in the accepted sense of the word, because it takes place entirely in the souls of poets and philosophers."

•

H.D.'s Romance then may have been—given the angels, the Christ of the mysteries, the doctrine of reality seen in vision and dream—false doctrine. The Roman Catholic and the established Protestant churches had cast out such heresies. By the nineteenth century to deal with such matters was to be a Rosicrucian or Theosophist or worse. "This is incantation," Fitts concludes in his attack on *Tribute to the Angels,* "but of an irresponsible, even perverse, kind." The rational and professional orthodoxy that had replaced the church authority concurred in outlawing Romance. So, the arbitrating voice of *The New Yorker* noted that "H.D.'s mysticism, once implicit in her Imagist poems dealing with Greek symbols, is rather thin and shrill in this collection of her later works, what with their Biblical background and their redemption-by-suffering theme"; and when Karl Shapiro and Richard Wilbur, two of the younger members of the new poem-writing caste, came to edit Untermeyer's *Anthology of British and American Poetry,* H.D.'s work was eliminated from the canon.

•

"Thoughts stir, inspiration stalks us"—the concept of a revealed poetry was not in tune with the mode of the great literary reviews of the forties. The new critics were partisans of what they called the rational imagination against whatever cults of experience—or the "irrational" as they put it. Poems were interpreted as products of sensibility and intelligence operating in language, solving problems and surpassing in tests in ambiguity and higher semantics, with special dispensations for exuberance as in Dylan Thomas. Back of it all was a model of the cultivated and urbane professor, of the protestant moderator victorious.

"Inspiration," "spell," "rapture"—the constant terms of The War Trilogy—are not accepted virtues in the classroom, where Dream or Vision are disruptive of a student's attentions. But more than that, these new professors of literature were descendants of those ministers of the seventeenth and eighteenth century, holding out against the magic of poetry as once they had held out—by burning or ridicule—against the magic-religion of the witch-cults, the theurgy of Renaissance Hermeticists, or the saint-worship of ecstatic Catholicism. "The fact is," John Crowe Ransom writes in "Why Critics Don't Go Mad," "that Brooks and I were about as alike as two peas from the same pod in respect to our native region, our stock (we were sons of ministers of the same faith, and equally had theology in our blood), the kind of homes we lived in, the kind of small towns. . . . "

•

The Rational Imagination then meant the respectable, bounded by the fears and proprieties of the townsman's uses and means. It excluded something else, some irrational imagination; it excluded heathenish ways; it excluded highfalutin' ideas, putting on airs.

•

"The dimness of the religious light," Ransom writes in that same essay, "is an anti-Platonic image which seems to me entirely Miltonic. And it is much to my own taste. I am hurt by the glare to which Plato's philosophers coming out of the human cave are subjected; or for that matter Dante's Pilgrim coming perilously close in his Heavenly Vision; even in imagination my eyes cannot take it in."

.

Randall Jarrell's "more than a little silly" may have been meant to re-prove the Platonic theosophy of H.D. Pound, Williams, and H.D. be-longed to Pagany; they brought back in their poetry the spirit of Eleusis; against theology and metaphysics, an art that sought routes in experi-ence to the divine. "Say it, no ideas but in things," Williams wrote in the earliest beginnings of *Paterson*. "Nothing but the blank faces of houses," he continues, but read further: "—into the body of the light."

.

The light of Dante or of Plato, the spiritual light whereby men saw in dreams or in thought, but also the matter of the ancient world, the mothering Life or Great Mother, the dark mysteries of the underworld, offended the Protestant ethos. *Seely* which had meant "spiritually blessed," "pious, holy, good" was shortened to *silly* as the interests of the mercantile and capitalist class took over the direction of society and profitable works won out against grace as a measure of value. All traces of the earlier numinous meaning of *seely-silly* were replaced by the meaning of "lacking in judgment or common sense; foolish, senseless, empty-headed" or "feeble-minded, imbecile." The small town closed round its marketplace and customs, closed round its mind against silly things, and grew fearful of man's inner nature as it grew fearful or grew from fear of the nature outside.

.

The New Criticism, from the generation of Ransom or Yvor Winters to the generation of Jarrell or James Dickey, the critical small-town reaction, must strive against the Romantic tradition. The gods of *The*

Cantos or of The War Trilogy are out of order for any monotheistic conviction. The immediate address to Thoth, to Amen-Father, to whatever eternal ones of the dream or of the imagination, must be unconvincing and offensive to the monotheistic cult of Reason as it had been to the monotheistic cult of Jehovah. The hint in H.D.'s persuasion that we might not be bound by the Covenant:

> not in the higher air
> of Algorab, Regulus or Deneb
>
> shall we cry
> for help—or shall we?

or Pound's broken prayer in *The Pisan Cantos* (LXXIX) "O Lynx keep watch on my fire," if they were not silly, were irresponsible and might be dangerous, a breaking thru of old ways. The prayers and invocations to angelic powers, as if they had a ground in reality, a validity, comparable to "God," and this "God"-ness in turn, when it was not a metaphysical proposition but an experienced reality—the Christ actually appearing in the bare meeting-room of the Dream in *The Walls Do Not Fall* or the Lady's Presence in *Tribute to the Angels*—such things exceed the tolerance of the right-minded critic: it was idolatry or presumption. Beyond Imagism H.D., like Pound, had traveled the dangerous courses of image and the Divine Image, of idea and Eidolon. The schoolmen of literary taste took their stand with the schoolmen of modern Protestantism; the ground of experience was in divorce from God. Hadn't modern science turned the earth to its uses? Nature was not a Mother.

.

So for Jarrell or Fitts words were not powers but "counters" Fitts called them. "Pretty, expected, shopworn" if they were not smartly turned out. "This search," H.D. had anticipated their reaction of ennui, "has been done to death before." And she had answered that she meant not to rehearse *the* search for spiritual realities but to communicate her own particular way:

but my mind (yours)
has its peculiar ego-centric

personal approach

.

Where words thought of as generative or as in *The Walls Do Not Fall*
mediative between the reality of Dream and Vision and the reality of
the actual, moving to give birth to feeling and thought, language is our
Mother-Tongue. We see not only gods but words anew: "their secret is
stored / in man's very speech, / in the trivial or / the real dream." This
sense that everything is meaningful if one learn to read must have drawn
H.D. to Freud as a teacher. Certainly, her belief that the poet does not
give meaning to the word but draws meaning from it, touches meaning
or participates in meaning there, must have deepened in the psycho-
analytic work. The power of the artist that Freud revered most was his
daring to work more than he knew. The unconscious Freud called the
source, but it was only in the world of consciousness that the depths of
this experience could be read: the dream, the story, the work of art, was
a manifest matter. Back of Freud was the tradition of earlier Jewish mys-
ticism that sought in every thing and even in the universe a revelation
of Being. Words were shop-worn only to shop-wearing eyes. "I know, I
feel," H.D. writes—it is a condition of method in *The Walls Do Not Fall:*

> the meaning that words hide;
>
> they are anagrams, cryptograms,
> little boxes, conditioned
>
> to hatch butterflies . . .

.

Against the idea of the mothering language in which our psyche is
continually reborn, the matrix of meanings, of evolving thought and
feeling, the critical reaction raises its semantic boundaries, its language
as gesture or equation or statement. "Discipline," "control," "responsi-
bility" assume prohibitive definition, striving to exorcize the medium.

.

The very mother tongue was *"l'éternelle Vénus"* for the man tormented by the conscience of Church dogma or of middle-class regulations. The Great Mother was *"une des formes séduisantes du diable."* The city limits surrounded the marketplace empty of God and filled with a rabble then where men contended to set up standards of trade and values. Outside, there was the countryside where caprice, hysteria, fantasy—a female whorishness—swarmed in Nature in place of Truth.

Chapter 10

What is the truth of the matter. The gospel truth. For the truth of what actually happened we need a jury, "the recollection of adults," which Freud in the early essay "Screen Memories" would call upon to test the truth of childhood memories. Fact is one kind of truth of the matter. But the facts of memories, Freud began to suspect, have been reassembled into a fiction of the living. Each psyche strives in its account of the facts to present its peculiar experience; here the facts are not true in themselves but become true as factors of the fiction to which they contribute. When we have assembled from a group of witnesses—Matthew, Mark, Luke, and John—an account of the facts, only an ardent faith can coordinate the historical evidence in which every recounted fact is gospel truth of an actuality and the spiritual evidence in which every parable and revelation is gospel truth of a dogmatic reality.

•

The life experience of any individual is not simply a matter of its actualities but of its realities. The man who would present himself without the dimensions of dream and fantasy, much less the experience of illusion and error, who would render the true from the false by voiding the fictional and the doubtful, diminishes the human experience. In the extreme state of such an anxiety for what truth can be held with certainty, he has left only the terms defined by logical positivism with which to communicate; the rest is poetry, the made-up world—the forging of the conscience of his race.

.

In classifying "the various worlds of deliberate fable"—the world of the *Iliad,* of *King Lear,* of *The Pickwick Papers*—with the various worlds of faith—the Christian heaven and hell, the world of the Hindoo mythology, the world of Swedenborg's *visa et audita*—William James proposes that such fictions must each be "a consistent system" within which certain definite relations can be ascertained. "It thus comes about that we can say such things as that Ivanhoe did not *really* marry Rebecca, as Thackeray *falsely* makes him do. The real Ivanhoe world is the one which Scott wrote down for us. *In that world* Ivanhoe does *not* marry Rebecca." It is curious, given his pluralism, that just here James cannot allow that after the Ivanhoe world of Sir Walter Scott another Ivanhoe world could have reality. The history of Christianity is a history of bloody persecutions and wars waged in the high mania of true against false doctrines of what Jesus was and what the Christ was.

In the classical case, there is a strong tradition in Greek thought that Homer falsified the story of Helen. The poet Stesichorus was blinded (blind like Homer to the truth) after writing his *Helen* and wrote then a recantation of *Palinôdia* of which only a fragment remains: "That tale was never true! Thy foot never stepped on the benched galley, nor crossed to the towers of Troy." Whereupon, as the legend goes, he recovered his sight. The historian Herodotus tells us that he learned from the priests in Egypt that Helen was given refuge at the court of Proteus in Memphis thruout the war. "Within the enclosure stands a temple, which is called that of Aphrodite the Stranger," Herodotus testifies: "I conjecture the building to have been erected to Helen, the daughter of Tyndarus." And at the conclusion of the Egyptian account, Herodotus proceeds to give his own reasons as an historian for finding this tradition convincing. So too, Helen in Euripides' great drama testifies that she was never at Troy: "Let me tell you the truth / of what has happened to me." (Following here Richmond Lattimore's translation that carries into our tongue something of high poetry):

But Hera, angry that she was not given the prize,
made void the love that might have been for Paris and me
and gave him, not me, but in my likeness fashioning
a breathing image out of the sky's air, bestowed
this on King Priam's son, who thinks he holds me now
but holds a vanity which is not I.

Euripides does not recant the Homeric account of Troy but imagines in his drama the fiction of an historical Helen and a spiritual Helen, the one in Egypt and the other in Troy, the one the real body and the other an eidolon.

.

Yet James would stress the definite and consistent within each system of reality. "Neptune's trident, e.g., has no status of reality whatever in the Christian heaven; but within the classic Olympus certain definite things are true of it, whether one believe in the reality of the classic mythology as a whole or not." "The various worlds themselves, however, appear to most men's minds in no very definitely conceived relation to each other," he continues, speaking here of the larger sub-universes of reality—the world of sense, the world of science, the world of ideal relations, as well as the world of creative fictions: "and our attention, when it turns to one, is apt to drop the others for the time being out of its account." But even within the world of fictions, as James's own trouble with Thackeray's Ivanhoe exhibits, men find it difficult to entertain contradictory accounts it would seem, much less to imagine new syntheses in which all accounts can be seen as contributing to the truth. Both the historical telling of Jesus and the spiritual account of the Christ in the New Testament present inconsistencies that must be held in one system, and a Robert Graves who is obsessed with reducing the variety of realities to what really happened must labor to establish a true Nazarene Gospel by clearing away what he would persuade us is false in the texts of Matthew, Mark, Luke, and John.

.

In the same year of James's *Psychology* (1890), Sir James Frazer in *The Golden Bough* began to advance another sense of supernatural systems, where in place of separate and discrete worlds or churches, nations or races of the spirit and mind, incomparable truths, self-consistent, he raised the picture of a field of religious order where Neptune's trident was no longer assumed to have no status of reality whatever in the Christian heaven. To the consternation of such a view, Frazer was to look for Neptune and trident in all other orders—"emblem of Hittite thunder-god, emblem of Indian deity . . . ," composing a language of persona, symbol, image, and emblem that would dissolve the pluralism of cultures and civilizations in the monism of a larger language of human meanings.

•

The exclusive truth that defines any individual order, in what it excludes, may be seen as false to the larger fabric of orders. Every factor of human experience has its own truth in its potency. It is more fluid, more interwoven with other realities than James allows. Neptune's trident that had no status of reality in the Christian heaven rose from the same ground, was child, as Heaven was, of man's imagination become most real. Toynbee in his *Study of History,* some fifty years after James's *Psychology,* would trace the Kingdom of Heaven back to the idea of a cloud kingdom as it appears in Aristophanes' fantasy of Cloudcuckooland. And if we look not in the upper world of Christian belief but in the lower world, we may find Neptune's trident in the pitchfork among the instruments of Hell's monitors.

•

Besides things as facts, there is another aspect of things as information, what sets up those widening circles of meaning and influence, what rings true. Neptune's trident that once seemed discordant, out of mode or system, now is heard in another, larger or higher sense of scale to be true. By the inspired subscription of the Council of Nicaea in 325 A.D. it is true and only it is true of Christ that he was the only begotten Son of God and was of the substance of God, who was incarnate, made Man, and suffered the Crucifixion. But by the inspired testament of *The Acts of John* the

Lord not only suffered but he did not suffer. The Christ of this Gnostic gospel is a Heraklitean Christ and His revelation is the suffering of the cross that is also the playing upon the Cross of the Contraries. "For you I call this cross of light," He says to Saint John: "now logos, now spirit, now Jesus, now Christ, now door, now way, now bread, now seed . . . " "God and the World," Whitehead proposes in *Process and Reality,* "are the contrasted opposites in terms of which Creativity achieves its supreme task of transforming disjoined multiplicity with its diversities in opposition, into concrescent unity, with its diversities in contrast."

•

I take the poem, any poem, as a product of this "Creativity" as the individual experiences it in language, to convey the transformation of a multiplicity of impressions into a unity of expression, that now becomes in its own order part of a new multiplicity of what poetry is, a pending material of the need for a new transformation.

•

Here, the poet's sense of the truth of his matter is not that it belongs to some previous system, that it happened or didn't happen in history, that it is defined as orthodox or heretical, but that it belongs to the work in which he is engaged. Here, his responsibility to the truth is to test the action of sound and sense in the process of its creation of its own definition. He must recognize what is going on. In his *Maximus,* Charles Olson insists the ear must listen, and he speaks in terms of sea depths; "a peak of the ocean's floor he knew so well the care / he gave his trade, his listening / at 17 to Callaghan (as Callaghan, / at 17, to Bohlen, / Bohlen to Smith), Olsen," as Olson in the language:

> could set his dories out
> as a landsman sows his fields
>
> and reap such halibut . . .

•

Gloucester, for Olson, is not a small town boundary for the mind, but a locus of the Earth. The continent and the sea are real, or elemental to the great reality. The nation or state of mind is another thing, a project of certain men to exploit the communities of other men. So there is "pejorocracy"; there is ownership of utilities—the sea or land or language—proprietorships men would make over truth or means to close off—the wondership, Olson calls it—the freedom any man has to take thought and to create in what he is.

•

"Evil was active in the land," is, in *The Walls Do Not Fall,* not only the War-Rule, usurping the creative will from each individual and forcing all action and language into its own terms, but it is also "tricked up like Jehovah," the Puritan ethos or its descendant the capitalist ethos or its ancestor the monotheistic ethos. "They were angry when we were so hungry / for the nourishment, God" refers not only to the Laws of Moses that ban certain actual foods, but to the banning of some food of the soul, of some experience. "They snatched off our amulets."

•

they whine to my people, these entertainers, sellers
they play upon their bigotries (upon their fears
Maximus cries.

•

At the end of the nineteenth century, when William James was writing his *Psychology* and James Frazer his *Golden Bough,* even intelligent men, men with something larger than small-town minds, still thought, not of all men being civilized in a variety of civilizations, but of "civilized" men and of "primitives" or savages, and of "advanced" civilizations and "retarded" civilizations. It was a late version of the old Christian sense of the City and the wilderness—heathen land or pagany; or back of that of the older division between the City and the barbarian world.

But today there are some, men in every field of thought and feeling who begin to picture in their work a species of humanity, a "we" where Australian bushman and Manhattan cityman each have community, where mud beehive forms and concrete tower forms are differing, contrasting but not opposing, expressions of being men. "There is no more striking general fact about language," Edward Sapir writes in

1921 in *Language,* "than its universality. One may argue as to whether a particular tribe engages in activities that are worthy of the name of religion or of art, but we know of no people that is not possessed of a fully developed language. The lowliest South African Bushman speaks in the forms of a rich symbolic system that is in essence perfectly comparable to the speech of the cultivated Frenchman. . . . Scarcely less impressive than the universality of speech is its almost incredible diversity. Those of us that have studied French or German, or, better yet, Latin or Greek, know in what varied forms a thought may run."

THE CHRIST AS PERSON OF THE POEM

Helen is at Troy; Helen is in Egypt. The spectral Helen in Marlowe's *Doctor Faustus* is desire "performed in twinkling of an eye," Beauty that would draw a man's soul forth from him. The Helena of Goethe's *Faust* is an intelligence, where Joy and Beauty are known in one and lost. One Helen *is* the other Helen. Herodotus will be concerned to find the historical Helen: the truth was, he tells us, she was in Egypt. The Trojan Helen was a wraith of men's minds. But the poetic truth has to do with the existence of a real unity or creation seeking its fullness in many personae, in many places, in many times. We will never understand the power of the mistress of Simon Magus if we believe her to be only a whore from Tyre, for it is an important part of her meaning that she is also the great Helen who was born from the egg of Leda, and was daughter of Zeus.

•

So too the *persona* of the Christos is continually created in the imagination. *Mythos* and *drômenon,* gospel and rite, are events first of poetry. This god Christ will not rest in an historical identity, but again and again seeks incarnation anew in our lives. The religious will takes the Divine as given, "uncreated," and seeks to use the god as an authority against any further creation of the idea of the god, drawing upon the spell of magic voice and action in which the Christ is real to convert, yet working thruout to establish prohibition and dogma to limit the creative energy to the immediate purpose. The powers that a Paul must use to set up one Church or one authoritative Christ in the place of many meanings and images, against the authors, come not from an historical Jesus where the truth of things can be located and done with but come from the fullness of a person that is hidden in the creative life, from a dangerous source. Creation and persuasion contend in the use. The cause must be drawn from the expression.

"Yet every cause," Burckhardt writes in *Force and Freedom*, "is in some way alienated and profaned by being expressed." "In the course of time, religion realizes how freely free art is behaving, moulding its material." The Church seeks to impose an unfree style, "the function of which is to represent only the sacred aspect of things, i.e., it must abandon the totality of the living object."

.

"Art is the most arrant traitor of all, firstly because it profanes the substance of religion," he continues. For the artist there is no established Truth, but events, ideas, things have their truth hidden in a form yet to be realized. "Secondly, because it possesses a high and independent selfhood, in virtue of which its union with anything on earth is necessarily ephemeral and may be dissolved at any time. And those unions are very free, for all that art will accept from religion or any other themes is a stimulus. The real work of art is born of its own mysterious life."

.

It is in the mystery-life of poem and novel, picture and drama, that Helen and Christ emerge as eternal persons of our human spirit, and again and again must be drawn from their conventions into their own life. Here the high and independent selfhood of each work of art is the vehicle of the reincarnation. H.D. working anew the Christos-Amen of her War Trilogy must free her figure from the predispositions of old ideas towards a life of its own. "The Christos-image / is most difficult to disentangle," she writes in *The Walls Do Not Fall*:

> from its art-craft junk-shop
> paint-and-plaster medieval jumble
>
> of pain-worship and death-symbol,

The difficulty of the separation coming into the operation of the poem, the medieval jumble and even the junk shop have been brought up and must haunt the picture then as a negative image. So Fitts finds his after-impression that the poem is "pseudo-medieval."

•

The Christ that is "the Presence . . . spectrum-blue, / ultimate blue ray" is not medieval but belongs to the Alexandrian orientalizing Greek world, to Gnostic doctrines of the Light Body and to neo-Platonic theories of the soul being moved spiritually thru the senses. This world of thought was revived by the Renaissance Platonists, following Pletho and Ficino. Sound was thought of as spiritually effective because it had movement, but color, though it came second to sound in order, was not primary because it was thought of as a static appearance. Following Newton's demonstration that white light could be broken up by a prism into the spectral colors red, orange, yellow, green, blue, indigo, and violet, theosophists identified the seven colors with the seven arch-angels, as before they had so identified the scale of seven tones. And following the early nineteenth century theories of color as vibration, the whole world of spirit was identified with a world of vibrations in which now color and sound were equally primary as spiritual forces. Kandinsky in *Concerning the Spiritual in Art* speaks theosophically as well as psychologically when he tells us that in the color blue "We feel a call to the infinite, a desire for purity and transcendence. *Blue is the typical heavenly color;* the ultimate feeling it creates is one of rest." "Rare as radium," H.D. describes her blue ray, "as healing."

It is a rarefied Christ H.D. would evoke here, the power of a pure color, the presentation of a dream where "deftly stage-managed" the bare, clean meeting-house interior suggests the spirituality of innerness, the language of inner light of the Moravian communion stripped bare of the morbid fascination with the wounds and blood of the Crucified. At last, it is the image from Velasquez that emerges and here where the terror and agony that would "stun us with the old sense of guilt" is hidden by lowered eye-lids, in the remove of high art, the figure is accepted.

•

But, "most difficult to disentangle," in its high and independent self-hood, the persona is haunted thruout by past lives. Long before the art-craft junk-shop of the nineteenth and twentieth centuries, before the dolls of Christ with up-rolled eyes, leaking piety from nailed palms, there was another Image that appeared in the Gothic world of Christ in torment. In a Christendom torn by savage wars of church against church and church against heresy the very ground of Christ was one of abject and evil suffering. With the great plagues of the fifteenth and sixteenth centuries sweeping the crowded populations of the new cities, not only wounds but sores ran from the Image. Is it against such Images, as if they were not true—against the Christ of Perpignan in the fifteenth century or the Christ of Grünewald in the sixteenth century—that H.D. would avoid the "medieval jumble / of pain-worship and death-symbol" and pose the Image of the Velasquez crucifixion?

.

If we compare the *Christ Carrying the Cross* of Bosch, contemporary with the crucified Christ of Grünewald, we see in the sixteenth century the expression of two contrasting images—the heterodox Quietist Master of Bosch and the orthodox Catholic Man of Grünewald. In the wholeness of the imagination they are magnetic alternates of one Image, having their life each in each. In their high and independent selfhood they are dependent upon each other. They exist in the range of a higher union, as, we may begin to see, H.D.'s Christos, rightly, exists in the disentangling she feels necessary, in the difficulty.

.

"And Heraclitus rebukes the poet who says, 'would that strife might perish from among gods and men.' They understand not how that which is at variance with itself agrees with itself. There is an attunement of opposite tensions, like that of the bow and the harp."

.

The crucifixion was not only a punishment (as those who judged Him saw it), not only a sacrifice, passion, and endurance, in the name of the world's sin (as the cult of pain-worship saw it), not only a compassion (as the cult of the Redeemer saw it), but also not a punishment, not a suffering, but, if one saw it as a thing in itself, a drama enacted, it was a play of revelation, or a dance. "To each and all it is given to dance," the Christ tells John at Ephesus: "He who joins not in the dance mistakes the event."

•

The eighteenth century Christ of the dream in The War Trilogy has its origins in the very figure we see in the work of Bosch and in the Gnostic Christ of St. John at Ephesus, in the heterodox tradition. The critical opposition—where those of orthodox persuasion considered The War Trilogy at all—had its origins too in the contentions raised against such a Christ of the Eternal Present, as if the truth of Grünewald's Christ must mean the falsity, the "irresponsible even perverse" and "naive" counter of Bosch. For the heretic sects, as often for mystics within the environs of the established Catholic and Protestant churches, the pain, death, and judgment of Christ were a dramatic reality in their own persecution, a ground for vision and meaning. He was a persona not of a contention in history but of an eternal event. The Christ of Bosch is not a victim but an actor in a mystery.

•

It is against the very idea of the Eternal that the critics of The War Trilogy strike. Jarrell's quip that "H.D. is History and misunderstands a later stage of herself so spectacularly that her poem exists primarily as an anachronism," [and] Fitts's outrage at the incantation (the music of the dance), knowingly or unknowingly echo the outrage and contempt of Church Fathers for deviate ideas of Christ outside the History of the Church.

Attacking the "Myth" of H.D.'s Christos-Amen, H.H. Watts wrote: "Whatever, then, the sources of the poet's view, it amounts to this: any man may, in his life, draw the inspired circle with a full sense that it coincides exactly with other circles drawn by past men, since they too were touched by the Vision that came from the Healer"—a view of H.D.'s sense of the past at work within the present that would seem to dismiss without consideration her insistence that each experience "differs from every other/in minute particulars." But Watts is concerned to dismiss, not to explore, the mythopoeic ground of H.D.'s thought.

Having established to his satisfaction that her method is mistaken, Watts expresses his contempt in his conclusion: "Very moving, if there be such a composite figure as Amen-Christos, such a fixed point, such an as-if. But one does not put a roof to bare ruined walls by means of an intensely felt metaphor or, to be quite fair, an emotional *aperçu* that is apparently the product of serious, extensive reading in comparative religion." Is there back of this the outrage of a man who in his own belief knows the true Christ, the one that really is, against the false images of the Christ that the human creativity raises? Or is there the outrage of the rational atheist who will have no traffic with things of the imagination at all?

•

H.D., Pound, and Lawrence, in their poetic vision saw the art-craft image as the god played false. Where what had been a passion is reduced to a lynching or a martyrdom as the social realist imagination sees the man as a victim, Christ beatnik or Christ under-dog. What goes false here is that these figures made real for the one-way literal mind, cleared of all intensely felt metaphor or as-if, act to block further activity of the imagination. The art-craft junk-shop and the scholastic criticism (biblical or literary) concur in their stand against the possibility of resonance and meaning.

•

This is not "our" Christos, H.D. insists. Her generation had a distaste for the warped emotionality of the cultivated sense of sin and suffering in the generation preceding theirs. The very aesthetic of the modern with its clean line and direct image was a reaction against morbidity. "This more or less masochistic and hell-breeding belief is always accompanied," Pound wrote in "Cavalcanti" of the prejudice against the body, "by bad and niggled sculpture (Angoulême or Bengal)."

•

They drew from everywhere it seemed, from "extensive reading in comparative religion," cooperative with many sources, to create a new composition that would stand against the public culture and its images. As Augustine had brought his City of God to stand in place of the actual

Rome, they brought inner images and evocations of the divine world to stand against the actual megalopolis. Not only H.D., but Lawrence, Pound, Joyce, and, for all his claim for orthodoxy, Eliot, strive for a composite art to embody the individual composite. "A man in himself is a city, beginning, seeking, achieving and concluding his life in ways which the various aspects of a city may embody," Williams proposes in *Paterson* and, for all his claim for the local against the international, Williams's America is a composite of times and places: "if imaginatively conceived—any city, all the details of which may be made to voice his most intimate convictions."

·

The Christs of public worship then that embody the convictions of Roman Catholic power or of Protestant capitalism, the art-craft gods of the manufacturers and consumers of commodities are false to the inner convictions of the poet. Pound and Joyce avoid Christ entirely, and Lawrence and H.D. must recreate Him. But the Christ of Lawrence and H.D. is of the same order as the Helios or the crystal body of Aphrodite in Pound's *Cantos,* or the Living God of Lawrence's last poems. The Divine Beings of our poets are presentations of their most intimate conviction—the creative imagination. Aphrodite and Pomona attend Pound in his Pisan cell as a higher reality. "I assure you that the eyes / of Velasquez' crucified," H.D. tells us:

> now look straight at you,
> and they are amber and they are fire.

I.

She had "gay blue eyes," William Carlos Williams tells us, and the Priestess of Isis in Lawrence's *The Man Who Died* who looks up at him "with her wondering blue eyes" may recall H.D. Not only readings in comparative religion but scenes from actual life enter into the composite to become the matter in which the divine presents itself. H.D., in picturing the confrontation of Mary Magdalene and Kaspar, and

Lawrence, in picturing the confrontation between his Man-Who-Died and the priestess, may each draw from their own confrontation in the Bloomsbury days, creating from each his model a new reality.

.

"Has Isis brought thee home to herself?" the woman asks the Christ of Lawrence's story. "I know not," he says.

"But the woman was pondering that this was the lost Osiris," Lawrence continues: "She felt it in the quick of her soul. And her agitation was intense." It was Orpheus that H.D. in her agitation saw Lawrence as; but Orpheus too was torn into many fragments and scattered.

.

It is Christ-Osiris in The War Trilogy whose eyes open, as in Lawrence's novella the eyes of the Man-Who-Died open "upon the other life, the greater day of the human consciousness." "To charge with meaning to the utmost possible degree," Pound had asked of the poem. For Lawrence, as for H.D. and Pound, the revulsion for the Christ as Sin-Bearer is a revulsion for the way He sees life. The Man Who Died rises from nausea and disillusion. The Christ-life had been a sickness, of soul and body: "I wanted to be greater than the limits of my hands and feet, so I brought betrayal on myself. And I know I wronged Judas, my poor Judas . . . But Judas and the high priests saved me from my own salvation." For Lawrence, the revelation was not in the Passion on the Cross but in the Man re-born. The priestess of Isis had been told: "Rare women wait for the re-born man. For the lotus, as you know, will not answer to all the bright heat of the sun. But she curves her dark, hidden head in the depths, and stirs not. Till, in the night, one of these rare, invisible suns that have been killed and shine no more, rises among the stars in unseen purple."

II.

Pound in the early period of The Spirit of Romance and the Cavalcanti essay, perhaps in his close association with Yeats, is concerned with an art that would "revive the mind of the reader . . . with some form of ecstasy, by some splendor of thought, some presentation of sheer beauty." In *The Cantos,* Cypris-Aphrodite, Dionysos, Kuthera, and Kore attend at Pisa, and in *Thrones,* "the boat of Ra-Set moves with the sun," but he will not let Christ move. Pound, mentor and monitor of *Kulchur,* bending his mind to furnish his "Chronology for school use," avoids the question of Christ and of the ecstatic.

•

In 1916 his mind was more open. "Christianity and all other forms of ecstatic religion," Pound writes in *Psychology and Troubadours,* "are not in inception dogma or propaganda of something called the *one truth* . . . their general object appears to be to stimulate a sort of confidence in the life-force." In "Cavalcanti" he writes again: "There is a residue of perception, perception of something which requires a human being to produce it. Which even may require a certain individual to produce it. This really complicates the aesthetic. You deal with an interactive force: the *virtu* in short."

•

Lawrence's *Man Who Died* and H.D.'s "over Love, a new Master" are creative projections, new images of a force or *virtu,* imagined along the line of interaction between the poet and the inspiring world, a life-force between percept and concept.

•

The personification that for Hulme was a literary device related to the conceit to heighten impression, to remove the thing seen from its common associations and to render it divergent and interesting:

    And saw the ruddy moon lean over a hedge
    Like a red-faced farmer

—for H.D. or for Lawrence was something quite different, coming into being along the route of a conversion, a feeling towards the deeper reality of the thing seen. They sought not originality but to recover a commune of spirit in the image. The "Make It New" that Pound took as his motto could stand for the old renewed as well as for the new replacing the old. Not only the experiment for novelty but also the psyche in its metamorphosis and the phoenix.

·

The truth here is the truth of what feeds the life of the organism where "prompted by hunger, / it opens to the tide-flow" but in its openness conservative of the poet's range of feeling. "But infinity? no," H.D. warns: "of nothing-too-much: I sense my own limit." As in *The Man Who Died,* Lawrence's persona resolves, "Now I know my own limits. Now I can live without striving to sway others any more. For my reach ends in my finger-tips and my stride is no longer than the ends of my shoes."

We sense it right away when a poet or painter is using a doll of Christ to project a given attitude, for the figure postures to present suffering or brotherly love and has no other life of its own. Even a master like El Greco, obsessed with attitude, will lose the persona. The doll of Christ becomes the occasion of a sanctified grievance that can easily be allied with the sanctions the artist or his patron would give to his own griev-ance. The exchange or interaction within What Is is closed off, and an inflation of attitude is drawn from the hubris involved.

In the exchange, the man makes a place for the God to be. In him-self—the stigmata of a Saint Francis appear in the intensity of the com-passion. Or the man as artist makes a place in his work for the God to be.

In the inflation, the man makes a place for his self, his grievance or guilt, to be deified in the doll.

·

We know the difference between the gods of vanity and the gods of desire. But my sense here is that in every event of his art man dwells in mixed possibilities of inflation and inspiration. Hence the constant warnings Dante must receive from Virgil and then from Beatrice. The locus of the Vision must be clearly given at the opening. The dark wood, the she-wolf, the leopard, and the lion may be allegorical figures of Dante's own times, of the Papal See, the city of Florence, and the

Royal House of France; but they are also, most certainly, real figures of Dante's own psyche, his acknowledgment of his own limits.

.

Dante's sense of his own place is the foundation of the Dream, the locus of its Truth. "Thou art my master and my author," he addresses Virgil—it is the Permission of the poet Dante in the man Dante. The glory is to be universal, not personal. The poet must not—it is the commandment of vision—usurp authority in his office. This is what Blake in turn means when he tells us "the authors are in eternity." Dante's master and author, Blake's authors, are counterparts of Thoth and the New Master, not only over Love but over the Poem, in H.D.'s Trilogy. These things, the poet testifies, I did not see by my own virtues, but they were revealed to me.

.

In the tenth circle of the *Inferno,* where the falsifiers of word and coinage contend, Dante loses his locus as poet. "I was standing all intent to hear them," he tells us—he had been lost in the contests of the damned; some personal wish of his feeding upon the wrathful spectacle: "when the Master said to me: 'Now keep looking, a little longer and I quarrel with thee!'" *"For the wish to hear it,"* Virgil adds, *"is a vulgar wish."*

.

All Paradise and Saint Peter wax red in a famous scene of the *Paradiso* at the thought of how Boniface VIII uses the Office of Pope as a personal power. "He who usurpeth upon earth my place, my place, my place," Peter exclaims: *"il loco mio, il loco mio, il loco mio."* It is the wrath of the Office misused.

.

Dante is about to witness in the Office of the Poet the splendor of God, the Rose Itself, and there may be a warning in this reminder of *il loco mio* that the poet too is to most remember his place. But the author and master of the *Divine Comedy,* the poet, has also his locus—it is the work itself. And Dante, to know his own place, but writes the work in service of, as agent of, that author.

III.

March 28, 1961. Tuesday.

There is, then, not only the order of *Paterson* and *The Cantos* in which we may consider The War Trilogy as a vision of our own times; but there is another order of dream or vision-poem disclosing the soul's journey from this world thru "Apocryphal fire," leaving "the-place-of-a-skull/ to those who have fashioned it"—How Virgil has to warn Dante to let Hell be—and coming at last into the presence of God in which works as various as *The Divine Comedy* or Bunyan's *Pilgrim's Progress* may be of a kind with H.D.'s Trilogy.

•

Dante, the heir of a cult in Christendom of Amor; Bunyan, a preaching seventeenth century Protestant convert, certainly no heir of a high poetic tradition; and H.D., late Imagist, versed in a Hermetic-Christian lore of the twentieth century. But to each the order or worth of this world is revealed in the light of another world. Man's spirit is seen more ardent, more in need. Angelic and daemonic spirits attend, and the narrative is in the terms of a religious convention the story of the individual soul's trials or stations in consciousness towards an authority or author who is God.

•

Each is a Dream-Vision. "I cannot rightly tell how I entered it," Dante tells us, "so full of sleep was I about the moment that I left the true way." The *selva oscura* is a dark passage of the Life-Dream, and the poet is moved by what Dante in the close of the Comedy calls his high fantasy.

•

In Bunyan's case he had, he tells us, set about to write an allegory. Well, no . . . he says:

> And thus it was: I writing of the Way
> And Race of Saints, in this our Gospel Day
> Fell suddenly into an Allegory
> About their Journey and the way to Glory.

·

To "fall into" an Allegory is, in this case, like falling in love or falling into a revery, to be compelled in the Work by a creative force—"in Eternity," Blake said that force was. Where what the imagination sees is acknowledged to be, not an unreal thing, nor an invention of the poet, but a higher reality revealed. The book itself becomes the Way. The journal, the daily return to the imagination of the book, becomes the journey.

·

"*In the similitude of a* DREAM," Bunyan subtitles the Progress.

·

Then there is, as in a fairy tale, the primary condition that the soul has lost the straight way and finds itself bewildered, having no way out except its angel or daimon direct. "Through the wilderness of this world," Bunyan has it. "So," H.D. tells us, "through our desolation / thoughts stir." "And they again began to multiply," Bunyan testifies, "Like sparks that from the coals of fire do fly."

·

It is like a dream but not a dream, this going out into the world of the poem, inspired by the directions of an other self. It has a kinship too with the séance of the shaman, and in this light we recognize the country of the poem as being like the shaman's land of the dead or the theosophical medium's astral plane. In the story of Orpheus there is a hint of how close the shaman and the poet may be, the singer and the seer.

·

Hermes in the old lore guides the poet in the underworld, as Virgil guides Dante in the Inferno. Briefly, in *The Cantos,* Plotinus appears to rescue Pound from the hell-mire of politicians and dead issues, but Pound is eager to interrupt the inspiration of his poem and to direct its course.

It is the originality of Pound that mars his intelligence. The goods of the intellect are communal; there is a *virtu* or power that flows from the language itself, a fountain of man's meanings, and the poet seeking the help of this source awakens first to the guidance of those who have gone before in the art, then the guidance of the meanings and dreams that all who have ever stored the honey of the invisible in the hive have prepared.

IV.

March 29, 1961. Wednesday.
From Bunyan's *Apology to Pilgrim's Progress:*

> Would'st read thy self, and read thou know'st not what
> And yet know whether thou art blest or not
> By reading the same lines? O then come hither,
> And lay my Book, thy Head, and Heart together.

—from this verse of Bunyan's we may go on to the close of H.D.'s poem "Good Frend," where H.D. calls upon Shakespeare as her author, with "Avon's Trinity":

> When one is Three and Three are One,
> The Dream, the Dreamer and the Song.

Chapter 11

Glimpses of the Last Day: In the West some intense fire burned, red in the evening. Fires were scattered over the landscape, descending suddenly as if cages or caps of flames had been clamped down from another realm above over men where they were, working in the fields or on their way home, or as if footsteps of angelic orders, fateful and yet oblivious of the individual, had burst into flame. At random the incendiary blows fell and yet with a purpose everywhere to charge the world with the realization of its last day. Just here, and then just here, blows shook the earth, fires broke out, and men swarmed to recover the ground.

The landscape was out of Bosch's *Temptation of Saint Anthony* or Brueghel's *Dulle Griet,* a countryside with fields and hamlets laid waste by war or by industry and mining. For I have never seen a city under fire, but hitch-hiking thru West Virginia and Pennsylvania, I have seen such desolate and wrathful landscapes at night where man's devastating work has raised great mountains of slag and left great pits in the earth, burning wastes and befouled rivers that appear an earthly Hell. In the dream, the visitation is, like these actual landscapes, a just rendering of some desire of man's fulfilled. One of the afterthoughts of the dream was that this Last Day had to do with all men coming into one reality out of the—*unreal,* I called it in the dream, when I was conferring with the Doctor at the spring. It would be many things for many men but for all at last, not just for men in Europe and Asia but for America too, there would be the fires, the laying waste. It was "the lightning shattered earth and splintered sky" of the poem I have kept as my text, the "zrr-hiss" of *Tribute to the Angels*.

·

The scene of the Flemish apocalyptic paintings was a pervasive reference. It had transformed or taken over the locus of San Francisco where the Flemish valley lay between Twin Peaks and the Bay, and the far-away incandescence glared out of the darkness of Playland-at-the-Beach, where the Pacific now meant the Abyss itself. The distant circle of burnings was the horizon. The spring, where the Doctor (Charles Olson) and I met to work the drawing of the waters in the primal direction, was in the East—it would have been the Berkeley hills. But here, the reference to my own city was gone (as too, there was no likeness to Olson's Gloucester). The Place of the Spring was in the high mountains. Yet even as I write this the sense of high mountains seems wrong. I saw the mist-cloud realm of Ibsen's Professor Rubek and Irene in *When We Dead Awaken,* as I saw those heights long ago reading the play, and then another high place from Ibsen's *Little Eyolf*—for a second, Allmer's "Upwards—towards the peaks. Towards the stars. And towards the great silence." Then, replacing the idea of high mountains, I see as I write that the Place of the Spring was a cleft of the Mother Earth between low-lying hills.

The Doctor was certainly Olson, but that certainty did not belong to my first recognition in the dream. The important thing at first was that he was Jewish, not the Messiah, but that other beneficent power, the hidden rabbi, the Zaddik. So I told myself in the dream he is Einstein, he knows the numbers of the cosmos. He may have been Freud—Freud, the new Master over Love in H.D.'s life, but also Freud the Master of dreams. But Freud did not occur to me in the dream itself. No, I thought, it is not Einstein, it's Charles. As I saw it was Charles, it was in his glance, how those familiar eyes beamed with the thought of our task together at the spring.

As, early in the dream, there had been another poet I knew. The youthful master of the incandescence was Robin Blaser. He existed on two levels or in two orders. In one, as a fellow in that earlier stage where all of us men sometimes courageously battled the fires that sprang up, sometimes cowered in panic, he told me of his dream concerning that incandescence. It was as he told me of it that I first saw that disk of fire. And then, thru his telling, thru his dream within my dream, I saw another Robin—Redbreast, I thought when I woke from the dream, and tried to figure: *Who killed Cock Robin?* Suggestions of an old rite seemed hidden in the dream figures. Along this line of half-waking digression I was led by that other haunting nursery rime, *The Hunting of the Wren.* "We will go to the wood, says Robin to Bobbin." There may have been some distant periphery where the Wren Boys made their rounds. The Robin of the dream may have been Robin Hood, a person of the life drama, like the Child in childhood or the Man in manhood. There was too, ever ready in my post-Freudian associations, "red Breast" and "cock robbing." But the fact of the dream or vision remains: for the disk was not of fire or flame or destruction but was a pool of heat and light that drew all of us men out of our selves into its incandescence. The Robin of my dream was the fire man I saw long ago in the séance at Woodstock before the War.

So there was the other pun: Blazer. The white that was also red-hot, that burned, that was-to-burn something of me into a black charcoal, and to fire something of me into a radiance, was a blaze, a blazon or sign or seal of God as a pure intensity. Robin Blaser was a shepherd of this place of seal. The incandescence may have been the Fleece then. He was the tender. Now it comes to me that within this radius, this blazon was the spot that flares up, the tender spot as well as the threatening spot.

I was afraid, I told him. As if there were some great pain or agony in the blaze, and yet knowing there was no pain, no agony—only radiance. Robin's dream made a bridge between the Last Day (my dream time) and the Blazon (his dream place) where it seemed I went to try the fear I had, for I did in the dream anticipate my burning up in the heat to a black clinker, my entering the light.

Yet, with this vision of what was at last, of lasting things, there remained the works of the last days. As Robin tended the region of the incandescence, but also related his dreaming of that place, so I had my work to do. I was among men fighting the fires that sprang up bewilderingly where the steps fell. I was terrified as they were, cowering and praying in the dream that these strokes pass over my head.

Then came the break-thru of astral forms, a streaming down into this landscape, where Bosch's vision and my own San Francisco were already mingled, of another world, a coming together of universes. Giants and monsters, phantasms of Norse and Greek gods from storybooks of childhood, images of past eras, Palaeozoic and Mesozoic, fell as if poured out of their imaginary being into this one time and one world. It was the sign in the dream whereby I knew what must be done. I had known from the beginning and told those about me that we were in the Last Days, in the Glory then. Now the change came.

"The astral worlds have fallen down," I told those about me. "We must redirect the spring" or "we must *draw* the springs in the first direction" or "the right direction."

The Doctor came into the picture then. We went together or we met at the spring to draw forth the waters once more. I told him about the fall of the giant orders into the world. "How can the unreal have as much effect as the real?" I asked.

He was Einstein, Doctor of the Cosmos, and then Olson. Where I see now the cover of Olson's *O'Ryan* with the giant Orion drawn in his stars by Jess. The falling of the astral worlds may be, then, the falling of the sky, where giant stars and dwarves, monstrous constellations and regents of the planets stream down in the collapse of time. Here, the Doctor and I must restore the Milky Way, the spring of stars that is our universe.

The Doctor had a key to the old science of the spring. I had to find the lock, but now it seems that I draw the waters forth by the physical magnetism of a shaman, witching, pulling invisible reins of the stream with my hands.

"You who are nearest to me," I said to the Doctor, "are unreal." I could see thru his form, yet just then he seemed most dear. A sentence of Heraklitus comes to mind now which had been a theme in Olson's

San Francisco evenings in 1957: "Man is most estranged from that which is most familiar."

The Doctor belonged to a supernatural order. At this moment of estrangement, there was a more powerful return. It was here that his eyes, most Charles's, beamed upon me, that I saw Charles in the Doctor or thru the Doctor, at once my superior and my companion in the work at the springs.

I.

To have a companion is a happiness. But these were not the springs of happiness but of meaning.

•

"The pursuit of happiness," of good fortune then, of *la bonne heure,* good time, that inalienable right that those merchants, bankers and farmers set high who made their Declaration of Independence for these United States, is a vanity, even a vice, when it blinds men to life as a work. *Le bonheur* comes as a gift. It is easy to think of good times as a gift, but bad times too are a gift. It is the hour itself that comes as a gift, the time of the Work; and the artist learns early that it is not happiness, but what is meaningful, an appointment, what verges upon the mystery of his being, that may be hard to bear, that opens once more, more than happiness or unhappiness, the joy or flower of life. It is not a chance on the wheel of fortune but a chance to work he must seek, where from the many roots of what he is and of what he has known streams of humanity, of animal life, of divine wish, flow towards the beauty that can be terrible, the flower, that precedes the good fruit.

•

"I shall have no peace until I get the subject off my chest," Pound wrote, sometime in 1932, in his *ABC of Economics.* He was never to have that peace. The subject itself was to lead him from the *claritas* of this little book, with its interweavings of ideal and practical views, on to the disturbed and then contentious pamphlets against those great windmills of the capitalist order—the usury of investment capital and the economy of war. "After about forty pages," he wrote in the *ABC*, "I shall not 'descend,' but I shall certainly go into, 'go down into' repetitions and restatements in the hope of reaching this clarity and simplicity." "'Capital' for the duration of this treatise implies a sort of claim on others, a sort of right to make others work. My bond of the X and Y railroad is capital. Somebody is supposed to earn at least 60 dollars a year and pay it to me because I own such a bond."

•

What he wanted was to restore time for the communal good. The necessary work must be distributed among all able to work. This would mean a shorter working day and time for creative work. It meant production for social needs, not for speculation. What Pound wanted was not the pursuit of happiness but the pursuit of the good. This taking thought toward the distribution of goods was an extension of early democratic thought in America. It meant finally that all men must be citizens, living in the imagination of the common good, against privilege. Which Adams saw "requires the continual exercise of virtue beyond the reach of human infirmity, even in its best estate."

•

"Any spare time not absolutely obsessed by worry can be the means to a 'better life'": this was the crux of Pound's concern. It was 1932. The Depression—the meaning of "worry"—was economic (as now it is psychological and becoming apocalyptic). For the poor, enslaved by want, idle hours meant jobless hours. For the rich, idle hours meant time to waste, money to waste, profit to waste. Men selling their hours, so that labor came to mean a commodity of so-much time and not a means towards some good, struggled to get more of the profits, to increase the price of work-time, or feared for their livelihood. We have left from the waxing twenties, fat after the holocaust of moneymaking in the war, records of what life was like for those who had lost the goods of the intellect for the commodities of a cultured sensibility: the deracinated drift of Scott Fitzgerald or the inhabitants of Eliot's *The Waste Land*.

Capitalist society, as Marx had rightly pointed out, exploited materials and men's labor towards a profit that was empty of meaning. The whole speculative possibility of the market grew up around panics of inflation and depression, sales-manias, war-manias, and time-wasting.

•

"Leisure is not gained by simply being out of work. Leisure is spare time *free from anxiety*": that was one side of Pound's sense, quickened by his knowledge of how men were wasted in the job-commodity market, by the spectacle of drifting rich and destitute poor in the early thirties. The corollary of such leisure as Pound wanted was not only time freed from wage-slavery by a shorter working day but time free for work, for what the artist, the poet of *The Cantos,* knew as his life work, as other men wanted time free for their households or hobbies. Hours that might be the means for poetry, for taking thought, for singing about the piano in the evening, for crafts, and for the variety of exercises—these leisure hours depend in turn upon hours devoted to the common goods, to the raising of food, the furnishing of clothes, houses, minds, workshops, to distribution and transportation. The two are interdependent. Where anything was done at all, vision and work cooperated in one act. Such leisure could not be earned or given; it could only be created. The rest was exploitation, or obsessional competition in which men strove for an evil or hold over other men, a politics and a business that drove the souls of all before them with threats of war and unemployment.

•

There is a sense in which men's hours are their souls. This buying of men's hours under the threat of poverty and war rises in the same history that saw the new order of the devil wherein Mephistopheles buys men's souls with the lure of happiness. In *The Zohar,* Moses of Leon in the thirteenth century sees a man's being as his space and time. Not only must a man care for and account for every cell of his body, but he must account for every second of his life. A man's being is not his but a communal property, for "his" body and "his" time are held in trust to be returned to God. These men, the Abrahams or Davids of *The*

Zohar, are creatures of a communal imagination. They have no right to themselves or right in themselves. They can not even, we read, judge; for the judgment was with God: it came from their communal identity.

.

What time is, what man is, what work is—these are elements of a use we make of living. Pound's thematic concern with the nature of economic evil and good must be ours too where we are concerned with evil and good at all.

.

In the late thirties, when I was just coming into young manhood, men still thought and talked about some total social good. Even while "Socialism," "Communism," and "Democracy" were written large on banners of contending nations in war, and total turned totalitarian, we had known—as younger men now have not known—a time when it seemed there could have been the choice for a peaceful economy. We had seen the good cast down and a convenient evil taken up and followed. Now in the "Communist" countries and "Democratic" countries alike a new era of military rule begins.

.

H.D., like Pound, shows scars of the experience men had during the Depression years. In 1933 she went to Freud to undertake a work or to become able again to return to work. She was in a depression. The term here is psychological, but the terms cross over—it is economic too. Thus: "obvious sentiment," she lists in her cross examination of her limits in *The Walls Do Not Fall*:

> folder round a spiritual bank-account,
>
> with credit-loss too starkly indicated,

.

There is a thematic continuity we must keep, a sense of the appointed work and its time, to which our imagination and our making or poetry must return, to release life from its disappointments. We too, if we would restore the streams of vitality that in the dream are called the spring in the first direction or the spring in the right direction, must know no peace but work in a scene of war, as once men worked in a scene of depression. My sense is not figurative here, for our world economy and politics moves now not by the threat of depression but by the threat or hope of war; and the work to be done—to bring back the place and time, the event or conjunction we have called in this study the Presence or the Present, or to bring ourselves to it—means a change at the roots of the world-order for the good in the place of an evil. As men came to know the depression on a psychological level, we will experience in our turn the war within the psyche.

∙

Where the hour, the work, and the body are thought of as terms of outer and inner economy, we begin to understand the burden of Pound's theme in *Thrones:*

> The temple is holy ⊥⊥⊥ because it is not for sale

and we see that it is not accidental that it follows upon:

> In a buck-board with a keg of money: Damn you, I
>   said I would get it (the wages).

∙

From the "Time is not money, but it is nearly everything else" of *ABC of Economics;* from "The temple is holy because it is not for sale" of *Thrones,* we may see deeper into the tenor of Pound's *Usura* theme. But now I would gather here another tenor of correspondences where economic practice is a key to spirit, so that to imagine a new spirit, we imagine a new economic practice. So, we've got to go to the roots of things, to find new terms or new orders. From H.D.'s:

> Let us measure defeat
> in terms of bread and meat,
>
> and continents
> in relative extent of wheat
>
> fields;

thru Olson's "Variations Done for Gerald Van de Wiele" which brings forward into the contemporary world Rimbaud's *Season in Hell:* "Le Bonheur! Sa dent, douce à la mort, m'avertissait au chant du coq,— *ad matutinum, au Christus venit,*—dans les plus sombres villes:" "what soul/ isn't in default?" Olson takes up Rimbaud's words in his own:

can you afford not to make
the magical study

which happiness is? do you hear
the cock when he crows? do you know the charge,

that you shall have no envy, that your life
has its orders, that the seasons

seize you too, that no body and soul are one
if they are not wrought

in this retort? . . .

•

In the dream of the spring it was the work itself that was the magical study.

•

This work, this sense of what happiness is, is somehow missed or mussed in American experience. The O.E.D. gives among the roots of the word: Old Norse *verkja, virkja,* to feel pain; Danish *virke,* to operate, act, weave. Greek *organon,* organ; *orgion,* orgy. Work then was once of the earth that brings forth in travail and is still, where the real work is done, where the fields are tilled and planted, the clothes are worked with pains-taking craft, the stone cut to fine measure, the sentences brought to their exacting senses. And we've to hold this happiness, against the prevailing sense in which happiness is when and where we do not suffer or take pains. As against that Declaration of Independence, we must remember now the communality we have with all men, our interdependence everywhere in life.

•

Is there *vir,* man, and *virtus,* manlinèss, in the word *virkja,* suffering? Is there *orgaeo,* to swell and teem with moisture; is there *orgeon,* "a citizen chosen from every demos, who at stated times had to perform certain sacrifices, being in fact a sort of priest"; is there *orge,* "one's temper, temperament, disposition, nature, heart"; is there *orgizo,* "to make angry, provoke to anger, irritate," among the roots of this idea of Work or Life, as the O.E.D. tells us there is *organon,* "an instrument for making or doing something" and *orgion,* "secret rites, secret worship"? What part has that Man-God upon the Cross that is also the Life Tree in our American right claimed as the pursuit of happiness?

·

In the Gospel of St. John at Ephesus, the Christ tells John: "And if thou givest ear to my round dance, behold thyself in me the speaker. And when thou seest what I do, keep my mysteries silent. If thou dancest, ponder what I do, for thine is this human suffering that I will suffer."

·

For most Christians of church faiths, their Master suffered for their sins, a surrogate. Here Christ is Redeemer. It is this truth: that in our concern to redeem, to save or keep alive the wholeness of what we are alive, we discover the work to do.

·

For the Gnostic Christians, their teacher was two—the one, the human Jesus, suffered, and the other, the divine Logos, did not suffer. Here again there is truth, for to know suffering as an act of the soul's drama is something other than suffering, is more than a happy thing. Ill hap or good hap, the happening or chance, belongs to the inertia of man's pleasure or displeasure. But in searching out what we suffer or enjoy not as happening to us or belonging to us but as belonging to a design or creation, taking our strength there, we discover a new person who does not suffer but who creates in our suffering, coming into an increase of meaning.

·

So, for the poet, for the man already transformed in making some work of art, for the carpenter, the meaning of the crucifixion scene is not the unhappiness of a lynching party nor the mere suffering of a passion, but it belongs to a poem in the actual world, the fulfillment of a prophecy or story-form. There is in the man and in the god a perfume and a radiance, a flower that portends; and in the passions of the two in One upon the cross or tree, we see the ripeness of what the story demands, the mystery of the whole thing in which nails, blood, and the cry, the *Eli, Eli, lama sabachthani* are designed to fit, to charge with meaning to the utmost degree, the crisis of the poem enacted.

•

In our work we lose our selves, our independence, the *Jesus* of each one, or it is fused and enters into the radiance of another power of the same being, another person we imagine in the community of language and our work there, that we call the poet. It is in passion, in suffering, that, even as we cry out, we become workers, organs, instruments of our Art that is fateful or formal. The Christ is the music, the sense of needed form, the "over Love, a new Master."

In the *Gospel of John* it is called the Round Dance. "If thou wouldst understand that which is me," the Christ says: "know this: all that I have said, I have uttered playfully—and I was by no means ashamed of it. I danced, but as for thee, consider the whole. . . . "

•

This being in suffering and in happiness and yet—and just there—being in the Dance or play is the experience of being in the poem, awakening to the demand of the language. We know it as longing unrequited, as our voluntary quest for fulfillment or fate or justice, which is not happiness, *la bonne chance,* nor the freak of chance that stands in Zen for the immediacy, but is Lord over all, the command of What Is that it come into Its Own, that has Beauty and fullness.

•

In the poem this fatefulness is the commanding sense of the form, of an inner course in action, a power then of the *orge,* of one's temper or nature or heart in action. The volition of the artist is to fulfill the form or will that he feels or discovers in the thing he is making.

·

The man's soulfulness disturbs the poet's spirit; and the poet stands above the cross of anger or of love-anguish, and yet will himself cry out, as the Christ says to John that He cried: "And if those whom thou seest by the cross have as yet no single form, then all the parts of him who descended have not been gathered together." It is in the poem that the parts of the poet are gathered together. Where in terms of the Egyptian mysteries, we see Isis as the Muse or Mother of the poet, gathering together, remembering (as in Greece, Mnemosyne was mother of the arts) the Osiris-Christ in the Horus, the sufferer and redeemer of the poem in the new work and its worker.

·

"Liberty" too is a demand of the anti-poetic. The poet cannot take liberties in the poem. For just there, where the arbitrary, self-expressive or self-saving, where the self-conscious voice comes, the *idiotes,* private howl or moan or the urbane sophisticated tone breaks or takes over from the communal voice. In the communal consciousness, the idiot is a member; is, in a sense, any and every individual member if he be separated from the imagination of the whole. But self-expression and likewise self-possession in verse would set up an "I" that is the private property of the writer in the place of the "I" in which all men may participate.

·

The "our," "my," "us," "we," "I," "me" of the poet's work, and the other "you," "your," "they," "them" are pronouns of a play, members or persons of a world drama in division. These are no more at liberty, no more seek liberty than they pursue happiness, for the sense of poetic justice or form that is history reveals them all as actors or chorus of a work that now we see is a self-creative drama at play. The ideals of the revolution are also its hubris. Under the banners or the oracles, the content of the dream must be played out to its resolution, which we see in the burned and smoking countryside of the dream.

•

"*All that I have said, I have uttered playfully,*" this god says.

II.

It was to unmask play that Freud set about his life task. "*Mein goldener Sigi,*" his mother still called him in her nineties, Jones tells us. "From his mother came, according to him, his 'sentimentality'." Had she given him his name *Sigmund?* For *Sigmund*—and Freud was to be a hero of the psyche-world—*Sigmund* belonged, not to the Jewish consciousness, but to the Germanic fairytale or play world. Freud was born with a caul; that was part of his mother's legend of him. "Thus," Jones writes, "the hero's garb was in the weaving at the cradle itself." Freud had genius, and to have genius is to be a member of the Dream, to be a creature of wish, of the mother's wish (incestuous wish, Freud was to say) or prophecy of a great man in her son. Freud was to call this Mother-world of wish and fulfillment or failure the realm of the Pleasure-Principle.

•

The whole play of Freud's mind, his true heroism, belongs to that source. His life task was to expose the fiction of dreams at work in man's reality, to show up wishers for what they really were. He could descend in this guise of the scientist upon the nursery world with a vengeance, as if there would be an end of childish things and a full confession of infantile guilts. "We will have none of that nonsense in here," we seem to hear some Victorian papa declare. Whatever phantasies attended the wetting of the bed, his father demanded an accounting for what really happened. "It was from such experiences," Jones relates, "that was born his conviction that typically it was the father who represented to his son the principles of denial, restraint, restriction, and authority; the father stood for the reality principle, the mother for the pleasure principle." But what, we might begin to ask, in this Freudian determination, did the child stand for? The father's voice and the mother's voice might direct Freud, but he agreed with the father that the child was wrong. There was to be no childish principle.

·

Among those childish things had been playing religion. There must have been the play of the name Sigmund, the incestuous hero of the Nibelungen saga. There had been too another plaything. Freud's nurse, Jones tells us, was a Czech: "and they conversed in that language, although Freud forgot it afterwards." He may have put it away; "repressed it" is the later Freudian term. "That prehistoric old woman," he called her later, meaning perhaps to deny that she belonged to his history. For she was Catholic, Jones tells us, and more importantly, "She implanted in him the ideas of Heaven and Hell, and probably also those of salvation and resurrection. After returning from church the boy used to preach a sermon at home and expound God's doings." There may then have been caustic, if not angry, reproof from Freud's liberal, free-thinking father at his infant son's taking up with such alien ideas.

Let only *Ananke* and *Logos* be our gods, he proposes in *The Future of an Illusion*, where in the name of Science he belabors religion—as wish, but then as failing to repress evil wishes. Sometimes seeming to uphold the child: "I think it would be a very long time before a child who was not influenced began to trouble himself about God and the things beyond this world. Perhaps his thoughts on these matters would then take the same course as they did with his ancestors; but we do not wait for this development; we introduce him to the doctrines of religion at a time when he is neither interested in them nor capable of grasping their import." It is never clear in *The Future of an Illusion* that there might have been a particular child protesting here that he had been led astray. But there had been a time when Freud's beloved nurse and he had formed just such a "we," talking a language together, Czech and Christian, foreign to the Jewish and rationalistic persuasion of his fathers, a vernacular eloquence such as Dante says "we acquire without any rule, by imitating our nurses," that provided the medium that nursery languages provide for children of making an other world, where Father and Mother, reality and pleasure principles, give way to the Child, to the principle of play or enacting what is, a sense of form that demands its creative ends over whatever reality or pleasure.

There must have been some moment of apology, of putting the blame off on Nurse, of recanting, that we see reflected in the plea: "Perhaps his thoughts on these matters would then take the same course as they did with his ancestors." For liberal and free-thinking as the senior Freud was, he must have, with humorous and kindly point perhaps, but with the severity of the nineteenth century Papa surely, reminded the infant Freud (he was barely two, or two and a half, Jones tells us) who disputed like the infant Jesus in the temple that this God of the Catholic faith was the enemy of his ancestors. If the nurse was Catholic, she plays the role in Freud's childhood of the heretic. Was she a Moravian Czech? H.D. did not know this story of Freud's old nurse, but along the lines of her own association in *Tribute to Freud* she drew the course religion had taken with her ancestors, the way of the Unitas Fratrum or Moravian Brotherhood, and the way she had taken in psychoanalysis into one design. "Livonia, Moravia, Bohemia—Count Zinzendorf, the founder of the renewed Bohemian brotherhood, was an Austrian, whose father was exiled or self-exiled to Upper Saxony, because of his Protestant affiliations. The Professor himself was an Austrian, a Moravian actually by birth."

Freud remembers that he gave his nurse all his pennies, and Jones remarks of the memory: "Perhaps it got connected with her dismissal for theft later on when he was two and a half years old." Did she play the Promethean role, stealing the fire that the father had forbidden the child, the fire of the soul's realms, Heaven and Hell, and of the soul's drama of salvation and resurrection, that Freud was to bring from the cathedral into the doctor's office in the name of scientific reason?

The Future of an Illusion is the book of a haunted mind, of a man divided against himself. "Certainly this is true of the man into whom you have instilled the sweet or bitter-sweet poison from childhood on." But this man is Freud himself, the man who followed his genius, his

Sigmund, to lay bare the incest-wish in the psyche, his life work with dream and play, his obsession with the City of God or Rome. "But what of the other, who has been brought up soberly?" he asks. This man is that other person of Freud, who lays down the conditions under which dreams and play can come into the question at all. There was truth, William James saw, in the worlds of fiction—it was the truth of religion and poetry in one. But for Freud that truth might be various was at times intolerable. It was his lasting communication that the heroic struggle for the reality principle took place in the earliest years. In the little scene some intolerable action takes place: the beloved Nurse is banished, the child surrenders childish things and undertakes his father's ways. But the "prehistoric old woman" that Freud tells us was ugly too is still to be banished from the thoughts of the Master in his seventy-first year. It was never to be done; the father was never entirely to win over the child in Freud. He wrote to Ferenczi while *The Future of an Illusion* was still in press: "Now it already seems to me childish; fundamentally I think otherwise; I regard it as weak analytically and inadequate as a self-confession." The dramatic fiction remained, the 'As If' reality could not be dismissed.

•

As it is played at the close of the second act of Wagner's *Die Walküre,* first produced in 1857 when Freud was a babe in arms.

Wotan, the Father-God, drives out Brunnhilda, his own Psyche or Sympathy. He had commanded, "Death to Sigmund! This be the Valkyrie's work." She defends Sigmund against the ancestral law. "In greatest need, I must falsely abandon the true one!" she cries. She becomes then an exile from the Father, dwelling in his wrath; and just there, she becomes Nurse or Muse of Sigmund in his incestuous love for Siglinda. The hero, shielded by his Valkyrie, strikes out to kill Siglinda's husband, but even as he aims his blow, Wotan as Father appears. "A reddish glow breaks through the clouds, heralding Wotan, who stands above Hunding" so that the son's sword is shattered and the husband's spear strikes home.

•

Did Freud never question or search out his namesake in that old story? There were, he argued, instinctual wishes "born anew with every child." These he believed most real and grievous—"such instinctual wishes are those of incest, of cannibalism, and of murder." But there were other wishes that appeared to Freud not with the reality of instincts but with the unreality of inhibitions or illusions. "Think of the distressing contrast between the radiant intelligence of a healthy child and the feeble mentality of the average adult," he is moved again to argue, thinking here of religious ideals as an adult contagion. Yet he can, identifying with the adult, view religion as a weakness of childhood in the same passage: "From this bondage I am, we are free. Since we are prepared to renounce a good part of our infantile wishes. . . . "

"I am reminded," he tells us proudly, "of one of my children who was distinguished at an early age by a peculiarly marked sense of reality. When the children were told a fairy tale, to which they listened with rapt attention, he would come forward and ask: Is that a true story? Having been told that it was not, he would turn away with an air of disdain."

Here we are reminded in turn of another scene that Freud does not recall, where Freud himself comes home from the cathedral, from the imaginative world of the Nurse-Mother, of the Christ and Sigmund, to enact before his father a play he had come to know. "To preach a sermon and expound God's doings," Jones tells us. But what of the ritual he had seen? In the charmed or incestuous circle of the nursery the mythos had been told. In the temple of the Child a mystery had been seen, the magic transubstantiation of the Mass. What confused, inspired gospel had our two and a half year old Freud to tell and to play out? Here it is not Freud's son, but Freud's father who is "distinguished by a peculiarly marked sense of reality"—for the senior Freud had a sense of being Jewish, a sense of being rational, before this insult of Christian fairy tales. "Bitter-sweet poisons," Freud was to call them later. It is the father who turns from the son "with an air of disdain."

•

Ananke ("external reality" Freud defines it as) is "force, constraint, necessity," Liddell & Scott tells us: "Fate, destiny"; "actual force, punishment." It is Freud's reality principle as a god. For the poets, the lexicon says, it stood for "bodily pain, anguish, suffering." It had then internal reality. It meant too "like Latin *necessitudo,* the tie of blood, relationship, kindred." And *Logos* is the Christ. Surely that Catholic or perhaps Moravian Nurse, among the bitter-sweet poisons that had included doctrines of Heaven and Hell must have told something of the Jewish Child who was the Logos, expounding the word of God in the temple among the rabbis. He had come to give a new dispensation from the Law of the Father.

Those gods over *The Future of an Illusion,* the Ananke and the Logos that appear as abstract, that Freud said must be the only gods of Science, had once been only a scornful and offended Victorian papa—well, yes, he was Jewish and he was Austrian, but the type was of the age not of nation or race in particular—and an imaginative and charming nurse seeking to save the child.

Like those instinctual wishes of incest, cannibalism, and murder that Freud thought most real, "born anew in every child," the inexorable will of the father and the lasting good wish of the nurse belong to the very stuff of fairy tale and god lore.

•

"Playfully," like poetically, can mean that things are not to be taken seriously. Yet, to charge the word with its utmost degree of meaning, there are seventeen columns under the word "Play" in the O.E.D. Like Pound's "time," it may not be money, but it is nearly everything else.

Among adults it is agreed that play is not to be taken seriously. "I thought we were only playing." But the play of the child is his very being where alone he is completely engrossed. It is the 'As If' world. And it is, where the child has survived in the life of the adult, the creative fiction of man's religions and arts.

•

The locus of Yeats's image of Michael Angelo where:

> With no more sound than the mice make
> His hand moves to and fro

is, back of the Vatican hall where the Renaissance master works, another room where the child Yeats sits in solitary play at making up a world:

> Like a long-legged fly upon the stream
> His mind moves upon silence.

And back of these images, we remember from *The Zohar*—that Yeats knew well in his occult studies—the Child Creator of the Universe playing with the letters of the alphabet.

·

The Christ then in a sense says to John that the Crucifixion is child's play. Unless you play with me, unless you are intent as I am in the thing, you will not understand what is going on. He had had, after all, only to surrender to the reality principle and to deny His role—cry out "*I am only a man!*" and Pilate would have let him go from His fate; he would have found his liberty. Or to have let the pleasure principle guide him.

But the play we are talking about has its own laws; it uses reality or pleasure as it will. This high play, like the high novel or high poetry, will not shape its ends to provide a happy or a likely consequence. It refuses the sensible.

·

The reality principle sees the Oedipus complex as a fixation where sexual wishes are in conflict with tribal custom, or even, as Freud does at times, as an instinct to incest and murder. The pleasure principle insists it would be best to let well-enough alone.

"Let me," Teiresias insists:

> go home. It will be easiest for us both
> to bear our several destinies to the end
> if you will follow my advice.

But Oedipus must, for the play's sake, climb up into the uneasiest state necessary for the moment at which the crisis of the play shows forth and we realize the fulfillment of the plot. Beyond the pleasure principle, beyond the reality principle, is the play principle seeking its passionate formal fulfillment. This is the only glory we know.

Oedipus, with the blood streaming down from his eyes, having come into the fullness of the knowledge of his play, is like Christ with the blood streaming down from his hands—eyes that looked with love upon his mother; hands that touched with love his fellow men.

The difference between the neurotic nursing his guilt or sin and the hero is the dramatic gesture, the formal imperative.

•

"Are we at the beginning of a great religious crisis?" Burckhardt wrote in 1871: "We shall be aware of ripples on the surface very soon." He saw that "even languages are traitors to causes" and quoted from Bacon: "whereas the meaning ought to govern the term, the term governs the meaning."

"Art, however," Burckhardt continues: "is the most arrant traitor of all, firstly, because it profanes the substance of religion, i.e., it robs men of their faculty for profounder worship, putting eyes and ears in its place, and substituting figures for feelings, which are only transiently deepened by them." Then he goes on to speak of the high and independent selfhood of art. "The real work of art," he concludes, "is born of its own mysterious life."

The figures of Child and of Christ in passion that we have drawn upon do not belong then to the world of religion; for what they are and undergo is not "for profounder worship" but "of its own mysterious life." They belong not to the Church, that has its gods or God to be worshipped, as the Church in turn must be obeyed, but to the Art. Both meaning and term are governed in the art by the apprehension of the form. The spirit and the letter of the law, the betrayal and the cause, appear as elements of a structure that is at play. What Burckhardt calls the Art's "high and independent selfhood" is not only the poet's form, but the underlying relation and meaning in the story of things. It is the selfhood of Poetry that makes of the writer's self no more and no other than a persona of the cast.

•

We have come a long way from that *Dream of the Last Day*. There were angels there, but there was no sign of Christ the Child or of Christ the Crucified. There was, instead, the turning back of the waters into their first courses. There may have been then an appearance of the reality principle, the inexorable will of the father, in the landscape that was the scene of modern war and the universal fear of—but it is also a wish for—total destruction. The turning of the waters at the spring may then have been the reviving of the mother-world, the Mutterrecht? But now, as the news comes from diggings in the first agricultural civilizations, in the very world of the Mothers, we see clearly that this is not the spring.

As the Father-World is a world of nations, the Mother-World was a world of cities. There was not one Mother, there were Mothers, and their crowns were armed citadels. Poets sang by heart long before there were cities, but the Mothers developed writing to keep their household records. Their soldiers went out from the hive to pillage the surrounding countryside and reduce its farmers and herdsmen to domestic order. "They culminated," Robert Adams tells us in "The Origin of Cities" (*Scientific American,* September 1960), "in the Sumerian city-state with tens of thousands of inhabitants, elaborate religious, political and military establishments, stratified social classes, advanced technology and widely-extended trading contacts." Universities, armies, industries, city administrations, political organizations belong to the realm of Mutterrecht.

No, the spring in the first direction refers to "that prehistoric old woman," to an age when all men worked at the sources of their life. The Age of the Maker where at Jarmo he shaped the stone vessels. The Age of the Nurse where plants and animals were brought into the human commune and man discovered the sowing of seeds and the breeding of herds. We have come back, along the path of the Christ of St. John at Ephesus and his Round Dance, to the Christ of the country man, to the spring that lies in the grain. For before He was the Logos, He was the grain-food. We have come back to the first talk I had, sprawled on the lawn of the campus at Berkeley, twenty-five years ago, in 1947, with Charles Olson, for we talked then of cities, and of how they exploited the first things, having to coerce the men of the countryside to supply them with food and the necessities of life. The root or spring was pagan. The heart of the god was in the work, the essential work of the material source.

We have come, back of the dream, to "Against Wisdom As Such," Olson's essay on my early work. In the dream I play again with wisdom, speaking of the last days and apprehending as I did that alternative of black-as-a-clinker and the pure light. But then a change comes, and there is something to be done. I must draw, not conclusions but beginnings, the stream of thought and feeling into life.

"There are only his own composed forms," Olson writes of the artist as a warning against the tendency of my thought, and the warning must remain: "each one solely the issue of the time of the moment of its creation, not any ultimate except what he in his heat and that instant in its solidity yield. That the poet cannot afford to traffick in any other 'sign' than his one, his self, the man or woman he is. Otherwise God does rush in"—does he mean Authority does rush in? He may mean, as I do here, that the God of the profounder worship is not to be mixed up with the art: "And art is washed away, turned into that second force, religion," Olson puts it. Then, driving home, he calls upon those forces of fire and water that reappear as elements of the landscape in my dream of the glowing disk and the spring.

"I said to Duncan," he continues: "'heat, all but heat, is symbolic, and thus all but heat is reductive.' I asked Duncan if it wasn't his own experience that a poem is the issue of two factors, (1) heat, and (2) time. How plastic, cries Wilhelm, is the thought of 'water' as seed-substance in the *T'ai I Chin Hua Tsung Chih*. And time is, in the hands of, the poet. For he alone is the one who takes it as the concrete continuum it is, and who practices the bending of it." So, in the dream I go with Olson to bend the waters.

"Rhythm is time (not measure, as the pedants of Alexandria made it). The root is 'rhein': to flow. And mastering the flow of the solid, time, we invoke others."

•

When, in that letter of 1916, H.D. writes to Williams of "your Spirit," she refers to this agency we know as the Poet who serves the selfhood of the poem and would bend time to its purposes. "A very sacred thing," she calls the "business of writing"; and again "real beauty is a rare and sacred thing in this generation."

The ardor or fire remains constant in her nature as a poet. Among the earliest poems, in "Pygmalion," she gives voice to this place in the fire or in the swirl of water where God does rush in and the artist begins to traffic with spirit in the matter:

> am I master of this
> swirl upon swirl of light?

Pygmalion is the Maker engrossed in the Making. He is no longer at liberty. His own has become confused with properties of the work itself:

> have I made it as in old times
> I made the gods from the rock?
>
> have I made this fire from myself?
> or is this arrogance?
> is this fire a god
> that seeks me in the dark?

.

In the dream I faltered but had to go on. I had to act in the nexus of belief and disbelief to draw the reins of the water. It was not belief or disbelief about the life-force of the waters that was at issue. I knew no other world but this universe of pulsations and exchanges. Everything existed by visible powers: the stars were radiant suns of energy that belonged too to the orders that wax and wane, that are born and die; the waters of the sea moved in tides drawn by the gravity of the moon and of the sun from the gravity of the earth—and we, too, who were animal, having the breath of life, had our origin in the alchemy of the cosmos where tides of the sun and tides of the sea cooperated under the aegis of the moon. "Earth-caused tides in the liquid Moon," Gamow tells us, "must have been eighty-one times higher than the lunar tides in our oceans."

The alchemist searching for the life-force in his alembic did not believe or disbelieve in the life-force. That nexus in which belief and disbelief become terms of our consciousness arises when we must act to direct those forces. To draw the reins of the horses, to draw the rains down into the circulations from which life first rose, is to draw upon our own life-force being to charge our self-consciousness. The self is surcharged. The consciousness raised to the testing point where it wavers between inspiration and inflation is seized by hopes and fears, beliefs and disbeliefs. Belief and disbelief are a protective order, the sense we have when we over-reach our limits.

·

This consciousness, this picture the human organism can make of what the cosmos is and of his operation there, is a special organ of life. It has evolved and is evolving, as all the other organs of our bodies have evolved. How close our common sense of the meaning of belief and disbelief is to our digestive tract. "I cannot swallow that" means that the consciousness resolutely resists trying the idea at all. "I cannot stomach that" means that the consciousness becomes sick with the idea and must throw it up. Then, when we take in certain facts about the universe or entertain new ideas, there will still be the sense that we cannot digest all the potentialities we sense are there—"I cannot take it all in."

The rest is "shit," "crap"—what the organism, the consciousness cannot draw upon at all in the fund of human ideas. The waste matter thrown off is not without virtue; it is just what we are unable as organisms to use. Or it is deadly—a ground of poisons that threaten, were we to take them in at all, the very structure of what we are.

In inspiration, this consciousness makes some organic leap. It sees the light or is struck by the light. Its whole relation to what is poisonous and what is nourishing changes, for its inner being or code-script has changed. The mind must conform to its seed-pattern, its identity or species, or die. But within a life, in a stroke of light, the mind can be in-formed. It can pass from one order into a new more complex order. It can come into a new species of mind.

For the uninspired, for all of us as we are our own selves, the urgency of our self-life commands the testing and tasting at its borders, filled with the apprehension a structure has that may or may not be able to tolerate this new food for thought. A matter of taste is an arbitrary thing, and we may be in error in our choice, but taste is all that preserves us from the chaotic possibilities beyond our ken. The real apprehension for the organism in what can be believed or tolerated is for its own survival in identity.

.

"This bitter-sweet poison," Freud called religion, unconsciously recalling the sweets his nurse had fed him, the bitter consequences, and the poison he had come to see them as after his father's counsel. He might have been converted, his mind poisoned by Catholicism against the way of his ancestors, but in the crisis his identity with his father was threatened. He was to keep faith all his life with that choice to affirm the way of his free-thinking Jewish father, but he was to imagine in psychoanalysis new terms in which Catholicism, Judaism, and free thought too, were to be translated into the language of an underlying humanity. An inspiration, a mutation, had come in thought that was more various to survive. Old intolerances gave way, and the range of man's food for thought was extended.

III.

So we've to see H.D.'s "prompted by hunger, / it opens to the tide-flow" and the retraction that follows:

but infinity? no,
of nothing-too-much:

I sense my own limit,

as referring to the survival of identity in the growth and evolution of the poet's mind, recapitulating the experience of those first cells of life in the primal waters. Some of those cells remained what they were, and they remain in our seas today, triumphs of species to adapt and survive. They escaped somehow from the magic, the pouring radiations of the stars that altered the code-script. They were not among the cells that came into the light and lost their selves in dream. For these other cells that mutated towards new forms, that were to lose what they were, prompted by hunger, opened to the tide-flow of the stars. They died and were re-born, caught in the alembic under the radioactive rays, they were flooded with what we call longing. Their inner order was disturbed, re-arranged, altered. Burned to a clinker in the sun-spot—that was the greatest chance—or enlightened.

•

This is the deeper sense, the life-force sense, of H.D.'s opening passages in *The Walls Do Not Fall*. Thinking of all the mutations in spirit, of the waste of millions in the process, we may read with new meaning:

O, do not pity them, as you watch them drop one by one,

for they fall exhausted, numb, blind
but in certain ecstasy,

for theirs is the hunger
for Paradise.

It is a theosophical poem, and theosophy, whether Hellenistic or Victorian, takes thought not from dogma but from speculations upon the nature of the cosmos as a divine revelation. Back of such thought is a concept of universal sympathies, correspondences, communications; the imagination of the whole of What Is as an experiencing entity. So that for the theosophical mind, even where Darwin's acausal evolution is accepted, evolution, the evolution of forms, is an experience. "The universe is one animal connected and contained by one life," Proclus argues in his *Commentary on Plato's "Timaeus"*: "For if this life were not common, there would not be a sympathy of the parts in it. For sympathy is effected through a participation of the same nature."

So the vision of the trilogy that sees history as the evolution of psychic forms sees the physical universe as vital:

where great stars pour down
their generating strength, Arcturus

or the sapphires of the Northern Crown.

•

But now let us see the "prompted by hunger, / it opens to the tide-flow" as referring to the poetic consciousness itself. The tide-flow of the poem's own compelling measures where rhymes and ratios have a felt relation to the sympathies within the total cosmos. Carlyle's sense that the heart of things is musical is of this order. The poem, H.D. would say, is generated just here, between the hunger—the opening of the organism to take in the world around it—and the sense of limits. Just this, she says, I could digest, incorporate, bring into my survival. The imagination might go beyond, but the biological reality is again and again asserted: "I am what I am" plays in counterpoint to a vision in which life is characterized not only by the limits of species but by the generation of new forms. "The Presence," then, of *The Walls Do Not Fall* xiii, "ultimate blue ray, / rare as radium," identified with the new Master over Love, may be rightly related to what we understand of the role mutation plays in the evolution of life-forms.

.

In the small-town integrity of John Crowe Ransom as he protests against Dante's *Divine Comedy* the sense of limits is all, the preservation from evolution of life-forms. For such an entity, holding its own in the constant danger of being lost in larger more complex forms, the battle against pathetic fallacy is a kind of magic to keep back the flood of sympathies. My mind returns to the cells that came into the dangerous currents of the light and were changed. Some of us dream of such a light and are even infatuated with the thought. So Proclus quotes from Orphic texts:

> The Gods admir'd, in ether when they saw
> A light unlook'd for, bursting on the view,
> From the immortal Phanes' glittering skin.

But we seem to have remembered too in the morphology of our psyche a panic, as if there could be a withdrawal from being taken over so, we seem to recapitulate some knowledge of the alternative in which millions of cells survived without being changed. "I am hurt by the glare," Ransom tells us, "even in imagination my eyes cannot take it." He is talking about the imagined glare of Dante's vision of God.

Touched by the disturbances that make for poetry, Ransom prayed from the beginning for protection against them. "Two evils, monstrous either one apart," he tells us in "Winter Remembered," "possessed me, and were long and loath at going."

> Think not, when fire was bright upon my bricks,
> And past the tight boards hardly a wind could enter,
> I glowed like them, the simple burning sticks,
> Far from my cause, my proper heat and center.

.

It is as if, in our phantasy of cells quickened in the primal seas by the light, some of them resisted the knowledge and could escape the rule of sympathies. A man could be touched by the genius of Poetry as Ransom was and then emerge magnificently free from the ravages of inspiration in what he would call his "proper heat and center." Finally the disease of poetry left Ransom's spiritual body, and he ceased having poèms in his mind. He could almost be at ease with his friend Brooks who had never lost his proper center. But we know Ransom had seen something in the light Plato saw by, for he tells us "I am hurt by the glare," and we know that he glowed in the fire of sympathetic fallacy, for he tells us not to think so. The physical sensation remains.

.

The planetary regents of *Tribute to the Angels* are not only figures reviving the lore of an old tradition in the drama of the present, but they are evoked as ministers of inner sympathies. The planets are influences—we have only to think of how interdependent those orbits and gravities are with our own terrestrial order in the solar system. And men, taking the wandering lights of the planets as elements of their thought, of their sky map and their cosmic imagination, have made them symbolic influences.

But H.D. is thinking of them, too, as star-beings, active intelligences. She returns again and again to the prayer for inspiration, for the "power between us" to inform the poem, just as Ransom turned his mind against the possibility of such identifications or projections. In her early childhood she had heard their names—Venus, Mars, Saturn, Jupiter. "Venus is very beautiful tonight," her father, Charles Doolittle of the Flower Observatory, would report. The planets were persons of her father's mysteries before they were persons of Greek myth. In time, in a lifetime of study, the divine powers of the ancient world would become more and more real in H.D.'s world, most particularly in their late Hellenistic syntheses, where astral cult and chthonic cult had merged with the poetry of what Festugière in *La Révélation d'Hermès Trismégiste* calls *les fictions littéraires*. "I say *fictions*," the Roman Catholic scholar writes, "because, for us, moderns, it is evident that the Hellenistic accounts of revelation carry no inner meaning of truth." So, too, we remember from Freud's *Future of an Illusion* when asked by his son who had a peculiarly marked sense of reality if a fairy tale were a true story, Freud replies, no.

But for H.D., as for the Romantics before her, for the masters of Rosicrucian and Hermetic romances in the Renaissance, or for the theosophists out of the Hellenistic period, the fairy tale could communicate the deepest truth. In *The Hedgehog* she tells us: "Bett made Madge understand that the stories weren't just stories, but that there was something in them like the light in the lamp that isn't the lamp. Bett would say to Madge, when she was a very little girl, 'Now what is the lamp side of the story and what is the light side of the story?' so Madge could see very easily (when she was a very little girl) that the very beautiful stories Bett told her, that were real stories, had double sorts of meanings." By the time of The War Trilogy, not only the stories of the old gods, but the great Hellenistic literary fictions of the New Testament, the Apocalypse, and the Gnostic gospels had come into H.D.'s realm of real stories and of double sorts of meaning.

At the same time, as we have traced in charade and *roman à clef,* H.D.'s life became more and more a story of her life. In the earliest poems, those close to her—Pound, Aldington, Lawrence, Bryher—were projected as persons of story and drama, and beyond these, as mythological persons. Life itself had double sorts of meanings. Did the flowering tree of The War Trilogy actually appear to her? In *The Walls Do Not Fall* v, she tells us that the track of the story will lead "from a plum-tree in flower / to a half-open hut-door" and in xxvi and xxvii she asks "of all the flowering of the wood" what flowering tree is to be our store. This is clearly the preparation of a fiction. In her notes to *Ion* she brought in the story of the burnt olive-tree of Pallas Athené, sending out a new shoot of frail silver life. "Pallas Athené, then, was not dead. Her spirit spoke quietly, a very simple message." The revival of the burnt out tree was an old theme of H.D.'s fiction.

Yet in *Tribute to the Angels,* her testimony comes with the verity of the actual, an event long awaited, long prepared. The fictional depth and the actual figure contend so that, as she tells us, we do not know whether "we were there or not-there," but:

> we saw the tree flowering;
>
> it was an ordinary tree
> in an old garden-square.

So, too, the dream-visitation of the Christ in *The Walls Do Not Fall* and of the Lady in *Tribute to the Angels* I take it are actual dreams. But just beyond, creatures of shadow and light, actuality and fiction, delusion and illusion, are the angelic beings. What we are forced to recognize is that she actually felt their presence. Ecstatic in the tide-flow she opened her mind to the invasion of the imagination. "Then came the break-through of astral forms, a streaming down into this landscape, where Bosch's vision and my own San Francisco were already mingled, of another world. . . . "

•

"More than a little silly," Jarrell wrote of H.D.'s critical vulnerability. Back of that word "silly" I find the sense in earlier meanings: *Seely,* "blissful, holy; innocent, harmless; deserving of pity, helpless, defenceless; often of the soul, as in danger of divine judgment; frail, worn-out, crazy; foolish." *Silly,* from: "deserving of compassion" to "feeble, insignificant; sorry; unsophisticated; feeble-minded; empty-headed; stunned, dazed as by a blow." As late as the fifteenth century, in the mind of Medieval Christendom, it had meant happiness; "said of persons, their condition or experiences" when blessed by God. For the sophisticated mind of the Age of Reason it meant what was most contemned.

The silly condition of the open soul was that there must have been so many freaks, frail worn-out crazy rebirths; so many deaths of meaning, relapses into chaotic matter; so many ecstatic explosions in the alembic. We sense it in the course of human genius. The fact of the risk of inspiration is recognized in the common sense of "touched." Where men have vision and courage for the experience of life itself, even where it exceeds the uses of understanding, beyond the preservation of the species, *silly* could mean blissful, and it was deserving of compassion, for it meant too to go in peril of the soul.

·

The landscape of the dream may be thought of, as I have thought of H.D.'s poem, as the alembic where radiant powers move. The incandescence is the sun-spot, the tender-spot, the conjunction of the script and the fire. Just here what we are not begins to take life in Us. "We have no map," H.D. writes in the closing lines of *The Walls Do Not Fall*. On the biological level, in Darwinian terms, the whole intricately evolved pattern of those who survive gives no map that will tell us the fate of man, for the orders of the living are inbound and informed by the orders of the cosmos that men call chaos or chance. "Possibly we will reach haven, / heaven," is the only resolution of the longing in us towards what is not ourselves but belongs to the current of possibilities in evolution. This "we" is no longer at liberty but serves the purpose that H.D. calls "*Paradise*" in The War Trilogy. "The seal of the jar was un-broken." Yes, and Kaspar was most aware of his cause, his proper heat and center. But, "no secret was safe with a woman."

·

Italicizing, H.D. draws into correspondence the two utterances: "*for many waters can not quench love's fire*" and:

but to an outcast and a vagabond,
to-day shalt thou be with me in Paradise.

There is a love in which we are outcast and vagabond from what we are that we call "falling in love." It appears an evil or a power over us, and can seize us, sweeping from us all sense of who we are. We know it as the cells must have known the first magic rays, as pain, as longing, as loss, as ecstasy; for we are estranged from ourselves in this love or light, and something evolves.

Where we preserve ourselves, ripening into our own forms or species, we must often pray against this "falling in love," the imperative that might carry us beyond ourselves. For there is the other love we know, the domestic and kindly love for what we are, our daily practice of love. In the highest vision they are one, but in the individual heart that enters the changes towards the higher vision so that "falling in love" may belong to the things we love, the changes are fearful.

It was this "falling in love," if we read Ransom's "Winter Remembered" rightly, that was Ransom's time of knowing the hurt or light or inspiration that made him begin his struggle to reduce Poetry to a domestic art. There was:

A cry of Absence, Absence, in the heart,
And in the wood the furious winter blowing.

Just for the moment he was in that very *selva oscura,* the desolation, where thoughts stir, in which the great adventure of the spirit in the *Divine Comedy* or *Pilgrim's Progress* or The War Trilogy begins.

But the great adventure of the spirit is in its evolution, in its surrender of itself and coming into the intention of God in the peril of the soul. Towards Paradise, heaven, the light—*that* has been the eternal promise. The promise that falling in love makes to the lover.

•

"*Quando m'apparve Amor subitamente,*" Dante says: "When suddenly Amor appeared to me, the memory of whose being maketh me shudder." And he tells us in his journal of the same event:

I thought I saw in my chamber a cloud of the hue of flame, within which I discerned the figure of a lord, of fearful aspect to one who should look on him. And he seemed to me of such gladness as to himself that a wondrous thing it was; and in his words he said many things which I understood not save a few, among which I understood these: *Ego dominus tuus.* I am your Master. In his arms I thought I saw one sleeping, naked, save that she seemed to me wrapped lightly in a crimson drapery; whom, gazing at very intently, I knew to be the lady of the salutation, who the day before had deigned to salute me. And in one of his hands I thought he held a thing that was all aflame; and I thought he said to me these words: *Vide cor tuum.* Behold thy heart. And when he had tarried a while, I thought he awoke her who slept and so wrought he by his art that he made her eat of that thing that was aflame in his hand, whereof she ate afeared. Thereafter, short time he abode ere his gladness was changed to bitterest weeping: and thus weeping, he gathered this lady up in his arms and with her I thought he went away heavenward: whereat I sustained so great anguish that my feeble little sleep could not endure, but broke and I was awake. And straightway I began to ponder and found that the hour in which this vision had appeared to me had been the fourth hour of the night: so that it manifestly appeareth that it was the first of the last nine hours of the night.

•

Wherever he names the time (*la bonne heure*) in *La Vita Nuova,* Dante finds it in terms of the number nine: "Nine times already since my birth had the heaven of light returned," "so that almost from the beginning of her ninth year she appeared to me and I beheld her almost at the end of my ninth"; again, Beatrice appears to Dante nine years later in the ninth hour of the day. The theme of the beginning in the end, of the first and the last is repeated in the design of nines, where in the first vision of Amor Dante finds the hour of the dream to have been "the first of the last nine hours of the night." The second vision of Amor is in the ninth hour of the day. A third comes on the ninth day of a painful illness. Hours, days, years—months along, the nine months of gestation, seem missing. Then, in accounting for the time of Beatrice's death Dante tells us, "because many times the number nine hath found place among the preceding words, whereby it appeareth that it is not without reason," he will discuss the meaning of the number. First, he must show how the number nine appears in her death: "I say that according to the Arabian style her most noble soul departed in the first hour of the ninth day of the month; and according to the Syrian style, it departed on the ninth month of the year—and according to our style, she departed in that year of our era, namely of the years of our Lord, wherein the perfect number was completed nine times in that century wherein she was placed."

In a series of revelations Dante has dangerously hinted that Beatrice is analogous first to Love, then in the Giovanna Primavera–Giovanni *prima verra* passage that she is analogous to *"la verace luce,"* the True Light or Christ. Now he tells us that nine has reason; first, because it denotes the astrological harmony of the nine spheres appropriate to her birth; then, "more subtly and according to infallible truth, this number was her very self," "This lady was accompanied by the number nine to give to understand that she was a nine, that is, a miracle whose root is the wondrous Trinity alone."

But Dante has prepared for the daring of this suggestion in his digression on the license of poets in their fictions from which I took my epigraph at the beginning of this day book. He seems to be explaining his license to a serious reader with a philosophic bias: "Here a person worthy of having all his difficulties made plain might be perplexed, for he might have a difficulty as to what I say concerning Love, as if he were a thing in himself and not only an intelligent being but a corporeal being. Which thing according to truth, is false; for Love exists not as a being in itself but as a quality of a being."

Things are not what they seem. But poets are allowed, Dante argues, a "greater license in speech" than composers in prose. "The poets have spoken to inanimate things as they had sense and reason and have made them speak together, and not only real things but unreal things." Is Amor then the creature of such a poetic license? Nor was the poet sincere in that high ardor of vision in which he saw Beatrice so exalted? "Deep shame were it to him," Dante writes: "who should rhyme under cover of a figure or of a rhetorical colour and, afterwards, being asked, knew not how to strip such vesture from his words, in such wise that they should have a real meaning." Is it philosophical error or theological heresy that the poet would cover for in his license? Is the real meaning beneath the vesture of the figures of Amor and Beatrice less than or more than the poet would tell us in the poem? In the first case he means to warn us that he praises Beatrice inordinately; in the second case, that she is in truth—"the glorious lady of my mind who was called Beatrice by many who knew not how she was called"—an other higher entity. In sections v and vi of the *Vita Nuova*, Dante tells us how midway between him and Beatrice there sat a lady "marvelling at my look which seemed to end in her," so that many mistook the object of his gaze. "Then I comforted me greatly being assured that my secret had not been made common that day to others by my look." "And straightway," he continues: "I thought to make this lady a screen of the truth."

•

From Apuleius's *The Golden Ass* or those *"fictions littéraires du logos de revelation,"* as Festugière would call them, to which the orthodox *Gospel of John* as well as the heretical *Acts of John* surely belongs, from the creative romanticism of the late Hellenistic age to Dante's *La Vita Nuova* in the transition to the Renaissance, even to H.D.'s War Trilogy written in our period which has relegated the terms of Christian vision as well as of pagan mystery or of daemonic or angelic hierarchies to the domain of illusion and delusion, the response to experience in the spirit of romance has been to seek out the deeper meaning or impact of the seizure that we know as falling in love. In each romance there is a transformation, a deprivation in which beyond the physical, a psychic and then a spiritual reality is revealed. Festugière is right, I think, in his pointing out that these revelations are *fictions littéraires,* for they come about in an art of fictions, a witchcraft of the Word. And their higher truth or reality remains poetic, a revelation of the power of the reality of man's language itself. "The end of my Love," Dante writes, "was once this lady's salutation [where *salute* may also mean salvation]; and therein dwelt my beatitude, for it was the end of all my desires. But since it hath pleased her to deny it to me, Love, my lord, by his grace, hath placed all my beatitude in that which cannot fail me . . . in those words that praise my lady."

•

To find the hour and the place, bringing into the fictive creation the particulars of the actual life, is part of the magic of self-transformation, so that the creative fiction enters the sense of actual reality. H.D., like

Dante, like John of Patmos, has no experience that is not meaning, that is not, by emblem or rubric, part of feeling beyond her feeling. The events of her life are not only personal, they are also hints of a great universe to which all man's fictions belong. Dante's astrological and numerological practices, reading the nine of his fictions into the times of his actual life, take creative thought in actuality as they take action in a creative fiction, akin to H.D.'s practice of astrology and angelology:

I had been thinking of Gabriel,
of the moon-cycle, of the moon-shell,

of the moon-crescent
and the moon at full:

It is taking thought where the poet begins to have a heightened sense of time and this life as informed by his Work. But our Work, which may have been the alchemical Work, or the Work in the Art, is now in a larger sense a Life-Work or evolution of Life in which we play our human phase. The poet begins to have a heightened sense of his involvement in a great work beyond his work.

•

Ananke, in Freud's *The Future of an Illusion,* the law of "in so far as external reality allows it," reflects all Freud's sense of how the soul in the throes of creative change was most likely to come thru "touched" or "silly," maimed or lost, in its new self. He had on his mind too how maimed, lost, silly, souls often were, who had gone thru the alembic of religious conversions.

But *Ananke* had a twin in *Logos. Ananke/Logos,* that Freud proposes to take the place of the old gods of the cathedral, is just, in one guise, the Hell-Heaven that his nurse had sown in his infant mind. *Ananke/Logos* might also be the Christ-Crucified/Christ-Child. He is Falling-in-Love/Loving. He is the inspiration, the feeling of a divine order that we sense in a directive that is not from our personal bias but from the self we have in a universal community. He is Amor. He is the evolutionary imperative.

"You would have the state of bliss to begin immediately after death";

Freud writes: "you ask of it the impossible, and you will not surrender the claim of the individual. Of these wishes our god *Logos* will realize those which external nature permits, but he will do this very gradually, only in the incalculable future and for other children of men. Compensation for us, who suffer grievously from life, he does not promise." The reality—this is Freud's sense here that seems most true—the deep reality of actual life is without consolation for the claim of the individual. Dante tells us that in deprivation of the actual Beatrice he wept and then fell asleep "like a beaten sobbing child." H.D. in the opening passages of *The Walls Do Not Fall* speaks of her "desolation" and inspiration "stalks" like a threatening hunter so that the poet trembles. Amor, in *La Vita Nuova,* appears as "a cloud of the hue of flame, within which I discerned the figure of a lord, of fearful aspect to one who should look upon him."

Yet the promise, wherever the pain has been known and received as a condition of the Work, is bliss. We had been talking of Kaspar, in H.D.'s poem, for he came to a moment when he knew in a way he was lost. "The seal of the jar was un-broken"—Kaspar was what he was; but "no secret was safe with a woman." Did he fall in love? He had a high sense of his cause, his proper heat and center:

> he drew aside his robe in a noble manner
> but the un-maidenly woman did not take the hint;

yet the epiphany of *The Flowering of the Rod* is his falling in love somehow, falling in with the stars, being inspired. "Kaspar did not recognize her," H.D. tells us:

> until her scarf slipped to the floor,
>
> and then, not only did he recognize Mary
> as the stars had told (Venus in the ascendant . . .

We begin to trace the line of an inspired seizure, from "as the stars had told"—Yes, he felt what Dante called the salutation of the Lady, he felt he had an appointment there, as eyes too may meet in a new light—thru the travail of desire, the courses of the stars:

and what he saw made his heart so glad
that it was as if he suffered,

his heart laboured so
with his ecstasy

in his seeing "the fleck of light":

like a flaw in the third jewel

to his right, in the second circlet,
a grain, a flaw or speck of light.

·

Dante tells us that in the vision of Amor, his heart or rather, "the vital
spirit which dwelleth in the most secret chamber of the heart" trembled
so that "it was horribly apparent in the least of my pulses"; even as "the
animal spirit which dwelleth in the high chamber to which the spirits
of sense carry their perceptions" began to marvel.

·

So that when he comes into the presence of the Christ-Child, Kaspar
is inspired to see or to present (for the fragrance that is the Divine
Presence is both the myrrh which he brings escaped from the unbroken
seal of the jar and also the Child born from the virgin woman) what we
have called the promise of falling in love or the revelation of the end of
desire. Which the Mother sees or knows is there:

she said, Sir, it is a most beautiful fragrance,
as of all flowering things together;

·

"It is really about the soul, or the primal intelligence, or the *Nous,* or
whatever we choose to call that link that binds us to the unseen and
un-created," John Gould Fletcher wrote in 1917, reviewing H.D.'s *Sea
Garden.* "A new cadence means a new idea," the Preface of *Some Imagist
Poets* in 1915 argued. Something Platonic and then neo-Platonic haunts
these passages, as it haunts Pound's definitions of *logopoeia, melopoeia* and

phanopoeia, with hints not only of a theosophy, a lore and wisdom of divine orders, but also a theurgy, an operation of divine orders.

Fletcher sees H.D.'s work in such terms and tells us we must read her as we read "Plotinus or Dionysius the Areopagite, or Paracelsus, or Behmen, or Swedenborg, or Blake, or any other of the mystics."

In the mixing ground of pre-War London where theosophical currents passed thru the talk of Yeats and the lectures of G. R. S. Mead into the main bloodstream of Pound's thought in *The Cantos* or, from some aftermath of Blavatsky's fantastic anthropology and cosmogony, were stored up by D. H. Lawrence to emerge in his *Fantasia of the Unconscious,* there must have been times when talk of metrics and cadence turned to old theurgic ideas of numbers and evocative measures, where cadence meant a means of vision; where idea, eidolon, and image were closely associated concepts. Allen Upward's *The Divine Mystery* with its exposition of poetic genius as shamanistic power and its doctrine that desire thru intuition operates in the actual was read and talked about by the literary following of *The Egoist* as well as the theosophical following of *The Quest.*

But H.D. is not a mystic philosopher. Her genius is fictive and dramatic, not philosophic. When she speaks of "where thought dwells, / and beyond thought and idea, / their begetter, / Dream, Vision," these— *thought, idea, dream, vision*—are not concepts or terms of a phenomenology but entities, *dramatis personae* of her universe. "Sword" and "Word" are poetic counterparts of daimonic beings in neo-Platonic hierarchies, having their creative necessity here in the plasticity of the immediate reality of the poem rather than in the requirements of a philosophic structure. She is searching out the quality of an experience coming into being. There is no reality in H.D.'s sense of things that is not involved in the physical and vital realities around us. "Dream" or "Vision" are creative forces at large, and the Word may enter, as Death enters Cocteau's world or Bergman's. Like Ficino or Pico della Mirandola, her sense of the reality of the gods is of a magic to inform the life of her art. She evokes the old gods, and then the new—Christ as Master, the Lady, or the Christ-Child—and attends the tutelary spirits of the hours, her angels, as actual figures of a dramatic intensity. The place "where thought dwells" has at least the reality of Shakespeare's coast of Bohemia.

She may interpret on many levels the meaning of their appearance or presence, but she does not present these persons of the poem as ethical or edifying figures. The War Trilogy or *Helen in Egypt* will not supply metaphysical or even psychological ideas on the nature of Love or of Evil, for H.D. seeks not terms of concept but terms of experience. There is no argument for the good of the union of all things but in the Child, the Mother at the close of the poem finds "a most beautiful fragrance, / as of all flowering things together."

.

In comparing The War Trilogy with *La Vita Nuova*, we must recognize that, while H.D. has Dante's concern for psychology, she does not have his philosophic interest: Dante is exploring the concept of Love as well as telling its story and evoking the reality of Love as an experience. Nor does H.D. have the moral concern of Bunyan in his allegory. But for all three, as poets, the primary concern is in the world of experience they create, whatever their philosophy, their morality or learning. It is of the essence that Amor too in *La Vita Nuova* is not a concept or an allegory but a presence of the poem, who can hold a burning heart in his hand, an eternal being of the dream. As for Bunyan too, who meant allegory, "in the similitude of a DREAM," Atheist and Ignorance appear with all the force of living creatures and his created world takes on the urgency and immediacy of revelation that the actual world has. It is in this, in our entering a made up reality, rather than in whatever concept, that the specifically *poetic* lies.

.

Every hour, every moment
has its specific attendant Spirit

belongs to the metaphysics of Hellenistic and Renaissance star cults that no longer make sense in our contemporary science. Astrology fell into such disrepairs as men no longer were concerned with the actual stars themselves and ceased to observe the precession of the equinoxes and as men were no longer concerned with picturing their nature but turned to telling fortunes. But in The War Trilogy the verses have to do with the stage directions of the drama H.D. means to unfold. In the enchantment in which the Spirits of hours and moments appear, we are led to an inner feeling of things that changes the world about us into the world of the poem. It resists metaphysical concern. Well, it does not rest at all on such a concern but upon a thing seen and heard:

> for it was ticking minute by minute
> (the clock by my bed-head,
>
> with its dim, luminous disc)

This is not, in a sense, artful writing, for no wit or sensibility of the poet must appear to distract us from the world of the poem:

> there was no door
> (this was a dream, of course),
>
> and she was standing there,
> actually, at the turn of the stair.

•

It is what is actual to the poem that concerns her. She may follow lines of association, opening new levels of what is happening, exciting reverberations. These unfold in the course of the poem from her deepened and heightened sense of its world, of what is happening. The core of the Imagist ethos is there thruout her work in the last years. "Direct treatment" remains; all the special effects, interesting or sensitive words, similes, metaphors, epithets have been eroded away by the attention to what is going on. The thing in itself had become by 1915 a thing in its surroundings and atmosphere. By the time of The War Trilogy, H.D. is most aware of a many-leveled experience. So, she is drawn back to the old mystery cults—to mystery not to mysticism—to the roots of the drama, back of Euripides, in the secret worships of the Mother, of Dionysos, and to the Christ and the Lady of the Christian mysteries. Where she makes definitions they are operative not logical. These gods or angelic orders are never speculative figures, propositions of God, or members of a metaphysical system; they are actors upon a stage that is the world.

"Bliss" is a state of the realized moment, as in *Bid Me to Live:* "walking for the first time, taking the first steps in her life, upright on her feet for the first time alone, or for the first time standing after death (daughter, I say unto thee) she faced the author of this her momentary psychic being, her lover, her husband. It was like that in these moments. She touched paradise."

Paradise, like the houses of the Zodiac, can no longer be placed in the dimensions of the physical universe; but all places and gods have entered the imagination and belong as surely to the feeling of things as they ever did, for we have only to step upon the stage of *The Tempest* to find that Ariel and Caliban are most real and in turn to awaken to such attendant servants about us in our actual life. The world-map of Dante is a curiosity, but the poet in the *Paradiso* looking deep into the profound and shining being of God, for all his theological schema of the trinity, sees "one by the second as Iris by Iris seemed reflected, and the third seemed a fire breathed equally from one and from the other" and it is not the theology that lasts but this seeming; for looking "entering through the ray of the deep light which in itself is true," Dante, who is full of discourse, found his vision "mightier than our discourse, which faileth at such sight." This Paradise, like H.D.'s, that once was a place in the physical universe, now is a place in feeling.

•

"The Tuscan demands harmony in something more than the plastic," Pound wrote in the Cavalcanti essay: "He declines to limit his aesthetic to the impact of light on the eye. It would be misleading to reduce his aesthetic to terms of music, or to distort the analysis of it by analogies to the art of sonority. Man shares plastic with the statue, sound does not require a human being to produce it. The bird, the phonograph, sing. Sound can be exteriorized as completely as plastic. There is the residue of perception, perception of something which requires a human being to produce it. Which even may require a certain individual to produce it." Then, the passage we have returned to before: "This really complicates the aesthetic. You deal with an interactive force: the *virtu* in short." "The conception of the body as perfect instrument of the increasing intelligence pervades."

"The truth having been Eleusis?" he writes in that same sense in *Kulchur*, "and a modern Eleusis being possible in the wilds of a man's mind only?"

•

The god that appears to bewilder H.D.'s Pygmalion is the *virtu*, the interactive force of a creativity between the man as he is a maker who experiences in his making and the world as it is a matter that informs as it is shaped. There is the sculptor's "own light," "own heat," "own fire"; the increasing intelligence is an increasing awareness of instrumentality in which the sense of the work is known as in-formed by the stone, the swirl on swirl of light, by the appearance out of the work. It is experience that is the fire in "does this fire carve me / for its use?" as thirty years later it is the experience of the poem that is the new Master over Love. There is no awareness or being above, beyond, outside of, the interaction of things we experience; and here, in the work of the poet the Master of the poem must be the experience of the Word, the Master of Rime. Our uses are our illuminations.

Appendix 1 *Preliminary Notes toward Book 3 of* The H.D. Book

EXCHANGES

August 31. reading of Euripides' *Helen* translated by Richmond Lattimore. "Introduction" quoted from the *Palinode* of Stesichorus (6th century):

> That story is not true.
> You never went away in the launched ships.
> You never reached the citadel of Troy.

We know no more than this fragment; we do not know where Helen did go, until Herodotus tells us he heard from the priests of Hephaestus in Memphis that Paris did steal Helen but, driven by winds to the Egyptian coast, he had to surrender Helen to the keeping of Proteus, King of Egypt, until her husband should claim her.

So that Menelaus and Agamemnon at Troy are told by the Trojans that they do not have Helen. The war that follows, for the Greeks do not believe the Trojans, is mistaken. Only after the fall of Troy do they find that the Trojans were telling the truth.

Menelaus sails for Egypt, collects Helen, and (after "disgracing himself and Greece by an illicit sacrifice involving two Egyptian boys") sails home.

In Homer's telling of Troy in the *Iliad* there had been magic substitution: when Diomedes lifting a great stone crushes the thigh of Aineias in battle, Aphrodite, the mother of Aineias, surrounds the hero and "spreads before his face a fold of her radiant vesture", fleeing with him from Diomedes' wrath. But Aphrodite, Homer tells us, has no warcraft (powers or mastery in war) "no Athena she nor Enyo, master of cities." Diomedes, pursuing her, attacks the goddess herself and wounds her hand: "straight through the ambrosial raiment that the Graces themselves had given her pierced the dart into the flesh, above the springing of the palm."

•

In H.D.'s narrative of *Helen in Egypt* there is a theme of a veil or a scarf. There had been in the magic of Mary Magdalene, setting into motion her glamour in which Kaspar has his "spiritual optical-illusion" or clairvoyance in *The Flowering of the Rod,* a first gesture that disarmed Kaspar: "and her scarf slipped to the floor." Not only does the scarf operate here to uncover her hair, but it operates too to put the Mage off guard:

He who was unquestionably
master of caravans,

stooped to the floor;
he handed her her scarf;

The disordered, the disheveled element is her hair—H.D. tells us Simon at the feast had seen Mary as a Siren and that she may have been—"wrecks followed the wake of such hair" Simon remembers where

she was deftly un-weaving

the long, carefully-braided tresses
of her extraordinary hair.

But it is the scarf that is exchanged in the magic "As he stooped for the scarf, he saw this"—the hair may be the revelation in the light "like moon-light on a lost river" and the scarf that seems incidental the magic apparatus that both distracts the man and engages him, and that reveals as it falls.

•

This must be an oldest and most common magic of women—the dropping of a glove or a kerchief or a scarf or fan, some hint of disclosure that must be acknowledged and returned. Here the scarf is lure.

.

In *Helen in Egypt* night after night Achilles had watched the phantom Helen on the walls of Troy signal with her scarf. The information here—between the fold of Aphrodite's radiant vesture in Homer's narrative, and the scarf-magic of Mary Magdalene in H.D.'s *The Walls Do Not Fall,* the everyday magic of women to cast lures in the way of would-be lovers, and the scarf of the phantom Helen that had captured Achilles' gaze and maybe his soul in H.D.'s *Helen in Egypt*—the pattern is musical. The cloak or veil or scarf of a woman may not be symbolic but thematic. In "Palinode" of *Helen,* book four, we are told: "The symbolic 'veil' to which Achilles had enigmatically referred now resolves itself down to the memory of a woman's scarf, blowing in the winter-wind". Crossing Lethe, Achilles loses his sense of the War: only the salt air and a gull hovering

> seemed real, and an old sailor
> who greeted me as a lost stranger,
> resting his gnarled hands
>
> on the oars, *where would you go?*
> I did not know,
> I saw her scarf
>
> as the wind caught it
> one winter day; I saw her hand
> through the transparent folds,

and:

> I only remember the turn
> of a Greek wrist,
> knotting a scarf

Achilles tells us later. And we remember the steps in the magic between Mary Magdalene and Kaspar (1) "and her scarf slipped to the floor,"

(2) "As he stooped for the scarf," (3) "and as he straightened," (4) "as his hand just did-not touch her hand," (5) "as she drew the scarf toward her," (6) "as he dropped his arm in the second half-second" and in the seventh step

> what he saw was a woman of discretion,
> knotting a scarf,

Style is an effort to exorcise or to control the magic or glamour of sound in music, stone in sculpture or evocation in words. The effort in style is to increase an awareness of the rationale of the works. Thinking now of the lure of women's hair and dress, we see that in periods of style women cut their hair or keep it most in place, and that style in dress means the effortful projection of effect—all aims at increasing our awareness of what is there as a thing in itself. Sorceresses wear their hair coiled and loosened, their robes flowing and with scarves and bracelets, pinpoints of jewel-light and beads, for they do and undo their hair and dress weaving their spells. Lure is the opposite of style; the sentence and thought must wander to distraction before the reader becomes hopelessly involved. And hopeless involvement is the underlying psychic need of the magician. Had magic intended power over all things it could have found power, but the deep desire the magician hides from himself is the bewilderment he seeks. Lucifer does not betray, he brings to light our secret wishes to be undone.

I

Aineias all but mortally wounded—the crushing of his thigh is itself a step in another magic—the crippling or anticipation of divine retribution (as in vaccination we anticipate the disease we fear)—cannot rise. "The darkness of night veiled his eyes" Homer tells us, and it is in this confusion of the selves, this breach of the war itself where Aineias is no longer aware of the war, that Aphrodite is able to spread this fold of her own vesture.

We are in this passage of Homer in some charged account of the most dangerous passages of one magic—Aphrodite's—entering the field of another magic—the War—where it has no powers. Aphrodite here is bereft. It is my sense here, not Homer's, that what happens is that Aineias is partly aware of the battle around him, partly in the deep night where his mother's power may help him; and in this partial awareness of the battle, he threatens his mother's art. Aphrodite herself becomes vulnerable wherever thru Aineias the reality of the battle may invade.

Wounded, with a great cry she lets fall her son: "him Phoebus Apollo took into his arms and saved him in a dusky cloud." The magic is the same magic Aphrodite had attempted but could not carry thru because Aineias was her son and she was undone in him. Apollo has no such psychic share and we see now the steps of this magic substitution as it parallels the substitution of Helen recounted first by Euripides.

The steps are these:

1. The god casts a glamour or vesture or sheath at a point of confusion in the human consciousness. As in the *Iliad*, Aphrodite can enter upon Aineias's swoon, where "the darkness of night veiled his eyes" and substitute for that darkness "a fold of her radiant vesture", and then in turn in the cry or dismay of the goddess, Apollo can take over "in a dusky cloud." So, too, perhaps less clearly than a swoon, but certainly a confusion, in the confusions of gossip and emotion after Paris's winning Helen and before his taking her—think how much this is like the confusion of falling in love that opens a place for daemonic interference—Hermes, in Euripides' *Helen,* spirits away the actual Helen.

> I myself was caught up by Hermes
> > sheathed away
> in films of air

2. The god moves the protégée from the breach to a refuge. In the *Iliad*, Aineias is removed from the battle to the temple of Apollo in Pergamos where he is glorified. In *Helen* of Euripides, Helen is set down in Egypt, having secretly the glory of marital honor.

> Yet I have heard
> from the god Hermes that I yet shall make my home
> in the famous plain of Sparta with my lord, and he
> shall know I never went to Ilium, had no thought
> of bed with any man.

3. The god creates a double to stand-in for the hero. Apollo "made a wraith like unto Aineias' self." Hera, in Euripides' play,

> angry that she was not given the prize,
> made void the love that might have been for Paris and me,

so Helen tells us:

> and gave him, not me, but in my likeness fashioning
> a breathing image out of the sky's air,

We note here that the double or doppelganger is a phantom cast upon the air, a mirage, an atmospheric seeming—related then is the clouding of consciousness in the first step of the magic. The shield of radiant vesture, dusky cloud or films of air, becomes the vehicle in which the hero is transported and at the same time is the medium in which the wraith appears.

•

This high magic, like the fascinations of the scarf, has its counterpoint in the magic of everyday life. It is the very nature of confusion that we are not in some sense ourselves; "it is not the true you," those about us say. We are shielded on our swooning or panicking or being upset or falling in love and in a way are not really there. When the time of confusion passes our true self seems to emerge, untouched by it all. And it is very difficult remembering our own composed accounts of acute trouble—to believe that we were really ourselves at all. Aineias torn in two between his craven terror as he is thrown to the ground and his heroic identity, and Helen torn in two between her faithfulness to her husband and her temptation for "the love that might have been for Paris and me" prepare a ground not extraordinary in human experience for magic to take hold.

·

The statement may be that tho the wraith of Aineias continued in battle, the real Aineias was to be glorified in refuge; tho the wraith of Helen continued in adultery and cause of the war, the real Helen was to be sought after but faithful—a counterpart of Penelope. The formula of the magic involved is on one side of the equation an unreal but apparent person in the real situation and on the other side a real but hidden person in an unreal or foreign refuge from the situation.

II

Not only Helen, then, in the narrative traditions of the Trojan war had a wraith so that behind the apparent truth of the war was a very different truth waiting for its own denouement. Aineias, himself, had a wraith, was in some sense duplicit. In his study *Folk Tale, Fiction and Saga in the Homeric Epics,* Rhys Carpenter relates the tradition of Helen of Egypt to a suspicion that the victory at Troy itself is a substitute for an Egyptian disaster:

> On the walls of the temple at Medinet Habu in Egypt is a series of reliefs depicting a great naval battle in which the forces of "the northern countries . . . who came from their lands in the islands in the midst of the sea" (as the accompanying hieroglyphic text declares) are being annihilated by the navy of Rameses III. The date is about 1190 B.C., almost precisely the year of the sack of Troy according to one of the most widely favored classical computations of that distant event. The often-quoted account in the Egyptian record may bear one more repetition here:
>
>> The Isles were restless, disturbed among themselves . . .
>> As for those who advanced together on the sea . . . a net was prepared to ensnare them . . . At the Nile mouths the full flame was in front of them, a stockade of lances surrounded them on the shore: they

were dragged, hemmed in, laid low on the beach, slain, made into heaps: their ships and their goods were as if fallen into the sea.

•

"True," Carpenter continues, "the Egyptian texts chronicle the utter defeat"—etc. to end of paragraph pp. 62–63.

•

There was at Troy a defeat hidden in the midst of triumph; a triumph hidden in the midst of defeat. In the *Iliad* where only hints of Egypt appear—Carpenter points out that the suspicion that Helen never went to Troy may haunt the *Odyssey,* if not the *Iliad.* Carpenter points out that Menelaus and Helen of the *Odyssey* go to Egypt after the fall of Troy—and that Ulysses-Odysseus upon his return in his account for his years to the old swineherd says he had been in Egypt seven years. The return of Odysseus from the fabulous victory at Troy is thru waters of a nightmare troubled sea towards the real homeland where he arrives having lost all men and ships. In the tradition of Hesiod, Stesichorus,— Herodotus and Euripides—the cause of the war was fraudulent.

•

So, too, we in our own time have seen two fraudulent wars and prepare now for a third, where no cause is raised but the threat of disaster. Freedom, Christianity, democracy—whatever wraith upon the walls to be defended or liberated—has not been in our lands since the beginning nor in the hands of the enemy, but spirited away to Egypt while we must be at it again to loose ourselves and our forces in the ruin of cities.

> this to drain our mother earth of the burden and the multitude
> of human kind

Helen says in Euripides' play.

> . . . fought for me (except it was not I but my name only)—

•

The tradition that Helen was in Egypt—the tradition in which out of Euripides (and, as we shall develop later, out of Goethe) H.D. takes her narrative dramatic poem is record of man's self-betrayal in love and in war. These two greatest of confusions are fields of deception—the issue in either must be as mixed as the ground of desires intolerably mixed that seeks its satisfaction there. In Helen we see the issue of love, the issue of war.

III

"Playing with fire," the common expression goes for the confusions of passionate love and for the confusions of war and we may live in a very confusion of war now for the threats and fears now on all sides: the expression has grown dreadful and trite, "You are playing with fire."

•

In the "Palinode" of *Helen in Egypt,* Achilles, drawn to the shores of Egypt because the magic of the scarf survives the waters of Lethe, finds Helen or she finds him—they meet upon a shore where he has been ship-wrecked from the Ship of Death and she had been waiting for the arrival of her soul-mate. In "Palinode" it is Achilles, but she knows it is also someone else. He gathers brushwood and builds her a fire. Then the playing with fire that follows the playing with the scarf begins.

Because a magic is here we watch, as we watched the scarf, how the scene is developed—but that was the scarf-magic of Mary Magdalene and Kaspar in *The Flowering of the Rod,* this other scarf magic lies ahead in the "Palinode," or it shows itself in the scene over the bonfire on the beach.

•

Achilles lights the fire with an old flint he finds in his pocket.

> "I thought I had lost that", he says and then:
> "I am ship-wrecked, I am lost,"
> "I am a woman of pleasure," Helen says.

•

He has come with the mistaken flame of the war in his eyes

> the bane of battle
> and the legions lost

and another "sea-enchantment in his eyes" of Thetis, his mother. He had kindled the fire for Helen, and now she seeks to use it, confusing herself with Thetis, his mother—and thru that confusing (as thru a scarf he had once seen her hand) showing her hand.

A night-bird flies up. "Strive not," Helen says to him when he questions:

> it is dedicate
> to the goddess here, she is Isis";
>
> "Isis," he said, "or Thetis," I said,

•

They are playing with fire, asking *who are you? where are we?* in such a way that the scene begins to throng with powers beyond their own persons. Feeding the fire with the presence of Thetis his mother and Zeus her father so that when she reaches for a blackened stick in the burning, she is not sure whether she reached to blacken her face, to mask herself among the dead or whether it was an ember.

•

The thought of "Helen, hated of all Greece" burns in him as an ember

> as the flint, the spark
> of his anger,

the poem tells us. There are not only persons but times that begin to throng now, and a magic rage possesses Achilles—it is the War that arrives here with all its hosts. The actual night-bird that "hooted past"—such is the pull of the magic to shape things towards its necessities—becomes anonymous even as it flies.

he started, "a curious flight,
a carrion creature—what—"
(dear God, let him forget);

What?—forget what? It is the name, *owl,* that he is prevented in the magic from reaching—and "a carrion creature" leads, as Helen saying "it is dedicate to the goddess here" leads us not to *owl-Athene* but to the fatal substitution *vulture-Isis,* "or Thetis" she adds, for the sea Achilles had been over was the sea of the dead, and had Helen blackened her face he would have seen the mask of the carrion-Mother. He does, even in her gesture see that face: "Hecate!" he cries.

●

By the actual night-bird, they evoke the vulture, bird of Isis; by the actual sea beyond the fire on the beach, they evoke Thetis; by the vulture and by Thetis and by the actual blackened stick they evoke Hecate and the hosts of the dead. So that all the human loss is there, the sea of the dead, the dead lost at sea in the war:

the fury of the tempest in his eyes
the bane of battle
and the legions lost

Now the fire on the beach is another fire.

consuming the Greek heroes;
it is the funeral pyre;

By the actual flint, he begins the playing with fire; by the actual ember they evoke his anger, but his anger is desire. Hatred of Helen, hatred of his mother, hatred of the carrion Isis, evokes the legions of the war as the Holocaust—the fire sweeping the whole of the man, consumed with passion. Achilles leaps forward to strangle Helen

what heart-break, what unappeasable
ache, burning within his sinews,

He leaps towards his own confusion, for there is a scarf about her neck
or, she tells us,

> it was they, the Holocaust,
> a host, a cloud or a veil
>
> who encircled, who sheltered me,
> when his fingers closed on my throat;

    •

Sept. 1 / 61
There were only these things to work with:

> the sea, the shore, the night
> as we walk, heel and sole
> leave our sandal-prints in the sand,
>
> though the wounded heel treads lightly
> and more lightly follow,
> the purple sandals

his limp then; the brushwood fagots, the flint, the fire, the blackened
sticks then and the ember, the night-bird, her purple sandals ("I am a
woman of pleasure," she could suggest), her scarf or veil, his "shield,
helmet, greaves."

    •

How to the carrion-bird vulture, Isis; hawk, Horus; and swan, Zeus
come! Mother, son, and Father gathering in along one line of associa-
tion. And in those wings of the night-bird greater wings of the war
itself, feathered with all of the dead, a thousand arrows and one—the
arrow in war that mortally wounded immortal Achilles. Thetis was to
blame for that, for the fatal vulnerable spot, the thousand ships. "This
is the spread of wings."

    •

In the poem to these actual things, where the man and the woman
huddle over a fire in the night on the beach, a gathering begins. This
is not the magic of symbols, but the magic that goes on in the practices

of psychoanalysis—the magic of associations until a host of incidents, impersonations, tendencies precipitate what is called "the content" and in the precipitation the crisis. Not those streams of consciousness that in Proust's magic opened out from one impression vistas of the past recaptured; but as if this magic were reversed and all the glowing and modulated fabric were to be called in from its dispersion to increase the pressures of a single moment.

•

They seek to draw themselves out of the fire—ash and ember; to look from the blackened mask, to flame forth anew out of the things at hand. They seek too to resurrect their old selves, to bring forth just what was intolerable—the spread of wings, the fascination of the veil. The spark must be the spark of war and love, Eros and Eris is one. The holocaust itself, the burnt offering of Iphigenia and the wholesale burning of the war-dead is needed for Achilles to be this Achilles, Helen to be this Helen.

•

"Never, never do I forget the host," Helen says:

the chosen, the flower

of all-time, of all-history;
it was they who struck,
as the flint, the spark

of his anger,

•

The host, the all, struck the spark; but the thousand-and-one darts were "a host, a cloud or a veil" we learn from Helen. It may be that the thousand-and-one associations—their lives—they had called up "encircled", "sheltered". *"Helena, which was the dream?"* Achilles asks her:

the rasp of a severed wheel,
the fury of steel upon steel,
the spark from a sword on a shield?

or the deathless spark
of Helena's wakening . . .
a touch in the dark?

•

There is the magic of the sword, the magic of everyday distraction, even to be beside oneself with grief. The attention is disarrayed and the attention returning is caught by the glance of an eye or the touch of a hand; for a moment we do not know where we are; we ourselves have lost track of ourselves—and we fish for clues. Along the lines of *what does it mean?* we may do and undo veils of the meaningful in which we mean to catch ourselves, that elude us and lure us on. *What will it mean to me?* reaches out toward new fate. *What would it have meant to me?* may be more really present in what we are than what happened.

But there come other moments, when we must ask Who are you? Where am I at last?

•

Describing Frederick Myers's work in an address for a meeting of the Society for Psychical Research in 1901, William James tells us: "he took a lot of scattered phenomena, some of them recognized as reputable, others outlawed from science, or treated as isolated curiosities; he made series of them, filled in the transitions by delicate hypotheses or analogies; and bound them together in a system by his bold inclusive conception of the subliminal self, so that no one can now touch one part of the fabric without finding the rest entangled with it. Such vague terms of apperception as psychologists have hitherto been satisfied with using for most of these phenomena, as 'fraud,' 'rot,' 'rubbish,' will no more be possible hereafter than 'dirt' is possible as a head of classification in chemistry or 'vermin' in zoology."

•

What James calls "the classic romantic" type of imagination had "a fondness for clean pure lines and noble simplicity in its constructions"— the proper realm of mentality, man's "normal" state was abstracted—"a sort of sunlit terrace was exhibited on which it took its exercise. But where that terrace stopped, the mind stopped; and there was nothing left to tell of in this kind of philosophy but the brain and the other physical facts of nature on the one hand, and the absolute metaphysical ground of the universe on the other."

"But of late years," James continues, "the terrace has been overrun by romantic improvers, and to pass to their work is like going from classic to Gothic architecture, where few outlines are pure and where uncouth forms lurk in the shadows." As in H.D.s "Palinode"

> we huddled over the fire,
> was there ever such a brazier?
> a night-bird hooted past,
>
> he sparked, "a curious flight,
> a carrion creature—what—"

·

We have seen already the role these questions—the why? the who? the what goes there? the what does it mean?—play in the psychoanalytic séance that had its beginnings in the same era of or context of hypnotism, suggestion, and association that furnished the ground for the Society of Psychical Research and for James's own Pluralistic philosophy, for Madame Blavatsky's theosophy and Frazer's bringing together of scattered phenomena in *The Golden Bough*.

"A mass of mental phenomena are now seen in the shrubbery beyond the parapet. Fantastic, ignoble, hardly human, or frankly non-human are some of these new candidates for psychological description. The menagerie and the madhouse, the nursery, the prison, and the hospital, have been made to deliver up their material. The world of mind is shown as something infinitely more complex than was suspected; and whatever beauties it may still possess it has lost at any rate the beauty of academic neatness."

·

Seen in light of the classic-academic, the conservative-institutional new, hysteria is a disease, a disturbance of mind—but mind here is the public peace. Hysteria is ominous with riot.

But hysteria is the very prophetic voice of Cassandra; cries woe and [illegible] of cities, and ravens for what it most fears. War-hysteria, love-hysteria.

 ringed and rayed with the word "beautiful";

    •

In areas of science that most avoided such thought, even the psycho-analytic subconscious of Freud much less the subliminal self of Myers—men, as if they did not know what they were doing, insured the great hysterical possibility of our time—the increase of pressures and explo-sion in the atom bomb, the radioactive aftermath that would riot in the chromosomic structure of man, that most would increase to a new power the meaning of the hysteric thing, this suffering in the womb.

 Oppenheimer and Fermi, Teller and Vannevar Bush enact two stages of one operation: in the first the hysteric cannot see the consequences to which he contributes—he knows not what he does. In the second, the hysteric is possessed by the sight of what he does, he knows what he does but his judgment of the consequences is perverted and his greatest enemy is the judgment at all of the consequences to which he contrib-utes. Or they take on the lure of fate, and all that leads away from those consequences appears malicious and hysterical.

    •

Wherever an "enemy appears" as now in the United States an enemy has appeared in Russia and even in the Castro regime in Cuba; or as in Russia an enemy has appeared in the United States, an hysterical crisis impends. All things about us become organized and useful to our hid-den "mate" or "enemy" or "holocaust"; life takes on tendency.

    •

 "lust—enough—" Achilles says.
 "I was afraid of evil,
 in an evil place."

    •

Had there never been the War, had Achilles never stooped to fasten a broken strap of his sandal and lost all, had so many not died and the walls of Troy fallen, had Helen not been so deeply hated—there had not been the spark. There may then have been all the incidents of the war preceding to give death this one possibility.

Every identity these two have is in the War. The wings of her father Zeus are feathered with its arms and dead hosts and the sails of its ships; the sea-enchantment of his mother is the cheat of its cause, dream of the phantom Helen.

•

As if only at last in the ruins and burning waste of the world we know could our desire be realized; so that there is an overwhelming threat and fear of those ruins and that holocaust.

> but without the Galaxy,
> the sails of the thousand ships,
> the Glory that encompassed me

> when I face his anger,
> we would have burnt out in a flash.

•

In *Final Impressions of a Psychical Researcher* (1909), William James notes in the medium "an odd *tendency to personate,* found in her dream life as it expresses itself in trance." "Most of us reveal such a tendency," he adds, "whenever we handle a 'ouija-board' or a 'planchet,' or let ourselves write automatically with a pencil. The result is a 'control,' who purports to be speaking." " . . . On such a view," he continues, "the medium's *will to personate* runs the whole show; and if spirits be involved in it at all, they are passive beings, stray bits of whose memory she is able to seize and use for her purposes, without the spirit being any more aware of it than the saltor is aware of it when his own mind is similarly tapped."

•

Sept. 2 / 61
In the primary magic of every day life we personate our selves, setting things into motion or emotion about us, telling them what they are.

Free association, it was once called; but Freudian analyses have shown that associations are not free but binding. In the process of personation the events about us are transformed into knots, possibility is tied to possibility until a net is woven writhing with the psychic energies that before had been oceanic.

•

Achilles and Helen seem in the opening scene on the Egyptian beach to be playing with fire, magic against magic. Later, we begin to see that there was a Command or commands; and as the great presences of Thetis and Zeus, sea-veil of Cytheraea and wing of eagle or swan, tend to form along the lines of the play, we feel Achilles and Helen are being moved, not moving.

•

"We are thrown, for our conclusions, upon our instructive sense of the dramatic probabilities of nature," James writes in *Psychical Researcher:* "My own dramatic sense tends instinctively to picture the situation as an interaction between slumbering faculties in the automatist's mind and a cosmic environment of *other consciousness* of some sort which is able to work upon them. If there were in the universe a lot of diffuse soul-stuff, unable of itself to get into consistent personal form, or to take permanent possession of an organism, yet always craving to do so, it might get its head into the air, parasitically, so to speak, by peopling weak spots in the armor of human minds, and slipping in and stirring up there the sleeping tendency to personate."

IV

In the third part of *Helen,* the "Eidolon," we learn that Egypt may have been dream, delirium, as Leuké, *l'isle Blanche* had been trance, ecstasy, and "Eidolon" the waking-dream or day-dream. Egypt—Leuké—Hades then is dreamland and the question that comes again and again: *which is the dream? which is the veil?* is the trick or key of what is happening. Helen and Achilles are fairies, figures of fairyland or the veil itself. The White Isle of Thetis is the white egg of Leda we learn, but it is the moon too.

•

Where Thetis, the sea-goddess, and Proteus, the sea-god who presents himself as King of Egypt, are, we recall, as we are ourselves in dreams shape-shifters. In our dreams, we are always being dreamt, as Alice learns in that first of all dream books.

·

"Come and look at him!" the brothers cried, and they each took one of Alice's hands, and led her up to where the King was sleeping.

"Isn't he a *lovely* sight?" said Tweedledum.

. . . "He's dreaming now," said Tweedledee: "and what do you think he's dreaming about?"

Alice said, "Nobody can guess that."

"Why, about *you*!" Tweedledee exclaimed, clapping his hands triumphantly. "And if he left off dreaming about you, where do you suppose you'd be?"

"Where I am now, of course," said Alice.

"Not you!" Tweedledee retorted contemptuously. "You'd be nowhere. Why, you're only a sort of thing in his dream."

·

"Now, Kitty," Alice says at the end, having wakened, yes; but she is still in the telling of the story: "Let's consider who it was that dreamed it all. This is a serious question, my dear, and you should *not* go on licking your paw like that—" ["The first automatic writing I ever saw was forty years ago," James writes: "I unhesitatingly thought of it as deceit, although it contained vague elements of supernormal knowledge. Since then I have come to see in automatic writing one example of a department of human activity as vast as it is enigmatic."] "as if Dinah hadn't washed you this morning! You see, Kitty, it *must* have been either me or the Red King. He was part of my dream, of course—but then I was part of his dream, too! *Was* it the Red King, Kitty? You were his wife, my dear, so you ought to know—" ["Every sort of person is liable to it, or to something equivalent to it; and whoever encourages it in himself finds himself personating someone else, either signing what he writes by a fictitious name, or spelling out, by ouija board or table-tips, messages from the departed."]

still she haunts me, phantomwise,

So Carroll tells us in his envoi to *Through The Looking Glass*:

> Alice moving under skies
> Never seen by waking eyes.

DREAMS

Is it of dream itself that Helen speaks then in the opening where "the old enchantment holds," where

> The potion is not poison,
> it is not Lethe and forgetfulness
> but everlasting memory—?

It may be. Where

> the breathing and breath-taking
> climb and fall, mountain and valley

betray the oceanic being of the Sleeper, the ground itself of the dream. The dream itself that Achilles sees as also the veil of Cytheraea may be the Amen-temple, where

Sept. 4th: / Helen tells us she is alone

> yet in this Amen-temple,

> I hear their voices
> there is no veil between us . . .

and the Dreamer, in the opening measures of the poem (it is the "Do not despair"), is presaged in Helen's sense that

> Amen (or Zeus we call him)
> brought me here;

> fear nothing of the future or the past,
> He, God, will guide you,
> bring you to this place,

In God, in the dream, there is no veil between us. As in *The Walls Do Not Fall* there was

and beyond thought and idea,
their begetter,

Dream,
Vision.

and the Dreamer could appear there as

Ra, Osiris, *Amen* appeared
in a spacious, bare meeting-house;

he is the world-father,
father of past aeons,

present and future equally;
beardless, not at all like Jehovah,

there was in life a Presence, as in Love a Master. We recall in the first so-called "Imagist" phase of H.D.'s work, in the poem "Pygmalion," published in 1917, the questions asked by the mask of the sculptor as artist engaged with the divine:

Now am I the power
that has made this fire
as of old I made the gods
start from the rocks?
am I the god
or does this fire carve me
for its use?

•

In poem after poem H.D. (as during the same brief period Lawrence and Pound also were speaking in personae) spoke in the persons of Chorus, nymph, prisoner, priest of Adonis, Pygmalion, Eurydice, and then Demeter, Thetis, Circe, Leda. From these poems we begin to see that the "Image", the "intellectual and emotional complex in an instant of time" was not simply an invention of the poet to convey vividly his impressions or sensibility in things but a form in poetry of trafficking with the daemonic and beyond the daemonic with the divine, the "swirl upon swirl of light?" of the poem "Pygmalion."

•

I

We learn in the novel *Bid Me to Live* that there had been an exchange in poetry between D. H. Lawrence and H.D. in the period of "Adonis" and "Eurydice" to which "Pygmalion" belongs, and an exchange in the dream. "You said, next morning, you heard me singing in a dream and found your face wet with tears," Julia writes Rico: "Is that true? How could you say that casually, while Elsa washed the breakfast things behind the screen?"

•

We are inhabitants of our dreams, and to wake is not to escape from the Dreamer for he remains to haunt us. These are the orders of the imagination: The poet in his imagination comes into a dimension beyond his invention or calling up where the imagination is received. In *Bid Me to Live,* "She felt curiously this room had been invented for her. It might have been said of her, from the moment of her entrance to this house, that she had felt the same of every room in this house. Every door, every shallow or steep step, every irregularity of passage-way, of door-sill held its peculiar and intimate reality. There was a charm over the house, of that she was certain." This is a realm in which the dream is most real and what we daily view as objects are subject to magic invasion. "The words themselves held inner words, she thought. If you look at a word long enough, this peculiar twist, its magic angle, would lead somewhere, like that Phoenician track, trod by the old traders." H.D. continues in Julia's delirium or reverie: "She was a trader in the gold, the old gold, the myrrh of the dead spirit. She was bargaining with each word."

•

As we in the course of this book, [illegible] have followed the lead of words or trying them to find a lead, "bargaining with each word—" "She brooded over each word, as if to hatch it" H.D. tells us of Julia-H.D.

But what we follow here is the lead of another time, twisting the "room" to tell us of this room as dream. "But I thought if you wanted me, you would ask me to come up to your room," Julia writes Rico: "How could I climb those stairs, not knowing what you wanted?"

> . . . "You said, next morning, you heard me singing in a dream and found your face wet with tears."

    •

"But I am aware of your spider-feelers, I am not walking into your net. I am not answering your questions. 'What room have you? What room has Vanio?'"

We are in the realm of magic now, what the psychiatrist or psychoanalyst calls the psychotic: "This house caused you no anxiety. It was easy to block in, the whole thing was familiar. I, a familiar would be drawn literally into your picture. How could I walk up those stairs?" It is trafficking in dreams. She furnishes one more key as to how it is done: "Once a Dakota poet I knew said systematic starvation was a sort of dope. I don't mean we starved actually. But doing without non-essentials leaves room, a room. I walked into it here."

    •

The great effort in the therapeusis of Freud was to avoid the psychotic possibility, to exorcise the room, to protect the integrity of the psyche against thoughts of invasion. The case histories of psychotic disorders carefully documented by orthodox Freudians are directly related to the particulars gathered by the Inquisitions in case histories of witchcraft: there was evidence in some of daemonic possession, but there was a wider practice in which human psyche invaded human psyche. Lawrence and H.D., Mary Butts or Yeats document in their work illnesses of a dangerously experimental course of the psyche. And Ezra Pound's late *idée fixe* upon the perversion of the monetary exchange in the practices of usury and profit-commodities may have a hidden ground in his brief exposure to the increases and depletions of the "image" game.

•

Just as in magic men manipulated the harmonics of the divine to produce disturbances of harmonics in what we call fascination; or disturbances of the divine correspondences to weave a net of circumstantial evidence, to "pull strings" as we sense it, playing with influences; so men cast spells. Poets cast images. And in this Lawrence's magic of casting the room or dream in *Bid Me to Live,* is located as a drawing: "You made it all up, Elsa's work-bag on the floor, the cups and saucers, the branch out of the window, when I thought you were writing. You were writing or you were painting rather, a branch out of the window, with the window-frame one side and the folds of the blue curtain the other. You drew the fanlight over the door, downstairs."

•

This is evil; "Old English yfel," the O.E.D. tells us: "usually referred to the root of *up, over.*" Where in the orders of the universe the services of craft or art become masterful in craft, crafty as artful; and the ease is dis-eased or mal-eased, we may pose as the Dreamer of our own dream or another's; man, beast, angel, god may pose as the creator of Creation and appear to have power over things.

•

Helen struggles with the true state of what is, as often we do in dreams, in terms of her own art in letters: In her magic exchange (involvement with) Achilles, she traffics also in a magic claim (power) over Achilles:

> I said, "there is mystery in this place,
> I am instructed, I know the script,
> the shape of this bird is a letter,
>
> they call it the hieroglyph;

•

(Writing on the Wall)

Freud, as H.D. tells us in *Tribute to Freud,* had viewed just this writing on the wall as "dangerous." "We can read my writing," she tells us (she is speaking of the writing that appeared on a wall to her in a vision, but it is also her own writing):

> "We can read my writing, the fact that there was writing, in two ways or in more than two ways. We can read or translate it as a suppressed desire for forbidden 'signs and wonders,' breaking bounds, a suppressed desire to be a Prophetess, to be important anyway, megalomania they call it—a hidden desire to 'found a new religion' which the Professor ferreted out in the later Moses picture. Or this writing-on-the-wall is merely an extension of the artistic mind, a *picture* or an illustrated poem, taken out of the actual dream or day-dream content and projected from within (though apparently from outside), really a high-powered *idea,* simply over-stressed, *over-thought,* you might say, an echo of an idea, a reflection of a reflection, a 'freak' thought that had got out of hand, gone too far, a 'dangerous symptom.'"

·

So Helen tries to confess the truth about letters.

> I said, I was instructed in the writ,
> but I had only heard of it,
> when our priests decried
>
> papyrus fragments,
> travelers brought back,
> as crude, primeval lettering—

what saves her, what saves H.D. is the "Do not despair" that whatever the art, it is "as if God made the picture"; by magic, by violation calling forth violence we try to read:

> no, I was not instructed, but I "read" the script,
> I read the writing when he seized my throat,

·

And in Helen we learn that not only she, but other inhabitants of the Dream, have a magic and seem to dream each others' dreams. To communicate at all, creature to creature, creation must be used as meaning; interpretation itself is a power over things. "I can not 'read' the hare, the chick, the bee," H.D.-Helena must confess for her own salvation. Here "the Sun,

> hidden behind the sun of our visible day."

is the Dreamer, Creator-Uncreated. "The invisible attunement is superior to the visible," Heraklitus tells us.

.

The dream may be the veil of Cytheraea, and the veil the fabric of Maya, and the Dreamer-Creator Brahma. For wherever in Western thought this dream in which we are dreamed appears as the world, we feel the Hindu influence.

In the years following The War Trilogy the theosophical and esoteric elements which had begun to operate in her poetics there increase. We are not on the wrong track to follow from Greece and Egypt to India.

> you may ask forever, you may penetrate
> every shrine, an initiate,
> and remain unenlightened at last.

she tells us:

> How does the Message reach me?
> do thoughts fly like the word
> of the goddess? a whisper—

she asks.

> (my own thought or the thought of another?)

.

So in "Palinode"—Proteus, "the legendary King of Egypt, reveals the future, the mystery or the legend." His is the enactment; "Nameless-of-many-Names he decrees". He is "Sun behind the sun of day", we learn in "Eidolon" I:3, Formalhaut. Is it formal-haut, highest-Form? Is it the star Formalhaut, the month of Pisces—Christos? Helen hears "a voice to lure, a voice to proclaim,

the script was a snare."

II

Helen In Egypt is a dream-fiction; it belongs not to the orthodox Freudian interpretation of the dream where the content speaks for the subconscious or the collective conscious; but the Dream of Helen-in-Egypt is the Dream of Alice-in-Wonderland, of consciousness that admits other consciousness. It is the situation, as James pictured it in 1901: "as an interaction between slumbering faculties in the automatist's mind and a cosmic environment of *other consciousness* of some sort which is able to work upon them." Formalhaut or Farmalhaut is the Red King.

·

Lewis Carroll is playing games of the psyche, we sense in *Alice*. Yes,

The dream-child moving through a land
　Of wonders wild and new,
In friendly chat with bird or beast—
　And half believe it true.

—we're only, of Helen too, half to believe it true. "From a Fairy to a Child" Dodgson wrote sending his work:

Lady dear, if Fairies may
　For a moment lay aside
Cunning tricks and elfish play,
　'Tis at happy Christmas tide.

·

It is not only for the Star, the Dreamer of the Dream, that Helen seeks to read the script—but she searches too for the Child: the Euphorion of the poem.

> O Child, must it be forever,
> that your father destroys you,
> that you may find your father?

•

It is along another line tho that I want to trace the relation between the work of Lewis Carroll and the work of H.D. [quote H.D. from "Writing on the Wall" page 80] For they have, we find, a common element in the fairyland-dreamland lore of the nineteenth century, that makes it seem so childish or childlike to grown up minds,

1. Éliphas Lévi (Alphonse Louis Constant), *The History of Magic.*
   quote: pg 141 from "The Romans . . . were great observers of dreams"—1888
2. *Esoteric Buddhism*
3. Blavatsky, *The Secret Doctrine* I. pg 279, I 309–10, I pg 691
4. Lewis Carroll 1893. Preface to *Sylvie and Bruno Concluded.*
   pg 463–464
5. George MacDonald 1895. *Lilith*

•

Sept. 11   The dream or trance is the summons of God where

> God's plan is other than the priests disclose;
> I did not know why
> (in dream or in trance)

> God had summoned me hither
> until I saw the dim outline
> grown clearer,

We are concerned in *Helen in Egypt* with the operations of the dream

"Zeus be my witness," I said,
"it was he, Amen dreamed of all this
phantasmagoria of Troy,

it was dream and a phantasy";

Dante's vision and the dreams of the *Vita Nuova* give background to the
tradition of phantasy we follow here: the revelation at nine years old,
childhood being the locus and the child the secret person then

"He commanded me many times that I should seek to behold this
most youthful angel: wherefore in my childhood often did I go seeking
her . . . "

the power of the poet being that of an *alta fantasia;* the world in the
Dream being the Divine World or Other world of the Dead in one—the
testimony is Orphic and Shamanistic.

> •

But it is more directly to certain dream workers of the nineteenth cen-
tury—to Lewis Carroll, to George MacDonald, and to theosophical
fantasts. Here the dream in its movement resembles more closely the
associations of Helen-in-Egypt. H.D. has no actual reference to Dante.
Pound and Eliot may have, in their so authoritative Danteism, turned
her aside, as she seems everywhere to have sought routes to experi-
ence outside the recommended charts. [She would, we surmise, have
followed, had she read Dante, the alternate readings, to search out the
curious heresy or more than Christian possibility in the imagination of
Amor and Beatrice.]

It is to the heterodoxy of *Alice-in-Wonderland* (or *Alice's Adventures
Underground*) and of *Phantastes* then that we would turn. Not because
H.D. read here and was "influenced"—but because, in the light of cer-
tain nineteenth century works, we may see *Helen in Egypt* with special
emphases.

> •

In the syncretic teachings of Éliphas Lévi, the revelations of Catholic Christianity, poetic testimony and magic tradition have a common ground in the Astral Light. "There is a composite agent," Lévi writes in his *History of Magic,*

> a natural and divine agent, at once corporeal and spiritual, an universal plastic mediator, a common receptacle for vibrations of movement and images of form, a fluid and a force which may be called, in a sense at least, the imagination of Nature. By the mediation of this force every nervous apparatus is in secret communication together; hence come sympathy and antipathy, hence dreams, hence the phenomena of second sight and extra natural vision.
>
> A particular phenomenon occurs when the brain is congested or over-charged by Astral Light; sight is turned inward, instead of outward; light falls on the external and real world, while fantastic brilliance shines on the world of dreams; even the physical eyes experience with a slight quivering and turn up inside the lids. The soul then perceives by means of images the reflection of its impressions and thoughts.

But this light in which we now see "the source of all apparitions, all extraordinary visions and all the intuitive phenomena peculiar to madness or ecstasy," where "it may be understood in a day to come that seeing is actually speaking and that the consciousness of the light is a twilight of eternal life in being," is, Lévi insists, "the word of God Himself," the "*Fiat Lux.*"; for "the soul enamoured with the pageantry of universal beauty, and fixing its attention on that luminous script of the endless book which is called things manifest, seems to cry on its own part, as God at the dawn of the first day, the sublime and creative words: *Fiat Lux.*"

•

Carried over into the schools of "Esoteric Buddhism," where theories of evolutionism after Darwin and of the ultimate wisdom of the Vedanta were added to the syncretic essay, the Astral world appears as the Kama-Loca. A. P. Sinnett, in 1884, pictured this astral realm, not as Lévi had—as the ground of high revelation—but as a lower *soul* ground contrasted with man's spiritual reality.

"The individual consciousness, it is argued, cannot be in two places at once," Sinnett writes in *Esoteric Buddhism*. "But first of all, to a certain extent, it can. As may be perceived presently, it is a mistake to speak of consciousness, as we understand the feeling in life, attaching to the astral shell or remnant; but nevertheless a certain spurious semblance may be reawakened in that shell, without having any connections with the real consciousness all the while gaining in strength and vitality in the spiritual sphere." "The consciousness even of the lower principles *during life* is a very different thing from the vaporous fleeting and uncertain consciousness, which continues to inhere in them when that which really is the life, the overshadowing of them, or vitalization of them by the infusion of the spirit, has ceased as far as they are concerned."

.

What *Alice's Adventures in Wonderland* in 1865 with its "*cunning tricks and elfish play*" and then in *Through the Looking Glass* in 1872 where "though the shadow of a sigh / May tremble through the story. . . .":

it shall not touch with breath of bale,
The pleasance of our fairy-tale.

What in these works of Carroll had shown in the operation of the story-book—the pluralistic universe where Alice, Red King, and Kitten too share in the identity of the Dream—now in the "childish" deliberations of theosophy shows again.

.

"Language cannot render all the facets of the many-sided idea intelligible at once any more than a plain drawing can show all sides of a solid object at once," Sinnett writes: "And at the first glance different drawings of the same object from different points of view may seem so unlike as to be unrecognizable as the same; but none the less, by the time they are put together in the mind, will their diversities be seen to harmonize. So with these subtle attributes of the invisible principles of man—no treatise can do more than discuss their different aspects separately. The various views suggested must mingle in the reader's mind before the complete conception corresponds to the realities of Nature." Sinnett and his mentor Madame Blavatsky presented an effort absurd in its dogma but admirable in its sense of the play of man's realities; the letting things mingle in the mind was the creative genius of theosophy. Éliphas Lévi had taught that Dante had triumphed over hell by inverting its dogma: "thanks to the pagan genius of Virgil, Dante emerges from that gulf above the door of which he had read the sentence of despair; he escapes by standing on his head, which means by reversing dogma." And Blavatsky in turn would play Humpty-Dumpty with the official orthodoxies of Church of England and Science of England alike. She labored the absurd, as Carroll played with it. Blavatsky questioned every establishment in the light of every heterodox dogma. Carroll, George MacDonald's son tells us, "the shy, learned mathematician who hated inaccuracy, loved to question the very multiplication-table's veracity."

Blavatsky delighted in correcting unverifiable spiritualization-tables. "The Earth was in her first Pûpa," she writes in *The Secret Doctrine:* "the essence of which is the Âkâshic Principle . . . that which is now known as, and very erroneously termed, Astral Light." Lévi should have added, she tells us, that the *Lux* "is the body of those Spirits themselves, and their very essence"—here she is speaking of the Elohim. "Our physical light is the manifestation on our plane."

•

In the teachings of theosophy this Astral Light was dreamland; but it was also fairyland or Wonderland. Outside whatever formed reality was an unseen lower and higher real, or (so that the Astral Light was thought of as the primal Egg of Leda from which Helen or the Moon, regent of dreams, was born) a globe or shell. "Our planet (like all we see)"—so the theosophical teaching went—"is adapted to the peculiar state of its human stock, that state which enables us to see with our naked eye the sidereal bodies which are coessential with our terrene plane and substance, just as their respective inhabitants, the Sorraus, Marhaus and others, can perceive our little world." The Earth belonged to a "Chain" or "String"; it was a note in a scale of planets. But if one could change the scale, that was the constant theme of theosophy, if one saw a "terrene" Mars in the String of Terra, in the String of Mars other planets, another earthly reality could appear. "If he," Sinnett is told in *Esoteric Buddhism:* "would perceive even the dim silhouette of one of such 'planets' on the higher planes, he has to first throw off even the thin clouds of astral matter that stand between him and the next plane."

•

The prospect delighted Carroll, where in his "Preface" to *Sylvie and Bruno Concluded* in 1893 we find him posing his humor in theosophical terms:

> It may interest some of my Readers to know the *theory* on which this story is constructed. It is an attempt to show what might *possibly* happen, supposing that Fairies really existed; and that they were sometimes visible to us, and we to them; and that they were sometimes able to assume human form; and supposing, also, that human beings might sometimes become conscious of what goes on in the Fairy-world—by actual transference of their immaterial essence, such as we meet with in 'Esoteric Buddhism'.
> I have supposed a Human being to be capable of various psychical states, with varying degrees of consciousness, as follows:
> (a) the ordinary state, with no consciousness of the presence of Fairies;
> (b) the "eerie" state, in which, while conscious of actual surroundings, he is *also* conscious of the presence of Fairies;
> (c) a form of trance, in which, while unconscious of actual surroundings, and apparently asleep, he (i.e. his immaterial essence) migrates to other scenes, in the actual world, or in Fairyland, and is conscious of the presence of Fairies.
> I have also supposed a Fairy to be capable of migrating from Fairyland into the actual world, and of assuming, at pleasure, a Human form; and also to be capable of various psychical states, viz.
> (a) the ordinary state, with no consciousness of the presence of Human beings;
> (b) a sort of "eerie" state, in which he is conscious, if in the actual world, of the presence of actual Human beings; if in Fairyland, of the presence of the immaterial essences of Human beings.

He proceeds to tabulate passages from the two volumes of *Sylvie and Bruno* where "abnormal states occur."

•

"And also, in the hope of suggesting, to them and to others," Carroll had written of his first *Sylvie and Bruno* volume and its child readers: "some thought that may prove, I would fain hope, not wholly out of harmony with the graver cadences of Life." The effort in theosophy too was to bring into harmony the seeming conflicts that appear between the graver cadences of Life that were orthodox in Christianity and other cadences of Life in other human religions.

·

The eerie voices of the Looking-Glass world do seem out of harmony with orthodox possibilities, but the key to its authenticity (and to the mis-take that parodies of Carroll must make) is that it does belong in its humor, not among trivial farces, but to the graver cadences of the human spirit in its heterodox possibilities. The cult of Childhood, in the work of Lewis Carroll and George MacDonald, as a realm bordering upon Fairyland or Wonderland and likewise upon the Kingdom of Heavens, the Child as revelation of the divine self and the Dream as revelation of the divine World; and in the Romance, the shifting impersonations of a faërie or phantasy mode: these orders reappear in our work by H.D.

Sept. 17
The proposition of Sinnett's *Esoteric Buddhism:* "The individual consciousness, it is argued, cannot be in two places at once. But first of all, to a certain extent it can," appealed, in a period when belief in the Christian world was newly challenged by developing sciences of geology and biology, to a childish make-believe in *Sylvie and Bruno,* the belief in the fairy world and the belief in the divine world stand in the same need of a child-like innocence of mind. The graver cadences more and more, like the fun of an open and inventive phantasy, must be carried by the imagination.

For the theosophists Wonderland, fairyland, dreamland are one in the realm of the Astral light. For Carroll, as a churchman, there is on the one side the letting go of the serious imagination where "God has become a myth, and heaven a poetic fancy" so that "the light of life is gone." More and more the reality of God seems to belong to the reality of dreams and child-like make-believe. Unless you become like little children, you shall not see the Kingdom of Heaven, took on new meaning. "Heaven" too was an "other" world.

．

So in MacDonald's *Lilith,* written in 1890, child, dream, sleep, being two places at once—and above all the imagined or fictive real—are keys to its structure.

．

"You see that large tree to your left, about thirty yards away?" [asked the Raven] "It stands on the hearth of your kitchen and grows nearly straight up its chimney. That rose-bush is close to the lady at the piano. If you could but hear the music! Those great long heads of wild hyacinth are inside the piano, among the strings of it, and give that peculiar sweetness to her playing."

"Pardon me: I forgot your deafness!"

"Two objects," I said, "cannot exist in the same place at the same time!"

"Can they not? I did not know. I remember how they do teach that to you. It is a great mistake—one of the greatest mistakes ever made! No man of the universe, only a man of the world could have said so."

．

Sept. 21

Back of *Helen in Egypt,* H.D. tells us, lies Stesichorus of Sicily's *Palinode* and Euripides' *Helen in Egypt* with the word of a phantom Helen at Troy and of the illusory reason for the War then. But Helen in the play of Euripides is not a magic power, we know nothing there of the real Helen's complicity in the War. The phantom is a thing of air, cast, not in Helen's desire but by Hera out of the vanity of Menelaus and Paris. Helen's hubris is in her deranged matronly propriety: against the memory of Aphrodite's singing with flute and drums that once had changed the grief of Demeter, and against the passionate orders of the Great Mother Herself; and then, so the chorus accuses Helen, against the abandon, "the whirled course of the wheel in the air."

The Helen of H.D.'s phantasia takes from this ancient tradition her other Helen, but she is a complice of that wraith at Troy. She was at once in Egypt and at Troy. The scene of Euripides' play, no more than Egypt before the house of Proteus, no more than King of Egypt, in H.D.'s *Helen in Egypt* has become likewise complex: for Egypt is dream-land and Proteus is the agency we find of the dreamer:

This is Formalhaut's temple,
not far from Athens,
not far from Eleusis,

yet Egypt; not far
from Theseus, your god-father,
not far from Amen, your father

but dedicated to Isis,
or if you will, Thetis;
not far from the blessèd isles,

the Hesperides, or from Amenti;
not far from life-in-death,
another portal, another symbol.

•

From the second century we hear news of another Helen. One Simon, who claimed to be an incarnation of "the Great Power," according to our legend, had learned a magic in Egypt and had found in that magic a Helen or *the* Helen. The Church Fathers said that Simon's Helen was a prostitute he had picked up at Tyre. But in the Gnostic circles, where thought moved not towards orthodoxy and dogma but towards a multiplicity of meanings and imagination, this Helen was not only a prostitute, she was the Moon, not only the Moon but also the World-soul; A. E. Waite in his edition of Lévi's *History of Magic* tells us that "it is said otherwise that she was Helen of Troy in a previous incarnation." This Sun-Logos-Simon and this Selene-Anima-Mundi-Helen were persons in magic of a charlatan and a prostitute. This magic, so the rumor went, was practiced in sexual intercourse, was something "known" in each other.

•

G.R.S. Mead in his discussion of Simon Magus tells us further there was something about a Fire and a Concealment; the spark and the veil of H.D.'s poem may have their origin in the Graeco-Egyptian Hellenistic world where after the conquests of Alexander a border upon India had been opened. It is the expansion of empire beyond the confines of "western" civilization—in the time of Alexander when the Greek world was exposed to the Indian world and in the time of Victoria, again, when the English world was exposed to the Indian world—that borderlines, not only of race and national character mix, but religions too, wherever thought is not rigidly defensive, fuse. The Alexandrian Helen of Tyre and the Helen of our text come to life and multiplicity of being not only out of the Egg of Leda but also from the sphere of Kama.

.

[from Eliade, *Yoga: Immortality and Freedom:* "And in a magical papyrus of the second century we find certain Hindu beliefs mentioned; Isis is compared to Māyā, name and personification of the Buddha's mother and also of the Great Illusion."]

.

The Simon Magus of Hellenistic Gnostic legend may have known something of the Kama-Loca and sought along the lines of an erotic magic in a proto-Kamasutra to find his apotheosis, his ascension, to become a star. In the *Acts of Peter* Simon gets high, or flies higher than the Saint.

.

And is brought down, deflated in Christian legend, to Hell, to be Simon the Magician. Where Helen is finally only a shadow. For in the rule of orthodoxy, the restrictions of truth between the fourth century and the breaking up of the Holy Roman Empire, all other thought and feeling existed in the extensions of falsehood. Gods became daemons, heroes became ghosts, priestesses became witches, magi became magicians. False faces and false names appear everywhere. If the magic is white you look into a crystal; if the magic is black you look into a mirror. We think of them now as doors to the future, "fortune telling," we call it. But the mirror-world is the world of *Through the Looking Glass* and of MacDonald's *Lilith*. What we see there is an illumination of things. "Of a familiar type," Edith Butler notes in *Ritual Magic*, "is the one in which a pure lad of about ten who has been born in wedlock looks into the stone whilst the Cabalist prays to St. Helena, the mother of Constantine, who was said to have rediscovered the cross of Christ."

●

For in the mirror one might have seen, not St. Helena, but Helena of Troy.

The Faust, we know, called up a wraith of Helen, "Spirits in the shape of Alexander the Great, of his paramour, and of Helen of Troy," the dramatis personae reads in Marlowe's play. "Be silent, then," Faustus says: "for danger is in words."

"[Music sounds, and Helen passeth over the stage]"

●

Is there some hint of the Helen of the shadows, the familiar of the Kama-Loka, in Marlowe's phantom? "To glut the longing of my heart's desire—" Faustus says he would have Helen for his paramour.

●

It is from this first Helen of our English tradition that H.D. draws certain themes. "Was this the face that launched a thousand ships" is immortal as "And burnt the topless towers of Ilium" somehow is not. And later in the same speech Faustus-Simon cries:

"Oh, thou art fairer than the evening air
Clad in the beauty of a thousand stars"

●

So "the legions lost" in H.D.'s *Helen in Egypt,* "the host," "the holocaust," are numbered. In "Palinode" II.2 "the thousand-petalled lily; / they are not many, but one;" in "Palinode" II.4 "all the thousand petals of the rose," but "the thousand sails," "the thousand feathered darts / that sped them home." In "Palinode" III.2: "can one weigh the thousand ships /

against one kiss in the night?" We recognize in passing the Thousand and One Nights of Shahárazád, "City-freer" Burton notes, told to rescue her sister Dunyázád, "World-freer" or Dinázád "Religion-freer."

•

"Sweet Helen, make me immortal with a kiss," Faustus demands or requests. [*Kisses her.*]

> Her lips suck forth my soul; see where it flies!—
> Come, Helen, come, give me my soul again.
> Here will I dwell, for Heaven is in these lips.

•

This kiss, and the dwelling in a kiss, is a wisdom of the Kamasutra. Or the eroticists or "kamatists" were wise to it. The tongue searches in all adult kisses for an electricity that a child's kiss has, or "thrill" that floods the body. Sexuality may feed upon this thrill, but—this is our concern here—Heaven feeds there too. We remember the passage in H.D.'s romance *Bid Me to Live* where the Hesperides, the *paradiso* is the locus or the presence of the husband where: "she faced the author of this her momentary psychic being, her lover, her husband. It was like that, in these moments. She touched paradise. He too. But he did not think of that." Had he thought of it, paradise would have touched her. The kiss, the touch, the coming together sought some ultimate exchange or reciprocity.

•

"He's looking for another book—the *Hesperides?* he's wandering. He's not here. No, he wasn't there. It was almost better when she was alone.
    "All of the *Hesperides* was there, nearer than the table, than the mantelpiece . . . "

•

"This star in the night" Helen calls it. Achilles springing forward in the spark of his anger, or is it pain of death?

mine, the one dart in the Achilles-heel,
the thousand-and-one, mine.

Is there some rumor that in a thousand spermatozoa one may be magic,
or as we call it, fecundating, one may be hers? He "covers her" we say
of birds; Achilles was no longer Achilles but from the realm of fathers,
the *pitaloka* the Hindus called it, the Father. Zeus then. "This is the
spread of wings," and the eternal angry or blood-reddened Fatherhead
giving up into the mothering womb its semen.

I read the writing when he seized my throat,

this was his anger,
they were mine, not his,
the unnumbered host;

mine, all the ships,
mine, all the thousand . . . .

That one strike, that one come home to Leuké, the white island, the
egg-sphere or prayer, the quickened circuits of the child.

•

It is the burning ember
that I remember
heart of the fire,

Helen tells us.

•

Is the "hieroglyph, repeated endlessly," that Helen tries to read the
code-script of the chromosomes? *My legions lost,* the father cries;

"the flower of all-time,
of all-history,
my children, my legions";

•

The "arrows" of Eris and then of Eros, the thousand, and the one that strikes home, brought me back then to Kama-Loca of the theosophists, to the Kama-Loka of the Hindus, as Zimmer in *Philosophies of India* told of him, Puspa-bāna "whose arrows are flowers," lord of the flower-shafts.

•

In "Palinode" III.4—the thousand is "a cloud in the night,"

> must I tell him again their name,
> the one name for the thousand lost,
> Eros, the Hawk Horus?

We begin to realize that the veil is the thousand and the spark that strikes is the one. "A touch in the dark," it is called in "Palinode" III.5. The veil, itself, may here be what we call "coming" in crude vulgar speech, more true to poetry than the scientific "orgasm" or "ejaculation." But "orgasm" had something to do with our spark of anger, and ejaculation with our throwing of the thousand and one arrows.

•

In VII of "Palinode" the Image of Eidolon of Thetis ["It is Thetis," H.D. tells us "(Isis Aphrodite)"] says:

> A woman's wiles are a net;
> they would take the stars
> or a grasshopper in its mesh;

The stars, the Galaxy, we learned earlier, are the thousand. And, like an echo here or a resonance from an untouched octave, we realize there was one star too.

> what unexpected treasure,
> what talisman or magic ring
> may the net find?

fishing for a clue or a child or particular star. Proteus reveals to Helen, the shape-shifter to the immortal face:

when they reach a certain degree

they are one, alike utterly,
though Achilles woke from the dark
and her Lord was cast

into the lowest depth

　　　•

Is Achilles, the mate, Simon the Magus, Faustus the Magician?
　　"Let Faustus live in hell a thousand years," Marlowe's Faustus asks,
and then for the thousand-and-one: "and—at last—be saved!"

　　　•

　　yet even Cimmerian embers,

H.D.'s Helen seems to reply

　　burnt out, extinguished and lost,
　　will flame anew if God
　　wills to re-kindle the spark;

　　　•

God may be the Thousand-and-one. In "Palinode" VII.6:

　　I have talked with Proteus—or—

　　another (whoever he be,
　　he manifests variously);
　　Nameless-of-many-Names he decrees

　　that *Helena* shall remain
　　one name . . . .

　　　•

H.D. was familiar with all this; as an initiate of Freud's in psyche-
analysis, she knew that the "lover" could be read everywhere in the
"higher." There was an encoding in the dreamscript that revealed
something going on in a realm of sexual phantasy.

　　　•

The old teaching was that "as above so below" might mean also the orders of the stars could be read in the spermatozoa, the anima mundi might be a common whore in the port-town of Tyre, the logos could be found in any word anywhere. Christ was not selective when he said the Kingdom is within you, or that we were gods. "Ye are gods," He said to the crowd. Now we begin to see galaxy upon galaxy, there may be as many suns as there ever have been men.

•

(Paris said, *why must you recall
the white fire of unnumbered stars,
rather than that single taper*

burning in an onyx jar),

"ART TO INCHANT"

It would seem that the human community itself has tides where even the most "independent" minds are swept along, even as the cells that have each "a unit-life centred on itself" *belong* to a body. Here we are creatures of a society, taking on life as units of a larger economy. We may migrate from one association to another depending upon our reality in the new economy—this is a transfer of functions: an automobile mechanic may be directly transferable to another society in which there are automobiles. But those of us who live as units in relation to the language of a society in its functions of suggestion, even as we become most aware of belonging to mankind at large, have come into this realization along the lines of a particular language. Nearing the center or centers of our own language—most aware of the Germanic *geist,* the Roman *spiritus,* the Greek *psyche* that meet in English along the pathways of invading peoples—we are more and more aware, more near, to circumferences of language. Drawn into the fascination of the language, beyond the little civilized or semantically defended area of defined *words,* we come into another area where meanings appear as design. There are no words in themselves, just as in the thought of the human body itself, transformed by passion and desire, there are no cells in themselves—but all local meanings, the threads of German, Latin, and Greek, and the knottings of individual words, save as bonds in a total illusion, an image of images in which the personae may appear: not only our own psyche-identities, our own experience that seems the most real, that is built up of the invisible actual in which the real life of the cells goes on; but the greater images in kind to which our own lives contribute, the roles in the drama of history as we come to play them— that may be ghosts or luminous spirits. The Helen and Achilles, Paris and Theseus of H.D.'s poem are in turn members not only of history (for the siege of Troy belongs still to historical memory) but of the love of mankind. They are Eternal Ones of the dream.

•

The design now is of such an order that all loci seem to contribute to their own loss of identity in the larger figure: the poet takes over as a higher person from the immediate social personality of the man who sits down to write.

•

So that Blake in his "personal" relations to his patron Hayley or his contemporaries Flaxman and Fuseli, may have all the petty annoyances, we call them, of daily life, all the individual originality of the actual closed cell, and write in irritation TO F[LAXMAN]

I mock thee not, tho' I by thee am Mockèd.
Thou call'st me Madman, but I call thee Blockhead.

•

"Blockd" would have been the cruder rime. Men in their contention dramatize the stupidity of cells in their place, some ever present quality of the locus to insist upon its own life independence to be a reality in itself, a closed form. But Blake in his contention is irritably aware of his belonging, to a design in the history of the visual imagination, one member of a figure in which the two other members are Fuseli and Flaxman. What we call movements in art are melodic figures in history, passages in which there is a tendency so that individual instances lose their immediate importance in the sense that something beyond is happening. The cells in all the complexity of their specialization and variation are alive because they are chemically unstable, factors not products of creation, creator-creatures. They come into, each into a form that is all and only his, what they are authorized in a melodic coherence that belongs to a coherence within and yet without what we can imagine. This imagination of what we are lies along our senses of belonging: kinship, meaning, and then the rarer sureness the artist knows of correspondences and harmonies belonging to scales we cannot define. "The authors," Blake wrote, "are in eternity," and in *All Religions Are One* he draws the following among principles:

> Principle 1st. That the Poetic Genius is the true Man, and that the body or outward form of Man is derived from the Poetic Genius. Likewise that the forms of all things are derived from their Genius, which by the Ancients was call'd an Angel & Spirit & Demon.

·

This Poetic Genius is our melody or movement to which notes in music or events in history come to belong. We may rationalize our existence, insist upon a rational, sensible personality, only as we increasingly dwell as if we were in ourselves sufficient and meaningful: electing the guarded manner of "science" to defend what we can know as fact against what we can only know as feeling, and beyond such knowledge against rank feeling and doubtful intuition.

·

Against which Blake wrote: "I. Man's perceptions are not bounded by organs of perception; he perceives more than sense (tho ever so acute) can discover.

"II. Reason, or the ratio of all we have already known, is not the same that it shall be when we know more."

·

May it not be that the reality that James called fictive has its illusion of the highest truth—the vividness of Lear or the sylph Ariel having a lasting quality of having happened that exceeds that of most inhabitants of the actual—includes finally the "scientific," because in the Poetic Genius man is inspired by or derives his vision from, not such eyes as sensible own cornea, retina, lens, and optical nerve are, but from the melody of seeing thruout the universe along which human eyes have evolved. The Poetic Genius having just that center and circumference, that "nowhere and everywhere" of Christian mystic definitions at which to communicate impulses of the whole in which we see more than we see.

·

Physics, our imagination of the universe in which we live, confronts, even as the poetic does, the ultimate mystery in which the melos imagines the melody; the cell imagines and lives to make vivid its body; the person imagines and lives to make vivid his manhood; the man imagines and lives to make vivid his poet; the poet like the scientist imagines and lives to make vivid his universe. The "our," "his" impersonates the belonging, the feeling of being along the line of some form or the longing for some other among others where we will become member among members of a divine feeling. In physics as in poetics reality unfolds in thematic developments, leadings, and harmonies in the light of which all previous "truths" take on new meaning.

·

We seem to have come to a point distant from the initial proposition of my chapter: "Art to Inchant." To sing upon or to sing into things so that lines of melodic coherence appear.

·

When we follow, for instance, the changes of astronomical physics and the corresponding shifts in metaphysics we may have the illusion of a science advancing towards a surer and surer picture of What Is, in more and more fitting corrections. Yet the facts remain, the reasons change—the factors remain, the ratios change—from Copernicus to Newton, from Newton to our modern physics the imagination of the universe proves delusive or illusive. In what scale can we find the ratios? It is the fascination, the communion a man's mind has in longing for the form of What Is thru the stars, that comes to belong to What Is—it is the being drawn toward, the quest or tendency that remains.

I

If the psychic life may be the Kama-Loca or Astral Light of theosophy, in turn the Leuké of *Helen in Egypt,* it is not What Is. It is not the source but the medium of the dream. So in our poem the veil appears as a secret of the whole: Helen may manipulate her veil as an agent of the veil in which she appears as a figure in a pattern. Thus, Helen draws Achilles, enchants him within the enchantment.

•

The haunting Helen has of being possessed by or speaking for Thetis and of seeing the signs of her father Zeus attendant upon Achilles her lover is the nexus in one note of a "higher" and "lower" melody. Helen *is* Thetis, just as a single actual tone may belong to more than one line of movement in musical pattern.

•

On the human level some pattern appears in which Helen, Clytaemnestra, Iphigenia, belong to one "theme." As in Wagner, the leitmotif recalls all. And the interplay of leit motifs may bring gods, men, and the ghosts of the dead into one melodic mingling. The leading that H.D. builds on—from association to association—is only incidentally reasonable in relation to what we already have established in the poem. For the poet, the poem is unfolding, not conforming to but tending towards "Formalhaut," its creator beyond, and the line of the gathering form itself.

•

In "Palinode" the line of Helen as Enchantress began in the opening lines: "the old enchantment holds." And in the foreword to "Palinode" III, the question "Is it possible that it all happened, the ruin—it could seem not only of Troy, but of the 'holocaust of the Greeks,' . . . in order that two souls or two soul-mates should meet?" may be translated into our language of musical reference where all the happenings of the whole establish the nexus each note might be of other tones. Significance springs along the line of preparedness, and in the enchantment of gathering melodic figuration everything before and after contributes to certain "moments." Thinking of the host lost in the war, "the holocaust," Helen in "Palinode" II.2 tells us: "I feel the lure of the invisible," where we may see too that she feels the lure of a lyric strain that moves to find its way in the passage from the thousand and one to the one Helen to the "another and another and another" that Helen and Theseus exchange.

·

In "Eidolon" I.8 Helen tells us:

> it was dream, a catafalque, a bier,
>
> a temple again, infinite corridors,
> a voice to lure, a voice to proclaim,

"Are you still subjugated? enchanted?," Paris had asked. "The script was a snare," Helen says. The difficulty of who and where that haunts Helen, the knowing-the-script and yet not being able to read where, as in *Palinode* II.2:

> I can not "read" the hare, the chick, the bee,

or in *The Walls Do Not Fall,* some fifteen years earlier:

> still the Luxor bee, chick and hare
> pursue unalterable purpose,

is the knowing as feeling yet not knowing to read that a factor has within a series of patterns where it may simultaneously function.

·

Who and where becomes confused in the increased possibilities of belonging that are awakened thru the act. Words in a poem must be exactly where and what they are—have a "Maximus" of life—not because they have independent reality, integrally themselves—but because they depend and tend everywhere in the poem, from a variety of patterns on which they function. The eloquent tendency and dependency *is* fascination, lure, the enchantment.

.

So, in "Eidolon" II.4, we find:

> What was the charm?
> a touch—so a hand
> brushes the lyre-strings;
>
> a whisper—a breath
> to invite the rose;

and:

> was Troy lost for a subtle chord,
>
> a rhythm as yet un-heard,
> was it Apollo's snare?
> was Apollo passing there?

And in II.6, the poet tells us: *Indeed it was 'Apollo's snare.' None other.* The war at Troy, Helen herself, the leap forward of Achilles to "fall in love" at last, the ships and souls of the holocaust, the stars of the galaxy were in order that Troy be sung, for the Song's sake. The passage of Helen from Egypt to Leuké, and then to her echo on the walls of Troy, from the command of Oenone, that "if you forget—Helen" of the Shepherd's hut on Mount Ida where "who will forget Helen attends," that passes in turn into the sessions in which Theseus and Helen recall what was— all these are passages of a music, in which the "Helen" recurs in the changes of changing environments of the music, as the same note may be recognized in new measures of the one song.

.

The song itself is felt thruout the song. "I tremble," Helen says in
"Eidolon" VI.6:

> I feel the same
> anger and sudden terror,
> that I sensed Achilles felt,

II

Oct. 29 / 61

The felt world, the world as it "moves" us, we say, where sympathies
and antipathies make things most intensely real, is one with the imag-
ined world—symphonic in its movement, where things are real in each
other. Or have "body," "substance," in each other. The human cell,
having its own autonomous life, must define its own most concrete
real, beyond which its role or function in the tissue to which it belongs
is more vaguely known. But in the higher orders, just as there are poets
who come to imagine—vaguely, obscurely, or abstractly to be sure—
their place in a larger order, might there be an imagination of the Man,
a formal apprehension in the cell?

·

In our manhood, we find the idea of the reality of the cell as trouble-
some to hold as the corresponding idea of our belonging in turn to some
larger order or happening. In *Helen in Egypt* Achilles had his autonomy
as a hero. Like Helen, he too is a collective or immortal person. Not
only has the image, the Imago of the Achilles or the Helen, been fed by
the imaginations of thousands who are participants—writers, readers,
and before them singers, listeners—in the poetry or *making,* but in turn
these fairies of the human dream, these likenesses in which the heroic,
the demonic or the divine may appear or move, have been fed by actual
men and women—models, actors, and impersonators. So, here, too,
there is a holocaust of war-dead who have contributed to the reality of
Achilles, a constellation of women who have gone up into the Helen.

·

What Nietzsche and then Cocteau from Nietzsche has called *The Eternal
Return,* reincarnation of certain fates or myths or plots in the lives of

those who do not know consciously their own story, so that unknowingly a ground is prepared once more for Helen and Achilles or, as in Cocteau's great movie, for Mark, Tristan, and Isolde to undergo again, to make new, their signatures, has a biological counterpart in the reincarnation of Man in each man. In the code-script of the genes, the cell is predestined or fated, under the human order or command, bears the imperative and lives towards the fulfillment of a person; as in the tradition or mythos or gospel persons in turn bear the imperative and lives towards the fulfillment of ideas, ideals or eìdola.

.

As "Associations" or memories they appear in the psychologies of our times. The stream of consciousness and the track of the analysand are modes of creating the past, following the cues or tendencies of the psychic worlds imagined by Bergson or Freud, and in the stream or along the track certain psychic entities arise. What any psychology is is a choreographic scheme in which its psyche may appear. This scheme is a map of time, a plot of event—as with the code-script of the genes, its form lies in its sequence. It is when our familiarity with time expands, so that we know not one history but many histories, that our human nature expands. The Imago of Helen comes into new powers as she comes into new understanding. As we come to find the Helena Dentritis, the Maiden or Helen's Tree of Rhodes, celebrated by Theocritus, our idea of Helen becomes more complex. We have only to form an allegiance to the worship of Rhodes, a complicity with Rhodes in our love of Athens.

.

As long as we are convinced of our unique claim to human respect and of the superstition, primitiveness, sillyness, ignorance, irrationality of all other (heterodox) human thought and feeling, our truth or worths will be measured most real against the fabrication of divine life. It is part of the sad story of monotheism that where it first forbade worship of other gods it divorced its people from the communion of the human spirit ("for the Lord thy God is a consuming fire, *even* a jealous God") and set over them a racial law. For the Jews, and after them, for the Christians and Moslems, all that was not lawful and in the book was error and falsehood. Just as the mixing of races was forbidden the Jews (so that ironically the anti-semite Hitler, because he was a racist, performed to the letter the will of Jehovah (Yahweh) as a consuming fire to cleanse the chosen race of its nephelium—those who had broken the laws) so all other traffic with images, dreams, sacred foods, arts was forbidden. "Behold, I set before you this day a blessing and a curse": so the commandments were laid down. Never again would the divine intrude, but the people under the law would know the divine only in the law: so, Moses is the last to see the Burning Bush.

•

Dec. 27/61   The narrative art is in weaving at once a story and a fabric, bringing into play whatever threads towards the full ground in which the figures become meaningful and tendencies become designful. But these "threads" are voices; the telling directive in verse or in prose shows in the way the immediate area is working. For the master of this art— for the art-full story teller, there is just this transformation of telling into spinning—there are those rare folk geniuses who can still spin a good yarn—for whom words pass into phrases like wool into thread, and threads fly into sentences. We gathered to hear the story, are following the thread. All of this is a voice—and if it isn't a voice, and then a voice into which other voices enter—there is no story. *Mythos* the Greeks called it, what the mouth uttered, and Aristotle said that *mythos* was plot.

Helen in Egypt belongs to the high art of the narrative. H.D. draws not only upon what Stesichorus in his *Palinode* told to be the truth of Homer but also upon how he told it. [Just as Plato or Herodotus praises Stesichorus for having seen the light and rendering Helen true to life, tell us too.] We learn from Plato or Herodotus that Stesichorus saw the light and told at last the true story of Helen; but we learn too from Greek historians of poetics the Stesichorus found a new way of the high art, alternating prose and choric verse in his narrative. He took up the story from the Homeric tradition and told it anew in the light of an alternate weave. "Truth" here is in the fitting figure, the turn of the plot that has the highest economy in complexity. The Helen on the ramparts of Troy being a wraith, the Helen in Egypt being the truth, fitted the truth of war and its causes. So in Euripides' *Helen*, we hear *Helen in Egypt* in a speech that has the warp of what happened in the Trojan war and a woof of what is happening in Athens' own phantasmagorical war with Sparta. And—this is the full magic of the art—we see anew our own war obsessions. It was all, Helen tells us:

> thus to drain our mother earth
> of the burden and the multitude of human kind—

and then:

> fought for me (except it was not I
> but my name only).

It is most fitting then that H.D. [illegible] the alternate tradition, where we fight for freedom and the Soviets for communism (these two: freedom and communism being the two vital expectancies of the human spirit in our time), but both in that delusion of the name only. Communism no more truthfully the cause of the Soviets than freedom the cause of the American forces.

•

But it is not for such a political persuasion that H.D. writes in *Helen in Egypt*. Plato's Socrates in referring to the *Palinode* of Stesichorus had been struck by the implication that the truth of Helen in Egypt gave the lie to the cause of the Greeks at Troy, but his concern here was not that of a pacifist seeking to discredit war, but that of a seer and teacher seeking to illuminate the nature of human life itself. Our greatest delusion is the lure of the ground in which we appear: our own liveliness is our wraith, we are not deluded by the false causes of the enemy but by our own.

•

It is not misfitting that in our common speech "to tell a story" has already the underthread and overthread of two meanings. We must always be in the full enchantment of the voicing, the telling phrases, the rhythmic successions that lead us on—aware that all the intensely alive thing is the one thing that is alive—the human voice or mythos. What they said. The rest of history is dust. And we are misled if we think the facts have this significance in them. War has terrible repercussions—all of a sudden in the fabric of the human community the threads of a thousand tendencies are realized. There is not only the *mythos* but there is the *dromenon*: men not only tell their story but they enact it. If men imitate in their arts, they imitate in their lives. And the intensely alive actor like the intensely alive narrator intends towards crisis. To have community with other men at all is to become a member of a communal peril beyond our individual fate. At the heart and from the heart of this awful communal mind the *mythos*, just like the *dromenon*, springs. The story teller begins and the dynamics of his art takes force from the compelling voice that transforms us from individually responsible men into listeners and leads us on—that's one charge of the tension that makes for attention—and from the alert mind that attends that voice and works to articulate and relate. There are only two living poets in our language of the stature of H.D.—William Carlos Williams and Pound. Both Edith Sitwell and Eliot at a crucial phase ceased to develop as poets and never entered the major phase of the man for whom all thought and feeling has become "poetic," transmuted into the medium of his art.

But it is not with Williams or Pound that I would compare *Helen in Egypt*. "We all know the story of Helen of Troy but few of us have followed her to Egypt" the prose of *Palinode* begins.

> Do not despair, the hosts
> surging beneath the Walls,
> (no more than I) are ghosts;
>
> do not bewail the Fall,
> the scene is empty and I am alone,

The antiphon of the verse takes up the theme. This art is of an unfolding, informing narrative, most aware from the first of its voice as a story. "I hear voices," Helen tells us in this opening passage

> there is no veil between us,
> only space and leisure

•

H.D.'s counterparts in contemporary writing are the Thomas Mann of *Joseph* and *Doctor Faustus* and the Malraux of *The Psychology of Art*. Here the writer is aware of his art as the central drama—rhyme, meter, number; stanza, chapter, book are articulations that provide possibilities of an intricate fabric of parts, kept moving, without conclusion. The depths of the art, tho it has crisis, are sounded in reverberations and correspondences—a whole structure. While each poem participates in the life of other poems.

The multiple phases of Helen—in Troy, in Egypt, phantom and actual; the other beings of Helen, the girl that Theseus knew, the young matron who "had lost her childhood or her child" in Sparta, the obsessional paramour of Paris who died thrown from the walls of Troy, the wise Helen who never was at Troy but lived under the protection of Proteus—all the imaginations of what she was are gathered up into the great Persona of Helen for whom only Achilles—the other great Persona of the War—can be mate.

    •

Yes, as we begin to see how these many articulations are moving, move as they do in-forming each other and in that unfolding a melody, we recognize that H.D. here and there is aware (as Shakespeare in *The Tempest* or Mann in *Doctor Faustus* is aware) that in this work the author seeks to reveal his/her identity. There is the personal signature, Hilda Doolittle's "H.D." in the Helena Dentritis, Helen of the trees. So, Helen, this dryad Helen, is the counterpart of another dryad, the H.D. of the very first poems. Everywhere in the world of this poem impersonation passes into our dwelling in and then living in one another. Phantom is complicit in the real: Helen "is both phantom and reality."

    •

Plato had read the truth of the Helen in Egypt to mean that men fought at Troy for an illusion, for a lie. "That story is not true," Stesichorus had written:

> You never went away in the launched ships.
> You never reached the citadel of Troy.

Only these 3 lines remain of his *Palinode*. There is a hint in the Greek Anthology that Pythagoras believed Homer lived anew in Stesichorus and at last, finding the truth of Helen, "saw," was no longer blind. The truth of Helen for Herodotus the historian and for Euripides the dramatist was the truth about the war. "Fought for me (except it was not I)," Helen says in Euripides' play: "but my name only."

Yet when we find Helen again in Goethe's play (where the Helen of Tyre that Simon Magus knew has been gathered into the Persona of Helen, as Achilles–Simon Magus has been gathered into the Faustus role) the abducted wife of Homer's epic, the phantom of Stesichorus's *Palinode* and Euripides' *Helen of Egypt,* the face that sank a thousand ships of Marlowe's show—all the illusion, the lure, the cause of war has become Beauty: At least, Goethe remarked, there was once a war that was fought for Beauty.

•

What in-forms the Helen of H.D.'s masterwork anew is the analysis of the psyche (H.D. being an initiate of Freud himself).

Appendix 2 *Composition and Publication History of* The H.D. Book

BOOK I: BEGINNINGS

Chapter 1: Written in 1960. Published in *Coyote's Journal* 5/6 (1966): 8–31.

Chapter 2: Written in 1960. Published in *Coyote's Journal* 8 (1967): 27–35.

Chapter 3, Eros: Written in 1961. Published in *Tri-Quarterly* 12 (Spring 1968): 67–82.

Chapter 4, Palimpsest: Written in 1961. Published in *Tri-Quarterly* 12 (Spring 1968): 82–98.

Chapter 5, Occult Matters: Written in 1961. Published in *Aion: A Journal of Traditional Science* (December 1964): 5–29; reprinted in *Stony Brook Poetics Journal* 1/2 (Fall 1968): 4–19.

Chapter 6, Rites of Participation: Written in 1961. Published in *Caterpillar* 1 (October 1967): 6–29, and *Caterpillar* 2 (January 1968): 124–54.

BOOK 2: NIGHTS AND DAYS

Chapter 1: Written March 10, 1961. Revised 1963. Published in *Sumac* 1, 1 (Fall 1968): 101–46.

Chapter 2: Written March 11, 1961. Revised 1963. Published in *Caterpillar* 6 (January 1969): 16–38.

Chapter 3: Written March 12, 1961. Revised 1963. Published in *Io* 6 (Summer 1969): 117–40.

Chapter 4: Written March 13, 1961. Revised 1964. Published in *Caterpillar* 7 (April 1969): 27–60.

Chapter 5: Written March 14, 1961. Revised 1963. Published in *Stony Brook Poetics Journal* 3/4 (Fall 1969): 336–47 [section I]; *Credences* 1, 2 (July 1975):

50–52 [extract from section II]; *Sagetrieb* 4, 2–3 (Fall/Winter 1985): 39–86 [complete].

Chapter 6: Written March 15, 1961; September 2, September 3, September 4 and 10, October 1, 1964. Published in *Southern Review* 21 (Winter 1985): 27–48.

Chapter 7: Written March 20, 1961; October 8, 1964. Published in *Credences* 1, 2 (July 1975): 53–67.

Chapter 8: Written March 21, 1961. Published in *Credences* 1, 2 (July 1975): 68–94.

Chapter 9: Written March 22, March 24, 1961. Published in *Chicago Review* 30 (Winter 1979): 37–88.

Chapter 10: Written March 25, March 28, March 29, 1961. Published in *Ironwood* 11, 2 [#22] (Fall 1983): 48–64.

Chapter 11: Written May 25, 1961. Published in *Montemora* 8 (1981): 79–113.

A selection of passages from Book 2, revised and supplemented with new material, appeared in *Origin* (second series) 10 (July 1963): 1–47, as "The Little Day Book."

BOOK 3 [APPENDIX I]

Part 1 ("Exchanges"): Written 1961. Published in *West Coast Line* 60 (42, 4) (2009): 100–117.

Part 2 ("Dreams" and "'Art to Inchant'"): Written 1961. Published in *The Capilano Review* 3, 9 (Fall 2009): 80–101.

Appendix 3 *A List of Works Cited by Robert Duncan in* The H.D. Book

In the course of writing *The H.D. Book,* Robert Duncan refers to hundreds and hundreds of texts. This is part of his summoning of a world and all its proliferating implications, as well as the incarnation of his conversation with the great minds of the world. This is a world of mind at work in the work of minds. Sometimes his references are substantial. Sometimes they are simply passing mentions of titles that illustrate a point. In compiling this list, we decided to include only those works which Duncan goes on to quote substantially or discuss. Where possible we have tried to cite the editions that he worked with, or at least the editions that were in his personal library or otherwise available to him at the time. We have not included works cited in Book 3 (Appendix 1).

Aldington, Richard. *Life for Life's Sake.* New York: Viking Press, 1941.

Ambelain, Robert. *La Kabbale Pratique.* Paris: Edition Niclaus, 1951.

Apuleius. *The Transformations of Lucius, Otherwise Known as "The Golden Ass."* Translated by Robert Graves. Harmondsworth, Eng.: Penguin, 1950.

Augustine, Saint, Bishop of Hippo. *The City of God.* London: Dent, 1945.

Baudelaire, Charles. *Mon coeur mis à nu.* Paris: J. Corti, 1949.

Bergson, Henri. *Evolution Créatrice.* Translated by Arthur Mitchell. New York: Modern Library, 1944.

Bettelheim, Bruno. "A Case History of a Schizophrenic Child Who Converted Himself into a 'Machine' Because He Did Not Dare Be Human." *Scientific American,* March 1959.

Blackwood, Algernon. *The Bright Messenger.* New York: E. P. Dutton and Co., 1921.

————. *The Centaur.* London: Macmillan, 1911.

————. *The Promise of Air.* London: Macmillan, 1918.

Blake, William. "Annotations to Lavater's *Aphorisms on Man.*" In *The Complete Poetry and Prose of William Blake.* Edited by David V. Erdman. New York: Anchor Books, 1965.

————. Letter to Thomas Butts, 22 Nov. 1802. In *The Complete Poetry and Prose of William Blake.*

————. Letter to John Flaxman, 21 Sept. 1800. In *The Complete Poetry and Prose of William Blake.*

————. Letter to William Hayley, 6 May 1800. In *The Complete Poetry and Prose of William Blake.*

Blavatsky, Helena Petrovna. *Isis Unveiled.* New York: J. W. Bouton, 1889.

————. *The Secret Doctrine.* London: Theosophical Society, 1908.

Bogan, Louise. Review of *The Walls Do Not Fall. The New Yorker,* October 21, 1944, p. 89.

Browning, Robert. *Dramatis Personae.* Hammersmith, Eng.: Doves Press, 1910.

Bryher, Winnifred. *Heart to Artemis.* New York: Harcourt, Brace and World, [1962].

Bunyan, John. *Pilgrim's Progress.* London: Dent, 1954.

Burkhardt, Jacob. *Force and Freedom: Reflections on History.* New York: Pantheon Books, 1943.

Butts, Mary. *Armed with Madness.* London: Wishart, 1928.

————. *Ashe of Rings.* New York: Albert and Charles Boni, 1926.

————. *The Death of Felicity Taverner.* London: Wishart, 1932.

————. *Imaginary Letters.* Paris: E. W. Titus [At the sign of the Black Manikin], 1928.

————. *Speed the Plow.* London: Chapman and Hall, 1923.

————. *Traps for Unbelievers.* London: Desmond Harmsworth, 1932.

Carlyle, Thomas. *On Heroes, Hero-Worship, and the Heroic in History.* New York: Macmillan, 1918.

Carroll, Lewis. *Sylvie and Bruno.* London and New York: Macmillan, 1889.

Cocteau, Jean. *Orphée: A Tragedy in One Act and an Interval.* Translated by Carl Wildman. London: Oxford University Press, 1933.

Corbin, Henry. *Avicenna and the Visionary Recitals.* London: Routledge and Kegan Paul, 1961.

Crow, W. B. *Mysteries of the Ancients.* Issues no. 1–18. London: Michael
Houghton, 1942–45. Includes: (1) Planets, Gods and Anatomical Organs;
(2) The Astrological Correspondences of Animals, Herbs & Jewels;
(3) The Planetary Temples; (4) Human Anatomy in Temple Architecture;
(5) Noah's Ark; (6) Astrological Religion; (7) The Calendar; (8) Seven
Wonders of the World; (9) The Mysteries; (10) The Cosmic Mystery
Drama; (11) The Historical Jesus—High Priest of the Mysteries; (12) The
Law of Correspondences; (13) The Symbolism of Chess and Cards;
(14) Druids and the Mistletoe Sacrament; (15) The Symbolism of the
Coronation; (16) Initiation; (17) The Nature Mysteries; (18) Appendices
to the Series.

Cumont, Franz. *The Mysteries of Mithra.* London: Kegan Paul, Trench and
Trübner, 1903.

———. *The Oriental Religions in Roman Paganism.* New York: Dover, 1956.

Dante Alighieri. *De Monarchia.* Translated by Herbert W. Schneider. New
York: Liberal Arts Press, [1957].

———. *De Vulgari Eloquentia.* In *A Translation of the Latin Works of Dante
Alighieri.* Translated by A. G. Ferrers Howell and Philip H. Wicksteed.
London: Dent, 1904.

———. *The Divine Comedy.* 3 vols. Translated by Charles S. Singleton.
Princeton: Princeton University Press, 1977.

———. *The Inferno.* London: J. M. Dent and Co., 1946. The Temple
Classics.

———. *The Paradiso.* London: J. M. Dent and Co., 1946. The Temple
Classics.

———. *The "Vita Nuova" and "Canzoniere" of Dante Alighieri.* London: J. M.
Dent, 1948.

Dewey, John. *Art as Experience.* New York: Capricorn Books, 1959 [orig.
pub. 1934].

Dodds, E. R. *The Greeks and the Irrational.* Berkeley: University of
California Press, 1951.

Eisler, Robert. *Orpheus the Fisher.* London: Watkins, 1921.

Eliot, T. S. *Four Quartets.* London: Faber and Faber, 1960.

———. *The Waste Land and Other Poems.* London: Faber and Faber, 1940.

Faure, Elie. *The History of Art: The Spirit of Forms.* New York and London:
Harper and Brothers, c. 1921–30.

Fenollosa, Ernest. *The Chinese Written Character as a Medium for Poetry.* [San
Francisco]: City Lights Books, [1936].

Festugière, A. J. *La Révélation d'Hermès Trismégiste*. 4 vols. Paris: J. Gabalda, 1949–54.

Fitts, Dudley. "Celebration of Man and God." *Saturday Review of Literature* 22 (February 1947): 19.

———. Review of *Tribute to the Angels*. *Partisan Review* 13 (Winter 1946): 113–20.

Flaubert, Gustave. *Trois Contes*. London: Harrap, 1959.

Fletcher, John Gould. Review of *Sea Garden*. *Egoist* 3 (December 1916): 183–84.

Frazer, James George. *The Golden Bough,* 3rd ed. 12 vols. New York: Macmillan, 1951.

Freud, Sigmund. *Civilization and Its Discontents*. London: Hogarth Press, 1957.

———. *The Future of an Illusion*. Garden City, N.Y.: Doubleday, 1957.

———. *The Interpretation of Dreams*. New York: Basic Books, 1959.

———. *Moses and Monotheism*. New York: Vintage Books, 1955.

———. "Screen Memories." In vol. 3 of *The Standard Edition of the Complete Psychological Works of Sigmund Freud*. 24 vols. London: Hogarth, 1953–74.

———. "Thoughts on War and Death." In vol. 4 of *Collected Papers*. Edited by Joan Riviere. 5 vols. New York: Basic Books, 1959.

———. *Three Contributions to the Theory of Sex*. New York: E. P. Dutton, 1920.

———. *Three Essays on the Theory of Sexuality*. Translated by James Strachey. New York: Basic Books, 1962.

Frobenius, Leo. *African Genesis*. New York: Stackpole Sons, 1937.

Giedion, Seigfried. *The Eternal Present: The Beginnings of Art*. New York: Pantheon, 1962. Bollingen Series 35.6.1.

Graves, Robert. *King Jesus*. New York: Creative Age Press, 1946.

———. *The White Goddess: A Historical Grammar of Poetic Myth*. New York: Vintage Books, 1958.

H.D. *Bid Me to Live*. New York: Grove Press, 1960.

———. *By Avon River*. New York: Macmillan, 1949.

———. *Choruses from "Iphigenia at Aulis" and the "Hippolytus" of Euripides*. London: The Egoist, 1919.

———. *Collected Poems*. New York: Boni and Liveright, 1925.

———. *Euripides' "Ion."* Boston and New York: Houghton Mifflin Co., 1937.

———. *The Flowering of the Rod*. London: Oxford University Press, 1946.

———. *The Hedgehog*. London: Brendin Publishing Co., 1936.

———. *Hedylus*. Boston and New York: Houghton Mifflin Co., 1928.

———. *Helen in Egypt*. New York: Grove Press, 1960.

———. *Hermetic Definitions*. [Newburyport: Frontier Press], 1971. Reprinted as *Hermetic Definition,* New York: New Directions, 1972.

———. *Hippolytus Temporizes*. New York: Houghton Mifflin, 1927.

———. *Kora and Ka / Mire-Mare*. Paris: Contact Editions, 1934.

———. "Narthex." In *Second American Caravan*. Edited by Alfred Kreymborg et al. New York: Macaulay Co., 1928.

———. *Nights*. Dijon: Darantiere, 1935.

———. *Palimpsest*. Paris: Contact Editions, 1926.

———. *Red Roses for Bronze*. New York: Random House, 1929.

———. "Sagesse." *Evergreen Review* 2, 5 (Summer 1958): 27–36.

———. *Tribute to Freud*. Boston: Godine, 1974.

———. *Tribute to the Angels*. London: Oxford University Press, 1945.

———. *The Usual Star / Two Americans*. Paris: Contact Editions, 1934.

———. *The Walls Do Not Fall*. London: Oxford University Press, 1944.

Harrison, Jane Ellen. *Prolegomena to the Study of Greek Religion*. Cambridge: Cambridge University Press, 1903.

———. *Themis*. Cambridge: Cambridge University Press, 1912.

Harvey, William. *Anatomical Disquisition on the Motion of the Heart and Blood in Animals*. London: Dent, [1908].

Hawthorne, Nathaniel. "The Birthmark." In *Mosses from an Old Manse*. New York: Crowell, 1902.

Hesiod. *Theogony*. Translated by Norman O. Brown. New York: Liberal Arts Press, [1953].

Hockett, Charles D. "The Origins of Speech." *Scientific American,* September 1960.

Hoffmann, E. T. A. "Don Juan, or A Fabulous Adventure That Befell a Music Enthusiast on His Travels." In *Tales from Hoffmann*. Edited by Christopher Lazare. New York: A. A. Wyn, 1946.

Hofmann, Werner. *The Earthly Paradise: Art in the Nineteenth Century*. New York: George Braziller, 1961.

Hugo, Victor. "Pleurs dans la nuit." In *Les Contemplations*. Paris: Nelson, [1935].

James, Henry. *The Wings of the Dove*. New York: Dell, 1958.

James, William. *Principles of Psychology*. New York: Dover, [1950].

Jarrell, Randall. Review of *Tribute to the Angels*. *Nation* 29 (December 1945): 741.

———. Review of *The Walls Do Not Fall*. *Partisan Review* 12 (Winter 1945): 120–26.

Jonas, Hans. *The Gnostic Religion*. Boston: Beacon Press, 1958.

Joyce, James. *Dubliners*. New York: Modern Library, 1954.

———. *Exiles*. New York: Viking Press, 1951.

———. *Finnegans Wake*. New York: Viking Press, 1957.

———. "I hear an army charging upon the land." In *Collected Poems*. New York: Viking Press, 1937.

———. *Portrait of the Artist as a Young Man*. New York: Viking Press, 1956.

———. *Ulysses*. New York: Random House, 1946.

Jung, Carl. *The Archetypes and the Collective Unconscious*. London: Routledge and Kegan Paul, 1959.

Kandinsky, Wassily. *Concerning the Spiritual in Art*. New York: Wittenborn, Schultz, 1947.

Kantorowicz, Ernst. *Frederick the Second, 1194–1250*. Translated by E. O. Lorimer. London: Constable and Co., 1931.

Kelly, Robert. "Notes on the Poetry of the Deep Image." *Trobar* 2 (1960): 14.

Lawrence, D. H. *Lady Chatterley's Lover*. Harmondsworth, Eng.: Penguin Books, 1960.

———. *The Man Who Died*. New York: New Directions, 1950.

———. "Surgery for the Novel—or a Bomb." *Literary Digest International Book Review*, April 1923.

Levertov, Denise. *The Jacob's Ladder*. New York: New Directions, 1961.

Lewis, Wyndham. *The Apes of God*. Harmondsworth, Eng.: Penguin Books, 1965.

———. *Time and Western Man*. Boston: Beacon Press, 1957.

Lowell, Amy. "Patterns." In *Complete Poetical Works*. Boston: Houghton Mifflin, 1955.

Lowell, Robert. *Land of Unlikeness*. Cummington, Mass.: The Cummington Press, 1944.

MacDonald, George. *Lilith*. London: G. Allen and Unwin, 1924.

Malraux, André. *The Metamorphosis of the Gods*. New York: Doubleday, 1960.

———. *Psychology of Art*. 3 vols. New York: Pantheon Books, 1949–50.

McAlmon, Robert. *Being Geniuses Together*. New York: Doubleday, 1968.

Mead, G. R. S. *Fragments of a Faith Forgotten*. London and Benares: Theosophical Society, 1906.

———. *Pistis Sophia*. London: John M. Watkins, 1949.

———. *Thrice-Greatest Hermes.* 3 vols. London: John M. Watkins, 1949.

Mechthild of Magdeburg. *The Revelations of Mechthild of Magdeburg: or, The Flowing Light of the Godhead.* Translated by Lucy Menzies. London: Longmans, 1953.

Moses de Leon. *Zohar (Sefer Sheqel haq Qodesh).* London, 1911.

Murray, Gilbert. *Five Stages of Greek Religion.* New York: Doubleday, 1955.

Nietzsche, Friedrich. *Beyond Good and Evil.* Chicago: H. Regnery Co., 1955.

Novalis. *Heinrich von Ofterdingen.* Oxford: Blackwell, 1959.

Olson, Charles. "Against Wisdom as Such." *Black Mountain Review* 1, 1 (Spring 1954): 35–39.

———. "As the Dead Prey upon Us." *Ark II / Moby I* (1956–57): 12–19.

———. "The Gate and the Center." *Origin* 1 (Spring 1951): 35–41.

———. *Maximus Poems.* New York: Jargon/Corinth, 1960.

———. *O'Ryan.* San Francisco: White Rabbit Press, 1965.

———. "Projective Verse." *Poetry New York* 3 (1950): 13–22.

Plato. *Lysis. Symposium. Gorgias.* Translated by W. R. M. Lamb. Cambridge, Mass.: Harvard University Press, 1961.

Plutarch. "The E at Delphi." In *Moralia,* vol. 5 of The Loeb Classical Library. Translated by Frank Cole Babbitt. Cambridge, Mass.: Loeb Classical Library, 1936.

———. "Isis and Osiris." In *Moralia,* vol. 5 of the Loeb Classical Library. Translated by Frank Cole Babbitt. Cambridge, Mass.: Loeb Classical Library, 1936.

Pound, Ezra. *ABC of Reading.* New York: New Directions, 1951.

———. "Aux Etuves de Wiesbaden." In *Pavannes and Divagations.* New York: New Directions, 1958.

———. *The Cantos 1–95.* New York: New Directions, 1956.

———. "Cavalcanti." In *The Spirit of Romance.* New York: New Directions, 1952.

———. "Genesis (after Voltaire)." In *Instigations of Ezra Pound.* New York: Boni and Liveright, 1920.

———. *Guide to Kulchur.* London: Faber and Faber, 1938.

———. *How to Read.* London: D. Harmsworth, 1931.

———. *Hugh Selwyn Mauberly.* London: Ovid Press, 1920.

———. *Make It New.* London: Faber and Faber, 1934.

———. "Religio." In *Pavannes and Divagations.* New York: New Directions, 1958.

——. "A Retrospect." In *Literary Essays*. New York: New Directions, 1954.

——. *Ripostes*. London: E. Matthews, 1915.

——. "The Serious Artist." In *Literary Essays*.

——. *Social Credit: An Impact*. London: P. Russell, 1951.

——. *The Spirit of Romance*. New York: New Directions, 1952.

——. *Thrones, 96–109 de los cantares*. New York: New Directions, 1959.

——. "The Tradition." In *Literary Essays*.

Proclus. *The Commentaries of Proclus on the "Timaeus" of Plato, in five books; containing a treasury of Pythagoric and Platonic physiology*. 2 vols. Translated by Thomas Taylor. London: Thomas Taylor, 1820.

Raine, Kathleen. *Blake and Tradition*. 2 vols. Princeton: Princeton University Press, 1968. Bollingen Series 35.11.

Ransom, John Crowe. "Why Critics Don't Go Mad." *Kenyon Review* 14: 331–39.

——. "Winter Remembered." In *Selected Poems*. New York: Alfred Knopf, 1963.

Rees, Alwyn and Brinley. *Celtic Heritage*. London: Thames and Hudson, 1961.

Reich, Wilhelm. *The Function of the Orgasm*. New York: Noonday Press, 1961.

Richardson, Dorothy. *Pilgrimage*. New York: A. A. Knopf, 1938.

Riding, Laura. *Collected Poems*. New York: Random House, 1938.

——. *Progress of Stories*. London: Constable and Co., 1935.

Rilke, Rainer Maria. Letter to Witold von Hulewicz, 1925. In vol. 2 of *Letters of Rainer Maria Rilke, 1910–1926*. Translated by J. B. Greene and M. D. Herter Norton. New York: Norton, 1947.

Roheim, Géza. *The Eternal Ones of the Dream*. New York: International University Press, 1945.

Sabartes, Jaime. *Picasso: An Intimate Portrait*. New York: Prentice Hall, 1948.

Santayana, George. *The Last Puritan*. New York: Scribner's, 1936.

Sapir, Edward. *Language*. New York: Harcourt, Brace and World, 1949.

Saurat, Denis. *Gods of the People*. London: J. Westhouse, 1947.

Scholem, Gershom. *Major Trends in Jewish Mysticism*. London: Thames and Hudson, 1955.

Schrödinger, Erwin. *What Is Life?* New York: Doubleday Anchor Books, 1956.

Seligmann, Kurt. *The Mirror of Magic*. New York: Pantheon Books, 1948.

Sessler, Jacob John. *Communal Pietism among Early American Moravians*. New York: Henry Holt, 1933.

Shelley, Percy Bysshe. "Hellas." In *The Complete Poetical Works*. Edited by Thomas Hutchinson. London: Oxford University Press, 1960.

Sinnett, Alfred Percy. *Esoteric Buddhism*. Boston: Houghton Mifflin, 1912.

Stein, Gertrude. "Composition as Explanation." In *Selected Writings of Gertrude Stein*. Edited by Carl Van Vechten. New York: Random House, 1946.

——. "Portraits and Repetition." In *Lectures in America*. Boston: Beacon Press, 1957.

Stravinsky, Igor. *Poetics of Music in the Form of Six Lessons*. New York: Random House, 1947.

Symonds, John. *The Lady with the Magic Eyes*. New York: T. Yoseloff, 1960.

Taliesin. *The Poems of Taliesin*. Translated by J. E. Caerwyn Williams. Dublin: Institute for Advanced Studies, 1968.

Tarn, W. W. *Hellenistic Civilisation*. London: Arnold, 1952.

Taylor, Henry Osborn. *The Mediaeval Mind*. Cambridge, Mass.: Harvard University Press, 1959.

The Tibetan Book of the Dead. Edited by W. Y. Evans-Wentz. Oxford: Oxford University Press, 1949.

Tieck, Ludwig. "The Elves." In *Tales by Musaeus, Tieck, Richter*. Translated by Thomas Carlyle. London: Chapman and Hall, 1874.

Upward, Allen. *The Divine Mystery*. Santa Barbara, Calif.: Ross-Erikson, 1976.

Vaughan, Thomas. *Anthroposophia theomagica, or a discourse on the nature of man and his state after death*. In *The Works of Thomas Vaughan*. Edited by Arthur Edward Waite. London: Theosophical Publishing House, 1919.

Vital, Hayyim. *The Tree of Life*. Northvale, N.J.: Jason Aronson, 1999.

Waite, A. E. *The Brotherhood of the Rosy Cross*. New York: University Books, 1961.

Walker, D. P. *Spiritual and Demonic Magic from Ficino to Campanella*. London: The Warburg Institute, 1958.

Watts, H. H. "H.D. and the Age of Myth." *Sewanee Review* 56 (1948): 317–21.

Werblowsky, R. J. Zwi. *Joseph Karo: Lawyer and Mystic*. Oxford: Oxford University Press, 1962.

Weston, Jessie. *From Ritual to Romance*. Garden City, N.Y.: Doubleday, 1957.

———. *The Quest for the Holy Grail*. London: G. Bell, 1913.

Whitehead, Alfred North. *Adventures of Ideas*. New York: Macmillan, 1956.

———. *Aims of Education*. New York: New American Library, 1949.

———. *Process and Reality*. New York: Macmillan, 1957.

Whitman, Walt. "As I Ponder'd in Silence." In *Leaves of Grass*. New York: New American Library, 1958.

———. "Preface." *Leaves of Grass,* 1855 edition. New York: Viking Press, 1959.

Williams, William Carlos. *Autobiography*. New York: New Directions, 1951.

———. *Collected Poems, 1921–1931*. New York: Objectivist Press, 1934.

———. *In the American Grain*. New York: New Directions, 1956.

———. *Kora in Hell*. San Francisco: City Lights Books, 1957.

———. *Paterson*. New York: New Directions, 1954.

———. *Selected Essays*. New York: Random House, 1954.

———. *Spring and All*. Dijon: Contact Editions, 1923.

———. *The Wedge*. Cummington, Mass.: The Cummington Press, 1944.

Woolf, Virginia. *The Waves*. New York: Harcourt, Brace and World, 1959.

Yeats, William Butler. *The Death of Cuchulain*. In *Last Poems and Plays*. London: Macmillan, 1940.

———. *A Packet for Ezra Pound*. Dublin: Cuala Press, 1929.

———. *Per Amica Silentia Lunae*. London: Macmillan, 1918.

———. *The Trembling of the Veil*. In *Autobiography: Consisting of "Reveries over Childhood and Youth," "The Trembling of the Veil," and "Dramatis Personae."* New York: Macmillan, 1953.

Zimmer, Heinrich Robert. *The King and the Corpse: Tales of the Soul's Conquest of Evil*. New York: Pantheon Books, 1951.

Zukofsky, Louis. *"A"* 1–12. Kyoto, Japan: Origin Press, 1959.

———. *Bottom: On Shakespeare*. Austin: Ark Press [for the Humanities Research Center, University of Texas], 1963.

Credits

ROBERT DUNCAN

Book 1, Chapter 1 originally published in *Coyote's Journal* 5/6 (1966): 8–31. Reprinted by permission.

Book 1, Chapter 2 originally published in *Coyote's Journal* 8 (1967): 27–35. Reprinted by permission.

Book 1, Chapter 3 originally published in *Tri-Quarterly* 12 (Spring 1968): 67–82.

Book 1, Chapter 4 originally published in *Tri-Quarterly* 12 (Spring 1968): 82–98.

Book 1, Chapter 5 originally published in *Aion: A Journal of Traditional Science* (December 1964): 5–29; reprinted in *Stony Brook Poetics Journal* 1/2 (Fall 1968): 4–19.

Book 1, Chapter 6 originally published in *Caterpillar* 1 (October 1967): 6–29, and *Caterpillar* 2 (January 1968): 124–54. Reprinted by permission.

Book 2, Chapter 1 originally published in *Sumac* 1, 1 (Fall 1968): 101–46.

Book 2, Chapter 2 originally published in *Caterpillar* 6 (January 1969): 16–38. Reprinted by permission.

Book 2, Chapter 3 originally published in *Io* 6 (Summer 1969): 117–40. Reprinted by permission.

Book 2, Chapter 4 originally published in *Caterpillar* 7 (April 1969): 27–60. Reprinted by permission.

Book 2, Chapter 5 originally published in *Stony Brook Poetics Journal* 3/4 (Fall 1969): 336–47 [section I]; *Credences* 1, 2 (July 1975): 50–52 [extract from section II]; *Sagetrieb* 4, 2–3 (Fall/Winter 1985): 39–86 [complete]. Reprinted by permission.

Book 2, Chapter 6 originally published in *Southern Review* 21 (Winter 1985): 27–48. Reprinted by permission.

Book 2, Chapter 7 originally published in *Credences* 1, 2 (July 1975): 53–67. Reprinted by permission.

Book 2, Chapter 8 originally published in *Credences* 1, 2 (July 1975): 68–94. Reprinted by permission.

Book 2, Chapter 9 originally published in *Chicago Review* 30 (Winter 1979): 37–88. Reprinted by permission.

Book 2, Chapter 10 originally published in *Ironwood* 11, 2 [#22] (Fall 1983): 48–64.

Book 2, Chapter 11 originally published in *Montemora* 8 (1981): 79–113.

Index

Brueghel, Peter, 187, 334, 547
Bryher (Annie Winifred Ellerman),
    209, 219–21, 241–45, 248–50, 257–
    60, 295–96, 576
Buddha, 126, 408
Buddhism, 129, 145, 146, 558, 618,
    620–21, 622, 624
Bunting, Basil, 356
Bunyan, John, 207, 544, 545, 546,
    579, 587
Burckhardt, Jacob, 404, 534, 567
Burne-Jones, Edward, 305, 390, 472
Burroughs, William S., 390
Bush, Vannevar, 606
Butler, Edith, 628
Butts, Mary, 5, 11, 193, 244, 216, 263,
    391, 488, 613; works by: *Armed with
    Madness*, 225; *Ashe of Rings*, 250;
    The Macedonian, 250; *Scenes from
    the Life of Cleopatra*, 250; *Speed the
    Plough and Other Stories*, 250; *Traps
    for Unbelievers*, 261, 448
By Avon River (H.D.), 207, 218

Caesar's Gate (Duncan), 1
Calder, Alexander, 172
Calliope, 111
Calvin, John, 364
Cammell, C.R., 143
canon, literary, 5, 11, 36, 37, 226, 518,
    522
capitalism, 36, 122, 175, 176, 183, 259,
    260, 336, 339, 516, 523, 532, 539,
    552, 553
Carlyle, Thomas, 73, 76, 216, 255, 307,
    379, 388, 434, 574
Carpenter, Rhys, 597–98
Carroll, Lewis, 205, 609–10, 617, 618,
    619, 621, 623–24
Castro, Fidel, 606
Catherine de Medici, 469
Catholicism, 94, 95, 143, 335, 467,
    476, 479, 507, 521, 522, 537, 539,
    562, 572, 620
Catullus, 185

Cavalcanti, Guido, 50, 51, 185, 306
Cavell, Stanley, 29–30n7, 29n4
Céline, Louis-Ferdinand, 61, 511
Celtic tradition, 56, 73–74, 95, 96, 98,
    289, 513
"Centaur Song" (H.D.), 285
Cézanne, Paul, 155, 168, 192, 305
"Chance Meeting" (H.D.), 260
chaos, 83, 84, 136, 146
childhood, 157–61, 171, 451, 494, 495,
    562, 564, 565, 566, 567, 568, 587,
    624, 625
Chinese language, 208, 443
Chowl, Hay, 296
Christianity, 269, 528, 530, 598, 624;
    and Eliot's work, 53; and Eros, 86–
    95; and esoteric tradition, 143; and
    H.D.'s War Trilogy, 304, 324, 353,
    437, 582, 588; and Lawrence's work,
    73; and Robert Lowell's work, 352–
    53; and Pound's work, 358
Christmas, 161
Christos, 122, 126, 143, 161, 183,
    269, 307, 324, 334, 346, 358, 388,
    400, 417, 472, 481–83, 519, 533,
    534, 536–38, 617. *See also* Jesus
    Christ
cinema. *See* film
"Circe" (H.D.), 259
"Cities" (H.D.), 44, 176–78, 181, 182,
    190, 191, 336, 393, 397
clairvoyance, 57, 130, 197, 198
Clarke, John, 30n8
Claudel, Paul, 61
Clement of Alexandria, Saint, 364
Close Up (periodical), 295–98
Clovis, 89
Coburn, Alvin Langdon, 313
Cocteau, Jean, 207, 229, 252, 272–73,
    419, 423, 434, 490, 586, 640–41
Cola di Rienzi, 212
Coleridge, Samuel Taylor, 30n9, 316–
    17, 321
Collected Poems (H.D.), 45, 96, 226,
    230, 285

collective unconscious, 102, 137, 316, 353, 489

Collins, Jess. *See* Jess

communism, 67, 122–23, 176, 336, 502, 554, 643

community, 21, 40, 67–68, 154, 157, 255, 310, 315, 316, 332, 335, 361, 363–66, 371, 455, 479, 504, 532, 558, 583, 633, 644

Confucius, 196, 288, 361

constellations, 203–6, 283, 299. *See also* stars

Contact Editions, 250

"The Contest" (H.D.), 421

Cook, Arthur Bernard, 96

Cooper, James Fenimore, 389, 390

Copernicus, Nicolaus, 636

Corbin, Henry, 9, 29n2, 128, 519–21

Corman, Cid, 23, 217

Cosimo Tura, 321, 471

Council of Nicaea, 530

Courbet, Gustave, 474

Coward, Noel, 225, 448

Crane, Hart, 216

Creeley, Robert, 204, 217, 221

Crow, W.B., 378

Crowley, Aleister, 142–43

Cuba, 606

Cubism, 167, 168

"Cuckoo Song" (H.D.), 258

Cummings, E.E., 372

Cumont, Franz, 286

Cupid, 80, 82, 94

Curie, Marie, 80, 187, 343, 345, 545

Curie, Pierre, 343, 345

Dalí, Salvador, 168, 293, 325

"The Dancer" (H.D.), 211

Dante Alighieri, 9, 28, 40, 48, 55, 73, 95, 96, 156, 186, 197, 207, 214, 370, 375, 376, 390–91, 416, 434, 504, 514, 516, 519, 521, 523, 579–85, 622; Pound on, 96, 197, 305, 306, 307, 321, 390; works by: *De Monarchia*, 370; *De Vulgari Eloquentia*, 367, 395, 492, 562; *The Divine Comedy*, 95,

184, 198, 321, 390, 411, 542–44, 546, 574, 579, 589; *La Vita Nuova*, 40, 203, 580, 582, 584, 587, 619

Darwin, Charles, 139, 154, 281, 309, 392, 573, 578, 620

Delphic oracle, 118, 119, 121, 382

Demeter, 96, 121, 145, 301, 490, 611, 625

democracy, 122, 123, 359, 362, 363, 510, 552, 554, 598

Demosthenes, 512, 513

Depression, Great, 147, 148, 210, 225, 261, 552, 554–55

Derain, André, 229

Dewey, John, 60, 304–5, 354

The Dial (periodical), 250, 360

Dickens, Charles, 354, 528

Dickey, James, 523

Dickinson, Emily, 437

Diogenes, 511, 512, 513

Dionysius the Areopagite, 48, 320, 586

Dionysus, 105, 119, 120, 122, 144, 243, 541, 588

Divus, Andreas, 440

Dodds, E.R., 513

Donnelly, Ignatius, 149

Doolittle, Charles (H.D.'s father), 117, 292, 576

Dostoyevsky, Fyodor, 60, 63

dreams, 66, 72, 97–99, 103, 105, 118, 125, 153, 188, 242, 251, 268, 280, 289, 310, 356, 368, 369, 397, 481, 525, 560, 578, 587, 608–26; Duncan's remembering of, 11, 147, 150–52, 265–67, 292–93, 428–31, 433, 438–39, 442–45, 547–51, 569, 570; and Roheim's *Eternal Ones of the Dream*, 162–66, 168, 171–72

Dryden, John, 355, 359, 506

Dull, Harold, 403

Dunsany, Lord, 73

Durkheim, Emile, 144, 315

ecology, 153, 281

The Egoist (periodical), 46, 176, 178,

Lawrence, D.H. *(continued)*
314; and World War I, 180, 189,
338, 352, 451; works by: *Fantasia
of the Unconscious*, 100, 586; *Lady
Chatterley's Lover*, 457–59, 461;
Love Poems and Others, 306; *The
Man Who Died*, 39, 73, 482, 483,
488, 539–42
Leda, 111, 533, 608, 611, 622, 627
Lemuria, 126, 137
Leonardo da Vinci, 196, 512
Letters (Duncan), 1
"Let Zeus Record" (H.D.), 248, 258
Levertov, Denise, 204, 221; works by:
"Hypocrite Women," 459; "The
Jacob's Ladder," 267–68; "Our
Bodies," 459
Lévi, Éliphas, 618, 620, 622, 626
Levy, Gertrude, 218
Lévy-Bruhl, Lucien, 155
Lewis, C.S., 390
Lewis, Wyndham, 47, 212, 235, 244,
302, 392
libido, 163–65, 466
Life and Letters Today (periodical), 211,
217, 250, 296, 377
Lilith, 89, 386, 387, 409, 459, 481, 490
literary canon, 5, 11, 36, 37, 226, 518,
522
The Little Review (periodical), 295,
296, 307, 308, 396, 457
logical positivism, 527
Logos, 6, 7, 121, 160, 324, 557, 565,
568, 583–84, 626
London, England, 211, 292; and H.D.'s
"Cities," 176–77; and H.D.'s *Palimp-
sest*, 106, 107, 108, 109, 379; and
H.D.'s "The Tribute," 178–82; and
H.D.'s War Trilogy, 270, 280–81,
339, 353, 365, 380, 463
Loos, Anita, 372
"lost" generation, 193–94, 261, 338
Lowell, Amy, 40–41, 42, 46–47, 53,
58, 59, 227, 395, 396
Lowell, Robert, 179, 352–53, 396
Lowes, John Livingstone, 434, 435

Loy, Mina, 5
Lucas van Leyden, 283, 334
Lucifer, 82, 137, 284, 306, 456, 489,
594
Luke, biblical book of, 87, 353, 496,
527, 529

MacDonald, George, 255, 268, 386,
489, 618, 619, 622, 624, 625, 628
Machen, Arthur, 143
MacLeish, Archibald, 226
Macpherson, Kenneth, 295, 297
madness, 127, 160, 355, 356, 359,
415, 417, 509, 620. *See also*
schizophrenia
Magdalene, Mary, 387, 388, 437, 460,
473, 481, 482, 483, 485, 486, 489,
495, 539, 592, 593, 599
mahjong, 148–49
Mallarmé, Stéphane, 392, 453
Malraux, André, 9, 155, 172–74, 304,
310, 645
Manicheanism, 91, 92, 390, 468
Mann, Thomas, 645
Mantegna, Andrea, 185
Mark, biblical book of, 496, 527, 529
Marlowe, Christopher, 533, 628, 632,
646
Mars, 117, 220, 241, 622
Marsden, Dora, 320
Martin, John, 16, 17
Marx, Karl, 127, 154, 274, 509, 510,
553
Marxism, 142, 502
Mary, Virgin, 476
Mass, Christian, 199, 356, 516, 564
Mathers, MacGregor, 142
Matisse, Henri, 63, 68
Matthew, biblical book of, 87, 199,
496, 527, 529
Maya, 290, 513, 616, 627
McAlmon, Robert, 193–94, 221, 244–
45, 247–48, 250, 258, 338, 372
Mead, G.R.S., 9, 96, 144, 145, 185,
302, 319, 586, 627
Mechthild of Magdeburg, 94

Olcott, Henry Steel, 130, 132
Oliver, George, 130
Olson, Charles, 255, 421, 455, 501,
531–32, 548, 550–51, 568–69; works
by: "Against Wisdom as Such,"
205, 278, 569; "As the Dead Prey
Upon Us," 218, 219; "The Gate
& the Center," 217–18; *Maximus
Poems,* 217, 531; *O'Ryan,* 204–5,
550; "Projective Verse," 188, 217,
272, 273, 328, 329–30, 332, 374,
400, 431, 432, 434; "Variations
Done for Gerald Van de Wiele,"
556
The Opening of the Field (Duncan), 12
Open Space (periodical), 403
Oppenheimer, J. Robert, 606
"Orchard" (H.D.), 195, 197
"Oread" (H.D.), 397
"Orestes Theme" (H.D.), 211
organic form, 164, 173, 270, 327–28,
331–32, 345, 359, 571
Origen, 319
Origin (periodical), 204, 217, 221
Orion, 204, 220, 284, 292, 293, 550
Orpheus, 86, 127, 185, 218, 243, 403,
414, 540, 545; and Cocteau's *Orphée,*
272–73, 277
Orphic tradition, 83, 96, 127, 145, 152,
286, 291, 377, 456, 507, 574, 619
Osiris, 82, 114, 115, 116, 117, 118,
120, 122, 123, 126, 278, 299, 324,
388, 483, 540, 559
Others anthology, 216, 235–36
Ovid, 203
Owen, Wilfred, 108, 181

pacifism, 4, 65, 336, 338, 643
Pagany (periodical), 250, 377
Palimpsest (H.D.), 100–123, 209, 220,
226, 242, 243, 249, 260, 379, 391,
422, 503
"Pallas" (H.D.), 182
Pallas Athene, 113–15, 118, 121, 211,
401, 577
Palmer, Samuel, 417

Pan, 89, 419
Paracelsus, 48, 153, 320, 586
Paradise, 86, 87, 90, 92, 184, 199, 391,
451, 464, 466, 501, 573, 578, 579,
589, 629
Parkinson, Thomas, 348
Parrish, Maxfield, 124–25, 127
Partisan Review (periodical), 281, 434,
517, 519
Pater, Walter, 305, 434, 435
patrons and patronage, 219, 241, 244,
248, 257–59, 634
Paul, Saint, 533–34
Pearson, Norman Holmes, 1, 2, 6, 13,
241, 435–36, 438
"Pear Tree" (H.D.), 51
Peire Cardenal, 185
Perdita, 209, 242, 244, 419
permission, poetic, 9, 384, 385, 406
Perrault, Charles, 418
Persephone, 96, 145, 152
Petrarch, 306
"Phaedra" (H.D.), 258–59
phantastikon, 105–6
Philippe le Bon, 257–58
Philo Judaeus, 103
Phosphorus, 284, 489
photography, compared to poetry, 313
Piaget, Jean, 155
Picasso, Pablo, 63, 229, 448, 467, 468;
works by: *Guernica,* 68, 405; *Woman
in the Mirror,* 60
Pico della Mirandola, 128, 300, 307,
586
Pietro di Borgo, 322
Pisanello, 322
planets, 575–76, 622–23. *See also*
astrology; stars
Plato, 9, 84–87, 154, 156, 159, 169–70,
176, 192, 286, 485, 523, 642, 643,
645
pleasure principle, 560, 561, 562, 566
Plethon, Gemistos, 300, 358, 535
Plotinus, 48, 128, 183, 214, 266, 307,
309, 320, 390, 508, 546, 586
Plutarch, 9, 103, 118–23, 128, 156

Poe, Edgar Allan, 223, 490
"The Poet" (H.D.), 211
poetic field, 151–52, 174, 188, 304,
  309, 330, 331, 332, 359, 374, 376,
  450, 492
poetic form, 3, 8, 9, 10, 11, 41–42,
  45, 52, 70–71, 83, 99, 122, 141, 150,
  166, 206, 208, 209, 222–23, 270,
  310, 314–15, 322, 323, 326–27, 328–
  29, 332, 359, 370, 374, 429, 500
poetic permission, 9, 384, 385, 406
Poetry (periodical), 46, 216, 226
Pompeii, 280, 283, 334, 353
"The Pool" (H.D.), 397
Porphyrius, 112
Porter, Katherine Anne, 193
Potocki, Jan, 355
Pound, Ezra, 2, 9, 11, 70, 76, 196,
  208, 210, 216, 229, 234–37, 239,
  245, 292, 296, 300–303, 305–10,
  313–23, 342, 374, 399, 406, 414,
  415, 434, 436, 437, 438, 476, 479,
  488, 490, 538, 539, 540, 576, 611,
  644; and anti-semitism, 510; and
  Browning's work, 103, 104–5;
  on Cavalcanti, 50, 51; and corre-
  spondence with Duncan, 272; and
  correspondence with Eliot, 223–
  24, 225; and correspondence with
  Williams, 366, 372, 395, 463, 515;
  and Dante's work, 96, 197, 305,
  306, 307, 321, 390; on democracy,
  362, 510; and dream-work, 368–69;
  on Eliot, 233; and fascism, 305;
  and Fenollosa's work, 208, 443; on
  Flaubert, 101; on Freud, 463, 509,
  510; on H.D., 45–46, 226, 241, 396,
  397, 420, 463, 469; and Imagism,
  45–50, 53, 54, 56, 57–59, 96, 100,
  125, 175, 198, 212, 226, 235, 236,
  241, 313, 314, 319, 420, 470; on
  Henry James, 306–7; on Lawrence,
  306, 363, 366; Wyndham Lewis on,
  392; and masculine speech, 372,
  373, 395, 516; on Milton, 306; on
  Moore, 395; and neo-Platonism,
48, 49, 100, 214, 307, 323, 358;
on *phantastikon,* 105–6; postwar
confinement of, 177, 212, 213, 357,
369, 539; on Provencal poetry, 91,
410, 411, 514; on rhetoric, 55–56;
on usury, 54, 179, 194, 306, 364,
365, 510, 552, 555, 614; and verna-
cular speech, 367–68, 373, 396; and
Vorticism, 51, 212, 235, 305, 373;
on Williams, 223; Williams on, 187,
396; and World War I, 180, 189, 338;
and World War II, 211–12; Yeats on,
321, 470–71; and Yeats's work, 214,
235, 291, 323, 358, 540, 586; works
by: *ABC of Economics,* 551–52, 555;
ABC of Reading, 47–48, 55, 56, 70,
100, 197, 309, 313, 356; "April,"
470; "Aux Etuves de Wiesbaden,"
198, 357; Canto I, 358; Canto III,
214; Canto VII, 139; Canto XIV,
364; Canto XXXIII, 440; Canto
XXXVI, 317; Canto XXXIX, 459;
Canto XLV (Usura Canto), 364,
365; Canto LXXII, 179; Canto
LXXIV, 178, 288; Canto LXXIX,
524; Canto LXXX, 288; Canto XCI,
214, 215, 509–10, 516; Canto CXV,
187, 307; Canto CXVI, 193, 509;
The Cantos, 47–48, 55, 56, 70, 100,
127, 176, 183–85, 212, 226, 235, 279,
291, 302, 305–8, 313, 318, 319, 321–
24, 354, 357–59, 361, 364, 368–69,
376, 390, 393, 435, 440, 470–71, 508,
510, 516, 524, 539, 541, 544, 546,
553, 586; *Cathay,* 367; "Cavalcanti,"
50, 51, 196, 301, 306, 309, 317, 319,
358, 411, 434, 538, 540, 541, 589;
Confucian Odes, 367; "Genesis (after
Voltaire)," 357; "A Few Don'ts," 45,
179, 384; *Guide to Kulchur,* 55, 235,
236, 321, 322, 323, 357, 368, 389,
541, 590; *How to Read,* 313; *Hugh
Selwyn Mauberley,* 175; "In a Station
of the Metro," 45, 53, 57–58, 313;
Instigations, 208; *Make It New,* 208;
The Pisan Cantos, 47–48, 55, 56, 70,

Rilke, Rainer Maria, 241, 336, 337, 389, 515
Rimbaud, Arthur, 556
Roheim, Géza, 10, 162–72, 477
Romance tradition, 36, 48, 71–73, 91, 95, 96, 97, 98, 100, 390, 411, 434, 519, 521, 582
Roman Empire, 89, 90, 191, 627
Romanticism, 100, 128, 140, 216, 253–54, 302, 346, 388, 434, 436, 467, 475, 523
Rome, 10, 137–38, 283, 339, 379, 427
Roots and Branches (Duncan), 12
Rosicrucianism, 5, 11, 79, 129, 214, 497, 576
Rossetti, Dante Gabriel, 214, 305, 519
Rougemont, Denis de, 390
Rubens, Peter Paul, 468
Rukeyser, Muriel, 292–93
Russia, 370, 371, 502, 504, 606, 643

Sabartes, Jaime, 468
Sade, Marquis de, 355
"Sagesse" (H.D.), 214–15, 240, 323
Saint-John Perse, 437
Sand, George, 247
San Francisco, California, 217, 278, 548, 577
San Francisco renaissance, 1
Santayana, George, 308
Sapir, Edward, 45, 96, 106, 155, 156–57, 191, 230, 532–33
Sappho, 105, 187, 196, 209, 249, 285, 378
Sarapion of Athens, 118
Satan, 89, 179, 306, 454, 456, 480
Satie, Erik, 229
Saturn, 117
"Saturn" (H.D.), 211
Saurat, Denis, 289–90
schizophrenia, 413–17
Scholem, Gershom, 164
Schrödinger, Erwin, 326–27, 329, 347, 493, 494, 500
science, 135–36, 142, 463, 501, 524, 635, 636

Scott, Sir Walter, 37, 528
screen memories, 451, 452, 495, 527
Sea Garden (H.D.), 45, 48, 227, 273, 320, 384, 585
"Sea Heroes" (H.D.), 182
"Sea Lily" (H.D.), 51, 421
"Sea Rose" (H.D.), 51, 74, 397
"Sea Violet" (H.D.), 51
"Secret Name" (H.D.), 101, 107, 109, 110–16, 209, 250, 251–52, 277, 325, 330
Sefiroth, 164–65
self, 3, 8, 115, 159, 160, 171, 240, 268, 280, 364, 489, 559, 569, 571, 583
Seligmann, Kurt, 469
Sessler, Jacob John, 499
sexuality, 85, 128, 164–65, 195–96, 197, 262, 302, 333, 360, 366, 371, 377, 385, 388, 406–7, 414, 438, 444, 453–57, 459–60, 465, 488–89, 499, 566, 626, 629, 632. See also eroticism
Shakespeare, William, 97, 98–99, 103, 128, 196, 199, 214, 318, 404, 405, 423, 506, 586; works by: Hamlet, 352; King Lear, 354, 528; Macbeth, 128, 199; The Tempest, 197, 404, 492, 589, 644
shamanism, 127, 128, 159, 216, 358–59, 408, 417, 473, 545, 550, 586, 619
Shapiro, Karl, 5, 522
Shekinah, 82, 162, 171, 174
Shelley, Percy Bysshe, 140, 141, 142, 367
"Sheltered Garden" (H.D.), 397
"The Shrine" (H.D.), 44, 228–29, 265, 397
Simon Magus, 93, 96, 215, 319, 533, 626–27, 632, 646
Sinclair, May, 226, 251, 391, 420
Sinnett, A.P., 129, 620–21, 622, 624
Sitwell, Edith, 2, 5, 11, 70, 216, 217, 296, 434, 436, 437, 462, 488, 644
Sitwell, Osbert, 241
Smith, Pamela Coleman, 470, 472
socialism, 67–68, 176, 502, 514, 554

unconscious, 52, 83, 102, 105, 131–32, 309, 316, 338, 368, 371, 375–77, 379, 386, 400, 466, 525, 606

Underhill, Evelyn, 143

underworld, 96, 125, 152, 291, 307, 379, 418, 449, 450, 480, 508, 523, 546

University of California at Berkeley, 225–26

Untermeyer, Louis, 5, 435, 522

Upanishads, 186

Upward, Allen, 358, 586

Uranus, 82, 291, 480

"The Usual Star" (H.D.), 260, 263, 291

usury, 176, 195, 351; Pound on, 54, 179, 194, 306, 364, 365, 510, 552, 555, 614

utilitarianism, 29n4, 183, 337

Valentino, Rudolph, 263

Valhalla, 176

Van Dongen, Kees, 391

Van Eyck, Hubert, 257, 258, 268, 277

Van Eyck, Jan, 220, 257, 258

Vanzetti, Bartolomeo, 122

Vaughan, Thomas, 449, 453, 496, 497

Velázquez, Diego de, 300, 304, 310, 467, 468, 499, 535, 536, 539

Venice, Italy, 247, 259, 260, 387

"The Venice Poem" (Duncan), 1, 271, 275, 429, 439–41

Venus, 90, 94, 109, 117, 284, 303, 324, 479–80, 489, 490, 514, 526

Verve (periodical), 283, 310

Vico, Giambattista, 173

Virgil, 307, 390–91, 521, 542, 543, 544, 546, 622

Vishnu, 100

Vital, Hayyim, 160, 161, 198

Vorticism, 51, 52, 212, 235, 305, 399

Wagadu, legend of, 176–77, 181, 185, 375

Wagner, Richard, 247, 255, 563, 637

Waite, A.E., 5–6, 30n9, 35, 143, 453, 470, 471, 626

Walker, D.P., 317

The Walls Do Not Fall (H.D.), 76–77, 114–15, 188, 210, 217, 219, 248, 269, 270–74, 280–83, 287–88, 292, 297, 304, 312, 319–20, 323–24, 329–30, 332–34, 336, 340, 342, 345–46, 351–52, 358, 363–64, 375–77, 380, 385–86, 399, 401–2, 408, 414, 424, 435, 464, 480, 482–84, 494, 496, 498, 514, 516, 524–25, 532, 534, 554, 573–74, 576–78, 584, 593, 611, 638

war, 65, 68, 175, 176, 183, 351, 353, 363, 365, 374, 455, 598, 606–7, 646. See also World War I; World War II

Warner, Lloyd, 167

Warren, Robert Penn, 434

The War Trilogy (H.D.), 23, 176, 196, 207, 210, 212, 217, 218, 235, 247, 270–71, 279, 286, 292, 296, 298, 299, 308, 313, 319, 320, 323–25, 329, 331, 334, 337, 343, 350, 351, 354, 361, 376, 384, 387–88, 398–401, 404–5, 422, 426, 435, 438–40, 471–72, 476, 480–82, 489, 498, 502, 514, 516, 519, 522, 524, 534, 537, 540, 544, 576, 578–79, 582, 587–88, 616

"Wash of Cold River" (H.D.), 50–51, 230

Watkins, John M., 143

Watts, H.H., 537–38

Weaver, Harriet, 258

Weber, Max, 258

Webern, Anton, 222

Werblowsky, R.J. Zwi, 161

Weston, Jessie, 96, 144–45, 237

Whistler, James Abbott McNeill, 323

Whitehead, Alfred North, 102, 347, 354; works by: Adventures of Ideas, 343, 497; Aims of Education, 139; Process and Reality, 114, 531

Whitman, Walt, 76, 100, 127, 316, 354, 434, 437, 488; "Chanting the Square Deific," 93

Whorf, Benjamin Lee, 155
Wilbur, Richard, 5, 435, 436, 522
Wilder, Alexander, 130, 132
Wilder, Thornton, 431
Willetts, Ronald Frederick, 381
William of Auvergne, 519, 521
Williams, Charles, 143, 390
Williams, Gertrude, 130
Williams, William Carlos, 2, 9, 11,
    76, 183, 186–88, 197, 210, 212–13,
    231–39, 292, 296, 319, 359, 361,
    375–76, 398, 406, 415, 436, 438,
    478, 479, 488, 490, 506, 516, 644;
    and correspondence with H.D.,
    231, 234, 238, 372, 389, 393, 394,
    569–70; and correspondence with
    Robert Lowell, 396; and correspon-
    dence with Pound, 366, 372, 395,
    463, 515; and correspondence with
    Stevens, 236; on Eliot, 186–87, 196,
    224, 226, 233, 396; on H.D., 45, 187,
    221, 231–33, 262, 265, 363, 384, 421,
    437, 469, 539; and Imagism, 47, 235,
    314; and masculine speech, 372, 373,
    395, 516; on "no ideas but in things,"
    188, 197, 315, 373, 523; on Pound,
    187, 396; Pound on, 223; works by:
    "Asphodel, That Greeny Flower,"
    215–16, 235; Autobiography, 186, 187,
    212, 220–21, 232–33, 265, 374–75,
    421, 437; The Clouds, 221; Desert
    Music, 218; In the American Grain,
    226; Journey to Love, 218, 435; Kora in
    Hell, 231, 233, 237–38, 372; "March,"
    319, 372–73, 389, 394, 396; Paterson,
    80, 81, 86, 187, 196, 212–13, 217,
    218, 221–22, 235, 308, 315, 320, 329,
    343, 345, 354, 374, 376, 396, 435,
    438, 454, 516, 523, 539, 544; "The
    Poem as a Field of Action," 188;
    "Postlude," 234; Selected Essays, 187;
    Spring and All, 221–23; "To Daphne
    and Virginia," 235; The Wedge, 221,
    374, 386
Winters, Yvor, 434, 523
"Wooden Animal" (H.D.), 211

Woolf, Virginia, 39, 72, 78, 457, 488,
    492–93, 494, 495–96, 503; works by:
    Between the Acts, 493; Mrs. Dalloway,
    492; The Waves, 73, 492
World War I, 57, 68, 108–9, 175, 178,
    180–82, 189–90, 339, 352, 362
World War II, 143, 176, 211, 216, 270,
    455
Wotan, 176
Wright, Frank Lloyd, 427
"The Writing on the Wall" (H.D.),
    207, 217

Xenophanes, 85, 285–86

Yeats, William Butler, 9, 11, 127, 151,
    250, 251, 265, 476, 514, 519, 565–66,
    613; Eliot on, 361; on Mallarmé,
    392, 453; on Pound, 321, 470–71;
    Pound's association with, 48, 73,
    185, 214, 235, 291, 302, 319, 321,
    323, 361, 540, 586; and relations
    with H.D., 2–3, 214–15; and Sym-
    bolism, 100, 141; and theosophy,
    73, 140–44, 244, 251, 358, 566,
    586; works by: Autobiography, 144;
    The Death of Cuchulain, 475; The
    Trembling of the Veil, 140, 143, 389,
    392, 453
Young, Ella, 74

Zen Buddhism, 146, 558
Zeus, 94, 111, 285, 440, 441, 475, 600,
    602, 607, 608, 630, 637
"Zeus-Provider" (H.D.), 211
Zimmer, Heinrich Robert, 290, 631
Zinzendorf, Nicolaus Ludwig von, 2,
    498, 499, 562
Zodiac, 136, 146, 218, 299, 321, 471,
    589
The Zohar, 82, 140, 158, 160, 174,
    294, 380, 507, 553–54, 566
Zoroastrianism, 176, 189, 485
Zukofsky, Louis, 216–17; works by:
    "A," 217, 311; Bottom: On Shake-
    speare, 217, 434

Designer: Nola Burger
Text: 10.75/14.5 Bembo
Display: Bembo, Benton Gothic
Compositor: BookMatters, Berkeley
Indexer: Andrew Joron

CPSIA information can be obtained
at www.ICGtesting.com
Printed in the USA
BVHW03s2133090318
510217BV00002B/56/P

9 780520 272620